An Introduction to Simulation Using GPSS/H

An Introduction to Simulation Using GPSS/H

Thomas J. Schriber
Professor of Computer and Information Systems
School of Business Administration
University of Michigan

John Wiley & Sons
WILEY New York • Chichester • Brisbane • Toronto • Singapore

Library of Congress Cataloging in Publication Data:

Schriber, Thomas J.
An introduction to simulation using GPSS/H / Thomas J. Schriber.
p. cm.

Includes bibliographical references.

QA76.9.C65S384 1990 003'.35133--dc20 90-36373
CIP

ISBN 0-471-04334-6
1. Digital computer simulation. 2. GPSS (Computer program language) I. Title.

Printed in the United States of America

10 9 8 7 6 5 4 3 2 1

for
Ann
Sarah, John, and Maria

Preface

For the Student.

Computer-based simulation modeling is an exciting, satisfying, and practical technique that can be used to experiment with various designs for complex systems in such areas as manufacturing, health care, transportation, communications, and computing. This book introduces building and experimenting with simulation models using a powerful, flexible, fast, and well-established simulation modeling language, GPSS/H (General Purpose Simulation System/H). GPSS/H is frequently used in industry, so you might find that knowledge of GPSS/H will be of direct benefit to you in your career. Even if you work eventually with an alternative simulation language similar in type to GPSS/H, you will find that the priniciples learned in this book can be readily used to develop an operational capability with the alternative language. Student DOS-GPSS/H is contained on a disk supplied with this book, so GPSS/H-based simulation is only as far away as the nearest DOS-based microcomputer.

You can use this book in a relatively formal way in a course on simulation, or you can use the book outside of formal coursework as the basis for self-study of the foundations of simulation using GPSS/H. Every attempt has been made to write the book in such a way that the ideas it contains can be mastered successfully without the need to rely on lectures, although lectures can enrich, extend, and speed up the learning of the material presented here.

Numerous exercises are built into the book. Most of them involve hands-on use of GPSS/H. Some of the exercises call for use and/or modification of GPSS/H models that are discussed in the book and supplied on a disk that comes with the book. Solutions to many of the exercises are presented in an appendix, so you can immediately check your thinking and your work against these solutions.

The book has two prerequisites. First, some familiarity with computer use is assumed. This familiarity can involve such things as the use of a computer for word processing, or text editing, or spreadsheeting, or filing, or database applications, or electronic mail. It need not include experience in computer programming. The computer-familiarity prerequisite is indicated because this book contains no introductory material on computer use as such.

The other prerequisite is a first course in probability and statistics. How does this material come into play? The types of system for which simulation models are built using GPSS/H can include components that behave in random but statistically predictable fashion. Incorporation of "statistical predictability" (which is explained in the book) in a model involves working with random numbers, random variables, and probability distributions. Furthermore, if one or more of the components of a simulation model varies at random, then values characterizing a model's behavior vary at random. An objective of simulation is to observe such values and then use the observed values to make inferences about long-run model behavior. This explains why a first course in probability and statistics is a prerequisite for successful use of this book. (Many students have told me that the study of simulation brings probability and statistics to life for them for the first time.) Fingertip knowledge of such material is not assumed, however. Instead, all such needed material is commented on and summerized (but not developed) in the book, and its use is illustrated with examples.

Except for the indicated basic background in probability and statistics, there are no mathematical prerequisites for use of this book. Simulations of the type we will study do not involve formulating and then solving sets of equations, as you will see.

So now you should be able to get started with your introduction to simulation using GPSS/H. You can go immediately to Chapter 1 and proceed from there. Best wishes for successful use of the book, and for enjoying yourself in the process.

For the Instructor.

This book can be used in a simulation course in a number of different ways. The alternatives depend on the purpose of the course, the instructor's approach to dealing with the material in the book, the duration of the academic term, and whether the course is to be based on a modeling language, with general principles of simulation playing a secondary role, or is to emphasize general principles of simulation, with use of a modeling language playing a secondary role. Several broad possibilities are suggested later.

As for the purpose of a first course in simulation, a distinction can be made between a course whose objective is to build a base of understanding for students who have no intention of going on to become practitioners of simulation (their goal may be to become informed consumers of results produced by practitioners), and a course being taken by students who might eventually become simulation practitioners. Students in BBA or MBA programs (especially those specializing in operations management, statistics and management science, or computer and information systems), for example, might fall into the former category. Industrial engineering students at all degree levels, operations research majors, and Ph.D. students (who might intend to use simulation methodology in their dissertation work) in operations management, operations research, in a range of engineering specializations, or in health-care management or public administration, for example, might fall into the latter category. Although students in the former category can be well served by a single course in simulation, those in the latter category cannot learn enough about simulation in a single course (in my opinion) to satisfy their needs. (See Section 8 of Chapter 1 in this regard.) Whether both types of students can be served equally well in one and the same first course is debatable. In any event, this book is designed for use in a first course, not in a two-course sequence. (Not many of us have the privilege of offering a two-course sequence in simulation, despite the importance of simulation in the view of both operations-research practitioners and educators. See Section 4 of Chapter 1 for documented insights into the importance of simulation.)

In my experience, both types of students just mentioned are strongly motivated by a first course that emphasizes a modeling language, with general principles playing a secondary role. (Let's face it, it is fun, challenging, satisfying, and stimulating to build simulation models, get them running correctly, and then perform experiments with them.) Simulation is a topic that shouldn't simply be "talked about," but that should be "done." (As someone has said, simulation, like football, is a contact sport.) In this approach, practice both informs and motivates an interest in theory, with a focus on practical problems leading to an interest in the more abstract considerations that provide results useful in coping with practical problems. Under ideal circumstances, an instructor can move back and forth with considerable success between practice on the one hand, and theoretical considerations on the other.

An instructor's approach to dealing with material of the type in this book can also influence the number of simulation topics covered in a first course, and helps determine how much time students must invest in the course outside of class. At the one extreme, an instructor might give detailed lectures on the material in this book and perhaps challenge the students with quick exercises to be done in class and then to be immediately discussed in class. This approach saves student time outside of class but doesn't leave much class time for other things. At the other extreme, an instructor might give brief overview lectures (or no lectures at all) on the material in this book, expecting students to master the material on their own and demonstrate mastery by handing in various GPSS/H modeling assignments. The time students must spend on a course can increase dramatically if this approach is taken. (The number of office hours that must be held to clarify issues that otherwise could have been methodically explained in lecture can also increase dramatically.) The class time freed up in this approach, however, can be used to extend the range of topics covered in the first course. In this approach, for example, an instructor might base the course on a general-purpose simulation textbook (see item 3 further on), and have the students use this GPSS/H book as an accompanying text whose contents are largely up to the student to master.

The rate at which material of the type in this book can be covered in lecture also depends on whether or not transparencies are used to support lectures. I can supply to adopters paper copies of transparencies that can be used in giving detailed lectures on the material in this book. (See below. For the most part, these transparencies are large-scale versions of figures and tables in the book.)

Keeping the preceding considerations in mind, here are some possible patterns for use of this book in a first course in simulation:

1. If an instructor gives detailed lectures on material in this book, and if these lectures *lead* the corresponding reading assignments, this book can be the basis for an entire course. The student time saved when lectures lead the reading can be spent doing more out-of-class hands-on exercises than might otherwise be reasonably required. In my experience using this approach, students can hand in about 12 modeling assignments during a 15-week term. (These assignments progress from simpler exercises up to the level of more demanding activities, the last of them, in my case, based on a current paper from the literature.) There is also time for students to extend their base of simulation literacy by reading and reporting on the simulation chapters in several operations research books and by studying and reporting on simulation applications they find by searching the literature. (See Exercises 1 and 4 in Section 11 of Chapter 1.) Time permitting, the instructor might also introduce students to detailed aspects of some GPSS/H capabilities that are beyond the scope of this book (see Chapter 17, and especially Section 28 of that chapter, in this regard), demonstrate Proof (the animation and presentation software produced by the vendor of GPSS/H), and perhaps teach some operational skills in the use of Proof to produce animations and presentations.

2. If an instructor limits himself or herself to giving overview lectures on the material in this book, then the book can also be the basis for an entire course. In this approach, students must spend more time outside of class studying the material in the book, but the book can be covered more quickly in lecture. This leaves more class time in the latter part of the term for additional activities of the type mentioned under item 1 and can also leave enough time for students to do a simulation project in the closing weeks of the term. (If a student project is assigned, then the instructor probably should introduce students to detailed aspects of some GPSS/H capabilities that are beyond the charter of this book. See Chapter 17, and especially Section 28 of that chapter, in this regard. Some instructors might choose to have their students pursue any needed additional details on their own, as a test of their ability to come to grips with new material in independent fashion.)

3. Another possibility is to base a simulation course on a general simulation text such as Banks and Carson (1984), Law and Kelton (1982, 2nd edition forthcoming in 1990), or Watson and Blackstone (1989) while using this book as an adjunct to introduce operational aspects of a modeling language. This book is written in such a style that it can be studied without being lectured on extensively (but with corresponding demands, of course, on the use of student time outside of class).

The three patterns just described are suggestive, not exhaustive. Various permutations of these patterns can be developed to suit the needs of instructors and their students.

For instructors who have learned or taught from *Simulation Using GPSS* (Schriber, 1974), it may be helpful to comment on the differences between that book and this one. Sometimes referred to as the Red Book or as Big Red, the 1974 book is extensive in covering the Blocks in IBM's GPSS/360 (a product of the late 1960s) and providing detailed examples of their use, but is not extensive otherwise. It contains no overview of simulation and no GPSS material relative to the statistical analysis of output, or variance reduction techniques, or selecting the probable best from two or more competing alternatives, for example. Furthermore, given the vintage of GPSS/360, the Red Book takes a batch-oriented approach in discussing the internal aspects of GPSS. In contrast, the present book is not as extensive with respect to the coverage of Blocks in the fast, extremely powerful implementation of GPSS known as GPSS/H. It provides an *introduction* to GPSS/H, not a comprehensive treatment of the language. But this book *does* contain an overview of simulation and material on statistical analysis of output, variance reduction techniques, and selecting the probable best from two or more competing alternatives, and shows by discussion and example how GPSS/H can be brought to bear in these important areas. Furthermore, this book uses an interactive approach to teach GPSS/H, with batch use not operationalized until Chapter 6, and with additional aspects of interactive use extending even beyond that point. Like the Red Book, this book explains and illustrates the data structures (Chains) and processing algorithms (including GENERATE-Block initialization, the Scan Phase, and the Clock Update Phase) on which GPSS/H is based, so that the student has the priceless satisfaction of understanding *how* a GPSS/H simulation proceeds. Whereas that material was dealt with largely in desktop fashion in a single dose in the Red Book, a much more satisfying and gradual hands-on, interactive approach is taken in dealing with that material here.

If you teach from this book, you might send me a note on your school's letterhead to tell me that (University of Michigan, Ann Arbor, MI 48109-1234). You will then receive instructional-support material. You are also encouraged to send me exercises you might compose for use with the book. Some of these might then be included (conditioned on your approval, and with credit given to you) in later editions of the book. Your general comments and innovative ideas for successful use of the book are also welcome.

Acknowledgments

Many people contribute to a book like this, both directly and indirectly. Encouragement, support, and/or ideas have come from Andy (Richard W.) Andrews and Gil (Dean Gilbert R.) Whitaker, Jr. (both of the University of Michigan); Jerry Banks (Georgia Institute of Technology); Dan Brunner, Bob Crain, Nancy Earle, Jim Harbour, Jim Henriksen, Roy Pafenberg, Elizabeth Tucker, and Lee Wightman (all of Wolverine Software Corporation); John Carson (Carson/Banks & Associates); Ed Dudewicz and Bob Sargent (both of Syracuse University); Dave Kelton (University of Minnesota); Averill Law (University of Arizona); Gerhard Niemeyer (University of Regensburg in Regensburg, Germany); Alan Pritsker (Pritsker Corporation and Purdue University); Steve Roberts (Regenstrief Institute and Purdue University); Lee Schruben (Cornell University); Ingolf Ståhl (Stockholm School of Economics in Stockholm, Sweden); John Sturgul (South Australian Institute of Technology in Ingle Farm, South Australia); Pandu Tadikamalla (University of Pittsburgh); Maurice Verhelst (University of Louvain in Louvain, Belgium); Franz Weinberg (Swiss Federal Technical University in Zurich, Switzerland); and Jim (James Reed) Wilson (Purdue University). Contributions and motivation have come from thousands of students with whom I have been privileged to work, principally in credit courses at the University of Michigan and in 5-day professional development courses in the United States and Europe. The support of information systems editor Joe Dougherty, senior copy editor Gilda Stahl, production supervisors Tomi Navedo and Gay Nichols, digital production supervisor Jennifer Dowling (who used Pagemaker on a Macintosh to produce this book from my Microsoft Word and MacDraw files), and others at John Wiley is also acknowledged with thanks. In the final analysis, though, it was my always understanding, supportive, and patient wife, Ann, who cleared the path for this book by saying "OK Tom, drop out of sight for as long as it takes and write the book."

THOMAS J. SCHRIBER
Ann Arbor
January 1990

Contents

1 A Perspective on Simulation and GPSS/H

1.1 Preview

This chapter provides several perspectives on the area of simulation. First, the general character of simulation is described. Then the application scope of simulation as a tool used to investigate the characteristics of systems is indicated, and the importance of simulation in operations research is pointed out. Some of the advantages and disadvantages of simulation are described. The steps involved in a simulation study are outlined, and the skills required of a simulation professional are discussed in light of these steps. Comments are then provided on the GPSS/H modeling language and its applications, and the objectives of this book are indicated. In the closing section of the chapter, readings are recommended for obtaining a broader-based overview of simulation. The closing section also calls attention to some articles in which successful applications of simulation are described.

Those interested in getting started as soon as possible with GPSS/H might choose to skim-read Chapter 1 at first and then proceed with detailed reading of Chapters 2 through 17. Whether Chapter 1 is carefully read at first, or is just skim-read, it can no doubt be reread profitably after some experience has been gained in building and running GPSS/H simulation models.

1.2 The General Character of Simulation

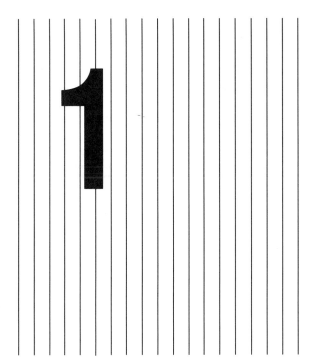

Simulation is a word with which many people are familiar, at least in a general way. A dictionary suggests that simulation involves imitation, or mimicking, "giving the appearance or effect of" or "taking on the characteristics of reality," and that simulation may involve a sham object, or a counterfeit, or a replica, or a model. Simulation brings to mind the idea of pretending, or feigning. When an architect builds a three-dimensional model showing the proposed design of a building, the model is an imitation of the building. Easier, faster, and much less expensive to build than the building itself, and much less costly to modify for the purpose of correcting mistakes or experimenting with possible changes in the design of the building, the model provides the architect with insights in terms of layout, feasibility, workability, and appearance. These same insights might not be available in two-dimensional drawings of the design (which are also simulations in their own right) or in attempts to visualize the design mentally. The model aids the architect himself or herself, provides the architect's client with an easily understood version of the design proposed for the building, and serves as a basis for communication (discussion) between the architect and client, making it more likely that each understands the other's intentions and that the two are in agreement on what the final outcome is to be.

The architect's model is an example of a physical, three-dimensional, and static simulation. The model is static (rather than dynamic) in the sense that people do not move through the building or use its facilities, elevators in the building do not go up and down, the heating and air-conditioning systems do not work, and so on.

Examples of physical, three-dimensional, dynamic simulation models also come to mind. For instance, a major elevator manufacturer has a physical model of a generalized elevator system in which elevators move up and down as time goes by. The user of this model decides how many floors and elevators to have in the system, sets the rates at which people on various floors come to take an elevator, indicates the floors to which these people want to move, selects the rules for elevator movement (such as specifying that some elevators will only stop at floor 20 or higher), and then puts the model into operation, watching clusters of waiting people (represented by lights and counters) form on various floors, watching elevators pick up these people and deliver them to their destinations, and then obtaining statistics indicating the average waiting time, average time required for people to reach their destination, and so on. By changing the arrival points and arrival rates of people and the number of elevators and the rules for their movement, the user can experiment informally with the model in "what if" fashion, searching for a design that balances performance on the one hand with cost on the other.

The elevator model involves not just physical aspects, but also logical aspects. The experimenter provides information that the model uses, both logically and computationally, to imitate the operation of an elevator system. Note that the model mimicks not just the operation of the elevator system, but also reflects the passage of time. In the model, simulated time might go by more quickly than it would in a real elevator system. For example, it might only take 1 second for the simulated elevator system to make the moves that would require 5 seconds in a real elevator system. The effect of this time compression is to speed up the rate of experimentation, making operation of the model more time efficient for the user.

Some dynamic simulations behave deterministically, whereas others contain probabilistic elements. In the model of an elevator system, for example, the time required for a moving elevator to travel between two consecutive floors might be some strictly determined value, such as 1 second. On the other hand, when an elevator stops at the lobby just before 8 A.M. on a workday, the number of people waiting for it might vary at random from simulated day to simulated day.

A great medium for simulations that entertain and often educate, too, is provided by personal computers. These computer-based simulations are not physical in the sense of a three-dimensional architectural model, but can be physical in the sense that aspects of a situation are often represented pictorially on a two-dimensional screen. And, like the dynamic model of an elevator system, they can have logical and computational aspects, and inputs from the user. They often go further than this, providing challenging interplay with the user. For example, consider flight simulators, in which the user sits at a simulated control panel in the cockpit of a plane (a Sopwith Camel, for example, or a Fokker triplane), with outside views shown through the windows of the cockpit. The user tries his or her skills at taking off, landing, climbing, diving, and banking and may crack up many times before developing the skills needed to control the plane successfully. After fundamental flying skills have been mastered, the user might then be ready to try dogfighting with enemy planes. This leads to a whole new set of learning experiences, while the user develops and experiments with a variety of dogfighting strategies to discover which ones seem to work and which ones don't.

Another example of simulation on personal computers involves a game in which the user designs and constructs the playing surface of a pinball machine, then plays pinball on the machine. A palette of pinball components is provided at the edge of the computer screen (flippers, spinners, bumpers of various shapes, energizers, holes, guiderails), and these can be selected and copied at will into places of choice on the playing surface of the pinball machine. The user can then experience the characteristics of the pinball game that he or she has designed by playing the game in simulated fashion, complete with realistic sound effects. Has one bumper been placed too close to another? Try moving one of the bumpers, and see what effect this has on the play of the game. Have so many flippers been provided that the player hardly ever loses a ball? Try removing some of the flippers, and see if this makes the game more challenging. Do balls disappear too often into holes on the playing surface? Try repositioning or eliminating some of the holes, or use bumpers to block some pathways to the holes. And so on. Such a simulation is capable of being very realistic, sometimes giving the feeling that it is not a simulation at all, but is the real thing.

Note that simulation does not necessarily involve specifying and then solving a set of equations. There are some types of simulation that are equation-based, but there are other types that are not. In the pinball simulation, for example, designing the layout of the playing surface does not involve the use of equations to describe relationships among the elements of the game. Beginning with Chapter 2, we will learn how to build simulation models that are *not based on equations*, but instead involve the use of other techniques to describe logical relationships among the elements involved in situations of interest.

1.3 The Application Scope of Simulation

Just as a person can use simulation to experiment with dogfighting stragtegies or design a pinball game and then experience its playing characteristics, so too can a person use simulation to investigate the characteristics of proposed designs or strategies for a wide range of situations of very practical importance. The use of simulation is not restricted to one or several narrow classes of problems. Instead, simulation is a versatile tool that has an enormous range of applications.

Some of the situations that have been the subject of simulation-based investigation are listed in Table 1.1.

The types of applications mentioned in Table 1.1, although suggestive, are by no means exhaustive.

Some of applications of simulation are made more specific in activity 4 of Section 1.11 in this chapter, where references are given to a sampling of articles reporting the successful use of simulation in a variety of situations. You might consider turning briefly to that point in this chapter now and reading several of the brief application overviews given there.

1.4 The Importance of Simulation in Operations Research

Simulation is just one of the techniques in the field of operations research and management science (OR/MS). These techniques have the overall objective of using the scientific method to help solve complex decision problems in organizational settings. Among the techniques are simulation, statistics, linear programming, stochastic processes, network analysis, decision theory, queuing theory, inventory control, and so on.

Simulation ranks very well among the other operations research techniques in terms of importance. This is consistently born out by numerous studies dating at least as far back as the mid-1960s. For example, consider Table 1.2, which is part of a larger table that appears in one of these studies (Harpell, Lane, and Mansour, 1989). In this study, questionnaires were sent to 250 educators and 250 practitioners selected at random from the ORSA membership directory in 1973 and then again (with new random selections each time) in 1978 and 1983. (Table 1.2 indicates the number of respondents in each case. For example, 89 educators and 96 practitioners responded to the 1983 questionnaire.) Three techniques consistently stand out as most important: statistics, linear programming, and simulation. As shown in Table 1.2, simulation moved up from rank 3 among educators and 4 among practitioners in 1973 and 1978 to rank 2 among both educators and practitioners in 1983.

In another study, Turban (1972) found that simulation was used in about 25 percent of operations research activities at the corporate level. And Cook and Russell (1976) found in a survey of *Fortune* 500 companies that only 11 percent of them did *not* use simulation in the decision process. (Updated Turban and Cook/Russell percentages would probably be even more favorable for simulation now than they were when these surveys were conducted, thanks to major improvements in simulation methodology and software, increased computer hardware performance, decreased computing costs, the advent of microcomputers, the growth in databases, and increased awareness of and education in simulation and its uses.)

Another insight into the relative importance and frequency of use of simulation is provided in the 1988 Harold Larnder Memorial Lecture, entitled "Operations Research: A Global Language for Business Strategy" and presented to the Canadian Operational Research Society by a distinguished operations researcher, Professor Harvey M. Wagner of the University of North Carolina (Wagner, 1988). Wagner "argues that the concepts and vocabulary of operations research have become a pervasive part of the thinking of modern American industrial managers and that the related models are playing important roles in informing the decisions that they

Table 1.1
Selected Applications of Simulation

Urban-social	
Emergency-response vehicle location	Facilities scheduling
Mass transit system design	Air pollution control
Garbage collection patterns	Population planning
Traffic light sequencing	Air traffic control
Police beat design	Airport design
Political redistricting	Urban development
Educational planning	Schoolbus routing
Political campaign strategies	Urban dynamics
U.S. and world economic conditions	Courtroom scheduling
Health Care	
Health care planning	Hospital admissions
Emergency room design	Blood bank management
Organ transplant strategies	Diet management
Hospital staffing	Ambulance crew scheduling
Disease control strategies	Patient flow
Drug interaction control policies	
Aerospace-military	
Space system reliability	Search and rescue strategies
Equipment replacement policies	Equipment distribution
War games/strategies	Space defense systems
Armed forces recruiting strategies	Satellite positioning
Service Industry	
Portfolio management	Fleet scheduling
Insurance and risk management	Bank teller scheduling
Professional sports draft strategies	Supermarket clerk scheduling
Auditing strategies	Telephone switching
Communication network design	Facility location
Feedlot management	
Industrial	
Food and chemical blending	Production scheduling
Inventory management	Product safety testing
Facility layout	Quality control
Repair crew scheduling	Tool crib personnel planning
Design of distribution channels	Labor negotiations

Source: Budnick, McLeavey, and Mojena (1988).

make." For purposes of his analysis, Wagner puts operations research activities into the five categories of mathematical programming models, discrete optimization, dynamic models, multivariate statistical models, and computer simulation models. On the topic of simulation, he states that "computer simulation models have enabled companies to test strategies before implementing them and thereby substantially reduce the risk of adopting an unworkable approach. The ambitious nature of these applications is impressive. Of all the techniques mentioned, computer simulation is the most

Table 1.2

Ranks of the 12 Quantitative Techniques Educators and Practitioners Believe Are Most Important to Teach Operations Research Majors According to Three Pairs of Questionnaires Sent to a Random Sample of ORSA[1] Members at Five-Year Intervals

	1973		1978		1983	
Technique	**Educator N = 106 Rank**	**Practitioner N = 92 Rank**	**Educator N = 98 Rank**	**Practitioner N = 88 Rank**	**Educator N = 89 Rank**	**Practitioner N = 96 Rank**
Statistics	1	1	2	1	3	1
Linear Programming	2	2	1	2	1	3
Simulation	3	4	3	4	2	2
Math Programming	4	7	10	5*	6	5
Probability	5	3	9	3	7	4
Stochastic Processes	6	–	4	7*	4*	8
Network Analysis (PERT)	7	–	6	11*	4*	–
Optimization	8	9*	–	5*	9	6
Dynamic Programming	9	–	–	–	10	–
Decision Theory	10*	9*	5	–	8	–
Queuing	10*	5*	8	7*	11	7
Inventory Control	10*	–	7	–	–	–

[1]ORSA: Operations Research Society of America.

* Indicates a tie.

– Indicates the technique was not ranked among the top 12.

resource intensive. Nevertheless, the number of applications of this approach probably *exceeds that of mathematical programming by a factor of 10 to 1."* (Italics have been added.) That simulation outpaces mathematical programming in its frequency of use by an estimated factor of 10 to 1 is remarkable, given the frequent application of linear programming and other mathematical programming techniques.

Simulation's high ranking among OR/MS techniques, and the frequency of its use, are testimony to the ability of this methodology to help develop effective, cost-saving solutions to realistic problems. It is no wonder that the field of simulation is as vigorous, dynamic, and growing as it is today.

1.5 Simulation Versus the Alternatives

Figure 1.1 displays a set of three alternative approaches that can be used in problem solving, or more specifically in the design and analysis of systems. At the left extreme in the figure is experimentation on the real system. At the right extreme is mathematical modeling. Positioned between these two extremes is simulation.

Let's illustrate the Figure 1.1 alternatives with a simple but instructive example set in the context of bows and arrows. Suppose 10 arrows are to be shot

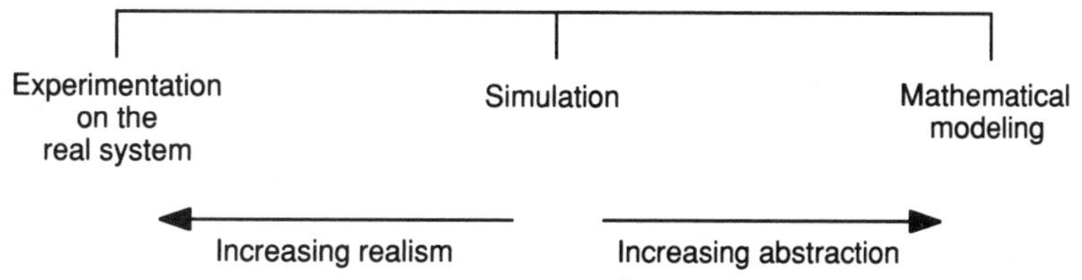

Figure 1.1 *Alternative Problem-Solving Approaches*

at a target. Assume that each arrow either hits or misses the target with probability 0.5. What then is the probability that an *even* number of hits (such as 0, or 2, or 4, etc.) will result? One way to *estimate* the answer to this question is to experiment with the real system, as indicated at the extreme left in Figure 1.1. This requires that we get a target, a bow, and some arrows and establish conditions such that each shot of an arrow has one chance in two of hitting the target. We then shoot 10 arrows at the target, one by one, and note whether an even number of hits occurs. We repeat this experiment many times and keep count of the number of times that an even number of hits results. The fraction of the experiments that result in an even number of hits can then be used as an *estimate* for the answer to the question originally posed.

Another way to answer this question is to approach the problem via mathematical modeling, applying some fundamental concepts from the field of probability. This approach is indicated at the extreme right in Figure 1.1. Letting p be the probability that an arrow hits the target, and P be the probability that an even number of hits occurs when ten arrows are shot at the target, then P and p are related by the equation

$$P = \sum_{k=0}^{5} \binom{10}{2k} p^{2k}(1-p)^{10-2k}$$

(The term in the first set of parentheses is the number of 10 things taken $2k$ at a time.) This equation can then be evaluated for $p = 0.5$, providing an *exact* answer to the question.

Simulation provides a third method that can be used to reply to the question we are dealing with about shooting arrows at a target. In the sense used here, and as suggested in Figure 1.1, simulation involves neither experimentation on the real system nor mathematical modeling. Instead, it involves experimenting with an alternative to the real system. If we either can't or don't want to shoot arrows at a target, we can faithfully mimic the process in a number of different ways. This requires that we come up with a scheme to interpret a random event of one kind or another as corresponding either to a hit or a miss in the simulated shooting of an arrow at the target. We could flip a fair coin, for example, interpreting "heads" as a hit and "tails" as a miss. Flipping the coin repeatedly and noting results appropriately, we could then simulate many times the process of shooting 10 arrows at a target. As when experimenting on the real system, the fraction of the experiments resulting in an even number of hits can then be used as an *estimate* for the answer to the question originally posed.

In the simulation approach, we *replace* the shooting of an arrow at a target with the flipping of a coin. Flipping a coin would be tedious, of course, and time consuming as well. In simulation, we're motivated as a result to *automate* the replacement device. This can perhaps best be done with computer-based simulation. But computers always behave predictably. How can the uncertain outcome of shooting an arrow at a target be incorporated into a computer simulation? Briefly, this can be done by the use of a computer-based scheme to produce "random numbers." For example, suppose we have a computer-based scheme for drawing a number *at random* from the set of all 16-digit decimal numbers uniformly distributed on the open interval ranging from 0.0 to 1.0. (An open interval is one that excludes its end points.) To simulate the shooting of an arrow at a target, a computer could draw a number at random from this 0–1 interval. If the number is 0.5 or less, this can be interpreted to mean the arrow hit the target; otherwise, the interpretation would be that the arrow missed the target. From here, it's an easy step for those who know how to program computers to write a program that simulates many times the process of shooting a set of 10 arrows at a target. Then, as when experimenting on the real system, the fraction of the experiments that results in an even number of hits can be used to provide an *estimate* for the answer to the question originally posed. Note that computer-based simulation would proceed much more quickly than either the coin-flipping simulation or the actual shooting of arrows at a target.

This simple example of shooting arrows at a target illustrates the nature of the differences between experimentation on the real system at the one extreme and mathematical modeling at the other extreme, with simulation occupying an intermediate position between these two extremes. Problems of real interest are more complex and serious than shooting arrows at a target, of course. These problems often *do not have* mathematical solutions, and usually involve a system that *does not exist* or cannot be used for experimentation, so that simulation might be the only feasible approach for dealing with such problems.

1.6 The Advantages and Disadvantages of Simulation

We comment briefly in this section on the advantages and disadvantages of real-system experimentation and mathematical modeling, then cite the relative advantages and disadvantages of simulation in more detail.

As indicated in Figure 1.1, realism is achieved by experimenting with the real system, which is the major advantage of this approach. The approach has numerous disadvantages, however. Among these are the fact that the real system must exist before experiments can be performed on it, whereas the objective might be to design a system that does not yet exist. If the system does exist and is in use, then for economic and/or political reasons it might not be feasible to interrupt its ongoing use for the purpose of experimentation. For example, if a manufacturing system is being used to build products, then it might be cost prohibitive to interrupt the production process to investigate the effects of making one or more proposed changes in the system. Even if the real system can be used for experimentation, large amounts of time are usually needed to carry out the experimentation. If an existing system must operate for days or weeks while it is being observed experimentally after a change has been applied to it, then perhaps only one or two alternatives can be investigated at most, and even then the results of the experimentation might not be available in timely fashion.

In addition, real-system experimentation does not produce *exact* answers to questions, but only *estimated* answers, as illustrated in the bows-and-arrows example of the preceding section.

Furthermore, there is no generality in the results observed by experimenting with a real system. The results apply only to the system in the state in which the experimentation was performed. (In the example of the preceding section, for example, what if the probability of an arrow hitting the target is changed from 0.5 to 0.2? Then the experimentation must be repeated under the changed conditions, because the results for the 0.5 case cannot be extended or generalized to the 0.2 case.) No explicit cause-and-effect relationships are derived from the experimentation, and it is difficult or impossible to generalize the findings. Nevertheless, some systems are so inherently complex that direct experimentation with them often must be resorted to, at least eventually. For example, to determine the effectiveness of a proposed new anticancer drug in a human biological system, direct experimental use of the drug on people might be necessary eventually.

Now let's consider the pros and cons of mathematical modeling. As indicated in Figure 1.1, mathematical modeling involves a high degree of abstraction. Mathematical models of systems result from abstracting properties of the systems and using equations to express quantitative and logical relationships among the elements of which systems are composed. Mathematical modeling falls into such Table 1.2 categories as linear programming, probability, stochastic processes, queuing, and inventory control. Such modeling benefits from the generality, elegance, and power of mathematics. The major advantage of mathematical models is that, subject to their underlying assumptions, they express in the form of equations the exact way in which the values of dependent variables of interest vary with alternative values of decision variables. This is evident in the equation in the preceding section, for example. If the probability of a hit is changed from 0.5 to 0.2, it's only necessary to substitute accordingly into that equation to compute the exact answer to the question about the probability of an even number of hits.

Mathematical models can also often be used to determine whether an optimal solution to a problem exists and, if so, whether the optimal solution is unique. In the arrows-and-target situation, for example, suppose it is asked what value of p (the probability that a shot hits the target) maximizes the value of P (the probability that an even number of hits occurs). In the mathematical approach, the equation relating P to p can be used to answer this question exactly. By way of contrast, consider how time consuming, inconvenient, and tedious it would be to use experimentation on the real system to develop an approximate answer to this question.

The major disadvantage of mathematical models and the mathematical methods on which they are based is that one or more important characteristics of a situation may have to be distorted or ignored if a model amenable to mathematical solution is to be developed. To the extent that the assumptions made in building a mathematical model fail to fit the conditions of the problem, the resulting model may not produce a solution to the original problem. In this regard, there is a saying that "The right solution to the wrong problem is the wrong solution." This disadvantage goes a long way toward explaining why simulation is so frequently used as an alternative to mathematical modeling.

Another potential disadvantage of mathematical modeling is that it can require a relatively high level of mathematical sophistication on the part of the problem solver. Even if a mathematical model exists for a given problem, the problem solver might be unaware of its existence, or might not understand the details of the model to the extent required to apply the model correctly to the situation at hand. And even if a valid mathematical model can be developed for the problem, such development might be beyond the capabilities of the person or group responsible for coming to grips with the problem.

Now consider simulation, which we regard here as "an experiment in which we attempt to understand how something will behave in reality by imitating its behavior in an artificial environment that approximates reality as closely as possible" (Shogan, 1988, p. 749). Positioned in Figure 1.1 between the two extremes of real-system experimentation and mathematical modeling, simulation has some of the advantages and disadvantages of the two extremes. Here are some of the advantages of simulation.

1. **Realism.** Simulation models can be realistic, in the sense of capturing the actual characteristics of the system being modeled. Because simulations of the type we deal with in this book are not equation based, such things as linearity, differentiability, time dependencies, and so on, are not the issues they can be in the realm of mathematical modeling, where it might be necessary to make unrealistic simplifying assumptions to support mathematical manipulation. The number of complex systems subject to realistic, simulation-based experimentation is much greater than the number subject to realistic mathematical modeling.

2. **Nonexistent systems.** The systems whose behavior is to be investigated need not actually exist to be subject to simulation-based experimentation. They only need to exist in the mind of the designer.

3. **Time compression.** Time can be compressed in simulation models. The equivalent of days, weeks, and months of real-system operation often can be simulated in only seconds, minutes, or hours on a computer. This means that, relative to real-system experimentation, a large number of simulated alternatives can be investigated, and results can be made available soon enough to influence the choice of a design for a system.

4. **Deferred specification of objectives.** Some types of mathematical modeling (e.g., linear and other types of mathematical programming) involve specifying an objective at the outset of the modeling activity and formulating this objective in mathematical terms. (For example, in a manufacturing system, the objective might be to maximize profit subject to a set of machine, manpower, and marketing constraints.) Subsequent development of the model is conditioned on this objective. No such initial formulation of an objective is required in simulation. This makes it possible for the modeler and client to keep their options open and search for a system design that eventually proves to be satisfactory in a multicriterion decision environment. (But see disadvantage 3, which appears later on.) This deferred specification of an objective or objectives can also be an advantage in circumstances when those for whom the modeling is being done cannot agree initially on the objective(s) or when the relative importance of various objectives isn't clear or is subject to continuing debate. For example, is it more important to maximize profits during the next 12 months or to avoid major disruptions in the work force that could result if some workers were laid off for the next 12 months?

5. **Experimental control.** In simulation, every variable can be held constant except the ones whose influence is being studied. As a result, the possible effect of uncontrolled variables on system behavior need not be taken into account, as often must be done when experiments are performed on a real system.

6. **Reproducibility of random conditions.** In simulations of systems composed of elements that exhibit random but statistically predictable behavior, it is possible to reproduce random events identically via sequences of pseudorandom numbers that, although perfectly predictable because of the pseudorandomness, can otherwise exhibit the characteristics of truly random numbers. This makes it possible to use variance reduction techniques to improve the precision with which system characteristics can be estimated for a given amount of simulation effort and to sharpen the contrast between alternative (competing) system designs. (The nature of pseudorandom numbers is taken up in Chapters 13 and 14. Selected variance-reduction techniques are explored in Chapters 15 and 16.)

7. **Training.** Simulation does not require as great a level of mathematical sophistication as does mathematical modeling. This makes it easier to train simulation practitioners than to train mathematical modelers. (But see Section 1.8 of this chapter in this regard.)

8. **Winning over the client.** Because the concept of simulation is fairly easily and almost intuitively understood, clients are likely to be more receptive to the use of simulation than to the use of mathematical modeling. As a result, clients are more likely to be inclined to implement simulation-based recommendations than those resulting from the use of models based on mathematics that they may not understand and whose results they may not trust.

9. **Inexpensive insurance.** It has been estimated that comprehensive simulation studies designed to estimate the characteristics of a proposed system can cost 2 percent or less of the capital outlay involved in building the system (Henriksen, 1983). For example, it might cost $250,000 or less for simulation studies designed to evaluate a manufacturing system involving a capital outlay of $12,500,000. In this sense, simulation provides inexpensive insurance against building systems that are underdesigned and so will not perform to specifications, or that are overdesigned and so expensively provide more capacity than needed.

Along with its many advantages, simulation is subject to important disadvantages. Among them are these:

1. **Failure to produce exact results.** Suppose a system is composed of one or more elements that are subject to random behavior. In a hospital system, for example, the time required for a doctor to examine a patient may vary at random. The various times required by a doctor to examine patients influence the waiting-time experiences of others waiting to be examined by the doctor. When a simulation is performed with a model of the system, the values of such variables as "the time a patient spends waiting to see the doctor" are recorded by the model, and the averages of these values are given in a postsimulation report. But the *average* in a sample of observed waiting times only provides an *estimate* of the *expected* (or long-run average) time that patients must spend waiting to see a doctor. In this sense, a simulation only provides estimates, not exact results.

2. **Lack of generality of results.** Simulation results apply only to the situation that was simulated and do not lend themselves to generalization. For example, suppose it is assumed in a manufacturing system that the manufacturing resources include three machines of Type A, five machines of Type B, and two machines of Type C. Suppose that a simulation study is performed on this basis, and the resulting manufacturing rate is estimated. What manufacturing rate will result if there is one less Type B machine or if one of the Type B machines is replaced with another Type C machine? The results from the simulation study already performed cannot be used to answer these questions. Instead, the model has to be modified to correspond to these changed conditions, and then simulation studies must be performed with the modified models to estimate the resulting manufacturing rates.

   By way of contrast, suppose a mathematical model has been built to express in the form of an equation or equations the manufacturing rate as a function of the number of Type A, B, and C machines. This model could be evaluated quickly and easily for all combinations of Type A, B, and C machines that might be of interest.

   Regression techniques can be used to fit a regression equation to the results produced by simulation studies performed for a series of alternative system conditions (such as the number of machines of various types in the preceding example). Used for interpolation (but not for extrapolation), the resulting equation can then be evaluated to estimate the results corresponding to system conditions for which simulations were not performed. A limited degree of generalization may be achieved in simulation modeling in this way, but not generalization of the type that results when cause-and-effect relationships are used in mathematical modeling.

3. **Failure to optimize.** Simulation is used to answer questions of the "what if" type, but not of the "what's best" type. In this sense, simulation is not an optimization technique. Consider the type of manufacturing system question posed earlier: "What combination of products should we produce if the objective is to maximize profit subject to the following machine, manpower, and marketing constraints?" Simulation can be

used to estimate the profit that will result when a given combination of products is produced. This involves a "what if" situation. In other words, "What if we produce this combination of products? What profit will result?" But simulation cannot be used to indicate which combination of products among *all feasible combinations* results in the *maximum* profit. This would involve a "what's best" situation. In other words, "What combination of products is best in the sense of maximizing profit?" In simulation, the only alternatives considered are those that are directly investigated. Simulation does not *generate* solutions; it only *evaluates* those that have been proposed. If six alternative combinations of products are investigated, then that alternative *among the six considered* that maximizes profit can be identified, but it is quite possible that one or more of the alternatives *not* considered result in larger profits than the best of the six that *are* considered.

4. **Long lead times.** A simulation study cannot be conducted over a weekend. *Months* of effort can be required to gather data; build, verify, and validate models; design experiments, and evaluate and interpret the results. (See Section 1.7 for an outline of the steps involved in a simulation study.) A simulation effort should be started well before the results are needed. In practice, unfortunately, the results of simulation are usually needed "yesterday." A simulation study may not be authorized until the project involving the system to be simulated becomes of urgent priority, and then there may not be adequate time to complete the study before the results are needed.

5. **Costs for providing a simulation capability.** Establishing and maintaining a simulation capability involves making a major and ongoing commitment with concomitant personnel, software, hardware, training, and other support costs. Many smaller organizations cannot afford to maintain a simulation capability. Some organizations may have one or two people who work on simulation projects from time to time. Such people may have to be supplemented by outside consultants on occasions when simulation projects are to be conducted. Other organizations may simply contract out their occasional simulation projects to consultants or firms specializing in simulation. They will then pay a premium to have a simulation study conducted and may wind up in a position of dependency and relative inflexibility if follow-on simulation efforts are required.

6. **Misuse of simulation.** There are many facets to a balanced, comprehensive simulation study. (See Section 1.7 for particulars.) As a result, a person should be educated in a variety of areas (e.g., analysis of input, design of experiment, analysis of output) before becoming a simulation practitioner. This fact is sometimes ignored, however, resulting in situations in which people who only know how to build simulation models and make runs with them are cast in the role of simulation professionals, even though their education and training may not have prepared them adequately for this designation or for these responsibilities. Such people may not be in a position to conduct balanced and comprehensive simulation studies. As a result, such studies may be incorrectly performed, or may be incomplete, or may fall short in other ways, perhaps resulting in failure of the simulation effort.

In conclusion, simulation is not a panacea. It offers powerful advantages, but suffers from major disadvantages as well. Fortunately, most of the disadvantages are diminishing in importance with time, thanks to improved simulation tools, methodology, education and computer performance, and decreasing computing costs. As we've seen, simulation ranks extremely well even now among the alternatives. And its relative merits should continue to improve over time.

1.7 Steps in a Simulation Study

The steps involved in a simulation study are outlined and discussed in this section. The objectives are to provide a broad-based perspective on the overall elements in a simulation study and to supply a framework that can be used to describe the goals of this book.

There are a number of ways to categorize the steps involved in a simulation study. We report and discuss the steps outlined by Law (1986). These steps are shown in flowchart form in Figure 1.2, where the boxes have been numbered for ease of reference. The discussion provided here is qualitative. References are occasionally made to later chapters in the book where there is discussion of operational details associated with some of the steps in Figure 1.2.

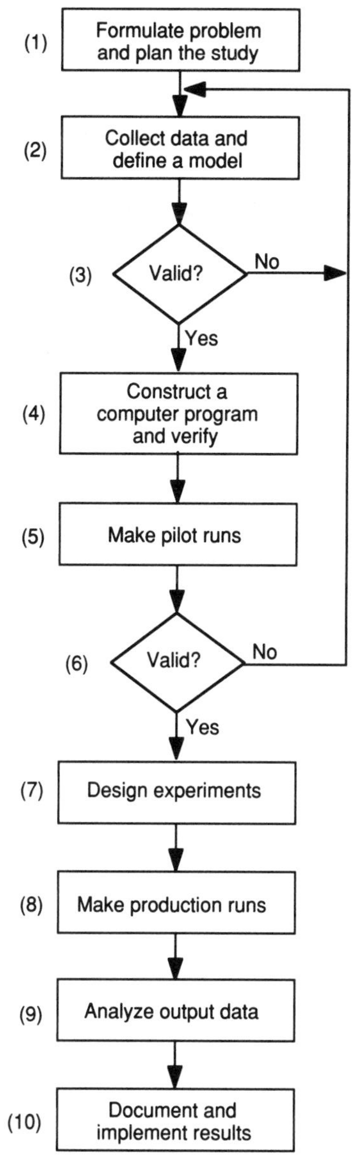

Figure 1.2 *The Steps in a Simulation Study*
Source: Law (1986)

1. **Formulate the problem and plan the study.** In this step, the simulation professional (modeler) and the client (decision maker) come together to discuss details of the situation or system that is the basis for the simulation study. (The client is the party or group on whose behalf the study is to be performed.) The modeler must become familiar in intimate detail with the characteristics and purpose of the system that is to be modeled, with any and all alternatives that are to be considered, and with the objectives of the simulation study as seen through the eyes of the client. The criteria for comparing alternative (competing) system designs must be determined, and the cost and time required to conduct each aspect of the study should be estimated and agreed upon. As a by-product of formulating the problem and planning the study, the modeler may have to educate the client with respect to those things that can be accomplished in simulation modeling and the information, data, support, and time required in this regard.

   Formulating the problem and planning the study will very likely require that the modeler and client get together on a number of occasions. Furthermore, the insights of both the modeler and the client will be sharpened as the work proceeds, and details of the study will have to be altered in all likelihood as a result. An objective of the modeler should be to keep the client well informed and appropriately involved on a continuous basis as the project proceeds. The probability that a simulation project (or any technical project, for that matter) will be successful will be increased significantly if time and attention are invested in the project by the client.

2. **Collect data and define a model.** Collection of the data needed to drive a model can begin at this stage of the study. In the context of a manufacturing system, for example, data can involve such things as machining times, tool change-over times, the running time of a freshly repaired machine until its next failure, and the time required to repair a failed machine. These data may be observable in an existing system, or they may have to be estimated if there is not yet an existing system that can be observed. If a model of an existing system is being built, then it is important to obtain data on its operation and performance for later use in validating the model. (See step 6 following.) More details regarding data estimation and the incorporation of data into GPSS/H models are provided in Chapter 13.

   Defining a model involves determining which aspects of the system to represent in the model, and at which levels of detail, versus system aspects that it is judged do not have to be included in the model. (Note that a conceptual model is involved at this point, not a computer model. See step 4 following.) For example, suppose that a system operates eight hours a day, from 8 A.M. until noon and from 1 P.M. until 5 P.M., five days a week. Is it important to model noon hours, midmorning and midafternoon breaks, and shift start-up and shutdown, or is it adequate, as a first approximation, to view a 40-hour workweek as consisting of 40 consecutive hours of uninterrupted operation? Should worker absenteeism be modeled, or is it sufficient to assume that employees always show up for work? Should machine breakdowns be modeled, or can it be assumed that machines never break down? If machine breakdowns are included, can it be assumed that it always takes a fixed amount of time, such as 16 hours, to repair a machine, or should variations in repairtime be reflected in the model? Answers to such questions as this will depend both on the objectives of the simulation study and on the experience and judgment of the model builder. In this sense, simulation is as much an art as a science.

3. **Valid?** A model is said to be valid if, for purposes of supporting the decision making at hand, it is a suitable representation of the system being modeled. If the production rate achieved in a manufacturing system is adversely affected during shift start-up and shutdown, for example, and if the objective of a simulation study is to estimate the production rate, then a model that fails to include shift start-up and shutdown considerations may not be valid for the purpose at hand. Similarly, if there are eight machines of a given type in a system and these are out of service about 25 percent of the time because of breakdowns, then a model that does not represent the individual breakdowns and their timings, but simply assumes there are just six machines of this type and that they never break down, will almost certainly be invalid for use in estimating the production rate.

   Model validation involves, among other things, the level and type of detail to be included in a model. We limit ourselves here to describing the meaning of validation, without trying to indicate how the validation process can be accomplished. In any event, the model validation done at step 3 is only preliminary. If this preliminary validation suggests that the conceptual model specified at step 2 is not suitable for decision making, given the objectives of the study, then the model must be respecified, as indicated by the return line from step 3 to step 2 in Figure 1.2.

   Several additional comments on model validation are provided later, in step 6.

4. **Construct a computer model and verify it.** In this step, the conceptual model specified in step 2 and accepted as valid on a preliminary basis in step 3 is put into computerized form. A specific modeling language such as GPSS/H is chosen for this purpose. The resulting computer model must be verified. That is, steps must be taken to determine whether the conceptual model specified at step 2 has been faithfully and accurately reflected in computerized form, or whether the modeler has made one or more logical errors in the building of the computer model.

   We are not simply talking here about working with the model until error messages no longer result when computer-based execution of the model is attempted. Low-level errors of this type must be eliminated before model verification can even begin. By model verification, we refer to the much higher-level issue of whether the computer model accurately captures the logic that it is our intention to capture in the model. For example, suppose that if a machine fails in a manufacturing system, work waiting for the machine is to be rerouted to other machines as a result. In the computerized model of the system, is this rerouting handled correctly? Or has the model been misbuilt, so that waiting work is not rerouted, but simply waits where it is until the failed machine has been repaired? Establishing that the model performs correctly in this regard reflects the spirit of model verification.

   It is interesting to note that synthetic data can be used for model verification. This is because verification focuses on the *logic* of the computerized model, not on the data used to drive the model. A practical consequence of this is that verification can precede or proceed in parallel with data collection. In fact, the model itself dictates the data that are needed to drive the model. This means that if timing is not a problem, it could be beneficial to delay data collection until the model has been built, and it has been determined exactly what data are needed to support operation of the model. In this regard, see Chapter 13 and the comments on data sensitivity analysis under step 5.

   Thanks to its interactive monitoring capability, the GPSS/H modeling language provides a powerful set of tools that can be used to support model verification. This interactive monitoring capability is given full treatment in this book, beginning in Chapter 2. Model verification can also be supported, at least in part, by animation of GPSS/H models. (Simulation animation uses computer graphics to produce screen-based displays of the movement of entities through a simulated system. See Section 27 of Chapter 17 for further comments.)

In concluding these step 4 comments, note that a careful distinction must be made between the terms *validation* and *verification*. The terms have different meanings, and they should not be used interchangeably. The distinction between the terms can be expressed in the following play on words. In validation we attempt to answer the question, "Are we building the **right model**?" (Are we formulating the correct *conceptual* model?) In verification we attempt to answer the question, "Are we building the **model right**?" (Are we correctly *computerizing* the conceptual model?) Note that it is possible to computerize an invalid conceptual model correctly(!), just as it is possible to computerize a valid conceptual model incorrectly(!).

5. **Make pilot runs.** As the name suggests, pilot runs are preliminary simulations performed with a model after it has been verified. Pilot runs have a number of purposes. First, they increase the modeler's experience in use of the simulation model and begin to set the modeler's expectations with respect to model output, both in qualitative and quantitative terms. Second, they provide results that can be used to plan various aspects of the later production runs. (See step 8. Also see Chapter 15.) Third, they provide results that can be used to help validate a model of an existing system. (See step 6.)

   Pilot runs can also be used to do sensitivity analysis with respect to the data that drive a model. Simulations corresponding to alternative assumed forms of the data can be carried out, and the resulting changes in the model's behavior can be observed. For cases in which model behavior is fairly insensitive to the form of the data, then the time, effort, and expense needed to collect highly accurate data can be reduced.

6. **Valid?** If the model has been built for an existing system, and if data and performance measures have been collected for this system, then the validity issue can be assessed by comparing the model's performance (as observed in the step 5 pilot runs) with the performance of the real system. (Simulating an *existing* system is often a prelude to simulating the effect of proposed changes in the existing system.) Is the model's behavior consistent with the known behavior of the system being modeled? If not, then the conceptual model must be respecified, as indicated by the return line from step 6 to step 2 in Figure 1.2.

7. **Design experiments.** In this step, the plan for experimental use of the simulation model is formulated. For how many alternatives are simulations to be performed? Under what conditions should each run be performed, and what should be the duration of a run? What degree of precision is required in the measures of system performance? How many simulation runs must be performed for each alternative to achieve this degree of precision? It is questions of this type that are asked and answered in planning the experimentation that is to be carried out with the simulation model. (See Chapters 14 through 17 for more details.)

8. **Make production runs.** This step involves making the simulation runs called for in the step 7 design of experiments.

   Whereas computer work up to this point might have been done most conveniently on a microcomputer or workstation, the production runs themselves might be carried out on a mainframe computer, to take advantages of its speed and large memory. In this regard, it is advantageous if the modeling language used to computerize the model runs on a variety of hardware platforms, so that models can be uploaded and downloaded with ease, and without the need for modification. (This is the case with GPSS/H, which exists in consistent, coherent implementations on machines ranging from microcomputers through engineering and scientific workstations to mainframes.)

9. **Analyze output data.** In this step, results of the step 8 production runs are analyzed statistically to estimate the values of system performance measures and to rank alternative (competing) system designs in terms of their relative goodness. (See Chapters 14, 15, and 16 for further details.)

10. **Document and implement results.** Documentation of the simulation study involves preparing a written report that describes all important aspects of the study, including objectives, assump-

tions made in forming the conceptual model, aspects of data collection, the transformation of the conceptual model into computerized form, steps taken to verify and validate the model, listings of the computerized model (complete with internal documentation in the form of explanatory comments carried on the statements making up the model), a machine-readable copy of the model, sample output, conclusions of the study, personnel involved in the project, and pertinent dates.

Preparation of such documentation, although perhaps tedious, has the benefit of further clarifying the insights and thinking of the modeler. Furthermore, it provides a clear trail that can be followed later (perhaps one or two or more years later) when another modeler is given the assignment to use the resulting model as the starting point in a follow-on simulation study. In the absence of documentation, the modeler who inherits someone else's model may throw up his or her hands in despair and start from scratch, resulting in an *enormous* waste of time, energy, and money.

Figure 1.2 implies that documentation is the last step in a simulation study. But this should not be the case. Documentation should be anticipated and prepared as the study proceeds, and should not be deferred until the end of the study, for then there is a good chance that it will not be done at all. For example, intramodel comments should be provided at the time a model is computerized, and should not simply be provided after the fact, almost as an afterthought. Preparation of these comments helps to clarify a modeler's thinking on the spot and as a result can reveal logical flaws in the model even as it is being developed. Furthermore, such comments will be of use to the modeler himself or herself as the computerization and use of a large model extends over weeks and weeks of time.

Another reason for documenting "as you go" is that a simulation study may involve multiple modelers and may extend over a long period of time. One modeler's documentation contributes immediately to other modelers' understanding as multiple modelers work in parallel on a study. Furthermore, one or more modelers originally assigned to a study may be reassigned to other activities before the study has been completed, and other modelers may be assigned to the work group to take their place. Such newcomers to a project can become effective work group members much more rapidly if the study is documented on an as-you-go basis. Documentation of this type is perhaps best accomplished in a work group setting by using an information system based on hypertext. Larger organizations might even standardize and facilitate documentation of simulation studies by providing ready-made documentation prototypes in a hypertext system.

Finally, it should be noted that documentation is time consuming and therefore expensive. (The cost of *not* documenting is even more expensive, however.) Documentation time should be included in step 1, when the time and cost of carrying out a simulation study is being estimated.

Implementing the results of a simulation study involves putting the conclusions into practice. This can take the form of building a new system, or of applying changes to an existing system. It's also possible that a simulation study will conclude that a proposed new system is not economically attractive or that for economic reasons it is more favorable to leave an existing system as is than to apply changes to it.

The steps in Figure 1.2 may seem to imply that simulation models (and the simulation studies of which they are a part) have fully served their purpose after step 10 has been accomplished. But this is not necessarily the case. Beyond step 10, a simulation model might be of assistance in operating a system on a postimplementation basis and can be of later use in studying the effect of proposed changes in the system. (The demands placed on a system will eventually change, leading to proposals to modify the system accordingly.) In fact, it is valid to talk about the life cycle of simulation models. For useful insights in this regard, see Musselman and Martin (1984).

1.8 The Skills and Work Environment of a Simulation Professional

Figure 1.2 makes it clear that the practice of simulation requires multifaceted skills on the part of a simulation professional, and is not limited to the simple process of building, checking out, and making a few runs with a computer model. In fact, building, checking out, and making runs with a computer model constitute perhaps only about 35-45% of what's involved in a complete simulation study. Skills in interacting and communicating with the client, collecting and analyzing data, defining and validating a conceptual model, computerizing, verifying, and further validating the model, animating the model, designing experiments, analyzing output, and documenting the results are all required of the simulation professional.

The point made in the preceding paragraph is reinforced in the following quote from Shannon et al. (1985).

> Today, in order to use simulation correctly and intelligently, the practitioner is required to have expertise in a number of different fields. This generally means separate courses in probability, statistics, design of experiments, modeling, computer programming, and a simulation language. This translates to about 720 hours of formal classroom instruction, plus another 1440 hours of outside study (more than one year of effort), and that is only to gain the basic tools. In order to really become proficient, the practitioner must then go out and gain real world, practical experience (hopefully under the tutelage of an expert).

Shannon et al. go on to speculate on the development of expert systems in support of simulation professionals, systems designed to lessen the burden involved in the practice of simulation.

As to the working conditions under which a simulation professional operates, Henriksen (1983) makes the point that "the availability of good software tools is vitally important to practitioners of simulation" and concludes that "there is great cause for optimism: it appears likely that simulation practitioners of the future will work in an *environment* composed of well-integrated software tools. The integrated software environment of the 1990s will make present state-of-the-art simulation software tools look as primitive as the building of simulation models entirely in high-level languages like Fortran looks today." Henriksen envisions a simulator's workbench whose proposed architecture includes a model editor, input preparation subsystem, facilities for statistics collection, experimental design, and output definition, a program editor, a compiler, a run-time support system, and a knowledge base.

Both the skills required of simulation professionals and the environment within which such professionals would ideally practice their trade are formidable. It's quite possible to talk about majoring or minoring in simulation at the master's or Ph.D. level, as part of a formal program of study. A reasonable *introduction* to simulation can be gained in a three-credit course or, better yet, in a sequence of two three-credit courses, but a person cannot reach a level of expertise in simulation simply by taking one or two university-level or professional development courses in the subject.

1.9 About the GPSS/H Modeling Language and Its Applications

The choice of a modeling language for use in step 4 of Figure 1.2 is vitally important. Such a language is used to put the conceptual model developed and validated in steps 2 and 3 into a computerized form that will then be verified, validated, and provide the basis for experimentation. There is no one modeling language that works equally well for all proposed simulation studies. Just as there are many diverse applications of simulation, so too is there a variety of alternative modeling languages that can be adopted to model these situations. Certain modeling languages apply especially well to certain types of situations, but not to others. And so, even though modeling languages are often based on common principles, it's not true that mastering a single language puts a person into a position to apply simulation to all situations of practical interest.

The modeling language we study in this book, GPSS/H, is an *outstanding* choice of language for modeling systems composed of *units of traffic that compete with each other for the use of scarce resources.* Numerous types of systems fit this description. Included are manufacturing systems, health care systems, transportation systems, communication networks, defense systems, civil systems, and queuing (waiting-line) systems in general.

For our purposes, a *system* is a collection of interrelated elements that work together to achieve a stated objective. A manufacturing system, for example, consists of people, machines, materials, spaces, procedures, information, and data that interact with the objective of building quality products in timely fashion and at acceptable rates. Similarly, a health care system consists of elements that can be described with such words as people, machines, materials, spaces, procedures, information, and data, where the objective is to maintain and/or restore the health of individuals at acceptable cost levels. The system being simulated may only be in the design stage, or it may already exist. (As pointed out earlier, simulating an *existing* system is often a prelude to simulating the effect of proposed changes in the existing system.)

In a manufacturing system, *units of traffic* might be units of work-in-process, and the scarce (limited) resources for which units of work-in-process compete include people, machines, space in the waiting areas at machines, and the equipment used to transport work-in-process from point to point in the system.

In a health care system, units of traffic might be people who have come to use the services provided by the system, and the resources for which these people (patients) compete are such things as space in the parking structure, wheelchairs, check-in clerks, nurses, doctors, examination rooms, X-ray machines, operating rooms, beds in intensive care units, and beds in general wards.

In a transportation system, units of traffic might be ships carrying cargo, and the resources for which these ships compete when they arrive at a harbor to unload their cargo are space in the harbor within which to wait for an unloading berth, unloading berths themselves, tugboats to use to get pulled into berth, personnel and unloading equipment at berthside, and tugboats to use to get pulled out of berth after the unloading has been completed.

GPSS/H is used for *discrete-event* simulation. A discrete-event simulation is one in which the state of a model (or of the system being modeled) changes at only a discrete, but possibly random, set of time points, known as event times. For example, an order arrives at an order-filling system. The arrival of the order is an event. It occurs at a point in time. Or, a doctor begins to examine a patient in a hospital's emergency room. The act of beginning the examination is an event. It occurs at a point in time. Later, the doctor finishes the examination. The act of bringing the examination to an end is an event, occurring at a point in time.[1]

[1]Discrete-event simulations contrast with *continuous* simulations. In a continuous simulation, one or more aspects of the state of a model change continuously over time. For example, suppose that a tanker pulls into a berth at an oil refinery and begins to pump crude oil into a tank on shore. The level of crude oil in the tank rises continuously while the pumping proceeds. The ongoing change in oil level can be modeled in continuous terms. (This would typically involve including a rate equation explicitly in the model.) Alternatively, the change in level could be interpreted as a series of discrete changes, each of finite size (and with no need to include a rate equation in the model). Because of the possibility of discretizing continuous processes, discrete-event simulation often can be used to model continuous systems successfully. The use of discrete approximations to model continuous systems is not taken up in this book, however.

As indicated earlier, and as we will see beginning in Chapter 2, GPSS/H models express the rules that govern the operation of a system and do not involve formulating and then solving sets of equations.

A GPSS/H model takes the form of a series of statements (or, initially and on paper, diagrams representative of these statements). The results of simulating with such a model are provided as information describing the current state of the model as it operates over time, and/or detailing the time-ordered set of states through which the model has moved in reaching its present state, and/or summarizing the model's performance in aggregate terms at the end of a simulation.

GPSS/H models do not automatically provide pictorial representations of the situation being modeled. Through the use of computer graphics and animation, however, GPSS/H models can be supplemented to extract such representations from them and provide visual insights both for the modelers of the system and the modelers' clients, and to serve as a communication medium between the modelers and the clients. (See Section 27 of Chapter 17 for comments on animation and "Proof," which is software that can be used to provide high-quality animation for models written in GPSS/H and other languages.)

Elements in a GPSS/H model can exhibit random, but statististically predictable, behavior. For example, a machine's "running time until its next failure" may be statistically predictable in the sense that it is uniformly distributed between 120 and 200 hours. After the *real* machine is put into operation, however, its "running time until its next failure" on this particular occasion won't be known until the machine actually breaks down. (As we will see, a machine's running time until its next failure is determined *in a simulation* by drawing a sample at random from the population of running times until failure.) Or the time required for a doctor to examine a patient may be statistically predictable in the sense that it is normally distributed with a mean of 15 minutes and a standard deviation of 3 minutes.

What is the background of GPSS/H? GPSS/H implements the world view (stylized way of visualizing a problem) originally implemented in the "GPSS" released by IBM (International Business Machines) in October 1961. That world view has proven to be so powerful and practical over the years that "GPSS" was chosen as 1 of 13 languages whose historical foundations have been recorded by ACM's SIGPLAN (the Association of Computing Machinery's Special Interest Group for Programming LANguages) in a book entitled *History of*

Table 1.3

Selected GPSS/H Hardware Platforms and Execution Speeds

Manufacturer	Model	Average Blocks per CPU Second	Technical Comments (e.g., Clock Rates, Chips)
Amdahl	5860	240,000	
Apollo	DN3500	6,600	16-MHz 68020 with 68881; SR10.1
Digital	MicroVAX II	4,760	VMS
	VAX 8600	28,800	VMS
Hewlett-Packard	9000/350	11,700	25-MHz 68020 with 25-MHz 68881
IBM	PC AT	980	Release 2.0 for DOS; 6-MHz 68881
	PS/2 Model 80	3,890	Release 2.0 for DOS; 16 MHz 80386 with 80387
	4381/13	71,000	
	3090-150	160,000	
	3090-200	330,000	
Silicon Graphics	IRIS 3xxx	8,800	16-MHz 68020 with FP hardware
	IRIS 4D/220	60,000	25-MHz R3000/R3010
Sun Microsystems	Sun-3	10,400	25-MHz 68020 with 20-MHz 68881
	Sun-4/110	14,000	SPARC

Programming Languages (Gordon, 1978). "GPSS" has been implemented and improved many times by many different parties over its 30-year history, and its powerful world view has been incorporated into a number of languages with names other than "GPSS" (Schriber, 1989). GPSS/H, first released by Wolverine Software Corporation in 1977 and enhanced substantially since then, is the state-of-the-art implementation of "GPSS" that runs on hardware ranging from DOS-based microcomputers through engineering and scientific workstations to mainframes.

Table 1.3 lists some of the various hardware platforms on which GPSS/H runs and shows the rates at which GPSS/H models execute under various circumstances, with the rates expressed in "Block executions per CPU second." (The concept of Block executions will be explained in Chapter 2.) The rates, which are specific to the particular model used to do this benckmarking, vary between about 1000 Block executions per CPU second on a PC AT to 330,000 Block executions per CPU second on an IBM 3090–200. Not shown is the fact that GPSS/H executes over 400,000 Blocks per CPU second on The University of Michigan's IBM 3090–600E mainframe! (A current and complete version of Table 1.3 can be obtained from Wolverine Software Corporation, 4115 Annandale Road, Annandale VA 22003–2500.)

One of the hallmarks of GPSS/H is that the numeric results it produces, although generally resulting from probabilistic modeling and so subject to "randomness," as explained in detail beginning in Chapter 2, are independent of the hardware platform on which GPSS/H is run (subject only to limitations in the precision of the hardware). This is a result of careful attention paid to hardware and other considerations in implementation of the GPSS/H random number generators as written in assembly language for IBM-compatible mainframes, and in C for other hardware platforms. (See Chapter 14 for discussion of the GPSS/H random number generators.) This consistency smooths the way for building and checking out GPSS/H models on desktop computers (steps 4 and 5, Figure 1.2) and, then uploading the models to a mainframe to take advantage of the mainframe's speed when making production runs (step 8, Figure 1.2).

The statements made in this section have often been quite general and are included only to provide a broad perspective on GPSS/H itself and the types of situations to which it applies. As indicated from time to time in this section, supporting details will be given at appropriate points throughout the book, beginning in Chapter 2.

1.10 The Scope of This Book

It is beyond the scope of this book to present the operational details involved in all aspects of a simulation study, but a healthy sampling is provided. Apart from the general overview of simulation given in this chapter, the book has the general objective of introducing fundamental operational details that apply when GPSS/H is used to build simulation models, perform interactive simulations with them to investigate their behavior, and describe and structure experiments to be performed with them in batch simulations whose results can be used to make inferences about model performance. More particularly, this general objective is achieved in the following way.

1. The highly successful world view incorporated by the GPSS/H modeling language is introduced and operationalized.
2. The GPSS/H capability of interactively monitoring an ongoing simulation is presented in fundamental terms. This deepens the understanding of the GPSS/H world view and facilitates the learning process by directly involving the student in the step-by-step details of ongoing simulations.
3. The underlying data structures and processing algorithms used by GPSS/H to support a simulation are explained. The effect is to take the mystery out of the process whereby the state of a model is methodically updated while simulated time goes by, and to put the modeler into the position of being able to build models that perform exactly as intended. Apart from enhancing the understanding of GPSS/H particulars, this material is also of interest in its own right in terms of the type of data structures and processing algorithms that can be applied in the context of a simulation modeling language.
4. Discussion of the GPSS/H interactive monitoring capability is extended to include more sophisticated use of this capability based on understanding the underlying data structures and processing algorithms that GPSS/H uses.
5. The incorporation of pseudorandom behavior into GPSS/H models is given due treatment. This is done by discussing the built-in sources of 0–1 uniform random numbers in GPSS/H; commenting on the exponential, normal, and triangular probability distributions and the built-in GPSS/H functions used to sample from these distributions; and explaining how user-defined GPSS/H functions can be specified to transform samples from 0–1 uniform sources into equivalent samples from empirical and/or theoretical distributions that may be of interest.
6. The method of replications is introduced as an experimental methodology that can be used in simulation to observe model behavior for the purpose of forming interval estimates for the expected values of simulation output variables of interest. Use of the method of replications in GPSS/H is illustrated. Confidence interval methodology for small and large sample sizes is reviewed to support this material.
7. The use of pilot simulations to estimate the variance of a point estimator is discussed, and the use of this estimated variance to determine (estimate) the sample size required to achieve a specified precision in an interval estimate of an expected value is reviewed. This material is supported by explaining how independent simulations can be specified in GPSS/H, so that an existing set of independent simulations can be supplemented with additional independent simulations.
8. The use of antithetic variates to achieve variance reduction in single-system studies is introduced, the way in which antithetic variates are specified in GPSS/H is explained, and the way this methodology is applied in GPSS/H experiments designed to reduce variance is illustrated.
9. The use of an uncorrelated paired-t comparison of two alternative (competing) system designs is discussed. GPSS/H-based design of experiments producing outputs that support this methodology is introduced and illustrated.
10. The use of common random numbers as a methodology for reducing the variance when comparing two alternative (competing) system designs is discussed. GPSS/H-based design of models and experiments producing outputs that support this methodology is introduced and illustrated.
11. The use of a sequential, two-stage methodology for selecting the probable best system from two or more competing alternatives is introduced,

discussed, and illustrated in the context of GPSS/H modeling.

In terms of the steps in a simulation study summarized in Figure 1.2, this book introduces and discusses fundamental material dealing with steps 4, 5, 7, 8, and 9.

Statistical material is not developed in this book, but is simply summarized and then its application in the setting of GPSS/H-based simulation is illustrated.

This book does not introduce all the GPSS/H modeling language, but only a subset. The subset is designed to be large enough to support the building of interesting models and to carry out meaningful statistical experiments with them. Furthermore, GPSS/H material is not introduced in black-box fashion. Instead, by discussing the data structures and processing algorithms on which GPSS/H is based, the foundation is carefully laid for the student to assimilate additional GPSS/H material available from other sources. A summary of GPSS/H capabilities not covered in this book and possibilities for further study of simulation using GPSS/H are provided in the last chapter (Chapter 17).

1.11 Activities

1. Textbooks on operations research and management science (or on quantitative methods in business) usually include a chapter on the topic of simulation as an operations research and management science technique. Such chapters, introductory in nature, often do a very nice job of providing a broad-based perspective on the nature of simulation, its characteristics, its advantages and disadvantages, its applications, various simulation methodologies, various modeling languages, and so on. Go to a library and read the simulation chapter in at least two textbooks of this type. There are dozens of such textbooks, so you should have a wide range of choices. (It is estimated that at least one new textbook on operations research and management science is written every year!) Because of rapid developments in the simulation area, you should choose books that have been published or updated fairly recently. Among these are the following:

ANDERSON, DAVID R., DENNIS J. SWEENEY, AND THOMAS A. WILLIAMS (1990). *Quantitative Methods for Business*, 4th ed. West, St. Paul, MN.

BUDNICK, FRANK S., DENNIS MCLEAVEY, AND RICHARD MOJENA (1988). *Principles of Operations Research for Management*. Richard D. Irwin, Homewood, IL.

COOK, THOMAS M. AND ROBERT A. RUSSELL (1990). *Introduction to Management Science*, 4th ed. Prentice Hall, Englewood Cliffs, NJ.

HILLIER, FREDERICK S., AND GERALD J. LIEBERMAN (1990). *Introduction to Operations Research*, 5th ed. McGraw-Hill, New York

KNOWLES, THOMAS W. (1989). *Management Science: Building and Using Models*. Richard D. Irwin, Homewood, IL.

LEE, SANG M., LAURENCE J. MOORE, AND BERNARD W. TAYLOR III (1990). *Management Science*, 3rd ed. Allyn & Bacon, Needham Heights, MA.

MARKLAND, ROBERT E. (1989). *Topics in Management Science*, 3rd ed. John Wiley, New York

RAVINDRAN, RAVI, DON T. PHILLIPS, AND JAMES J. SOLBERG (1987). *Operations Research: Principles and Practice*, 2nd ed. John Wiley, New York

SHOGAN, ANDREW W. (1988). *Management Science*. Prentice Hall, Englewood Cliffs, NJ.

TAHA, HAMDY A. (1987). *Operations Research*, 4th ed. Macmillan, New York

TAYLOR III, BERNARD W. (1990). *Introduction to Management Science*, 3rd ed. Allyn & Bacon, Needham Heights, MA.

2. Read one or more of the articles in the following five-part series. (Although these articles are set in the context of manufacturing systems, they contain many valuable insights that apply to simulation in general.)

CARSON, JOHN S. (1986). "Convincing Users of Model's Validity Is Challenging Aspect of Modeler's Job." *Industrial Engineering*, June 1986, pp. 74–85.

GRANT, JOHN W., AND STEVEN A. WEINER (1986). "Factors to Consider in Choosing a Graphically Animated Simulation System." *Industrial Engineering*, August 1986, pp. 37–40 and 65–68.

HAIDER, S. WALI, AND JERRY BANKS (1986). "Simulation Software Products for Analyzing Manufacturing Systems." *Industrial Engineering*, July 1986, pp. 98–

103. (Also see the errata for this article appearing on pp. 98–103 of *Industrial Engineering*, September 1986.)

KELTON, W. DAVID (1986). "Statistical Analysis Methods Enhance Usefulness, Reliability of Simulation Models." *Industrial Engineering*, September 1986, pp. 74–84.

LAW, AVERILL M. (1986). "Introduction to Simulation: A Powerful Tool for Analyzing Complex Manufacturing Systems." *Industrial Engineering*, May 1986, pp. 46–63.

3. Read one or more of the following articles.

COOK, THOMAS M., AND ROBERT A. RUSSELL (1976). "A Survey of Industrial OR/MS Activities in the 70's." *Proceedings of the 8th Annual Conference of The American Institute for Decision Sciences*, Decision Sciences Institute, Atlanta, GA, pp. 122–128.

GORDON, GEOFFREY (1978). "The Development of the General Purpose Simulation System (GPSS)." *Proceedings of the ACM SIGPLAN History of Programming Languages Conference*, published as *SIGPLAN Notices*, Vol. 13, no. 8, pp. 183–198. (These *Proceedings* were subsequently published in a hard-cover edition by the Association for Computing Machinery, New York.)

HARPELL, JOHN L., MICHAEL S. LANE, AND ALI H. MANSOUR (1989). "Operations Research in Practice: A Longitudinal Study." *Interfaces*, Vol. 19, no. 3, May–June 1989, pp. 65–74.

HENRIKSEN, JAMES O. (1983). "The Integrated Simulation Environment (Simulation Software of the 1990s)." *Operations Research*, Vol. 31, no. 6, November–December 1983, pp. 1053–1073.

MUSSELMAN, KENNETH J., AND DAVID L. MARTIN (1984). "Simulation in the Life Cycle of Flexible Manufacturing Systems." *Proceedings of the First ORSA/TIMS Special Interest Conference on Flexible Manufacturing Systems* (The Institute of Management Sciences, Providence, RI), pp. 154–167.

SCHRIBER, THOMAS J. (1989). "Perspectives on Simulation Using GPSS." *Proceedings of the 1989 Winter Simulation Conference*, Society for Computer Simulation, San Diego, CA, pp. 115–128.

SHANNON, ROBERT E., RICHARD MAYER, AND HEIMO H. ADELSBERGER (1985). "Expert Systems and Simulation." *Simulation*, Vol. 44, no. 6, June 1985, pp. 275–284.

TURBAN, EPHRAIM (1972). "A Sample Survey of Operations Research Activities at the Corporate Level." *Operations Research*, Vol. 20, no. 3, May–June 1972, pp. 708–721.

WAGNER, HARVEY M. (1988). "Operations Research: A Global Language for Business Strategy." *Operations Research*, Vol. 36, no. 5, September–October 1988, pp. 797–803.

4. Articles reporting successful applications of simulation often appear in the literature. References for some of these articles are given here, along with a brief indication of the nature of the simulation application. These applications include but are not restricted to the type of situations to which GPSS/H can be applied. Go to the library and read one or more of these articles that involve situations you think might be of interest to you. In a course setting, you could be asked to prepare a written summary of the application, and/or to make an oral presentation on the application. (An activity of this type probably could be carried out with more insight toward the end of a course in simulation than at the beginning of such a course.)

1. Reference

DAVIS, SAMUEL G., ET AL. (1986). "Strategic Planning for Bank Operations with Multiple Check-Processing Locations." *Interfaces*, Vol. 16, no. 6, November–December 1986, pp. 1–12. (Also summarized in Knowles, 1989, pp. 903–904.)

Overview

In check transactions, the amount for which a check has been written must be magnetically encoded on the check to support computer-based handling of the check from that point forward. This encoding is done at the first bank in the chain of banks through which the check moves. Special encoding equipment is needed for this purpose, along with personnel trained to operate the equipment. When a bank holding company has multiple branches, it might provide the encoding capability at some of the branches, but not all, with a resultant savings in capital investment and personnel costs. But this means checks must travel from some branches to others for encoding, and the time this takes delays receipt of funds on the part of the bank in some cases. And so a trade-off is involved in balancing the cost of delayed funds availability on the one hand versus a relatively small number of encoding locations on the other.

This article reports on the findings of a simulation-based study conducted by BancOhio to determine how many check-processing centers to have in its branch-banking system. In early 1984, after a major expansion made possible by deregulation of the banking industry, BancOhio processed checks at 22 of its 266 branches. In the interest of consolidating its check processing activities, BancOhio commissioned simulation studies to determine how many processing centers it should have, where they should be located, and what branches they should serve. On the basis of these studies, the number of check processing centers was reduced from 22 to 7, resulting in an annual savings of $1.6 million.

2. References

GOLOVIN, LEWIS B. (1979). "Product Blending: A Simulation Case Study in Double-Time." *Interfaces*, Vol. 9, no. 5, November 1979, pp. 64–76; and Golovin, Lewis B. (1985). "Product Blending: A Simulation Case Study in Double Time: An Update." *Interfaces*, Vol. 15, no. 4, July–August 1985, pp. 39–40. (Also summarized in Knowles, 1989, pp. 839–840.)

Overview

Gasoline is produced by blending (combining) various distilled components of petroleum. These components have varying octane ratings. The individual octane ratings, and the proportion of components used in the blending process, determine the octane rating of the resulting gasoline. An objective in blending various grades of gasoline is to achieve the octane levels corresponding to the grades. Within reason, the difference between realized and target octane levels could be compensated for at one time by adding tetraethyl lead (TEL) to the gasoline. But that was before the use of TEL was banned in California (and eventually in the entire United States) in the interest of reducing air pollution.

The banning of TEL by the state of California gave the Exxon Corporation only two months to change its gasoline-blending operations at its Benicia, California, refinery in such a way as to compensate for the pending inability to include TEL in gasoline. In the absence of TEL, greater volumes of high-octane components are needed to offset the low-octane ratings in other components. This translates into issues of providing adequate component-production capabilities and storage capacities for both higher- and lower-octane components and gasoline itself in the face of equipment failures, occasional alternative uses of equipment, varying levels of demand, and irregular schedules for filling barges and tank trucks with gasoline. It was tentatively concluded from a preliminary mathematical analysis that Exxon would have to add at least two component storage tanks and one or two more tanks for finished gasoline to offset the loss of flexibility that the use of TEL provided. It was then determined through simulation studies that only one more component tank and one more tank for finished product would have to be added to the system if changes were made in the way existing tanks were used. This resulted in a savings to Exxon of at least $1.4 million.

But the good news does not end here. The simulation model used for the TEL study has been put into the form of a multistage facilities model used by Exxon to study "refineries, chemical plants, distribution terminals, marine harbors, coal mines, and synthetic fuel plants" (quoted from Golovin, 1985, p. 39). Tens of millions of dollars have been saved in some uses of the model!

3. Reference

HUBBARD, HERBERT B. (1978). "Terminal Airspace/Airport Congestion Delays." *Interfaces*, Vol. 8, no. 2, February, 1978, pp. 1–14. (Also summarized in the 3rd edition of Cook and Russell, 1990, pp. 520–521.)

Overview

This article describes a simulation study undertaken at United Airlines to reduce air traffic delays at O'Hare Airport in Chicago. Findings from the study were used to reduce the average holding delays of inbound planes by from 2 to 3 minutes. Although this result seems modest, its effect has been to save United Airlines in excess of $1.2 million *per year* in its operations at O'Hare Airport. In broader terms, it is estimated that minimizing air traffic delays due to airport congestion results in savings for the U.S. airline industry of up to 5 million barrels of jet fuel per year.

4. Reference

KOLESAR, PETER (1984). "Stalking the Endangered CAT: A Queueing Analysis of Congestion at Automatic Teller Machines." *Interfaces*, Vol. 15, no. 6, November–December 1984, pp. 16–26. (Also summarized in Budnick, McLeavey, and Mojena, 1988, pp. 801–810.)

Overview

This article reports not on an application of simulation, but on an application of queueing theory (mathematical modeling). Reference to the article is included here to highlight the fact that simulation need not always be resorted to in dealing with realistic problems. If a problem can be solved with mathematical modeling, then so much the better (to gain the power, flexibility, and elegance of mathematics). Note that mathematical modeling and simulation can sometimes be used in parallel or in tandem, too. (See items 6 and 10 below.)

This study was done for the retail division of a large commercial bank and involves the issue of supplying sufficient capacity at automatic teller machines (ATMs) with the objective of serving the bank's customers in satisfactory but cost-effective fashion. Here, "capacity" refers both to the number of ATMs provided at a given location and the size of the lobby space within which the ATMs are used. The hypothesis is that *potential* ATM users will simply walk on by and *not* wait to use an ATM if the waiting area is full (especially in bad weather), or if there are otherwise too many others already in line for use of an ATM. This situation could be modeled very nicely with GPSS/H-based simulation, but mathematical modeling was adequate to the task, making simulation unnecessary. The term CAT appears in the title of the article because the ATMs in this study are sometimes called customer-activated terminals (CATs). When the demand for a CAT is very high, the CAT is said to be "endangered."

5. Reference

MARKLAND, ROBERT E. (1970). "A Simulation Model for Determining Scrap Decision Rules in the Metal Processing Industry." *Production and Inventory Management*, Vol. 11, no. 1, 1st Quarter 1970, pp. 29–35. (Also summarized in Markland, 1989, pp. 620–631.)

Overview

The setting of the problem described in this article involves a company that cuts large sheets of metal into smaller sizes on a to-order basis. Scrap pieces of metal result from this process. The question then is whether to sell these scrap pieces at a loss, getting only their salvage value for them, or whether to put the scrap pieces back into inventory with the possibility that they might be large enough in some cases to be usable in filling future orders. An intermediate approach can be taken, putting scrap pieces of large enough size back into inventory and selling smaller pieces for their salvage value. But at what point is a scrap piece "large enough" to make it potentially worthwhile to put it back into inventory? Simulation was used as a methodology to investigate the answer to this and other questions. In this late 1960s application, the simulation model was written in Fortran.

6. Reference

MONARCHI, DAVID E., THOMAS E. HENDRICK, AND DONALD R. PLANE (1977). "Simulation for Fire Department Deployment Policy Analysis." *Decision Sciences*, Vol. 8, no. 1, January 1977, pp. 211–227. (Also summarized in Watson and Blackstone, 1989, pp. 46–47.)

Overview

How many fire stations should a city provide, and where should they be located? This question was raised by city fathers in Denver, Colorado, at a time when Denver had 44 fire stations. Mathematical modeling and simulation studies were authorized to determine whether the existing system could be changed with the effect of saving money without reducing service levels. The mathematical model indicated that the system could be reduced by five fire stations. Simplifying assumptions had to be made in the mathematical modeling, however, and so a simulation model was used to evaluate the situation under a set of more realistic assumptions. The simulation study also indicated that 5 fire stations could be removed from the system. This was subsequently done, providing a cost reduction of about $2.3 million over a seven-year period, with continuing annual cost savings of about $1.2 million.

7. Reference

MCHUGH, MARY LYNN (1989). "Computer Simulation as a Method for Selecting Nurse Staffing Levels in Hospitals." *Proceedings of the 1989 Winter Simulation Conference*, Society for Computer Simulation, San Diego, CA, pp. 1121-1129.

Overview

This article reports on the use of GPSS/H-based simulation to examine the effect on wage costs and staffing adequacy of varying nurse staffing levels. Three psychiatric care units in a large Veterans Administration hospital served as models for the study. The staffing patterns tested were at 40%, 50%, 60%, and 80% of maximum work load. The conclusion reached in this Ph.D. dissertation study was that staffing level performance was acceptable at both the 50% and 60% levels. At the 80% staffing level, direct wage costs would be 8% higher than at the 50% level, and 11.6% overstaffing would result as compared with 0.2% overstaffing at the 50% level. The 50% level produced 0.9% understaffing as compared with 0.3% understaffing for the 80% level.

8. Reference

RICCIO, LUCIUS J., AND ANN LITKE (1986). "Making a Clean Sweep: Simulating the Effects of Illegally Parked Cars on New York City's Mechanical Street-Cleaning Efforts." *Operations Research*, Vol. 34, no. 5, September–October 1986, pp. 661–666. (Also elaborated on in the form of a parallel problem in Shogan, 1988, pp. 764–770.)

Overview

About 95% of street litter lies within 18 inches of the curb. To facilitate removal of this litter, parking regulations in New York City make it illegal for cars to park at certain times along the sides of streets that are scheduled for mechanical street cleaning. (If a mechanical sweeper must move away from the curbside to avoid an illegally parked car, it cannot sweep up the litter along the corresponding stretch of curb.) This article reports on a simulation study used to quantify how much more effective street cleaning would be in New York City if there were better compliance with parking regulations.

9. Reference

SCHERER, WILLIAM T., AND CHELSEA C. WHITE III (1986). "A Planning and Decision-Aiding Procedure for Purchasing and Launching Spacecraft." *Interfaces*, Vol. 16, no. 3, May-June 1986, pp. 31–40. (Also summarized in Budnick, McLeavey, and Mojena, 1988, p. 863.)

Overview

This application involves Intelsat, a cooperative commercial organization that provides satellite communication services to over 100 countries. Among other things, Intelsat must plan for replacement of old satellites with more sophisticated ones to keep up with the growth in demand for communication services. With satellites costing tens of millions of dollars, an appropriate balance must be struck between cost containment, on the one hand, and adequate future communication capacity, on the other. The article describes a simulation model used by Intelsat to help evaluate alternative upgrade strategies.

10. Reference

SCHRIBER, THOMAS J., AND KATHRYN E. STECKE (1988). "Machine Utilizations Achieved Using Balanced FMS Production Ratios in a Simulated Setting." *Annals of Operations Research*, Vol. 15, 1988, pp. 229–267.

Overview

This article illustrates how simulation can be used as an adjunct to mathematical modeling. Simplifying assumptions made in mathematical modeling can be relaxed in a simulation model and system performance predicted by the mathematical model can be compared with system performance achieved in the more realistic simulation model. The relative validity of the mathematical model can then be assessed in light of the performance differences.

Specifically, Stecke developed mathematical programming (MP) models for determining, from a set of part types on order, the production ratios (part types to be produced next, and their proportions) that maximize overall machine utilization by balancing machine work loads in a flexible manufacturing system (FMS). The MP models make simplifying assumptions by ignoring such things in the FMS as contention for transportation resources, travel time for work-in-process, contention for machines, finite buffer space, and the rules used to dispatch work to machines. This article reports on the use of GPSS/H simulation to investigate machine utilizations in the absence of these simplifying assumptions. It is found that machine utilizations are adversely impacted when the simplifying assumptions are relaxed, ranging from 9.1% to 22.9% below those predicted by the MP models.

11. Reference

SWART, WILLIAM, AND LUCA DONNO (1981). "Simulation Modeling Improves Operations, Planning and Productivity of Fast Food Restaurants." *Interfaces*, Vol. 11, no. 6, December, 1981, pp. 35–47. (Also summarized in Watson and Blackstone, 1989, pp. 41–43.)

Overview

This article reports on a simulation study undertaken to investigate the effects of alternative procedures, staffing, equipment, and layouts for fast, efficient customer service in Burger King restaurants. The study involved building about a 2500 statement GPSS model that is now used on a regular basis at Burger King.

12. Reference

WYMAN, F. PAUL (1977). "Simulation of Tar Sands Mining Operations." *Interfaces*, Vol. 8, no. 1, part 2 (Special Practices issue), November 1977, pp. 6–20. (Also summarized in Watson and Blackstone, 1989, pp. 38–40.)

Overview

This article describes the application of simulation to study two alternative systems proposed for the open-pit mining of oil-bearing tar sands in the Athabasca Tar Sands region of Alberta, Canada. One proposed system involved filling large buckets by dragging them through the sand, then lifting the buckets and emptying them onto a pile for subsequent movement of the sand by conveyor to a train, and then to a plant for extraction of the oil from the sand. The other proposed system, called bucketwheel excavation, involved attaching a wheel of revolving buckets to the end of a long boom, scooping sand into the revolving buckets, then dumping the sand onto a conveyor, and so on. Bucketwheels had been used successfully for operations of this type in the past, but the dragline approach had never been tried. The effect of extremely cold weather on equipment availability was one of the complicating factors that had to be considered. A combined GPSS-Fortran model for the alternative operations was built, using 2200 GPSS and 2100 Fortran statements. Results of the modeling indicated that either the bucketwheel or the dragline approach could be used successfully. Because lower capital costs were associated with the dragline scheme, it was chosen for implementation. The dragline approach worked successfully. Even after installation of the dragline system, the simulation model continued to be used to refine the ongoing operation of the system. (This application of GPSS won a prize in 1977 from the TIMS College for the Practice of Management Science.)

5. As implied by several of the references in activity 4, an excellent source of simulation application articles is *Interfaces*, a joint periodic publication of the Operations Research Society of America (ORSA) and The Institute of Management Sciences (TIMS). Consult this source to find at least three such articles other than those described in activity 4. In a course setting, you might be asked to prepare a written summary and/or make an oral presentation on one or more of the applications.

6. The *Proceedings of the 19XX Winter Simulation Conference* (XX = 90, 89, 88, etc.) are another excellent source of simulation application articles. If these conference proceedings are available in your library, consult this source to find at least three such articles in areas of interest to you. In a course setting, you might be asked to prepare a written summary and/or make an oral presentation on one or more of the applications. (To the extent that they are not yet out of print, these circa 1000-page proceedings can be obtained from the Society for Computer Simulation, P.O. Box 17900, San Diego, CA 92117, phone: 619-277-3888. Per copy prices range from \$50 to \$100.)

7. If you know how to program a computer, outline a procedure that could be programmed to simulate the process of shooting arrows at a target, as described in Section 1.5. Assume the availability of a "random number generator." That is, assume the program you prepare can draw numbers *at random* from the set of all 16-digit decimal numbers uniformly distributed on the open interval ranging from 0.0 to 1.0. Your program should input the probability that a single shot results in a hit, and the number of times the experiment is to be performed. It should output the fraction of the time that an even number of hits resulted when the experiment was simulated the indicated number of times. Time and interest permitting, and assuming that a "random number generator" is indeed available to you, you might even implement the program you design and make several runs with it.

8. When fair dice are tossed, the total number of points on the two upturned faces ranges from 2 to 12. The following activities refer to outcomes that occur when fair dice are tossed. Parts a, b,

and c call for use of fundamental ideas from the area of probability and statistics.

(a) Compute the expected result (that is, the long-run average). (Answer: 7.)

(b) Compute the relative frequency with which the expected result will occur when the dice are tossed one time. (Answer: 1/6.)

(c) Compute the relative frequency with which snake eyes ("2") will occur when the dice are tossed one time. (Answer: 1/36.)

(d) Assume you don't know how to do the computations called for in parts a, b, and c. Describe how you could experiment with the dice to estimate the values requested in parts a, b, and c.

(e) Suppose you don't have dice with which to experiment in part d. Develop plans for noncomputerized simulations you could carry out to estimate the values requested in parts a, b, and c. What replacement device do you use to simulate the tossing of the dice? Try your hand at this *before* reading the following hint.

Hint: You can simulate the tossing of a single die two consecutive times to get the effect of tossing a pair of dice one time. When a single fair die is tossed, the six alternative results (the integers 1 through 6) occur with equal likelihood. If you have a digital watch that ticks off seconds, you can divide the 60 seconds into six uniformly sized sets of numbers and assign one result to each set. For example, seconds readings of 1, 7, 13, 19, 25, 31, 37, 43, 49, and 55 could correspond to getting a "1" when a die is tossed. And so on. If you look at the seconds reading on your watch at random times, you can then interpret what you see in the context of having tossed a die. Not much fun. (Can you come up with a better noncomputerized way to simulate tossing a die, or to simulate tossing a pair of dice?)

(f) Suppose again that you don't have dice with which to experiment in part d. If you know how to program a computer, sketch out procedures that could be programmed to estimate the values requested in parts a, b, and c. Assume the availability of a "random number generator." That is, assume the program(s) you prepare can draw numbers *at random* from the set of all 16-digit decimal numbers uniformly distributed on the open interval ranging from 0.0 to 1.0.

9. The noncomputerized simulation described in Section 1.5 for shooting arrows at a target is very simple. The following sources contain detailed descriptions of more complicated noncomputerized simulations. Consult one or more of these sources and study the noncomputerized simulations they present. (Incidentally, a noncomputerized simulation of sorts is also presented in Section 2.5 of Chapter 2 in this book.)

1. Law, Averill M. (1986). "Introduction to Simulation: A Powerful Tool for Analyzing Complex Manufacturing Systems." *Industrial Engineering*, May 1986, pp. 46–63.

In Section 1.2 of this article, pp. 47–51, Law provides a noncomputerized simulation for a one-line, one-server queuing system. The server is a machine, and the units of traffic that use the machine are jobs moving through a manufacturing system. Jobs arrive at the machine at random points in time, and the time required by the machine to process a job varies at random from job to job.

2. Markland, Robert E. (1989). *Topics in Management Science*, 3rd ed. John Wiley, New York.

On pp. 613–619 in this book, Markland provides the details for noncomputerized simulations for waiting line, inventory control, and travel-network situations.

3. Ravindran, Ravi, Don T. Phillips, and James J. Solberg (1987). *Operations Research: Principles and Practice*, 2nd ed. John Wiley, New York.

In this book, the authors present on pp. 383–396 noncomputerized simulations for the performance of a baseball hitter, operation of a tool crib (a one-line, one-server system), and production-line maintenance.

4. Shogan, Andrew W. (1988). *Management Science*. Prentice Hall, Englewood Cliffs, NJ.

Shogan presents noncomputerized simulations on pp. 754–758 of this book in the setting of an equipment-replacement problem and on pp. 771–779 in the setting of a machine-repair problem.

2 Transactions: Their Creation, Movement, and Destruction

2.1 Preview

This chapter provides the base for our study of GPSS/H. The stylized way of approaching the building of a GPSS/H model is introduced, along with the concept of Transactions and fundamental aspects of their creation, movement, and destruction. Supporting material includes Blocks, the simulated clock, interarrival time, Block Diagrams, Model Files, and the interplay between the user and GPSS/H in carrying out Test-Mode simulations with models. The material involves a blend of concepts from the general area of discrete-event simulation, on the one hand, and the particulars of their representation in GPSS/H models, on the other.

Hands-on use of GPSS/H is not called for in this chapter until the first exercise section is reached (Section 2.24). Those interested in installing Student DOS GPSS/H (which comes with this book) and making one or two test runs now with a GPSS/H model can turn immediately to Appendix A and carry out the installation and test run instructions that are given there.

2.2 Approach to Model Building in GPSS/H

A GPSS/H model can be expressed as a **Block Diagram**, or as the statement equivalent of a Block Diagram. GPSS/H modelers sometimes start the modeling process by constructing a Block Diagram of the model. Statements corresponding to the Blocks in a Block Diagram (**Block Statements**) are then prepared and are supplemented with additional types of statements known as **Control Statements**, and perhaps with other types of statements known as **Compiler Directives**. These additional statements provide supporting information about the model and describe the plan for its experimental use. The resulting collection of statements, known as a **Model File**, is then executed by GPSS/H under computer control.

A Block Diagram is a collection of figures (Blocks) with one-way paths connecting them. The paths are shown as directed line segments. (A directed line segment is a line with an arrowhead at one end of it.) Each type of Block plays a particular role in a model. There are more than 60 Block types in GPSS/H, each with its own distinctive shape.

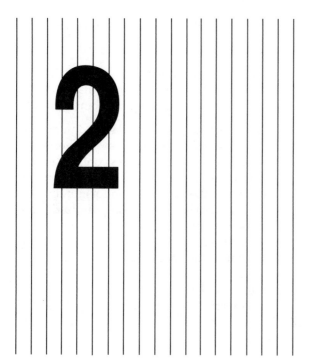

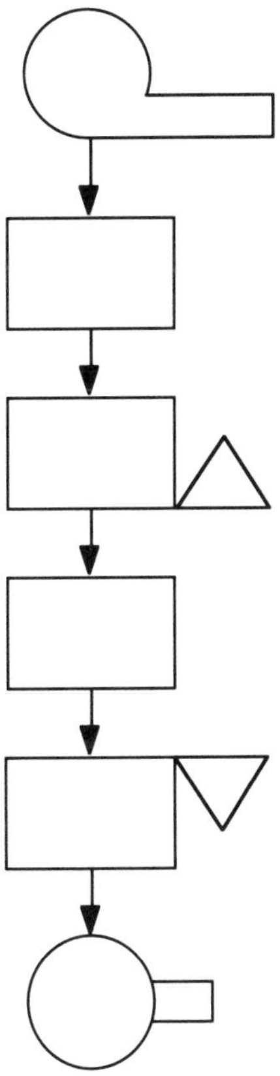

Figure 2.1 *A Silhouette of a Block Diagram*

Units of traffic move along the one-way paths in a Block Diagram. The name **Transaction** is given to a unit of traffic in GPSS/H. (Many everyday terms, such as "Transaction" and "Block," have specialized meanings in GPSS/H. Such terms are capitalized to emphasize their specialized use.) The movement of Transactions from Block to Block as a simulation proceeds is a vital part of a GPSS/H simulation.

A model is built by selecting appropriate Blocks from the available types and sequencing them in a Block Diagram to form patterns corresponding to patterns in the system being modeled. The Blocks are used to represent such things as system resources, information-gathering, and decision-making capabilities. The physical and logical aspects of the system being modeled, and the type of information that the model is to provide, determine which Blocks are used in constructing the model. When the model is executed by a computer, it is the movement of units of traffic from Block to Block that is analogous to (simulates) the movement of traffic through the system being modeled.

The silhouette of a simple Block Diagram is shown in Figure 2.1. A sequence of six Blocks appears in the figure, with five different Block shapes used. Information that usually appears in a Block Diagram has been excluded from Figure 2.1, the intent being to provide a first glimpse of a Block Diagram for the sake of perspective.

The silhouette of a more complicated Block Diagram appears in Figure 2.2. In this case, the Block Diagram consists of two unconnected segments. (In general, a Block Diagram can consist of any number of segments). Ten types of Blocks appear in Figure 2.2. Several types appear more than one time. One of the Blocks has two paths leading into it, and one of the Blocks has two paths emerging from it.

Two types of Blocks will be discussed in detail in this chapter. Additional Block types will be introduced in succeeding chapters to support building fundamental models and then models of increasing complexity. (If the entire set of 60^+ GPSS/H Blocks is mastered, models of very complicated systems can be built with surprising ease.)

2.3 Transactions: Units of Traffic in GPSS/H Models

As indicated, GPSS/H views the world as consisting of units of traffic (they're called **Transactions** in GPSS/H, or **Xacts** for short) that move along paths from Block to Block in a model as a simulation proceeds. Each Block represents an action to be performed whenever the Block is executed. In general, it is the movement of a Transaction into a Block that causes the Block to be executed.

Because Xacts simulate units of traffic, they represent whatever the corresponding units of traffic are in the system being modeled. In an air traffic control system, for example, some Xacts might represent planes that move through a sequence of control zones as the planes travel from one airport to another. In a manufacturing system, some Xacts might represent units of work-in-process that move from point to point in the system as machining steps are performed on them to convert units of raw material to units of finished product. In a hospital system, some Xacts might represent people who come to the emergency ward to be treated for accidents requiring immediate medical attention. In an information system, some Transactions might represent units of information that move from processing point to processing point in the system. And so on.

It's evident, then, that Xacts can have a great range of possible alternative meanings in models.

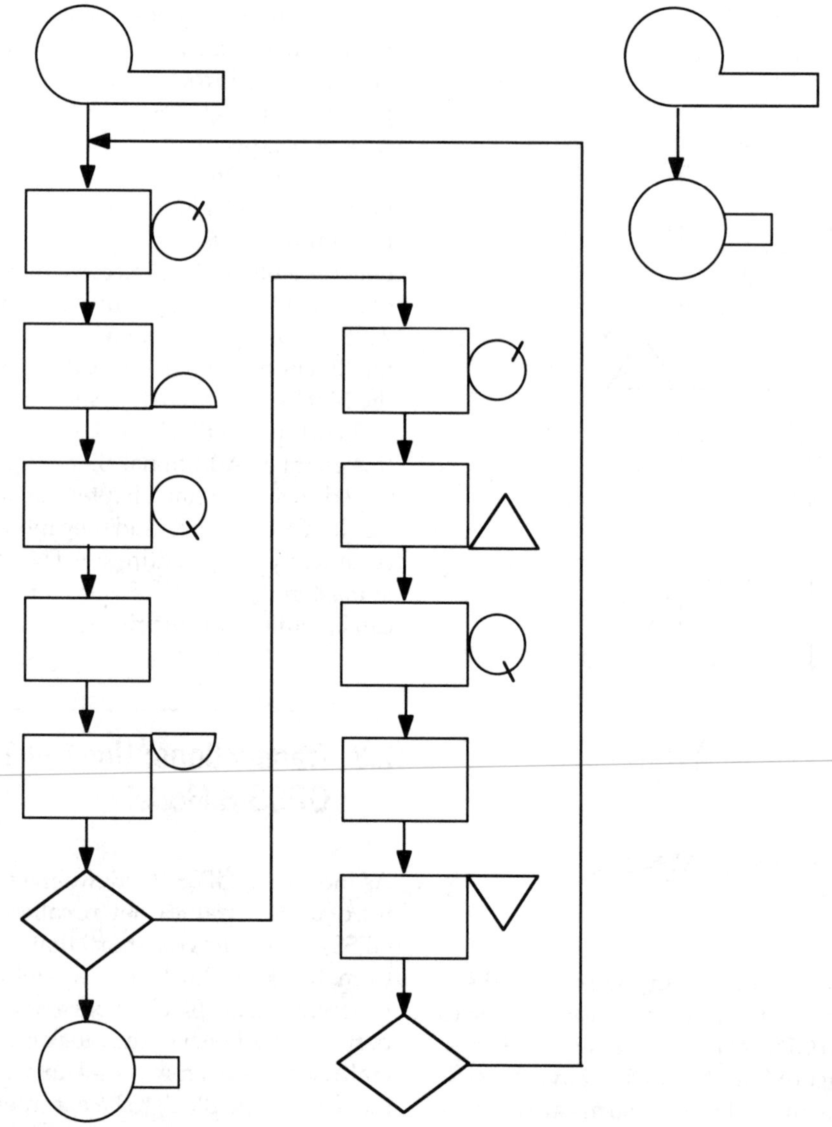

Figure 2.2 *Another Silhouette of a Block Diagram*

It's also evident that in some cases, Transactions represent people, and in other cases, represent things. And it's not necessary that all Xacts in a model represent either persons or things. In an inventory control system, for example, some Xacts might represent people who check inventory levels to determine whether conditions call for placing replenishment orders, whereas other Xacts might represent replenishment orders on the way from distributors to retailers.

For learning purposes, it is useful to get in mind a picture, or icon, for a Transaction. Because Xacts sometimes represent people and, like people, move from point to point, an Xact can be thought of as a stickperson. A set of three stickpersons is shown in Figure 2.3. More than one stickperson is shown to emphasize the fact that there can be many different Xacts in a model at a time (just as there can be many different units of traffic in a system at a time). A unique number is written on the head of each of the three stickpersons in Figure 2.3, because each Xact

Figure 2.3 *Transactions Shown as Stickpersons*

in a model has a unique identification number. A Transaction's **id number** is a positive integer. More is said about Xact id numbers later in this chapter.

2.4 The Nature of Transaction Movement in a Model

When a simulation begins, no Xacts exist in a model. As the simulation proceeds, Xacts are created and introduced into the model from time to time, according to the logic built into the model. Similarly, Xacts leave the model (are destroyed) from time to time. The number of Xacts in a model usually varies during the course of a simulation.

Transactions reside within the Blocks making up a model. In general, each Xact in a model has a **Current Block** (the Block it is currently in) and a **Next Block Attempted** (the Block the Xact will attempt to move into next). Between its time of creation and eventual destruction, a Transaction goes through a life cycle, usually consuming simulated time in the process. During its life cycle, an Xact moves through a sequence of Blocks. For example, a Transaction might move through three Blocks in the first part of its life cycle, then stop moving temporarily, then move through another five Blocks at a later simulated time, then stop moving temporarily, then move through some additional Blocks at an even later simulated time, then stop moving temporarily again, and so on, until it eventually moves into a Block that destroys the Xact, which brings its life cycle to an end.

There usually are many Xacts in a model, but only one Xact moves at a time. When it becomes a Transaction's turn to try to move, it tries to move from its Current Block into its Next Block Attempted. If the attempted move can be made, the Xact goes into its Next Block (which becomes its new Current Block), carrying out the action corresponding to that Block. The Xact then (in general) immediately tries to move from its new Current Block into its new Next Block Attempted, and so on. The Xact's movement continues in uninterrupted fashion until it experiences one of three alternative conditions that force it to stop moving for the time being:

1. The Xact moves into a type of Block whose purpose is to **hold the Xact** in the Block for a prescribed interval of **simulated** time. In this case, the Xact temporarily remains within this Block.

2. The Xact's Next Block Attempted **blocks the Xact** (refuses for the time being to let the Xact move into it). In this case, the blocked Xact remains in its Current Block. The Xact will later retry to move into its Next Block Attempted. As model conditions change, one of the Xact's later retries generally will be successful, meaning that the Transaction can resume its movement in the model.

   There are only five types of Blocks in GPSS/H that are capable of blocking a Transaction. The first of these types is introduced in Chapter 6. Until we reach Chapter 6, then, Xact blocking will not be an issue. For now, whenever an Xact tries to move into its Next Block, it will be able to do so.

3. The Xact moves into a type of Block that **destroys the Xact**. In this case, the Xact is permanently removed from the model.

When a Transaction is forced to stop moving, it will be some other Transaction's turn to try to move from its Current Block into its Next Block Attempted, and so on, until one of the three earlier conditions comes about and forces that Xact to stop moving. And so on.

Certain insights can now be drawn from the Block Diagram silhouettes in Figures 2.1 and 2.2. For example, one Block in Figure 2.1 and two in Figure 2.2 are "sources"; that is, no path leads into them. These Blocks, identical in shape, are of the type that creates Transactions and introduces them into a model. (They are **birth Blocks.**) Similarly, one Block in Figure 2.1 and two in Figure 2.2 are "sinks"; that is, the path on which they lie does not extend beyond them. These Blocks, identical in shape, are of the type that destroys a Transaction when it moves into such a Block. (They are **death Blocks.**) Finally, Figure 2.2 consists of two disconnected sets of Blocks. When a simulation takes place, action occurs in the set of Blocks containing the moving Xact. The next Xact to move may be located in a different set of Blocks, which results in a switch of the action to that part of the model. The action can skip about in a Block Diagram, then, during the course of a simulation.

2.5 The Simulation Clock

Time passes as events occur in real systems. For example, a unit of work-in-process arrives at a machine in a manufacturing system and requests use of the machine. When its turn comes, the machine begins to carry out a step on the unit. Still later, the machining step is finished, and the unit of work-in-process moves on in the system. If such events are to be represented in a simulation model, they must occur with respect to the simulated elapsing of time. As a consequence, GPSS/H provides a **simulated clock** that it uses to record the passing of time.

The simulated clock registers values in the form of positive **decimal numbers** (also known as real numbers, or floating point numbers). The smallest value the clock can register is 0.0. Examples of possible simulated clock values are 0.0, 0.7, 1.2, 241.6, and 12345.6. Except in computer printouts, simulated clock times usually will be given to 1 decimal place in this book. In computer printouts, clock values are given to 4 decimal places. (Internally, simulated clock times are carried to about 16 decimal digits and can become at least as large as about 10 to the 35th power and at least as small as about 10 to the -35th power.)

The modeler chooses the simulated clock's **base time unit** for a model. For example, if 1 minute is chosen as the base time unit, then a clock value of 10.1 corresponds to simulated time 10.1 minutes (10 minutes and 6 seconds) in the simulation, a clock value of 75.0 corresponds to simulated time 75 minutes (1 hour and 15 minutes) in the simulation, and a clock value of 480.0 corresponds to the end of the 8th simulated hour (480 is 8 hours, expressed in minutes).

The value registered by the simulated clock can only increase as a simulation proceeds. It's not possible to go backward in time in a GPSS/H simulation.

When a simulation begins, the clock's value is 0.0. GPSS/H starts the simulation by creating one or more Xacts at clock time 0.0 and determining the simulated times at which they are to be introduced into the model. The clock is then set to the earliest simulated time at which a Transaction is to come into the model. This Xact is then given a chance to move and, starting at its "birth Block," moves as far along its path as possible. (Any other Xacts that might be coming into the model at this simulated time will be given their turn (one at a time) to move as far along their paths as possible, too.)

Eventually, no Xacts will be able to move any farther at the current simulated time. GPSS/H will then advance the clock to the earliest future (simulated) time at which one or more Xacts have been scheduled to move. (This time might correspond to the introduction of a new Xact into the model, and/or it might correspond to the completion of an Xact's holding time in the type of Block that holds an Xact for a prescribed interval of simulated time.) Each qualifying Xact will then be given its turn to move

Table 2.1

A Possible Sequence of Events in a Drill-and-Castings System

Order of Events	Event	Real Time of Occurrence[1]	Simulated Time of Occurrence[2]
1	the shift begins	8:00.00 A.M.	0.0
2	casting 1 arrives; the drilling of casting 1 begins	8:22.30 A.M.	22.5
3	casting 2 arrives and begins to wait for the drill	8:36.12 A.M.	36.2
4	casting 3 arrives and begins to wait for the drill	8:40.18 A.M.	40.3
5	the drilling of casting 1 ends; the drilling of casting 2 begins	8:42.36 A.M.	42.6

[1]expressed in hours:minutes.seconds (e.g., 8:22.30 is 22 minutes and 30 seconds after 8 A.M.)

[2]expressed in minutes, relative to a base of 0.0 at 8:00.00 A.M.

at this new simulated time. Eventually, no Xacts will be able to move further at the current simulated time, so the simulated clock will be advanced again, and so on. It is in this way that Xact movement proceeds in a simulation.

The use of a technique known as "event scheduling" is implied in the preceding paragraphs. To schedule an event is to make arrangements to have it occur at some future time. In GPSS/H, an arrival event is scheduled by creating an Xact, determining its future time of arrival, and then, when that future time is reached, taking steps to cause that arrival to occur. (Detailed aspects of such event scheduling are explored in Chapter 4.) The technique of event scheduling is often heavily used in simulation.

An example will shed more light on this overall process. Consider a simple system consisting of a drilling machine. Castings come to this machine to have a hole drilled in them. An 8-hour work shift begins at simulated time 0.0, which corresponds (let's agree) to 8:00 A.M. in the real system. Assume that no castings are waiting to be drilled at the start of the shift, so the drill is idle when the shift begins. Let 1 unit of simulated time correspond to 1 minute of real time in the system. Table 2.1 shows the times and types of the first several actions that we assume take place early in the shift and which are discussed below, clock reading by clock reading.

Clock Time 0.0

When the simulation begins at time 0.0, a casting-Transaction is created ("casting 1"). Let's assume this casting is scheduled to come to the drill at future simulated time 22.5 (corresponding to 22.5 minutes after 8 in the morning).

Clock Time 22.5

The simulated clock is then advanced to 22.5, and casting 1 is introduced into the model. (See 2 under "Order of Events" in Table 2.1.) A successor casting-Transaction ("casting 2") is created and scheduled to come to the drill at future time 36.2 (let's assume). Meanwhile casting 1, finding the drill idle at time 22.5, takes control of the drill, and drilling begins. That is, the casting-1 Transaction moves forward in the model at time 22.5, Block by Block, capturing the drill and then moving into a Block that will hold the casting-Transaction until future time 42.6 (let's assume), to simulate drilling time.

Clock Time 36.2

The simulated clock is then advanced to 36.2, the earliest future time at which a Transaction has been scheduled to move. (This corresponds to casting 2 arriving at the drill.) Casting 2 is introduced into the model. (See 3 under "Order of Events" in Table 2.1.) A successor casting-Transaction ("casting 3") is created and scheduled to come to the drill at simulated time 40.3. Meanwhile casting 2, finding the drill is busy working on casting 1, begins to wait its turn to use the drill.

Clock Time 40.3

The clock is then advanced to 40.3, the earliest future time at which a Transaction has been scheduled to move. (This corresponds to casting 3 arriving at the drill.) Casting 3 is introduced into the model. (See 4 under "Order of Events" in Table 2.1.) A successor casting-Xact ("casting 4") is created and scheduled to come to the drill at future simulated time 55.1. Meanwhile, casting 3 finds the drill is busy (still working on casting 1) and so begins to wait its turn to use the drill.

Clock Time 42.6

The clock is then advanced to 42.6, the earliest future time at which a Transaction has been scheduled to move. (This corresponds to completion of the drilling of casting 1. See 5 under "Order of Events" in Table 2.1.) Casting 1 becomes the moving Xact, gives up control of the drill, and leaves the model (is destroyed). Casting 2 then becomes the moving Xact and captures the drill, and the drilling of this casting begins. Casting 3 then tries to move but finds it can't (casting 2 now controls the drill, and casting 3 must continue to wait its turn to be drilled), and so on.

It is clear how closely coupled the elapsing of simulated time is with the sequence of events that takes place in a simulation. GPSS/H automatically advances the simulated clock as required by the logic incorporated into a model and is a "next event" simulator. That is, after the state of the model has been updated at the current simulated time, the clock is advanced to the earliest future simulated time at which a Xact has been scheduled to move. Potential clock times are jumped over when no Xacts have been scheduled to move at those simulated times.

Care must be taken to distinguish between the elapsing of **simulated** time and the elapsing of **real** time. After the simulated clock is advanced to its next value, that value (simulated time) remains temporarily constant while real time goes by as the computer updates the simulated state of the model. In rare circumstances, it may require minutes of computer time to move models of some highly detailed systems through minutes of simulated time. On the other hand, experiments equivalent to weeks, months, or even years of simulated time can often be conducted in only seconds or minutes of computer time. Such **time compression** is one of the potential advantages of experimenting with systems by simulating them on a computer.

2.6 The Structure of Blocks

Each Block in a model occupies a specific Location, has an Operation word, and has zero or more Operands. This general Block structure is shown in Figure 2.4, which repeats the Figure 2.2 Block Diagram silhouette, but with general Block details supplied as appropriate. The nature of these details will now be discussed under the Location, Operation, and Operands headings.

1. Location. Each Block occupies a unique **Location** in a model. Block Locations are numbered 1, 2,

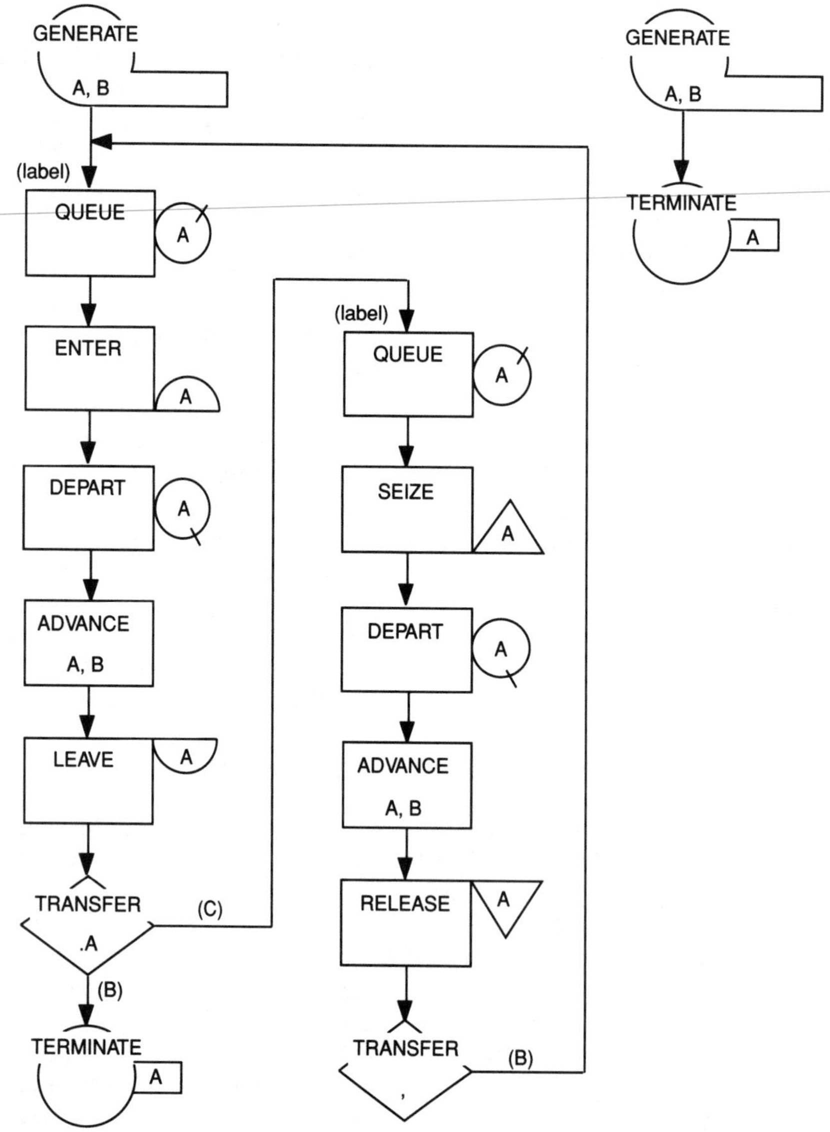

Figure 2.4 A Repetition of Figure 2.2, with General Block Details Shown

3, and so on. The first Block in a model occupies Location 1, the second Block occupies Location 2, and so on.

The modeler does not provide **Block Location Numbers.** When GPSS/H executes a Model File, it assigns Location Numbers to Blocks in the top-down order of their appearance in the Model File.

The model builder has the option of **labeling** one or more Blocks in a model. A **Block Label** identifies the Location that a Block occupies. Attaching a label to a Block makes it easy to refer to that Block from elsewhere in the model.

In Figure 2.4, for example, Labels are attached to the two "QUEUE" Blocks. These labels are shown there in general form as "(label)." The directed line segments connecting the Figure 2.4 "TRANSFER" Blocks to the nonsequential QUEUE Blocks imply that the TRANSFER Blocks make reference to (point to) the QUEUE Blocks. As we will see later, this referencing (pointing) is done via the labels attached to the QUEUE Blocks.

2. Operation. A Block's **Operation** is a key word indicating the role that type of Block plays in the modeling process. Each Block type is characterized by a unique Operation word. The Operation words GENERATE, TERMINATE, QUEUE, DEPART, ADVANCE, SEIZE, RELEASE, ENTER, LEAVE, and TRANSFER all appear in Figure 2.4. When a Block statement is prepared, the Block's Operation must be specified. The Operation word can be abbreviated with its first four characters. For example, GENERATE can be shortened to GENE, TERMINATE can be shortened to TERM, and so on.

3. Operands. Most Blocks have one or more **Operands**. A Block's Operands provide information on which the Block's action is based.

   The number of Operands a Block has depends on the Block type. Many Blocks use only one or two Operands. Others use as many as nine. Several Blocks use no Operands. Block Operands are represented in general as A, B, C, D, and so on. Block Operands are shown in this general fashion in Figure 2.4.

   For some Blocks, values of all Operands must always be supplied explicitly. For other Blocks, no Operand values need be supplied explicitly; **default values** can be used instead. And there are intermediate cases in which values for some of a Block's Operands must be supplied explicitly, whereas default values can be used for other Operands.

2.7 Creating Transactions: The GENERATE Block

Actions in a GPSS/H model are based on the movement of Xacts through Blocks. And so we begin detailed Block considerations with the type of Block used to create Xacts and introduce them into a model, the GENERATE Block. This section introduces the GENERATE Block and explains how the Block's A and B Operands specify the timing with which GENERATE Blocks create Xacts and introduce them into a model.

In the following discussion, it will be helpful to distinguish between (1) creation of a Transaction and (2) movement of that Xact into and then out of its GENERATE Block and into its Next Block, and so on. As we will see, a Transaction is created at one simulated time, but in general does not move into and then out of its GENERATE Block and into its Next Block until some later simulated time.

Consider the idea of having a series of Xacts move from a GENERATE Block into their Next Block, one by one, as simulated time goes by. Suppose a Transaction moves out of a particular GENERATE Block and into its Next Block at simulated time 16.7, then another Xact moves out at time 31.0, and yet another moves out at time 48.8, and so on. These hypothesized times at which Xacts move from this GENERATE Block into their Next Block, and go on from there, are shown in Figure 2.5. Simulated time is shown on a horizontal time line, and the times at which Xacts move from the GENERATE Block into their Next Block are marked accordingly.

The times between movement of consecutive Transactions from a particular GENERATE Block are termed **interarrival times.** The first Xact to come out of the GENERATE Block in the Figure 2.5 example has an interarrival time of 16.7 (relative to the start of the simulation at clock time 0.0), as shown in Figure 2.5. The second Xact to come out has an interarrival time of 14.3 with respect to its predecessor (31.0 - 16.7 = 14.3); the third Xact has an interarrival time of 17.8 (48.8 - 31.0 = 17.8); and so on.

As suggested in the example, the times between movement of Xacts from a GENERATE Block usu-

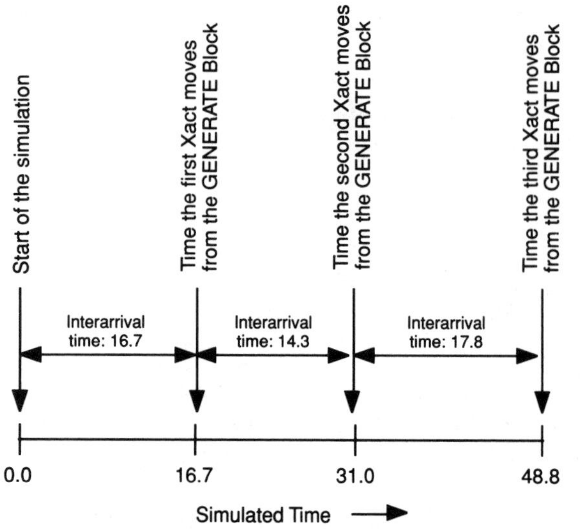

Figure 2.5 *Hypothesized Times at Which Transactions Move from a Particular GENERATE Block into Their Next Block*

ally vary at random. In other words, interarrival time is usually a **random variable**. The interarrival time applying to each Xact is usually determined by sampling from a distribution of interarrival times supplied by the modeler. We will now explain how **uniformly distributed** interarrival times can be specified at a GENERATE Block.

A **uniform** distribution can be described by indicating its **average** value and the **half-width of the range** (the half-range) over which its values vary. Suppose a continuous random variable is uniformly distributed on the open interval centered at 15.0 and having a half-range of 4.5. (An **open** interval is one that excludes its end points.) Then the random variable can take on values in the open interval 15.0 ± 4.5. (Read "±" as "plus or minus.") That is, the random variable can take on values in the open interval ranging from 10.5 (15.0 - 4.5 = 10.5) to 19.5 (15.0 + 4.5 = 19.5). (The end points of 10.5 and 19.5 are not included in the interval.) In theory, there is an infinite number of distinct interarrival-time values in this interval. In GPSS/H, in excess of **2 billion** unique interarrival-time values can be sampled from an interval. (Particulars are provided in Chapter 13.)

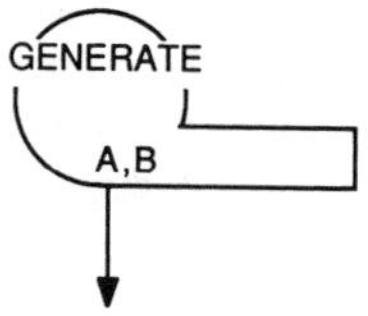

Operand	Significance	Default Value or Result
A	Average interarrival time	0.0 (zero)
B	Half-range of the uniformly distributed interarrival time random variable	0.0 (zero)

Figure 2.6 *The GENERATE Block, with Its A and B Operands*

When interarrival times are uniformly distributed, the average interarrival time is indicated by the GENERATE Block's A Operand, and the half-range is indicated by the B Operand. These facts are summarized in Figure 2.6, where a GENERATE Block is shown with its A and B Operands in generalized form.

Figure 2.7 shows a specific GENERATE Block, with 15.0 as its A Operand and 4.5 as its B Operand. Interarrival times at the Figure 2.7 GENERATE Block are uniformly distributed in the open interval ranging from 10.5 to 19.5.

If a GENERATE Block's A Operand is greater than zero and its B Operand equals its A Operand, then interarrival times of zero cannot occur. This is a consequence of the fact that A ± B describes an **open** interval. For example, interarrival times of zero cannot occur at the Block "GENERATE 25,25", or "GENERATE 7.2,7.2".

A GENERATE Block's B Operand cannot be larger than its A Operand. Otherwise, a **negative** interarrival time could occur, requiring that the simulated clock be set back to an earlier time, which GPSS/H does not do. For example, the Block "GENERATE 50,60" is invalid.

We've seen that it's easy to specify uniformly distributed interarrival times in GPSS/H. To express more complicated interarrival-time distributions, the modeler either uses built-in GPSS/H Functions (for sampling from such distributions as the exponential, normal, and triangular) or defines customized Functions and then refers to them from A and/or B Operand positions at GENERATE Blocks. Specification of nonuniformly distributed interarrival times at GENERATE Blocks is intro-

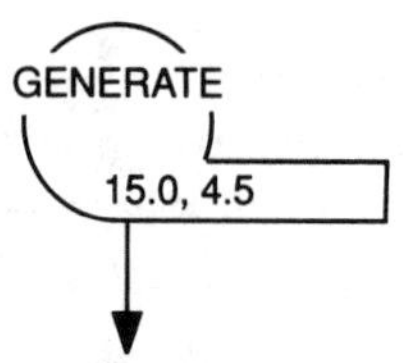

Figure 2.7 *A GENERATE Block with an A Operand of 15.0 and a B Operand of 4.5*

duced in Chapter 13. For now, we'll use uniform distributions so we can concentrate our time and energy initially on more important aspects of discrete-event modeling and GPSS/H.

In the Figure 2.7 GENERATE Block, the A and B Operand values are supplied as decimal numbers. If a GENERATE Block's A and/or B Operands are whole numbers, then the value or values can be indicated either with or without keying a decimal point. For example, "GENERATE 15,4.5" is a valid alternative to "GENERATE 15.0,4.5".

Now consider the behavior of the Figure 2.7 GENERATE Block in the context of a model. When GPSS/H initializes the model at simulated time 0.0, it will create a Transaction and schedule it to move into the model from this GENERATE Block at some future simulated time. To determine that time, GPSS/H **draws a sample** from the interarrival-time distribution indicated at the GENERATE Block. Suppose the sampled value is 16.7. GPSS/H then creates a Transaction at time 0.0 and schedules it to move from this GENERATE Block at future time 16.7 (initialization time 0.0 + interarrival time 16.7 = future time 16.7). Later, at time 16.7, this Xact will move from this GENERATE Block. In response, GPSS/H will then (at time 16.7) create another Xact to be the first Xact's successor and will schedule this successor to come out of this GENERATE Block at some future time. The successor's interarrival time will be determined by sampling from the 15.0 ± 4.5 distribution. Let's assume that the sampled value will be 14.3. This means GPSS/H will schedule the successor to move from the GENERATE Block at future time 31.0 (current time 16.7 + interarrival time 14.3 = future time 31.0). When simulated time 31.0 is eventually reached, this Xact will move from the GENERATE Block into its Next Block, and so on. In response, GPSS/H will create another Transaction to be its successor and will schedule this successor to move from this GENERATE Block at some future simulated time. And so on. The particulars of the example in this discussion correspond to those shown in Figure 2.5.

It should be clear from the preceding discussion that when an Xact moves from a GENERATE Block, this causes the Block to create another Xact and schedule it for future movement from the GENERATE Block. In other words, the arrival process at a GENERATE Block is self-perpetuating (self-sustaining).

As shown in Figure 2.6, GENERATE Block A and/or B Operand values do not have to be supplied explicitly. **Default values** of 0.0 apply to both of these Operands. Figure 2.8 shows a GENERATE Block whose A Operand is 10.0 and whose B Operand is 0.0 (by default). Interarrival times at the Figure 2.8 GENERATE Block are then uniformly distributed over the open interval 10.0 ± 0.0. That is, interarrival times at the Block are always exactly 10.0. This is an example of **deterministic** (that is, nonrandom) interarrival times.

Assume the Figure 2.8 GENERATE Block is part of a model. When initializing the model at simulated time 0.0, GPSS/H will create an Xact and schedule it to come out of the GENERATE Block at simulated time 10.0 (initialization time 0.0 + interarrival time 10.0 = future time 10.0). Later, at time 10.0, this Xact will come out of the GENERATE Block. In response, GPSS/H will create another Xact to be this first Xact's successor, arranging for it to arrive at future time 20.0 (current time 10.0 + interarrival time 10.0 = future time 20.0). This arrival pattern will be in effect throughout the simulation. In other words, Xacts will come out of the Figure 2.8 GENERATE Block at simulated times 10.0, 20.0, 30.0, 40.0, 50.0, and so on.

There can be any number of GENERATE Blocks in a model. In the Figure 2.4 Block Diagram, for example, there are two GENERATE Blocks. Each GENERATE Block operates in self-contained fashion. That is, the various GENERATE Blocks in a model are independent of each other.

2.8 Transaction id Numbers

Transactions have individual properties, or attributes, just as the individual units of traffic moving through a real system often have individual properties. In a manufacturing system, for example, units of work-in-process might have properties such as a job number, a customer number, and a due date. Information of this sort can be attached to Xacts to support modeling systems in which units of traffic have individual characteristics.

We limit ourselves here to the idea that each Xact in a model has a unique identification number (**id**

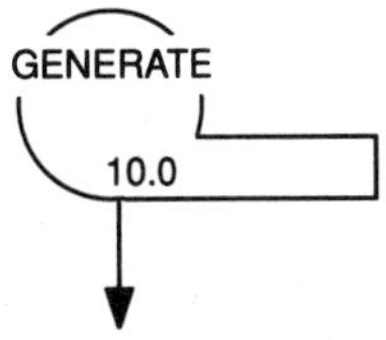

Figure 2.8 A GENERATE Block with an A Operand of 10.0 and with a Default B Operand of 0.0

number). Xact id numbers are automatically attached to Xacts at the time of their creation. Xacts are numbered serially from 1 forward in the order in which they are created, **independent of the GENERATE Block that creates them**. The first Xact to be created in a model is numbered 1, the second to be created is numbered 2, the next to be created after that is numbered 3, and so on.

Xact id numbers are important in tracing Xact movement, as we will begin to see later in this chapter. Xact id numbers are also used internally by GPSS/H, and they sometimes appear in reports that GPSS/H produces at the end of a simulation.

2.9 Destroying Transactions: The TERMINATE Block and the Model's Termination Counter

A type of Block known as a **TERMINATE Block** is used to destroy Transactions (remove them from a model). A TERMINATE Block never denies entry to a Transaction. When a moving Xact takes a TERMINATE Block as its Next Block, the Xact proceeds without delay into the TERMINATE Block, and is destroyed. There can be any number of TERMINATE Blocks in a model.

A TERMINATE Block and its A Operand are shown in Figure 2.9. A TERMINATE Block's A Operand, which is integer valued, is a **decrement** for the **model's Termination Counter**. That is, a TERMINATE Block's A Operand indicates the amount by which the value of a counter in the model (called the model's Termination Counter, or **TC** for short) is to be reduced each time a Transaction destroys itself by moving into the TERMINATE Block.

The model's Termination Counter is an integer-valued variable that is initialized with a value of 1 or more (via the START Control Statement, to be discussed in Section 2.14) when the Transaction-movement part of a simulation starts. As the simulation proceeds, Xacts move into TERMINATE Blocks from time to time, potentially reducing the value of the model's Termination Counter. When the value of the Termination Counter has been reduced to zero (or less), the simulation stops immediately.

TERMINATE Block execution can cause the value of the model's Termination Counter to become less than zero. For example, if the model's TC has a value of 1 when a Transaction executes a "TERMINATE 2" Block, the TC value will be reduced to -1 (1 - 2 = -1). Models are usually designed to reduce the value of the Termination Counter to exactly zero.

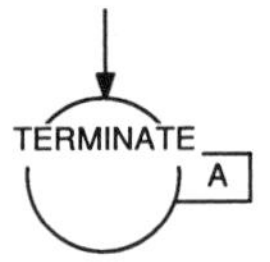

Operand	Significance	Default Value or Result
A	Decrement for the model's Termination Counter	0 (zero)

Figure 2.9 *The TERMINATE Block and Its A Operand*

As indicated in Figure 2.9, the default value of a TERMINATE Block's A Operand is 0 (zero). If a Transaction moves into a TERMINATE Block whose A Operand is zero, the value of the model's Termination Counter is reduced by zero, which means its value doesn't change at all.

TERMINATE Blocks play a **dual role** in a model. On the one hand, they are used to destroy Xacts. This is their primary role. On the other hand, a by-product of destroying Xacts with TERMINATE Blocks is that the value of the model's Termination Counter is potentially reduced. This is the secondary role of TERMINATE Blocks. This secondary role provides the modeler with a tool for controlling the duration of a simulation. (See Exercise 8 of Section 2.23.)

A model can contain any number of TERMINATE Blocks, but the model has only one Termination Counter. Transaction movement into any of a model's TERMINATE Blocks causes the value of the model's Termination Counter to be potentially decremented.

2.10 A Two-Block GPSS/H Model

Figure 2.10 shows a simple but complete two-Block GPSS/H model consisting of a GENERATE Block followed by a TERMINATE Block. When a simulation is performed with this model, a Transaction will come out of the GENERATE Block every 15.0 ± 4.5 time units and move immediately into the TERMINATE Block, destroying itself and decreasing the value of the model's Termination Counter by 1. The model is not intended to correspond to a real system. It does provide a basis for discussing

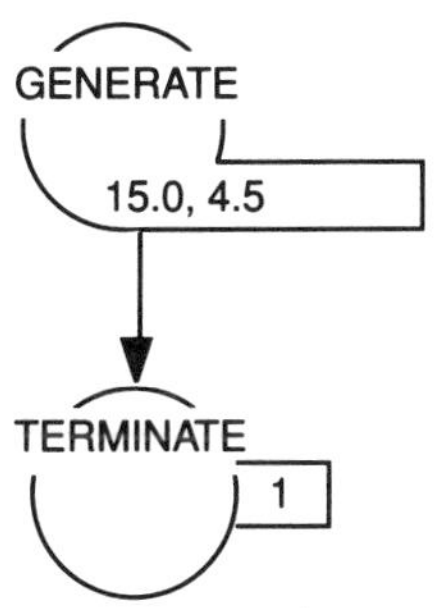

Figure 2.10 *A Two-Block GPSS/H Model*

Model Files, however, and will be used for demonstration purposes later in this chapter.

2.11 Block, Control, and Comments Statements and Model Files

To perform a simulation with a model, the statement version of the Blocks in the model must be prepared and then supplemented with additional types of statements known as **Control Statements**. The resulting collection of statements must then be arranged in an appropriate order in a file (a Model File) and can then be submitted to GPSS/H for execution.

In addition to containing Block and Control Statements, a Model File can include **Comments Statements**. (It can also contain another type of statement, Compiler Directives, which are introduced later in the book.)

The nature of Block, Control, and Comments statements can be summarized as follows:

1. Block Statements. Block Statements are the statement form of Blocks in a model. They are the only type of statement that directly corresponds to Blocks. Block Statements are only executed at the time Transactions move into Blocks.

2. Control Statements. There are several types of Control statements. For example, some Control Statements are used to control the overall execution of a Model File. Others are used to define certain features of model components. Still others are used to read input into and write output from GPSS/H models. And so on.

   Control Statements do not correspond to Blocks, and so they are not shown as part of a Block Diagram. Furthermore, Transactions do **not** "move into" Control Statements. Transactions only move from Block to Block. The concept of Transaction movement from Control Statement to Control Statement is **not valid**.

3. Comments Statements. Comments Statements provide the modeler with a means for including intramodel documentation (comments) as part of a Model File. Comments Statements provide commentary for people who work with the Model File and do not supply information that GPSS/H itself uses in performing simulations with the Model File. Use of Comments Statements, although optional, is strongly recommended.

2.12 The Structure of Control Statements

Control and Block Statements are similar in structure. Like Blocks, Control Statements have up to three characteristics: a Label (sometimes referred to as a Location in the case of Blocks), an Operation, and Operands. These are described in general terms as follows:

1. Label. In some Control Statements, a **Label** is required. (A Label is usually just an identifier for a particular Control Statement.) In others, a Label is optional. In yet others, the use of a Label is not allowed. The use of Labels in Control Statements is introduced later in the book.

2. Operation. A Control Statement's **Operation** is a key word suggestive of the effect resulting from execution of that type of Control Statement. Examples of Control Statement. Operation words are **SIMULATE**, **START**, and **END**. (Each of these Control-Statement types is discussed in Section 2.15.) When Control Statements are put into a Model File, each Control Statement's Operation word **must** be specified.

3. Operands. Control Statements have zero or more **Operands**. A Control Statement's Operands provide information on which the Control Statement's action is based.

   The number of potential Operands a Control Statement has depends on the type of Control-Statement. Operands are represented in general with the letters A, B, C, D, and so on.

   Values must be supplied explicitly for certain Operands on certain types of Control Statements. In many cases, however, it's possible to default in the use of Control Statement Operands.

2.13 The Format of GPSS/H Statements

Each type of GPSS/H statement is composed of one or more pieces of information. A piece of information is expressed as a sequence of one or more consecutive characters. For example, the statement-equivalent of a TERMINATE Block is composed of up to three pieces of information: an optional Block Label, a required Operation word (TERMINATE), and an optional value for the A Operand. The format of a statement refers to the positions in the statement that the pieces of information making up the statement can or must occupy.

Block and Control Statements are formatted identically. Corresponding to its Label (or Location), Operation, and Operands, a statement consists of three fields. (A "field" is a sequence of consecutive columns in a statement.) It is convenient to use a fixed format when keying GPSS/H statements. Table 2.2 shows a suggested format. In this format, a statement's Label (or Location), if any, is entered (in consecutive columns) beginning in **column 2**. Its Operation word is entered beginning in **column 11**. And its Operands, if any, are entered beginning in **column 22**, and not extending beyond column 72. In the case of two or more Operands, consecutive Operands are separated by commas, without any blanks in between.

The **first blank column** appearing in a statement's Operand's field marks the end of that field. Explanatory comments can be keyed to the right of this first blank to help document the model. **Comments should not extend beyond column 80 in a statement.**

If an **asterisk (*)** is entered in column 1 of a statement, GPSS/H treats the statement as a Comments Statement. Comments Statements provide the modeler with a method for documenting models with lengthy comments, and/or with the capability of leaving nearly blank lines between what might otherwise be consecutive nonblank statements making up a Model File. Used appropriately, these nearly blank lines can make it easier for a person to read a listing of a Model File.

For the format described in Table 2.2, columns 10 and 21 will always be blank. (This is because a Label cannot exceed 8 characters, as will be explained later, and so cannot extend into column 10, and because no Operation word started in column 11 is long enough to extend into column 21.) A minimum of one blank column will then always separate the Label (Location) and Operation fields, and the Operation and Operands fields, in the Table 2.2 format.

To illustrate the Table 2.2 format, the Block statements for the two Blocks in Figure 2.10 are shown in Figure 2.11. A template has been supplied in the background in Figure 2.11 with horizontal lines separating consecutive statements, and with a header and vertical lines identifying statement columns 1, 10, and 21, and the Label, Operation, and Operands fields, making it easy to see that the formatting is consistent with Table 2.2.

The Blocks in Figure 2.10 are not labeled, so the respective Label fields in Figure 2.11 have been left blank. Comments have been appended to the two Block statements. Note the use of one or more blanks in Figure 2.11 to separate a Block's Operands from the start of the comments appended to the Block statement. Two Comments Statements have also been included in Figure 2.11. These accommodate the relatively long comment that begins on the second of the Block statements.

Any alphabetic characters that are part of the Label, Operation, and Operands fields must be in UPPER CASE, as they are in Figure 2.11. In contrast, documentation characters can be lower and/or upper case (as they are in Figure 2.11).

The format of Table 2.2 will be used throughout this book, but it does not have to be used in general. *Free format can be used in GPSS/H. In free format, only one blank need separate the Label, Operation, Operands, and Comments fields.*

Table 2.2

A suggested (but optional) fixed format for GPSS/H statements

Statement Columns Making Up the Field	Type of Information Entered into the Field	
2-9	Label[1]	(if any)
11-20	Operation	
22 et seq.	Operands	(if any)
> (last Operand's last column, + 1)	Comment	(if any)

[1] In the case of Blocks, sometimes referred to as Location or Block identifier.

1	Label (2 - 9)	Operation (11 - 20)	Operands (22 - 72) →	
		GENERATE	15.0,4.5	Transactions arrive, one by one
		TERMINATE	1	Transactions are destroyed,
*				one by one, each reducing the
*				value of the model's TC by 1

Figure 2.11 An Example of Block Statements in the Format of Table 2.2

2.14 The SIMULATE, START, and END Control Statements

A Model File almost always contains a SIMULATE Statement and one or more START Statements, and must contain exactly one END Statement. These three types of Control Statements are introduced in this section. The following section then shows how Block statements and these three types of Control Statements are arranged in a basic GPSS/H Model File.

2.14.1 The SIMULATE Control Statement

Figure 2.12 shows the general form of the **SIMULATE Control Statement,** displayed on a template like the one used in Figure 2.11. The SIMULATE Statement is never labeled. Its Operation word is SIMULATE. Its optional A Operand is discussed next.

The SIMULATE Statement tells GPSS/H to put a Model File into execution after it has been compiled (that is, after it has been put into an internal form suitable for execution). In the absence of a SIMULATE Statement, a Model File will only be compiled. Saving a model in its compiled state will not be of interest in this book.

The SIMULATE Statement's optional A Operand is a **Time Limit Operand.** This Operand puts a limit on the total amount of computer time (CPU time) GPSS/H is permitted to use in compiling and executing a Model File. Use of the Time Limit Operand can prevent a "runaway simulation" from consuming excessive amounts of computer time. (A runaway simulation is one performed with a model that fails to include an effective means for bringing the simulation to an end. See Exercise 2 of Section 2.25.)

DOS GPSS/H ignores the SIMULATE Statement's Time Limit Operand. The Time Limit Operand is introduced here, however, for users (or eventual users) of non-DOS GPSS/H.

The Time Limit Operand, which can be an integer or decimal constant, has default units of **minutes.** If **seconds** are intended, the last character in the A Operand must be S (for Seconds).

If the SIMULATE statement's Time Limit Operand is used in non-DOS GPSS/H and the time limit is reached, GPSS/H stops the simulation and issues an Error Message.

1	Label (2 - 9)	Operation (11 - 20)	Operands (22 - 72) →
	never used	**SIMULATE**	**A**

Label or Operand	Significance	Default Value or Result
Label	Never used	Must Default (Compile-time error otherwise)
A	Time Limit Operand (integer or decimal number; units are CPU minutes unless followed by an S, then units are CPU seconds)	No internal Time Limit will be set

Figure 2.12 The SIMULATE Control Statement and Its A Operand

	Label (2 - 9)	Operation (11 - 20)	Operands (22 - 72) ⟶
1			
		SIMULATE	**3S Example 1 (3 second CPU Time Limit)**
		SIMULATE	**0.5 Example 2 (0.5 minute CPU Time Limit)**
		SIMULATE	**Example 3 (no Time Limit)**

Figure 2.13 *Examples of the SIMULATE Control Statement*

Several examples of SIMULATE Statements are given in Figure 2.13. The SIMULATE Statement in Example 1 uses the Time Limit Operand to set a time limit of 3 seconds. In Example 2, the Time Limit Operand is used to set a time limit of 0.5 minutes. In Example 3, the Time Limit Operand is not used, so no time limit is imposed by GPSS/H.

If the Time Limit Operand is used, at what value should it be set? The answer depends on such things as the size of the Model File, the number of Block executions required by the simulation, and the computer being used. The computer being used determines the Block execution rate. DOS GPSS/H typically executes **one thousand** or more Blocks per CPU second. Used on a mainframe computer, GPSS/H executes as many as **four hundred thousand** or more Blocks per CPU second. The models in this book execute under DOS GPSS/H in from less than 1 second up to several minutes. The same models execute on an IBM 3090-600E mainframe in not more than 1 to 2 seconds. For users of non-DOS GPSS/H, experience is the best guide in deciding the level at which to set time limits.

Because DOS GPSS/H ignores the Time Limit Operand, we will not make use of it in this book.

2.14.2 The START Control Statement

When a **START Control Statement** is executed, three things happen:

1. The model's Termination Counter is given an initial value.
2. The model's GENERATE Blocks are initialized. (That is, at each GENERATE Block in a model, START Statement execution causes a Transaction to be created and scheduled to be brought into the model from that GENERATE Block at an appropriately determined simulated time.)
3. Block-to-Block movement of Transactions begins.

Figure 2.14 shows the format of the START Statement and its A Operand. The Operationword is START. The START Statement's A Operand specifies the **initial value of the model's Termination Counter.** The A Operand must have a value of 1 or more. Failure to specify a value for the A Operand results in an error.

As indicated in Figure 2.14, a START Statement can be labeled. We'll have no occasion to label START Statements in this book.

	Label (2 - 9)	Operation (11 - 20)	Operands (22 - 72) ⟶
1			
	see below	**START**	**A**

Label or Operand	Significance	Default Value or Result
Label	START-statement identifier	Unlabeled statement
A	Initial value of the model's Termination Counter	Defaulting results in a compile-time error

Figure 2.14 *The START Control Statement and Its A Operand*

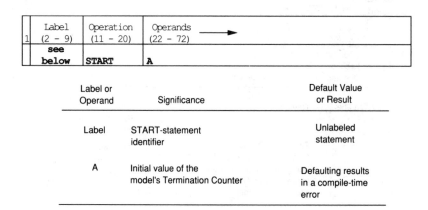

1	Label (2 - 9)	Operation (11 - 20)	Operands (22 - 72) ——▶
		START	**25 Example 1 (initial TC value: 25)**
		START	**1 Example 2 (initial TC value: 1)**
		START	**100 Example 3 (initial TC value: 100)**

Figure 2.15 *Examples of the START Control Statement*

Several examples of START Statements are shown in Figure 2.15. In Example 1, the initial value specified for the model's Termination Counter is 25. In Examples 2 and 3, the model's Termination Counter will be initialized with values of 1 and 100, respectively.

2.14.3 The END Control Statement

The END Control Statement plays two roles in a Model File: (1) its presence indicates the physical end of the Model File, and (2) its execution causes GPSS/H to stop executing the Model File and give control back to DOS (or, in general, to the operating system).

Figure 2.16 shows the format of an END Control Statement. The statement's Operation word is END. The statement has no Operands, either required or optional. Use of a Label on the statement is optional.

As implied, each GPSS/H Model File should contain exactly one END Statement. This statement should always be the last statement in the Model File.

2.15 The Top-Down Order of Statements in a Basic GPSS/H Model File

The suggested top-down order of statements in a basic GPSS/H Model File is shown in Figure 2.17. First comes a SIMULATE Control Statement, then the Block Statements for the model, then a START Control Statement, and finally an END Control Statement.

Comments Statements are not shown in Figure 2.17. Comments Statements can be interspersed throughout a Model File.

2.16 A Complete GPSS/H Model File

A complete GPSS/H Model File corresponding to the simple two-Block model in Figure 2.10 is shown in Figure 2.18. The Model File statements have been superimposed on a background similar to that used in Figures 2.11, 2.12, and 2.13, making it easy to see how the statements have been formatted. And for discussion purposes, a column of statement numbers has been provided at the left edge of the figure. The order of statements in the Model File corresponds to the statement order given in Figure 2.17. First there is a SIMULATE Statement (statement 1), then Block statements (statements 7 and 8), then a START Statement (statement 16), and finally an END Statement (statement 19).

Statements 2 through 6 in Figure 2.18 are Comments Statements that provide a banner for the Block-Statement portion of the Model File. Similarly, statements 11 through 15 are Comments Statements that provide a banner for the Control-Statement section of the Model File. Statements 9 and 10

1	Label (2 - 9)	Operation (11 - 20)	Operands (22 - 72) ——▶
	see below	**END**	

Label or Operand	Significance	Default Value or Result
Label	END-statement identifier	Unlabeled statement

Figure 2.16 *The END Control Statement*

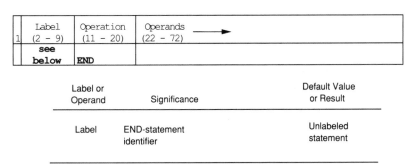

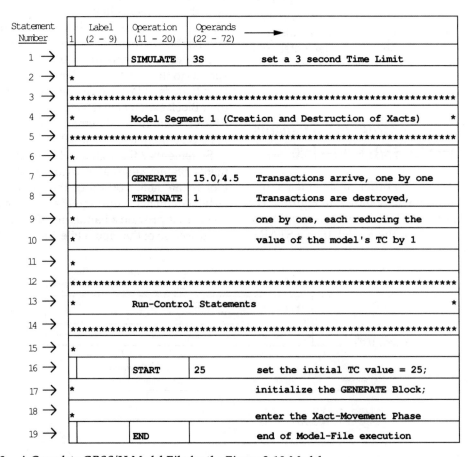

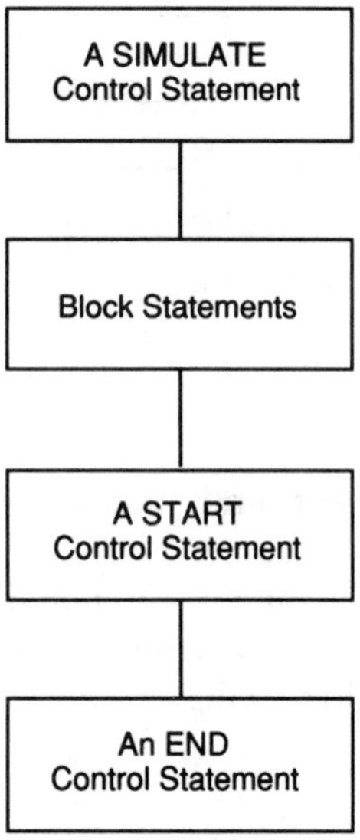

Figure 2.17 *The Top-Down Order of Statements in a Basic GPSS/H Model File*

are Comments Statements used to help carry the relatively long comment appended to the TERMINATE-Block Statement (statement 8).

2.17 Keying GPSS/H Model Files

Before a Model File can be executed, it must be created in the form of an ASCII text file. Any text editor (or a word processor that can save a file in ASCII format) can be used to build a Model File. Use of a visual (full-screen) editor is recommended. The DOS line editor EDLIN will work, but a visual editor is much easier to use in the case of larger Model Files. Many computer users already have a favorite editor they will prefer for the building of Model Files.

The GPSS/H statement format described in Table 2.2 is very practical for keying Model Files. Tab

Statement Number	1	Label (2 - 9)	Operation (11 - 20)	Operands (22 - 72) →
1 →			SIMULATE	3S set a 3 second Time Limit
2 →	*			
3 →	**			
4 →	*			Model Segment 1 (Creation and Destruction of Xacts) *
5 →	**			
6 →	*			
7 →			GENERATE	15.0,4.5 Transactions arrive, one by one
8 →			TERMINATE	1 Transactions are destroyed,
9 →	*			one by one, each reducing the
10 →	*			value of the model's TC by 1
11 →	*			
12 →	**			
13 →	*		Run-Control Statements	*
14 →	**			
15 →	*			
16 →			START	25 set the initial TC value = 25;
17 →	*			initialize the GENERATE Block;
18 →	*			enter the Xact-Movement Phase
19 →			END	end of Model-File execution

Figure 2.18 *A Complete GPSS/H Model File for the Figure 2.10 Model*

stops can be set at columns 11, 22, and 33 (say), corresponding, respectively, to the start of the Operation, Operands, and Comments fields, and the keying can proceed accordingly.

Those who do not have a preferred editor, and who aren't familiar with available editors, should ask a computer counselor in their organization to outline possibilities for them. Good shareware editors are available for personal computers. In a course, instructors may want to recommend an editor to the students.

Remember that except for comments, GPSS/H statements must be in UPPER CASE. The keyboard's Caps Lock key (or equivalent) can be useful in this regard.

2.18 Batch-Mode Versus Test-Mode Use of GPSS/H

GPSS/H Model Files can be executed in Batch Mode or in Test Mode. In Batch Mode, the user prepares a Model File, submits it to the computer for execution, and then gets the results after the run is finished. For example, the user can initiate a Batch run from a personal computer, directing the results to the computer screen for immediate viewing or to a disk file for later viewing.

When a GPSS/H run takes place in Test Mode, the user can interact in a number of ways with the ongoing simulation. For example, the user can specify conditions under which model execution is to be temporarily suspended (interrupted) while the user displays information about the state of the model. Test-Mode use of GPSS/H provides a powerful tool for troubleshooting and checking out models and coming to a detailed understanding of their operation.

The use of GPSS/H in Test Mode is introduced later in this chapter. Batch Mode use of GPSS/H is introduced in Chapter 6. The steps carried out by GPSS/H in executing Model Files in both Batch and Test Mode are described in the next two sections.

2.19 The Steps Followed by GPSS/H in a Batch-Mode Simulation

The steps followed by GPSS/H in executing a Model File in Batch Mode are shown in Figure 2.19. The figure will be discussed in terms of the numbered boxes of which it is composed.

(1) Model Compilation and Compiler Report

After reading a Model File, GPSS/H first goes into the **Model Compilation** Phase and compiles the model (Box 1, Figure 2.19). That is, it puts the Model File into an internal form suitable for execution.

As part of compilation, GPSS/H produces a report that includes an enhanced copy ("Source Echo") of the Model File, Warning and Error Messages if appropriate, and other information not of interest to us now. (See the comments attached to Box 1 in Figure 2.19.)

There is an important distinction between Warning and Error Messages. A Warning Message, which is just an advisory, calls the modeler's attention to some aspect of the model about which the modeler might have been unaware. For example, if the modeler labels a Block, and then does not refer to this labeled Block from some other point in the model, a Warning Message will be issued. Did the modeler **intend** to refer to this labeled Block, and then forget to do so? This is the spirit of Warning Messages. Even if there are Warning Messages, the processing of a Model File will continue.

On the other hand, an Error Message is just that: a message describing an error found in the model. If a word such as GENERATE or TERMINATE has been keyed incorrectly, for example, this results in an Error Message. Or if a START Statement fails to contain its required A Operand, this results in an Error Message. If the compiler detects one or more errors in a Model File, corresponding Compile-Time Error Messages will be displayed, and control will be returned to DOS (or to the operating system).

Even if compilation is successful, processing of the Model File will then stop if the file does not start with a SIMULATE statement. (See the line labeled "Compile-Time Error(s), or no SIMULATE," coming from Box 1 in Figure 2.19.)

Otherwise, execution of the compiled Model File will begin, as indicated by the line segment labeled "SIMULATE" coming from Box 1 in Figure 2.19.

(2) Control-Statement Execution

When GPSS/H enters the **Control-Statement Execution** Phase for the first time (see the path from Box 1 to Box 2 in Figure 2.19), it executes Control Statements in their top-down order of appearance in the Model File. The first post-

SIMULATE Control Statement in the Figure 2.17 basic GPSS/H Model File is START. Its execution initializes the model's Termination Counter and GENERATE Block or Blocks, and then sends GPSS/H out of Control-Statement Execution and into the Transaction Movement Phase (as indicated by the line labeled "START" connecting Box 2 to Box 3 in Figure 2.19).

As indicated in Box 2 of Figure 2.19, Warning Messages might also be issued during Control-Statement Execution.

(3) Transaction Movement (Block-Statement Execution)

Transactions only move in a model (and Blocks are only executed) during a **Transaction-Movement** Phase. During this phase, Xacts are created and brought into the model from time to time, move along their path from Block to Block, and may eventually be removed from the model (destroyed).

As indicated in Box 3 of Figure 2.19, Warning Messages might also be issued during the Transaction-Movement Phase.

The Transaction-Movement Phase continues until the value of the model's Termination Counter is reduced to zero (or less). When this happens, GPSS/H produces a Postsimulation Report (as indicated by the line labeled "TC ≤ 0" connecting Box 3 to Box 4 in Figure 2.19).

(4) Postsimulation Report

As part of the **Postsimulation Report** (Box 4), GPSS/H produces information summarizing what happened in the model during the preceding Transaction-Movement Phase. This information includes the value of the simulated clock, counts of the number of times each Block in the model was executed, and information about many aspects of a GPSS/H simulation to be discussed later. Postsimulation Reports will be of interest to us beginning in Chapter 6.

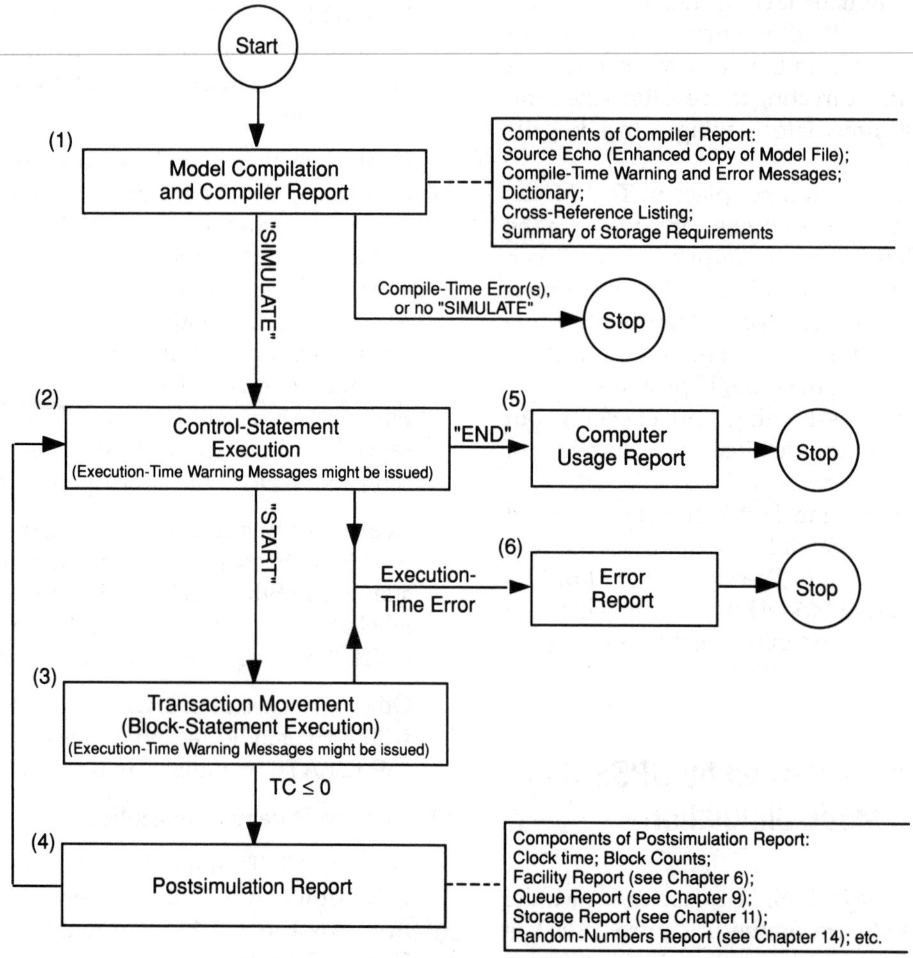

Figure 2.19 *The Steps Followed by GPSS/H in Executing a Model File in Batch Mode*

As indicated by the return line from Box 4 to Box 2 in Figure 2.19, GPSS/H then resumes Control-Statement execution, beginning with the Control Statement following the most recently executed START Statement. The next Control Statement after the one START Statement in the basic GPSS/H Model File in Figure 2.17 is END. Execution of the END Statement causes GPSS/H to produce a Computer-Usage Report (as indicated by Box 5, Figure 2.19), and then return control to DOS (or to the operating system).

(5) Computer-Usage Report

The GPSS/H **Computer-Usage Report** summarizes aspects of the use of computer memory, time, and effort in execution of the Model File. This report indicates the current, average, and maximum use of a type of GPSS/H computer memory known as COMMON. (The importance of COMMON is explored at several points later in the book, and in Section B.2 of Appendix B.) It indicates how many Blocks were executed in total during the simulation, and how much CPU time was required per Block execution on average. It also provides a breakout on the CPU time used in various phases of Model-File processing.

Except for the brief foregoing comments, the Computer-Usage Report will not be further discussed in this book.

After producing the Computer-Usage Report, GPSS/H stops executing the Model File and control is returned to DOS (or to the operating system).

(6) Error Report

Execution Errors can occur during Control-Statement execution and during Xact movement. If an Execution Error occurs, GPSS/H exits the phase it is in and produces an Error Report (see the lines labeled "Execution-Time Error" leading from Boxes 2 and 3 in Figure 2.19). In a Batch-Mode simulation, GPSS/H then stops executing the Model File.

2.20 The User's Role in a Test-Mode Simulation

A basic view of the interplay between the user and GPSS/H in a Test-Mode simulation is shown in Figure 2.20. The lines in the figure have been numbered for reference. The figure only provides a broad overview of the user's role when carrying out Test-Mode simulations. (Specific Test-Mode commands that the user can issue are introduced later. Furthermore, Figure 2.20 has been simplified by assuming that no Execution Errors occur and that the user quits the Test-Mode simulation before the model's Termination Counter has been decremented to zero.)

Figure 2.20 will now be discussed in terms of its numbered lines.

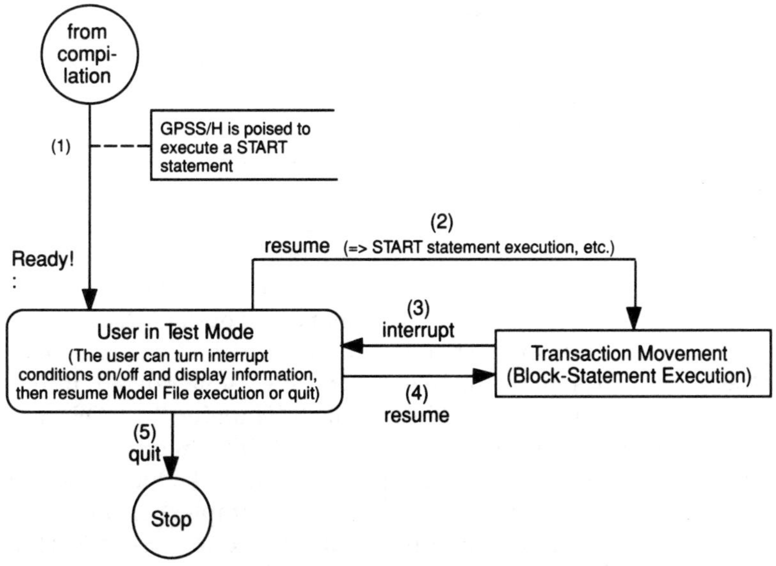

Figure 2.20 *A Basic View of the Interplay Between the User and GPSS/H in a Test-Mode Simulation*

Line (1)

It is assumed in Figure 2.20 that model compilation has been completed successfully, that Control-Statement execution is proceeding, and that GPSS/H is about to execute a START Statement. At this point, GPSS/H temporarily suspends (interrupts) execution, writes a "Ready!" message to the screen, and gives control to the user, displaying a colon (:) to prompt the user to enter a Test-Mode command. (See Line 1 in Figure 2.20, connecting "from compilation" to the "User in Test Mode" box.)

Line (2)

The user now (optionally) issues one or more Test-Mode commands to describe conditions under which GPSS/H is later to suspend (interrupt) temporarily the simulation and return control to the user. (The types of Test-Mode commands that the user can issue are described in Section 2.22, and in Chapters 3 and 4.) The user then issues a command to GPSS/H to resume the simulation. (See Line 2 in Figure 2.20, connecting the "User in Test Mode" box to the "Transaction Movement" box.)

Line (3)

GPSS/H then resumes the simulation, executing the START Statement and going into the Transaction Movement Phase. The simulation proceeds until an interrupt condition comes about. GPSS/H then suspends the simulation, displays a message on the screen telling the user the conditions under which the simulation is being interrupted, and gives control to the user, displaying a colon (:) to prompt the user to enter a Test-Mode command. (See Line 3 in Figure 2.20, connecting the "Transaction Movement" box to the "User in Test Mode" box.)

Line (4)

The user now (optionally) issues one or more Test-Mode commands to change the set of interrupt conditions in effect (perhaps establishing some new interrupt conditions, and/or deleting some old interrupt conditions). Commands can also be issued to display information about various aspects of the model. The user then issues a command to resume the simulation. (See Line 4 in Figure 2.20, connecting the "User in Test Mode" box to the "Transaction Movement" box.)

Lines (3) and (4) (alternating)

GPSS/H then resumes the previously interrupted simulation, proceeding until an interrupt condition comes about again. At this point, another message is displayed on the screen to describe the interrupt condition, and control is given back to the user (Line 3).

The user then optionally issues one or more Test-Mode commands to alter the interrupt conditions and/or to display information about the model, and then issues a command to resume the simulation (Line 4).

This back-and-forth process shown as Lines 3 and 4 in Figure 2.20 continues until the user has accomplished the purpose of the Test-Mode simulation. The user then issues a command to stop (Line 5).

As noted within the "User in Test Mode" box in Figure 2.20, the Test-Mode user can turn interrupt conditions on and back off, display information, and cause the simulation to be resumed. (The Test-Mode command used to display information is introduced in Chapter 3.)

The Test-Mode user cannot make any changes in the Model File with which the simulation is being performed. To do that, it's necessary to quit the Test-Mode session, use an editor to make Model File changes, and then recompile and start another Test-Mode session.

2.21 Running GPSS/H Under DOS

After a Model File has been prepared, an operating system command must be issued to direct GPSS/H to execute the Model File. This command indicates that GPSS/H is to be used, provides the name of the computer file containing the Model File, specifies whether the run is to be in Batch or Test Mode, and can provide other optional information as well.

The particulars of the operating system command and options depend on the operating system under which GPSS/H is being used. Appendix B provides generalized information for running GPSS/H under PC-DOS (the Disk Operating System for IBM microcomputers) and MS-DOS (the Microsoft Disk Operating System).

For example, here are two DOS commands that can be used to run GPSS/H in **Test Mode**:

```
gpssh filename.gps tv type nowarn
gpssh filename.gps tvtnw
```

In such DOS commands, **gpssh** is always required. In ***filename*.gps**, ***filename*** represents the name of the Model File, and **gps** is the file extension. (If the extension is not specified, **gps** is assumed.)

Options are indicated in the remaining information supplied in the two preceding examples of **gpssh** commands. Options expressed on the first of these two command lines are **tv** (which signals that the run is in Test Mode, not Batch Mode, and that the computer screen is to be split into three windows, as to be explained and illustrated in Section 2.22), **type** (which means the Postsimulation Report is to be typed on the screen), and **nowarn** (which means that if Compile-Time Warning Messages occur, they are not to be displayed on the screen). The second command line is identical in effect to the first, but expresses the options in the compressed form of **tvtnw** (**tv**, **t**ype, **nowarn**). Because of its compactness, the second command line is more convenient than the first.

Examples of DOS commands for running GPSS/H in Batch Mode are given both in Appendix B and in Chapter 6, where the use of Batch Mode is first illustrated.

If further particulars about running GPSS/H under DOS are of interest now, consult Appendix B.

2.22 Tracing Transaction Creation and Destruction in Test Mode

The first Test-Mode command we introduce is the **step** command. In its simplest form, this command consists only of the word **step**. A step command means "resume the simulation, proceed to the point that one more Block has been executed, and then interrupt the simulation." And so a step command both establishes an interrupt condition and causes the simulation to be resumed. The resume-the-simulation aspect of **step** corresponds to Lines 2 and 4 in Figure 2.20. (As we will see in Chapter 5, there are also other Test-Mode commands that correspond to Lines 2 and 4.)

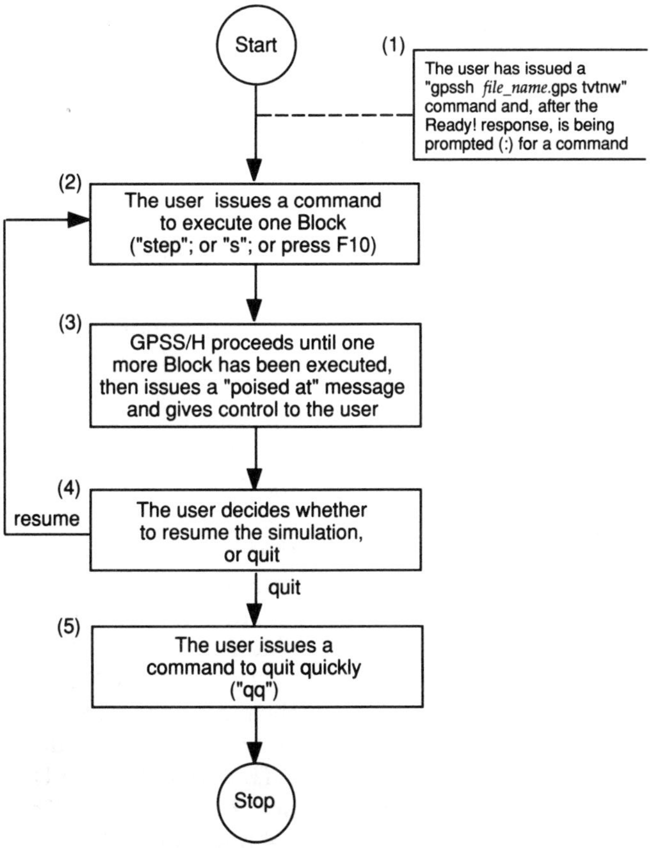

Figure 2.21 *Stepping Through a GPSS/H Simulation, One Block Execution at a Time*

When issuing a step command, **step** can be abbreviated as **ste**, or **st**, or just as **s**. Another way to issue a step command is to press the F10 key.

Let's now use the step command to trace the movement of two Transactions through the two-Block model shown in the Figure 2.10 Block Diagram and the Figure 2.18 Model File. With the simple step command, we **single-step** our way through model execution, proceeding at the rate of just one Block execution at a time. The overall procedure is outlined in Figure 2.21.

We first issue a DOS command to run GPSS/H in Test Mode with the Model File of interest. (See the comment labeled (1) in Figure 2.21.) GPSS/H compiles the Model File, proceeds to the point where it is ready to execute the START Statement, and returns control to us, writing a "Ready!" message to the screen and then a colon (:) to prompt us for a command. We then issue a **step** command to tell GPSS/H to start the simulation and proceed until a single Block has been executed (Box 2). GPSS/H does this, then interrupts the simulation, and returns control to us (Box 3), printing out a message and prompting us for another command. If we want GPSS/H to resume the simulation (Box 4), we issue another **step** command (Box 2). We repeat the process until we are ready to quit. At this point (Box 4), we tell GPSS/H to quit the simulation (Box 5) and return to DOS.

Figure 2.22, parts (a) through (g), shows a sequence of seven consecutive computer screens that result when we single-step our way through execution of the Figure 2.18 Model File. Discussion of this screen sequence follows. (In Exercise 1 of Section 2.24, you are asked to reproduce this screen sequence on your computer.)

Screen 1 (Figure 2.22, part a)

Screen 1 is produced in response to issuing this DOS command:

```
gpssh fig218.gps tvtnw
```

The file that contains the Figure 2.18 Model File is "fig218.gps". "tvtnw" is short for "tv type nowarn," as has been indicated in Section 2.21.

At the bottom of Screen 1, we see the Ready! message and the colon (:) marking the transition from Box 1 to Box 2 in Figure 2.21. The various labels in Screen 1 are explained in the discussion of Screen 2.

Screen 2 (Figure 2.22, part b)

Screen 2 results when we respond to Screen 1 by keying in and sending a **step** command. Having executed this command, GPSS/H has printed out this message:

```
XACT 1 POISED AT BLOCK 2. RELATIVE CLOCK: 12.9327
```

(This message is explained further below.) GPSS/H then has printed out a colon to prompt us for more input. (See the last several lines at the bottom of Screen 2.)

The **step** command is the first example we've seen of a GPSS/H Test-Mode command. Test-Mode commands are only issued while running in GPSS/H in Test Mode. These commands are **not** to be made part of the content of Model Files. Furthermore, **Test-Mode commands can be keyed in lower, upper, or mixed case.** (This contrasts with statements in GPSS/H Model Files that, with the exception of comments, must be in UPPER CASE.)

Before proceeding with the interpretation of screen information, we now pause to describe the composition of the screens themselves.

The screens in Figure 2.22 are divided into three parts, or windows. These are called the Source, Status, and Dialog Windows. These windows are shown in Figure 2.22bb, which boxes in and labels the three windows in Figure 2.22(b). Discussion follows.

Source Window

The **top window** in Figure 2.22bb is the **Source Window**. The rightmost part of the Source Window shows the name of the Model File (fig218.gps) and the label **SOURCE CODE**. Under the SOURCE CODE label are displayed up to five consecutive Block Statements in the Model File. In the Figure 2.22bb Source Window, both Block Statements in the Model File ("GENERATE 15.0,4.5" and "TERMINATE 1") are shown.

The left part of the Source Window consists of columns labeled **BLOCK**, **CURRENT**, and **TOTAL**. The **BLOCK** column shows the Locations in the model occupied by the Blocks appearing in the right part of the window. In this case, the GENERATE and TERMINATE Blocks are in Locations 1 and 2, respectively. The **CURRENT** and **TOTAL** columns show Transaction counts for the corre-

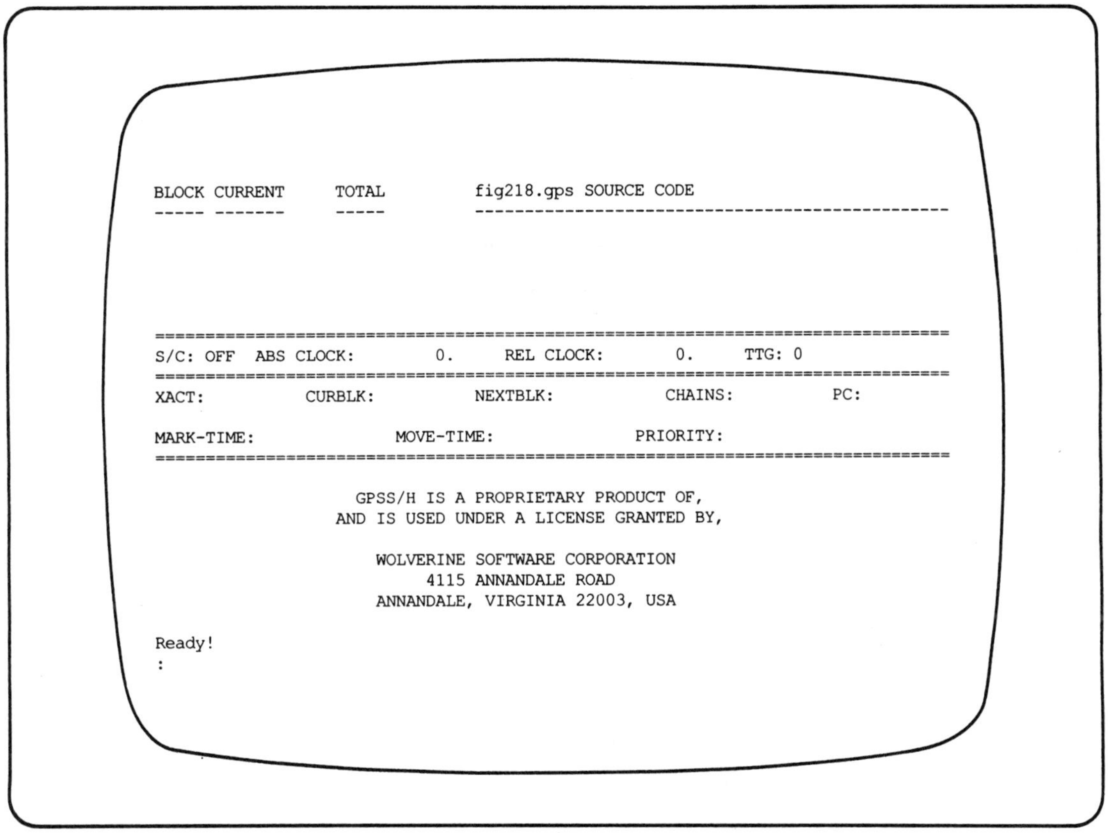
BLOCK CURRENT TOTAL fig218.gps SOURCE CODE
S/C: OFF ABS CLOCK: 0. REL CLOCK: 0. TTG: 0
XACT: CURBLK: NEXTBLK: CHAINS: PC:
MARK-TIME: MOVE-TIME: PRIORITY:
GPSS/H IS A PROPRIETARY PRODUCT OF,
AND IS USED UNDER A LICENSE GRANTED BY,
WOLVERINE SOFTWARE CORPORATION
4115 ANNANDALE ROAD
ANNANDALE, VIRGINIA 22003, USA
Ready!
:

Figure 2.22 *Seven Computer Screens Resulting When the Figure 2.18 Model File Is Run in Test Model (a) Screen 1*

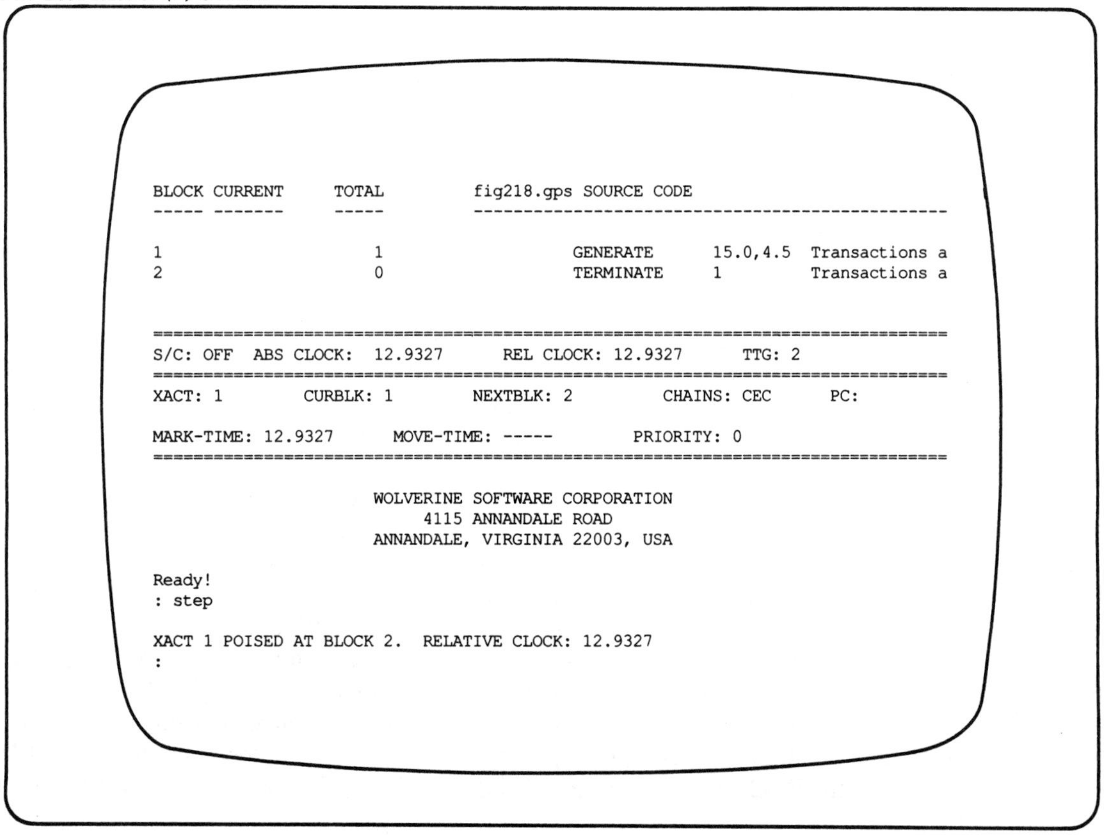
BLOCK CURRENT TOTAL fig218.gps SOURCE CODE
1 1 GENERATE 15.0,4.5 Transactions a
2 0 TERMINATE 1 Transactions a
S/C: OFF ABS CLOCK: 12.9327 REL CLOCK: 12.9327 TTG: 2
XACT: 1 CURBLK: 1 NEXTBLK: 2 CHAINS: CEC PC:
MARK-TIME: 12.9327 MOVE-TIME: ----- PRIORITY: 0
WOLVERINE SOFTWARE CORPORATION
4115 ANNANDALE ROAD
ANNANDALE, VIRGINIA 22003, USA
Ready!
: step
XACT 1 POISED AT BLOCK 2. RELATIVE CLOCK: 12.9327
:

Figure 2.22 (b) *Screen 2*

```
BLOCK CURRENT     TOTAL         fig218.gps SOURCE CODE
----- -------     -----         ---------------------------------------------

1                   1                  GENERATE      15.0,4.5  Transactions a
2                   0                  TERMINATE     1         Transactions a

                              Source Window
```

```
S/C: OFF  ABS CLOCK:  12.9327      REL CLOCK: 12.9327       TTG: 2
================================================================================
XACT: 1        CURBLK: 1        NEXTBLK: 2          CHAINS: CEC       PC:

MARK-TIME: 12.9327      MOVE-TIME: -----         PRIORITY: 0

                              Status Window
```

```
                       WOLVERINE SOFTWARE CORPORATION
                            4115 ANNANDALE ROAD
                       ANNANDALE, VIRGINIA 22003, USA

Ready!
: step

XACT 1 POISED AT BLOCK 2.  RELATIVE CLOCK: 12.9327
:
                              Dialog Window
```

Figure 2.22bb *A Repetition of Figure 2.22b, with the Source, Status, and Dialog Windows Boxed in and Labeled*

sponding Blocks. The CURRENT count indicates how many Xacts are currently in the Blocks, and the TOTAL count indicates how many times the Blocks have been executed so far in the simulation. The GENERATE Block in Screen 2 has been executed one time, and the TERMINATE Block hasn't yet been executed. And so the GENERATE TOTAL count is 1, and the TERMINATE TOTAL count is "blank," which corresponds to zero. (Instead of printing a count of zero, GPSS/H leaves the position blank instead.)

The CURRENT column in the Figure 2.22bb Source Window contains blanks (zeros) for the GENERATE and TERMINATE Blocks, even though the moving Xact, Xact 1, is currently in the GENERATE Block. GPSS/H does not update the CURRENT counts *until the moving Xact cannot move any further*, which explains why the CURRENT count at the Figure 2.22bb GENERATE Block is zero, not 1, even though Xact 1 is in the Block at the moment.

Status Window

The **middle window** in Figure 2.22bb is the **Status Window**, which shows information describing the current status of the model.

In row 1 of the Status Window, the **S/C** label isn't important for us now. **ABS CLOCK** and **REL CLOCK** are labels for the current values of the **Absolute Clock** and **Relative Clock**, respectively. These clocks show the current simulated time (12.9327 in Figure 2.22bb). The distinction between the Absolute and Relative Clocks isn't important for us here. In this book, the value registered by the Absolute Clock will always match the value registered by the Relative Clock.

TTG is the label for the current value of the model's Termination Counter. The START statement in the Figure 2.18 Model File specifies an initial value of 2 for the Termination Counter, consistent with **TTG: 2** in Figure 2.22bb. The TERMINATE Block hasn't been executed yet even a first time, so the initial value of the Termination Counter is still in effect.

Rows 2 and 3 of the Status Window provide information about the currently moving Xact (or, during interludes when there is not a moving Xact, about the Xact that was most recently moved). In row 2, **XACT** labels the id number of the Transaction. **CURBLK** and **NEXTBLK** label this Transaction's Current Block and Next Block Attempted (with the information displayed in terms of Block Location Numbers). **CHAINS** labels the "cha n" on which this Transaction is resident. **CEC** s short for **Current Events Chain**. The Current Events Chain is composed of Transactions scheduled to move along their path in the model at the current simulated time. More will be said about the Current Events Chain in Chapters 4 and 7. The **PC** label isn't important for us now.

In row 3 of the Status Window, **MARK-TIME** labels the Absolute Clock time at which the moving (or most recently moved) Xact came out of its GENERATE Block. **MOVE-TIME** labels the simulated time at which this Xact is moving. (When this value is shown as "-----," as in Figure 2.22bb, Move Time matches the ABS CLOCK value shown in the Status Window.) And **PRIORITY** labels the Priority Level of this Xact. (Priority Level, not important for us now, is introduced in Chapter 3.)

Dialog Window

The **bottom window** in Figure 2.22bb is the **Dialog Window**. The Dialog Window shows Test-Mode commands keyed in by the user and the resulting messages and prompts issued by GPSS/H. Information in the Dialog Window automatically scrolls (shifts) upward to make room for new lines being added at the bottom of this window.

Compare the Dialog Windows in Screens 1 and 2. The first several dialog lines in Screen 1 have scrolled off the top of the Dialog Window in Screen 2 to make room for the several new lines at the bottom of the Screen 2 window.

Having now finished describing the makeup of the screens, we resume with the interpretation of the screen information in the context of the model that GPSS/H is processing.

Toward the bottom of the Screen 2 (Figure 2.22b) Dialog Window, we see the **step** command that the user issued in responding to the prompt at the bottom of Screen 1. Then we see this message issued in return by GPSS/H:

```
XACT 1 POISED AT BLOCK 2. RELATIVE CLOCK: 12.9327
```

A "**poised at**" message **always** means that a moving Xact is about to try to move into the Block at which the Xact is poised. (When the simulation is later resumed, the action begins with this moving Xact trying to move into the Block at which it is poised.)

The "poised at" message tells us that Xact 1 is the moving Transaction (we also see that information in the Status Window) and that this Xact is about to try to move into the Block in Location 2 in the model (the TERMINATE Block). By moving from its GENERATE Block, Xact 1 **has triggered execution of the GENERATE Block**, resulting in a **TOTAL** execution count of 1 for that Block (as indicated in the Source Window). This Xact movement is taking place at simulated time 12.9327.

The **CURRENT** column in the Source Window contains blanks, for reasons explained earlier.

Screen 3 (Figure 2.22, part c)

Screen 3 results when we respond to Screen 2 by keying in and sending another **step** command. This command tells GPSS/H to resume the simulation and proceed until one more Block has been executed. Having executed the **step** command, GPSS/H has displayed this message:

```
XACT 1 DESTROYED AT BLOCK 2. RELATIVE CLOCK: 12.9327
```

and then has printed out a colon to prompt us for more input. (See the last several lines in the Screen 2 Dialog Window.)

It's easy to understand what happened to produce Screen 3. Resuming the simulation, GPSS/H moved Xact 1 from its Current Block (the GENERATE Block in Location 1) into its Next Block (the TERMINATE Block in Location 2). The TERMINATE Block destroyed this Xact and reduced the value of the model's Termination Counter by 1. (In the Status Window, note that **TTG** now has a value of 1, whereas in the Screen 2 Status Window, it had a value of 2.)

Screen 4 (Figure 2.22, part d)

Screen 4 results when we respond to Screen 3 by keying in and sending another **step** command. Having executed this command, GPSS/H has printed this message:

```
XACT 2 POISED AT BLOCK 2. RELATIVE CLOCK: 27.9268
```

```
BLOCK CURRENT     TOTAL         fig218.gps SOURCE CODE
----- -------     -----         ------------------------------------------

1                 1                       GENERATE      15.0,4.5  Transactions a
2                 1                       TERMINATE     1         Transactions a


================================================================================
S/C: OFF  ABS CLOCK:  12.9327      REL CLOCK: 12.9327      TTG: 1
================================================================================
XACT: 1        CURBLK: 1        NEXTBLK: 2         CHAINS:           PC:

MARK-TIME: 12.9327      MOVE-TIME: -----         PRIORITY: 0
================================================================================
                      ANNANDALE, VIRGINIA 22003, USA

Ready!
: step

XACT 1 POISED AT BLOCK 2.  RELATIVE CLOCK: 12.9327
: step

XACT 1 DESTROYED AT BLOCK 2.  RELATIVE CLOCK: 12.9327
:
```

Figure 2.22 (c) *Screen 3*

```
BLOCK CURRENT     TOTAL         fig218.gps SOURCE CODE
----- -------     -----         ------------------------------------------

1                 2                       GENERATE      15.0,4.5  Transactions a
2                 1                       TERMINATE     1         Transactions a


================================================================================
S/C: OFF  ABS CLOCK:  27.9268      REL CLOCK: 27.9268      TTG: 1
================================================================================
XACT: 2        CURBLK: 1        NEXTBLK: 2         CHAINS: CEC       PC:

MARK-TIME: 27.9268      MOVE-TIME: -----         PRIORITY: 0
================================================================================
: step

XACT 1 POISED AT BLOCK 2.  RELATIVE CLOCK: 12.9327
: step

XACT 1 DESTROYED AT BLOCK 2.  RELATIVE CLOCK: 12.9327
: step

XACT 2 POISED AT BLOCK 2.  RELATIVE CLOCK: 27.9268
:
```

Figure 2.22 (d) *Screen 4*

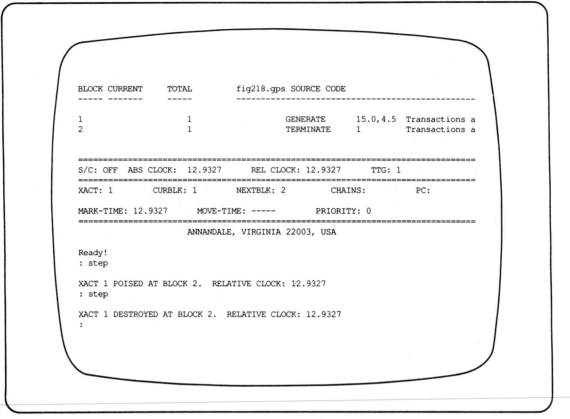

and then has printed a colon to prompt us for more input.

What happened to produce Screen 4? Resuming the simulation, GPSS/H advanced the simulated clock to the earliest future simulated time at which a Transaction was scheduled to try to move. The Xact in question has id number 2. This Xact is the next to enter the model from the Location 1 GENERATE Block. Its time of model entry is 27.9268, as we see in row 1 of the Screen 4 Status Window. Xact 2 has executed the GENERATE Block (note in the Screen 4 Source Window that the **TOTAL** execution count for the GENERATE Block is now 2) and, as the message says, is poised to move into Block 2 (the TERMINATE Block).

Recall, GPSS/H does not update the CURRENT count until the currently moving Xact cannot move any further. This explains why the CURRENT count at the GENERATE Block in the Screen 4 Status Window is blank (zero), even though Xact 2 is currently in that Block.

Screen 5 (Figure 2.22, part e)

Screen 5 results when we respond to Screen 4 by keying in and sending another **step** command. GPSS/H has responded by executing one more Block, then printing the message

```
REQUESTING OUTPUT IN (CONTROL) STATEMENT NUMBER 16.
RELATIVE CLOCK: 27.9268
```

and then printing a colon to prompt for more input.

What occurred to produce Screen 5? Resuming the simulation, GPSS/H moved Xact 2 from its Current Block (the GENERATE Block in Location 1) into its Next Block (the TERMINATE Block in Location 2). The TERMINATE Block destroyed this Xact (note that no "destroyed" message was issued in this case) and reduced the value of the model's Termination Counter by 1. (In the Status Window, note that **TTG** now has a value of 0, whereas in the Screen 4 Status Window it had a value of 1.) This reduction of the TC value to zero concludes the Transaction-Movement Phase. GPSS/H is now ready to go into the Postsimulation Report Phase corresponding to Box 4 in Figure 2.19. (When running in Test Mode, the Postsimulation Report is not automatically produced; instead, the user must ask to see it.)

The START Statement whose execution led into the Transaction-Movement Phase that has now come to an end is Statement 16 in the Model File. This explains why the Screen 5 message says, in part,

```
REQUESTING OUTPUT IN (CONTROL) STATEMENT NUMBER 16.
```

Screen 6 (Figure 2.22, part f)

Screen 6 results when we respond to Screen 5 by keying in (but not yet sending) a **qq** command. "qq" is short for "Quit Quickly." When a **qq** command is issued, GPSS/H will immediately return control to DOS, without displaying the Postsimulation Report.

If it **is** of interest to see the Postsimulation Report when running in Test Mode, the user can issue another **step** command in response to the **REQUESTING OUTPUT** message at the bottom of Screen 5, and the Postsimulation Report will then be displayed. The user can then issue a **qq** command to return to DOS.

Screen 7 (Figure 2.22, part g)

Screen 7 results when we send the **qq** command keyed in at the bottom of Screen 6. In Screen 7, both the Source and Status Windows have disappeared. Screen 7 shows the complete Dialog Window and ends with the DOS prompt C:>.

2.23 Logging the Dialog Window in a Disk File

In a course, the instructor may ask students to hand in a paper copy of information displayed in the Dialog Window when exercises are carried out in Test Mode. This can be done by logging the Test-Mode Dialog Window in a disk file, then later printing out the disk file. To log a Test-Mode Dialog Window in a disk file, initiate the Test-Mode session by issuing a DOS command having this form:

```
gpssh filename.gps tv nowarn
```

Note that, *importantly*, the **type** option is not specified.

Then, in response to the Ready! prompt, issue this Test-Mode command:

```
BLOCK CURRENT     TOTAL          fig218.gps SOURCE CODE
----- -------     -----          ---------------------------------------------

1                   2                      GENERATE       15.0,4.5  Transactions a
2                   2                      TERMINATE      1         Transactions a


================================================================================
S/C: OFF  ABS CLOCK:  27.9268     REL CLOCK: 27.9268      TTG: 0
================================================================================
XACT: 2         CURBLK: 1        NEXTBLK: 2          CHAINS:            PC:

MARK-TIME: 27.9268       MOVE-TIME: -----         PRIORITY: 0
================================================================================
: step

XACT 1 DESTROYED AT BLOCK 2.  RELATIVE CLOCK: 12.9327
: step

XACT 2 POISED AT BLOCK 2.  RELATIVE CLOCK: 27.9268
: step

REQUESTING OUTPUT IN (CONTROL) STATEMENT NUMBER 16.  RELATIVE CLOCK: 27.9268
:
```

Figure 2.22 (e) *Screen 5*

```
BLOCK CURRENT     TOTAL          fig218.gps SOURCE CODE
----- -------     -----          ---------------------------------------------

1                   2                      GENERATE       15.0,4.5  Transactions a
2                   2                      TERMINATE      1         Transactions a


================================================================================
S/C: OFF  ABS CLOCK:  27.9268     REL CLOCK: 27.9268      TTG: 0
================================================================================
XACT: 2         CURBLK: 1        NEXTBLK: 2          CHAINS:            PC:

MARK-TIME: 27.9268       MOVE-TIME: -----         PRIORITY: 0
================================================================================
: step

XACT 1 DESTROYED AT BLOCK 2.  RELATIVE CLOCK: 12.9327
: step

XACT 2 POISED AT BLOCK 2.  RELATIVE CLOCK: 27.9268
: step

REQUESTING OUTPUT IN (CONTROL) STATEMENT NUMBER 16.  RELATIVE CLOCK: 27.9268
: qq
```

Figure 2.22 (f) *Screen 6*

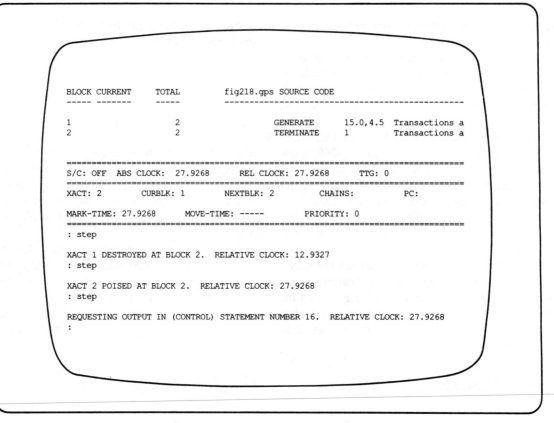

```
Simulation begins.

                    GPSS/H IS A PROPRIETARY PRODUCT OF,
                  AND IS USED UNDER A LICENSE GRANTED BY,

                      WOLVERINE SOFTWARE CORPORATION
                           4115 ANNANDALE ROAD
                      ANNANDALE, VIRGINIA 22003, USA

Ready!
: step

XACT 1 POISED AT BLOCK 2.  RELATIVE CLOCK: 12.9327
: step

XACT 1 DESTROYED AT BLOCK 2.  RELATIVE CLOCK: 12.9327
: step

XACT 2 POISED AT BLOCK 2.  RELATIVE CLOCK: 27.9268
: step

REQUESTING OUTPUT IN (CONTROL) STATEMENT NUMBER 16.  RELATIVE CLOCK: 27.9268
: qq

C:>
```

***Figure 2.22** (g) Screen 7*

```
set tlog on
```

Now proceed with the session. The Source, Status, and Dialog Window information will be displayed on your screen, as usual. In addition, information displayed in the Dialog Window will be copied into the file named ***filename*.lis** in the directory containing the ***filename*.gps** file. DOS will create the ***filename*.lis** file if it does not already exist. If this listing file already exists and is nonempty, new lines coming into the file will overwrite old lines.

For example, suppose you want to conduct a Test-Mode session with the model in the **mymodel.gps** file, and log the resulting Dialog Window information in a disk file. You can do this by issuing this DOS command to initiate the session:

```
gpssh mymodel.gps tv nowarn
```

In response to the Ready! prompt, issue the Test-Mode command **set tlog on**. The Dialog Window information will then be logged in the **mymodel.lis** file.

You probably do not want to **set tlog on** if you specify **type** as an option on the DOS **gpssh** command line. Reason: If **type** is specified, no use is made of a ***filename*.lis** file; instead, all information is typed on the screen. Each Dialog-Window line will then appear *two times* in the Dialog Window and will not appear at all in a disk file.

If you follow the preceding steps to log the Dialog Window, then list the log file, the listing will contain not only the Dialog-Window information, but also the Source Echo, Dictionary, and Cross-Reference Listing. (See the "components of compiler report" comment attached to Box 1 in Figure 2.19.) These will precede the Dialog-Window information. To avoid having the often lengthy Source Echo, Dictionary, and Cross-Reference Listing appear in the log file, initiate the Test-Mode session by issuing this DOS command:

```
gpssh filename.gps tv nowarn nos nodict noxref
```

This form is similar to the one given earlier in this section, except that it additionally include **nos**, **nodict**, and **noxref** as options. These options specify that **no** source (**nos**), **no dictionary** (**nodict**), and **no** cross-**ref**erence listing (**noxref**) are to be included in the *filename*.**lis** file.

2.24 Exercises

In this series of exercises, you're invited to carry out a variety of simulations in Test Mode, using the **step** command.

If compilation or execution errors occur as you do these exercises and you are not automatically returned to DOS, return to DOS by issuing a **qq** ("quit quickly") command. Then use an editor to correct the Model File, and issue another DOS command to have GPSS/H execute the corrected Model File in Test Mode.

Solutions to and/or comments on selected exercises throughout the book are given in Appendix C. An asterisk appears next to the numbers of the exercises for which this is the case.

1. If you have not yet done so, install your copy of Student DOS GPSS/H on your computer and make two test runs with it. Do this by carrying out the steps described in Appendix A.

2. The file named fig218.gps (contained on the supplementary disk included with this book) contains the Model File shown in Figure 2.18. ("fig218" = **figure 2.18**; we use this file-naming pattern consistently for files containing models shown as figures in the book.) Using the DOS command **gpssh fig218.gps tvtnw**, perform a simulation with the Figure 2.18 Model File in Test Mode, stepping through the simulation one Block execution at a time, as shown in Figure 2.22. Compare the information coming up on your screen with the information shown in Figure 2.22. (Your results should match those shown in Figure 2.22. For this to be true, interarrival times sampled in your simulation must match those sampled in the Figure 2.22 simulation. This will be the case, because the samples are not drawn in truly random fashion, but in "pseudorandom" fashion. This situation is discussed in detail in Chapter 14 of the book.)

3. (a) Repeat Exercise 2, but now log the Dialog Window in the **fig218.lis** file. (See Section 2.23.) Initiate the Test-Mode simulation with a **gpssh fig218.gps tv nowarn** command. Get a printout of the **lis** file on paper. Find the Dialog-Window information near the bottom of the listing. The Source Echo, Dictionary, and Cross-Reference Listing appear first in the printout. These can be ignored for now. (Details of the Source Echo are discussed in Chapter 6 of the book. Details of the Dictionary and Cross-Reference Listing are not discussed in the book.)

   (b) Issue a DOS command to erase the **fig218.lis** file from part (a). Then repeat part (a), but specify **nos nodict noxref** after **tv nowarn** on the **gpssh** command used to initiate the Test-Mode simulation. Get a printout of the **lis** file on paper. Note that the Source Echo, Dictionary, and Cross-Reference Listing do not appear in the printout.

   (c) Speculate on what the contents of the **fig218.lis** file in part (b) would be if you had not erased that file. Check out your thinking by repeating part (a), and then doing part (b) without erasing the **lis** file.

*4. Copy the fig218.gps file to a new file. Use an editor to change the A Operand in the START Statement in the copy from 2 to 5. Carry out a Test-Mode simulation with this model, stepping through the simulation one Block execution at a time. At what simulated times do the Xacts with id numbers 3, 4, and 5 come out of their GENERATE Block?

*5. Copy the fig218.gps file into a new file. Use an editor to change the GENERATE Block's A and B Operands in the copy from "15.0,4.5" to "3.75,1.25", and change the A Operand in the START Statement from 2 to 5. Carry out a Test-Mode simulation with this model, stepping through the simulation one Block execution at a time. At what simulated times do the Xacts with id numbers 1, 2, 3, 4, and 5 come out of their GENERATE Block?

*6. Build a Model File for this two-Block model:

```
GENERATE  100
TERMINATE 1
```

Use an A Operand of 3 in the START Control Statement. At what simulated times will Xacts come out of the GENERATE Block? At what time will the simulation stop? Check out your predictions by carrying out a Test-Mode simulation with the model.

(The Block statements shown have not been displayed on a template similar to the one used in Figures 2.11, etc. In general, templates will not be used from this point forward in the book. This is because the Label, Operation, Operands, and Comments fields in a statement always appear in left-to-right order and are self-evident.)

*7. Build a Model File for this four-Block model:

```
          GENERATE  50
          TERMINATE 1
*
          GENERATE  35
          TERMINATE 1
```

Use an A Operand of 3 in the START Control Statement. At what simulated times will Xacts come out of the two GENERATE Blocks, and what will their id numbers be? At what time will the simulation stop? Check out your predictions by carrying out a Test-Mode simulation with the model.

*8. Build a Model File for this four-Block model:

```
          GENERATE  50
          TERMINATE 1
*
          GENERATE  35
          TERMINATE 0
```

Use an A Operand of 3 in the START Control Statement. At what simulated times will Xacts come out of the two GENERATE Blocks, and what will their id numbers be? At what time will the simulation stop? Check out your predictions by carrying out a Test-Mode simulation with the model.

*9. Transactions come out of a GENERATE Block every 25 ± 10 time units, and then are destroyed immediately. Build a model for this situation. Design the model so that the Transaction-Movement Phase stops at time 480.0 exactly. Perform a simulation with the model in Test Mode. How many Xacts have come out of the "GENERATE 25,10" Block when the Transaction-Movement Phase ends? (Hint: Use two GENERATE/TERMINATE sequences in the model.)

*10. Build a Model File for this four-Block model:

```
          GENERATE  60,30
          TERMINATE 1
*
          GENERATE  50,25
          TERMINATE 2
```

Use an A Operand of 5 in the START Control Statement. Perform a Test-Mode simulation with the model. At what simulated times do Xacts come out of the GENERATE Blocks, and what are their id numbers? At what time does the simulation stop? What is the value of the model's Termination Counter when the simulation stops?

2.25 More About the User's Role in a Test-Mode Simulation

The Figure 2.20 basic view of the user's role in a Test-Mode simulation is repeated in an extended form in Figure 2.23. Lines 1 through 5 in Figure 2.23 are identical to those in Figure 2.20, whereas Lines 6 through 10 are new. Lines 6 through 10 will now be discussed.

Line (6)

Line 6 shows the path followed if the simulation proceeds to the point that the model's Termination Counter is decremented to a value of zero (or less). If this condition occurs, GPSS/H issues an "output pending" message and returns control to the user, as Line 6 indicates. (We've already seen this situation come about in Section 2.22, Screen 5.)

Lines (7) and (8)

If the user, in response to the Line 6 "output pending" message, issues a command (such as **step**) to resume the simulation, GPSS/H will display the postsimulation report. This is indicated by Line 7 in Figure 2.23. After the report has been produced, control is returned to the user, as indicated by Line 8. The beginning user who chooses the Line 7 path

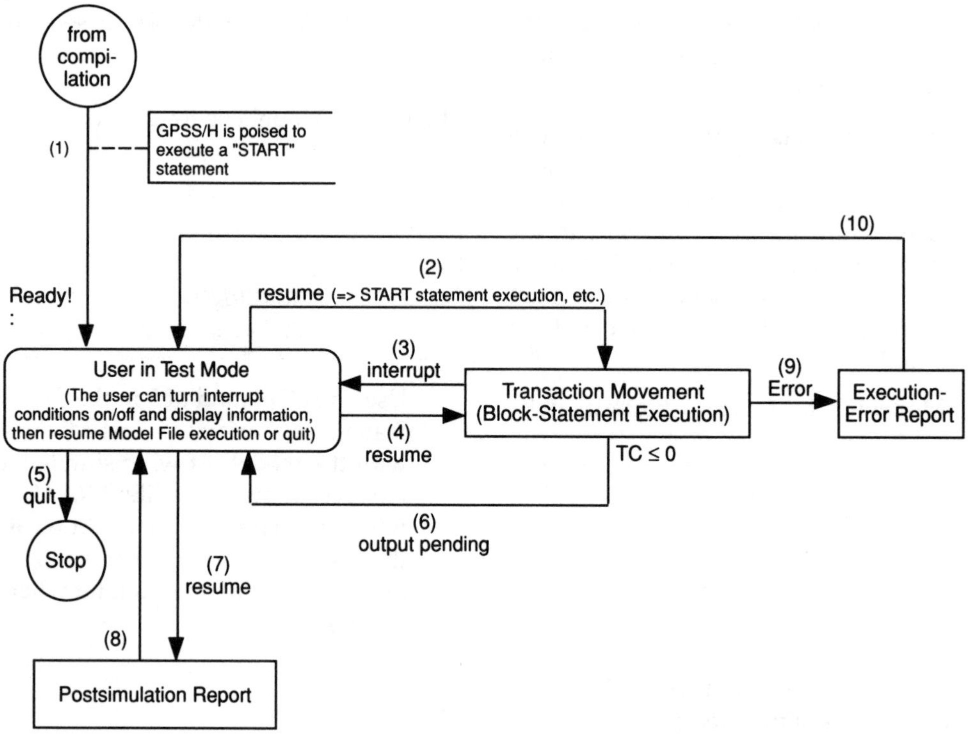

Figure 2.23 An Extended View of the Interplay Between the User and GPSS/H in a Test-Mode Simulation

in response to the Line 6 message then normally chooses to end the simulation (per Line 5 in Figure 2.23). On many occasions, the user might immediately choose to end the simulation (Line 5) in response to the Line 6 message. (This is what we did in the Section 2.22 Test-Mode simulation.)

Lines (9) and (10)

If an execution error occurs during the Transaction-Movement Phase, GPSS/H displays an Error Message in the Dialog Window and then returns control to the Test-Mode user. This is indicated by Lines 9 and 10 in Figure 2.23. (This is what will happen when doing the "bug clinic" exercises in the next section.) At this point, the user normally stops the simulation (Line 5). (Remember that to correct errors in the Model File, the user must go back to DOS, use an editor to change the Model File, and then recompile the changed Model File by issuing another **gpssh** command.)

2.26 Bug Clinic

GPSS/H has high-quality error-detection capabilities. To illustrate types of modeling errors and the reaction of GPSS/H to them, this book provides "bug clinic" sections from time to time. A bug clinic consists of exercises involving models that contain errors of one kind or another. The response of GPSS/H to these errors can be determined by carrying out simulations with these models.

In doing these exercises, it will be useful to distinguish between Compile-Time and Execution-Time Warning and Error Messages. See Figure 2.19 in this regard.

Remember that it's always possible to return from GPSS/H to DOS by issuing a **qq** command in response to a colon (:) prompt.

It is also useful to know that when GPSS/H is being run interactively, **model execution can be interrupted at any point by typing CTRL-BREAK** (that is, by simultaneously pressing the keyboard's CTRL and BREAK keys). If this is done in a Test-Mode simulation, GPSS/H will display the word **ATTENTION!**, and then issue a colon (:) to prompt for a command.

Finally, remember that throughout the book an asterisk next to the number of an exercise indicates that Appendix C contains a solution for and/or comments on that exercise.

*1. Build a Model File for this two-Block model:

```
        GENERATE   20,30
        TERMINATE  1
```

Use an A Operand of 5 in the START Statement. What is the problem with this model? What do you think will happen if a simulation is performed with the model? Do you think a Compile-Time or Execution-Time Error Message will be issued? Check out your predictions by simulating with the model in Test Mode.

*2. Build a Model File for this two-Block model:

```
        GENERATE   100
        TERMINATE  0
```

Use an A Operand of 1 in the START Statement. What is the problem with this model? What do you think will happen if a simulation is performed with the model? Do you think a Compile-Time or Execution-Time Error Message will be issued? Check out your predictions by carrying out a Test-Mode simulation with the model.

*3. Consider this Model File:

```
        SIMULATE
*
        GENERATE   35,15
        TERMINATE  1
*
        GENERATE   20,10
*
        START      3
*
        END
```

What is wrong with the model in the Model File? Do you think a Compile-Time or an Execution-Time Error Message will be issued? Build the Model File and carry out a simulation with it in Test Mode to see what happens.

*4. Consider this Model File:

```
        SIMULATE
*
        GENERATE   35,15
*
        GENERATE   20,10
        TERMINATE  1
*
        START      3
*
        END
```

What is wrong with the model in the Model File? Build the Model File and carry out a simulation with it in Test Mode to see what happens. Is a Compile-Time or an Execution-Time Error Message issued?

*5. Apply a correction of your choice to the problem in the Model File of Exercise 4. Then create a new problem by deleting the START statement from the Model File. Initiate a Test-Mode simulation with the Model File. How does GPSS/H respond to the absence of a START statement?

3 More About Transaction Creation and Movement

3.1 Preview

The elements of Transaction creation, movement, and destruction were taken up in Chapter 2 in terms of GENERATE and TERMINATE Blocks. In Chapter 3, a type of Block (ADVANCE) that temporarily suspends Transaction movement is introduced. Further aspects of Transaction creation at GENERATE Blocks are then considered. Finally, a type of Block (TRANSFER) used to direct Transactions to a nonsequential Next Block is described. The operation of ADVANCE is demonstrated with a Test-Mode simulation, and the use of ADVANCE, extended GENERATE, and TRANSFER Blocks in appropriate contexts is considered.

3.2 Suspending Transaction Movement for a Specified Time: The ADVANCE Block

When traffic moves in a system, it often reaches points at which it pauses and spends time before resuming its movement. These points frequently correspond to locations in a system at which traffic receives service. For example, it takes time for a machine to drill a hole in a casting. When a casting (a unit of traffic moving through a manufacturing system) captures a drill (a resource in the manufacturing system), it spends time at the drill while a hole is drilled in the casting. Similarly, it takes time for a doctor to examine a patient in the emergency ward of a hospital. When a patient (a unit of traffic moving through the emergency ward) is examined by a doctor, time goes by while the examination proceeds.

In the two examples just given, time goes by while a unit of traffic remains **in place** at a fixed point in the system while receiving service. Time also goes by while traffic **moves** from point to point in a system. For example, it takes time for a conveyor to transport a casting from point A to point B. After a casting has been put on the conveyor, it spends time on the conveyor while moving from the conveyor's on-point to its off-point. Similarly, it takes time for a patient in a hospital to be moved from an examining room in the emergency ward to an X-ray room. After a patient has been put onto a rolling bed, the patient spends time on the bed while being rolled from the examining room to the X-ray room.

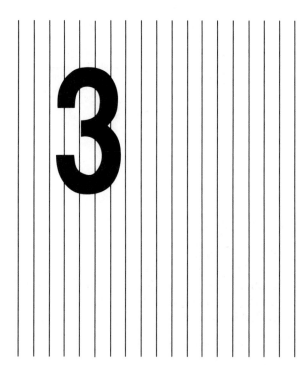

There are many occasions in GPSS/H modeling when it is appropriate to have a Transaction move into a Block and then remain in that Block for a while to simulate either the time required to receive service at a fixed point in a system or to be moved between two points in a system. The ADVANCE Block provides this capability. When a Transaction moves into an ADVANCE Block, a simulated time lag is applied to the Transaction. Only after a specified amount of simulated time has gone by will the Transaction try to move from the ADVANCE Block (its Current Block) into the following Block (its Next Block Attempted).

Holding time at an ADVANCE Block, like interarrival time at a GENERATE Block, often varies at random from Transaction to Transaction. (For example, it may take longer to drill a hole in one casting than to drill a hole in another casting.) For this reason, ADVANCE-Block holding time is treated as a random variable in the general case. Just as the A and B Operands at a GENERATE Block are used to specify the distribution followed by an interarrival-time random variable, so too are the A and B Operands at an ADVANCE Block used to specify the distribution followed by a holding-time random variable.

The ADVANCE Block, and its A and B Operands, are shown in generalized form in Figure 3.1. When holding times at an ADVANCE Block are to be **uniformly distributed**, the average holding time is indicated by the ADVANCE Block's A Operand, and the half-range over which the holding time varies is indicated by the B Operand. These facts are summarized in Figure 3.1. Note that the ADVANCE Block's A and B Operands play the same role for

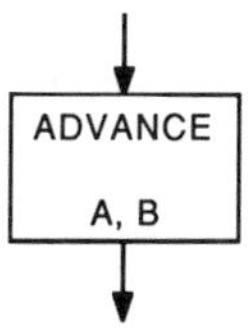

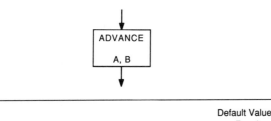

Operand	Significance	Default Value or Result
A	Average holding time	0.0 (zero)
B	Half-range of the uniformly distributed holding time random variable	0.0 (zero)

Figure 3.1 *The ADVANCE Block, with its A and B Operands*

uniformly distributed holding times as played by the GENERATE Block's A and B Operands for uniformly distributed interarrival times.

For example, suppose a simulation is taking place, and assume that the moving Transaction has "ADVANCE 25.5,3.0" as its Next Block at simulated time 50.4. **An ADVANCE Block never denies entry to a Transaction.** The Transaction, therefore, moves without delay into the ADVANCE Block and executes it. A sample is drawn from the uniform distribution 25.5 ± 3.0. Let's assume that the sampled value is 26.5. Then the Transaction will stop moving, remaining in this ADVANCE Block for 26.5 simulated time units, or until future time 76.9 (current time 50.4 + holding time 26.5 = future time 76.9). When time 76.9 is reached, the Transaction will try to move from the ADVANCE (its Current Block) into the sequential Block (its Next Block Attempted), and so on.

It is easy, then, to specify uniformly distributed holding times at ADVANCE Blocks. To express more complicated interarrival-time distributions, the modeler either uses built-in GPSS/H Functions (for sampling from such distributions as the exponential, normal, and triangular), or defines such Functions, and then refers to them from A and/or B Operand positions at ADVANCE Blocks. Specification of nonuniformly distributed holding times at ADVANCE Blocks is taken up later, in Chapter 13.

Like the GENERATE Block's A and B Operands, the ADVANCE Block's A and B Operands take values of 0.0 **by default**. For example, suppose a simulation is in progress, and assume the moving Transaction has "ADVANCE 15.0" as its Next Block at simulated time 120.3. The Transaction then moves into the ADVANCE Block and executes it. The holding time is 15.0, exactly (15.0 ± 0.0). The Transaction stops moving, remaining in this ADVANCE Block for 15.0 simulated time units, or until future time 135.3 (current time 120.3 + holding time 15.0 = future time 135.3). Because holding times at this ADVANCE Block are always exactly 15.0, this is an example of a **deterministic** (that is, nonrandom) **holding time**.

What happens if a Transaction moves into the Block "ADVANCE 0" (or "ADVANCE 0,0" or simply "ADVANCE")? The holding time at these ADVANCE Blocks is **zero**, deterministically, and so a simulated time lag of zero is applied to the Transaction. Without simulated delay, then, **the Transaction immediately tries to move** from the ADVANCE Block into the sequential Block, and so on. We will see occasions later when an ADVANCE time of zero can be of use in modeling.

```
          SIMULATE
*
          GENERATE  50
          ADVANCE   60
          TERMINATE 1
*
          START     1
*
          END
```

Figure 3.2 A Model File for Tracing ADVANCE-Block Operation

3.3 Tracing ADVANCE-Block Operation in Test Mode

In this section, we use GPSS/H in Test Mode to trace the movement of two Transactions in the simple three-Block model shown in Figure 3.2. Figure 3.3, parts (a) through (e), shows a sequence of five computer screens that result when we single-step our way through execution of the Figure 3.2 model. Discussion of this screen sequence follows. (In Exercise 1 of Section 3.4, you are asked to reproduce this screen sequence on your computer.)

Screen 1 (Figure 3.3, part a)

Screen 1 results after the DOS command

```
gpssh fig32.gps tvtnw
```

has been executed and a **step** command has been executed one time. At the bottom of the Screen 1 Dialog Window, GPSS/H has displayed the message

```
XACT 1 POISED AT BLOCK 2. RELATIVE CLOCK: 50.0000
```

and then has displayed a colon to prompt us for more input. We are at time 50.0, and the first Transaction of the simulation (Xact 1) is about to move into the ADVANCE Block.

Screen 2 (Figure 3.3, part b)

Screen 2 results when we respond to Screen 1 by keying in and sending another **step** command. Having executed one more Block, GPSS/H has displayed the message

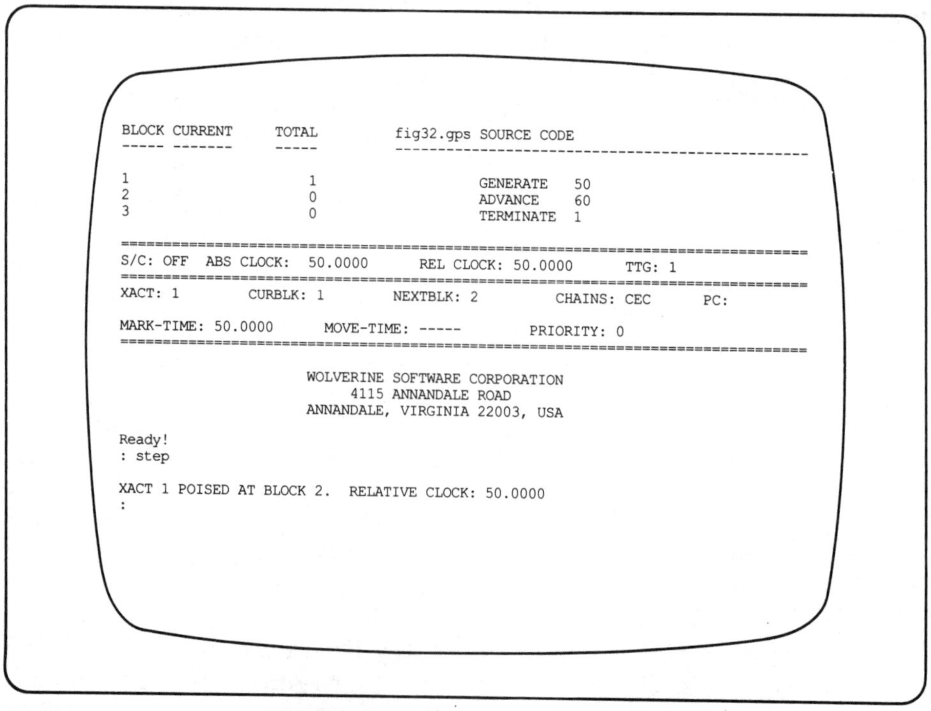

Figure 3.3 Five Computer Screens Resulting When the Figure 3.3 Model File Is Run in Test Mode (a) Screen 1

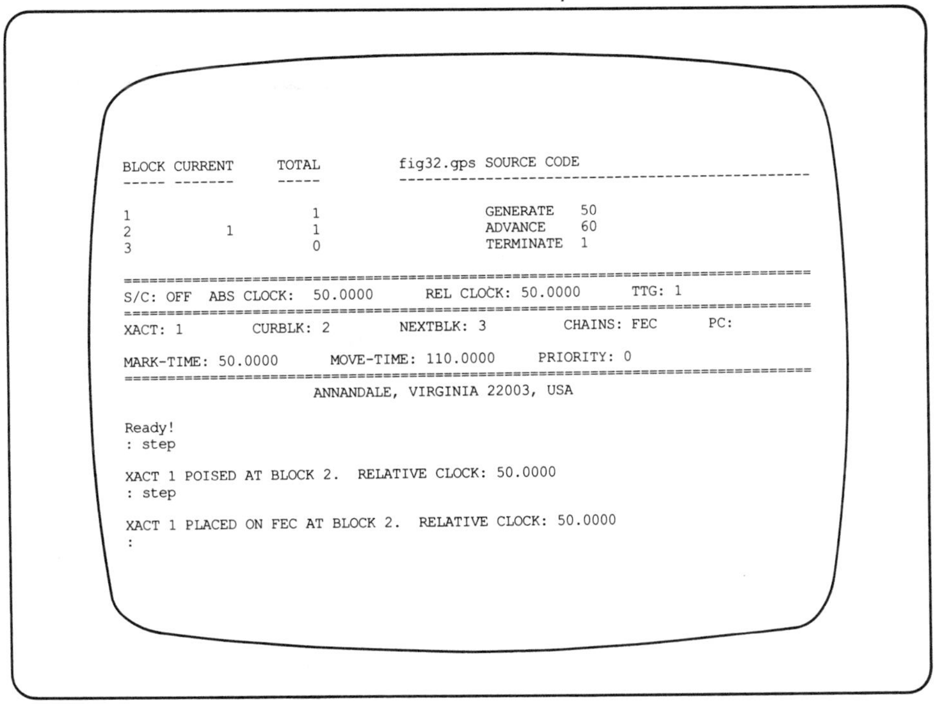
BLOCK CURRENT TOTAL fig32.gps SOURCE CODE
1 1 GENERATE 50
2 1 1 ADVANCE 60
3 0 TERMINATE 1
S/C: OFF ABS CLOCK: 50.0000 REL CLOCK: 50.0000 TTG: 1
XACT: 1 CURBLK: 2 NEXTBLK: 3 CHAINS: FEC PC:
MARK-TIME: 50.0000 MOVE-TIME: 110.0000 PRIORITY: 0
ANNANDALE, VIRGINIA 22003, USA
Ready!
: step
XACT 1 POISED AT BLOCK 2. RELATIVE CLOCK: 50.0000
: step
XACT 1 PLACED ON FEC AT BLOCK 2. RELATIVE CLOCK: 50.0000
:

Figure 3.3 (b) *Screen 2*

```
XACT 1 PLACED ON FEC AT BLOCK 2. RELATIVE CLOCK: 50.0000
```

and then has displayed a colon to prompt for another command. (See the last several lines in the Screen 2 Dialog Window.)

What happened to produce Screen 2? Resuming the simulation, GPSS/H moved Xact 1 from its Current Block (the GENERATE Block) into its Next Block (the ADVANCE Block). The ADVANCE Block responded by "placing Xact 1 on the FEC." **FEC** is an abbreviation for **Future Events Chain**. The Future Events Chain is composed of Transactions scheduled to resume movement along their path at a known **future** simulated time. The ADVANCE Block has placed Xact 1 on the Future Events Chain, where it will remain until future time 110.0 (current time 50.0 + holding time 60.0 = future time 110.0.) (Recall that the **Current Events Chain**, mentioned briefly in Chapter 2, consists of Transactions scheduled to try to move along their path in the model at the **current** simulated time.) More will be said about the Current and Future Events Chains in Chapter 4.

In the Screen 2 **Source Window**, the ADVANCE Block has a **CURRENT** count of 1. (There is currently one Xact in the ADVANCE Block, the Xact with id number 1.) Also notice in the Source Window that the ADVANCE Block has a **TOTAL** count of 1. (It has been executed one time).

In the Screen 2 **Status Window**, we see that the **CURBLK** (Current Block) for Xact 1 is Block 2 (ADVANCE) and that its **NEXTBLK** (Next Block) is the Block in Location 3 (TERMINATE). We also see that Xact 1 is on the Future Events Chain (**CHAINS: FEC**). Xact 1's **MARK-TIME** (the time it moved out of its GENERATE Block) is 50.0, and it's **MOVE-TIME** (the time Xact 1 will resume its movement in the model) is future time 110.0 (50.0 + 60.0 = 110.0).

Screen 3 (Figure 3.3, part c)

Screen 3 results when we respond to Screen 2 by keying in and sending another **step** command. Having executed this command, GPSS/H has displayed the message

```
XACT 2 POISED AT BLOCK 2. RELATIVE CLOCK: 100.00
```

and then has displayed a colon to prompt for another command.

What happened to produce Screen 3? Resuming the simulation, GPSS/H advanced the simulated clock to 100.0, the earliest future time at which a

Transaction was scheduled to try to move. (Xact 1 has a MOVE-TIME of 110.0, as we have seen. And Xact 2, the successor to Xact 1 at the GENERATE Block, has a MOVE-TIME of 100.0. And so between these **two** scheduled moves, the earliest of them is scheduled for future time 100. This is the first occasion we have seen when more than one move has been scheduled for future time.) GPSS/H then moved Xact 2 until it triggered one Block execution. Xact 2 has executed the GENERATE Block (note in the Screen 3 Source Window that the **TOTAL** execution count for the GENERATE Block is now 2) and is poised at Block 2 (ADVANCE).

Screen 4 (Figure 3.3, part d)

Screen 4 results when we respond to Screen 3 by issuing a **step** command. Having executed this command, GPSS/H has displayed the message

```
XACT 2 PLACED ON FEC AT BLOCK 2. RELATIVE CLOCK: 100.0000
```

and then has displayed a colon to prompt for another command.

What happened to produce Screen 4? Resuming the simulation, GPSS/H moved Xact 2 from its Current Block (GENERATE) into its Next Block (ADVANCE). The ADVANCE Block responded by "placing Xact 2 on the FEC," where it will be until future time 160.0 (current time 100.0 + holding time 60.0 = future time 160.0).

There are now two Xacts in the ADVANCE Block. (Xact 1, with a MOVE-TIME of 110.0, is still in the ADVANCE Block; and now Xact 2, with a MOVE-TIME of 160.0, is also in the ADVANCE Block.) This fact is confirmed by the ADVANCE Block's **CURRENT** count (2), as shown in the Screen 4 **Source Window**.

You should now inspect the Screen 4 **Status Window** and determine that you agree with the information shown there.

Screen 5 (Figure 3.3, part e)

Screen 5 results when we respond to Screen 4 by issuing another **step** command. GPSS/H has responded by executing one more Block, then displaying the message

```
REQUESTING OUTPUT IN (CONTROL) STATEMENT NUMBER 7.
RELATIVE CLOCK: 110.0000
```

and then displaying a colon to prompt for another command.

What happened to produce Screen 5? Resuming the simulation, GPSS/H advanced the simulated clock to 110.0, the earliest future simulated time at which a Transaction was scheduled to move. (Xacts 1 and 2, both in the ADVANCE Block, have MOVE-TIME's of 110.0 and 160.0, respectively, as we have seen. And Xact 3, the successor to Xact 2 at the GENERATE Block, has a MOVE-TIME of 150.0. And so, among these **three** scheduled moves, the earliest of them is scheduled for future time 110.0.) GPSS/H then moved this Xact (Xact 1) until it triggered one Block execution. Xact 1 has executed the TERMINATE Block (note in the Screen 5 Source Window that the **TOTAL** execution count for the TERMINATE Block is now 1). This concluded the Transaction-Movement Phase, producing the transition into the Postsimulation Report Phase. The START statement whose execution led into the Transaction-Movement Phase is Statement Number 7 in the Model File. This explains why the Screen 5 message says, in part,

```
REQUESTING OUTPUT IN (CONTROL) STATEMENT NUMBER 7.
```

At this point, the command **qq** (quit quickly) was issued (not shown in Figure 3.3), bringing the demonstration to an end.

3.4 Using a Step Count with the Step Command

In general, the **step** command takes the form

```
step step_count
```

where ***step_count*** stands for a positive integer. ***Step_count*** indicates **how many Block executions are to take place** before GPSS/H returns control to the interactive user. For example, if the command **step 5** is issued, GPSS/H will resume the simulation and proceed until five more Block executions have taken place. Then it will return control to the user, displaying an appropriate message and prompting the user for another command.

The default value of ***step_count*** is 1. This explains why use of the **step** command without a ***step_count*** results in "single-stepping" through simulations.

```
BLOCK CURRENT     TOTAL         fig32.gps SOURCE CODE
----- -------     -----         -----------------------------------------------

1                   2                     GENERATE   50
2           1       1                     ADVANCE    60
3                   0                     TERMINATE  1

================================================================================
S/C: OFF  ABS CLOCK:  100.0000     REL CLOCK: 100.0000     TTG: 1
================================================================================
XACT: 2        CURBLK: 1        NEXTBLK: 2         CHAINS: CEC      PC:

MARK-TIME: 100.0000     MOVE-TIME: -----         PRIORITY: 0
================================================================================
: step

XACT 1 POISED AT BLOCK 2.  RELATIVE CLOCK: 50.0000
: step

XACT 1 PLACED ON FEC AT BLOCK 2.  RELATIVE CLOCK: 50.0000
: step

XACT 2 POISED AT BLOCK 2.  RELATIVE CLOCK: 100.0000
:
```

Figure 3.3 (c) *Screen 3*

```
BLOCK CURRENT     TOTAL         fig32.gps SOURCE CODE
----- -------     -----         -----------------------------------------------

1                   2                     GENERATE   50
2           2       2                     ADVANCE    60
3                   0                     TERMINATE  1

================================================================================
S/C: OFF  ABS CLOCK:  100.0000     REL CLOCK: 100.0000     TTG: 1
================================================================================
XACT: 2        CURBLK: 2        NEXTBLK: 3         CHAINS: FEC      PC:

MARK-TIME: 100.0000     MOVE-TIME: 160.0000      PRIORITY: 0
================================================================================
: step

XACT 1 PLACED ON FEC AT BLOCK 2.  RELATIVE CLOCK: 50.0000
: step

XACT 2 POISED AT BLOCK 2.  RELATIVE CLOCK: 100.0000
: step

XACT 2 PLACED ON FEC AT BLOCK 2.  RELATIVE CLOCK: 100.0000
:
```

Figure 3.3 (d) *Screen 4*

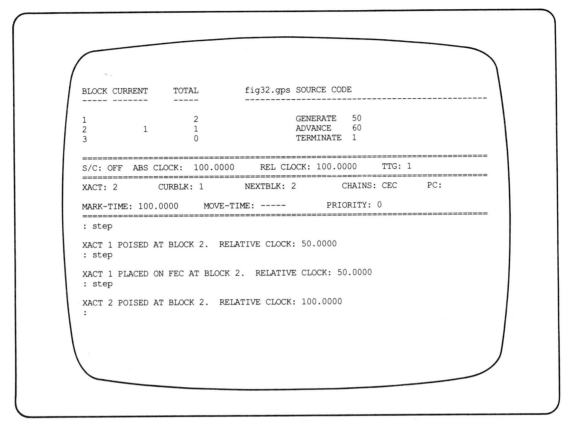

```
BLOCK CURRENT     TOTAL         fig32.gps SOURCE CODE
----- -------     -----         ------------------------------------------------
1                   2                    GENERATE   50
2          1        2                    ADVANCE    60
3                   1                    TERMINATE  1

=============================================================================
S/C: OFF  ABS CLOCK:  110.0000      REL CLOCK: 110.0000       TTG: 0
=============================================================================
XACT: 1        CURBLK: 2        NEXTBLK: 3         CHAINS:            PC:

MARK-TIME: 50.0000       MOVE-TIME: -----         PRIORITY: 0
=============================================================================
: step

XACT 2 POISED AT BLOCK 2.  RELATIVE CLOCK: 100.0000
: step

XACT 2 PLACED ON FEC AT BLOCK 2.  RELATIVE CLOCK: 100.0000
: step

REQUESTING OUTPUT IN (CONTROL) STATEMENT NUMBER 7.  RELATIVE CLOCK: 110.0000
:
```

Figure 3.3 (e) *Screen 5*

Use of a STEP count with the **step** command may be useful in the last several exercises in the following section.

3.5 Exercises

1. The supplied fig32.gps file contains the Model File shown in Figure 3.2. Use GPSS/H to perform a Test-Mode simulation with this Model File, stepping through the simulation one Block execution at a time. Compare the information coming up on your screen with the information shown in Figure 3.3. (Your results should exactly match the results shown in Figure 3.3.)

*2. Use an editor to change the A Operand in the START statement from 1 to 3 in a copy of the fig32.gps file. Can you predict the time a simulation performed with this model will stop? Carry out a Test-Mode simulation with the model, stepping through the simulation one Block execution at a time. At what time does the simulation stop? Was your prediction correct?

*3. Copy fig32.gps to a new file. Change the GENERATE Block's A and B Operands from "50" to "25,20" and change the ADVANCE Block's A and B Operands from "60" to "100,10". Also change the A Operand in the START statement from 1 to 5. Carry out a Test-Mode simulation with this model, stepping through the simulation one Block execution at a time. What is the largest number of Xacts ever in the ADVANCE Block at any one time? At what time or times does this condition occur? At what time does the simulation stop?

*4. Build a Model File for this three-Block model:

```
GENERATE  50
ADVANCE   250,250
TERMINATE 1
```

Use an A Operand of 5 in the START statement. Perform a simulation with the model in Test Mode. At what simulated times do Xacts move into the TERMINATE Block, and what are their id numbers? Are there any occasions when one Xact "passes" another in the ADVANCE Block? (Xact B "passes" Xact A in an ADVANCE Block if Xact B goes into the ADVANCE after Xact A does, and then comes out of the ADVANCE before Xact A does.)

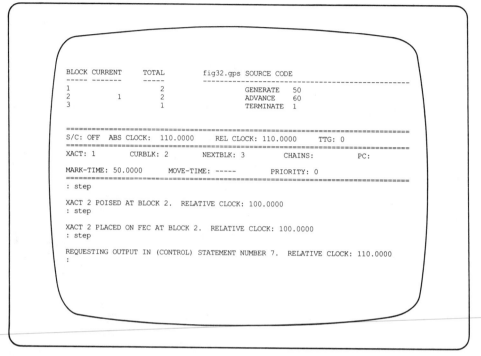

5. Build a Model File for this four-Block model:

```
        GENERATE   100,50
        ADVANCE    125,110
        ADVANCE    75,40
        TERMINATE  1
```

Use an A Operand of 5 in the START statement. Perform a simulation with the model in Test Mode. At what simulated times do Xacts move into the TERMINATE Block, and what are their id numbers? At what time does the simulation stop? Are there any occasions when one Xact passes another in an ADVANCE Block? (See Exercise 4.)

*6. In Exercise 5, do you think the two consecutive ADVANCE Blocks are logically equivalent to this single Block: "ADVANCE 200,150"? (In the single ADVANCE Block, the A Operand results from forming the sum of the A Operands in the two consecutive ADVANCE Blocks. The same is true for the B Operand in the single ADVANCE Block.) Why or why not?

*7. Build a Model File for this three-Block model:

```
        GENERATE   100
        ADVANCE    0
        TERMINATE  1
```

Use an A Operand of 3 in the START statement. At what simulated times will Xacts move into the TERMINATE Block? At what time will the simulation stop? Check out your predictions by carrying out a Test-Mode simulation with the model, stepping through model execution one Block at a time.

*8. Build a Model File for this six-Block model:

```
        GENERATE   50
        ADVANCE    50
        TERMINATE  1
*
        GENERATE   75
        ADVANCE    0
        TERMINATE  1
```

Use an A Operand of 3 in the START statement. At what time does the simulation stop? Will the first or second TERMINATE Block be the one whose execution brings the simulation to an end? Check out your predictions by carrying out a Test-Mode simulation with the model.

*9. A casting arrives at the put-on point of a conveyor every 200 ± 50 time units. It then takes the casting 500 time units to travel to the point at which it is taken off the conveyor (the take-off point). Build a GPSS/H model for this situation, letting Transactions simulate castings. Perform a simulation with the model in Test Mode. How long does it take in this simulation to convey five castings from the put-on point to the take-off point? At what times do they arrive at the take-off point?

10. In Exercise 9, **moving** castings are simulated by Transactions which are **at rest** in an ADVANCE Block. Why is this a valid way to represent movement in a model? Discuss this situation.

11. Extend Exercise 9 as follows. The conveyor moves castings to a drilling machine, which is located at the conveyor's take-off point. When a casting reaches the take-off point, the drill operator removes the casting from the conveyor (which takes 5 ± 3 time units) and drills a hole in the casting (which takes 75 ± 10 time units), which then leaves the system. The drill operator has no responsibilities other than those described. (Note that the timings are such that the drill operator will always be idle when a casting reaches the take-off point of the conveyor, so castings never have to compete with each other for use of the operator.) Build a model for this system. Simulate with the model until 50 castings have left the system. At what time does the simulation stop?

3.6 The GENERATE Block's Offset-Interval and Limit-Count Operands

In addition to having A and B Operands, the GENERATE Block has optional C and D Operands. The GENERATE Block and its A, B, C, and D Operands are shown in Figure 3.4.

As indicated in Figure 3.4, a GENERATE Block's **C Operand** is the **Offset-Interval** Operand. The Offset Interval, if used, indicates the **simulated time** at which the **first** Xact is to come into the model from that GENERATE Block. The times at which the second, third, and so on. Xacts will come into the model from that GENERATE BLOCK will then be determined in the usual way, by sampling from the interarrival-time distribution specified with the Block's A and B Operands.

If no Offset Interval is used at a GENERATE Block, then the times that **all** Xacts (including the first) come into the model from that GENERATE Block are determined by sampling from the interarrival-time distribution specified with the Block's A and B Operands.

The GENERATE Block's **D Operand** is the **Limit-Count** Operand. The Limit Count, if used, puts a limit on the total number of Xacts which are to come into the model from that GENERATE Block. If and when the Limit Count is reached, the GENERATE Block stops producing Transactions. If no Limit Count is specified, the GENERATE Block produces Transactions throughout a simulation.

Examples showing the effect of using GENERATE Blocks with Offset Intervals and/or Limit Counts are left to the exercises in the next section.

3.7 Exercises

*1. Build a Model File for this two-Block model:

```
GENERATE  100,,25
TERMINATE 1
```

Use an A Operand of 3 in the START statement. What is the value of the GENERATE Block's B Operand? At what simulated times will Xacts come out of the GENERATE Block? At what time will the simulation stop? Check out your predictions by carrying out a Test-Mode simulation with the model.

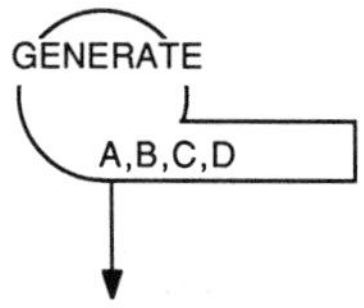

Operand	Significance	Default Value or Result
A	Average interarrival time	0.0 (zero)
B	Half-range of the uniformly distributed interarrival time random variable	0.0 (zero)
C	Offset Interval (deterministic time of first Xact arrival)	No Offset is in effect
D	Limit Count (maximum number of arrivals)	No Limit Count is in effect

Figure 3.4 The GENERATE Block, with its A, B, C, and D Operands

*2. Build a Model File for this two-Block model:

```
GENERATE  25,,25
TERMINATE 1
```

Use an A Operand of 3 in the START statement. What is the value of the GENERATE Block's B Operand? At what simulated times will Xacts come out of the GENERATE Block? At what time will the simulation stop? Check out your predictions by carrying out a Test-Mode simulation with the model.

*3. Build a Model File for this three-Block model:

```
GENERATE  100,50,25
ADVANCE   50
TERMINATE 1
```

Use an A Operand of 3 in the START statement. Carry out a Test-Mode simulation with the model. At what times do Xacts come out of the GENERATE Block? At what time does the simulation stop?

*4. Build a Model File for this three-Block model:

```
GENERATE  100,,0
ADVANCE   100
TERMINATE 1
```

Use an A Operand of 3 in the START statement. At what simulated times will Xacts come out of the GENERATE Block? At what time will the simulation stop? Check out your predictions by carrying out a Test-Mode simulation with the model.

*5. Build a Model File for this five-Block model:

```
   GENERATE  100,,,1
   ADVANCE   700
   TERMINATE 1
*
   GENERATE  250
   TERMINATE 1
```

Use an A Operand of 3 in the START statement. At what simulated times will Xacts come out of the GENERATE Blocks, and what will their id numbers be? At what time will the simulation stop? Check out your predictions by carrying out a Test-Mode simulation with the model.

*6. Build a Model File for this four-Block model:

```
          GENERATE  25,,5,2
          TERMINATE 1
*
          GENERATE  20
          TERMINATE 1
```

Use an A Operand of 5 in the START statement. At what simulated times will Xacts come out of the GENERATE Blocks, and what will their id numbers be? At what time will the simulation stop? Check out your predictions by carrying out a Test-Mode simulation with the model.

3.8 Bug Clinic

*1. Build a Model File for this two-Block model:

```
          GENERATE  50,25,-10
          TERMINATE 1
```

Use an A Operand of 5 in the START statement. What is the problem with this model? What do you think will happen if a simulation is performed with the model? Do you think a compile-time or an execution-time error will result? Check out your predictions by trying to carry out a Test-Mode simulation with the model.

*2. Build a Model File for this two-Block model:

```
          GENERATE  100,,,4
          TERMINATE 1
```

Use an A Operand of 5 in the START statement. What is the problem with this model? What do you think will happen if a simulation is performed with the model? Do you think a compile-time or an execution-time error will result? Check out your predictions by carrying out a Test-Mode simulation with the model.

*3. Consider this Model File:

```
          SIMULATE
*
          GENERATE  20,10
          ADVANCE   10,15
          TERMINATE 1
*
          START     3
*
          END
```

What is wrong with the model? Do you think a compile-time or execution-time error will result? Check out your predictions by building the Model File, then carrying out a Test-Mode simulation with the model.

3.9 When Two or More Transactions Move at the Same Simulated Time

In the simple models we've worked with so far, only one Xact has tried to move at any one simulated time. In the model of Figure 2.18 in Chapter 2, for example, Xact 1 moved at time 12.9327, then Xact 2 moved at time 27.9268, then the simulation stopped. In such simple cases, the order in which Xacts move simply corresponds to the increasingly later simulated times at which they've been scheduled to move.

What happens when two or more Transactions move **at one and the same simulated time**? For example, suppose Xacts 3 and 4 are both to move at time 60.0. Transactions move **one at a time**. Will Xact 3 move first, and then Xact 4? Or will Xact 4 move first, and then Xact 3? In what order do Xacts move in cases like this?

Let's begin to explore the answer to this question by considering a simulation performed with the model shown in Figure 3.5. Single Xacts will move from the first and second GENERATE Blocks at time 25. When two or more Xacts are to move at the same **simulated** time, they are said to be **time-tied**. Which of the two time-tied Xacts will be the first to move at time 25.0? **You should now perform a simulation in Test Mode with this model and answer this question for yourself.**

If you simulated with the Figure 3.5 model, you discovered that Xact 1 (the Xact with id number 1)

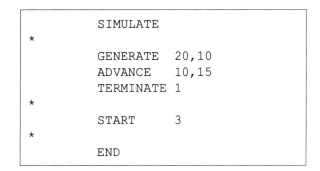

```
        GENERATE  25   first Block
        TERMINATE 1
*
        GENERATE  25   second Block
        TERMINATE 1
```

Figure 3.5 *A Model in which Two Transactions Move at the Same Simulated Time*

moves from the first GENERATE Block at time 25.0, and then Xact 2 moves from the second GENERATE Block at time 25.0. Why do these Xacts move in this order? The answer is that, in the absence of a consideration to be discussed in the next section, time-tied Xacts move in the order in which the **scheduling** of their moves took place. When the two GENERATE Blocks in the Figure 3.5 model are initialized at time 0.0, they are initialized in the **top-down order** of their appearance in the Model File. And so the move from the first GENERATE was scheduled before the move from the second GENERATE was scheduled. This explains the order in which the moves in the Figure 3.5 model occur.

3.10 Exercises

*1. If you haven't already done so, build a Model File for the model in Figure 3.5. Use an A Operand of 6 in the START statement. In what order will the time-tied Xacts move at times 25.0, 50.0, and 75.0, and what will their id numbers be? Check out your predictions by carrying out a Test-Mode simulation with the model.

*2. Repeat Exercise 1, except now use an A Operand of 7 on the START statement. What do you think will happen at time 100.0? Check out your prediction by carrying out a Test-Mode simulation with the model.

*3. Consider the following model, which is in the file s310x3.gps.

```
        SIMULATE
*
        GENERATE  50
        TERMINATE 0
*
        GENERATE  100
        TERMINATE 1
*
        START     1
*
        END
```

At what clock time will two or more Transactions move? What will their id numbers be? Which of the two will be the first to move? How many times will the first TERMINATE Block have been executed when the simulation stops? Check out your predictions by simulating with the model in Test Mode.

*4. Consider the following model, which is in the file s310x4.gps.

```
        SIMULATE
*
        GENERATE  25
        ADVANCE   25
        TERMINATE 1
*
        START     2
*
        END
```

At what earliest clock time will two or more Transactions move? What will their id numbers be? Which of the two will be the first to move? At what next earliest clock time will two or more Xacts move? What will their id numbers be? Which of the two will be the first to move? Check out your predictions by simulating with the model in Test Mode.

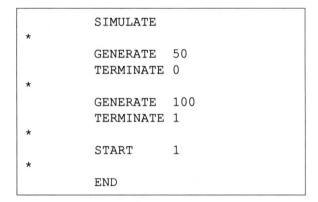

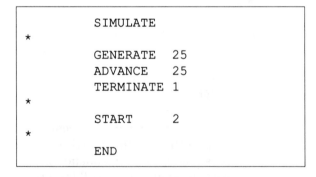

3.11 The GENERATE Block's Priority-Level Operand

The order in which time-tied Transactions move can be controlled by making use of Transaction **Priority Level**. (Control of this order can be extremely important in modeling, as we will see later.) Priority Level is an attribute, or characteristic, of every Transaction. A Transaction's Priority Level takes the form of a **signed integer** that can range in value from about -2,000,000,000 (minus 2 billion) to about +2,000,000,000 (plus 2 billion). Despite the considerable range of Priority Levels, modelers usually work with relatively small numbers when specifying Priority Levels. Examples of valid Transaction Priority Levels taking the form of relatively small numbers are 0, 1, 5, 100, 225, -1, -10, and -30.

A Transaction's **initial** Priority is determined at the time the Transaction is created. The GENERATE Block's **E Operand** indicates the Priority to be given to Transactions created when that GENERATE Block is executed. The default value of the E Operand is 0 (zero). These facts are indicated in Figure 3.6, which provides a summary of GENERATE Block characteristics introduced so far.

The Priority of the moving Transaction is shown in the **Status Window** when a simulation is being performed in Test Mode, where it is labeled **PRIORITY**. For example, see any of Screens 2 through 6 in Figure 2.22, where the moving Transaction always has a default Priority of zero.

(It is possible to change a Transaction's Priority while the Transaction goes through its life cycle. This is done by use of the PRIORITY Block, which is introduced later, in Chapter 12.)

What role does a Transaction's Priority play in a simulation? Priority determines the order in which time-tied Transactions move. The higher a time-tied Transaction's Priority, the sooner it moves with respect to other Transactions involved in the time-tie. For example, suppose Xacts 2 and 5 are time-tied at time 34.6, and suppose Xact 2 has Priority 9, whereas Xact 5 has Priority 2. Xact 2 will then move before Xact 5 does.

To illustrate the role of Priority by example, consider the model in Figure 3.7, which is a simple variation of the Figure 3.5 model. In the Figure 3.5 model, the two GENERATE Blocks have E Operands with default values of zero. In the Figure 3.7 model, however, Xacts created by the first and second GENERATE Blocks have Priority Levels of 5 and 10, respectively. (Note the use of four consecutive commas in both GENERATE Blocks to take default values for the B, C, and D Operands.) A Transaction will move from the first GENERATE Block at time 25.0, and a Transaction will also move from the second GENERATE Block at time 25.0. Which of these time-tied Xacts will be the first to move at time 25.0? You should now think through the answer to this question (perhaps verifying your answer with a Test-Mode simulation).

If you simulated with the Figure 3.7 model, you discovered that Xact 2 (the Xact with id number 2) moves from the second GENERATE Block at time 25.0, and then Xact 1 moves from the first GENERATE Block at time 25.0. These time-tied Xacts move in this order because Xact 2 has a higher Priority than does Xact 1 (and despite the fact that Xact 1 was the first of these two Xacts to be created and scheduled for movement at time 25.0).

The way Priority distinctions determine the order in which time-tied Transactions move is further explored in the following set of exercises.

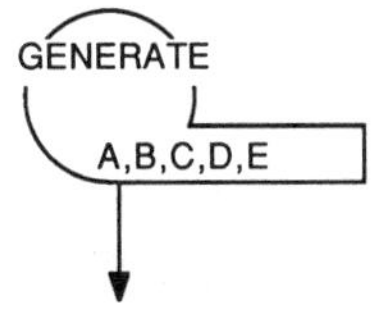

Operand	Significance	Default Value or Result
A	Average interarrival time	0.0 (zero)
B	Half-range of the uniformly distributed interarrival time random variable	0.0 (zero)
C	Offset Interval (deterministic time of first Xact arrival)	No Offset is in effect
D	Limit Count (maximum number of arrivals)	No Limit Count is in effect
E	Xact Priority Level	0 (zero)

Figure 3.6 *The GENERATE Block, with its A, B, C, D, and E Operands*

```
        GENERATE  25,,,,5
        TERMINATE 1
*
        GENERATE  25,,,,10
        TERMINATE 1
```

Figure 3.7 *A Variation of the Figure 3.5 Model*

3.12 Exercises

*1. If you haven't already done so, build a Model File for the model in Figure 3.7. Use an A Operand of 6 in the START statement. In what order will the time-tied Xacts move at times 25.0, 50.0, and 75.0, and what will their id numbers be? Check out your predictions by carrying out a Test-Mode simulation with the model.

*2. Repeat Exercise 1, except now use an A Operand of 7 on the START statement. What do you think will happen at time 100.0? Check out your prediction by carrying out a Test-Mode simulation with the model.

*3. Build a Model File for this four-Block model:

```
          GENERATE   50,,,,3
          TERMINATE  1
*
          GENERATE   25,,,,7
          TERMINATE  1
```

Use an A Operand of 6 in the START statement. At what simulated times will Xacts come out of the two GENERATE Blocks, and what will their id numbers be? At what time will the simulation stop? Check out your predictions by carrying out a Test-Mode simulation with the model.

3.13 The Labeling of Blocks

It can be of interest to refer to one Block from another Block in a model. This is done by the two-step process of (1) **labeling** the Block and then (2) referring to the Block by its Label. A Block's Label is an identifier for the **Location** that the Block occupies (and in this sense is an identifier for the **Block** in that Location). In the statement for a labeled Block, the Label is entered in the Label (Location) field.

The modeler composes Block Labels using from 1 to 8 alphanumeric characters, the first of which must be alphabetic. Labels should (but don't have to) begin with a **minimum of three alphabetic characters** to avoid having them accidentally match or begin with a GPSS/H **reserved word**. (A reserved word is a sequence of characters having a predefined meaning. If a Block Label does match or begin with a reserved word, GPSS/H will issue a compile-time Error Message.) Examples of valid Block Labels are BYPASS, DETOUR, ROUTE66, BACKUP, and HIGHWAY9.

As an example of the form that the statement for a labeled Block takes, suppose we want to use CONVEYOR to label the Block "ADVANCE 250." The corresponding Block statement takes the form shown in Figure 3.8.

Recall that each Block occupies a **numbered Location** in a model. GPSS/H assigns Location numbers to **Blocks** serially in the top-down order of their appearance in a Model File. The first Block is in Location 1, the second Block is in Location 2, and so on. A Block's Label is simply a symbol for the **number** of the **Location** occupied by the Block in a model. If the Figure 3.8 ADVANCE Block happens to occupy Location 35 in a model, for example, then the Label CONVEYOR has the fixed value 35 in the model.

3.14 Nonsequential Movement of Transactions in a Model

In the simple models we've worked with so far, a Transaction's Next Block has always been sequential to its Current Block. Sometimes a Transaction needs to take a **nonsequential** Block as its Next Block. The unconditional TRANSFER Block can be used for this purpose.

The unconditional TRANSFER Block is shown in Figure 3.9. In unconditional mode, the TRANSFER

1	Label (2 - 9)	Operation (11 - 20)	Operands (22 - 72) →
	CONVEYOR	**ADVANCE**	250

Figure 3.8 An Example of the Statement-Form of a Labeled Block

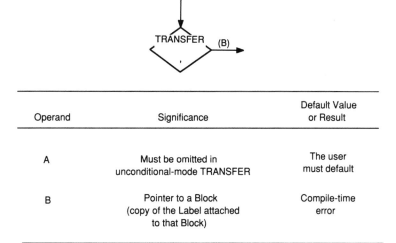

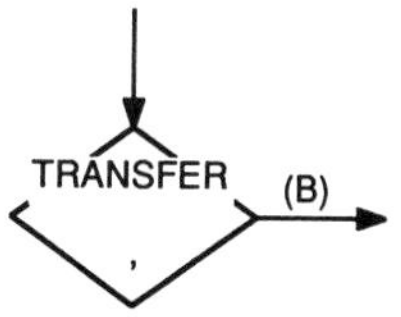

Operand	Significance	Default Value or Result
A	Must be omitted in unconditional-mode TRANSFER	The user must default
B	Pointer to a Block (copy of the Label attached to that Block)	Compile-time error

Figure 3.9 *The TRANSFER Block in Unconditional-Transfer Mode*

Block's A Operand is **not used**. (In its several other usage modes, the TRANSFER Block's A Operand is used. Other TRANSFER modes are discussed later in the book.) The B Operand "points" to the Next Block Attempted for Transactions that move into the unconditional TRANSFER Block. The pointing is accomplished by (1) labeling the Next Block Attempted and (2) using that label as the TRANSFER Block's B Operand.

There are other types of Blocks in GPSS/H that use one or more Operands to point to other Blocks in a model. When these Blocks are shown in a Block Diagram, the convention is to put parentheses around the corresponding Operands, even though these parentheses are **not included** in the statement form of the Block. Note the parentheses around the B Operand in Figure 3.9.

Use of the unconditional TRANSFER Block is shown in the simple conveyor-system model in Figure 3.10. In the conveyor system, objects arrive at a conveyor's on-point from two different sources. Objects from one source arrive at times 15, 45, 75, and so on. Objects from the other source arrive at times 30, 60, 90, and so on. Arriving objects are placed immediately on the conveyor and are conveyed to the off-point. Conveying time takes 250 time units.

In the Figure 3.10 model, the ADVANCE Block has been labeled CONVEYOR, and this label has been used as the TRANSFER Block's B Operand. A default has been taken on the TRANSFER Block's A Operand by preceding the B Operand with a comma. (This comma corresponds to the comma shown in the body of the TRANSFER Block in Figure 3.9.) Comments have also been provided to the right of the Operands in the model.

3.15 Exercises

*1. The Figure 3.10 model is contained in the file fig310.gps. Simulate with the model in Test Mode. What is the state of the model when the Transaction-Movement Phase ends? How many objects have been put onto the conveyor from each source? How many objects are on the conveyor? (Hint: You can speed up the simulation with commands like **step 25**.)

*2. Repeat Exercise 1, except design the model so that the Transaction-Movement Phase ends at time 1000 exactly. (See Exercise 7, Section 2.23.) Perform a simulation with the model in Test Mode. What is the state of the model when the Transaction-Movement Phase ends?

*3. Consider the following model:

```
          GENERATE  10,,,4
 REPEAT   ADVANCE   40,10
          TRANSFER  ,REPEAT
*
          GENERATE  200
          TERMINATE 1
```

Build a corresponding Model File, supplying a value of 1 for the START statement's A Operand. At what times will the four Transactions coming from the first GENERATE Block move into the ADVANCE Block? What will their id numbers be? Will they leave the ADVANCE Block in the order in which they enter it? Verify

```
          SIMULATE
*
          GENERATE  30,,15      objects arrive from source 1
          TRANSFER  ,CONVEYOR   go onto a conveyor
*
          GENERATE  30          objects arrive from source 2
 CONVEYOR ADVANCE   250         conveying time
          TERMINATE 1           conveyed objects leave system
*
          START     25          initialize the model's TC
*                               and the GENERATE Blocks;
*                               start the Xact-Movement Phase
          END                   end of Model-File execution
```

Figure 3.10 *A Model of a Simple Conveyor System*

your thinking by simulating with the model in Test Mode. At what time does the Total Count at the ADVANCE Block become 5? 6? 7? 8?

*4. In the Model File of Exercise 3, label the TRANSFER Block WHYDOIT. Initiate a Test-Mode simulation with this Model File. What is the response of the GPSS/H compiler to this unnecessary labeling of a Block? Does the response come at compile time, or at execution time? Does it take the form of a Warning Message or an Error Message?

3.16 Bug Clinic

*1. Copy the fig310.gps Model File to a new file. Delete the TRANSFER Block from the copy. What is wrong with the resulting model? Perform a simulation with the model in Test Mode, proceeding until an Error Message is displayed by GPSS/H. Is this a compile-time or an execution-time error?

*2. In the model in Exercise 3 of Section 3.15, move the label REPEAT from the ADVANCE Block to the first GENERATE Block. Does the resulting model make sense to you? Check out your intuition by putting the model into a Model File and then simulating with the model in Test Mode. What happens?

*3. Consider either this model:

```
          ADVANCE   25,5
          GENERATE  60,20
          TERMINATE 1
```

or this model:

```
          GENERATE  60,20
          TERMINATE 1
          ADVANCE   25,5
```

It can be argued that neither model makes sense, because there is no path into the ADVANCE Block. Build a Model File for either of the preceding models, using 5 as the A Operand in the START statement. Simulate with the model in Test Mode. Does GPSS/H issue either a compile-time or an execution-time Warning Message, or does the simulation run to completion? Is the result consistent with what you might have expected?

*4. Consider this Model File:

```
          SIMULATE
*
          GENERATE  75,40
          TRANSFER  ,ZAPPO
*
          GENERATE  35,5
          ADVANCE   10
          TERMINATE 1
*
 ZAPPO    START     5
*
          END
```

What is there about this Model File that doesn't make sense? What do you think the GPSS/H reaction will be to this Model File? Perform a simulation with the Model File and see what happens.

*5. In Exercise 4, move the ZAPPO label from START to END. Do you think the Model File makes sense now? Why, or why not?

*6. In Exercise 3 of Section 3.15, change the Label REPEAT to RN3. Try to perform a simulation with the resulting Model File. What Error Message results? (RN3 is a "reserved word" used to make reference to built-in random-number generator 3 in GPSS/H. It, therefore, cannot be used to label a Block. The GPSS/H random-number generators are discussed in Chapters 13 and 14.)

*7. Repeat Exercise 6, except change the Label REPEAT to RN3PATH. Try to perform a simulation with the resulting Model File. What Error Message results? (RN3 is a reserved word, as indicated in Exercise 6. Identifiers cannot consist of a reserved word, nor can they even begin with the characters that constitute a reserved word.)

4 How Transactions Are Managed by GPSS/H

4.1 Preview

Some insights into the operation of GPSS/H have been provided in Chapters 2 and 3 via discussion, exercises, and Test-Mode simulations. The insights are still incomplete, however. For example, the order in which time-tied Transactions move has been indicated, and the use of Transaction Priority Level to control this order has been described, but the specific actions of GPSS/H in these regards have not been completely explained. These matters are best understood by considering how GPSS/H organizes information about Xacts and by studying the logic GPSS/H follows to update information about Xacts and about the state of a model. Careful understanding of these issues speeds up the later study of GPSS/H, enhances the user's ability to check out models with Test-Mode simulations, and gives the modeler the understanding needed to build models that perform as intended.

This chapter deals with fundamental aspects of the information management and logic of GPSS/H. At the level of information management, the Transaction lists called the Current and Future Events Chains will be explained, and reference will be made to three other categories of Transaction chains in GPSS/H. At the level of logic, the algorithms (step-by-step procedures) followed by GPSS/H to initialize GENERATE Blocks and conduct the Transaction-Movement Phase based on information contained in the Current and Future Events Chains will be described and illustrated with flowcharts and Test-Mode demonstrations.

4.2 Transaction Chains

Much of the logic of GPSS/H can be understood by considering the approach used by GPSS/H to keep track of the location and status of the various Transactions in a model. The **external view** (the user's view) of Transaction location, as introduced in Chapters 2 and 3, keys on the concepts of **Current Block** and **Next Block Attempted**. The **internal view** (the software's view) of Transaction location, to be introduced now, keys on the concept of **chains**.

A "chain" is a **list of Transactions.** At any given time, each Transaction in a model is resident on exactly one of several alternative chains (and at the same time is located in a Block). In general, a Transaction moves from chain to chain (as well as moving from Block to Block) as a simulation proceeds.

A GPSS/H chain has a front end (front of the chain, or head of the list) and a back end (back of the

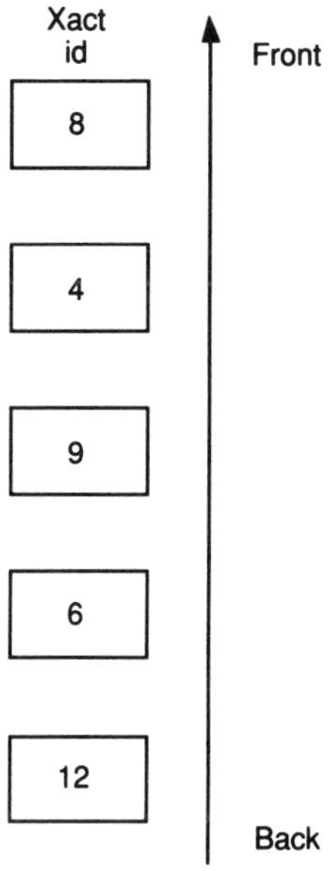

Figure 4.1 *A Representation of a Transaction Chain*

chain, or tail of the list). As a chain resident, a Transaction occupies a specific location in the chain. A Transaction might be at the front of the chain, or at the back of the chain, or at some intermediate point in the chain. As we will see, a Transaction's relative chain location is closely related to the order in which it will become that Transaction's turn to try to move again.

Figure 4.1 shows a stylized way of representing a GPSS/H chain in simple terms. The front-to-back orientation of the chain is indicated by use of a directed line segment, and with the words "front" and "back." Each of the five Xacts on the chain is shown as a rectangle. Each rectangle contains a number, which is the id number of the corresponding Xact. Xact 8 is at the front of the chain, Xact 4 is next to the front of the chain, Xact 12 is at the back of the chain, and so on.

There are five categories of chains:

1. Current Events Chain
2. Future Events Chain
3. User Chains
4. Interrupt Chains
5. MAG Chains (Match, Assemble, and Gather Chains)

There is always exactly **one** Current Events Chain and **one** Future Events Chain. There can be **zero or more** User Chains, Interrupt Chains, and MAG Chains. Only the Current and Future Events Chains will be considered in this chapter.

4.3 The Current Events Chain

The **Current Events Chain (CEC)**, sometimes simply called the **Current Chain**, is composed of all Transactions that want to move along their path at the **current** simulated time. Included in general among these Transactions are those that are currently **blocked**, that is, whose Next Block Attempted is temporarily denying entry to them. (The first of five Block types in GPSS/H that can deny entry to a Transaction will be introduced in Chapter 6.) Although a **blocked** Transaction **wants** to move from its Current Block into its Next Block Attempted, and so on, at the current simulated time, it will not be able to move until it is no longer blocked, and that may be at some later simulated time.

Transactions are arranged from front to back on the Current Events Chain in order of **decreasing Priority** (or, in case of Priority ties, in order of **nonincreasing** Priority). At each clock time, the order in which Transactions try to move corresponds to their **front-to-back** order on the CEC. The higher the Priority of a Transaction on the Current Chain, the higher the Transaction is in the pecking order in terms of which Transaction will be the next to be able to try to move. This is consistent with the statements made in Chapter 3 about the order in

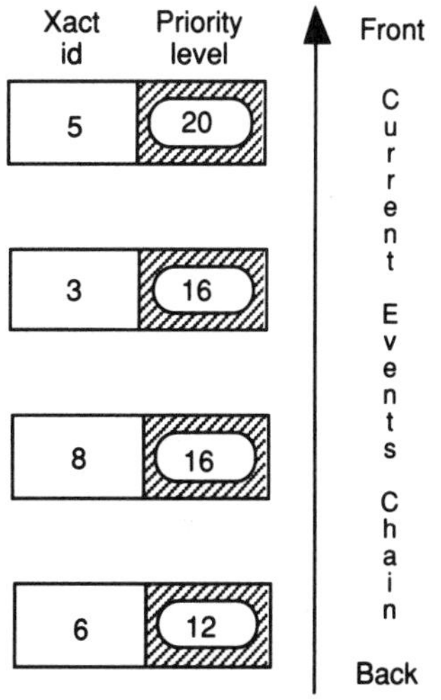

Figure 4.2 *A Representation of the Current Events Chain in a Specific Example*

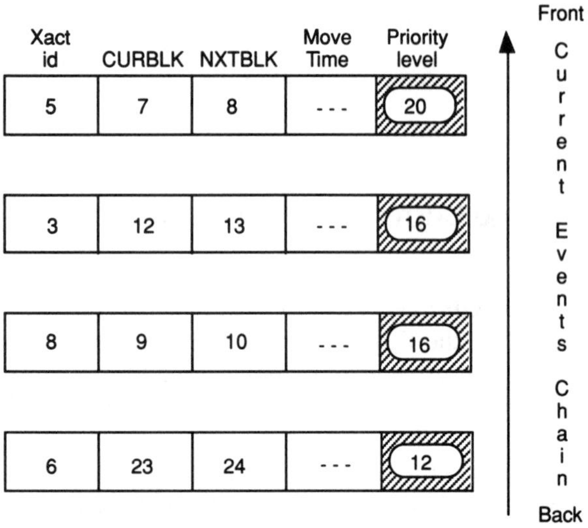

Figure 4.3 An Expanded View of the Current Events Chain

which time-tied Transactions having differing Priority Levels try to move.

Consider the example of the Current Events Chain in Figure 4.2. Each of the four Transactions on the chain is shown as a two-compartment rectangle. Each compartment contains a number. As indicated in Figure 4.2, the number in the first (left) compartment is the id number of the Transaction. The number in the second (right) compartment is the Transaction's Priority Level. Xact 5, at the front of the CEC, has Priority 20; Xact 3, second from the front, has Priority 16. And so on. Priority Levels have been highlighted in Figure 4.2 to emphasize that they form the basis for ordering Transactions on the CEC.

Xacts 3 and 8 in the Figure 4.2 CEC each have Priority 16. How are Priority ties like this resolved in arranging Xacts on the Current Chain? When a Transaction is put into the CEC, it is merged in as **last** (in front-to-back terms) **among other CEC residents having the same Priority Level.** Because Xacts on the CEC try to move in their top-down CEC order, this means Xacts **with the same Priority** try to move in FCFS (first-come, first-served) order. (In other words, they try to move in the chronological order in which they were put on the CEC.)

The fact that Transactions in a model are resident both **on a chain** and **in a Block** is emphasized in Figure 4.3, which repeats the Figure 4.2 Current Events Chain, but now shows each Transaction as a five-compartment rectangle. Two of the new compartments for each Transaction show the Transaction's **Current Block** and its **Next Block Attempted.** The labels used in Figure 4.3 for Current Block and Next Block Attempted are **CURBLK** and **NXTBLK**. (This is consistent with the labels used in **chain** displays produced by GPSS/H, as we will see. In the Test-Mode Status Window, however, Next Block Attempted is abbreviated as NEXTBLK, not NXTBLK.)

The third new compartment for each Transaction in Figure 4.3 shows the Transaction's **Move Time,** that is, the simulated time at which the Xact will try to move from its Current Block into its Next Block. By definition, the Move Time of all Xacts on the Current Chain is "now" (the current simulated time). For this reason, the Move Time for Xacts on the Current Chain is shown as dashes (-----) in Figure 4.3. This is also the way Move Time is shown in the Test-Mode Status Window for Xacts on the CEC.

As in Figure 4.2, Priority Levels have been highlighted in Figure 4.3 to emphasize that they form the basis for ordering Transactions on the CEC.

Discussion of the role of the Current Events Chain is continued later in this chapter, after the Future Events Chain has been described.

4.4 The Future Events Chain

The **Future Events Chain (FEC),** sometimes simply called the **Future Chain,** is composed of Transactions that won't try to move from their Current Block into their Next Block, and so on, until some known **future** simulated time has been reached. One or the other of two alternative conditions applies to a Transaction on the Future Events Chain:

1. The Transaction has been scheduled to come into a model from a GENERATE Block when a known future time is reached.
2. The Transaction has an ADVANCE Block as its Current Block and will not try to move into its Next Block until a known future time is reached.

Transactions are arranged from front to back on the Future Chain in order of **increasing Move Time** (or, in case of Move-Time ties, in order of **nondecreasing** Move Time). A Transaction's Move Time is the time at which the Transaction will try to move from its Current Block into its Next Block Attempted, and so on.

A Transaction that has been scheduled to come eventually into a model from a GENERATE Block **does not have a Current Block.** Such a Transaction is simply "on its way to the model" via the GENERATE Block whose execution created the Transaction. The

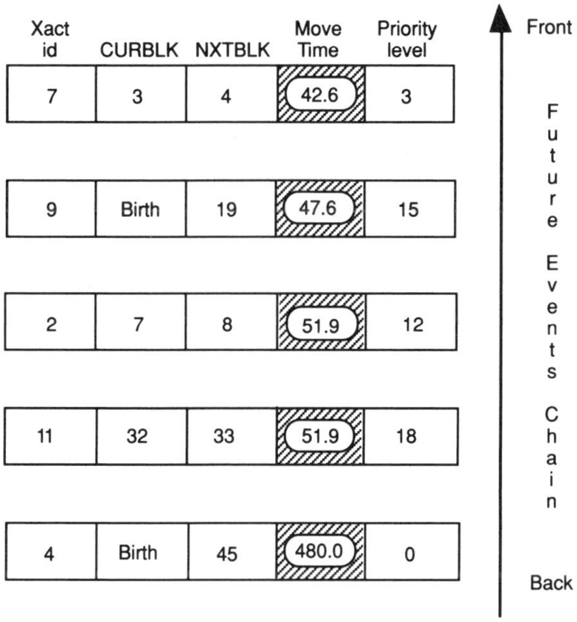

Figure 4.4 *A Representation of the Future Events Chain in a Specific Example*

Next Block for such a Transaction is the GENERATE Block from which it will come into the model. Strictly speaking, the GENERATE Block is such a Transaction's **First Block** (not its "Next" Block, because such a Transaction hasn't yet moved into **any** Block).

Consider the example of a Future Events Chain in Figure 4.4. Each of the five Transactions on the chain is shown as a five-compartment rectangle, as in the Figure 4.3 view of the Current Events Chain. The Xact with the smallest Move Time (42.6) in Figure 4.4, Xact 7, is at the front of the Future Chain; behind (beneath) it is the Xact with the next smallest Move Time, Xact 9; and so on. Move Times have been highlighted in Figure 4.4 to emphasize that they form the basis for ordering Transactions on the FEC.

Among the five Xacts pictured in Figure 4.4, two (Xacts 9 and 4) are on their way to the model via GENERATE Blocks, and three (Xacts 7, 2, and 11) are in ADVANCE Blocks. This statement results from looking at the **CURBLK** attribute of these Transactions. The **CURBLK** for Xacts 9 and 4 is shown as **Birth**, because these two embryonic Xacts are not currently in any Block. (Use of the word Birth is consistent with chain printouts produced by GPSS/H, as we will see later in this chapter.) In contrast, Xacts 7, 2, and 11 each have a Current Block. The Current Blocks for Xacts 7, 2, and 11, which are 3, 7, and 32, respectively, are ADVANCE Blocks.

Xacts 2 and 11 in the Figure 4.4 FEC each have a Move Time of 51.9. How are Move Time ties like this resolved in arranging Xacts on the Future Chain? When an Xact is put into the Future Chain, it is merged in as **last** (in front-to-back terms) **among other FEC residents having the same Move Time**. Priority Level is not used to break such ties. Notice that Xact 2 is ahead of Xact 11 in the Figure 4.4 FEC, even though the Priority of Xact 2 (12) is lower than that of Xact 11 (18).

When Move Times are determined by sampling from a probability distribution (such as a distribution of interarrival times, or of ADVANCE times), it is **very unlikely** that Move-Time ties will result, simply because more than **2 billion** different values can be sampled from a distribution in GPSS/H. On the other hand, if interarrival times or ADVANCE times are deterministic, then no sampling is involved, and the likelihood of Move-Time ties, although still small in many cases, increases substantially.

4.5 A Broad View of Transaction Movement

This section presents a broad view of the logic followed by GPSS/H in using information found on the Current and Future Events Chains as a basis for

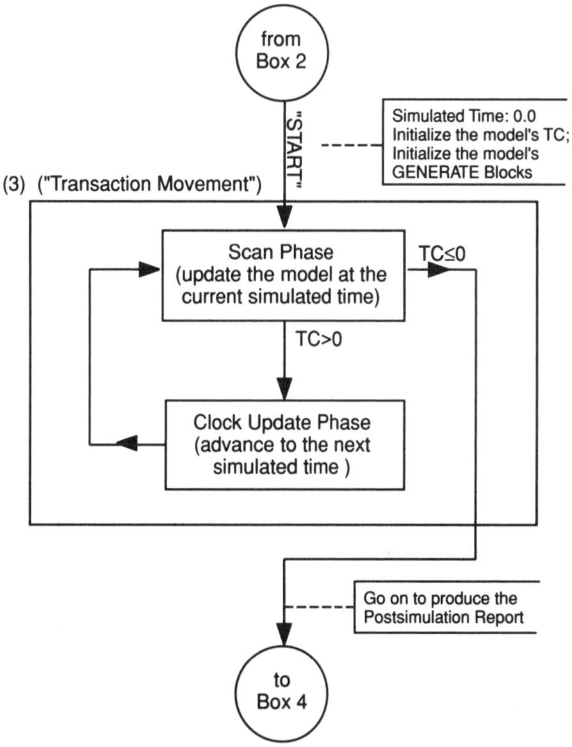

Figure 4.5 *An Expanded View of Box 3 ("Transaction Movement") in Figure 2.19*

moving Transactions. In following sections in this chapter, this broad view is then refined by presenting more specific details.

We have seen in Figure 2.19 that Xact movement begins when a START statement is executed and continues until the value of the model's Termination Counter is reduced to zero (or less). These aspects of Transaction movement are shown in Figure 4.5, which repeats Box 3 ("Transaction Movement") from Figure 2.19 but expands in more detail on the contents of Box 3. As indicated by the comments attached to the START statement in Figure 4.5, and as we've seen earlier, START-statement execution causes the model's Termination Counter to be initialized and the model's GENERATE Blocks to be initialized as well. GPSS/H then proceeds into the Box 3 Transaction-Movement Phase.

As the contents of Box 3 in Figure 4.5 indicate, the Transaction-Movement Phase consists of two subphases: the Scan Phase and the Clock Update Phase. The Scan Phase updates the state of the model at the current simulated time. The Clock Update Phase advances the clock to the earliest future time at which a Transaction has been scheduled to move. The Scan and Clock Update Phases are performed repeatedly (in alternating order) by GPSS/H as the overall Xact-Movement Phase proceeds. The Xact-Movement Phase eventually ends when the model's Termination Counter has been reduced in value to zero or less. (Things might not reach this point, of course, if the user quits during Test-Mode use of a model.)

As shown in Figure 4.5, the Xact-Movement Phase **begins with a Scan Phase**. Its purpose is to update the state of the model (if necessary) at the clock's first value, 0.0. Then the Clock Update Phase is performed a **first** time to advance the clock to the earliest future time at which one or more Transactions have been scheduled to move. Then the Scan Phase is performed again to update the state of the model at the clock's new value. Then the Clock Update Phase is performed again to advance the clock again. Then it's another Scan Phase, another Clock Update Phase, another Scan Phase, and so on, until the model's Termination Counter is reduced in value to zero (or less). At this point, the Xact-Movement Phase comes to an end, and the Postsimulation Report is produced.

The finer details of GENERATE-Block initialization, and of the Scan and Clock Update Phases, and the corresponding use of the Current and Future Events Chains are explained and illustrated in the following sections.

4.6 GENERATE-Block Initialization

The steps followed in initializing GENERATE Blocks are shown in Figure 4.6, in which the boxes have been numbered for discussion purposes. Study Figure 4.6, paying particular attention to these points:

1. GENERATE-Block initialization takes place at simulated time 0.0, per the comment attached to the line between Start and Box 1 in Figure 4.6. This means that during GENERATE-Block initialization, future times are determined relative to a current time of 0.0.

2. GENERATE Blocks are initialized in the **top-down** order of their appearance in a Model File (Box 1).

3. For each GENERATE Block, one and only one Transaction is created to initialize the Block (Box 2).

4. Transaction id numbers are assigned serially in a model from 1 forward, in the chronological order in which Transactions are created. (See the comment attached to Box 2). For example, the first GENERATE Block will be initialized with the Xact whose id is 1, the second GENERATE Block will be initialized with the Xact whose id is 2, and so on.

5. A Transaction's initial Move Time (the simulated time when the Xact will first begin to move in the model) is set equal to the value of the Offset Interval at its GENERATE Block (Box 4). If no Offset Interval has been supplied, the Move Time is set equal to the value sampled from the interarrival-time distribution specified by its GENERATE Block's A and B Operands (Box 5). (If interarrival time is deterministic, sampling is not required and does not take place.) This setting of initial Move Time is justified by the fact that the GENERATE-Block initialization is taking place at time 0.0.

6. If a Transaction's Move Time equals 0.0, the Xact is put onto the Current Events Chain (Box 7). This is because the Xact wants to move in the model "now," that is, at the current simulated time, which is 0.0. Such an Xact belongs on the Current Chain.

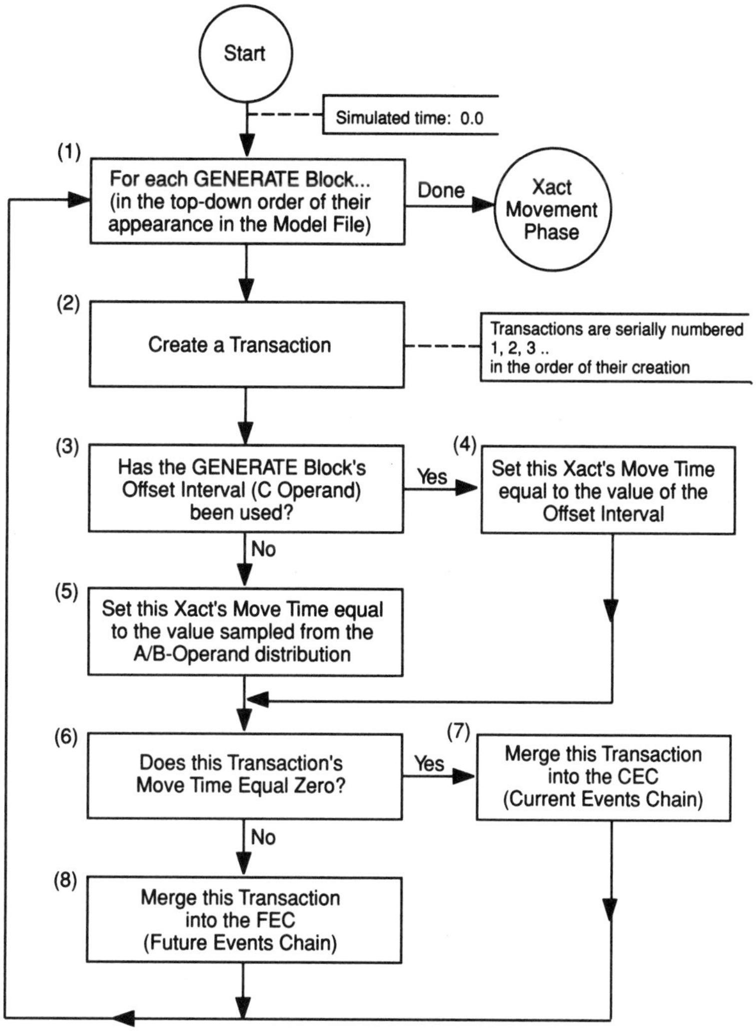

Figure 4.6 The Steps Followed to Initialize a Model's GENERATE Blocks

On the other hand, if an Xact's Move Time is greater than 0.0, the Xact is put onto the Future Events Chain (Box 8). This is because the Xact does not want to move in the model until some future simulated time is reached. Such an Xact belongs on the Future Chain.

In either case, a Transaction created to initialize a GENERATE Block has no Current Block, and its Next (First) Block is the GENERATE Block that created it. Recall from Figure 4.4 that the CURBLK for such an Xact is shown as "Birth."

In Section 4.9, we'll illustrate the Figure 4.6 logic with a Test-Mode simulation. But first we need to introduce the Test-Mode command that can be used to display the Current and Future Events Chains and indicate how we can use that command right after GENERATE Block initialization has taken place.

4.7 The Test-Mode Display Command

Figure 2.20 of Chapter 2 indicates that in Test Mode, the user can display information about the state of the model. Until now, information provided to the user has been limited to the messages GPSS/H produces when an interrupt occurs. The user can ask for other information by issuing one or more Test-Mode **display** commands. The display command takes this general form:

```
display info_type
```

where ***info_type*** represents the user's choice of a modifier indicating the type of information to be displayed.

Table 4.1
Selected types of information which can be displayed in Test Mode

Display Modifier	Information Displayed
blo	Current and Total Block Counts
cec	Current Events Chain
clocks	Absolute and Relative clock values
fec	Future Events Chain
xact=*xact_id*	the properties of the Xact whose id is *xact_id* (e.g., xact=25)

Table 4.1 lists some of the modifiers that can be used with the **display** command. For example, issuing the command **display blo** will cause all Current and Total Block Counts to be displayed, **display cec** will cause the Current Events Chain to be displayed, and **display xact=25** will cause the properties of Xact 25 to be displayed. (In the **display xact=*xact_id*** command, one or more blanks can be substituted for the equals sign (=). For example, **display xact 25** is an alternative to **display xact=25**.)

The minimal abbreviation for **display** is **d**. Issuing the command **d xact=31**, for example, would cause the properties of Xact 31 to be displayed.

Types of information other than that listed in Table 4.1 can be displayed. More modifiers for the **display** command will be introduced later.

It's possible to use two or more modifiers with the **display** command, listing them in any order after the key word **display** and separating them with one or more blanks. For example, when the command **display cec fec** is issued, both the Current and the Future Events Chains will be displayed.

Use of the **display** command to display the Current and Future Events Chains is illustrated in Section 4.9.

4.8 The Test-Mode "Trap Scan" Command

As shown in Figure 4.5, within the overall Xact-Movement Phase GPSS/H moves back and forth repeatedly between the Scan Phase and the Clock Update Phase. It's convenient on occasion for a Test-Mode user to be given control whenever GPSS/H is just about to begin a Scan Phase. At this point, for example, the user might want to issue a **display cec fec** command and study the composition of the Current and Future Events Chains just as a Scan Phase is about to begin.

To tell GPSS/H that we want to be given control at the beginning of each Scan Phase, we issue this command in response to the Ready! prompt at the beginning of a Test-Mode simulation:

```
trap scan
```

Unlike issuing a **step** command, issuing a **trap** command does **not** cause GPSS/H to resume the simulation. It simply establishes an interrupt condition, that is, a condition under which control is to be returned to the interactive user after the simulation has been resumed. (See the "User in Test Mode" box in Figure 2.20.) The user can resume the simulation by issuing this command:

```
run
```

When a **run** command is issued, GPSS/H simply resumes the simulation. (Resuming the simulation corresponds to Lines 2 and 4 in Figure 2.20.)

It may be useful to compare and contrast the **step** command with the **trap/run** combination. A **step** command has the *dual* effect of establishing an interrupt condition *and* causing the simulation to resume. A **trap** command has the *sole* effect of establishing an interrupt condition. A **run** command has the *sole* effect of causing the simulation to resume. (More complicated forms of the **trap** and **run** commands exist but won't be considered now.)

A **trap scan** command can be issued whenever the user has control during a Test-Mode simulation. From that point forward, the user will then be given control whenever a Scan Phase begins. In this sense, a **scan** trap is *semipermanent*. It remains in effect unless and until the user undoes the trap. The user can turn off a **scan** trap by issuing this command:

```
untrap scan
```

The effect of issuing an **untrap** command is simply to undo an effect previously established by issuing a corresponding **trap** command. (We'll learn in Chapter 5 and beyond that **trap** commands can be used in a number of different ways and aren't limited to setting a **scan** trap.)

In the next section, we'll use the **trap scan** command in a Test-Mode simulation to verify the details of GENERATE-Block initialization illustrated in Figure 4.6. We'll set a **scan** trap then issue a **run** command and be given control just as the first Scan Phase is about to begin, before any Blocks have been executed. We can then issue a **display cec fec** command, inspect the Xacts on the Current and Future Events Chains, and satisfy ourselves that GENERATE-Block initialization has taken place in accordance with the logic of Figure 4.6.

4.9 A Test-Mode Demonstration of GENERATE-Block Initialization

We now illustrate the Figure 4.6 logic of GENERATE-Block initialization and relate it to the Future and Current Events Chains with a Test-Mode simulation. We perform the simulation with the Model File shown in Figure 4.7.

The two GENERATE Blocks in the Model File have been arbitrarily labeled BLOCK1 and BLOCK3 to support discussion. (It's all right to label Blocks, even if the labels aren't necessary to support the logic of the model. In such cases, however, a compile-time Warning Message is issued. Such a Warning Message states that "The following entities have been defined but not explicitly referenced" and then lists such Block Labels. This type of message calls the modeler's attention to a characteristic of the model that might result from an unintentional oversight. After such a warning has been issued, compilation of the model continues.)

Inspecting the Figure 4.7 model, we know that the Xacts with id's 1 and 2 will be used to initialize the BLOCK1 and BLOCK3 GENERATE Blocks, respectively. Furthermore, we know Xact 1 will be put on the Future Chain, because its minimum feasible Move-Time exceeds zero. With its deterministic Move Time of 0 (because 0 is used as the Offset Interval for its GENERATE Block), Xact 2 will be put on the Current Chain. This understanding on our part will be validated in the following demonstration.

```
         SIMULATE
*
 BLOCK1  GENERATE  25,10
         TERMINATE 1
*
 BLOCK3  GENERATE  50,20,0
         TERMINATE 1
*
         START     2
         END
```

Figure 4.7 A Model File to Demonstrate GENERATE-Block Initialization

Figure 4.8 shows eight computer screens resulting when a simulation is performed with the Figure 4.7 Model File in Test Mode. Discussion of this screen sequence follows. (In Exercise 1 of Section 4.11, you are asked to reproduce this screen sequence on your computer.)

Screen 1 (Figure 4.8, part a)

Screen 1 was produced as follows. First, the command

```
gpssh fig47.gps tvtnw
```

was issued. Then **trap scan** and **run** commands were issued, as shown in the Screen 1 Dialog Window. This resulted in the GPSS/H message at the bottom of the Screen 1 Dialog Window

```
"SCAN" TRAP TAKEN (SYSTEM POISED TO BEGIN CEC SCAN).
```

The phrase "scan trap taken" simply means that the scan interrupt condition has come about. At this point, the model's GENERATE Blocks have been initialized, and the first Scan Phase is about to begin. As indicated in the Screen 1 Status Window, the simulated time (ABSCLOCK and REL CLOCK) is 0.0.

Note in Screen 1 that the Source Window is still empty. This window would normally be centered on the Block at which the currently moving Xact is poised, but there is not yet a currently moving Xact in the model.

Although there is not yet a currently moving Xact, the Screen 1 Status Window displays information about a type of Xact known as a "System Xact." Its id is $SYS, it does not have a CURBLK or a NEXTBLK, and it has a very large Priority. System Xacts are not ones that move through a model, but that instead are used for internal purposes to support model execution. They're not of direct importance to us, so nothing more will be said about them in this book.

Screen 2 (Figure 4.8, part b)

Screen 2 results when we issue a **display cec** command. Responding to this command, GPSS/H has

```
BLOCK CURRENT     TOTAL          fig47.gps SOURCE CODE
----- -------     -----          ----------------------------------------------



==============================================================================
S/C: OFF  ABS CLOCK:  0.           REL CLOCK: 0.           TTG: 2
==============================================================================
XACT: $SYS     CURBLK:            NEXTBLK:            CHAINS: CEC+SYS  PC:

MARK-TIME:              MOVE-TIME: -----         PRIORITY: 2147483647
==============================================================================
                        WOLVERINE SOFTWARE CORPORATION
                              4115 ANNANDALE ROAD
                        ANNANDALE, VIRGINIA 22003, USA

Ready!
: trap scan
: run

"SCAN" TRAP TAKEN (SYSTEM POISED TO BEGIN CEC SCAN).
:
```

Figure 4.8 *Eight Computer Screens Resulting When the Figure 4.8 Model File Is Run in Test Mode (a) Screen 1*

```
BLOCK CURRENT     TOTAL          fig47.gps SOURCE CODE
----- -------     -----          ----------------------------------------------



==============================================================================
S/C: OFF  ABS CLOCK:  0.           REL CLOCK: 0.           TTG: 2
==============================================================================
XACT: $SYS     CURBLK:            NEXTBLK:            CHAINS: CEC+SYS  PC:

MARK-TIME:              MOVE-TIME: -----         PRIORITY: 2147483647
==============================================================================

"SCAN" TRAP TAKEN (SYSTEM POISED TO BEGIN CEC SCAN).
: display cec

CURRENT EVENTS CHAIN

XACT      CURBLK   NXTBLK   CHAINS  SDPGFT**  MARK-TIME  MOVE-TIME  PRIORITY

2         BIRTH    BLOCK3   CEC                  ---        0.             0
:
```

Figure 4.8 (b) *Screen 2*

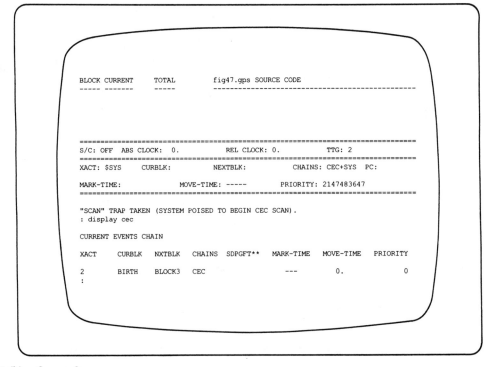

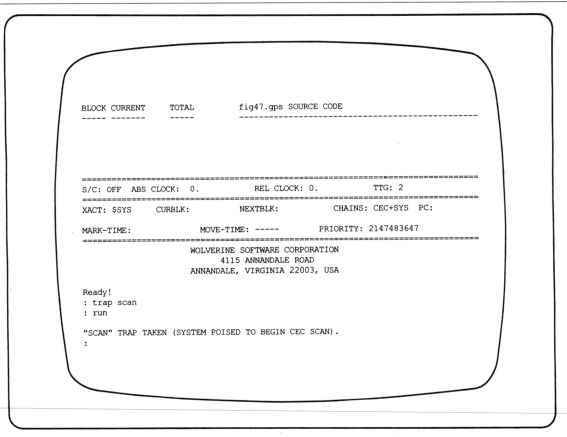

displayed the Current Events Chain in the Dialog Window. Each Xact on a chain is represented by two rows of information. The first row consists of labels, and the second shows the values corresponding to the labels. We see at the bottom of Screen 2 that there is one Xact on the Current Events Chain. This is **XACT 2** (column 1) with **BIRTH** as its **CURBLK** (column 2) and **BLOCK3** as its **NXTBLK** (column 3). Xact 2 is in pending birth status, on its way into the model via the GENERATE Block in the BLOCK3 Location. It doesn't yet have a Current Block (hence the BIRTH label), and its Next (First) Block is the BLOCK3 GENERATE.

In Screen 2, **CHAINS** (column 4) indicates which chain the Xact is on. **CEC** indicates the Current Events Chain. The **SDPGFT**** column (column 5) is not of interest to us now. **MARK-TIME** (column 6), as we know, is the time an Xact moves out of its GENERATE Block. Xact 2 has not yet moved into its GENERATE Block, let alone out of it, and so its **MARK-TIME** has not yet been given a value. This explains why its **MARK-TIME** entry is shown as dashes (-----) in Screen 2.

Column 7 in Screen 2 shows a **MOVE-TIME** value of 0.0 for Xact 2. This value is consistent with the Offset Interval of 0 specified at Xact 2's BLOCK3 GENERATE. The Move Time of 0.0 matches the current simulated time of 0.0, which is shown in the Status Window.

The rightmost column in Screen 6, column 8, shows Xact **PRIORITY**. Xact 2 has a Priority of 0, consistent with the default value of the Priority Operand (E Operand) at its BLOCK3 GENERATE Block.

Screen 3 (Figure 4.8, part c)

Screen 3 results when we issue a **display fec** command. We see in Screen 3 that Xact 1 is on the FEC. Its Current Block is BIRTH; its Next (First) Block Attempted is the BLOCK1 GENERATE Block. Its Move Time is 20.4059, which was determined by sampling from the 25±10 interarrival-time distribution at the BLOCK1 GENERATE, and it has a (default) Priority of 0.

If a chain is empty when a command is issued to **display** it, GPSS/H simply replies with a colon (:), prompting the user for another command. *No message is issued stating that the chain is empty.* This situation doesn't occur in this demonstration of GENERATE-Block initialization, but it will occur in some of the Section 4.11 exercises that follow.

In summary, after initialization of the GENERATE Blocks in the Figure 4.7 model, there is one Xact on the Current Events Chain and one on the Future Events Chain. The existence of these two Xacts and their various properties such as Current Block, Next Block Attempted, Move Time, and Priority, are consistent with the GENERATE-Block initialization logic of Figure 4.6.

Even though the objective of this demonstration has been reached, we'll continue briefly with the demonstration to show how to switch back and forth between use of the screen to display three windows (Source, Status, and Dialog) on the one hand, and use of the entire screen for the Dialog Window on the other hand.

Screen 4 (Figure 4.8, part d)

If we issue a **display cec fec** command, then GPSS/H will display both the Current and Future Events Chains. But these two chains are usually too long (in top-to-bottom terms) to be completely contained in the Dialog Window, meaning that part of the chain information will scroll off the top of the window. To reduce this problem, we can dedicate the entire screen to the Dialog Window, eliminating the Source and Status Windows for the time being. This is done by executing a **set tv off** command. We see this command keyed in (but not yet sent) at the bottom of Screen 4. (As we'll see in Section 4.10, pressing the F2 key is an alternative way to issue a **set tv off** command.)

Screen 5 (Figure 4.8, part e)

Screen 5 results when we send (and GPSS/H executes) the **set tv off** command keyed in at the bottom of Screen 4. Screen 5 has neither a Source nor a Status Window but is entirely dedicated to the Dialog Window, showing as much of the past dialog as fits onto the screen. Note that both the Current and Future Events Chains, as displayed earlier, are visible in Screen 5. Also note that GPSS/H has erased the **set tv off** command itself from the screen.

Screen 6 (Figure 4.8, part f)

Screen 6 results from issuing a **display cec fec** command in response to the colon (:) prompt at the bottom of Screen 5. Both the Current and Future Events Chains are displayed consecutively at the bottom of Screen 6. These chains haven't changed, of course, since the time they were displayed in

```
BLOCK CURRENT      TOTAL          fig47.gps SOURCE CODE
----- -------      -----          -----------------------------------------------



=============================================================================
S/C: OFF  ABS CLOCK:  0.           REL CLOCK: 0.            TTG: 2
=============================================================================
XACT: $SYS      CURBLK:            NEXTBLK:            CHAINS: CEC+SYS  PC:

MARK-TIME:                 MOVE-TIME: -----         PRIORITY: 2147483647
=============================================================================

2         BIRTH    BLOCK3    CEC                      ---         0.              0
: display fec

FUTURE EVENTS CHAIN

XACT      CURBLK   NXTBLK    CHAINS   SDPGFT**   MARK-TIME   MOVE-TIME   PRIORITY

1         BIRTH    BLOCK1    FEC                      ---         20.4059         0
:
```

Figure 4.8 (c) *Screen 3*

```
BLOCK CURRENT      TOTAL          fig47.gps SOURCE CODE
----- -------      -----          -----------------------------------------------



=============================================================================
S/C: OFF  ABS CLOCK:  0.           REL CLOCK: 0.            TTG: 2
=============================================================================
XACT: $SYS      CURBLK:            NEXTBLK:            CHAINS: CEC+SYS  PC:

MARK-TIME:                 MOVE-TIME: -----         PRIORITY: 2147483647
=============================================================================

2         BIRTH    BLOCK3    CEC                      ---         0.              0
: display fec

FUTURE EVENTS CHAIN

XACT      CURBLK   NXTBLK    CHAINS   SDPGFT**   MARK-TIME   MOVE-TIME   PRIORITY

1         BIRTH    BLOCK1    FEC                      ---         20.4059         0
: set tv off
```

Figure 4.8 (d) *Screen 4*

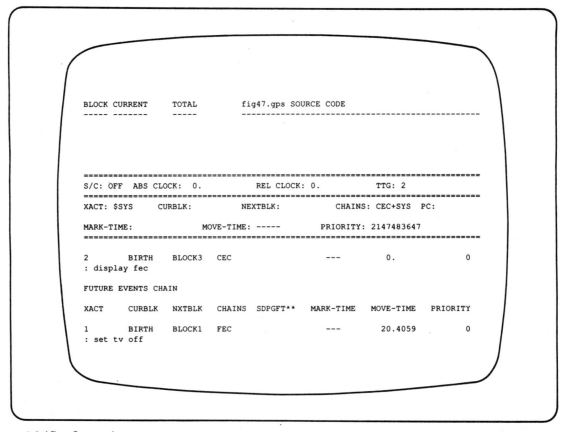

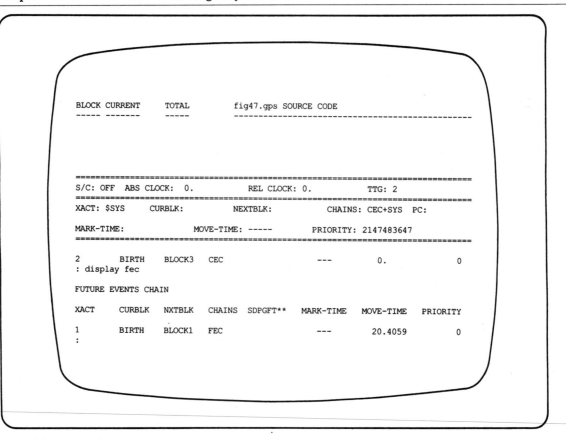

```
                  WOLVERINE SOFTWARE CORPORATION
                      4115 ANNANDALE ROAD
                  ANNANDALE, VIRGINIA 22003, USA

Ready!
: trap scan
: run

"SCAN" TRAP TAKEN (SYSTEM POISED TO BEGIN CEC SCAN).
: display cec

CURRENT EVENTS CHAIN

XACT    CURBLK   NXTBLK   CHAINS  SDPGFT**   MARK-TIME   MOVE-TIME   PRIORITY

2       BIRTH    BLOCK3   CEC                   ---         0.              0
: display fec

FUTURE EVENTS CHAIN

XACT    CURBLK   NXTBLK   CHAINS  SDPGFT**   MARK-TIME   MOVE-TIME   PRIORITY

1       BIRTH    BLOCK1   FEC                   ---         20.4059         0
:
```

Figure 4.8 (e) *Screen 5*

```
XACT    CURBLK   NXTBLK   CHAINS  SDPGFT**   MARK-TIME   MOVE-TIME   PRIORITY

2       BIRTH    BLOCK3   CEC                   ---         0.              0
: display fec

FUTURE EVENTS CHAIN

XACT    CURBLK   NXTBLK   CHAINS  SDPGFT**   MARK-TIME   MOVE-TIME   PRIORITY

1       BIRTH    BLOCK1   FEC                   ---         20.4059         0
: display cec fec

CURRENT EVENTS CHAIN

XACT    CURBLK   NXTBLK   CHAINS  SDPGFT**   MARK-TIME   MOVE-TIME   PRIORITY

2       BIRTH    BLOCK3   CEC                   ---         0.              0

FUTURE EVENTS CHAIN

XACT    CURBLK   NXTBLK   CHAINS  SDPGFT**   MARK-TIME   MOVE-TIME   PRIORITY

1       BIRTH    BLOCK1   FEC                   ---         20.4059         0
:
```

Figure 4.8 (f) *Screen 6*

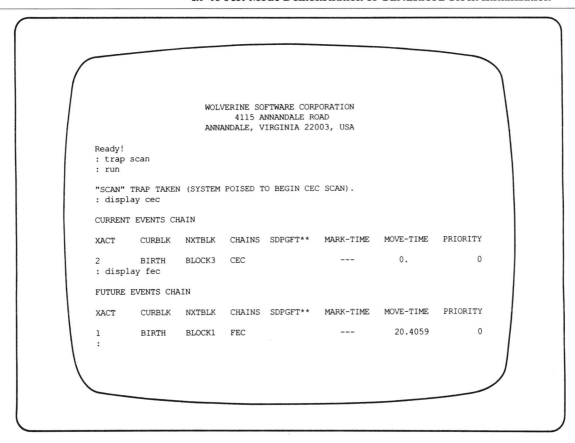

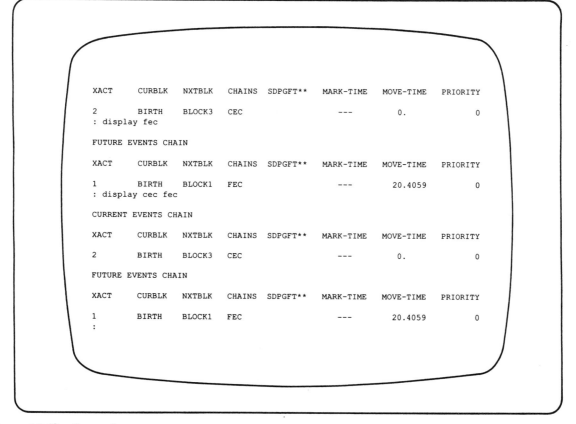

Screens 2 and 3. Most of the earlier displays of these chains are still visible in the upper part of Screen 6.

Screen 7 (Figure 4.8, part g)

Now let's return to use of the screen to display the Source, Status, and Dialog Windows. To do this, we use a **set tv on** command. The command is shown at the bottom of Screen 7, keyed in but not yet sent. (As we'll see in Section 4.10, pressing the F4 key is an alternative way to issue a **set tv on** command.)

Screen 8 (Figure 4.8, part h)

Screen 8 results after the **set tv on** command at the bottom of Screen 7 has been sent to GPSS/H and executed. The usual Source, Status, and Dialog Windows appear in Screen 8. The state of the simulation in Screen 8 matches that in Screens 1 through 7. The model's GENERATE Blocks have been initialized and the first Scan Phase is about to begin. No Blocks have been executed, because no Xact movement has yet taken place.

This concludes the demonstration of GENERATE-Block initialization.

4.10 The Use of Arrow and Function Keys to Scroll

Moving from Screen 4 to 5 in Figure 4.8, we **set tv off** to increase the size of the Dialog Window, with the disadvantage of giving up the Source and Status Windows. The benefit in doing this is that old Dialog Window information is retained on the screen longer, without disappearing under the Status Window. In another approach, old Dialog-Window information can be brought back onto the screen by scrolling backward in the Dialog Window. The keyboard's **up-arrow key** can be used for this purpose. The keyboard's **down-arrow key** can be used to scroll forward again in the Dialog Window.

We will see later that it can also be useful to scroll to the right (and then later scroll back to the left) in the Dialog Window. (This is because some GPSS/H information displays are wider than the screen itself.)

```
XACT      CURBLK    NXTBLK    CHAINS  SDPGFT**   MARK-TIME   MOVE-TIME   PRIORITY

2         BIRTH     BLOCK3    CEC                   ---          0.             0
: display fec

FUTURE EVENTS CHAIN

XACT      CURBLK    NXTBLK    CHAINS  SDPGFT**   MARK-TIME   MOVE-TIME   PRIORITY

1         BIRTH     BLOCK1    FEC                   ---        20.4059          0
: display cec fec

CURRENT EVENTS CHAIN

XACT      CURBLK    NXTBLK    CHAINS  SDPGFT**   MARK-TIME   MOVE-TIME   PRIORITY

2         BIRTH     BLOCK3    CEC                   ---          0.             0

FUTURE EVENTS CHAIN

XACT      CURBLK    NXTBLK    CHAINS  SDPGFT**   MARK-TIME   MOVE-TIME   PRIORITY

1         BIRTH     BLOCK1    FEC                   ---        20.4059          0
: set tv on
```

Figure 4.8 (g) *Screen 7*

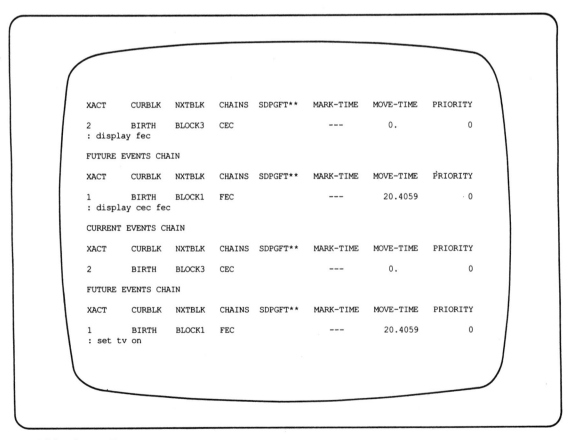

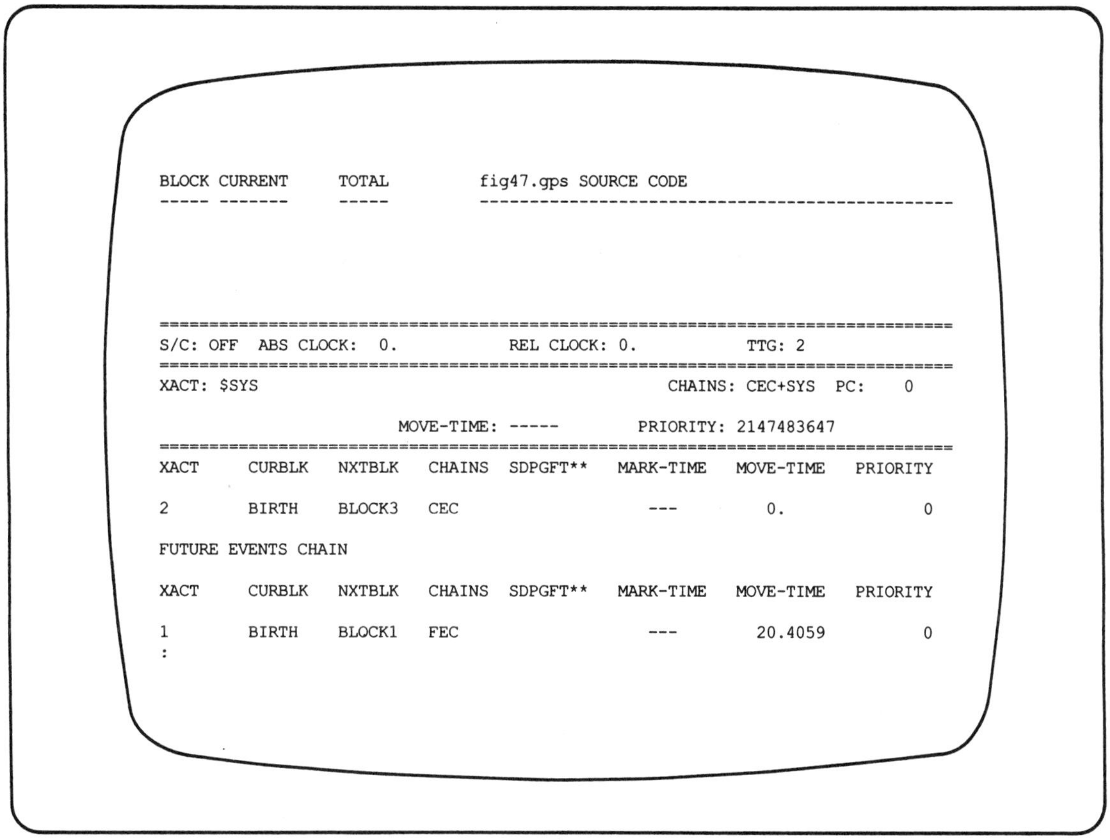

Figure 4.8 (h) *Screen 8*

The keyboard's **left- and right-arrow keys** can be used for this purpose. These keys provide left-and-right scrolling not just in the **Dialog Window**, but also in the **Block-image portion** of the **Source Window**. (Current and Total Block Counts displayed in the Source Window do not scroll left or right, however.)

The left- and right-arrow keys provide left and right scrolling in both the Dialog and Source windows, but the up- and down-arrow keys provide backward and forward scrolling *only in the Dialog Window.*

The ability to scroll up or down in the **Source Window** is of interest, because this window is only large enough to show the images of **five** consecutive Blocks at a time. To see the images of Blocks not currently in the Source Window, the keyboard's Function Keys **(F** keys) can be used. The Function Keys can also be used to scroll in the Dialog Window.

Table 4.2 shows how scrolling in the Source and/or Dialog Windows can be accomplished using the Function Keys. **F7** and **F9** can be used to scroll up and down, respectively, in the Source Window. Pressing either of these keys one time causes the Source Window to scroll by just one line. By "riding" either key, it's possible to scroll continuously in either direction.

Table 4.2

The role of the Function keys in scrolling

Function Key	Effect
F1	Zoom to the topmost line of dialog still in computer memory
F3	Zoom to the bottom (most recent) line of dialog
F5	Scroll 20 columns to the left in the Dialog and Source Windows
F6	Scroll 10 columns to the right in the Dialog and Source Windows
F7	Scroll up (one line) in the Source Window
F9	Scroll down (one line) in the Source Window

F1 can be used to zoom to the **topmost** line of dialog still in memory. (As the simulation proceeds, old dialog lines will be displaced methodically from computer memory.) **F3** can be used to zoom to the **bottom** (most recent) line of dialog. **F5** can be used to scroll 20 columns to the left in the Dialog and Source Windows. And **F6** can be used to scroll 10 columns to the right in the Dialog and Source Windows.

It's a challenge at first to remember which F keys have which effect. To jog the memory, the following command can be entered when in Test Mode:

```
display pf
```

GPSS/H will then summarize the effect of pressing the F keys. Among the effects already mentioned in the book, but not included in Table 4.2, are these:

1. Press **F2** to issue a **set tv off** command.
2. Press **F4** to issue a **set tv on** command.
3. Press **F10** to issue a **step 1** command.

The user can issue a single command to center the Source Window on a Block of choice. The command takes this form:

```
ds Block_identifier
```

where ***Block_identifier*** represents the Label attached to a Block or the number of the Location occupied by a Block. For example, the command **ds ROUTE101** (or **ds route101**) would center the Source Window on the Block labeled **ROUTE101**, and the command **ds 395** would center the Source Window on the Block in Location 395. The **ds** command is of help in moving around rapidly in large Model Files. (Think of "ds" as meaning "display source.")

4.11 Exercises

1. The file fig47.gps contains the Model File shown in Figure 4.7. Initiate a Test-Mode simulation with this Model File and reproduce the screen sequence shown in Figure 4.8.

*2. Consider this model, which is in the file s411x2.gps.

```
          SIMULATE
*
 BLOCK1   GENERATE   50,25
          TERMINATE  1
*
 BLOCK3   GENERATE   10,5
          TERMINATE  1
*
          START      5
          END
```

When the GENERATE Blocks in this model are initialized, what will be the id numbers of the corresponding Xacts? Immediately after GENERATE-Block initialization, which of these Xacts will be on which chains? If the two Xacts involved are both on the same chain, what will be the id number of the Xact at the front of the chain? Check your reasoning by building the Model File and initiating a Test-Mode simulation with it. Issue **trap scan** and **run** commands, then display the Current and Future Events Chains to determine the answers to these questions. (Caution: remember that if a chain is empty when a command is issued to **display** it, GPSS/H simply prints out a colon, prompting the user for another command. GPSS/H does not provide a message stating that the chain is empty.)

*3. Consider this model, which is in the file s411x3.gps.

```
          SIMULATE
*
 BLOCK1   GENERATE   10,5
          TERMINATE  1
*
 BLOCK3   GENERATE   50,25
          TERMINATE  1
*
          START      5
          END
```

Note that the Model File matches that of Exercise 2, except that the GENERATE Blocks (but not their Labels) have been interchanged. For this modified Model File, answer the questions posed in Exercise 2. As in Exercise 2, experiment with the model in Test Mode to check out your thinking.

*4. Consider this model, which is in the file s411x4.gps.

```
          SIMULATE
*
 BLOCK1   GENERATE  0,,,1
          TERMINATE 1
*
 BLOCK3   GENERATE  75,40
          TERMINATE 0
*
 BLOCK5   GENERATE  0,,,4
          TERMINATE 0
*
          START     5
          END
```

When the GENERATE Blocks in this model are initialized, what will be the id numbers of the corresponding Xacts? Immediately after GENERATE-Block initialization, which of these Xacts will be on which chains? What will be the relative order of these Xacts on these chains? Check your reasoning by building the Model File and initiating a Test-Mode simulation with it. Issue **trap scan** and **run** commands, then display the Current and Future Events Chains to determine the answers to these questions.

*5. Consider this model, which is in the file s411x5.gps.

```
          SIMULATE
*
 BLOCK1   GENERATE  0,,,1
          TERMINATE 1
*
 BLOCK3   GENERATE  75,40
          TERMINATE 0
*
 BLOCK5   GENERATE  0,,,4,5
          TERMINATE 0
*
          START     5
          END
```

Note that the Model File matches that of Exercise 4, except that an E Operand (Priority Operand) of 5 has been supplied on the BLOCK5 GENERATE. For this modified Model File, answer the questions posed in Exercise 4. As in Exercise 4, experiment with the model in Test Mode to check out your thinking.

*6. Consider this model, which is in the file s411x6.gps.

```
          SIMULATE
*
 BLOCK1   GENERATE  75,,,,5
          TERMINATE 1
*
 BLOCK3   GENERATE  75,,,,15
          TERMINATE 0
*
 BLOCK5   GENERATE  75,,,,20
          TERMINATE 0
*
          START     5
          END
```

When the GENERATE Blocks in this model are initialized, what will be the id numbers of Xacts in their front-to-back order on the Future Events Chain, and what will the Xact Priorities be? Check your reasoning by building the Model File and initiating a Test-Mode simulation with it. Issue **trap scan** and **run** commands, then display the Future Events Chain to determine the answers to these questions. Also issue a **display cec** command and note that GPSS/H will not respond with a message indicating that the CEC is empty, but will simply respond by displaying a colon (:).

*7. Consider this model, which is in the file s411x7.gps.

```
          SIMULATE
*
 BLOCK1   GENERATE  75,,0,,5
          TERMINATE 1
*
 BLOCK3   GENERATE  75,,0,,15
          TERMINATE 0
*
 BLOCK5   GENERATE  75,,0,,20
          TERMINATE 0
*
          START     5
          END
```

Note that the Model File matches that of Exercise 6, except that an Offset Interval of zero has been specified at each GENERATE Block. When the GENERATE Blocks in this model are initialized, what will be the id numbers of Xacts in their front-to-back order on the Current Events Chain, and what will the Xact Priorities be? Check your reasoning by building the Model File and initiating a Test-Mode simulation with it. Issue **trap scan** and **run** commands, then display the Current Events Chain to determine the answers to these questions. Also issue a **display fec** command and note that GPSS/H will not respond with a message indicating that the FEC is empty, but will simply respond by displaying a colon (:).

*8. Consider this model, which is in the file s411x8.gps.

```
          SIMULATE
*
 BLOCK1   GENERATE   100,50,,,5
 BLOCK2   TERMINATE 1
*
 BLOCK3   GENERATE   25,10
 BLOCK4   TERMINATE 1
*
 BLOCK5   GENERATE   35,,0
 BLOCK6   TERMINATE 1
*
 BLOCK7   GENERATE   0,,,1,25
 BLOCK8   TERMINATE 1
*
          START      5
          END
```

When the GENERATE Blocks in this model are initialized, what will be the id numbers of the corresponding Xacts? Immediately after GENERATE-Block initialization, which of these Xacts will be on which chains? If two Xacts are on the same chain, what will be the id number of the Xact at the front of the chain? Check your reasoning by building the Model File and initiating a Test-Mode simulation with it. Issue **trap scan** and **run** commands, then display the Current and Future Events Chains to determine the answers to these questions. Also practice use of the arrow keys and of the Function keys in carrying out this exercise.

*9. Suppose that in response to the Ready! prompt during a Test-Mode simulation, the user issues a **trap scan** command and then issues a series of **run** commands. At what points during the simulation will the user be put into control?

*10. Suppose that in response to the Ready! prompt during a Test-Mode simulation, the user simply issues a **run** command (without issuing a **trap scan**) command first. What do you think will happen? Check out your thinking by doing this with the model for Exercise 8 (or for any of the models in this section).

*11. Suppose that a simulation is resumed when *two or more* interrupt conditions have been established. Then the simulation will proceed until whichever interrupt condition occurs first, returning control to the interactive user at that time. In response to the Ready! prompt in the model of Exercise 5, for example, suppose the user issues a **trap scan** command, which establishes one interrupt condition, and a **step 1** command, which establishes another interrupt condition and causes the simulation to be resumed. Which of the two interrupt conditions will come about first? At what clock time? What will the state of the model be at that time? How many Blocks will have been executed? Check out your thinking by carrying out the corresponding Test-Mode simulation with the model in Exercise 5.

4.12 Updating the State of a Model at the Current Simulated Time: The Scan Phase

As illustrated in Figure 4.5, the Transaction-Movement Phase consists of two sub-phases: the Scan Phase, and the Clock Update Phase. The Scan Phase updates the state of the model at the current simulated time. To do this, during the Scan Phase GPSS/H gives each Xact *on the Current Events Chain* a chance to move as far forward as it can along its path in the model. The logic of the Scan Phase is summarized in the Figure 4.9 flowchart, where the boxes have been numbered to support the following discussion.

As the first Scan Phase step, GPSS/H checks to see if a **scan** trap has been set. If it has, then as we already know, GPSS/H gives control to the Test-Mode user. This is indicated in Figure 4.9 with the comment provided in Box 1.

As the next step in the Scan Phase, GPSS/H checks to see if there is an Xact at the front of the Current Events Chain. If there isn't, then the Cur-

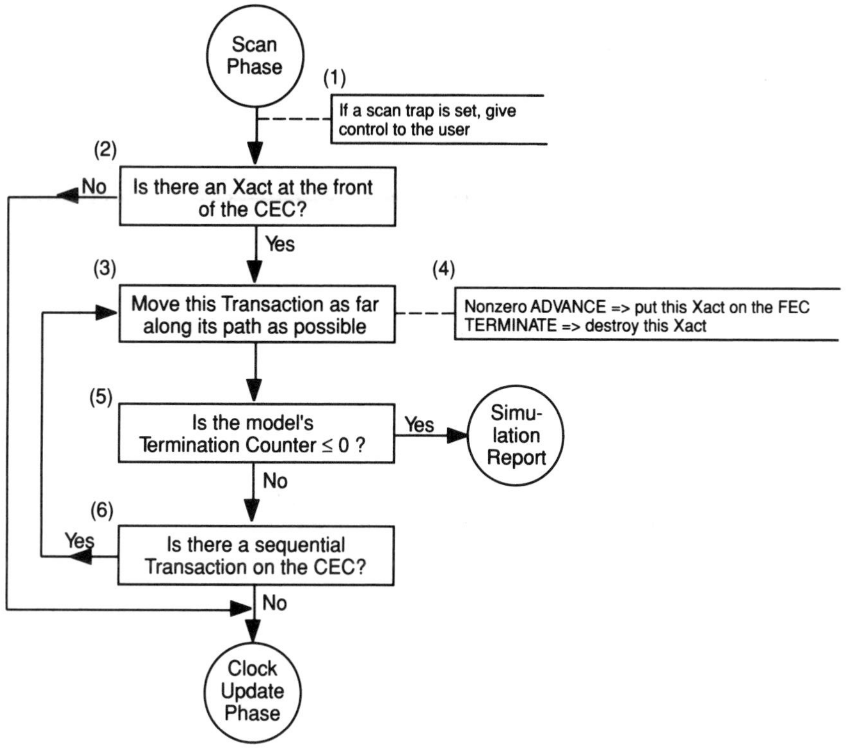

Figure 4.9 *A Simplified Form of the Logic Followed in the Scan Phase*

rent Chain is empty, and GPSS/H leaves the Scan Phase and goes into the Clock Update Phase, as indicated by the line labeled "No" coming from Box 2 in Figure 4.9. This condition occurs at time 0.0 if no Xacts were put on the CEC during GENERATE-Block initialization. This condition cannot otherwise occur at the *beginning* of a Scan Phase, as we will see later.

Assuming now that the CEC is not empty, GPSS/H picks up the Xact at the front of the CEC and moves it as far as possible, per Box 3 in Figure 4.9. As indicated by the Box 4 comments, this Xact stops moving either by going into an ADVANCE Block where a nonzero simulated time lag is applied to it, or by going into a TERMINATE Block. If this Xact terminates and reduces the model's TC value to zero or less, this ends both this Scan Phase and this overall Xact-Movement Phase, and GPSS/H produces the Postsimulation Report. (See the line labeled "Yes" coming from Box 5 in Figure 4.9. Also see Figure 4.5.)

If the model's TC still exceeds zero, GPSS/H then checks to see if there is an Xact on the CEC sequential to the Xact that just stopped moving. (See Box 6 in Figure 4.9.) If there is such an Xact, GPSS/H moves it as far as possible, and so on. (See the line labeled "Yes" connecting Box 6 to Box 3 in Figure 4.9.) Otherwise, the Scan Phase is finished and, leaving the Scan Phase, GPSS/H goes on to perform the next Clock Update Phase. (See the line labeled "No" coming from Box 6.)

What happens to the moving Xact itself during a Scan Phase when it can't move any further? The answer depends on **why** the Xact can't move any further. If the Xact moves into a **TERMINATE** Block, then the Xact is destroyed. In this case, the Xact is removed from the Current Events Chain and eliminated from the model. No Xact having this id number will be created during the rest of the simulation.

On the other hand, if the Xact moves into an **ADVANCE** Block, then the Xact will be held in that Block during some interval of simulated time. (This statement assumes the ADVANCE time is not zero. See the next paragraph in this regard.) A sample is drawn from the ADVANCE holding time distribution, and a new Move Time is computed for the Xact by adding the sampled value to a copy of the clock. For example, if the clock is 25.5, and the sampled holding time is 4.5, then the Xact's new Move time will be 30.0 (25.5 + 4.5 = 30.0). This means the Xact will not try to move from the ADVANCE (its Current Block) into the sequential Block (its Next Block Attempted) until some known **future** time (future time 30.0 in the example). This also means that the Xact should no longer be on the **Current** Chain now;

it should be on the **Future** Chain until the known future time comes when it will try to move again. And so the ADVANCE Block **transfers the Xact from the Current to the Future Chain**. This brings the movement of the Xact at the current clock time to an end.

What happens if an Xact moves into an ADVANCE where the holding time is **zero**? (The holding time would be zero at each of these ADVANCE Blocks: "ADVANCE 0"; "ADVANCE 0,0"; or just plain "ADVANCE", with no Operands.) In such a case, the Xact remains on the Current Chain and **immediately** tries to move from the ADVANCE into the sequential Block. It is **not** transferred from the Current to the Future Chain.

As the Figure 4.9 caption indicates, a *simplified* form of the Scan Phase logic is given in that figure. The Figure 4.9 logic is valid for Blocks of the type we've studied so far. After two additional types of Blocks have been introduced in Chapter 6, the Scan Phase logic will be refined and extended in Chapter 7.

4.13 Moving Ahead in Simulated Time: The Clock Update Phase

After the model's state has been updated at the current simulated time, GPSS/H advances the clock to the earliest future time at which an Xact has been scheduled to try to move. Each Xact waiting for its scheduled Move Time to come is on the Future Chain. Furthermore, Xacts are arranged on the FEC in order of increasing (nondecreasing) Move Time. The Xact at the **front** of the FEC is therefore the one scheduled to try to move at the earliest future time. Its Move Time determines what the clock's new value will be.

And so the Clock Update Phase advances the clock to match the Move Time of the Xact at the front of the FEC. The time for this Xact to try to move has come, so this Xact now belongs on the Current Chain. The Clock Update Phase therefore **removes the Xact from the front of the FEC and merges it into the CEC**. The merge point of this newcomer to the CEC is determined on the basis of its Priority. (Remember that Xacts are arranged on the CEC in order of decreasing Priority. Ties are resolved by putting the newcomer last among its CEC Priority peers.)

What about **Move-Time ties**? Assume that when a Clock Update Phase begins, the Move Time of the **second** Xact on the FEC matches the Move Time of the Xact at the **front** of the FEC. (This happens, for example, at time 25 in the model of Figure 3.5, "A model in which two Transactions move at the same simulated time.") Then the time for this second FEC Xact to try to move has now also come, and so this Xact now also belongs on the Current Chain. In this case, the Clock Update Phase **removes both of these Xacts from the FEC, one by one, and merges them into the CEC**. The Priority Level of the second time-tied Xact **on the FEC** might be higher than that of the first Xact. In this case, the second Xact winds up closer to the front of the **CEC** than the first. This is the way it should be. (It doesn't matter that Priority Level isn't used to break Move Time ties on the Future Chain, because Priority differences do prevail later when a Clock Update Phase moves the time-tied Xacts to the CEC.)

It follows that if there are **three** time-tied Xacts at the front of the FEC, then the Clock Update Phase will transfer all three of these Xacts from the FEC to the CEC. And so on. Such a situation will be demonstrated in Section 4.19.

Assuming the Future Chain is not empty at the beginning of a Clock Update Phase (see the next paragraph in this regard), a *minimum* of one Xact is put onto the Current Chain when a Clock Update takes place. This guarantees that the Current Chain *will not be empty* when the *following* Scan Phase starts. Of course, the *first* Scan Phase is not preceded by a Clock Update Phase. (See Figure 4.5.) This means the Current Chain *can* be empty when the first Scan Phase starts. In fact, the Current Chain will be empty when the first Scan Phase starts if GENERATE-Block initialization fails to put one or more Xacts on it.

What if the Future Chain is **empty** when a Clock Update Phase **begins**? Then there is no basis for advancing the clock. In this case, Execution Error Message 410, "No next event in system," is issued, and the simulation stops.

The Clock Update Phase logic described above is summarized in the form of a flowchart in Figure 4.10. In contrast with the Scan Phase steps in Figure 4.9, the Clock Update Phase details shown in Figure 4.10 **are complete** and won't be refined later.

The Clock Update Phase **moves Xacts**. But this Xact movement is **from chain-to-chain, not from Block-to-Block**. A Clock Update Phase moves one or more Xacts from the Future to the Current Chain. The purpose is to position this Xact (or these Xacts) on the CEC so that it (or they) can attempt Block-to-Block movement during the following Scan Phase.

The Scan Phase also moves Xacts, principally from Block to Block, but also **potentially** from Chain to Chain. As indicated in the Box 4 comment in Figure 4.9, chain-to-chain Xact movement occurs during a Scan Phase if and when an Xact moves into

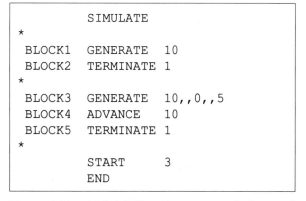

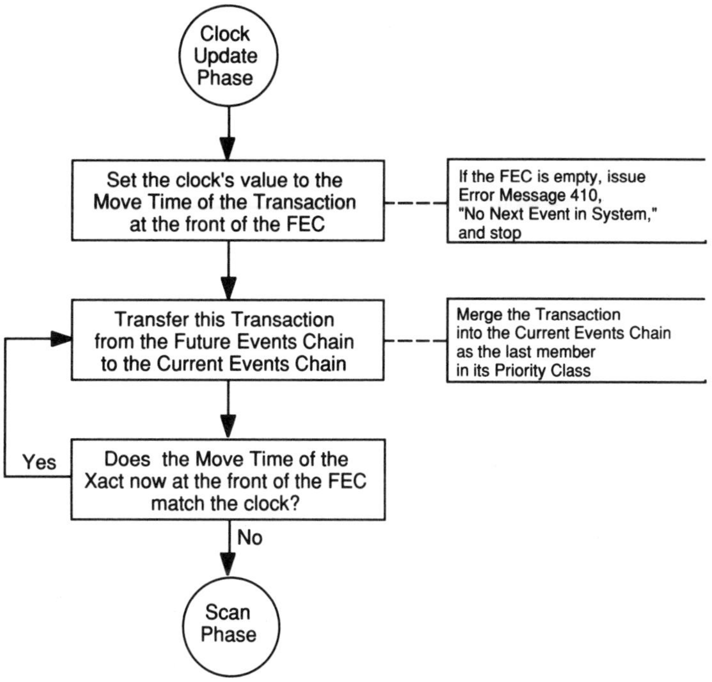

Figure 4.10 *The Logic of the Clock Update Phase*

a nonzero ADVANCE. Such an Xact is transferred by the Scan Phase from the Current to the Future Chain, where it will remain until the known future time has come for it to try to move again.

4.14 A Test-Mode Demonstration of the Scan and Clock Update Phases

Now we'll perform a simulation in Test Mode to demonstrate aspects of the Scan Phase and the Clock Update Phase. We'll do this using the Model File of Figure 4.11, where each Block has been labeled to support discussion.

Figure 4.12 shows eight computer screens resulting when a Test-Mode simulation is performed with the Figure 4.11 Model File. Discussion of this screen sequence follows. (In Exercise 1 of Section 4.15, you are asked to reproduce this screen sequence on your computer.)

Screen 1: GENERATE-Block Initialization (Figure 4.12, part a)

Screen 1 was produced by issuing **gpssh fig411.gps tvtnw**, **trap scan** and **run** commands, resulting in the message

```
"SCAN" TRAP TAKEN (SYSTEM POISED TO BEGIN CEC SCAN).
```

At this point, the model's GENERATE Blocks have been initialized, and the first Scan Phase is about to begin.

Screen 2: Display of Xacts Created During GENERATE-Block Initialization (Figure 4.12, part b)

Screen 2 results from issuing **set tv off, display clocks** and **display cec fec** commands. The

```
        SIMULATE
*
 BLOCK1 GENERATE  10
 BLOCK2 TERMINATE 1
*
 BLOCK3 GENERATE  10,,0,,5
 BLOCK4 ADVANCE   10
 BLOCK5 TERMINATE 1
*
        START     3
        END
```

Figure 4.11 *A Model File to Demonstrate the Scan and Clock Update Phases*

```
BLOCK CURRENT     TOTAL          fig411.gps SOURCE CODE
----- -------     -----          ------------------------------------------------




================================================================================
S/C: OFF  ABS CLOCK:  0.           REL CLOCK: 0.           TTG: 3
================================================================================
XACT: $SYS      CURBLK:          NEXTBLK:             CHAINS: CEC+SYS  PC:

MARK-TIME:               MOVE-TIME: -----         PRIORITY: 2147483647
================================================================================
                      WOLVERINE SOFTWARE CORPORATION
                           4115 ANNANDALE ROAD
                      ANNANDALE, VIRGINIA 22003, USA

Ready!
: trap scan
: run

"SCAN" TRAP TAKEN (SYSTEM POISED TO BEGIN CEC SCAN).
:
```

Figure 4.12 *Eight Computer Screens Resulting When the Figure 4.11 Model File Is Run in Test Mode (a) Screen 1*

```
                     ANNANDALE, VIRGINIA 22003-2500, USA

Ready!
: trap scan
: run

"SCAN" TRAP TAKEN (SYSTEM POISED TO BEGIN CEC SCAN).
: display clocks

RELATIVE CLOCK: 0.        ABSOLUTE CLOCK: 0.
: display cec fec

CURRENT EVENTS CHAIN

XACT      CURBLK   NXTBLK   CHAINS  SDPGFT**   MARK-TIME   MOVE-TIME   PRIORITY

2         BIRTH    BLOCK3   CEC                   ---         0.              5

FUTURE EVENTS CHAIN

XACT      CURBLK   NXTBLK   CHAINS  SDPGFT**   MARK-TIME   MOVE-TIME   PRIORITY

1         BIRTH    BLOCK1   FEC                   ---       10.0000           0
:
```

Figure 4.12 (b) *Screen 2*

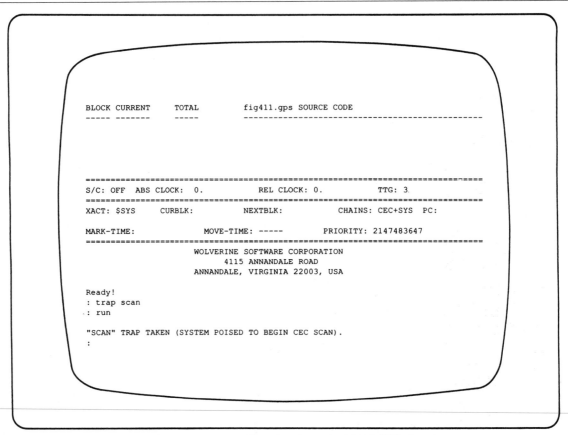

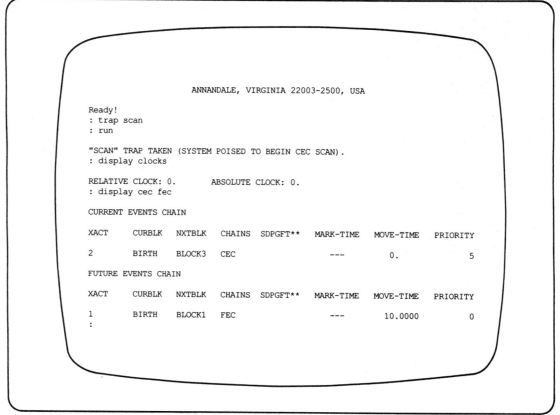

Dialog Window now occupies the entire screen (from which GPSS/H has erased the **set tv off** command) and as we see, the simulation is at clock time 0.0, and the Current and Future Events Chains each contain one Xact. Review the information provided for these CEC and FEC Xacts in Screen 2 until you are satisfied that the state of the model is consistent with the Figure 4.11 Model File.

Screen 3: Start of First Scan Phase (Figure 4.12, part c)

We start in Screen 3 by issuing a **step** command. This causes an interrupt condition to be established and the simulation to be resumed. In addition to the **step** interrupt condition ("interrupt as soon as there has been one more Block execution)," the **scan** interrupt condition ("interrupt when a Scan Phase begins") is still in effect, of course, so now GPSS/H must take into account the possibility of two interrupt conditions. What will GPSS/H do? Recall that when multiple interrupt conditions have been established, the simulation will proceed until whichever interrupt condition occurs first, returning control to the interactive user at that time. (See Exercise 12 of Section 4.11.)

In the simulation at hand, several Block executions will occur during the ongoing Scan Phase before the first Clock Update Phase and the following **scan** interrupt occur. (For the reverse of this situation, see Screen 5 which follows.) When the Screen 3 **step** command is issued, the first Scan Phase resumes. GPSS/H moves Xact 2 into the BLOCK3 GENERATE and then, in response to Xact 2's imminent escape from this GENERATE, executes the GENERATE to create and schedule a successor for Xact 2. GPSS/H then returns control to us at the terminal because the **step** interrupt has occurred.

We respond in Screen 3 by issuing a **display cec fec** command. In the resulting Screen 3 display of the Current Chain, we see that Xact 2 now has the BLOCK3 GENERATE as its Current Block, with the BLOCK4 ADVANCE as its Next Block Attempted. Xact 3, the successor to Xact 2, has been created and placed on the Future Chain. Its Current Block is BIRTH, its Next (First) Block Attempted is the BLOCK3 GENERATE, and its Move Time is 10.0. Xact 3 has been merged into the FEC behind Xact 1, with which it is involved in a Move-Time tie. Xact 3 is behind Xact 1 on the FEC, even though Xact 3's Priority is 5, whereas Xact 2's Priority is 0. (Recall that Priority is not used to resolve Move-Time ties on the Future Events Chain.)

Screen 4: Completion of First Scan Phase (Figure 4.12, part d)

Screen 4 results when we issue another **step** command, then **display cec fec**. When the **step** command is issued, the first Scan Phase continues through one more Block execution. GPSS/H moves Xact 2 from the BLOCK3 GENERATE into the BLOCK4 ADVANCE. This causes Xact 2's Move Time to be updated from 0.0 to 10.0 and Xact 2 to be transferred from the Current to the Future Chain, where it is merged in last relative to those with whom it is involved in a Move-Time tie. Note the message in response to the **step** command

```
XACT 2 PLACED ON FEC AT BLOCK 4 (BLOCK4). RELATIVE CLOCK: 0.
```

Also note Xact 2's position on the FEC in Screen 4, where it is last among the three time-tied Xacts there.

In Screen 4, a display of the CEC (as well as of the FEC) was requested. But the CEC is now empty. Note in Screen 4 that no information appears about the CEC. Recall, in response to a command to display an empty chain, GPSS/H provides no message reporting that the chain is empty, but simply replies with a colon (:), prompting the user for more input.

The first Scan Phase has been completed. (No other Xacts want to try to move at clock time 0.0.) The first Clock Update Phase comes next.

Screen 5: First Clock Update Phase (Figure 4.12, part e)

At the top of Screen 5, we issue another **step** command, calling for one more Block execution. With the Scan Phase finished at time 0.0, however, GPSS/H must perform the first Clock Update Phase and start the following Scan Phase before coming to the point of executing another Block. But a **scan** trap has been set. And so, after the first Clock Update Phase is finished and just as the second Scan Phase is about to start, the interrupt condition corresponding to the **scan** trap occurs. (See Box 1 in Figure 4.9.) In response, GPSS/H returns control to us with the Screen 5 message

```
"SCAN" TRAP TAKEN (SYSTEM POISED TO BEGIN CEC SCAN).
REMAINING STEP COUNT = 1
```

In addition to telling us that a CEC scan is about to begin, the "REMAINING STEP COUNT = 1" part of this message lets us know that the simulation fell

```
XACT     CURBLK    NXTBLK    CHAINS  SDPGFT**   MARK-TIME   MOVE-TIME   PRIORITY

1        BIRTH     BLOCK1    FEC                   ---       10.0000          0
: step

XACT 2 POISED AT BLOCK 4 (BLOCK4).  RELATIVE CLOCK: 0.
: display cec fec

CURRENT EVENTS CHAIN

XACT     CURBLK    NXTBLK    CHAINS  SDPGFT**   MARK-TIME   MOVE-TIME   PRIORITY

2        BLOCK3    BLOCK4    CEC                   0.          0.             5

FUTURE EVENTS CHAIN

XACT     CURBLK    NXTBLK    CHAINS  SDPGFT**   MARK-TIME   MOVE-TIME   PRIORITY

1        BIRTH     BLOCK1    FEC                   ---       10.0000          0

XACT     CURBLK    NXTBLK    CHAINS  SDPGFT**   MARK-TIME   MOVE-TIME   PRIORITY

3        BIRTH     BLOCK3    FEC                   ---       10.0000          5
:
```

Figure 4.12 (c) *Screen 3*

```
1        BIRTH     BLOCK1    FEC                   ---       10.0000          0

XACT     CURBLK    NXTBLK    CHAINS  SDPGFT**   MARK-TIME   MOVE-TIME   PRIORITY

3        BIRTH     BLOCK3    FEC                   ---       10.0000          5
: step

XACT 2 PLACED ON FEC AT BLOCK 4 (BLOCK4).  RELATIVE CLOCK: 0.
: display cec fec

FUTURE EVENTS CHAIN

XACT     CURBLK    NXTBLK    CHAINS  SDPGFT**   MARK-TIME   MOVE-TIME   PRIORITY

1        BIRTH     BLOCK1    FEC                   ---       10.0000          0

XACT     CURBLK    NXTBLK    CHAINS  SDPGFT**   MARK-TIME   MOVE-TIME   PRIORITY

3        BIRTH     BLOCK3    FEC                   ---       10.0000          5

XACT     CURBLK    NXTBLK    CHAINS  SDPGFT**   MARK-TIME   MOVE-TIME   PRIORITY

2        BLOCK4    BLOCK5    FEC                   0.        10.0000          5
:
```

Figure 4.12 (d) *Screen 4*

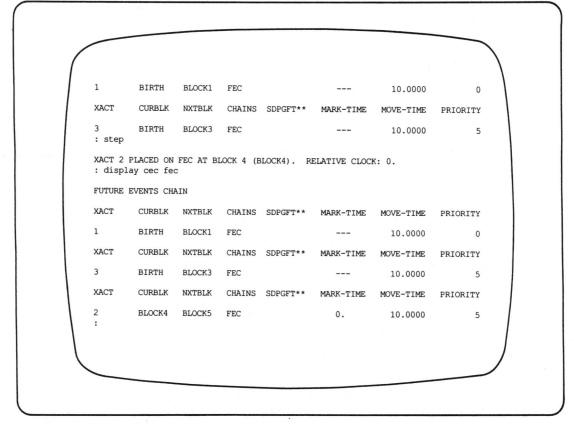

```
: step

"SCAN" TRAP TAKEN (SYSTEM POISED TO BEGIN CEC SCAN).
REMAINING STEP COUNT = 1
: display clocks

RELATIVE CLOCK: 10.0000    ABSOLUTE CLOCK: 10.0000
: display cec fec

CURRENT EVENTS CHAIN

XACT    CURBLK   NXTBLK   CHAINS  SDPGFT**  MARK-TIME  MOVE-TIME  PRIORITY

3       BIRTH    BLOCK3   CEC                   ---      10.0000         5

XACT    CURBLK   NXTBLK   CHAINS  SDPGFT**  MARK-TIME  MOVE-TIME  PRIORITY

2       BLOCK4   BLOCK5   CEC                    0.      10.0000         5

XACT    CURBLK   NXTBLK   CHAINS  SDPGFT**  MARK-TIME  MOVE-TIME  PRIORITY

1       BIRTH    BLOCK1   CEC                   ---      10.0000         0
:
```

Figure 4.12 (e) *Screen 5*

one Block execution short of fulfilling the **step** command that caused the simulation to resume. (In a more complicated case, for example, if a **step 5** command were issued to resume a simulation, and an interrupt condition occurred after only two more Blocks had been executed, then a "REMAINING STEP COUNT = 3" message would result.)

When the simulation is later resumed, GPSS/H ignores any remaining step count in effect when the preceding interrupt occurred. That is, the remaining step count is *not* enforced when the simulation is later resumed.

In Screen 5, we respond to the springing of the **scan** trap by issuing **display clocks** and **display cec fec** commands. As shown in Screen 5, the clock has been advanced to simulated time 10.0, corresponding to the Move Time of the Xact at the front of the Screen 4 FEC (Xact 1). Because they were involved in a three-way time tie with Move Times of 10.0, each of Xacts 1, 2, and 3 has been transferred by the Clock Update Phase from the Future to the Current Events Chain, as we see in Screen 5. These Xacts are arranged in Priority order on the CEC, with Xacts 3 and 2 (Priority 5) preceding Xact 1 (Priority 0). (Recall from Screen 4 that Xact 1 was ahead of Xacts 3 and 2 on the FEC, so the relative order of these Xacts on the CEC differs from what it was on the FEC.)

No Blocks were executed in moving from Screen 4 to Screen 5. Recall that a Clock Update Phase only advances the clock and transfers one or more Xacts from the Future to the Current Chain. No Blocks are ever executed during a Clock Update Phase.

Screen 6: Second Scan Phase (Figure 4.12, part f)

We proceed to step our way through the second Scan Phase, one Block execution at a time, without displaying chains in the process. This is accomplished by issuing a sequence of five consecutive **step** commands, as shown in Screen 6.

With the first two **step** commands in Screen 6, we step Xact 3 through its BLOCK3 GENERATE and into the BLOCK4 ADVANCE, where it is placed on the Future Events Chain for the time being.

Then, with the third Screen 6 **step** command, we move Xact 2 from the BLOCK4 ADVANCE into the BLOCK5 TERMINATE, where it is destroyed.

Finally, with the last two **step** commands in Screen 6, we step Xact 1 through its BLOCK1 GENERATE and into the BLOCK2 TERMINATE, where it is destroyed.

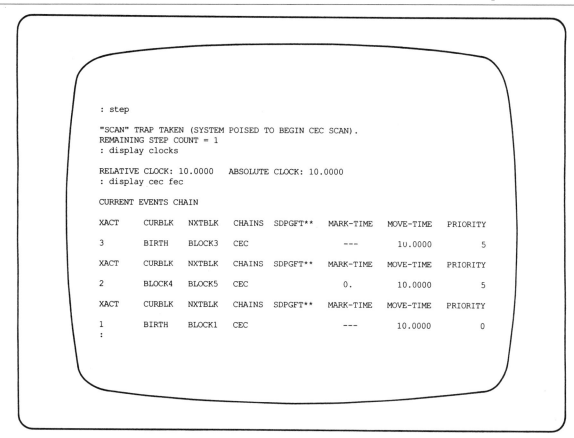

```
XACT      CURBLK    NXTBLK    CHAINS   SDPGFT**    MARK-TIME    MOVE-TIME    PRIORITY

2         BLOCK4    BLOCK5    CEC                       0.        10.0000           5

XACT      CURBLK    NXTBLK    CHAINS   SDPGFT**    MARK-TIME    MOVE-TIME    PRIORITY

1         BIRTH     BLOCK1    CEC                      ---        10.0000           0
: step

XACT 3 POISED AT BLOCK 4 (BLOCK4).  RELATIVE CLOCK: 10.0000
: step

XACT 3 PLACED ON FEC AT BLOCK 4 (BLOCK4).  RELATIVE CLOCK: 10.0000
: step

XACT 2 DESTROYED AT BLOCK 5 (BLOCK5).  RELATIVE CLOCK: 10.0000
: step

XACT 1 POISED AT BLOCK 2 (BLOCK2).  RELATIVE CLOCK: 10.0000
: step

XACT 1 DESTROYED AT BLOCK 2 (BLOCK2).  RELATIVE CLOCK: 10.0000
:
```

Figure 4.12 (f) *Screen 6*

In summary, the Screen 6 messages show the processing of the three Xacts that were resident on the CEC when the Scan Phase began at time 10.0.

Screen 7: Display of Chains after Completion of the Second Scan Phase (Figure 4.12, part g)

In Screen 7, we issue a **display cec fec** command to display the impact of the second Scan Phase (Screen 6) on the composition of the Current and Future Events Chains. No information is shown about the CEC in Screen 7, and so we conclude that it is empty. Xacts 4, 3, and 5 are shown in that order on the FEC. These Xacts each have a Move Time of 20.0 and so are involved in a three-way time tie. This means they appear on the FEC in the chronological order in which they were placed there. At the front of the FEC, Xact 4 is the successor to Xact 3 at the BLOCK3 GENERATE. Then comes Xact 3 itself, which is in the BLOCK4 ADVANCE. Finally, Xact 5 is at the back of the FEC, where it is the successor to Xact 1 at the BLOCK1 GENERATE.

The second Scan Phase has been completed. The second Clock Update Phase comes next.

Screen 8: Second Clock Update Phase (Figure 4.12, part h)

Now we issue a sixth **step** command. The first Scan Phase is finished, so GPSS/H resumes by performing the second Clock Update Phase, then gives control back to us because a scan trap is set. See the messages near the top of Screen 8 indicating "SCAN" TRAP TAKEN and REMAINING STEP COUNT = 1.

Then we issue **display clocks** and **display cec fec** commands. As shown in Screen 8, the clock has been advanced to simulated time 20.0, corresponding to the Move Time of the Xact at the front of the Screen 7 FEC (Xact 4). Because they were involved in a three-way time tie with Move Times of 20.0, each of Xacts 4, 3, and 5 has been transferred by the Clock Update Phase from the Future to the Current Events Chain, as we see in Screen 8. These Xacts are arranged in Priority order on the CEC, with Xacts 4 and 3 (Priority 5) preceding Xact 5 (Priority 0). These three Xacts happened to be in Priority order on the Screen 7 FEC, so their Screen 8 CEC order matches their Screen 7 FEC order.

Of course, no Blocks were executed in moving from Screen 7 to Screen 8.

```
XACT 2 DESTROYED AT BLOCK 5 (BLOCK5).  RELATIVE CLOCK: 10.0000
: step

XACT 1 POISED AT BLOCK 2 (BLOCK2).  RELATIVE CLOCK: 10.0000
: step

XACT 1 DESTROYED AT BLOCK 2 (BLOCK2).  RELATIVE CLOCK: 10.0000
: display cec fec

FUTURE EVENTS CHAIN

XACT   CURBLK   NXTBLK   CHAINS  SDPGFT**  MARK-TIME  MOVE-TIME  PRIORITY

4      BIRTH    BLOCK3   FEC                  ---       20.0000         5

XACT   CURBLK   NXTBLK   CHAINS  SDPGFT**  MARK-TIME  MOVE-TIME  PRIORITY

3      BLOCK4   BLOCK5   FEC                10.0000     20.0000         5

XACT   CURBLK   NXTBLK   CHAINS  SDPGFT**  MARK-TIME  MOVE-TIME  PRIORITY

5      BIRTH    BLOCK1   FEC                  ---       20.0000         0
:
```

Figure 4.12 (g) *Screen 7*

```
: step

"SCAN" TRAP TAKEN (SYSTEM POISED TO BEGIN CEC SCAN).
REMAINING STEP COUNT = 1
: display clocks

RELATIVE CLOCK: 20.0000   ABSOLUTE CLOCK: 20.0000
: display cec fec

CURRENT EVENTS CHAIN

XACT   CURBLK   NXTBLK   CHAINS  SDPGFT**  MARK-TIME  MOVE-TIME  PRIORITY

4      BIRTH    BLOCK3   CEC                  ---       20.0000         5

XACT   CURBLK   NXTBLK   CHAINS  SDPGFT**  MARK-TIME  MOVE-TIME  PRIORITY

3      BLOCK4   BLOCK5   CEC                10.0000     20.0000         5

XACT   CURBLK   NXTBLK   CHAINS  SDPGFT**  MARK-TIME  MOVE-TIME  PRIORITY

5      BIRTH    BLOCK1   CEC                  ---       20.0000         0
:
```

Figure 4.12 (h) *Screen 8*

In conclusion, the Figure 4.12 screens show GENERATE-Block initialization and then trace the results produced during the first two Scan Phases and the first two Clock Update Phases of a simulation performed with the Figure 4.11 Model File.

4.15 Exercises

In this section, you're asked to reinforce your understanding of the Transaction-Movement Phase of a simulation by carrying out some exercises in Test Mode.

1. The Figure 4.11 model is contained in the file fig411.gps. Initiate a Test-Mode simulation with this model, and repeat the screen sequence shown in Figure 4.12. Then go beyond the Figure 4.12 demonstration, carrying out two more Scan Phases and two more Clock Update Phases, displaying the Current and Future Events Chains as you proceed. Try to predict actions that will take place as you go along, then check your predictions against the evidence shown in the various GPSS/H messages and in the chain printouts.

*2. Perform a Test-Mode simulation with s415x2.gps, which contains this Model File:

```
          SIMULATE
*
 BLOCK1   GENERATE   100,50,0
 BLOCK2   ADVANCE    20,5
 BLOCK3   TERMINATE  1
*
          START      3
          END
```

Set a scan trap, then use **step** and **display cec fec** commands to move through the simulation until you get the "output pending" message. (If you prefer, use **F10** as an alternative for **step**.) Closely examine the CEC and FEC when you display them. Interpret what you see in terms of GENERATE Block initialization and of Scan Phase and Clock Update Phase logic. (If necessary or desirable, **set tv off** and/or scroll backward and forward in the Dialog Window to see all of the chain information that may be of interest.) Be certain your understanding of the logic of the Scan Phase and Clock Update Phase is consistent with the information displayed on the screen.

When comparing your findings against those shown in Appendix C, note the form of the table used there to summarize the results. *You might want to use a similar table to summarize your results for each of the remaining exercises in this section.*

*3. Perform a Test-Mode simulation with s415x3.gps, which contains this Model File:

```
          SIMULATE
*
 BLOCK1   GENERATE   100,50,75
 BLOCK2   ADVANCE    20,5
 BLOCK3   TERMINATE  1
*
          START      3
          END
```

Set a scan trap, then use **step** and **display cec fec** commands to move through the simulation until you get the "output pending" message. Closely examine the CEC and FEC when you display them. Interpret what you see in terms of GENERATE Block initialization and of Scan Phase and Clock Update Phase logic. (If necessary or desirable, **set tv off** and/or scroll backward and forward in the Dialog Window to see all of the chain information that may be of interest.) Be certain your understanding of the logic of the Scan Phase and Clock Update Phase is consistent with the information displayed on the screen.

(Comment: The Exercise 3 and Exercise 2 models match, except that the Offset Interval in Exercise 2 is 0, and in Exercise 3 is 75. In Exercise 2, Xact 1 is on the Current Chain after GENERATE Block initialization, and so the first Block executions occur at time 0.0, during the **first** Scan Phase and before the first Clock Update Phase has occurred. In Exercise 3, Xact 1 is on the Future Chain after GENERATE Block initialization, and the Current Chain is empty. (There are no Xacts on the CEC to be moved during the first Scan Phase.) And so in Exercise 3, the first Block executions do not occur until time 75.0, after the first Clock Update Phase has been performed and when the **second** Scan Phase is taking place.)

4. Perform a Test-Mode simulation with s415x4.gps, which contains this Model File:

```
         SIMULATE
*
BLOCK1   GENERATE  100,50,0
BLOCK2   ADVANCE   0
BLOCK3   ADVANCE   20,5
BLOCK4   TERMINATE 1
*
         START     3
         END
```

Set a scan trap, then use **step** and **display cec fec** commands to move through the simulation until you get the "output pending" message. Closely examine the CEC and FEC when you display them. Interpret what you see in terms of GENERATE Block initialization and of Scan Phase and Clock Update Phase logic. Be certain your understanding of the logic of the Scan Phase and Clock Update Phase is consistent with the information displayed on the screen.

(Comment: The Exercise 4 and Exercise 2 models match except for the presence in Exercise 4 of the "ADVANCE 0" Block. This exercise gives you a chance to investigate the behavior of such an ADVANCE Block. For all practical purposes, the presence of this Block does not cause the two models to behave differently. Times of arrival at the GENERATE Blocks are the same, holding times at "ADVANCE 20,5" are the same, and the time when the Transaction-Movement Phase ends is the same.)

5. Perform a Test-Mode simulation with s415x5.gps, which contains this Model File:

```
         SIMULATE
*
BLOCK1   GENERATE  100,50,0
BLOCK2   ADVANCE   15,10
BLOCK3   ADVANCE   20,5
BLOCK4   TERMINATE 1
*
         START     3
         END
```

Set a scan trap, then use **step** and **display cec fec** commands to move through the simulation until you get the "output pending" message. Closely examine the CEC and FEC when you display them. Interpret what you see in terms of GENERATE Block initialization and of Scan Phase and Clock Update Phase logic. Be certain your understanding of the logic of the Scan Phase and Clock Update Phase is consistent with the information displayed on the screen.

(Comment: The arrival times at BLOCK1 match those in Exercise 2 for the first two arrivals, but then differ from those in Exercise 2. This is because only **one** random number generator is being used to sample from the **three** distributions in the Exercise 5 model. (In Exercise 1, the same random number generator was being used to sample from that model's **two** distributions.) And so the use to which specific random numbers are put in Exercise 5 eventually differs from the use to which the same random numbers are put in Exercise 2. It's not important to fully understand this point now. The GPSS/H random number generators are discussed in Chapters 13 and 14.)

6. Perform a Test-Mode simulation with s415x6.gps, which contains this Model File:

```
         SIMULATE
*
BLOCK1   GENERATE  100,50
BLOCK2   ADVANCE   20,5
BLOCK3   TERMINATE 1
*
         START     3
         END
```

Set a scan trap, then use **step** and **display cec fec** commands to move through the simulation until you get the "output pending" message. Closely examine the CEC and FEC when you display them. Interpret what you see in terms of GENERATE Block initialization and of Scan Phase and Clock Update Phase logic. Be certain your understanding of the logic of the Scan Phase and Clock Update Phase is consistent with the information displayed on the screen.

(Comment: The Exercise 6 and Exercise 2 models match, except that no Offset Interval is used in Exercise 6. In Exercise 2, the time Xact 1 comes into the GENERATE Block is deterministic, whereas in Exercise 6, the time Xact 1 comes into the GENERATE Block is probabilistic. The sequence in which random numbers are used in Exercise 6, therefore, differs from the sequence in which random numbers are used in Exercise 2. This means that sampled interarrival and holding time values differ between the two models. Verify this by comparing Exercise 6 results with Exercise 2 results.)

*7. Perform a Test-Mode simulation with s415x7.gps, which contains this Model File:

```
          SIMULATE
*
 BLOCK1   GENERATE   100,50,0
 BLOCK2   ADVANCE    20,5
 BLOCK3   TRANSFER   ,BLOCK2
*
 BLOCK4   GENERATE   100
 BLOCK5   TERMINATE  1
*
          START      1
          END
```

Set a scan trap, then use **step** and **display cec fec** commands to move through the simulation until you get the "output pending" message. Closely examine the CEC and FEC when you display them. Interpret what you see in terms of GENERATE Block initialization and of Scan Phase and Clock Update Phase logic. Be certain your understanding of the logic of the Scan Phase and Clock Update Phase is consistent with the information displayed on the screen.

8. Perform a Test-Mode simulation with s415x8.gps, which contains this Model File:

```
          SIMULATE
*
 BLOCK1   GENERATE   25,,,,25
 BLOCK2   ADVANCE    20,5
 BLOCK3   TERMINATE  1
*
 BLOCK4   GENERATE   25,,,,50
 BLOCK5   ADVANCE    20,5
 BLOCK6   TERMINATE  0
*
          START      2
          END
```

Set a scan trap, then use **step** and **display cec fec** commands to move through the simulation until you get the "output pending" message. Closely examine the CEC and FEC when you display them. Interpret what you see in terms of GENERATE Block initialization and of Scan Phase and Clock Update Phase logic. Be certain your understanding of the logic of the Scan Phase and Clock Update Phase is consistent with the information displayed on the screen.

4.16 The Timing of GENERATE-Block Execution

In general, it is the movement of an Xact **into** a Block that causes the Block to be executed. However, the **GENERATE Block is a major exception to this point.** In GPSS/H, a GENERATE Block does **not** execute when a Transaction **moves into** the Block, but when a Transaction **is able to move out of** the Block into its Next Block.

The reason for this unusual timing in GENERATE-Block execution can be understood as follows. The purpose of GENERATE Block execution is to create and schedule a successor for an Xact moving into the model from its GENERATE Block. In a sense, an Xact hasn't yet made it into the model until it moves from its GENERATE Block into its Next Block. And so a successor isn't created and scheduled until the predecessor can "make it into the model" by moving from its GENERATE into the sequential Block.

A GENERATE Block is an Xact's first Block. If an Xact moves into and out of its GENERATE Block at one and the same simulated time, then whether this triggers GENERATE-Block execution when the Xact moves into or out of the Block doesn't really matter. The point becomes of some interest, however, if the Block following a GENERATE can **deny entry** to a Transaction. We'll return to this point in Chapter 7, after introducing in Chapter 6 a type of Block that can conditionally deny entry to Transactions. We'll also refer to the timing of GENERATE Block execution in the next section, where we explain how zero interarrival times at a GENERATE Block are handled during a Scan Phase.

4.17 Zero Interarrival Times at a GENERATE Block

An interarrival time of zero can apply at a GENERATE Block in either or both of two different contexts: when the GENERATE Block is being **initialized** and/or when the GENERATE Block is being **executed during a Scan Phase**. In either case, the created Xact is **put immediately on the Current Events Chain** when its interarrival time is zero (in terms of GENERATE-Block **initialization**, see Boxes 6 and 7 in Figure 4.6.) The reason is that the freshly created Xact wants to move "now," at the simulated time of its creation.

In general, an interarrival time of zero results in a situation in which **two or more Xacts** can come from a given GENERATE Block, one by one, at **the same simulated time**. This need not be the case, however.

For example, consider this GENERATE Block:

```
GENERATE 0,,,1
```

Interarrival time is zero at this Block, and the Offset Interval has not been used, but the Limit Count has. When this Block is initialized, a Transaction will be created and put on the CEC. Then the Scan Phase at time 0.0 will move this Xact into the GENERATE (its First Block), and from there into the model. But this Xact's movement from its GENERATE Block won't cause the GENERATE to be executed, of course, because the Block's Limit Count of 1 will already have been satisfied.

On the other hand, consider this GENERATE Block:

```
GENERATE 0,,,2
```

When this Block is initialized, a Transaction will be created and put on the CEC, as in the preceding example. Then the Scan Phase at time 0.0 will move this Xact into its GENERATE and from there into the model. This Xact's movement from its GENERATE Block **will** trigger GENERATE Block execution, because the Block's Limit Count of 2 isn't yet satisfied. The successor's interarrival time is zero, and so the successor will be **put immediately onto the Current Events Chain.** As always, an Xact is merged into the CEC as the last among its CEC Priority peers. The successor has the same Priority as its predecessor. (In this example, both have a Priority of zero, by default.) And so the successor is **somewhere behind its predecessor** on the CEC. The successor will then eventually be dealt with during the Scan Phase at the simulated time in question (time 0.0 in this example) and will be moved into the GENERATE (its First Block), and from there into the Next Block, and so on

Prior to this section, we'd only seen **two** ways for putting Transactions onto the CEC:

1. **GENERATE-Block initialization** puts an Xact onto the CEC if the interarrival time is zero.
2. The **Clock Update Phase** puts one or more Xacts onto the CEC (with the more-than-one case applying if Move-Time ties are involved).

Neither of these two ways involves the Scan Phase. We've now seen that Xacts can be put onto the CEC **during a Scan Phase**, too. This happens if a GENERATE Block is executed during a Scan Phase, and if zero interarrival time applies to the Xact that the GENERATE Block creates.

The steps followed by GPSS/H in handling zero interarrival times at a GENERATE Block will be demonstrated in Section 4.19.

4.18 A Chain-Oriented View of a Transaction's Location

An Xact is both on a chain and in a Block. (An exception involves Xacts that are "on their way" to a model via a GENERATE Block. As we have seen, these Xacts aren't yet in a Block. Their CURBLK is BIRTH.) Our understanding of GPSS/H has now been extended to include the role played by the Current and Future Chains. In terms of these two chains, a Transaction's location can be interpreted as shown in Figure 4.13. You should study this figure, which speaks for itself.

Although Figure 4.13 is complete for our purposes now, it is not complete for all of GPSS/H. For one thing, the other three categories of GPSS/H chains (User Chains, Interrupt Chains, and MAG Chains) are not included in Figure 4.13. For another thing, Figure 4.13 implies that Xacts eventually move into a TERMINATE Block and are destroyed, but we have seen that this does not have to be the case. (See the model in Figure 4.14 in the next section, for example.)

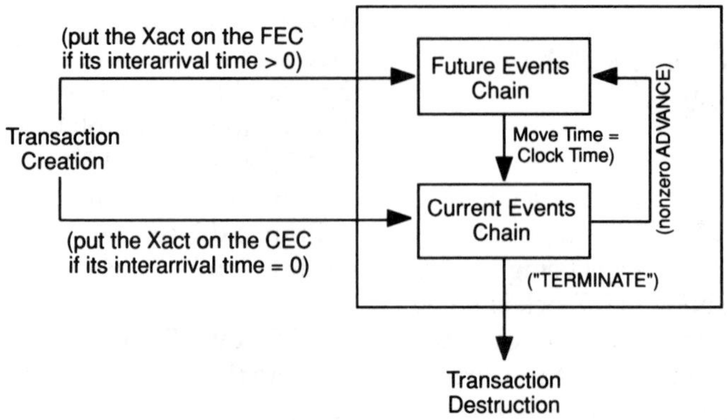

Figure 4.13 *A Chain-Oriented View of a Transaction's Location*

4.19 A Test-Mode Demonstration of Zero Interarrival Times at a GENERATE Block

Now we'll perform a simulation in Test Mode to demonstrate zero interarrival times at a GENERATE Block. We'll do this using the Model File of Figure 4.14, where the Block Labels BLOCK1 and BLOCK4 have been used to support discussion.

Figure 4.15 shows nine computer screens resulting when a Test-Mode simulation is performed with the Figure 4.14 Model File. Discussion of this screen sequence follows. (In Exercise 1 of Section 4.19, you are asked to reproduce this screen sequence on your computer.)

Screen 1: GENERATE-Block Initialization (Figure 4.15, part a)

Screen 1 was produced by issuing **gpssh fig414.gps tvtnw**, **trap scan** and **run** commands, resulting in the familiar "SCAN" TRAP TAKEN message. At this point, the model's GENERATE Blocks have been initialized, and the first Scan Phase is about to begin.

```
          SIMULATE
*
 BLOCK1   GENERATE   0,,,3
 REPEAT   ADVANCE    40,10
          TRANSFER   ,REPEAT
*
 BLOCK4   GENERATE   200
          TERMINATE  1
*
          START      1
          END
```

Figure 4.14 *A Model File to Demonstrate Zero Interarrival Times at a GENERATE Block*

Screen 2: Display of Xacts Created During GENERATE-Block Initialization (Figure 4.15, part b)

Screen 2 results from issuing **set tv off**, **display clocks** and **display cec fec** commands. The Dialog Window now occupies the entire screen (from which GPSS/H has erased the **set tv off** command) and as we see, the simulation is at clock time 0.0 and the Current and Future Events Chains each contain one Xact. Review the information provided for these CEC and FEC Xacts in Screen 2 until you are satisfied that the state of the model is consistent with the Figure 4.14 Model File.

Screen 3: Step One in the First Scan Phase (Figure 4.15, part c)

Screen 3 results when we issue a **step** command, then **display cec fec**. When this first **step** command is issued, the first Scan Phase begins. GPSS/H moves Xact 1 into the BLOCK1 GENERATE and then, in response to Xact 1's imminent escape from this GENERATE, executes the GENERATE to create and schedule a successor for Xact 1. In the display of the Current Chain, we see that Xact 1 now has the BLOCK1 GENERATE as its Current Block, with REPEAT ADVANCE as its Next Block Attempted. Xact 3, the successor to Xact 1, has been created and, with its interarrival time of 0.0 and its (default) Priority of 0, has been placed on the Current Chain behind Xact 1. Its Current Block is BIRTH, its Next (First) Block Attempted is the BLOCK1 GENERATE, and its Move Time is 0.0.

```
BLOCK CURRENT     TOTAL          fig414.gps SOURCE CODE
----- -------     -----          ----------------------------------------------




================================================================================
S/C: OFF  ABS CLOCK:  0.          REL CLOCK: 0.          TTG: 1
================================================================================
XACT: $SYS      CURBLK:           NEXTBLK:            CHAINS: CEC+SYS  PC:

MARK-TIME:               MOVE-TIME: -----         PRIORITY: 2147483647
================================================================================
                      WOLVERINE SOFTWARE CORPORATION
                            4115 ANNANDALE ROAD
                      ANNANDALE, VIRGINIA 22003, USA

Ready!
: trap scan
: run

"SCAN" TRAP TAKEN (SYSTEM POISED TO BEGIN CEC SCAN).
:
```

Figure 4.15 *Nine Computer Screens Resulting When the Figure 4.14 Model File Is Run in Test Mode (a) Screen 1*

```
Ready!
: trap scan
: run

"SCAN" TRAP TAKEN (SYSTEM POISED TO BEGIN CEC SCAN).
: display clocks

RELATIVE CLOCK:  0.0000   ABSOLUTE CLOCK:  0.0000
: display cec fec

CURRENT EVENTS CHAIN

XACT     CURBLK   NXTBLK   CHAINS  SDPGFT**   MARK-TIME   MOVE-TIME   PRIORITY

1        BIRTH    BLOCK1   CEC                   ---         0.              0

FUTURE EVENTS CHAIN

XACT     CURBLK   NXTBLK   CHAINS  SDPGFT**   MARK-TIME   MOVE-TIME   PRIORITY

2        BIRTH    BLOCK4   FEC                   ---       480.0000          0
:
```

Figure 4.15 (b) *Screen 2*

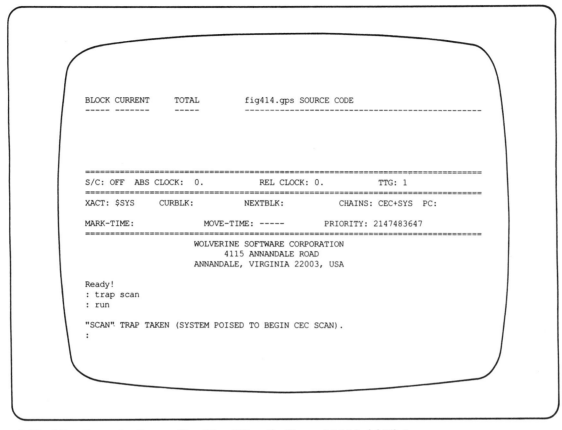

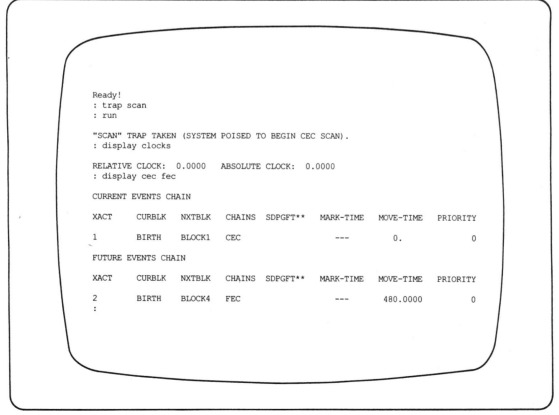

```
XACT    CURBLK   NXTBLK   CHAINS  SDPGFT**  MARK-TIME   MOVE-TIME   PRIORITY

2       BIRTH    BLOCK4   FEC                   ---      480.0000          0
: step

XACT 1 POISED AT BLOCK 2 (REPEAT).  RELATIVE CLOCK: 0.
: display cec fec

CURRENT EVENTS CHAIN

XACT    CURBLK   NXTBLK   CHAINS  SDPGFT**  MARK-TIME   MOVE-TIME   PRIORITY

1       BLOCK1   REPEAT   CEC                    0.          0.            0

XACT    CURBLK   NXTBLK   CHAINS  SDPGFT**  MARK-TIME   MOVE-TIME   PRIORITY

3       BIRTH    BLOCK1   CEC                   ---          0.            0

FUTURE EVENTS CHAIN

XACT    CURBLK   NXTBLK   CHAINS  SDPGFT**  MARK-TIME   MOVE-TIME   PRIORITY

2       BIRTH    BLOCK4   FEC                   ---      480.0000          0
:
```

Figure 4.15 (c) *Screen 3*

Screen 4: Step Two in the First Scan Phase (Figure 4.15, part d)

Screen 4 results when we issue another **step** command, then **display cec fec**. When this second **step** command is issued, GPSS/H resumes the movement of Xact 1, transferring it from its BLOCK1 GENERATE into the REPEAT ADVANCE Block and issuing the message

```
XACT 1 PLACED ON FEC AT BLOCK 2 (REPEAT). RELATIVE CLOCK: 0.
```

Xact 1 appears on the Screen 4 FEC with a Move Time of 35.4.

Screen 5: Step Three in the First Scan Phase (Figure 4.15, part e)

Screen 5 results when we issue a third **step** command, then **display cec fec**. Movement of Xact 1 was completed in Screen 4. In response to the third **step** command, the Scan Phase proceeds with the sequential Xact on the Current Chain, Xact 3. GPSS/H picks up Xact 3, moves it into the BLOCK1 GENERATE and then, in response to Xact 3's imminent escape from this GENERATE, executes the GENERATE to create and schedule a successor for Xact 3. GPSS/H then issues the message

```
XACT 3 POISED AT BLOCK 2 (REPEAT). RELATIVE CLOCK: 0.
```

In the Screen 5 display of the Current Chain, we see that Xact 3 now has the BLOCK1 GENERATE as its Current Block, with the REPEAT ADVANCE as its Next Block Attempted. Xact 4, the successor to Xact 3, has been created and, with its interarrival time of 0.0 and its (default) Priority of 0, has been placed on the Current Chain behind Xact 3. Its Current Block is BIRTH, its Next (First) Block Attempted is the BLOCK1 GENERATE, and its Move Time is 0.0.

Screen 6: Step Four in the First Scan Phase (Figure 4.15, part f)

Screen 6 results when we issue another **step** command, then **display cec fec**. When this fourth **step** command is issued, GPSS/H resumes the movement of Xact 3, transferring it from its BLOCK1 GENERATE into the REPEAT ADVANCE Block and issuing the message

```
XACT 3 PLACED ON FEC AT BLOCK 2 (REPEAT). RELATIVE CLOCK: 0.
```

```
XACT    CURBLK   NXTBLK   CHAINS  SDPGFT**   MARK-TIME   MOVE-TIME   PRIORITY

2       BIRTH    BLOCK4   FEC                  ---        480.0000          0
: step

XACT 1 PLACED ON FEC AT BLOCK 2 (REPEAT).  RELATIVE CLOCK: 0.
: display cec fec

CURRENT EVENTS CHAIN

XACT    CURBLK   NXTBLK   CHAINS  SDPGFT**   MARK-TIME   MOVE-TIME   PRIORITY

3       BIRTH    BLOCK1   CEC                  ---          0.              0

FUTURE EVENTS CHAIN

XACT    CURBLK   NXTBLK   CHAINS  SDPGFT**   MARK-TIME   MOVE-TIME   PRIORITY

1       REPEAT   3        FEC                  0.          35.4059          0

XACT    CURBLK   NXTBLK   CHAINS  SDPGFT**   MARK-TIME   MOVE-TIME   PRIORITY

2       BIRTH    BLOCK4   FEC                  ---        480.0000          0
:
```

Figure 4.15 (d) *Screen 4*

```
: step

XACT 3 POISED AT BLOCK 2 (REPEAT).  RELATIVE CLOCK: 0.
: display cec fec

CURRENT EVENTS CHAIN

XACT    CURBLK   NXTBLK   CHAINS  SDPGFT**   MARK-TIME   MOVE-TIME   PRIORITY

3       BLOCK1   REPEAT   CEC                  0.          0.              0

XACT    CURBLK   NXTBLK   CHAINS  SDPGFT**   MARK-TIME   MOVE-TIME   PRIORITY

4       BIRTH    BLOCK1   CEC                  ---          0.              0

FUTURE EVENTS CHAIN

XACT    CURBLK   NXTBLK   CHAINS  SDPGFT**   MARK-TIME   MOVE-TIME   PRIORITY

1       REPEAT   3        FEC                  0.          35.4059          0

XACT    CURBLK   NXTBLK   CHAINS  SDPGFT**   MARK-TIME   MOVE-TIME   PRIORITY

2       BIRTH    BLOCK4   FEC                  ---        480.0000          0
:
```

Figure 4.15 (e) *Screen 5*

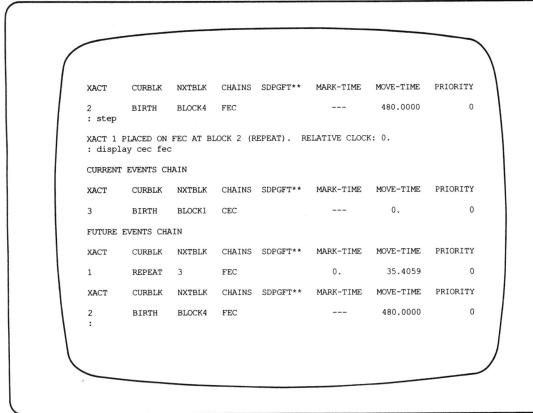

```
: step

XACT 3 PLACED ON FEC AT BLOCK 2 (REPEAT).  RELATIVE CLOCK: 0.
: display cec fec

CURRENT EVENTS CHAIN

XACT      CURBLK    NXTBLK    CHAINS   SDPGFT**    MARK-TIME    MOVE-TIME     PRIORITY

4         BIRTH     BLOCK1    CEC                     ---           0.               0

FUTURE EVENTS CHAIN

XACT      CURBLK    NXTBLK    CHAINS   SDPGFT**    MARK-TIME    MOVE-TIME     PRIORITY

1         REPEAT    3         FEC                      0.         35.4059            0

XACT      CURBLK    NXTBLK    CHAINS   SDPGFT**    MARK-TIME    MOVE-TIME     PRIORITY

3         REPEAT    3         FEC                      0.         39.9871            0

XACT      CURBLK    NXTBLK    CHAINS   SDPGFT**    MARK-TIME    MOVE-TIME     PRIORITY

2         BIRTH     BLOCK4    FEC                     ---        480.0000            0
:
```

Figure 4.15 (f) *Screen 6*

Xact 3 appears on the Screen 6 FEC with a Move Time of 39.9. Xact 3 has been merged into the FEC between Xacts 1 and 2, which have smaller and larger Move Times, respectively, than Xact 3.

Screen 7: Step Five in the First Scan Phase (Figure 4.15, part g)

Screen 7 results when we issue a fifth **step** command, then **display cec fec**. Movement of Xact 3 was completed in Screen 6. In response to the fifth **step** command, the Scan Phase proceeds with the sequential Xact on the Current Chain, Xact 4. GPSS/H picks up Xact 4 and moves it into the BLOCK1 GENERATE. In response to the imminent escape of Xact 4 from its GENERATE Block, GPSS/H executes the GENERATE (bringing its TOTAL COUNT to 3) but *does not* create and schedule a successor for Xact 4 in the process. Reason: Xact 4 is the third Xact to be introduced into the model from the BLOCK1 GENERATE Block, and this satisfies the Block's Limit Count of 3.

The Screen 7 Current and Future Events Chains are consistent with this analysis. Note that there is no successor to Xact 4 on the Current Chain in Screen 7.

Screen 8: Step Six in the First Scan Phase (Figure 4.15, part h)

Screen 8 results when we issue a sixth **step** command, then **display cec fec**. When this **step** is issued, GPSS/H resumes the movement of Xact 4, transferring it from its BLOCK1 GENERATE into the REPEAT ADVANCE Block and issuing the message

```
XACT 4 PLACED ON FEC AT BLOCK 2 (REPEAT). RELATIVE CLOCK: 0.
```

Xact 4 appears on the Screen 8 FEC with a Move Time of 44.7. Xact 4 has been merged into the FEC between Xacts 3 and 2, which have smaller and larger Move Times, respectively, than Xact 4.

Screen 9: The First Clock Update Phase (Figure 4.15, part i)

Now we issue a seventh **step** command. The first Scan Phase is finished, so GPSS/H resumes by performing the second Clock Update Phase, then gives control back to us because a scan trap is set. See the messages near the top of Screen 9 indicating "SCAN" TRAP TAKEN and REMAINING STEP COUNT = 1.

```
: step

XACT 4 POISED AT BLOCK 2 (REPEAT).  RELATIVE CLOCK: 0.
: display cec fec

CURRENT EVENTS CHAIN

XACT      CURBLK    NXTBLK    CHAINS  SDPGFT**   MARK-TIME   MOVE-TIME   PRIORITY

4         BLOCK1    REPEAT    CEC                   0.          0.             0

FUTURE EVENTS CHAIN

XACT      CURBLK    NXTBLK    CHAINS  SDPGFT**   MARK-TIME   MOVE-TIME   PRIORITY

1         REPEAT    3         FEC                   0.       35.4059           0

XACT      CURBLK    NXTBLK    CHAINS  SDPGFT**   MARK-TIME   MOVE-TIME   PRIORITY

3         REPEAT    3         FEC                   0.       39.9871           0

XACT      CURBLK    NXTBLK    CHAINS  SDPGFT**   MARK-TIME   MOVE-TIME   PRIORITY

2         BIRTH     BLOCK4    FEC                  ---      480.0000           0
:
```

Figure 4.15 (g) *Screen 7*

```
2         BIRTH     BLOCK4    FEC                  ---      480.0000           0
: step

XACT 4 PLACED ON FEC AT BLOCK 2 (REPEAT).  RELATIVE CLOCK: 0.
: display cec fec

FUTURE EVENTS CHAIN

XACT      CURBLK    NXTBLK    CHAINS  SDPGFT**   MARK-TIME   MOVE-TIME   PRIORITY

1         REPEAT    3         FEC                   0.       35.4059           0

XACT      CURBLK    NXTBLK    CHAINS  SDPGFT**   MARK-TIME   MOVE-TIME   PRIORITY

3         REPEAT    3         FEC                   0.       39.9871           0

XACT      CURBLK    NXTBLK    CHAINS  SDPGFT**   MARK-TIME   MOVE-TIME   PRIORITY

4         REPEAT    3         FEC                   0.       44.7954           0

XACT      CURBLK    NXTBLK    CHAINS  SDPGFT**   MARK-TIME   MOVE-TIME   PRIORITY

2         BIRTH     BLOCK4    FEC                  ---      480.0000           0
:
```

Figure 4.15 (h) *Screen 8*

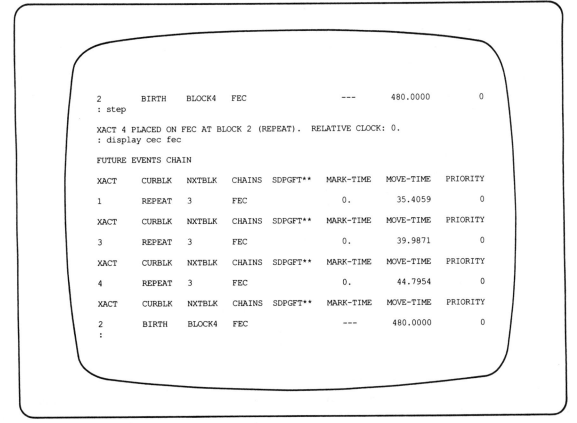

```
: step

"SCAN" TRAP TAKEN (SYSTEM POISED TO BEGIN CEC SCAN).
REMAINING STEP COUNT = 1
: display clocks

RELATIVE CLOCK: 35.4059    ABSOLUTE CLOCK: 35.4059
: display cec fec

CURRENT EVENTS CHAIN

XACT      CURBLK    NXTBLK    CHAINS  SDPGFT**    MARK-TIME    MOVE-TIME    PRIORITY

1         REPEAT    3         CEC                        0.      35.4059           0

FUTURE EVENTS CHAIN

XACT      CURBLK    NXTBLK    CHAINS  SDPGFT**    MARK-TIME    MOVE-TIME    PRIORITY

3         REPEAT    3         FEC                        0.      39.9871           0

XACT      CURBLK    NXTBLK    CHAINS  SDPGFT**    MARK-TIME    MOVE-TIME    PRIORITY

4         REPEAT    3         FEC                        0.      44.7954           0

XACT      CURBLK    NXTBLK    CHAINS  SDPGFT**    MARK-TIME    MOVE-TIME    PRIORITY

2         BIRTH     BLOCK4    FEC                       ---     480.0000           0
:
```

Figure 4.15 (i) *Screen 9*

Then we issue **display clocks** and **display cec fec** commands. As shown in Screen 9, the clock has been advanced to simulated time 35.4059, corresponding to the Move Time of the Xact at the front of the Screen 8 FEC (Xact 1). And Xact 1 has been transferred from the Future to the Current Chain.

In conclusion, the Figure 4.15 screens trace the process whereby three Xacts, each having a zero interarrival time, are introduced into a model by one GENERATE Block during a single Scan Phase. In the Figure 4.15 demonstration, the Scan Phase took place at time 0.0. The same principles apply, of course, no matter the time at which the Scan Phase is taking place. With respect to the Block "GENERATE 0,,100,4", for example, the same principles would be followed at time 100.0.

4.20 Exercises

1. Using the fig414.gps file, conduct a Test-Mode simulation and reproduce the screen sequence shown in Figure 4.15.

2. In a copy of the fig414.gps file, change the GENERATE Block to "GENERATE 0,,100,4". Initiate a Test-Mode simulation with the resulting model. In response to the Ready! prompt, issue a **trap scan** and **run** command, then a **display cec fec** command. Then issue **step** and **display cec fec** commands repeatedly until the third Scan Phase is about to begin. Examine the Current and Future Chains as you go along, and satisfy yourself that you understand the information that they provide. Note that the principles of Figure 4.15 apply in this exercise, but that it is during the *second* Scan Phase (at time 100.0) that these principles are in effect, and that four Xacts (not three) are being brought into the model with zero interarrival times from a single GENERATE Block.

3. Consider this two-Block model:

```
GENERATE   0
TERMINATE  1
```

(a) Put this model into a Model File, using 2 as the A Operand in the START statement. Go into a

Test-Mode simulation with the Model File. Issue a **step** command. At what simulated time will control be returned to you? Will Xact 2 (the successor to Xact 1 at the GENERATE Block) have yet been created? If so, what chain will it be on? How many other Xacts will be on this chain? Where will the successor to Xact 1 be among them? What will its Move Time Be? Issue a **display cec fec** command to check out your predictions.

(b) Now issue a **step 2** command. When control is returned to you, will Xact 3 (the successor to Xact 2 at the GENERATE Block) have yet been created? If so, what chain will it be on? What will its Move Time be? Issue a **display cec fec** command to check out your predictions.

(c) Finally, issue another **step** command. What will be the value of the model's Termination Counter when control is returned to you? What will the CEC look like at this point? What will the FEC look like? Issue a **display cec fec** command to check out your predictions.

4. Repeat Exercise 3, but change the GENERATE Block to "GENERATE 0,,25".

*5. Consider this four-Block model:

```
 BLOCK1   GENERATE   0
 BLOCK2   TERMINATE  1
*
 BLOCK3   GENERATE   0
 BLOCK4   TERMINATE  1
```

(a) Put this model into a Model File, using 2 as the A Operand in the START statement. Go into a Test-Mode simulation with the model. Issue a **step 1** command without issuing a **trap scan** command. When control is returned to you, will the successor to Xact 1 at the first GENERATE Block have yet been created? If so, what will its id number be? What chain will it be on? What will its Move Time be? Issue a **display cec fec** command to check out your predictions.

(b) Now issue a **step 2** command. When control is returned to you, will the successor to Xact 2 at the second GENERATE Block have yet been created? If so, what will its id number be? What chain will be it on? What will its Move Time be? Issue a **display cec fec** command to check out your predictions.

(c) Finally, issue another **step** command. What will the value of the model's Termination Counter be after this command is executed? What will the CEC look like at this point? What will the FEC look like? Issue a **display cec fec** command to check out your predictions.

*6. Build a Model File for this four-Block model:

```
 BLOCK1   GENERATE   0
 BLOCK2   TERMINATE  1
*
 BLOCK3   GENERATE   0
 BLOCK4   TERMINATE  0
```

Use an A Operand of 3 in the START statement. How many Xacts will have come out of the BLOCK1 GENERATE by the end of the simulation, and what will their id numbers be? Answer this same question for the BLOCK2 GENERATE. Check out your predictions by carrying out a Test-Mode simulation with the model.

*7. Build a Model File for this four-Block model:

```
 BLOCK1   GENERATE   0,,,,5
 BLOCK2   TERMINATE  1
*
 BLOCK3   GENERATE   0,,,,8
 BLOCK4   TERMINATE  1
```

Use an A Operand of 3 in the START statement. What will the id numbers be of Xacts coming out of the two GENERATE Blocks? At what time will the simulation stop? Check out your predictions by carrying out a Test-Mode simulation with the model.

5 Additional Test-Mode Capabilities

5.1 Preview

We've now used the **step 1** command in isolation on a number of occasions to move slowly through a simulation, Block-execution by Block-execution. We've also seen that a **trap scan/run** combination can be used in isolation to move fairly briskly through a simulation, clock-time by clock-time. In this chapter, additional GPSS/H Test-Mode capabilities will be introduced, making it possible to move through a simulation at two other rates of speed. We'll see how it's possible to move through a simulation Xact by Xact, which is faster than Block-execution by Block-execution but is slower than clock-time by clock-time. And we'll see how it's possible to move nonstop through a simulation until a specified simulated time has first been reached or exceeded. These various approaches don't have to be used in isolation, of course, but can be combined by the modeler to achieve his or her objectives in a Test-Mode simulation.

5.2 Stepping Through a Simulation, Transaction by Transaction

It's possible to move through Test-Mode simulations on an **Xact by Xact** basis. The user can be put in control each time an Xact **starts to move**, and the user can be put back in control whenever the moving Transaction **cannot move any farther** for the time being. For example, suppose an Xact starts to move, executes five Blocks, and then has to stop moving. If we use **step 1** commands to monitor this Xact's movement on a Block by Block basis, the simulation will be interrupted five times (one time per Block execution). On the other hand, if we monitor Xact movement on an Xact by Xact basis, the simulation will only be interrupted two times when this Xact moves. (We'll be put in control just before the Xact executes the first Block; and then we won't be put into control again until the Xact has executed the fifth Block and stops moving.)

To tell GPSS/H that we want to monitor Xact movement on an Xact by Xact basis, we can issue a trap command taking this form:

```
trap next system
```

This **trap** command sets both a **next** trap and a

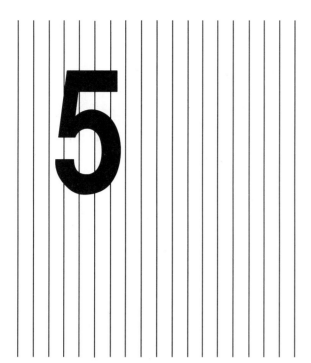

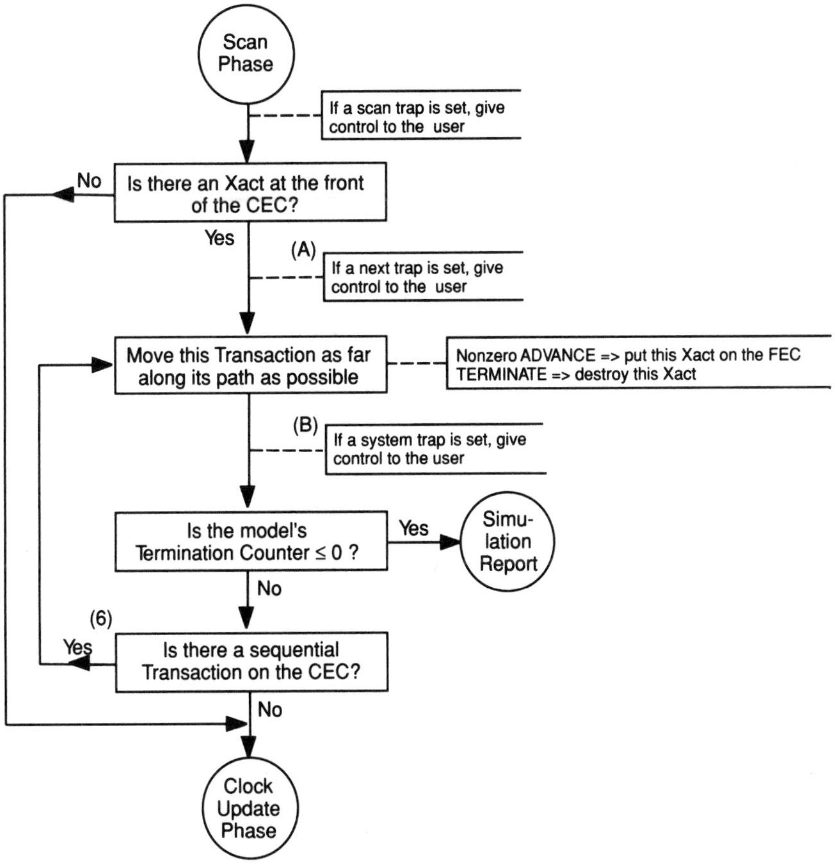

Figure 5.1 *A Repetition of Figure 4.9, With Boxes A and B Added to Show the Point at Which **Next** and **System** Traps Are Sprung*

system trap. When a **next** trap is set, GPSS/H gives control to the user each time any Transaction is about to try to move. When a **system** trap is set, the user is given control whenever the moving Xact can't move any farther for the time being.

Note that **next** and **system** traps are sprung (occur) only during a Scan Phase (because it's only during a Scan Phase that Transactions move from Block to Block).

The timing with which **next** and **system** traps are sprung is shown in Figure 5.1, which repeats the Scan Phase flowchart of Figure 4.9 but extends that flowchart with comments indicating exactly when **next** and **system** traps are sprung. In Figure 5.1, the Box A comment identifies the Scan Phase point at which a **next** trap is sprung. Similarly, the Box B comment identifies the point in a Scan Phase at which a **system** trap is sprung.

The words "pick up" are used in indicating when a **next** trap is sprung. During a Scan Phase, when GPSS/H "picks up" (focuses on) a Transaction in the process of starting to try to move it, the user is given control if a **next** trap is set.

Similarly, the term "drop" is used to indicate when a **system** trap is sprung. During a Scan Phase, when GPSS/H "drops" (puts down) a Transaction because it can't move any farther, the user is given control if a **system** trap is set.

As we saw in Chapter 4 with **trap scan**, issuing a **trap** command does not cause GPSS/H to resume a simulation. A trap command simply specifies one or more interrupt conditions. The user can resume the simulation by issuing a **run** command. Or, as we have seen in the Figure 4.12 and 4.15 demonstrations in Chapter 4, the user can alternatively resume the simulation by issuing a **step** command, in which case this also has the effect of specifying another interrupt condition.

The procedure involved in stepping through a GPSS/H simulation, Xact by Xact, is outlined in the Figure 5.2 flowchart, where boxes have been numbered to support discussion.

We now illustrate the Figure 5.2 procedure and the **trap next system** command by performing a Test-Mode simulation with the Model File shown in Figure 5.3.

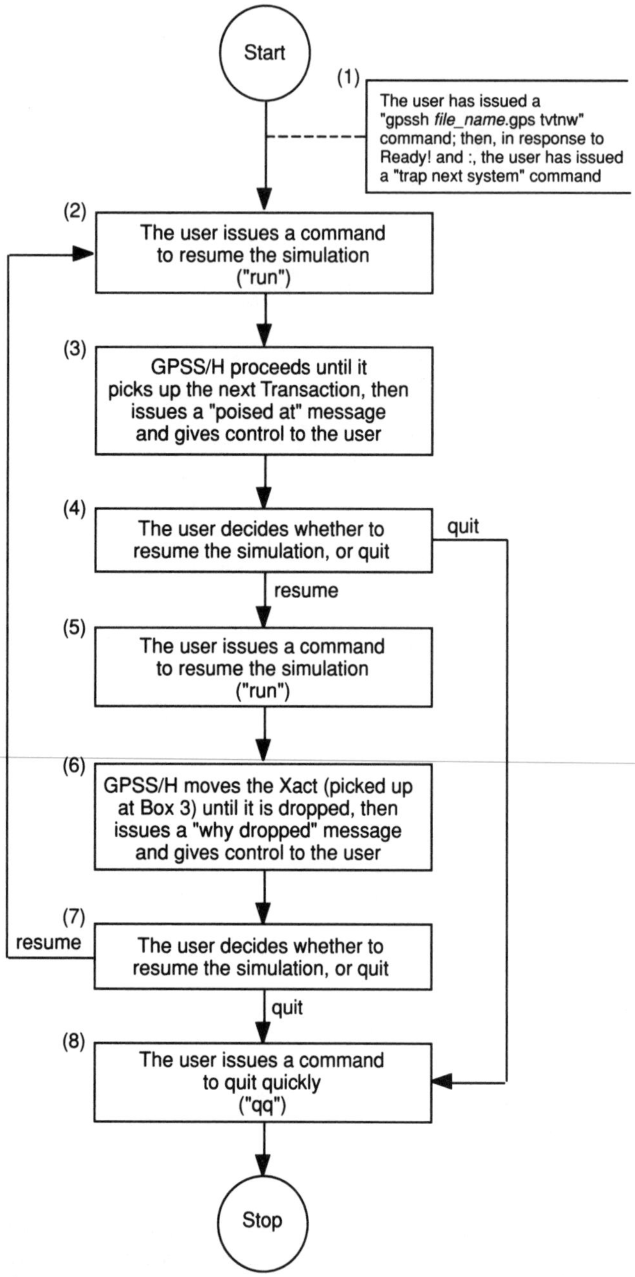

Figure 5.2 *The Steps Involved in Moving Through a Simulation, Xact by Xact (Basis: Interrupts Occur Whenever an Xact is Picked Up and Whenever an Xact is Dropped)*

Figure 5.4 shows six computer screens resulting from this simulation. Discussion of this screen sequence follows. (In Exercise 1 of Section 5.3, you are asked to reproduce this screen sequence on your computer.) Throughout the discussion, reference is made to the numbered Boxes in Figure 5.2.

Screen 1 (Figure 5.4, part a)

Screen 1 results after the steps shown in Boxes 1, 2, and 3 in Figure 5.2 have been carried out. DOS has executed a **gpssh fig53.gps tvtnw** command (Box 1). Then GPSS/H has executed a **trap next system** command (Box 1) and a **run** command (Box 2), has proceeded to the point of picking up an Xact (Box 3) and has displayed the message

```
XACT 2 POISED AT BLOCK 4 (BLOCK4). RELATIVE CLOCK: 29.9742
```

What led to the foregoing message? Having established **next** and **system** traps, GPSS/H re-

```
          SIMULATE
*
 BLOCK1   GENERATE  40,15
 BLOCK2   ADVANCE   25,10
 BLOCK3   TERMINATE 1
*
 BLOCK4   GENERATE  30,20
 BLOCK5   ADVANCE   20,5
 BLOCK6   TERMINATE 1
*
          START     5
          END
```

Figure 5.3 *A Model File Used to Demonstrate Next and System Traps*

sponded to the **run** command by executing the START statement and proceeding to the point of "picking up" an Xact for the first time. This required going through the first Scan Phase at time 0.0 (empty CEC), then the first Clock Update Phase (which advanced the clock from 0.0 to 29.9+, per the Screen 1 Status Window, and transferred Xact 2 from the FEC to the CEC). The second Scan Phase then began. GPSS/H went to the front of the CEC and picked up Xact 2. At this point, the **next** trap was sprung. Before starting to move Xact 2, GPSS/H then wrote out the XACT 2 POISED AT BLOCK 4 interrupt message and returned control to us.

In Screen 1, no Block executions have yet taken place in the simulation. Xact 2 hasn't moved yet, but is poised to start to move.

Note from Figure 5.1 that if a **scan** trap (as well as **next** and **system** traps) had been set in response to the Ready! prompt in Screen 1, then two "SCAN" TRAP TAKEN interrupts would have occurred before the simulation reached the point of issuing the XACT 2 POISED AT BLOCK 4 interrupt message in Screen 1. In other words, three interrupts would have occurred in total to bring us to this point in the simulation, even though no Blocks have yet been executed.

Screen 2 (Figure 5.4, part b)

Screen 2 results when we key in and send a **run** command (Box 5, Figure 5.2) in response to the prompt at the bottom of Screen 1. When this second

```
BLOCK CURRENT     TOTAL         fig53.gps SOURCE CODE
----- -------     -----         ---------------------------------------------
2                     0          BLOCK2   ADVANCE     25,10
3                     0          BLOCK3   TERMINATE   1
4                     0          BLOCK4   GENERATE    30,20
5                     0          BLOCK5   ADVANCE     20,5
6                     0          BLOCK6   TERMINATE   1
=============================================================================
S/C: OFF  ABS CLOCK:  29.9742       REL CLOCK: 29.9742        TTG: 5
=============================================================================
XACT: 2        CURBLK: BIRTH     NEXTBLK: BLOCK4     CHAINS: CEC       PC:

MARK-TIME:               MOVE-TIME: -----        PRIORITY: 0
=============================================================================
                      WOLVERINE SOFTWARE CORPORATION
                            4115 ANNANDALE ROAD
                      ANNANDALE, VIRGINIA 22003, USA

Ready!
: trap next system
: run

XACT 2 POISED AT BLOCK 4 (BLOCK4).  RELATIVE CLOCK: 29.9742
:
```

Figure 5.4 *Six Computer Screens Resulting When the Figure 5.3 Model File is Run in Test Mode (a) Screen 1*

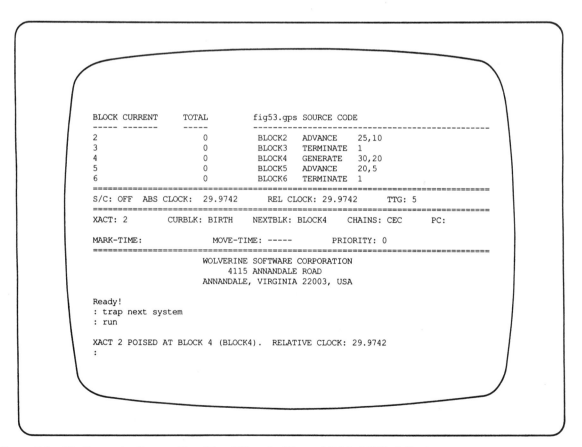

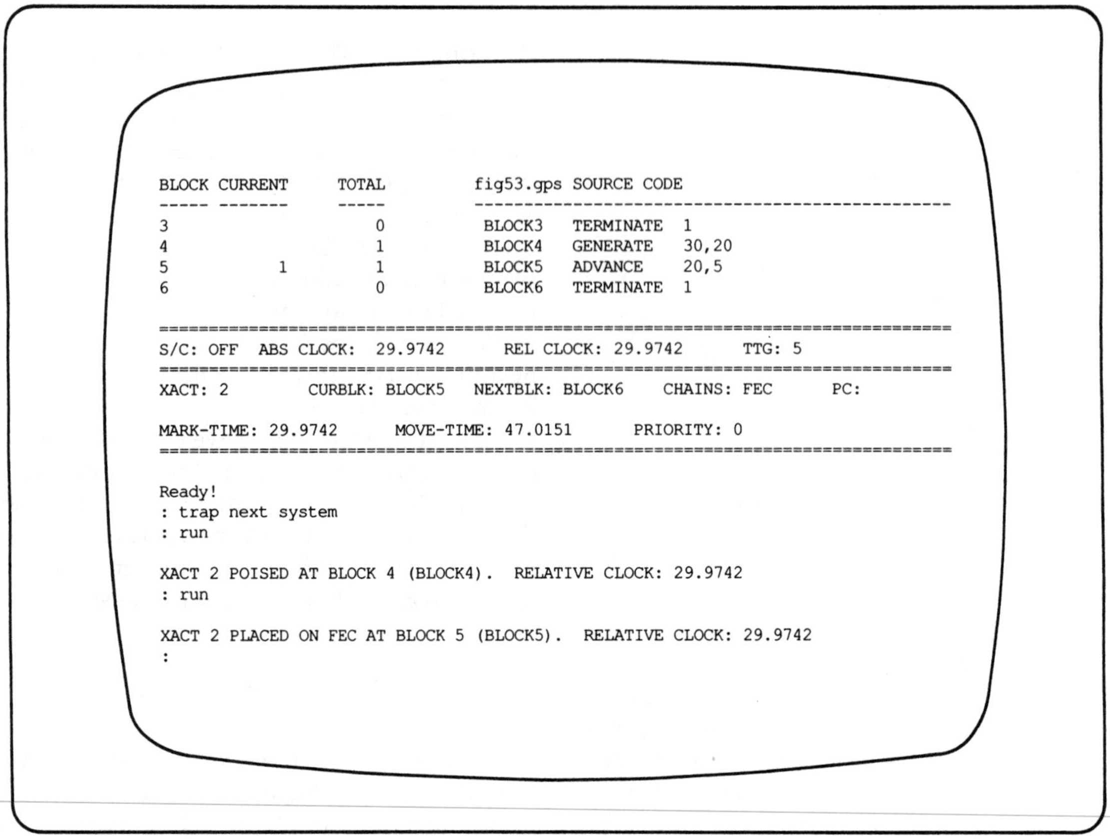

Figure 5.4 (b) *Screen 2*

run command was issued, GPSS/H resumed with Xact 2, moving it as far as possible before dropping it. (This involved only a two-Block move: GENERATE and ADVANCE.) At this point, the **system** trap was sprung. GPSS/H then wrote out the "why dropped" message at the bottom of Screen 2, XACT 2 PLACED ON FEC AT BLOCK 5.

Screen 3 (Figure 5.4, part c)

Screen 3 results when we key in and send another **run** command (Box 2, Figure 5.2) in response to the prompt at the bottom of Screen 2. When this third **run** was issued, GPSS/H proceeded to the next point of picking up an Xact. The second Scan Phase had come to an end at the bottom of Screen 2 with the placing of Xact 2 on the FEC. As its next step, then, GPSS/H performed the second Clock Update Phase, advancing the clock (from 29.9+ to 33.1+ per the Screen 3 Status Window) and transferring Xact 1 from the FEC to the CEC. The second Scan Phase then began, with GPSS/H going to the front of the CEC and picking up Xact 1, which is poised at its GENERATE Block (BLOCK1). At this point, the **next** trap was sprung. Before starting to move Xact 1, GPSS/H wrote out the XACT 1 POISED AT BLOCK 1 interrupt message and returned control to us.

Screen 4 (Figure 5.4, part d)

Screen 4 results when we key in and send another **run** command (Box 5, Figure 5.2) in response to the prompt at the bottom of Screen 2. When this fourth **run** command was issued, GPSS/H resumed with Xact 1, moving it as far as possible before dropping it. (This involved only a two-Block move: GENERATE and ADVANCE.) At this point, the **system** trap was sprung. GPSS/H then wrote out the "why dropped" message at the bottom of Screen 4, XACT 1 PLACED ON FEC AT BLOCK 2.

Screen 5 (Figure 5.4, part e)

Screen 5 results when we key in and send another **run** command (Box 2, Figure 5.2) in response to the prompt at the bottom of Screen 4. When this fifth **run** was issued, GPSS/H proceeded to the next point of picking up an Xact. The third Scan Phase had come to an end at the bottom of Screen 4 with

```
BLOCK CURRENT     TOTAL         fig53.gps SOURCE CODE
----- -------     -----         -----------------------------------------------


1                   0           BLOCK1   GENERATE   40,15
2                   0           BLOCK2   ADVANCE    25,10
3                   0           BLOCK3   TERMINATE  1
===============================================================================
S/C: OFF  ABS CLOCK:  33.1089      REL CLOCK: 33.1089      TTG: 5
===============================================================================
XACT: 1        CURBLK: BIRTH    NEXTBLK: BLOCK1    CHAINS: CEC      PC:

MARK-TIME: 0.             MOVE-TIME: -----         PRIORITY: 0
===============================================================================
: run

XACT 2 POISED AT BLOCK 4 (BLOCK4).  RELATIVE CLOCK: 29.9742
: run

XACT 2 PLACED ON FEC AT BLOCK 5 (BLOCK5).  RELATIVE CLOCK: 29.9742
: run

XACT 1 POISED AT BLOCK 1 (BLOCK1).  RELATIVE CLOCK: 33.1089
:
```

Figure 5.4 (c) *Screen 3*

```
BLOCK CURRENT     TOTAL         fig53.gps SOURCE CODE
----- -------     -----         -----------------------------------------------

1                   1           BLOCK1   GENERATE   40,15
2           1       1           BLOCK2   ADVANCE    25,10
3                   0           BLOCK3   TERMINATE  1
4                   1           BLOCK4   GENERATE   30,20
===============================================================================
S/C: OFF  ABS CLOCK:  33.1089      REL CLOCK: 33.1089      TTG: 5
===============================================================================
XACT: 1        CURBLK: BLOCK2   NEXTBLK: BLOCK3    CHAINS: FEC      PC:

MARK-TIME: 33.1089       MOVE-TIME: 63.4776       PRIORITY: 0
===============================================================================
: run

XACT 2 PLACED ON FEC AT BLOCK 5 (BLOCK5).  RELATIVE CLOCK: 29.9742
: run

XACT 1 POISED AT BLOCK 1 (BLOCK1).  RELATIVE CLOCK: 33.1089
: run

XACT 1 PLACED ON FEC AT BLOCK 2 (BLOCK2).  RELATIVE CLOCK: 33.1089
:
```

Figure 5.4 (d) *Screen 4*

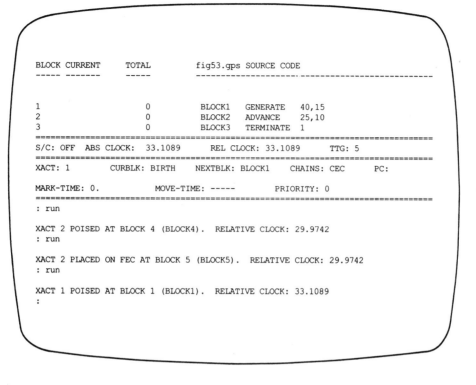

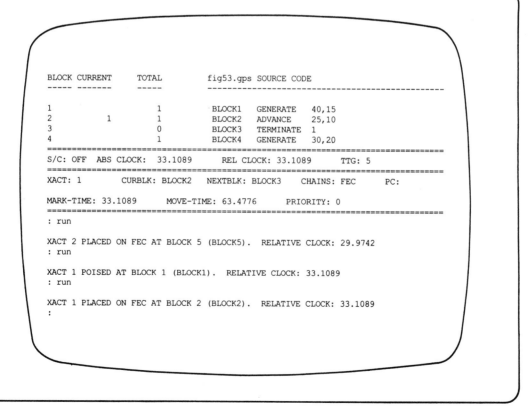

```
BLOCK CURRENT     TOTAL        fig53.gps SOURCE CODE
----- -------     -----        ---------------------------------------------
4                     1         BLOCK4   GENERATE   30,20
5            1        1         BLOCK5   ADVANCE    20,5
6                     0         BLOCK6   TERMINATE  1


================================================================================
S/C: OFF  ABS CLOCK:  47.0151       REL CLOCK: 47.0151       TTG: 5
================================================================================
XACT: 2         CURBLK: BLOCK5   NEXTBLK: BLOCK6    CHAINS: CEC       PC:

MARK-TIME: 29.9742      MOVE-TIME: -----        PRIORITY: 0
================================================================================
: run

XACT 1 POISED AT BLOCK 1 (BLOCK1).  RELATIVE CLOCK: 33.1089
: run

XACT 1 PLACED ON FEC AT BLOCK 2 (BLOCK2).  RELATIVE CLOCK: 33.1089
: run

XACT 2 POISED AT BLOCK 6 (BLOCK6).  RELATIVE CLOCK: 47.0151
:
```

Figure 5.4 (e) *Screen 5*

the placing of Xact 1 on the FEC. As its next step, then, GPSS/H performed the third Clock Update Phase, advancing the clock (from 33.1+ to 47.0+ per the Screen 5 Status Window) and transferring Xact 2 from the FEC to the CEC. The fourth Scan Phase then began, with GPSS/H going to the front of the CEC and picking up Xact 2, which is poised at a TERMINATE Block (BLOCK6). At this point, the **next** trap was sprung. GPSS/H then wrote out the XACT 1 POISED AT BLOCK 1 interrupt message and returned control to us.

Screen 6 (Figure 5.4, part f)

Screen 6 results when we key in and send another **run** command (Box 2, Figure 5.2) in response to the prompt at the bottom of Screen 5. When this sixth **run** command was issued, GPSS/H resumed with Xact 2, moving it into the BLOCK6 TERMINATE. At this point, the **system** trap was sprung. GPSS/H then wrote out the "why dropped" message at the bottom of Screen 6, XACT 2 DESTROYED AT BLOCK 6.

The user then quit quickly by issuing a **qq** command (Box 8, Figure 5.2). (This step is not shown in Figure 5.4.)

In conclusion, in Figure 5.4 we've demonstrated the springing of **next** and **system** traps during Scan Phases two, three, and four with the model of Figure 5.3. Only one **next** and one **system** trap were sprung in each of these Scan Phases, simply because there was only one Xact to be moved in each Scan Phase. In more complex models, two or more Xacts might be moved per Scan Phase. In such cases, **next** and **system** traps will be sprung multiple times per Scan Phase if these traps are set.

5.3 Exercises

1. Perform a Test-Mode simulation with file fig53.gps, which contains the Figure 5.3 Model File. Issue a **trap next system** command and then a series of **run** commands to repeat the Figure 5.4 simulation. Then continue the simulation by issuing six or more additional **run** commands. (Remember that two consecutive **run** commands will be required to deal with each moving Transaction.) Interpret the GPSS/

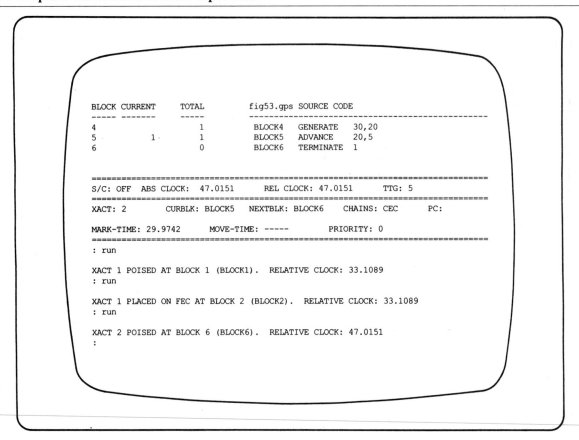

```
BLOCK CURRENT     TOTAL        fig53.gps SOURCE CODE
----- -------     -----        ------------------------------------------------
4                     1         BLOCK4    GENERATE   30,20
5                     1         BLOCK5    ADVANCE    20,5
6                     1         BLOCK6    TERMINATE  1


================================================================================
S/C: OFF  ABS CLOCK:  47.0151       REL CLOCK: 47.0151        TTG: 4
================================================================================
XACT: 2         CURBLK: BLOCK5   NEXTBLK: BLOCK6     CHAINS:            PC:

MARK-TIME: 29.9742       MOVE-TIME: -----          PRIORITY: 0
================================================================================
: run

XACT 1 PLACED ON FEC AT BLOCK 2 (BLOCK2).  RELATIVE CLOCK: 33.1089
: run

XACT 2 POISED AT BLOCK 6 (BLOCK6).  RELATIVE CLOCK: 47.0151
: run

XACT 2 DESTROYED AT BLOCK 6 (BLOCK6).  RELATIVE CLOCK: 47.0151
:
```

Figure 5.4 (f) *Screen 6*

H messages in terms of Scan Phase and Clock Update Phase logic.

2. Repeat Exercise 1, except **display cec fec** just before issuing each **run** command. Review the information in the resulting chain displays, and satisfy yourself that this information is consistent with your understanding of the state of the model as the simulation proceeds.

3. Perform a Test-Mode simulation with the model for Exercise 3 of Section 3.15. Issue a **trap next system** command; then issue **run** commands repeatedly until you get the "output pending" message. Interpret the messages that GPSS/H produces. Are these messages consistent with your understanding of what should be happening in the simulation? If anything is unclear, consider displaying the Current and Future Events Chains each time GPSS/H gives control to you, and use the resulting information to solidify your understanding of the steps taking place as the simulation proceeds.

4. Perform a Test-Mode simulation with the model in Figure 4.14, which is in the file fig414.gps. (This is the model in which three Xacts come out of a GENERATE Block, one by one, during the Scan Phase at time 0.0.) Issue a **trap next system** command and then a series of **run** commands until the first Clock Update Phase has occurred. Relate the information in the messages produced by GPSS/H to your understanding of what happens in this model during the time 0.0 Scan Phase. If necessary or desirable, issue a **display cec fec** each time you are in control.

*5. Suppose a user has initiated a Test-Mode simulation with a model.

(a) Assume the user issues these three commands in sequence in response to the Ready! prompt: **trap scan**, **trap next system**, and **run**. What interrupt condition will cause control to be returned to the user for the first time? (Hint: see Figure 5.1.) At what clock time will the interrupt occur? What message will GPSS/H issue? Check out your thinking by carrying out these steps on the computer with the fig53.gps model.

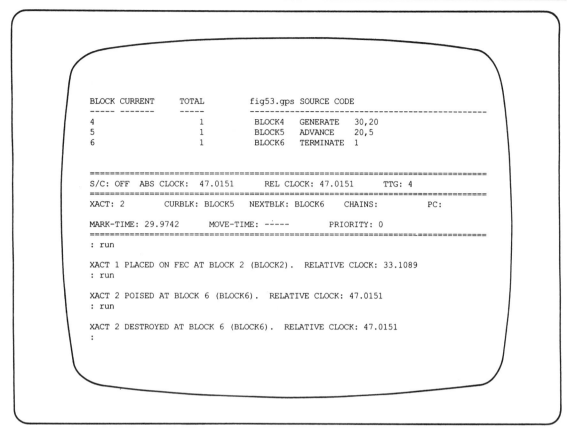

(b) Now assume that the user continues by issuing a series of consecutive **run** commands. What types of interrupts will occur? Will it ever happen that two traps will be sprung at the same time? If so, how do you think GPSS/H will respond when this happens? Check out your thinking by doing corresponding experimentation with the fig53.gps model.

*6. Suppose a user has initiated a Test-Mode simulation with a model.

(a) Assume the user issues these two commands in response to the Ready! prompt: **trap next system** and **step 1**. What interrupt condition will cause control to be returned to the user for the first time? What message(s) will GPSS/H issue? Check out your thinking by carrying out these steps on the computer with the fig53.gps model.

(b) Now assume that the user continues by issuing a series of consecutive **step 1** commands. What types of interrupts will occur? Will it ever happen that two traps will be sprung at the same time? If so, how do you think GPSS/H will respond when this happens? Check out your thinking by doing corresponding experimentation with the fig53.gps model.

5.4 More About Test Mode

In this section, we make some additional comments about the Test-Mode commands introduced so far.

To save keying time, minimal abbreviations can be used for all the Test-Mode commands (including commands yet to be discussed). We saw earlier that **step** can be shortened to **ste**, or **st**, or even to **s**. Similarly, **trap** can be shortened to **tra**, or **tr**, or **t**, and **run** can be shortened to **ru** or **r**.

There is no need to remember the abbreviations that are acceptable for Test-Mode commands or to be hesitant to try abbreviations. If an attempted abbreviation is unacceptable, GPSS/H simply displays an INVALID COMMAND message, then issues a colon to prompt the user for more input.

The Test-Mode command **display cec fec** is a compound form of the two commands **display cec** and **display fec**. Similarly, the Test-Mode command **trap next system** is a compound form of the two commands **trap next** and **trap system**. If **trap next** is used to set just a **next** trap, GPSS/H will give control to the user whenever an Xact is picked up (but not when an Xact is dropped). Similarly if a **trap system** is used to set just a **system** trap, GPSS/H will give control to the user whenever the moving Xact is dropped (but not when an Xact is picked up).

The user may want to set a **next** and/or **system** trap, then disable (turn off) one or both of these traps at a later point in the experimentation. Remember that after a trap has been set it can be disabled by use of the **untrap** command. For example, **untrap next** disables the **next** trap, **untrap system** disables the **system** trap, and **untrap next system** disables both the **next** and the **system** traps.

The minimal abbreviation for **untrap** is **unt**.

An asterisk (*) can be used as a wild card in the **untrap** command. That is, issuing an **untrap *** command causes *all* trap conditions to be disabled.

In longer Test-Mode sessions, the user may not always be able to remember which traps, if any, are set. (As we will see later, **next**, **system** and **scan** are not the only trap conditions that can be set.) The user can use the **display** command, however, to find out which traps are set. Used for this purpose, the **display** command takes this form:

```
display traps
```

Some interrupt conditions are *semipermanent*, remaining in effect unless or until they are later turned off by command. For example, a **next** trap remains in effect until an **untrap next** command is issued. This is also true for **scan** and **system** traps. Other interrupt conditions are *temporary* in the sense that they are *automatically turned off* the next time control is returned to the user *for any reason*. The only command of this type that we have seen is **step**.

5.5 Exercises

1. Repeat Exercise 1 of Section 5.3, but just issue a **trap next** command (not a **trap next system** command) and then a series of consecutive **run** commands until Xacts have been moved on six or eight occasions. Notice that control is returned to you by GPSS/H only half as often as in Exercise 1 of Section 5.3.

2. Repeat Exercise 1 of Section 5.3, but just issue a **trap system** command (not a **trap next system** command) and then a series of consecutive **run** commands until Xacts have been moved on six or more occasions. Notice that control is re-

turned to you by GPSS/H only half as often as in Exercise 1 of Section 5.3.

3. Using the Model File in fig53.gps, start a simulation in Test Mode by issuing a **trap next** command, and then issue a series of four or more **step 1** commands. Explain the meaning of the messages that GPSS/H writes out.

4. Using the Model File in fig53.gps, start a simulation in Test Mode by issuing a **trap next** command, and then issue a series of six or more **step 1** commands. Explain the meaning of the messages that GPSS/H writes out.

5. Using the Model File in fig53.gps, start a simulation in Test Mode by issuing a **trap system** command. Then issue a series of six or more consecutive **step 1** commands. Explain the meaning of the messages that GPSS/H writes out.

*6. Compose a Model File of your own choosing. Simulate with the Model File in Test Mode, using all the Test-Mode commands introduced up to this point. Try to introduce as many complications into the model as possible, including having Move-Time ties, Priority Level differences among Transactions, and two or more Transactions on the Current Events Chain when a Scan Phase begins. Be sure your understanding of the way your model *should* be operating (in terms of which Xacts move at which times) is consistent with the information provided in messages produced when interrupts occur.

   If you're taking a course, get together with some other students in the course and compare your Model File with theirs. What form does the most imaginative Model File take?

5.6 Specifying a Clock-Based Interrupt Condition

We've now seen how to proceed in a Test-Mode simulation in these three ways:

1. Block by Block. This is accomplished by issuing a series of consecutive **step 1** commands, as we have seen starting in Chapter 2 of this book.
2. Xact by Xact. This is accomplished by setting a **trap next system** command and then issuing a series of consecutive **run** commands, as we have seen in Section 5.2.
3. Clock-Time by Clock-Time. This is accomplished by setting a **trap scan** command and then issuing a series of consecutive **run** commands. See Exercise 9 of Section 4.11.

It's also possible for the user to specify that a Test-Mode simulation is to be interrupted when a specified clock time is first reached or exceeded. This is accomplished by setting a clock trap.

A clock trap is set by issuing the command

```
trap clock=clock_time
```

where ***clock_time*** stands for the user's choice of a simulated time for which the clock trap is being set (for example, **trap clock=100**).

The equals sign (=) can be replaced by one or more blanks in a **trap clock** command. For example, **trap clock=100** and **trap clock 100** are equivalent.

As is always true, issuing a **trap** command does not cause GPSS/H to resume a simulation. After setting one (or more) trap conditions, the user can resume the simulation by issuing a **run** or a **step** command.

The point at which a clock trap is sprung during a Scan Phase is indicated in Figure 5.5, which repeats and extends the Scan Phase flowchart of Figure 4.9 by adding comment Box A to indicate the point at which a clock trap is sprung. As indicated by Box A, a clock trap is sprung at the beginning of a Scan Phase if there is at least one Xact on the Current Chain and if clock time equals or exceeds the clock-trap time. (Recall that there will always be at least one Xact on the CEC at the start of a Scan Phase, except possibly at time 0.0.) Springing the **clock** trap has the effect of disabling the trap. The message produced when a **clock** trap is sprung will be shown farther on.

As just stated, a clock trap is sprung at the beginning of a Scan Phase if clock time equals *or exceeds* the clock-trap time. It's unlikely in general that the clock will happen to register a value that exactly *equals* a clock-trap time, and this explains the appropriateness of the *or exceeds* qualifier in the foregoing statement. For example, suppose that in a given simulation the time series of values registered by the clock is 0.0, 57.1, 124.7, 159.2, 201.3, 233.5, and so

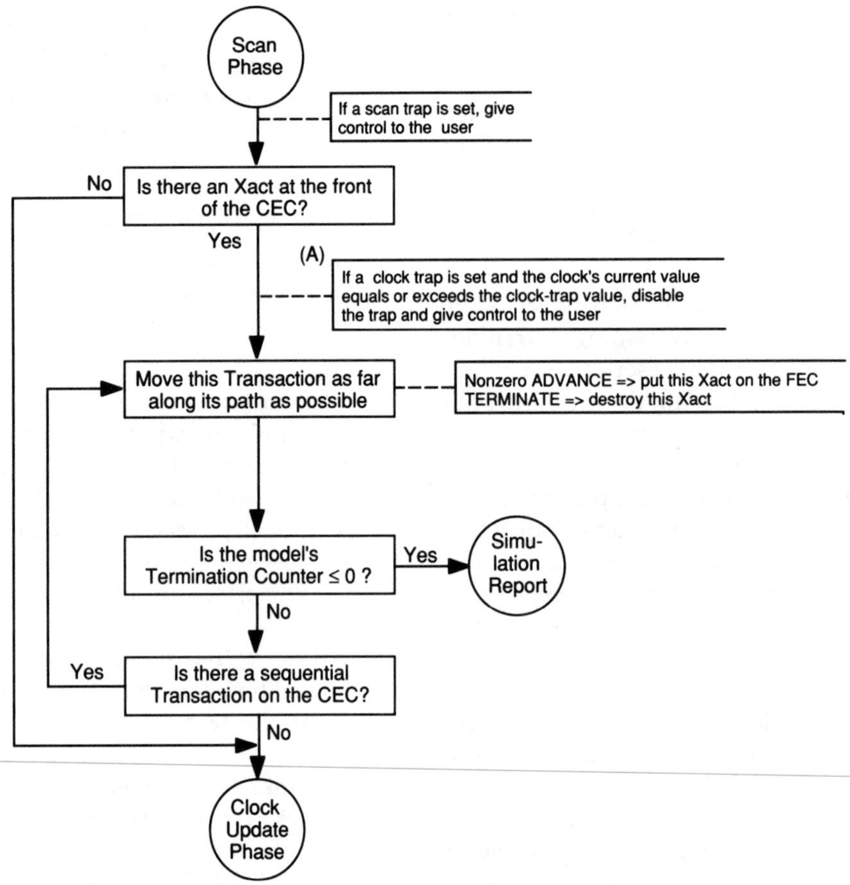

*Figure 5.5 A Repetition of the Figure 4.9 Scan Phase Logic, With Comment Box A Added to Show the Point at Which a **Clock** Trap is Sprung*

on. Suppose further that in a Test-Mode simulation, the user issues a **trap clock=175.0** command at time 0.0. Then the **clock** trap will be sprung at the beginning of the Scan Phase at time 201.3. Clock time jumps over the trap value of 175.0 in the Clock Update Phase that carries the clock's value from 159.2 to 201.3. There is no reason for the clock to register a value of 175.0. (There doesn't happen to be an Xact on the Future Chain whose Move Time equals 175.0.)

A **clock** trap remains in effect *until the clock trap has been sprung* or until it is turned off through use of an **untrap** command, which takes the form **untrap clock**. In other words, if some other interrupt condition occurs before a clock trap is sprung, then the clock trap remains in effect. But after a clock trap has been sprung, the user must issue another **trap clock=*clock_time*** command to establish another clock trap.

Only one clock trap can be in effect at a time. GPSS/H writes out an appropriate message if an attempt is made to set a clock trap when one is already set. To change a clock trap before it has been sprung, the user must **untrap** it first, then set the new trap value.

We'll now use the Figure 5.3 Model File in a Test-Mode simulation to demonstrate use of the **trap clock** command. The demonstration is shown in Figure 5.6.

Screen 1 (Figure 5.6, part a)

Screen 1 results after the DOS command **gpssh fig53.gps tvtnw** and the GPSS/H commands **trap clock 50** and **run** have been executed. Control has been returned to the user in Screen 1 with the clock-based interrupt message

```
XACT 4 POISED AT BLOCK 1 (BLOCK1).
RELATIVE CLOCK: 61.7289
CLOCK >= 50.0000 BREAKPOINT.
```

We see that the clock has reached a value of 61.7, which exceeds the value of 50.0 at which the **clock** trap

```
BLOCK CURRENT     TOTAL         fig53.gps SOURCE CODE
----- -------     -----         ----------------------------------------------

1                   1           BLOCK1   GENERATE   40,15
2           1       1           BLOCK2   ADVANCE    25,10
3                   0           BLOCK3   TERMINATE  1
==============================================================================
S/C: OFF  ABS CLOCK:  61.7289      REL CLOCK: 61.7289       TTG: 4
==============================================================================
XACT: 4         CURBLK: BIRTH     NEXTBLK: BLOCK1     CHAINS: CEC      PC:

MARK-TIME:               MOVE-TIME: -----         PRIORITY: 0
==============================================================================
                              4115 ANNANDALE ROAD
                         ANNANDALE, VIRGINIA 22003, USA

Ready!
: trap clock 50
: run

XACT 4 POISED AT BLOCK 1 (BLOCK1).  RELATIVE CLOCK: 61.7289
CLOCK >= 50.0000 BREAKPOINT.
:
```

Figure 5.6 Four Computer Screens Resulting When the Figure 5.3 Model File Is Run in Test Mode (a) Screen 1

```
Ready!
: trap clock 50
: run

XACT 4 POISED AT BLOCK 1 (BLOCK1).  RELATIVE CLOCK: 61.7289
CLOCK >= 50.0000 BREAKPOINT.
: display cec fec

CURRENT EVENTS CHAIN

XACT     CURBLK    NXTBLK    CHAINS  SDPGFT**   MARK-TIME   MOVE-TIME   PRIORITY

4        BIRTH     BLOCK1    CEC                   ---        61.7289          0

FUTURE EVENTS CHAIN

XACT     CURBLK    NXTBLK    CHAINS  SDPGFT**   MARK-TIME   MOVE-TIME   PRIORITY

1        BLOCK2    BLOCK3    FEC                 33.1089      63.4776          0

XACT     CURBLK    NXTBLK    CHAINS  SDPGFT**   MARK-TIME   MOVE-TIME   PRIORITY

3        BIRTH     BLOCK4    FEC                   ---        69.5650          0
:
```

Figure 5.6 (b) Screen 2

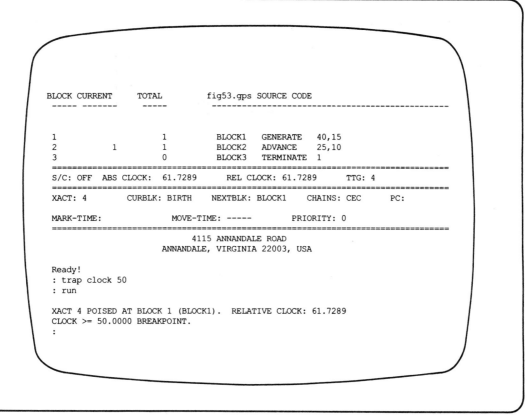

was set. (The immediately preceding clock time must have been less than 50.0.) The Scan Phase at time 61.7 is just beginning. Xact 4 has been picked up and is poised to move into its BLOCK1 GENERATE.

We have no direct way to know how many Scan and Clock Update Phases took place between time 0.0 and the return of control to us in Screen 1. With use of the **clock** trap, we are moving through the simulation in larger-scale terms than we did with use of **step**, **trap next**, and **trap system** commands.

Screen 2 (Figure 5.6, part b)

Screen 2 results when we proceed from Screen 1 by issuing **set tv off** and **display cec fec** commands. The Screen 2 Current Chain shows that Xact 4 is in the process of coming into the model via its BLOCK1 GENERATE, as we already know from the Screen 1 clock-trap message. The Future Chain in Screen 2 shows that Xact 1 is in the BLOCK2 ADVANCE and that Xact 3 is on its way to the model via the BLOCK4 GENERATE.

Screen 3 (Figure 5.6, part c)

Screen 3 results when we proceed from Screen 2 by issuing **set tv on, trap clock 75** and **run** commands. Control has been returned to us in Screen 3 with the clock-based interrupt message

```
XACT 3 POISED AT BLOCK 6 (BLOCK6).
RELATIVE CLOCK: 85.4904
CLOCK >= 75.0000 BREAKPOINT.
```

We see that the clock has reached a value of 85.4, which exceeds the value of 75.0 at which the **clock** trap was set. The Scan Phase at time 85.4 is just beginning. Xact 3 has been picked up and is poised to move from the BLOCK5 ADVANCE into the BLOCK6 TERMINATE.

Screen 4 (Figure 5.6, part d)

Screen 4 results when we proceed from Screen 3 by issuing **set tv off** and **display cec fec** command. The

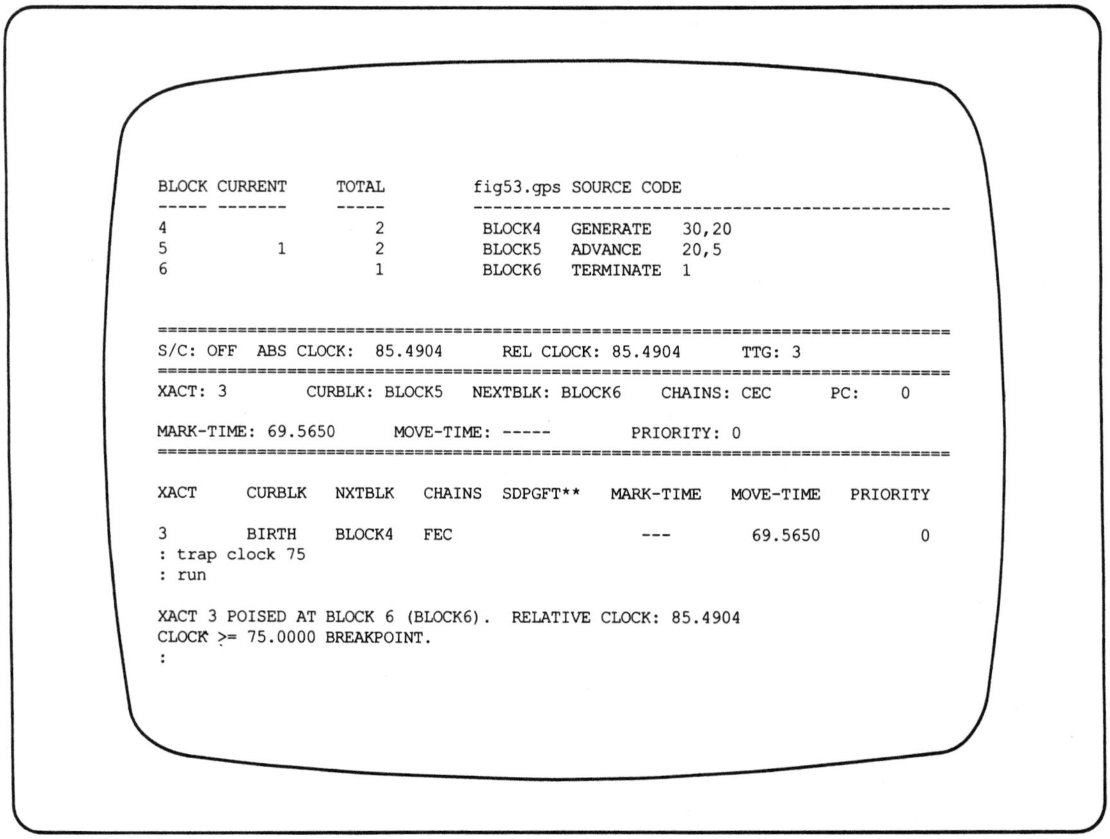

```
BLOCK CURRENT     TOTAL          fig53.gps SOURCE CODE
----- -------     -----          -----------------------------------------------
4                   2             BLOCK4    GENERATE    30,20
5           1       2             BLOCK5    ADVANCE     20,5
6                   1             BLOCK6    TERMINATE   1

==============================================================================
S/C: OFF  ABS CLOCK:  85.4904       REL CLOCK: 85.4904        TTG: 3
==============================================================================
XACT: 3         CURBLK: BLOCK5    NEXTBLK: BLOCK6     CHAINS: CEC       PC:     0

MARK-TIME: 69.5650       MOVE-TIME: -----           PRIORITY: 0
==============================================================================

XACT      CURBLK   NXTBLK   CHAINS   SDPGFT**   MARK-TIME   MOVE-TIME   PRIORITY

3          BIRTH   BLOCK4   FEC                    ---        69.5650          0
: trap clock 75
: run

XACT 3 POISED AT BLOCK 6 (BLOCK6).  RELATIVE CLOCK: 85.4904
CLOCK >= 75.0000 BREAKPOINT.
:
```

Figure 5.6 (c) *Screen 3*

```
XACT 3 POISED AT BLOCK 6 (BLOCK6).  RELATIVE CLOCK: 85.4904
CLOCK >= 75.0000 BREAKPOINT.
: display cec fec

CURRENT EVENTS CHAIN

XACT     CURBLK   NXTBLK   CHAINS  SDPGFT**  MARK-TIME   MOVE-TIME   PRIORITY

3        BLOCK5   BLOCK6   CEC                 69.5650     85.4904          0

FUTURE EVENTS CHAIN

XACT     CURBLK   NXTBLK   CHAINS  SDPGFT**  MARK-TIME   MOVE-TIME   PRIORITY

4        BLOCK2   BLOCK3   FEC                 61.7289     93.9180          0

XACT     CURBLK   NXTBLK   CHAINS  SDPGFT**  MARK-TIME   MOVE-TIME   PRIORITY

5        BIRTH    BLOCK1   FEC                   ---       99.9407          0

XACT     CURBLK   NXTBLK   CHAINS  SDPGFT**  MARK-TIME   MOVE-TIME   PRIORITY

6        BIRTH    BLOCK4   FEC                   ---      111.2596          0
:
```

Figure 5.6 (d) *Screen 4*

Screen 3 Current Chain shows that Xact 3 is in the process of moving from BLOCK5 to BLOCK6, as we already know from the Screen 3 interrupt message. The Future Chain in Screen 4 shows that Xact 4 is in the BLOCK2 ADVANCE and Xacts 5 and 6 are on their way to the model via the BLOCK1 and BLOCK4 GENERATEs, respectively.

This concludes the demonstration of clock-based traps, the objective having been to see the type of message produced when a clock-based trap is sprung and to show the state of a model immediately after a clock-based trap has been sprung by displaying the Current and Future Events Chains at those times.

Now that we've discussed and illustrated the characteristics of clock traps, let's conclude this section by describing two of their possible applications. Clock traps can be useful in *model debugging* and in *exploring model operation* to assure that a model is behaving as intended. These aspects of clock-trap use will now be outlined.

Model Debugging. Assume that a large GPSS/H model has just been built, and that a series of verification or pilot runs (see Boxes 4 and 5 in Figure 1.2 of Chapter 1) is being made with the model. During a Batch-Mode simulation in one of these runs, suppose that an error condition comes about. When an error occurs, GPSS/H always issues a message indicating the *currrent clock time* and, if there is a moving Xact, its id number, the Block it is trying to move from, and the Block it is trying to move into. If the circumstances leading to the error aren't immediately evident, the modeler may want to repeat the simulation, starting at the beginning and simulating "full speed ahead" up to the beginning of the Scan Phase at which the error occurs. (The ability to reproduce a previous simulation exactly is one of the advantages of working with pseudorandom number generators.) At that point, the user can display the Current Events Chain and study the information it contains, then slow things down, stepping carefully through the Scan Phase, perhaps one Block execution at a time, monitoring Xact movement and watching the developments that lead to the error. The process of investigating model behavior at this level of detail often brings into focus the circumstances that produce the error. The changes that should be made in the model to eliminate the conditions leading to such an error often become evident as a byproduct of this investigation.

Use of a **clock** trap under the circumstances just presented is straightforward. Suppose, for example, that an error condition occurs in a Batch-Mode run at simulated time 123456.7890. The modeler can then initiate a Test-Mode run with the model and, in response to the Ready! prompt, issue **trap clock=123456.7890** and **run** commands. The simulation will then proceed without interruption until the beginning of the Scan Phase at time 123456.7890. The clock trap will be sprung at that point, and the user can proceed to step slowly through the Scan Phase up to the occurrence of the error, displaying various aspects of the state of the model while proceeding.

Exploring Model Operation. Even if no error conditions occur while making verification runs with a model, the model builder should assure himself or herself before making production runs (see Box 8 in Figure 1.2 of Chapter 1) that the behavior of the model is logically correct. This can be done, in part, by starting a simulation, letting it proceed nonstop up to the beginning of a Scan Phase at some arbitrarily chosen simulated time, then monitoring Xact movement on a Block by Block basis as the Scan Phase proceeds. Are the moves made by Xacts logically consistent with the state of the model at that time? If not, then the model has been built incorrectly and will have to be modified before production runs are made.

The procedure just described can be accomplished by initiating a Test-Mode simulation, setting a **clock** trap for some arbitrarily chosen simulated time, and issuing a **run** command. The simulation will then proceed without interruption until the beginning of the first Scan Phase to take place after the clock-trap time has been reached or exceeded, and detailed monitoring of model behavior can begin at that point.

This technique should not be used for just one arbitrarily chosen simulated time, of course, but should be applied at a number of simulated times.

The full importance of being able to use **clock** traps in the two preceding settings may be difficult to appreciate at this point, because we're not far along in our study of GPSS/H. As a result, it may not be easy to envision the potential complexities of the modeling process and the challenges of model debugging and model verification now. Nevertheless, it should be clear that clock traps and various other types of traps and interrupt conditions provide powerful tools for use in model development and checkout.

5.7 Exercises

1. The file fig53.gps contains the Model File shown in Figure 5.3. Initiate a Test-Mode simulation with this Model File and reproduce the screen sequence shown in Figure 5.6.

2. Repeat Exercise 1, except **display cec fec** just before issuing each **run** command. Review the information in the resulting chain displays. Satisfy yourself that this information is consistent with your understanding of the state of the model as the simulation proceeds.

3. The file s411x8.gps contains the Model File shown in Exercise 8 of Section 4.11. Initiate a Test-Mode simulation with this Model File, then use a series of **clock** traps and **run** commands to move through the simulation. Select small enough clock-trap times so that at least five interrupts will occur before the "output pending" message is produced. You may have to do some experimentation in this regard. Display the Current and Future Events Chains each time you are given control, and use the information provided in these chain displays to satisfy yourself that you completely understand what is happening.

4. The file s57x4.gps contains the following Model File.

```
          SIMULATE
*
 BLOCK1   GENERATE   40,15
 BLOCK2   ADVANCE    25,10
 BLOCK3   ADVANCE    50,20
 BLOCK4   TRANSFER   ,BLOCK6
*
 BLOCK5   GENERATE   30,20
 BLOCK6   ADVANCE    20,5
 BLOCK7   TRANSFER   ,BLOCK2
*
 BLOCK8   GENERATE   500
 BLOCK9   TERMINATE  1

          START      1
          END
```

Initiate a Test-Mode simulation with this Model File, then use a series of **clock** traps and **run** commands to move through the simulation. Select small enough clock-trap times so that at least five interrupts will occur before the "output pending" message is produced. You may have to do some experimentation in this regard. Display the Current and Future Events Chains each time you are given control, and use the information provided in these chain displays to satisfy yourself that you completely understand what is happening.

5. This exercise involves experimenting to see how GPSS/H responds to two invalid commands.

(a) Initiate a Test-Mode simulation with the fig53.gps Model File. Set a **clock** trap of your own choosing. Then, without issuing a **run** command, try to set another **clock** trap. How does GPSS/H respond?

(b) Initiate a Test-Mode simulation with the fig53.gps Model File. Set a **clock** trap at time 75, then issue a **run** command. When you are in control again, issue another command to set a **clock** trap at time 75. How does GPSS/H respond?

*6. Discuss the similarities and differences between **scan** and **clock** traps.

*7. There was a time when GPSS/H did not have a **trap scan** command. In the absence of this command, the user could make do with **trap clock** commands in a Test-Mode simulation to gain control at the beginning of *each* Scan Phase (except for the time 0.0 Scan Phase if the CEC was empty at that time). Explain how **trap clock** commands can be used to achieve this purpose. Is it necessary to make any assumptions in this regard? Do the **trap clock** and **trap scan** techniques seem to be equally satisfactory for this purpose? If not, which technique seems to be superior, and why?

6 Fundamental Modeling of Single Servers

6.1 Preview

This chapter describes the principal method used in GPSS/H to model single servers. Two new types of Blocks, SEIZE and RELEASE, are introduced for this purpose. The properties of the SEIZE and RELEASE Blocks are discussed and related to the logic involved in modeling single servers in general. The fundamental use of these Blocks is then illustrated. (More imaginative modeling of single servers is presented in Chapter 8.)

6.2 The Nature of Servers

In simplest terms, a server is a person or thing (or perhaps a combination of the two, working as an integrated unit) that provides service of one kind or another. Here are some examples of servers who are people:

1. An assembly-line worker
2. A repairperson
3. A tool crib clerk
4. A doctor
5. A barber

Here are some examples of servers that are things:

1. A drilling machine
2. An automated guided vehicle (AGV) for transporting work-in-process from point to point in a manufacturing system
3. A berth used by a ship to load or unload cargo
4. A printer attached to a computer system
5. An operating room in a hospital

Servers are usually components of systems. Servers are **resources**. Because servers are often limited in number, they usually are **scarce** resources (**constrained** resources) in systems.

The term **server** (or the phrase **single server**) is used here to describe a resource that can only respond to **one request for service at a time**. For example, some drilling machines can only drill holes in one casting at a time. Only one ship at a time can use a berth to load or unload cargo. A printer attached to a computer can only print one file at a time. A barber only cuts one person's hair at a time.

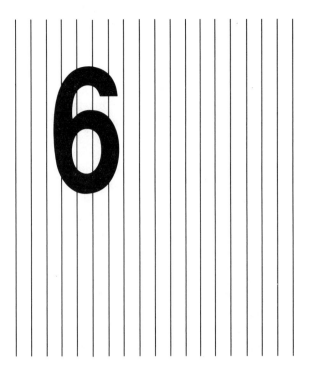

Whether a server can be **expected** to provide service depends on whether the server is **on duty** and **in working order**. For example, suppose a tool crib clerk works from 8 A.M. until noon, then gets a one-hour lunch break, and then works from 1 P.M. until 5 P.M. While on duty (from 8 A.M. until noon and 1 P.M. until 5), the clerk is expected to provide service on request. While off duty, however (from noon until 1 P.M.), the clerk is on his or her own time and is not responsible for providing service. Similarly, suppose that after a period of use, a machine breaks down. The machine then cannot provide service until after it has been repaired. As another example, even though a machine has not broken down, its services might be withdrawn temporarily to carry out preventive maintenance on it. While the preventive maintenance is taking place, the machine cannot be expected to provide service.

Even when a server can be expected to provide service on request, the server may not be able to respond **immediately** when asked to do so. For example, if a server is providing service to an earlier requestor when one or more new requests for service are made, the new requestors probably will have to wait their turn to be served.

In some systems, **preemptive** use of some servers is permitted. Preemption involves having a requestor come along and take a server away from someone (or something) else, even though the someone (or something) else is not yet finished using the server. For example, suppose you are sitting in a professor's office, getting help with an assignment. The phone rings. The professor interrupts the conversation with you, and answers the phone. Thinking of the professor as a server and the person on the other end of the phone as a requestor, this new requestor has just taken the server away from you, even though you aren't yet done being served!

Suppose a server finishes a service when two or more other requestors are waiting their turn to be served. The server must then decide whom to serve next. A number of alternative rules might be used to make this decision. The rule used is called the **service rule**, or the **queue discipline**, and the order in which requestors are served is called the **service order.** Here are some examples of service rules and service orders:

1. First-Come, First-Served. When the service rule is "first-come, first-served" (FCFS, sometimes known as "first-in, first-out," or FIFO), requestors are served in the **chronological order** in which the requests are made.

2. First-Come, First-Served, within Priority Level. In this variation on first-come, first-served, priority levels are assigned to the individual requestors. (For example, a person with appendicitis might be given higher priority for operating room use than a person waiting to use the operating room for routine exploratory surgery.) Highest-priority requestors are served first (using a FCFS service rule to break ties among these highest-priority requestors); then requestors at the next lower Priority Level are served (again using a FCFS service rule to break ties); and so on. The simple FCFS service rule is a degenerate case of the "first-come, first-served within priority level" service rule. (FCFS within priority level is simply FCFS when all requestors have one and the same priority.)

3. Shortest Processing Time. In the shortest processing time (SPT) service rule, requestors are prioritized on the basis of their **expected** service time (that is, on the basis of the **average** amount of time required to serve them; in general, the time their service will **actually** require is a random variable whose value is not known until after the service has been completed). The **smaller** the expected service time, the **higher** the priority given to the requestor. The next requestor to be served is the one with the smallest expected service time. (For example, jobs waiting for a printer in a computing system might be given priority levels that are inversely proportional to the number of pages to be printed. A job requiring the printing of only 5 pages will get higher priority than will a job involving the printing of 100 pages.) The SPT service rule is a simple form of the first-come, first-served within priority level service rule, a form in which expected service time is used as the basis for determining priority level.

Not all requestors wait for a server until their turn comes. For example, if there are already many waiting requestors, a newly arriving **potential** requestor might **balk**, that is, change plans and follow some other course of action. It's also possible that, having waited for some time, a requestor might decide to **renege**, that is, stop waiting and follow another course of action.

Some of the resources in a system might take the form of single servers, and others might take the form of groups of **two or more identical** servers. In a hospital, for example, there might be two general surgeons on the staff. These two surgeons might be identical in terms of their characteristics as surgeons. Two or more identical servers can be modeled as individual single servers or can be modeled on a grouped basis (that is, collectively).

Only general comments have been made so far in this section about the nature of servers. We now outline GPSS/H capabilities in terms of the foregoing ideas. In GPSS/H, single servers can be modeled individually, and such servers can be made subject to preemption. The servers in a group of identical servers can be modeled either on a grouped basis or individually. And, whether modeled individually or collectively, servers can be moved back and forth between "on-duty" ("in working order") and "off-duty" ("not in working order") states. Almost any service order can be modeled in GPSS/H. (The **default service order** is first-come, first-served within priority level, as we will see.) Finally, both balking and reneging can be modeled in GPSS/H.

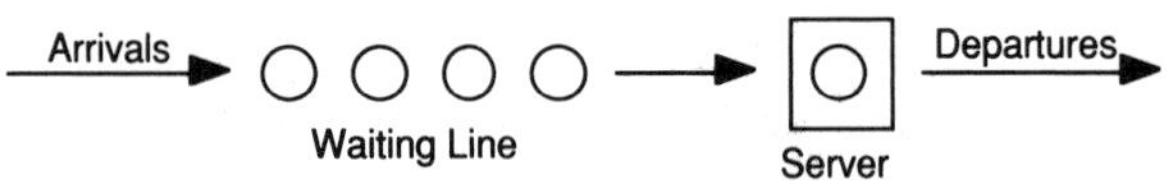

Figure 6.1 *A Spatial Representation of a Single-Server Queuing System*

6.3 Logical Considerations Involved in Modeling a Single Server

A single-server system can be visualized in spatial terms as shown in Figure 6.1, where circles are units of traffic (such as customers or work-in-process) that have come to be served, the square is the server, and the circle within the square is a unit of traffic being served. The line formed by units of traffic waiting for service is often called a **queue**. The combination of the server, the unit of traffic being served, and those waiting for service is termed a **queuing system**. For example, the server might be a drilling machine in a manufacturing system, and the units of traffic might be castings (units of work-in-process) that need to have a hole drilled in them by the machine.

Instead of visualizing a single-server system spatially, as in Figure 6.1, it is useful to take a **time-oriented view** of such a system. In a time-oriented view of a system through which traffic moves, we imagine a typical unit of traffic and identify the steps it takes as it works its way through the system. We arrange these steps in chronological order, and we then mark them off in general terms on a time axis.

To illustrate the time-oriented view of a single-server system, suppose we want to be served by a single server, such as the clerk at an express checkout counter in a supermarket. We go through five steps in the process, as shown in Figure 6.2. In step 1, we arrive at the express checkout lane, requesting

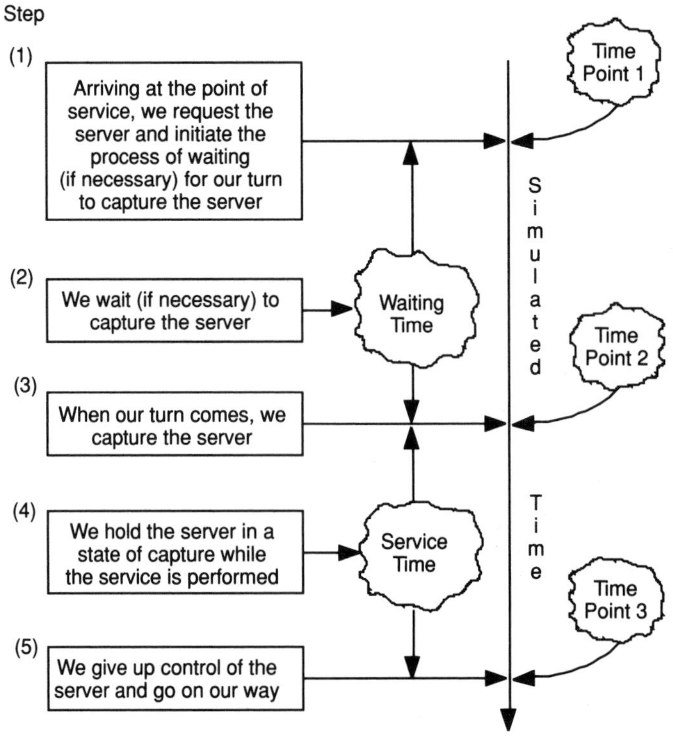

Figure 6.2 *The Five Steps Involved in Using a Single Server*

the clerk and **initiating** the process of waiting (if necessary) to take control of the clerk. This step occurs at a **point in time**, shown as Time Point 1 in Figure 6.2. In step 2, we wait (if necessary) to capture the server. This step in general consumes an **interval of time** ("Waiting Time"), as shown in Figure 6.2. In step 3, we capture the clerk (that is, we take control of the clerk). This step occurs at a **point in time**, shown as Time Point 2 in Figure 6.2. This step **ends** the Waiting Time interval, and **initiates** the process of receiving service. In step 4, we hold the clerk in a state of capture while we are being served. This step consumes an **interval of time** ("Service Time"), as shown in Figure 6.2. Finally, in step 5, when we are finished being served, we give up control over the clerk, **ending** the step 4 Service Time interval, and move on. Step 5 occurs at a **point in time**, shown as Time Point 3 in Figure 6.2.

If the server can be captured **immediately** when service is requested, Time Point 1 will coincide with Time Point 2 in Figure 6.2. Waiting Time is zero in this case.

The preceding discussion involves logic that must be taken into account one way or another, no matter what language or medium is used to model a single server. GPSS/H supports the modeling of single servers by providing types of Blocks corresponding to steps 3 and 5 in Figure 6.2. (The ADVANCE Block of Chapter 3 can be used to model step 4.) These two Block types are introduced in the next section.

6.4 Modeling Servers Individually: The Facility Entity

A GPSS/H **entity** is a tool (or an integrated set of tools) that can be used to accomplish frequently occurring objectives in modeling. For example, GPSS/H provides **Transactions** as a type of entity that can be used to model the discrete units of traffic that move through many types of systems. GPSS/H provides several dozen types of entities for use in building simulation models. The set of tools corresponding to most entity types, or classes, usually involves one or more **types of Blocks** having characteristics that support common objectives in the building of models.

GPSS/H provides the **Facility entity** as a tool for modeling single servers. The Facility entity provides two types of Blocks for use in modeling several important aspects of the Figure 6.2 logic. One type of Block (the SEIZE Block) supports the logic called for in step 3 (and, indirectly, in steps 1 and 2). The other type of Block (the RELEASE Block) supplies the logic called for in step 5.

When the Facility entity is used to model a single server, Transactions are used to model the requestors who use the single server. For example, if a Facility models the clerk working at an express checkout counter, then Transactions will be used to model the shoppers who are served by the clerk. The five-step process in Figure 6.2 is then implemented in GPSS/H by providing a sequence of Blocks through which Xacts (one Xact per user of the single server) move to simulate the five-step process.

To request control of a single server and initiate a waiting process if necessary (Time Point 1 and step 1, Figure 6.2), an Xact **tries** to move from its Current Block into a SEIZE Block (its Next Block Attempted). If the server is under the control of some other Xact at the time, the requesting Xact is **denied entry** to the SEIZE Block (it encounters a **blocking condition**) and remains in its Current Block. That is, the requesting Xact is **forced to wait** its turn to take control of the server (Step 2, Figure 6.2). When the requesting Xact's turn later comes, the Xact moves from its Current Block into the SEIZE, executing the SEIZE and taking control of the server (Time Point 2 and step 3, Figure 6.2). And to give up control of the server later, the Xact executes a RELEASE Block (Time Point 3 and step 5, Figure 6.2).

Having executed a SEIZE at Time Point 2, an Xact then controls the single server until it eventually executes a RELEASE at Time Point 3. An Xact simply **takes control** of the server by executing the SEIZE; it doesn't have to remain in the SEIZE to remain in control of the server.

SEIZE is the first example of a Block type that can **conditionally deny entry** to a Transaction. As stated earlier, there are only five types of GPSS/H Blocks that have this characteristic. These Blocks are often used to **control access to scarce resources.** (This is true of the SEIZE Block, for example, which controls access to a single server by forcing Xacts to **wait until** their turn comes to be served.) More generally, they can be used to force Xacts to wait at selected points in a model until the state of the model permits them to move forward once again.

The general form of SEIZE and RELEASE Blocks is shown in Figure 6.3. Each of these Block types has an A Operand. The role of the A Operand is to identify the particular single server ("Facility") that an Xact requests control of by trying to execute a SEIZE Block or gives up control of by executing a RELEASE Block.

A **specific** Facility (server) must be identified at SEIZE and RELEASE Blocks, because there may be

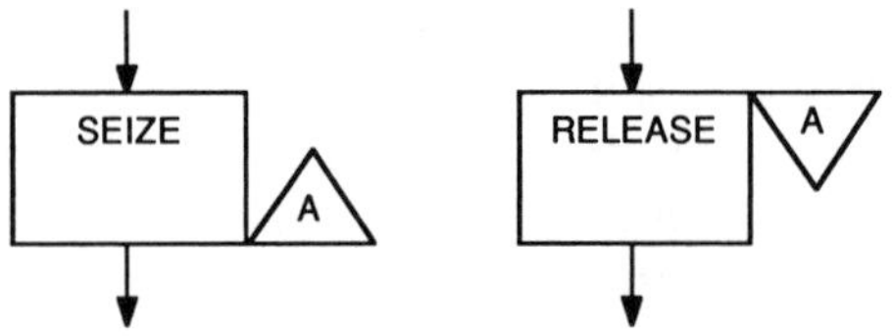

Operand	Significance	Default Value
A	The identifier for the Facility being requested/captured (at the SEIZE) or being given up (at the RELEASE)	No Default

Figure 6.3 *The SEIZE and RELEASE Blocks and Their A Operand*

two or more Facilities in a model (just as there may be two or more single servers in a system). This makes it necessary to indicate at a SEIZE Block **which** Facility is being requested, and at a RELEASE Block **which** Facility is being returned to a state of idleness. (We are using the term "Facility" as a synonym for "single server.") Distinctions are made among Facilities by giving each its own unique **identifier**, or **name**. Examples of such identifiers are DRILL, TUGBOAT, JENNIFER, JOE, DOCTOR21, and AGENT007.

Symbolic identifiers consist of from one to eight

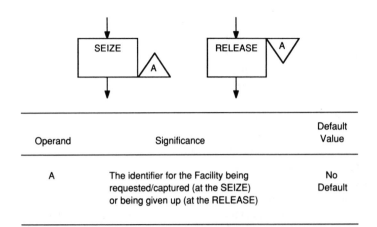

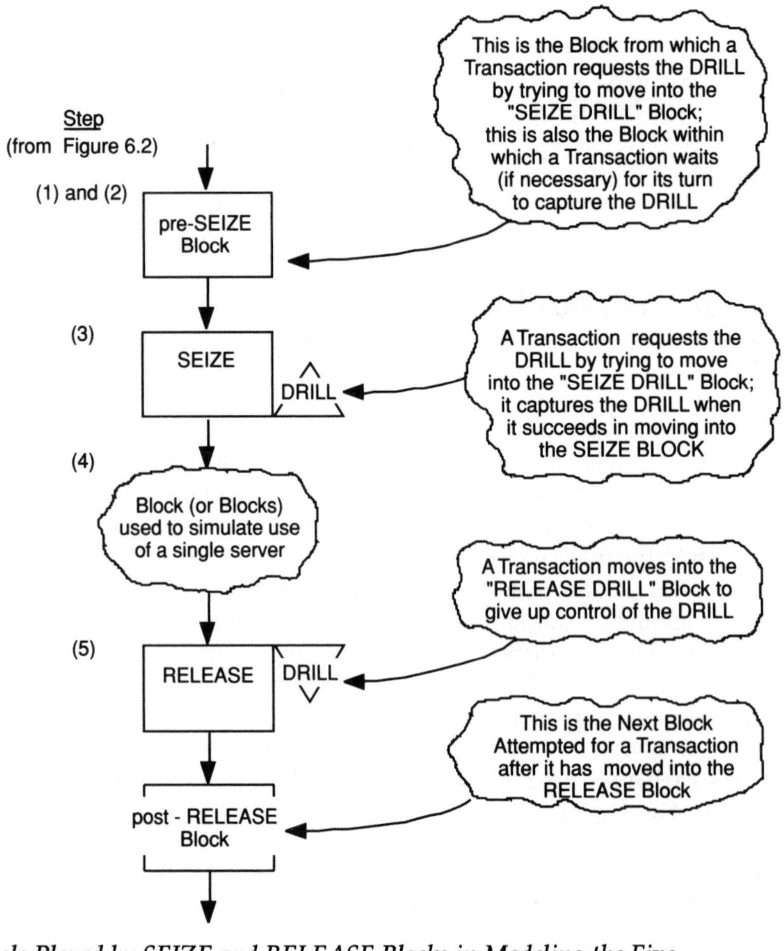

Figure 6.4 *The Role Played by SEIZE and RELEASE Blocks in Modeling the Five Steps Involved in Using a Single Server*

alphanumeric characters, the first of which must be alphabetic. Symbolic identifiers should (but don't have to) begin with a **minimum of three alphabetic characters** to avoid having them accidentally match or begin with a GPSS/H **reserved word**. (A reserved word is a sequence of characters that has a predefined meaning.) The rule for forming Facility identifiers is the same as for forming Block Labels (Block identifiers).

(**Caution:** Do not use the same identifier for a Facility as for a Block. The reason for this is that dual use of an identifier for a Block and a Facility may force GPSS/H to use more computer memory than would be used otherwise. It is beyond the scope of this book to explain this situation in detail.)

Facility identifiers can also be positive whole numbers, such as 1, or 5, or 12. Models that identify Facilities symbolically are much more readable than are those that use numbers for this purpose. For example, if a Facility simulates a drill, then it is better to refer to the Facility as DRILL than as Facility 9. Only symbolic identifiers will be used in this book.

Now assume that a drilling machine is a server in a manufacturing system, and that Xacts simulating castings ("casting-Xacts") come to this machine to have a hole drilled in them. Using DRILL as the identifier for a Facility, Figure 6.4 shows how SEIZE and RELEASE Blocks can be positioned in a model to provide the logic called for in steps 1, 2, 3, and 5 of Figure 6.2. As indicated, an Xact requests a Facility by trying to move into a SEIZE Block whose A Operand identifies the Facility being requested. The Xact making this request is in some other Block at the time (shown as the "pre-SEIZE Block" in Figure 6.4) and makes the request by trying to move from this Block (its Current Block) into a SEIZE Block (its Next Block Attempted). If the indicated Facility is **idle** (not captured), the requesting Xact executes the SEIZE Block without delay, putting the Facility into a state of capture. In contrast, if the Facility is under the control of some other Xact at the time, the requesting Xact is denied entry (blocked) by the SEIZE Block. It then stops moving for the time being, remaining in its Current Block, the "pre-SEIZE Block."

A pre-SEIZE Block can be any type of Block. The pre-SEIZE is simply the requesting Xact's Current Block. An Xact's first attempt to move from its pre-SEIZE Block into a SEIZE establishes a request on the part of that Xact for control of the indicated Facility. If the Facility is under another Xact's control at the time, the pre-SEIZE Block provides a Current Block within which the requesting Xact can wait until its turn comes to capture the Facility. It is the pre-SEIZE Block within which an Xact spends the "Waiting Time" shown as step 2 in Figure 6.2.

What eventually becomes of the Xact (or Xacts) that is (are) blocked by a SEIZE and temporarily remains in a pre-SEIZE Block? When the Xact controlling the Facility gives up control of it, this has the effect of **unblocking** these waiting Xacts. GPSS/H therefore "writes a note to itself" as a reminder that it must **later (but at the same simulated time)** turn its attention to these now-unblocked Xacts. (The method GPSS/H uses to "write a note to itself" is described in the next chapter.) When GPSS/H later turns its attention to these Xacts, they will be given a chance, one by one, to retry to take control of the Facility. The **first** such Xact to retry will move into the SEIZE, taking control of the Facility and proceeding on its way from there. When any remaining Xacts are given their turn to retry to move into the SEIZE, they will find the Facility has already been captured by another Xact (the first to retry), so they will continue to be blocked and continue to remain temporarily within the pre-SEIZE Block.

From a **Block-oriented** point of view, Xacts are in a pre-SEIZE Block while waiting their turn to take control of a Facility. From a **chain-oriented** point of view, these Xacts are on the **Current Chain**, waiting until they can resume movement. We know that Xacts are arranged on the CEC in order of decreasing (nonincreasing) Priority. We also know that during a Scan Phase, Xacts on the CEC are dealt with in front-to-back order. And we have seen that the order in which unblocked Xacts retry to move into a SEIZE Block determines which Xact is the next to capture the server. In terms of ideas discussed so far, it follows that retries take place in the order of **first-come, first-served within Priority Level**, which is the default service order in GPSS/H.

What happens to an Xact after it takes control of a Facility by executing a SEIZE? The Xact continues to move along its path from Block to Block until it can move no farther at that simulated time. In other words, having moved into a SEIZE Block, the Xact immediately tries to move from the SEIZE (its new Current Block) into the sequential Block (its new Next Block Attempted), and so on. The one or more Blocks following the SEIZE specify the logic for the Xact's use of the Facility it now controls. This is indicated as step 4 in Figure 6.4. In general, the logic for an Xact's use of a server can be quite complicated. For now, we indicate in Figure 6.4 that the step 4 "cloud" contains the "Block (or Blocks) used to simulate use of the single server." (In simple cases, the content of the step 4 cloud will be an

ADVANCE Block used to simulate service time.)

After an Xact has gained control of and used a Facility, it gives up control (returning the Facility to a state of idleness) by executing a RELEASE Block. This use of a RELEASE by an Xact is shown as step 5 in Figure 6.4. It is when an Xact executes a RELEASE that GPSS/H "writes a note to itself" as a reminder that it must later (but at the same simulated time) turn its attention to any Xacts that have become unblocked as a result.

When an Xact captures a Facility, GPSS/H remembers the id number of the capturing Xact. When an Xact executes a RELEASE, GPSS/H checks the id number of the releasing Xact to make certain that this Xact is the one that currently holds the Facility in a state of capture. If it isn't, an execution error results, an Error Message is written out, and the simulation is stopped.

It follows that if an Xact tries to RELEASE a Facility that is not currently captured, an error condition occurs, an Error Message is written out, and the simulation is stopped.

What happens to an Xact after it has given up control of a Facility by executing a RELEASE? The Xact immediately tries to move from the RELEASE Block (its Current Block) into the sequential Block (its Next Block). The Block sequential to the RELEASE is shown in general as a "post-RELEASE Block" in Figure 6.4. This "post-RELEASE Block" can be almost any type of Block. In practice, the post-RELEASE Block will be the first in a sequence of Blocks used to simulate the next series of moves the Xact wants to make. (In simple cases, the post-RELEASE Block might be a TERMINATE.)

SEIZE and RELEASE are **logically complementary** Blocks. Execution of the second Block in the pair undoes the effect of execution of the first in the pair. When a SEIZE is executed, a Facility is put into a state of capture; in complementary fashion, when a corresponding RELEASE is executed, the Facility is put back into a state of idleness. Many GPSS/H Blocks take the form of complementary pairs.

6.5 Other Blocks for the Facility Entity

It was pointed out in Section 6.2 that servers can be moved back and forth between "on-duty" ("in working order") and "off-duty" ("not in working order") states in GPSS/H. This is done by making use of a logically complementary pair of Blocks for which the Operation words are FAVAIL (for "Facility available") and FUNAVAIL ("Facility unavailable"). (In GPSS/H, "available" means "on duty," or "in working order," whereas "unavailable" means "not on duty," or "not in working order.") If these types of Blocks are not used in a model, then each Facility in the model is "on duty" ("available") 100 percent of the time. Each Facility in a model is initially in an "idle and on-duty" state. If a model contains no FAVAIL or FUNAVAIL Blocks, then each Facility in the model will be "on duty" 100 percent of the time. (This book doesn't go into operational details of FAVAIL and FUNAVAIL use.)

It was also pointed out in Section 6.2 that single servers can be made subject to preemption in GPSS/H. This is done by making use of a logically complementary pair of Blocks for which the Operation words are PREEMPT and RETURN. If these types of Blocks are not used in a model, then no Facilities in the model are subject to preemption, and no preemptive use will be made of them. (This book doesn't go into operational details of PREEMPT and RETURN use.)

6.6 Facility Reports

During a simulation, GPSS/H gathers information for each Facility in a model and then produces a postsimulation report for each Facility. Figure 6.5 provides an example of a Facility Report for a Facility named OVEN. (This report is produced at the

(1)	(2)	(3)	(4)	(5)	(6)	(7)	(8)	(9)	(10)
	--AVG-UTIL-DURING--								
FACILITY	TOTAL TIME	AVAIL TIME	UNAVL TIME	ENTRIES	AVERAGE TIME/XACT	CURRENT STATUS	PERCENT AVAIL	SEIZING XACT	PREEMPTING XACT
OVEN	.800			240	8.000	AVAIL	100.0	5	

Figure 6.5 *An Example of a Facility Report*

end of the simulation in Case Study 6A, presented in Section 6.10.) In Figure 6.5, numbers in parentheses have been placed over each column in the report. (These column numbers are not part of the report, but have been added to support discussion.) The information in each column will now be discussed by column number.

(1) The **FACILITY** column indicates the **identifier** used for the Facility.

(2) **– –AVG-UTIL-DURING– – TOTAL TIME** shows the fraction of **total** simulated time the Facility was in a state of capture. (This entry is .800 in Figure 6.5, corresponding to 80 percent OVEN utilization.)

(3) **– –AVG-UTIL-DURING– – AVAIL TIME** shows the fraction of **available** simulated time the Facility was in a state of capture. A Facility's "available simulated time" is the amount of simulated time the Facility was "on duty" ("in working order"), per the discussion of that concept in Section 6.2. In this book, each Facility used in a model will **always** be "on duty" throughout a simulation, and so "available simulated time" will always equal total simulated time. In such cases, the column 3 entry equals the column 2 entry and is not printed.

(4) **– –AVG-UTIL-DURING– – UNAVL TIME** shows the fraction of **unavailable** simulated time the Facility was in a state of capture. A Facility's "unavailable simulated time" is the amount of simulated time the Facility was "off duty" ("not in working order"). In this book, "unavailable simulated time" for Facilities will always be zero. In such cases, the conceptual entry in column 4 of the report for Facilities is also zero, but this zero is not printed. The column is left blank instead.

(5) **ENTRIES** indicates the number of times the Facility was put into a state of capture during the simulation. We will sometimes use **Capture Count** as a synonym for ENTRIES. The Figure 6.5 report indicates the OVEN was captured on 240 occasions.

If ENTRIES for a Facility is zero, **no report will be produced** for that Facility.

(6) **AVERAGE TIME/XACT** shows the average holding time per capture of the Facility. For example, if a Facility's Capture Count (ENTRIES) is 3, and if the Facility was held for 50, 100, and 60 simulated time units during captures 1, 2, and 3, respectively, then the average holding time per capture is 70 simulated time units ((50 + 100 + 60)/3 = 70). The average holding time per OVEN capture in the Figure 6.5 report is 8.000 time units.

(7) **CURRENT STATUS** indicates the Facility's "on-duty" ("in working order") versus "off-duty" ("not in working order") status at the time the report was produced. **AVAIL** means "on duty" ("in working order"), whereas **UNAVAIL** means "off duty" ("not in working order"). In models in which Facilities are always "on duty," the column 7 entry in Facility Reports will always be AVAIL, as in Figure 6.5. This will be the case throughout this book.

(8) **PERCENT AVAIL** shows the fraction of the total simulated time that the Facility was "on duty" ("in working order"). In models in which Facilities are always "on duty," this entry will be 100.0 percent, as in Figure 6.5. A value of 100 percent will be displayed in this column throughout this book.

(9) **SEIZING XACT** shows the **id number** of the Transaction (if any) that has the Facility captured at the time the report is produced. In the Figure 6.5 report, Xact 5 holds the OVEN in a state of capture. If a Facility is not captured, the SEIZING XACT column is blank.

A Facility's CURRENT STATUS (column 7) can be AVAIL ("available") even though the Facility is in a state of capture (even though the SEIZING XACT column is nonblank). This sounds like a contradiction, but it isn't. A server (or resource) can be **both** "on duty" ("available") **and** captured ("seized") at one and the same time. (The apparent contradiction in the phrase **available and captured** arises because, in everyday terms, the word "available" often means "not busy now," or "not tied up now," but in GPSS/H the word "available" has the **restricted and specialized meaning** of "on duty" ("in working order") and has nothing to do with the concept of "idle" versus "captured.")

(10) **PREEMPTING XACT** shows the **id number** of the Xact (if any) holding the Facility in a state of preemption at the time the report is produced. A Facility is put into a state of preemption if an Xact takes the Facility away from another Xact

and begins to use it itself, as discussed in Section 6.2. In models that do not provide for the possibility of preemptive Facility use, column 10 in Facility Reports will always be blank, as in Figure 6.5. This column will always be blank throughout this book.

In addition to being provided as part of postsimulation output, Facility Reports can be displayed by the user in Test Mode. This is done by using the **display fac** command, where **fac** means Facility.

6.7 More About the Steps Followed by GPSS/H in a Batch Simulation

In Section 6.10, we will show the use of a Facility in a simulation carried out in Batch Mode. Before reaching this point, it will be useful to review and extend somewhat the steps followed by GPSS/H in a Batch simulation. These steps were presented in Figure 2.19 of Chapter 2 to provide the basis for introducing the idea of a Test-Mode simulation. For convenience, Figure 2.19 is repeated and slightly extended here as Figure 6.6. You should now review Figure 6.6 and, if necessary, reread the Section 2.19 discussion of these steps.

The slight difference between Figures 6.6 and 2.19 involves the response of GPSS/H to an execution error. The initial response is to write an Error Report (see Box 6 in either figure). In Figure 2.19, GPSS/H then stops. This is what will happen if the user is not on-line at the time. For example, if the user submits a long job to be executed on a mainframe computer overnight (when billing rates are low, and/or when the load on the system is relatively light), then the user will not be on-line when the Batch simulation takes place.

In contrast, Figure 6.6 shows that after an execution Error Report is written at Box 6, GPSS/H usu-

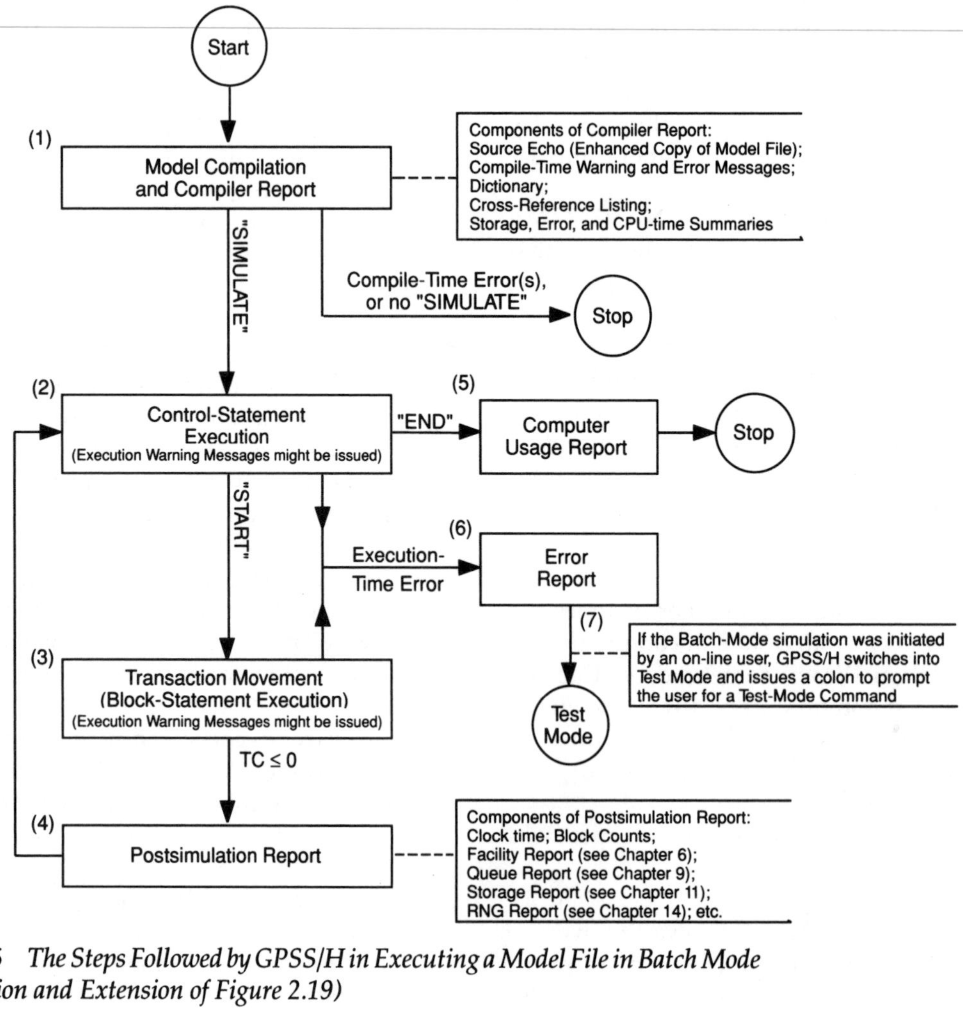

Figure 6.6 *The Steps Followed by GPSS/H in Executing a Model File in Batch Mode (a Repetition and Extension of Figure 2.19)*

ally goes into Test Mode if the user is on-line. GPSS/H displays an "unplanned entry to GPSS/H debug" message at this point, then prompts the on-line user to enter a Test-Mode command. The user then assumes control, and can use the **display** command, for example, to investigate the state of the model, if desirable, before quitting the simulation. (Remember that to change the model itself, however, the user must quit GPSS/H, edit the model, and then recompile.)

The user of DOS GPSS/H will be sitting at a computer when making Batch runs, and so will be on-line if and when an execution error occurs. Figure 6.6 consequently applies in this case. If an execution error occurs, an Error Message will be displayed on the screen; then GPSS/H will enter Test Mode; and so on.

6.8 Running GPSS/H in Batch Mode Under DOS

The simplest DOS command that can be used to make a Batch run takes this form:

```
gpssh file_name.gps
```

In ***file_name*.gps**, ***file_name*** represents the name of the Model File, and **gps** is the file extension. (If the extension is not specified, **gps** is assumed.) This command matches the one used to carry out Test-Mode simulations, except that the Test-Mode command additionally specifies **test** (either spelled out as such, or included in an abbreviated form such as **tvtnw**).

Output produced by GPSS/H during a Batch simulation is put into the file ***file_name*.lis**, where ***file_name*** stands for the name of the Model File. When the DOS command shown is used, this output will include the Compiler Report (see the comments attached to Box 1 in Figure 6.6), any execution Warning Messages (see Boxes 2 and 3 in Figure 6.6), the Postsimulation Report (see the comments attached to Box 4 in Figure 6.6), and either the Computer Usage Report (see Box 5) or the Error Report (see Box 6). If the user is on-line, any Warning Messages and the Error Report (if there is one) will also be displayed at the user's computer screen.

For an example of the foregoing DOS command, the model in Case Study 6A (to be presented in Section 6.10) was run by issuing this DOS command:

```
gpssh model6a.gps
```

The output produced when DOS executed this command was put into the output file **model6a.lis**. (Options for looking at this output after completion of the simulation are reviewed in Section 6.11.)

6.9 Documentation Pattern for Case Studies

Ten case studies are presented in this book to illustrate features of GPSS/H. A case study is a complete example of a GPSS/H model and the results produced by a Batch simulation performed with it.

Following are the documentation components provided with each case study:

1. Statement of the Problem. This component provides a sufficiently detailed description of the problem so that a GPSS/H model for the system can be built and run. (A person studying this book should be able to read the Statement of the Problem and then build the model without reading further, using material presented up to the point of the case study.)

2. Approach Taken in Building the Model. This section explains how the system described in the problem has been put into the form of a GPSS/H model. The intention is to explain the thinking behind the approach used.

3. Table of Definitions. In building GPSS/H models, analogies are formed between GPSS/H entities, on the one hand, and elements in the system being modeled, on the other hand. Good model documentation includes a description of the analogies chosen by the modeler. The Table of Definitions provides this description. The Table of Definitions is a listing of the various GPSS/H entities and entity members used in the model, with a brief indication of what it is they represent in the system being modeled. The base time unit chosen by the modeler is indicated. Then the interpretation given to Xacts is provided. After that, alphabetic order is followed for the other entity classes and entity members and their interpretations.

4. Block Diagram. A Block Diagram is given for each case study. In a Block Diagram, a person quickly

sees what Blocks have been used in a model, and how they have been arranged to form the model. Brief comments are placed next to the Blocks in the Block Diagram to indicate what the Blocks simulate, or help to simulate, in the system being modeled.

5. **Modified Source Echo.** A Source Echo is an enhanced listing of the Model File that the compiler produces. The features of a Source Echo are described in Case Study 6A. We won't use all the information provided in a Source Echo, and so only a modified form of the Source Echo is presented in general in the case studies. (Details are provided in Case Study 6A.)

6. **Postsimulation Report.** Selected components of the Postsimulation Report that GPSS/H produces are shown to provide results of the simulation and as a basis for discussion. On occasion, the Postsimulation Report is only summarized.

7. **Discussion.** Discussion of a case study may involve model logic, model implementation, and the Postsimulation Report.

   Model Logic. When appropriate, features of the Block Diagram are discussed to relate them to aspects of the problem itself or to the particular approach taken for interpretation of the problem in a GPSS/H context.

   Model Implementation. This part of the discussion deals with Control Statements and other non-Block aspects of the Model File.

   Postsimulation Report. The Postsimulation Report may be evaluated from time to time in terms of the answers it provides to questions asked or implied in the problem statement. A major purpose of the case studies, however, is to show how to build and run GPSS/H models. Detailed discussion of the Postsimulation Report is not always necessary to support this purpose.

6.10 Case Study 6A: Modeling a Widget Manufacturing System

1. Statement of the Problem

A two-step process is required to build widgets in a manufacturing system. In the first step, an assembly step, a worker puts together the pieces of material making up a widget. This takes 30 ± 5 minutes. In the second step, the same worker then uses an oven to heat-treat the widget. This takes 8 ± 2 minutes. After heat treating, the widget is finished, and the worker begins the process of building another widget.

Because ovens are expensive, there is only one oven in the system. Workers compete with each other for use of this oven, which can only heat-treat one widget at a time. Service order for oven use is first-come, first-served.

Workers work independently of each other. And workers always heat-treat the widget they are currently building before beginning to assemble another widget.

Figure 6A.1 shows the movement of work-in-process through the system. Four assembly stations are shown in the figure, which implies that there can be as many as four workers in the system.

Assuming that there are four workers and there is never a shortage of material for building widgets, construct a model for this system. Let Xacts simu-

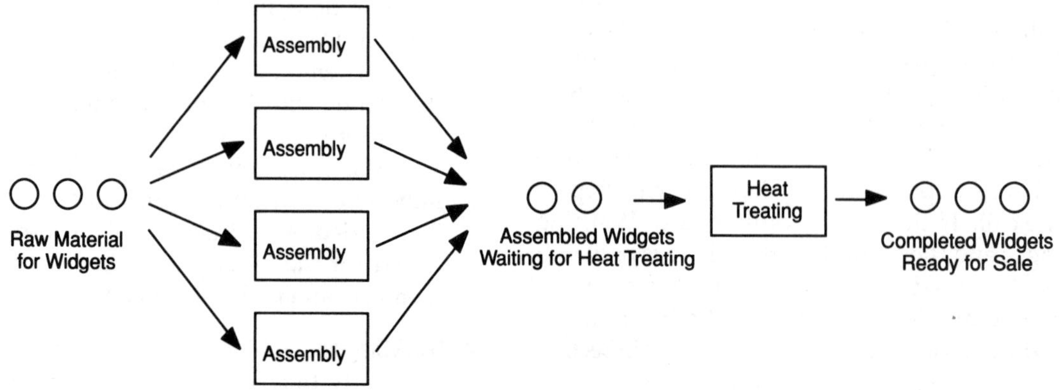

Figure 6A.1 A Flow Schematic for Case Study 5A

late the workers, and use the Facility OVEN to simulate the heat-treat oven. Use a base time unit of 1 minute. Assume that when the simulation starts, each of the four workers is at the point of starting to assemble another widget.

Design the model to simulate for 40 hours. This corresponds to five 8-hour shifts. Lunch breaks, breaks of other kinds, shift start-up, shift shutdown, and interruptions between shifts are to be ignored in the model. Whether the system operates 1, 2, or 3 shifts a day does not matter in the building of the model.

Perform a simulation with the model. In your simulation, how many widgets does the system produce in 40 hours? What part of the Postsimulation Report do you use to answer this question? Assuming that there is never any delay in use of the oven, carry out desk calculations to determine how many widgets the system can produce in 40 hours. Compare this ideal production rate to the one realized in the simulation.

You should now try your hand at building a model for this system before reading further.

2. Approach Taken in Building the Model

Here is a good approach to use in building GPSS/H models:

1. First, identify the *constraints* in the system to be modeled.
2. Then, make a decision about which GPSS/H entities to use to simulate these constraints in the model itself.

In the widget system, there are two constraints. First, there is only one oven. Second, there is some fixed number of workers who work in the system. It is natural to choose a Facility to simulate the oven (as suggested in the Statement of the Problem). And it is practical in this case to let Transactions simulate workers (as also suggested in the problem statement). Then, even as the workers can be thought of as circulating through the system as they move repeatedly through the assemble/heat-treat cycle, the worker-Xacts can loop repeatedly through the GPSS/H model of the system.

In this approach, there is no explicit representation of widgets as they move through the system. Widgets are indirectly represented by the workers who build them. The current state of a widget in the process of being built corresponds to the position of the worker-Xact at the time. (The worker-Xact might be in an ADVANCE and on the FEC, simulating assembly time; or in the same ADVANCE and on the CEC, waiting for the heat-treat oven; or in another ADVANCE and on the FEC, simulating heat-treat time. The corresponding widget is then being assembled, or is waiting for heat-treating, or is in the process of being heat-treated.) In an exercise later in the book, you'll be asked to build an alternative model for this system, letting Xacts explicitly simulate widgets and using another approach to model the workers. (See Exercise 1 of Section 11.20.)

In the system itself, after each worker takes a finished widget from the oven, the worker goes back to begin another assembly. In the model of the system, after a worker-Xact has released the OVEN Facility, it can be routed back via a TRANSFER to the ADVANCE that is used to simulate assembly time. And the Limit Count (D Operand) at the GENERATE Block that creates the worker-Xacts during the Scan Phase at time 0.0 can be used to fix the total number of worker-Xacts that loop through the model. Note that none of the worker-Xacts ever leave the model. (They never move into a TERMINATE Block.)

It's an easy matter to end Xact movement after 40 simulated hours. This only requires bringing in an Xact at the end of the fortieth hour and having it "TERMINATE 1". If Xact movement was initiated by executing a "START 1" statement, this brings Xact movement to an end. The Xact that carries out this task can be thought of as a "control-Xact." It does not represent an element in the system being modeled. Its purpose is to control the duration of the simulation. (You were asked to come up with a similar scheme in Exercise 7 of Section 2.23.)

3. Table of Definitions

The Table of Definitions for Case Study 6A is shown in Table 6A.1.

Table 6A.1

Table of definitions for Case Study 6A

Base Time Unit: 1 minute	
GPSS/H Entity	**Interpretation**
Transactions	
Model Segment 1	Workers
Model Segment 2	A control-Xact
Facilities	
OVEN	The heat-treating oven

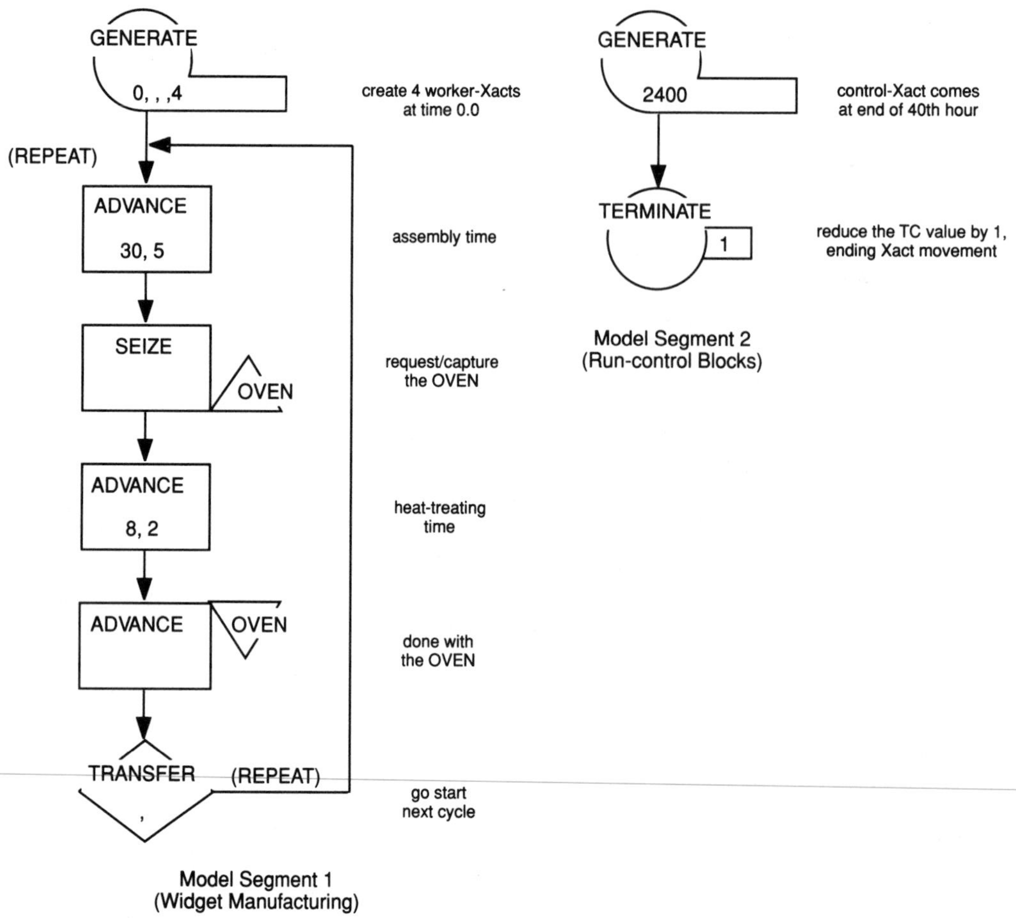

Figure 6A.2 *Block Diagram for Case Study 6A*

4. Block Diagram

The Block Diagram for Case Study 6A is shown in Figure 6A.2.

5. Modified Source Echo

The *unmodified* Source Echo of the Case Study 6A Model File is shown in Figure 6A.3. Numbers in parentheses have been placed over each column in the Source Echo. (These column numbers are not part of the Source Echo, but have been added to support discussion.) The information in each column will now be discussed by column number.

(1) The LINE# column shows the numbers of lines in the Model File. These numbers can sometimes be of use with editors which have a line-numbering capability. We won't use these numbers in this book.

(2) The STMT# column shows the number of each GPSS/H statement in the Model File, Comments Statements included. We'll refer to these numbers on occasion to support discussion of non-Block statements in the Model File.

(3) The IF column gives the current nesting depth of IF Control Statements. (IF Control Statements are not discussed in this book.)

(4) The DO column gives the current nesting depth of DO Control Statements. (DO statements are introduced in Chapter 14.)

(5) The BLOCK# column shows the number of the Location occupied by the corresponding Block in the model. In Figure 6A.3, note that the GENERATE Block is in Location 1, the ADVANCE Block labeled REPEAT is in Location 2, and so. (This means that the Block-Location identifier REPEAT has a fixed value of 2 in the Case Study 6A model.)

```
(1)    (2)   (3) (4)  (5)     (6)      (7)           (8)              (9)
LINE# STMT#   IF DO  BLOCK#   *LOC    OPERATION  A,B,C,D,E,F,G     COMMENTS

   1     1                              SIMULATE                                      Case Study 6A
   2     2                       *                                     A Widget-Manufacturing System
   3     3                       *                                          Base Time Unit: 1 Minute
   4     4                       ***********************************************************************
   5     5                       *          Model Segment 1 (Widget Manufacturing)                    *
   6     6                       ***********************************************************************
   7     7                       *
   8     8                  1               GENERATE    0,,,4        create 4 worker-Xacts at time 0.0
   9     9                  2     REPEAT    ADVANCE     30,5         assembly time
  10    10                  3               SEIZE       OVEN         request/capture the OVEN
  11    11                  4               ADVANCE     8,2          heat-treating time
  12    12                  5               RELEASE     OVEN         done with the OVEN
  13    13                  6               TRANSFER    ,REPEAT      go start next cycle
  14    14                       *
  15    15                       ***********************************************************************
  16    16                       *          Model Segment 2 (Run-Control Xact)                        *
  17    17                       ***********************************************************************
  18    18                       *
  19    19                  7               GENERATE    2400         control-Xact comes at end of 40th hour
  20    20                  8               TERMINATE   1            reduce the TC value by 1,
  21    21                       *                                   ending Xact movement
  22    22                       *
  23    23                       ***********************************************************************
  24    24                       *          Run-Control Statements                                    *
  25    25                       ***********************************************************************
  26    26                       *
  27    27                                  START       1            set TC = 1;  start Xact movement
  28    28                       *
  29    29                                  END                      end of Model-File execution
```

Figure 6A.3 *Source Echo of the Case Study 6A Model*

(6) Beginning in the *LOC column, columns 1–72 of each line in the Model File are displayed verbatim (that is, without modification) in the Source Echo. LOC corresponds to the Location field in each statement.

(7) OPERATION corresponds to the Operation field in each statement.

(8) A, B, C, D, E, F, G correspond to a statement's Operands.

(9) COMMENTS corresponds to the Comments field in each statement.

The fact that a Model File is a subset of a Source Echo is made clear in Figure 6A.4, where the Figure 6A.3 unmodified Source Echo is repeated, with a box drawn around the Model File itself.

The LINE#, IF, and DO columns in a Source Echo aren't of interest in this book. As a result, we'll eliminate these columns from Source Echoes, displaying a Modified Source Echo. The Modified Source Echo corresponding to the Figure 6A.3 Source Echo is shown in Figure 6A.5.

6. Postsimulation Report

The Postsimluation Report for Case Study 6A is shown in Figure 6A.6.

7. Discussion

Model Logic. The Case Study 6A model uses straightforward logic of the type that has been discussed extensively up to this point in the book. The following might be noted:

1. The basic structure of Model Segment 1, Figure 6A.2, corresponds to that shown for use of a single server in Figure 6.4. The pre-SEIZE Block of Figure 6.4 is "ADVANCE 30,5" in Figure 6A.2. The Blocks at Steps 3, 4, and 5 in Figure 6.4 are SEIZE/ADVANCE/ RELEASE in Figure 6A.2. The post-RELEASE Block of Figure 6.4 is "TRANSFER ,REPEAT" in Figure 6A.2. Instead of continually creating new Xacts to use the server in Figure 6A.2, the model causes one and the same set of four Xacts to use the server repeatedly. (In Exercise 8 of Section 6.12, you're

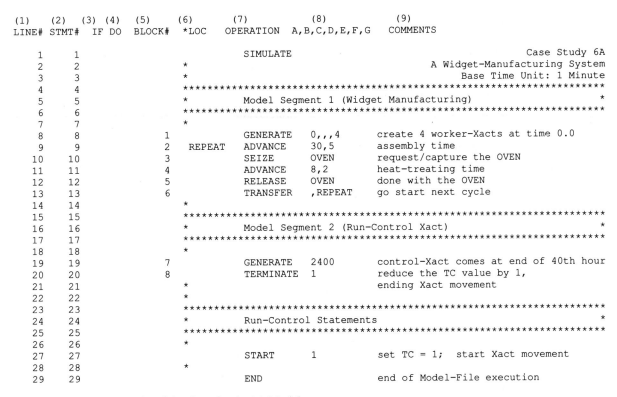

asked to build a model which continually creates new Xacts to use a server, with no Xact using the server more than one time.)

2. The way GPSS/H handles zero interarrival times at the GENERATE Block in Location 1 (see Figure 6A.5) has been discussed in Chapter 4.
3. A model similar to this one (but without use of a Facility) is presented in Exercise 3 of Section 3.15.
4. The Block Label REPEAT has a fixed value of 2 in this model. (Note from Figure 6A.5 that REPEAT labels a Block which occupies Location 2 in the model.)
5. Worker-Xacts waiting to use the OVEN are in an ADVANCE Block and on the CEC, waiting to move into Block 3 (SEIZE). From the point of view of Block Counts, these worker-Xacts contribute to the Current Count at Block 2 (ADVANCE), even though their holding time at the ADVANCE has already elapsed.

Model Implementation. The decision variable in the problem (the number of workers to hire) is reflected in the model in the form of the Limit Count on the Block 1 GENERATE. To simulate with other values of the decision variable, it's necessary at this point in the book to use an editor to change the Limit Count, then simulate with the changed Model File. (You're asked to do this in the exercises that follow.) A method for automating this process within the confines of a single Model File will be introduced in Chapter 14.

The GENERATE/TERMINATE sequence in Locations 7 and 8 in the model alternatively could be shifted to Locations 1 and 2, with the Blocks now occupying Locations 1 through 6 shifting down to Locations 3 through 8. Repositioning the Blocks in this way would have no effect on the logic of the model.

Comments Statements have been used in the Model File (see the Figure 6A.4 Source Echo) to provide banners for the two block segments of which the model is composed and for the "Run-Control Statements." These banners are arbitrary, of course, but they do assist the human reader of the Model File by visually segmenting its components.

Postsimulation Report. The Postsimulation Report produced at the end of the Xact-Movement Phase is shown in Figure 6A.6. Components of the report have been labeled part (a), part (b), and so on, to accommodate the following discussion.

Figure 6A.6(a) shows the values of the simulated clocks when the report was produced. Both the Relative and Absolute Clocks have identical values,

```
(1)    (2)   (3) (4)   (5)      (6)       (7)          (8)           (9)
LINE# STMT#   IF DO  BLOCK#   *LOC   OPERATION  A,B,C,D,E,F,G    COMMENTS

  1     1                          SIMULATE                                     Case Study 6A
  2     2                   *                                       A Widget-Manufacturing System
  3     3                   *                                            Base Time Unit: 1 Minute
  4     4                   ***********************************************************************
  5     5                   *       Model Segment 1 (Widget Manufacturing)                        *
  6     6                   ***********************************************************************
  7     7                   *
  8     8              1           GENERATE    0,,,4       create 4 worker-Xacts at time 0.0
  9     9              2    REPEAT ADVANCE     30,5        assembly time
 10    10              3           SEIZE       OVEN        request/capture the OVEN
 11    11              4           ADVANCE     8,2         heat-treating time
 12    12              5           RELEASE     OVEN        done with the OVEN
 13    13              6           TRANSFER    ,REPEAT     go start next cycle
 14    14                   *
 15    15                   ***********************************************************************
 16    16                   *       Model Segment 2 (Run-Control Xact)                            *
 17    17                   ***********************************************************************
 18    18                   *
 19    19              7           GENERATE    2400        control-Xact comes at end of 40th hour
 20    20              8           TERMINATE   1           reduce the TC value by 1,
 21    21                   *                              ending Xact movement
 22    22                   *
 23    23                   ***********************************************************************
 24    24                   *       Run-Control Statements                                        *
 25    25                   ***********************************************************************
 26    26                   *
 27    27                          START       1           set TC = 1;  start Xact movement
 28    28                   *
 29    29                          END                     end of Model-File execution
```

Figure 6A.4 *A Repetition of the Figure 6A.3 Source Echo, with the Model File Boxed In*

```
STMT#  BLOCK#  *LOC    OPERATION  A,B,C,D,E,F,G   COMMENTS

    1                  SIMULATE                               Case Study 6A
    2          *                                  A Widget-Manufacturing System
    3          *                                       Base Time Unit: 1 Minute
    4          ****************************************************************
    5          *       Model Segment 1 (Widget Manufacturing)                 *
    6          ****************************************************************
    7          *
    8       1          GENERATE    0,,,4       create 4 worker-Xacts at time 0.0
    9       2   REPEAT ADVANCE     30,5        assembly time
   10       3          SEIZE       OVEN        request/capture the OVEN
   11       4          ADVANCE     8,2         heat-treating time
   12       5          RELEASE     OVEN        done with the OVEN
   13       6          TRANSFER    ,REPEAT     go start next cycle
   14          *
   15          ****************************************************************
   16          *       Model Segment 2 (Run-Control Xact)                     *
   17          ****************************************************************
   18          *
   19       7          GENERATE    2400        control-Xact comes at end of 40th hour
   20       8          TERMINATE   1           reduce the TC value by 1,
   21          *                               ending Xact movement
   22          *
   23          ****************************************************************
   24          *       Run-Control Statements                                 *
   25          ****************************************************************
   26          *
   27                  START       1           set TC = 1;  start Xact movement
   28          *
   29                  END                     end of Model-File execution
```

Figure 6A.5 *Modified Source Echo Corresponding to the Source Echo of Figure 6A.3*

2400. (The distinction between these two clocks is not important to us now.)

Figure 6A.6(b) shows Block Counts. This Block Count information appears in three columns, labeled BLOCK, CURRENT, and TOTAL. (We're already familiar with Block Count information displayed in the Source Window when a simulation is run in Test Mode.)

Shown in the BLOCK column are Block Location numbers. (Block Location numbers are also given in the BLOCK# column in the Source Echo. See Figure 6A.5.)

Shown in the CURRENT column are the counts of Xacts located in the corresponding Blocks when the report is produced. Shown in the TOTAL column are the counts of the total number of Xacts that moved into the corresponding Blocks, including those still in the Blocks (if any).

For example, the Total Count at Block 1 in Figure 6A.6(a) is 4, meaning four worker-Xacts came into the model from the Location 1 GENERATE Block. Similarly, the Total Count at REPEAT (Block 2) is 243, meaning there were 243 occasions when widget assembly was initiated.

The Current Count of 3 at REPEAT means three worker-Xacts are in the ADVANCE Block. We have no way to know at this point whether all three of these Xacts are on the FEC, simulating assembly time, or whether one or more of them are on the CEC, waiting their turn to use the OVEN. The Current Count at Block 4 (ADVANCE) indicates that one worker-Xact is in the process of heat-treating a widget.

The Total Count at Block 5, RELEASE, is 239. This means that four workers built 239 widgets during the course of the simulated 40-hour week. (If workers never had to wait for the oven, four workers could build 256 widgets on average in a 40-hour week. You should check this calculation.)

The information provided by Block Counts can be useful, especially for large, complicated models. For example, the Total Counts are a measure of traffic intensity along various paths in a model. If the Total Count for each Block in a series of consecutive Blocks is **zero**, then no Xacts ever moved along

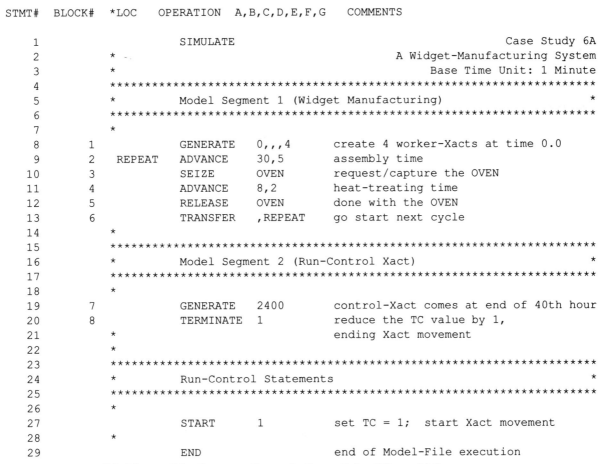

```
RELATIVE CLOCK:     2400.0000  ABSOLUTE CLOCK:     2400.0000
```

(a)

BLOCK	CURRENT	TOTAL
1		4
REPEAT	3	243
3		240
4	1	240
5		239
6		239
7		1
8		1

(b)

FACILITY	--AVG-UTIL-DURING-- TOTAL TIME	AVAIL TIME	UNAVL TIME	ENTRIES	AVERAGE TIME/XACT	CURRENT STATUS	PERCENT AVAIL	SEIZING XACT	PREEMPTING XACT
OVEN	.800			240	8.000	AVAIL	100.0	5	

(c)

RANDOM STREAM	ANTITHETIC VARIATES	INITIAL POSITION	CURRENT POSITION	SAMPLE COUNT	CHI-SQUARE UNIFORMITY
1	OFF	100000	100483	483	0.90

(d)

Figure 6A.6 *Postsimulation Report for Case Study 6A. (a) Clock values. (b) Block counts. (c) Facility Report. (d) RNG (Random Number Generator) Report*

that path in the model. If the model builder does not expect or cannot explain this situation, this may mean that the model has been built incorrectly.

If the Current Count at one or more Blocks is relatively large (such as, say, 6 or 8 or 10 more), then this situation may be worth investigating. Why aren't the corresponding Xacts able to move into their Next Block without having this kind of buildup occur? Is it reasonable to expect such traffic buildups, or have oversights been made in building the model or specifying the system?

Figure 6A.6(c) shows the OVEN Facility Report. This report matches the one in Figure 6.5 of Section 6.6, where Facility Reports are discussed. Reading Figure 6A.6(c) in left-to-right order, we see that the OVEN was in use 80.0 percent of the time; that it was captured 240 times; and that the average capture time was 8.0 time units (minutes), which by coincidence equals the expected value of the heat-treat-time random variable (8 ± 2).

Figure 6A.6(d) shows a Random-Number Generator (RNG) Report for the **random-number generator (RANDOM STREAM 1)** used during the simulation to sample from the model's assembly and heat-treat distributions. In the SAMPLE COUNT column of Figure 6A.6(d), we see that RANDOM STREAM 1 was used 483 times to support the simulation. Referring to Total Counts in Figure 6A.6(b), we see that 243 assemblies were initiated (Total Count at the REPEAT Block) and 240 heat-treatings were initiated (Total Count at the Block 4 ADVANCE). The sum of these two Total Counts, 483, equals the number of random numbers used in the simulation. (Matters of this type are taken up in detail in Chapters 13 and 14, where the GPSS/H random-number generators and RNG Reports are discussed.)

6.11 Displaying the Postsimulation Report

As pointed out in Section 6.8, the Postsimulation Report resulting from a Batch simulation goes by default into a DOS file. The Postsimulation Report in Case Study 6A, for example, was written by GPSS/H into the file **model6a.lis**. This report can be displayed on the computer screen by issuing this DOS command:

```
type model6a.lis
```

Some lines in a Postsimulation Report may be more than 80 characters wide, however. For example, a Facility Report is more than 80 characters wide. As a result, not all GPSS/H output can be seen by copying the Postsimulation Report to the screen. And DOS itself does not provide a scrolling capability, so it's not possible to scroll through a long, wide-line report on the screen. Alternative possibilities for viewing a long, wide-line Postsimulation Report are suggested here.

6.11.1 Use of GPSS/H in Test Mode

A Test-Mode run can be initiated with a Model File. In response to the Ready! prompt, the user can then issue a **run** command, without setting any interrupt conditions. The simulation then proceeds without interruption until the "output pending" message appears at the end of the Xact-Movement Phase. If another **run** command is then issued, the Postsimulation Report will be displayed on the screen. The user can then use the arrow and/or Function keys to scroll right, left, up, and down through the report.

In this Test-Mode approach, it's best to use the entire screen as the Dialog Window. (The Source and Status Windows then don't have to be supported as the simulation proceeds, and the size of the viewing area for the Postsimulation Report is maximized.) This can be done by using this DOS command to initiate the simulation:

```
gpssh model_file.gps test type
```

In this command **test** means, of course, that the simulation is to be in Test Mode, and **type** means that the Postsimulation Report is to be displayed **on the screen** (not in a **lis** file). The screen will not be split into three windows, but will only be used as a Dialog Window. The absence of **nowarn** means any Warning Messages will be displayed on the screen.

The disadvantage of this Test-Mode approach is that the Postsimulation Report is not put into a **lis** file, and so it's not possible to direct the report to paper as a by-product of the simulation. (Output can be printed one screen at a time using a print-screen key or function, but this approach is awkward if the report is lengthy.) On the other hand, this approach is perhaps most time efficient for the user when the objective is simply to browse through output without intermediate use of an editor (see the next subsection) and without waiting for output to be produced on a printer.

6.11.2 Use of an Editor

A visual (full screen) editor can be used to scroll right and left as well as up and down through textual material displayed on the screen. One possibility for viewing a Postsimulation Report is to use such an editor to view the **lis** file that GPSS/H produces as part of a Batch simulation. The editor chosen for building Model Files might also be used for viewing Postsimulation Reports.

6.11.3 Use of a Printer

If the printer attached to your DOS machine can be set to print lines of width up to 132 characters, then a DOS **print** command can be used to get a copy of the GPSS/H listing file on this printer, for example.

```
print model6a.lis lpt1
print model6a.lis prn
```

6.11.4 Use of a Sideways Utility

DOS prints output in a **portrait** orientation (that is, prints lines across the **width** of the printer paper). But DOS utilities (programs) are available which print in a **landscape** orientation (that is, print lines along the **length** of the printer paper). Such a utility can be used to print wide-line output even if the printer's maximum print span is 80 characters.

6.12 Exercises

1. The supplied file model6a.gps contains the Model File for Case Study 6A. Perform a Batch simulation with this Model File. (Simply issue a **gpssh model6a.gps** command.) Use a technique of your choice to display the Postsimulation Report on your computer screen, or get a listing of it on paper. Compare clock times, Block Counts, and information in

the Facility Report to the values given in Figure 6A.6. Corresponding values should match.

(Note: In the Batch run, the Compiler Report will include (by default) not only a Source Echo, but also a Dictionary and a Cross-Reference Listing. In addition to the Postsimulation Report, there will also be a Computer Usage Report. See Figure 6.6. Those types of output haven't been explained and can be ignored.)

2. Repeat Exercise 1, but now run in Test Mode. Use the technique described in Section 6.11.1 to browse through the Postsimulation Report on the screen.

*3. Copy the model6a.gps file to a new file; then change the model in the new file so that its base time unit is 0.5 minutes (instead of 1 minute as in Case Study 6A). Run the changed model. Compare its outputs with those in Case Study 6A. Are there any numeric differences in the output, even if only small ones? How do you account for these differences?

*4. Perform a Test-Mode simulation with the Case Study 6A model to answer these questions:

(a) At what times do the four workers, respectively, finish their first widget assembly?
(b) How long does the second worker who finishes a widget assembly have to wait to use the heat-treat oven?
(c) At what time does the worker simulated by the Xact with id number 5 finish assembling a widget for the third time?
(d) Are there any Move-Time ties at time 480 (the time that Xact movement ends)?
(e) Of the three worker-Xacts in the Block 3 ADVANCE at the end of the simulation, how many are on the CEC, waiting their turn to use the OVEN?

*5. In Case Study 6A, assume a fixed daily oven cost of $100, a worker's salary (including fringe benefits) of $85 per day, a $20 cost for the material in a widget, and a finished goods value of $30. In the Case Study 6A simulation, what average daily profit is realized? Only include **finished** widgets in your computation. (Assume that work-in-process has no economic cost or benefit.)

*6. Use modified forms of the Case Study 6A model to perform single 40-hour simulations with three workers and five workers. Then use the economic information in Exercise 5 to compute the average daily profit realized for the alternative cases of three, four, five and six workers. What number of workers maximizes the estimated average daily profit in these specific simulations?

(**Caution:** It would not be acceptable to use these single simulations to draw firm conclusions about which number of workers maximizes the average daily profit in this system. See Chapters 14, 15, and 16 for more particulars.)

7. In the system of Case Study 6A, assume that the timings given do **not** include the time needed for a worker to walk from an assembly station to the heat-treat oven, or from the heat-treat oven back to an assembly station and get the raw material needed for the next assembly. Suppose these times are 30 ± 15 and 180 ± 60 seconds, respectively. Providing these timings in the model, repeat the Case Study 6A simulation, and those of Exercise 6. What number of workers now maximizes the estimated average daily profit in these specific simulations? By how much do these additional time requirements decrease the average daily profit in these specific simulations for the cases of 3, 4, 5, and 6 workers?

*8. Castings are put onto a conveyor every 9.0 ± 4.5 minutes (uniformly distributed) and are then conveyed to a drill where a hole is drilled in them. It takes 6.0 minutes to convey a casting to the drill. Drilling time is 9.0 ± 1.25 minutes (uniformly distributed). After a casting has had a hole drilled in it, the casting leaves the system. The service order at the drill is FCFS.

(Note: When a casting reaches the end of the conveyor, it moves into a waiting space next to the drill. Assume the time required for a casting to move from the end of the conveyor into the waiting space is negligibly small and that the time required for a casting to move from the waiting space onto the drilling machine is also negligibly small. You are asked to relax these simplifying assumptions in Exercise 11.)

Model this system in GPSS/H, using 1 minute as the base time unit. Compare the structure of your model with that of Figure 6.4. What have you used as a pre-SEIZE Block? As a post-RELEASE Block? Now perform a Batch simulation with the model, simulating until 500 castings have had a hole drilled in them. Discuss the output produced at the end of the simulation.

*9. At the end of the Exercise 8 simulation, Current Counts in the Postsimulation Report show that three Xacts are in the "ADVANCE 6.0" Block. One or more of these Xacts might still be on the conveyor, or might already have reached the end of the conveyor and be waiting to capture the DRILL. Carry out a Test-Mode simulation with the model of Exercise 8 to determine what the state of affairs is in this regard.

*10. Modify the model of Exercise 8 so Xact movement will end after 480.0 simulated minutes (that is, at the conclusion of an 8-hour shift). Perform a Batch simulation with the changed model. Display the Postsimulation Report on your computer screen, or get a listing of it on paper. Analyze Block Counts and the Facility Report. Is a casting being drilled when the simulation ends? If so, what is the id number of the casting-Xact? How many castings were put on the conveyor? How many castings have left the system?

11. Simplifying assumptions in Exercise 8 are that the times required for a casting to move from the end of the conveyor into the waiting space next to the drill, and from the waiting space onto the drill, are both negligibly small. Suppose these times are 6 seconds and 12 seconds, respectively. Modify the model of Exercise 8 to include these 6- and 12-second times. Continue to use a base time unit of 1 minute in the model. Assume a casting can always move immediately from the end of the conveyor into the waiting space. (It cannot move from the waiting space onto the drill until it has captured the drill.) Carry out a Batch simulation with the revised model. How long does it take in this simulation to drill holes in 500 castings?

12. Suppose the conveying and drilling system modeled in Exercise 8 is extended as follows. Drilled castings move by conveyor to a deburring machine, where they are deburred and then leave the system. It takes 2.5 minutes to convey the castings from the drilling machine to the deburring machine. It takes 7.5 ± 2.5 minutes to deburr a casting.

    Change the Exercise 8 model to correspond to the above extension of the system. Carry out a Batch simulation with the changed model. At what time does the simulation stop? How many castings have been drilled by the end of the simulation? Is a casting being drilled when the simulation stops? How many castings are waiting to be drilled? How many are waiting to be deburred?

6.13 Bug Clinic

Each of these exercises calls for a Batch simulation. Remember that if and when an execution error occurs, an Error Message will be displayed at the screen and GPSS/H will usually give you control. (See Figure 6.6.) You can then display additional information of your choice, if you like, before quitting the simulation.

*1. Modify a copy of the Case Study 6A model (in the model6a.gps file) by eliminating the RELEASE Block. What is wrong with the resulting model? How do you think GPSS/H might respond if a simulation is performed with this model? Carry out a Batch simulation with the model and see what happens.

*2. Modify a copy of the model for Exercise 8 of Section 6.12 by eliminating the RELEASE Block. How do you think GPSS/H might respond if a simulation is performed with this model? Carry out a Batch simulation with the model and see what happens. Is a compile-time or an execution-time Error Message issued?

*3. Modify a copy of the Case Study 6A model by eliminating the SEIZE Block. What is wrong with the resulting model? How do you think GPSS/H might respond if a simulation is performed with this model? Carry out a Batch simulation with the model and see what happens. Is a compile-time or an execution-time Error Message issued?

*4. Modify a copy of the Case Study 6A model by eliminating the TERMINATE Block. What is wrong with the resulting model? How do you think GPSS/H might respond if a simulation is performed with this model? Carry out a Batch simulation with the model and see what happens. Is a compile-time or an execution-time Error Message issued?

*5. In Exercise 8 of Section 6.12, castings arrive every 9 minutes on average, and it takes 9 minutes on average to drill a casting. And so the drill is just able to keep up in the long run with the work expected of it. If mean casting interarrival time were anything less than 9.0, then the system would be **explosive** in the sense that work would accumulate without end over time. This would eventually lead to an impossible situation in the real system.

Perform the following experiment. Modify a copy of the Exercise 8 model, changing the GENERATE Block's A Operand from 9.0 to 3.0 and changing the B Operand from 4.5 to 1.5. You then have a model for an explosive situation. If you perform a simulation with this model, what do you think will eventually happen? (There seem to be two possibilities: either the simulation will run to completion, leaving a large buildup of casting-Xacts waiting their turn to be drilled, or GPSS/H will reach its internal limit on the maximum number of Xacts that can exist simultaneously. This internal limit is subject to user control in all GPSS/H implementations, but only to a limited extent in Student DOS GPSS/H, which supports a maximum of about 85 Xacts. See Section B.2 in Appendix B.) Put the model into Batch execution. What happens?

7 More About How Transactions Are Managed by GPSS/H

7.1 Preview

The method used by GPSS/H to organize and process information about Transactions was introduced in Chapter 4. The discussion of the Scan Phase in that chapter did not include considerations involving Transaction blocking. In this chapter, the Scan Phase logic presented earlier is extended to take into account complications resulting when Blocks such as SEIZE can deny entry to Transactions. Understanding this extended Scan Phase logic enhances the modeler's ability to simulate in Test Mode and paves the way for more efficient study and use of additional aspects of GPSS/H.

This chapter introduces the model's Status Change Flag, the concept of unique blocking, and a scheme involving putting Xacts to sleep on the Current Events Chain, and then eventually waking them back up. These aspects of a GPSS/H simulation are demonstrated in Test Mode, and exercises are provided for use in reinforcing the ideas involved.

7.2 Restarting the Scan During a Scan Phase

In terms of material discussed so far, Transactions waiting their turn to execute a SEIZE Block do their waiting on the Current Events Chain. One of them will be able to execute a SEIZE after some other Xact executes a corresponding RELEASE. That is, when the Xact currently controlling the Facility (server) executes a RELEASE, one of these waiting Xacts will be able to move into (execute) the SEIZE and go on from there. The waiting Xacts are **blocked**. The Xact that unblocks them by executing a RELEASE is an **unblocker**.

Picture this situation in a specific example in terms of the Block sequence shown in Figure 7.1 and the Current Events Chain shown in Figure 7.2. Figure 7.1 shows the pre-SEIZE/ SEIZE/ADVANCE/RELEASE/ post-RELEASE pattern with respect to the use of a Facility named DRILL. Assume that two blocked Xacts are in the pre-SEIZE Block and on the Current Chain, waiting their turn to execute the "SEIZE DRILL" Block. Meanwhile, the Xact that controls the DRILL is in the ADVANCE Block (while drilling time is elapsing) and on the Future Chain. Then a Clock Update Phase advances the clock to the Move Time of the controlling Xact and transfers it from the Future to the Current Chain, merging it in as last in its Priority Class. If the Priority Level of the controlling Xact equals that of the blocked Xacts, then it **goes behind them** on the Current Events Chain. This situation is shown in Figure 7.2, where Xacts 8 and 9 are the **blocked** Xacts and Xact 7 is the Xact that currently controls the DRILL.

Now the next Scan Phase begins. Can you see a potential problem shaping up in terms of the ar-

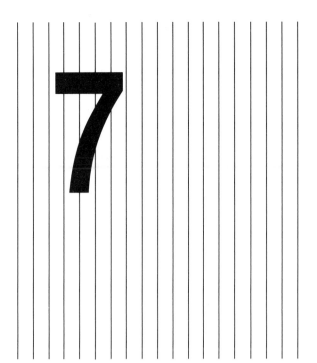

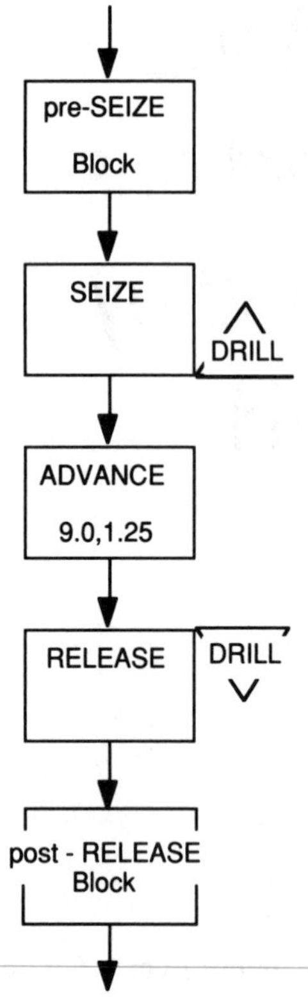

Figure 7.1 *A Block Sequence for Use of a Single Server*

rangement of Xacts on the Figure 7.2 CEC? The Scan Phase deals with Xacts **from front to back** on the CEC. Xact 8 is dealt with first but is still blocked. (Xact 7 hasn't yet been dealt with, and so hasn't yet put the DRILL into a state of idleness.) Xact 9 is dealt with next but is also still blocked. Xact 7 is then dealt with. It executes the RELEASE (with the side effect of unblocking Xacts 8 and 9) and continues to move until it can't move any farther (that is, until it moves into a TERMINATE and is destroyed, or moves into an ADVANCE and is placed on the FEC, or finds itself blocked and so remains in its Current Block and in its current position on the CEC).

What happens next? Xact 7, already moved, was last on the CEC when the scan began. And so all Xacts on the CEC have been dealt with. But **the state of the model hasn't yet been fully updated at the current clock time.** If GPSS/H **goes back to the front of the CEC** and **retries** to move Xact 8, the retry will be successful. (Xact 8 has been unblocked and can now move.) And so GPSS/H **restarts the scan** at the current clock time. Going back to the front of the CEC, it moves Xact 8 from the pre-SEIZE Block into "SEIZE DRILL" in Figure 7.1 and then into the ADVANCE, where it puts Xact 8 on the FEC. The restarted scan then proceeds to Xact 9, but this Xact is blocked (it was actually unblocked by Xact 7 and then reblocked by Xact 8!), and so it remains in the pre-SEIZE Block. There is no next Xact on the CEC, and so the model is now fully updated at the current simulated time. This means a Clock Update Phase will be performed next, and so on.

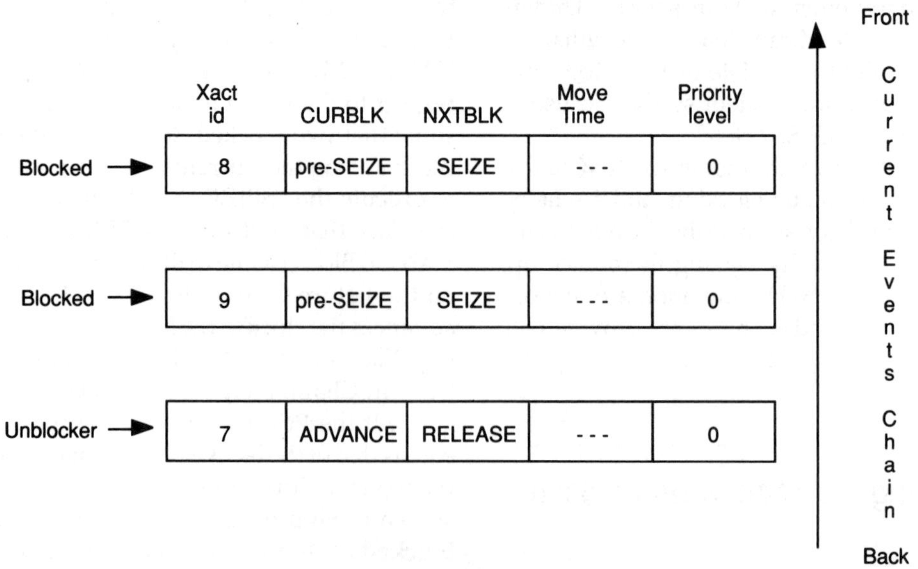

Figure 7.2 *A Current Events Chain Containing Two Blocked Xacts and One Unblocker Xact*

7.3 The Model's Status-Change Flag

In the Section 7.2 scenario, how does GPSS/H know that it should restart the scan after Xact 7 stops moving? It uses the **model's Status Change (S/C) Flag** for this purpose. The model's Status Change Flag has two possible settings: **on**; and **off**. During a Scan Phase, whenever the moving Xact executes a Block that **changes the status** of an entity member in a model in a potentially important way, GPSS/H **turns on** the model's Status Change Flag. Then, after eventually dropping the moving Xact, the next step GPSS/H carries out is to **test the Status Change Flag.** If the flag is **off**, GPSS/H proceeds to the **sequential Xact** on the CEC. If the flag is **on**, GPSS/H turns the flag back off and **restarts the scan** of the Current Chain. "Restarting the scan" means returning to the **front** of the CEC and starting to scan over again, as though the Scan Phase were just beginning. The purpose in restarting the scan is to retry to move any previously blocked Xacts that might have become unblocked because of the change of status of an entity member in a model.

As indicated, GPSS/H turns the model's Status Change Flag on whenever the moving Xact executes a Block that **changes the status** of a GPSS/H entity member in a potentially important way. For example, when an Xact executes a RELEASE, this **changes the capture status** of a Facility. Whereas the Facility was previously **captured**, the RELEASE execution has now made it **idle**. Why is this change in Facility status potentially important? Because, as we have seen in the preceding section, it may have the effect of **unblocking one or more Xacts** that are closer to the front of the CEC than the unblocker is. And so, when a RELEASE is executed, GPSS/H "writes a note to itself" (turns on the model's Status Change Flag) as a reminder that it must **later (but at the same simulated time)** restart the scan of the CEC to give any unblocked Xacts a chance to try to move forward again along their path.

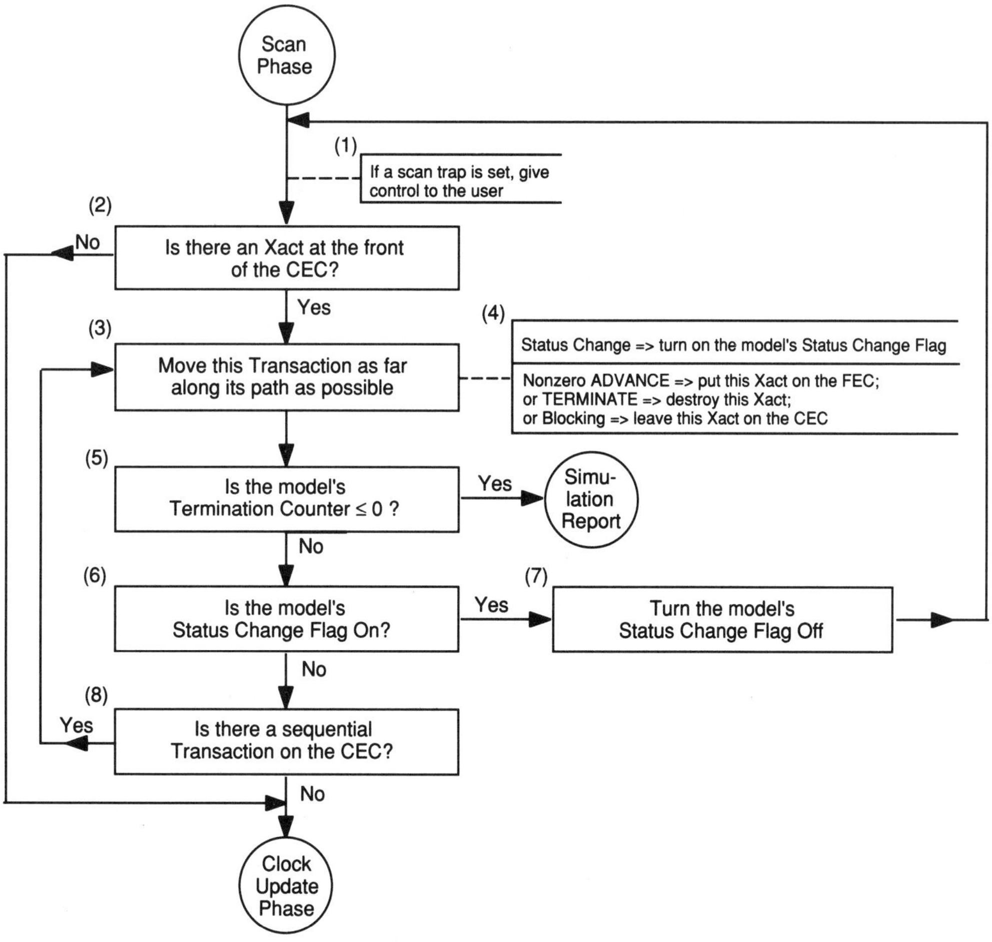

Figure 7.3 *Role of the Model's Status Change Flag in the Logic of the Scan Phase*

The role of the model's Status Change Flag in the logic of the Scan Phase is shown in the Figure 7.3 flowchart, which repeats and extends the Scan Phase flowchart of Figure 4.9. Boxes in Figure 7.3 have been numbered to support discussion.

In studying Figure 7.3, take note first of comments Box 4. This box contains two new entries relative to the corresponding box in the flowchart of Figure 4.9. First, it's indicated in Box 4 that if the moving Xact executes a Block (such as a RELEASE) that changes the status of an entity (such as a server) in the model, the model's Status Change Flag is to be turned on ("Status Change => turn on the Status Change Flag"). Second, the list of alternative reasons for which GPSS/H drops the moving Xact has been extended from two ("Nonzero ADVANCE => put this Xact on the FEC" and "TERMINATE => destroy this Xact") to three ("Blocking => leave this Xact on the CEC"). And so the fact that the moving Xact can experience a blocking condition, first pointed out in Chapter 6 in terms of the SEIZE Block, is formalized in Figure 7.3.

Box 6 in Figure 7.3 indicates that if the most recently dropped Xact made a move that turned the model's Status Change Flag on, that flag is to be turned back off (Box 7) and the scan is to be restarted (see the line leading from Box 7 back up to Box 2). If the **scan** trap is set, then control is given to the user at this point, as indicated by the Box 1 comment. In other words, if a **scan** trap is set, a user will be given control *not just when a Scan Phase begins, but also each time the scan is restarted during an ongoing Scan Phase.*

When a RELEASE Block is executed, GPSS/H always turns on the model's Status Change Flag, **whether or not any Xacts become unblocked as a result.** (It's not wrong to restart the scan of the CEC, even if there weren't one or more blocked Xacts waiting for another Xact to execute the RELEASE.)

As made clear in Figure 7.3, a status change does not result in an **immediate** restarting of the scan of the CEC. Instead, it results in an **eventual** restarting of the scan. Even after the model's Status Change Flag has been turned on, the moving Xact **continues to move** until it can move no farther (Box 3). **Then** GPSS/H tests the model's Status Change Flag (Box 6) and, finding it on, turns it back off (Box 7) and restarts the scan.

7.4 Blocks Whose Execution Turns on the Model's Status Change Flag

We've seen that execution of a RELEASE turns on the model's Status Change Flag. There are 13 types of Blocks in GPSS/H whose execution has this effect. The purpose in turning on the Status Change Flag **always** is to bring about an eventual restart of the scan at the current clock time, for reasons of the type illustrated earlier.

The **SEIZE** Block is among those whose execution turns on the model's Status Change Flag. This is because SEIZE execution changes the capture status of a Facility from **idle** to **captured.** Why eventually restart the scan of the CEC in response to the *capturing* of a Facility? Can one or more Xacts be blocked, waiting for a Facility to be captured? The answer is **yes.** There is a type of Block (GATE) that can deny entry to an Xact until a specified Facility is put into a state of capture. (Such an Xact doesn't want to capture the Facility itself, but has the task of taking responsive action when another Xact captures the Facility.) As a result, whenever a SEIZE is executed, GPSS/H turns on the model's Status Change (S/C) flag. (Operational details of the GATE Block will not be discussed in this book, but additional comments are provided in Chapter 17.)

In addition to SEIZE and RELEASE, other Blocks considered in this book whose execution turns on the Status Change Flag are ENTER and LEAVE (Chapter 11), and PRIORITY (Chapter 12).

7.5 Unique Blocking and a Transaction's Scan-Skip Indicator

If an Xact is blocked by a SEIZE, the blocking will continue until some other Xact executes a corresponding RELEASE. For example, if an Xact tries to "SEIZE DRILL" and finds itself blocked, it will remain blocked until some other Xact executes a "RELEASE DRILL." Such an Xact is said to be **uniquely blocked,** because the **only** resolution (the **unique** resolution) for the blocking is the execution of a "RELEASE DRILL" Block. (Not all types of blocking are unique, as we'll see in Chapter 12.)

If an Xact is uniquely blocked, there is no point trying to move it during Scan Phases until **after** the blocking condition has been removed. It wouldn't be wrong to try to move such an Xact, but there's no point in trying while the blocking condition is in effect. The motivation for **not** trying to move a blocked Transaction is to save the computer time that otherwise would be used in fruitlessly trying to move it.

Motivated by potential computer-time savings, GPSS/H takes advantage of unique blocking as follows. GPSS/H attaches to **each Xact** a flag known as a **Scan-Skip Indicator.** A Transaction's Scan-Skip

Indicator has two possible settings: **on** and **off**. If the moving Xact encounters unique blocking, GPSS/H **turns on the Xact's Scan-Skip Indicator.** The blocked Xact remains in its Current Block and in its current position on the CEC, so there is nothing new in this regard. The uniquely blocked Transaction has simply been flagged (marked) to signal that it is uniquely blocked. We will now describe how GPSS/H uses this signal.

When focusing on a CEC Xact during a Scan Phase, GPSS/H first **tests the Xact's Scan-Skip Indicator (SSI).** If the SSI is on, the Xact is uniquely blocked, and there is no point trying to move it. As a result, GPSS/H goes **immediately** to the sequential CEC Xact. But if the Xact's Scan-Skip Indicator is off, then the Xact is not uniquely blocked, and GPSS/H tries to move it from its Current Block into its Next Block, and so on.

Xacts whose Scan-Skip Indicator is **on** are **scan inactive,** because GPSS/H **skips over** such Xacts during the Scan Phase. Such Xacts are **asleep** on the Current Chain. In contrast, Xacts whose Scan-Skip

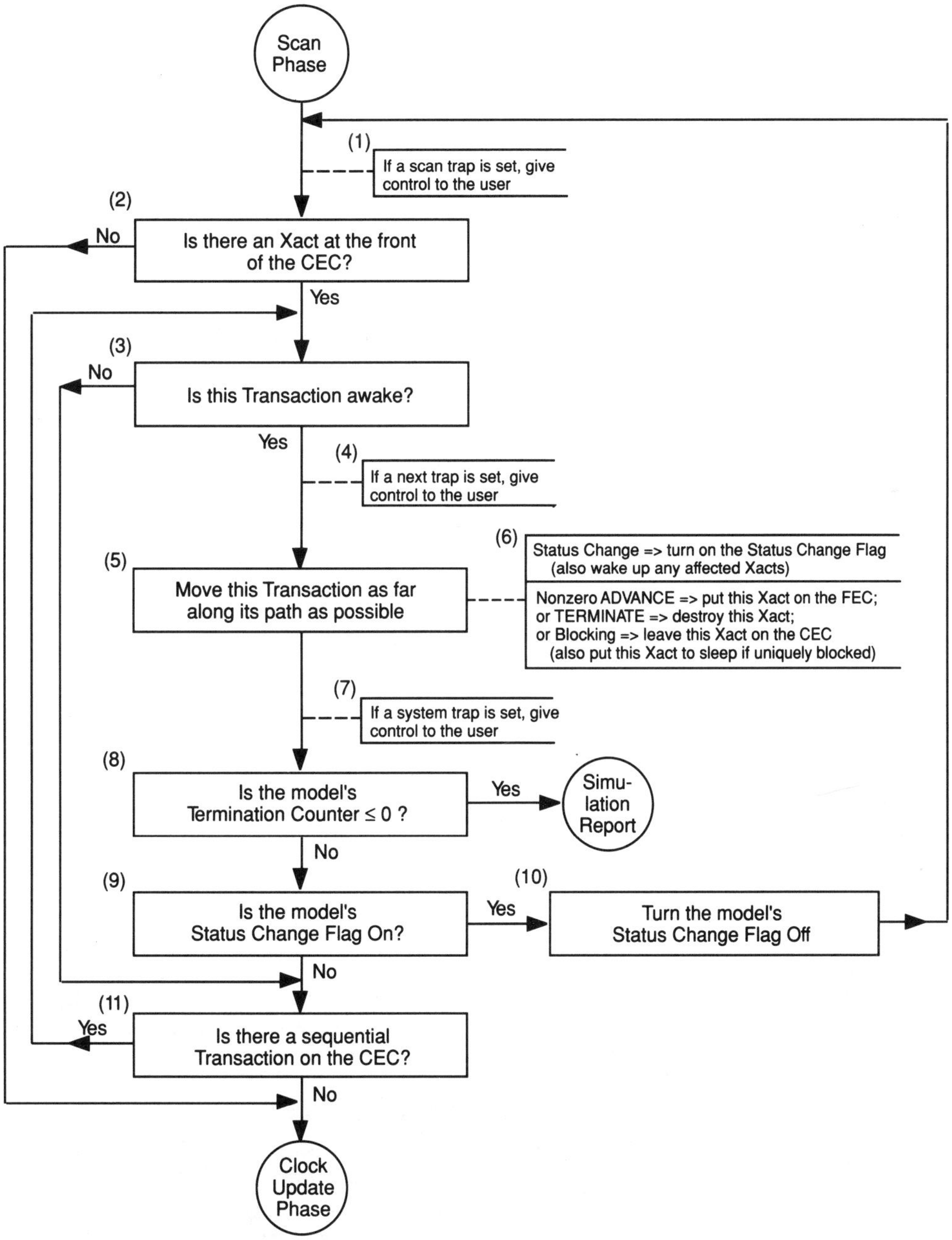

Figure 7.4 Role of the Awake or Asleep Status of Transactions in the Logic of the Scan Phase

Indicator is **off** are **scan active**, because when their turn comes to try to move, GPSS/H **does try to move them** from their Current Block into their Next Block, and so on. These Xacts are **awake** on the Current Chain. In these terms, an Xact is **put to sleep** on the CEC by turning its Scan-Skip Indicator **on**, and an Xact is eventually **reawakened** by turning its Scan-Skip Indicator back **off**.

After an Xact has been put to sleep, it is reawakened when the cause of its blocking is removed. For example, suppose one or more Xacts are asleep, with "SEIZE DRILL" as their Next Block. When another Xact executes a "RELEASE DRILL," GPSS/H wakes these Xacts back up by **turning off their Scan-Skip Indicators**. In addition, GPSS/H **also turns on the model's Status Change Flag**, as discussed in Section 7.3. After the *unblocker* Xact can move no farther, GPSS/H restarts the scan of the Current Chain, giving each of the *unblocked and reawakened* Xacts its turn to try to move into its Next Block, and so on.

The role of an Xact's Scan-Skip Indicator (and the awake or asleep status of Transactions) in the logic of the Scan Phase is summarized in Figure 7.4, which repeats the Scan Phase logic of Figure 7.3 but extends this logic to show how GPSS/H **skips over** CEC Transactions during a Scan Phase when they are asleep. The Boxes in Figure 7.4 have been numbered to support the following discussion.

In studying Figure 7.4, note first of all that when GPSS/H focuses on an Xact during a Scan Phase, the first thing done is to determine if the Xact is awake or asleep (Box 3). If the Xact is awake, then an attempt will be made to move it (Box 5). But if the Xact is asleep, then GPSS/H will not try to move it, but instead will immediately switch its focus to the sequential Xact (if any) on the Current Chain (Box 11).

Take note next of comments Box 6 in Figure 7.4. This box contains two new parenthetical entries relative to the corresponding box in the flowchart of Figure 7.3. First, it's indicated in Box 6 that if the moving Xact makes a move that turns on the model's Status Change Flag, all affected sleeping Xacts (if any) on the Current Chain are to be reawakened ("also wake up any affected Xacts"). Second, it's indicated in Box 6 that if the moving Xact is dropped because of unique blocking, then it is to be put to sleep ("also put this Xact to sleep if uniquely blocked").

It's important to realize that when a RELEASE executes, **each** Xact (if any) that is unblocked as a result will be reawakened. In general, only **one** of the unblocked Xacts will be able to be moved by the eventually restarted scan. In Figure 7.2, for example, **two** Xacts (Xacts 8 and 9) are asleep, waiting for Xact 7 to "RELEASE DRILL". When Xact 7 executes the RELEASE Block (in Figure 7.1), Xacts 8 and 9 are **both** reawakened. After Xact 7 can't move any farther and the scan is restarted, Xact 8 will execute the "SEIZE DRILL" Block of Figure 7.1, going from there into the ADVANCE and onto the FEC. The scan will then try to move Xact 9, but it is **still blocked** (has been reblocked, actually, by Xact 7's execution of the SEIZE). Still uniquely blocked by "SEIZE DRILL," Xact 9 will be **put back to sleep**. It will sleep until the next time a "RELEASE DRILL" is executed, when it will again be awakened and given a chance to try to "SEIZE DRILL". And so on. If an Xact starts to wait for a Facility when there are many other Xacts waiting ahead of it, then the Xact will be put to sleep, then be awakened, then be put back to sleep, then be awakened again, and so on, a large number of times before its turn eventually comes to capture the Facility.

Finally, Figure 7.4 indicates clearly the conditions under which a **next** trap will be sprung during a Scan Phase. See Box 4 in this regard. Note that GPSS/H does not spring a **next** trap each time it focuses on *any* Xact during a Scan Phase, but only does so if the Xact is *awake*. Xacts that are asleep on the Current Chain are incapable of causing traps to be sprung.

7.6 A Test-Mode Demonstration of the Status Change Flag and Scan-Skip Indicators

In this section, we use a Test-Mode simulation to demonstrate the operation of the model's Status Change Flag and of each Transaction's Scan-Skip Indicator. The Model File shown in Figure 7.5 is used for this purpose.

The model corresponds to this system:

> Castings are put onto a conveyor every 15 time units and are then conveyed to a drill where a hole is drilled in them. It takes 10 time units to convey a casting to the drill. Drilling time is 30 time units. After a casting has had a hole drilled in it, the casting leaves the system.

Corresponding comments have been attached to Block Statements in the Model File.

In the system described, castings are brought to the drill faster than the drill can handle them. Such a system is said to be **explosive**. (See Exercise 4 in Section 6.13.) This would eventually result in an

```
        SIMULATE
*
 BLOCK1  ADVANCE   15,,,2   a casting arrives every 15 time units
*
 BLOCK2  ADVANCE   10       conveying time
*
 BLOCK3  SEIZE     DRILL    request/capture the drill
 BLOCK4  ADVANCE   30       drilling time
 BLOCK5  RELEASE   DRILL    give up the drill
*
 BLOCK6  TERMINATE 1        the finished casting leaves the model
*
         START     2
         END
```

Figure 7.5 *A Model File to Demonstrate a Model's Status Change Flag and Each Transaction's Scan-Skip Indicator*

impossible situation in a real system, but suits our purposes here, where we want to watch the model's Status Change Flag, each Transaction's Scan-Skip Indicator, and scan restarts at work early in the simulation.

Where will casting-Transactions be in the Figure 7.5 model while waiting their turn to be drilled? The pre-SEIZE Block is the BLOCK2 ADVANCE, so it's in this ADVANCE that these casting-Xacts will accumulate while waiting to capture the DRILL.

A Limit Count of 2 has been used on the BLOCK1 GENERATE in the Figure 7.5 model. (This simplifies the demonstration by reducing the number of Xacts involved in chain displays.)

Figure 7.6 shows nine computer screens resulting from the early stages of a simulation with the Figure 7.5 model. Discussion of this screen sequence follows. (In Exercise 1 of Section 7.7, you are asked to reproduce this screen sequence on your computer.)

Screen 1 (Figure 7.6, part a)

In Screen 1, after the DOS **gpssh** command has been executed, we've first set a clock trap at time 40.0 and then have issued a **run** command. This brings the simulation to the beginning of the Scan Phase at time 40.0. Because the model is deterministic (no interarrival or ADVANCE times are random), we can reason out the exact state of the model at this point. The first casting-Xact came into the model at time 15.0, reached the DRILL at time 25.0, and will be done with the drilling step at time 55.0. The second casting-Xact came into the model at time 30.0 and is just about to reach the DRILL at time 40.0. This is consistent with the Screen 1 message

```
XACT 2 POISED AT BLOCK 3 (BLOCK3).
RELATIVE CLOCK: 40.0000
CLOCK >= 40.0000 BREAKPOINT.
```

Xact 2, simulating the second casting-Xact, is in the BLOCK2 ADVANCE and on the Current Chain and is about to try to move into the "SEIZE DRILL" Block. The first casting has the DRILL captured, of course, and so the **SEIZE will now deny entry to this second casting-Xact**.

We now want GPSS/H to tell us **when it stops moving Xact 2, and why**. And so in Screen 1 we set a **system** trap and issued a **run** command. Resuming the simulation by trying unsuccessfully to move Xact 2 from ADVANCE into SEIZE, GPSS/H then wrote out the message:

```
XACT 2 UNIQUELY BLOCKED AT BLOCK 3 (BLOCK3).
RELATIVE CLOCK: 40.0000
```

Note how the term **unique** is used in this message (because blocking at a SEIZE is unique).

Also note that Xact 2 will **remain in its ADVANCE Block** and **on the Current Chain** for some **unknown** interval of simulated time (until its turn comes to capture the drill). This situation can come about whenever the Block sequential to an ADVANCE can block an Xact, as in the Figure 7.5 model. There is nothing wrong with this. In this model, the BLOCK2 ADVANCE serves from time to time as the Current Block within which casting-Xacts wait their turn to capture the drill.

```
BLOCK CURRENT      TOTAL         fig75.gps SOURCE CODE
----- -------      -----         ----------------------------------------------
1                    2            BLOCK1    GENERATE    15,,,2    a casting arrives
2          1         2            BLOCK2    ADVANCE     10        conveying time ela
3                    1            BLOCK3    SEIZE       DRILL     request/capture th
4          1         1            BLOCK4    ADVANCE     30        drilling time elap
5                    0            BLOCK5    RELEASE     DRILL     give up the drill
================================================================================
S/C: OFF   ABS CLOCK:   40.0000        REL CLOCK: 40.0000          TTG: 2
================================================================================
XACT: 2           CURBLK: BLOCK2    NEXTBLK: BLOCK3     CHAINS: CEC        PC:

MARK-TIME: 30.0000         MOVE-TIME: ----            PRIORITY: 0
================================================================================
: trap clock=40.0
: run

XACT 2 POISED AT BLOCK 3 (BLOCK3).  RELATIVE CLOCK: 40.0000
CLOCK >= 40.0000 BREAKPOINT.
: trap system
: run

XACT 2 UNIQUELY BLOCKED AT BLOCK 3 (BLOCK3).  RELATIVE CLOCK: 40.0000
:
```

Figure 7.6 Nine Computer Screens Resulting When the Figure 7.5 Model File Is Run in Test Mode (a) Screen 1

```
BLOCK CURRENT      TOTAL         fig75.gps SOURCE CODE
----- -------      -----         ----------------------------------------------
1                    2            BLOCK1    GENERATE    15,,,2    a casting arrives
2          1         2            BLOCK2    ADVANCE     10        conveying time ela
3                    1            BLOCK3    SEIZE       DRILL     request/capture th
4          1         1            BLOCK4    ADVANCE     30        drilling time elap
5                    0            BLOCK5    RELEASE     DRILL     give up the drill
================================================================================
S/C: OFF   ABS CLOCK:   40.0000        REL CLOCK: 40.0000          TTG: 2
================================================================================
XACT: 2           CURBLK: BLOCK2    NEXTBLK: BLOCK3     CHAINS: CEC        PC:

MARK-TIME: 30.0000         MOVE-TIME: -----           PRIORITY: 0
================================================================================
: run

XACT 2 UNIQUELY BLOCKED AT BLOCK 3 (BLOCK3).  RELATIVE CLOCK: 40.0000
: display fac

            --AVG-UTIL-DURING--
FACILITY   TOTAL  AVAIL   UNAVL       ENTRIES     AVERAGE   CURRENT  PERCENT  SEIZING
            TIME   TIME    TIME                  TIME/XACT   STATUS   AVAIL     XACT
   DRILL   0.375                            1      15.000    AVAIL                 1
:
```

Figure 7.6 (b) Screen 2

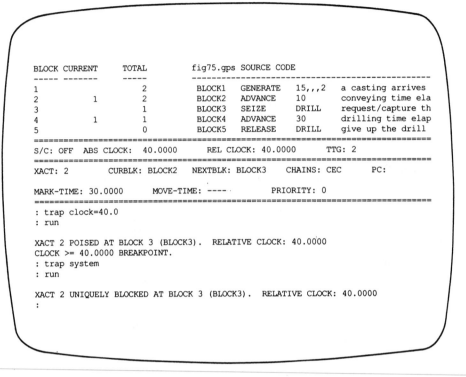

In the Screen 1 Source Window, the presence of Xact 2 in the BLOCK2 ADVANCE causes the Current Count at that Block to be 1. (The Current Count of 1 in the BLOCK4 ADVANCE reflects the presence of the current user of the drill.)

Screen 2 (Figure 7.6, part b)

In Screen 2, we issue a **display fac** command. The resulting Facility report indicates that the DRILL is captured by Xact 1 (note that SEIZING XACT is 1), consistent with our expectations. The --AVG-UTIL-DURING-- TOTAL TIME of 0.375, the ENTRIES of 1, and the AVERAGE TIME/XACT of 15.000 all check out.

Screen 3 (Figure 7.6, part c)

Now that Xact 2 is uniquely blocked, its Scan-Skip Indicator should be on. To demonstrate this, we **display cec** in Screen 3. There we see that Xact 2's CURBLK is BLOCK2, and its NXTBLK is BLOCK3. (This same information about Xact 2 can also be found in the Screen 2 Status Window.)

Now look at the column labeled SDPGFT** toward the bottom of Screen 2. **Each** of the letters **S** through **T** in this label represents a **flag** on the corresponding Transaction. In general, whenever the entry in one of these columns is **blank**, the corresponding flag is **off**. Whenever the entry in one of these columns **matches the column label,** the corresponding flag is **on**.

The column labeled **S** (the first column in SDPGFT**) shows the setting of the Transaction's **Scan-Skip Indicator**. At the bottom of Screen 2, we see an **S** in the **S** column. And so Xact 2's Scan-Skip Indicator is on, consistent with the fact that Xact 2 is uniquely blocked.

We won't talk about the other Transaction flags (DPGFT**) in this book.

Screen 4 (Figure 7.6, part d)

We now want to skip forward to the time when Xact 1 will RELEASE the DRILL. This will be the earliest future action in the model. (No new casting is scheduled to arrive, because the Limit Count of 2 at the

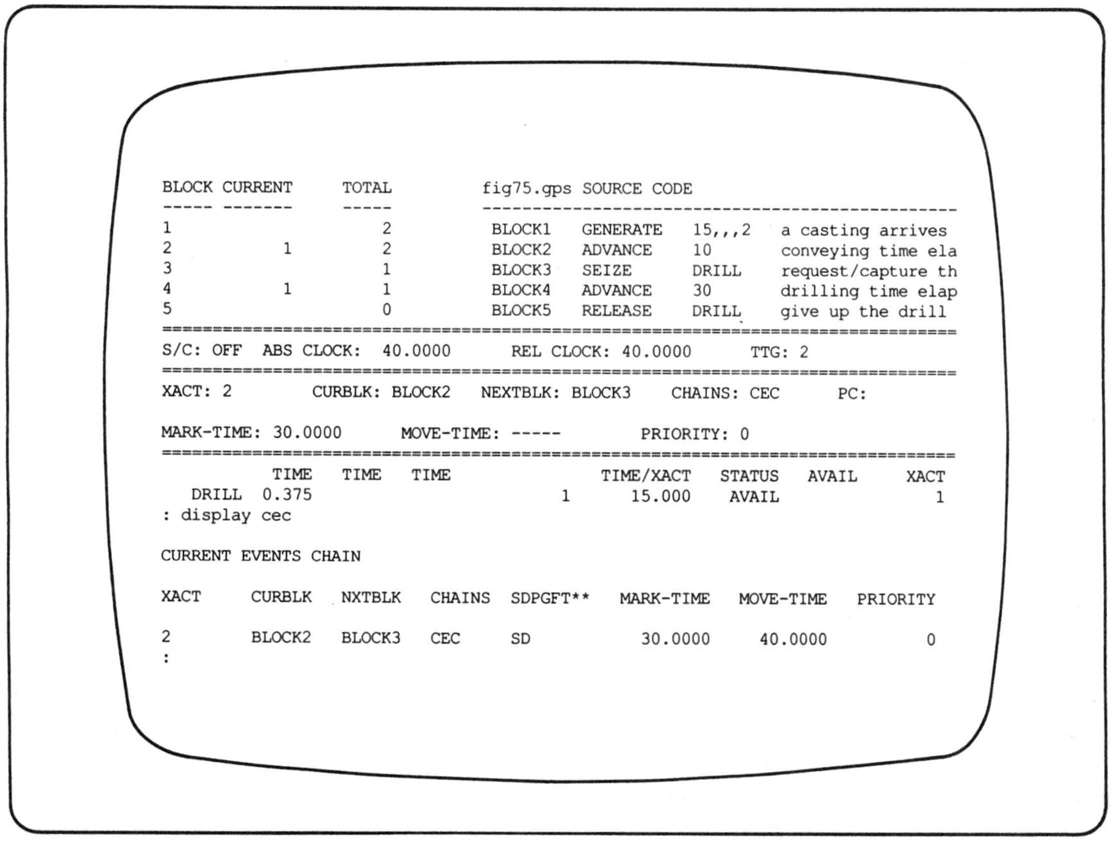

```
BLOCK CURRENT     TOTAL         fig75.gps SOURCE CODE
----- -------     -----         --------------------------------------------
1                   2            BLOCK1   GENERATE   15,,,2   a casting arrives
2           1       2            BLOCK2   ADVANCE    10       conveying time ela
3                   1            BLOCK3   SEIZE      DRILL    request/capture th
4           1       1            BLOCK4   ADVANCE    30       drilling time elap
5                   0            BLOCK5   RELEASE    DRILL    give up the drill
==============================================================================
S/C: OFF  ABS CLOCK:  40.0000      REL CLOCK: 40.0000      TTG: 2
==============================================================================
XACT: 2         CURBLK: BLOCK2  NEXTBLK: BLOCK3   CHAINS: CEC      PC:

MARK-TIME: 30.0000      MOVE-TIME: -----         PRIORITY: 0
==============================================================================
          TIME   TIME   TIME               TIME/XACT  STATUS  AVAIL     XACT
   DRILL  0.375                        1     15.000   AVAIL                1
: display cec

CURRENT EVENTS CHAIN

XACT     CURBLK   NXTBLK   CHAINS  SDPGFT**   MARK-TIME   MOVE-TIME   PRIORITY

2        BLOCK2   BLOCK3   CEC     SD           30.0000     40.0000          0
:
```

Figure 7.6 (c) *Screen 3*

```
BLOCK CURRENT      TOTAL          fig75.gps SOURCE CODE
----- -------      -----          ----------------------------------------------
3                      1           BLOCK3   SEIZE      DRILL     request/capture th
4            1         1           BLOCK4   ADVANCE    30        drilling time elap
5                      0           BLOCK5   RELEASE    DRILL     give up the drill
6                      0           BLOCK6   TERMINATE  1         the finished casti

=================================================================================
S/C: OFF  ABS CLOCK:  55.0000      REL CLOCK: 55.0000      TTG: 2
=================================================================================
XACT: 1        CURBLK: BLOCK4   NEXTBLK: BLOCK5    CHAINS: CEC       PC:

MARK-TIME: 15.0000      MOVE-TIME: -----         PRIORITY: 0
=================================================================================
CURRENT EVENTS CHAIN

XACT      CURBLK    NXTBLK    CHAINS  SDPGFT**   MARK-TIME   MOVE-TIME   PRIORITY

2         BLOCK2    BLOCK3    CEC     SD           30.0000     40.0000          0
: trap next
: run

XACT 1 POISED AT BLOCK 5 (BLOCK5).  RELATIVE CLOCK: 55.0000
: display cec
```

Figure 7.6 (d) *Screen 4*

BLOCK1 GENERATE has already been reached.) So in Screen 4 we set a **next** trap, then issue a **run** command. GPSS/H goes through the next Clock Update Phase, brings the following Scan Phase to the point of being about to try to move a scan-active Transaction, then gives us control with this message:

```
XACT 1 POISED AT BLOCK 5 (BLOCK5).
RELATIVE CLOCK: 55.0000
```

This message is consistent with our expectations. Xact 1, the first casting-Xact to use the drill, has been brought back to the CEC (from the FEC) at time 55.0 and is poised to RELEASE (BLOCK5) and TERMINATE.

For discussion purposes, we now want to **display cec**. And so we key in that command at the bottom of Screen 4 (with the result of sending this command seen in the Dialog Window on Screen 5).

Screen 5 (Figure 7.6, part e)

In Screen 5 we see the Current Events Chain displayed as a result of sending the **display cec** command keyed in at the bottom of Screen 4. Xact 2 is at the **front** of the CEC, and Xact 1 is behind it. As we know from Screen 4, Xact 2 is asleep. This explains why it is Xact 1 (not Xact 2) which is poised to try to move in response to the **run** command at the bottom of Screen 4. When an Xact is asleep, GPSS/H will not try to move it. *Xacts asleep on the CEC are incapable of causing interrupt conditions to occur.*

Screen 6 (Figure 7.6, part f)

In response to the prompt at the bottom of Screen 5, we issue a **step** command in the Screen 6 Dialog Window. Resuming the simulation, GPSS/H moves Xact 1 into BLOCK5 (RELEASE), then displays the message

```
XACT 1 POISED AT BLOCK 6 (BLOCK6).
RELATIVE CLOCK: 55.0000
```

Execution of the RELEASE Block changes the status of the DRILL Facility from captured to idle, turns on the model's Status Change Flag, and awakens Xact 2. The setting of the Status Change Flag (S/C) is reported in the Status Window, where it is labeled **S/C**. In the upper row of the Screen 6 Status Window, we now see

```
BLOCK CURRENT     TOTAL          fig75.gps SOURCE CODE
----- -------     -----          ----------------------------------------------
3                     1           BLOCK3   SEIZE      DRILL     request/capture th
4           1         1           BLOCK4   ADVANCE    30        drilling time elap
5                     0           BLOCK5   RELEASE    DRILL     give up the drill
6                     0           BLOCK6   TERMINATE  1         the finished casti

================================================================================
S/C: OFF  ABS CLOCK:  55.0000      REL CLOCK: 55.0000       TTG: 2
================================================================================
XACT: 1        CURBLK: BLOCK4   NEXTBLK: BLOCK5    CHAINS: CEC       PC:

MARK-TIME: 15.0000      MOVE-TIME: -----        PRIORITY: 0
================================================================================
CURRENT EVENTS CHAIN

XACT     CURBLK   NXTBLK   CHAINS  SDPGFT**   MARK-TIME    MOVE-TIME    PRIORITY

2        BLOCK2   BLOCK3   CEC     SD           30.0000      40.0000           0

XACT     CURBLK   NXTBLK   CHAINS  SDPGFT**   MARK-TIME    MOVE-TIME    PRIORITY

1        BLOCK4   BLOCK5   CEC                  15.0000      55.0000           0
:
```

Figure 7.6 (e) *Screen 5*

```
BLOCK CURRENT     TOTAL          fig75.gps SOURCE CODE
----- -------     -----          ----------------------------------------------
4                     1           BLOCK4   ADVANCE    30        drilling time elap
5                     1           BLOCK5   RELEASE    DRILL     give up the drill
6                     0           BLOCK6   TERMINATE  1         the finished casti


================================================================================
S/C: ON   ABS CLOCK:  55.0000      REL CLOCK: 55.0000       TTG: 2
================================================================================
XACT: 1        CURBLK: BLOCK5   NEXTBLK: BLOCK6    CHAINS: CEC       PC:

MARK-TIME: 15.0000      MOVE-TIME: -----        PRIORITY: 0
================================================================================

2        BLOCK2   BLOCK3   CEC     SD           30.0000      40.0000           0

XACT     CURBLK   NXTBLK   CHAINS  SDPGFT**   MARK-TIME    MOVE-TIME    PRIORITY

1        BLOCK4   BLOCK5   CEC                  15.0000      55.0000           0
: step

XACT 1 POISED AT BLOCK 6 (BLOCK6).  RELATIVE CLOCK: 55.0000
: display cec
```

Figure 7.6 (f) *Screen 6*

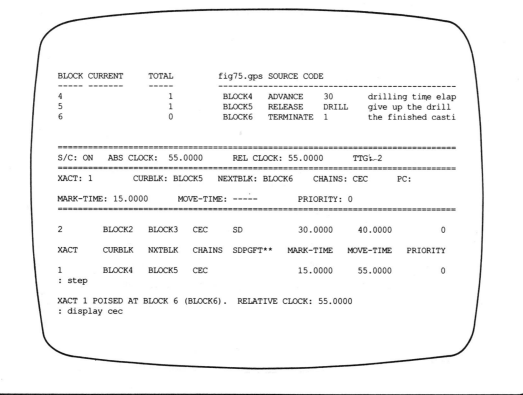

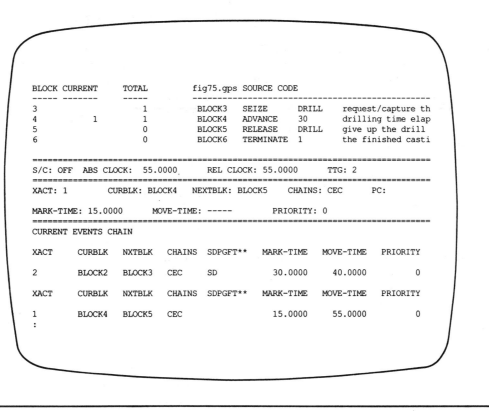

```
S/C: On
```

This is the first time the model's Status Change Flag has been turned on in this simulation. (Look back at Screens 1 through 5 in Figure 7.6, where **S/C: Off** consistently appears.)

To verify that RELEASE Block execution has awakened Xact 2, we key in **display cec** at the bottom of Screen 6, then send that command to produce Screen 7.

Screen 7 (Figure 7.6, part g)

Looking at Xact 2 on the Current Events Chain in Screen 7, we see that it is now awake. (Under its SDPGFT** label, the **S** column is blank, so Xact 2's Scan-Skip Indicator is off; Xact 2 is scan active.)

Screen 8 (Figure 7.6, part h)

Now we issue another **step** command. GPSS/H pushes the moving Xact, Xact 1, into its Next Block, BLOCK6 (TERMINATE), and Xact 1 is destroyed, as the message at the bottom of the Screen 8 Dialog Window verifies.

Screen 9 (Figure 7.6, part i)

We begin in Screen 9 by issuing a **run** command. GPSS/H turns the model's Status Change Flag off, restarts the scan, and focuses on Xact 2. Because a **next** trap is set and Xact 2 is awake, control is then given to us with the message

```
XACT 2 POISED AT BLOCK 3 (BLOCK3).
RELATIVE CLOCK: 55.000
```

And so Xact 2 is about to try (successfully) to execute the SEIZE Block and take control of the DRILL. We issue another **run** command. GPSS/H resumes with the movement of Xact 2, which executes the SEIZE and then the ADVANCE, where it stops moving for the time being. Because a **system** trap is set, control is then given to us with the message

```
XACT 2 PLACED ON FEC AT BLOCK 4 (BLOCK4).
RELATIVE CLOCK: 55.000
```

This concludes the demonstrated operation of unique blocking, of the model's Status Change Flag, of each Xact's Scan-Skip Indicator, and of scan restarts.

Congratulations! You've now completed study of the way GPSS/H organizes and processes infor-

```
BLOCK CURRENT     TOTAL        fig75.gps SOURCE CODE
----- -------     -----        ---------------------------------------------
4                     1         BLOCK4   ADVANCE    30        drilling time el
5                     1         BLOCK5   RELEASE    DRILL     give up the dril
6                     0         BLOCK6   TERMINATE  1         the finished cas

===============================================================================
S/C: ON   ABS CLOCK:  55.0000        REL CLOCK: 55.0000        TTG: 2
===============================================================================
XACT: 1          CURBLK: BLOCK5   NEXTBLK: BLOCK6    CHAINS: CEC        PC:

MARK-TIME: 15.0000        MOVE-TIME: -----           PRIORITY: 0
===============================================================================
CURRENT EVENTS CHAIN

XACT      CURBLK    NXTBLK    CHAINS   SDPGFT**    MARK-TIME    MOVE-TIME    PRIORITY

2         BLOCK2    BLOCK3    CEC        D          30.0000      40.0000            0

XACT      CURBLK    NXTBLK    CHAINS   SDPGFT**    MARK-TIME    MOVE-TIME    PRIORITY

1         BLOCK5    BLOCK6    CEC                   15.0000      55.0000            0
:
```

Figure 7.6 (g) *Screen 7*

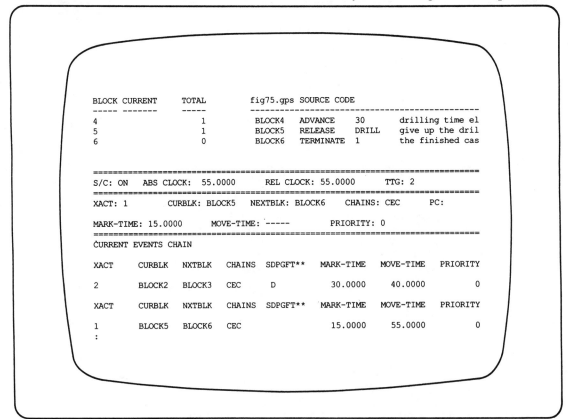

```
BLOCK CURRENT     TOTAL        fig75.gps SOURCE CODE
----- -------     -----        ----------------------------------------------
4                     1         BLOCK4   ADVANCE    30       drilling time elap
5                     1         BLOCK5   RELEASE    DRILL    give up the drill
6                     1         BLOCK6   TERMINATE  1        the finished casti

==============================================================================
S/C: ON   ABS CLOCK:  55.0000      REL CLOCK: 55.0000      TTG: 1
==============================================================================
XACT: 1         CURBLK: BLOCK5   NEXTBLK: BLOCK6    CHAINS:           PC:

MARK-TIME: 15.0000      MOVE-TIME: -----        PRIORITY: 0
==============================================================================

2        BLOCK2   BLOCK3   CEC      D           30.0000     40.0000          0

XACT     CURBLK   NXTBLK   CHAINS  SDPGFT**   MARK-TIME   MOVE-TIME   PRIORITY

1        BLOCK5   BLOCK6   CEC                 15.0000     55.0000          0
: step

XACT 1 DESTROYED AT BLOCK 6 (BLOCK6).  RELATIVE CLOCK: 55.0000
:
```

Figure 7.6 (h) *Screen 8*

```
BLOCK CURRENT     TOTAL        fig75.gps SOURCE CODE
----- -------     -----        ----------------------------------------------
2                     2         BLOCK2   ADVANCE    10       conveying time ela
3                     2         BLOCK3   SEIZE      DRILL    request/capture th
4          1          2         BLOCK4   ADVANCE    30       drilling time elap
5                     1         BLOCK5   RELEASE    DRILL    give up the drill
6                     1         BLOCK6   TERMINATE  1        the finished casti
==============================================================================
S/C: ON   ABS CLOCK:  55.0000      REL CLOCK: 55.0000      TTG: 1
==============================================================================
XACT: 2         CURBLK: BLOCK4   NEXTBLK: BLOCK5    CHAINS: FEC      PC:

MARK-TIME: 30.0000      MOVE-TIME: 85.0000      PRIORITY: 0
==============================================================================
: step

XACT 1 DESTROYED AT BLOCK 6 (BLOCK6).  RELATIVE CLOCK: 55.0000
: run

XACT 2 POISED AT BLOCK 3 (BLOCK3).  RELATIVE CLOCK: 55.0000
: run

XACT 2 PLACED ON FEC AT BLOCK 4 (BLOCK4).  RELATIVE CLOCK: 55.0000
:
```

Figure 7.6 (i) *Screen 9*

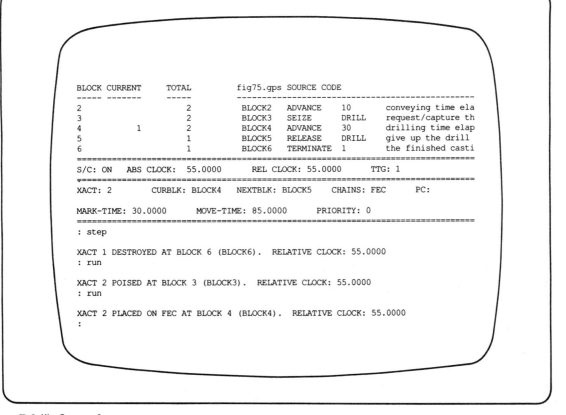

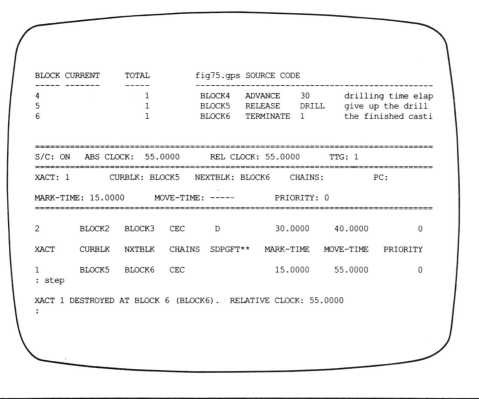

mation about Transactions in fundamental models. Having mastered this material, you'll find the remaining study of GPSS/H Blocks and Block interactions will proceed very smoothly.

7.7 Exercises

1. The file fig75.gps contains the Figure 7.5 Model File. Using this file, reproduce the screen sequence shown in Figure 7.6.

*2. The file s77x2.gps contains this Model File:

```
         SIMULATE
*
         GENERATE  0,,,5
         ADVANCE   0
         SEIZE     POWER
         ADVANCE   10
         RELEASE   POWER
         TERMINATE 1
*
         START     5
         END
```

(a) After completion of the Scan Phase at time 0.0, in which Block and on which chain will Xact 1 be, and what will its Move Time be? Answer this same question for Xacts 2, 3, 4, and 5. Will Xacts 2, 3, 4, and 5 be asleep (scan inactive) or awake (scan active)?

(b) Discuss this statement: "After completion of the Scan Phase at time 0.0, the future time of Xact 1's next attempted move is **known** to GPSS/H, but the future time of the next attempted moves of Xacts 2, 3, 4, and 5 is **unknown** to GPSS/H."

(c) Now suppose that Xact 1 has just executed RELEASE and TERMINATE at time 10.0. Will the model's Status Change Flag be on or off? In which Block and on which chain will Xacts 2, 3, 4, and 5 be? Will these Xacts be asleep or awake?

(d) After completion of the Scan Phase at time 10.0, in which Block and on which chain will Xact 2 be, and what will its Move Time be? Answer this same question for Xacts 3, 4, and 5. Will Xacts 3, 4, and 5 be asleep (scan inactive) or awake (scan active)?

(e) Ask yourself questions similar to those in (c) and (d) relative to times 20.0, 30.0, 40.0, and 50.0.

(f) Now perform a Test-Mode simulation with the model in the s77x2.gps file and issue commands designed to produce information you can use to confirm your answers to the foregoing questions. If one or more of your predicted answers are incorrect, think things through to the point of understanding why your reasoning was wrong.

You're asked in the remaining exercises in this section to indicate whether a given statement is true or false and to explain the reasoning behind your answer.

*3. "Whenever an Xact executes a RELEASE, GPSS/H *immediately* restarts the scan of the Current Chain." True or false? Explain your reasoning.

*4. "Whenever an Xact executes a RELEASE, GPSS/H *eventually* restarts the scan of the Current Chain." True or false? Explain your reasoning.

*5. "When an Xact executes a "RELEASE POWER" Block, GPSS/H will turn on the model's Status Change Flag even if no Xacts are blocked at a "SEIZE POWER" Block. True or false? Explain your reasoning.

*6. "When an Xact executes a "RELEASE POWER" Block and two or more Xacts are blocked at a "SEIZE POWER" Block, the Scan-Skip Indicator of *only one* of the blocked Xacts will be turned off (that is, only one of the blocked Xacts will be awakened, or made scan active)." True or false? Explain your reasoning.

*7. "It is possible for one or more Xacts to spend simulated time in an ADVANCE Block *and* on the Current Events Chain." True or false? Explain your reasoning.

*8. "If there is currently an Xact in an ADVANCE Block, this ADVANCE Block will deny entry to any other Xacts that take it as their Next Block Attempted." True or false? Explain your reasoning.

8 More Imaginative Modeling of Single Servers

8.1 Preview

The fundamental use of SEIZE and RELEASE Blocks to model single servers was introduced in Chapter 6. Additional possibilities for use of these Blocks in the modeling of single servers are considered in this chapter. Included in the discussion are the use of identical Blocks at multiple points in a model, simultaneous control of two or more resources by a Transaction, the use of consecutive Blocks that can deny entry, the use of overlapping SEIZE/RELEASE Blocks, and the use of dummy Facilities. The consequences of following a GENERATE Block with a type of Block that can deny entry are also considered.

8.2 When the Block Following GENERATE Can Deny Entry

It has been stated several times that a Block is executed when a Transaction **moves into** the Block. Whether or not the Transaction can then immediately **move out of** the Block into its Next Block does not matter. The Transaction's Current Block has already been executed, even if the Transaction must remain in the Block for some interval of simulated time.

As pointed out in Section 4.16, however, the **GENERATE Block** is a **major exception** to the point made in the preceding paragraph. In GPSS/H, a GENERATE Block does **not** execute when a Transaction moves **into** the Block. Instead, a GENERATE Block executes when a Transaction moves **out of** the Block into its Next Block.

In the great majority of cases, the GENERATE Block is followed by a type of Block that never denies entry to a Transaction. (In Case Study 6A, for example, the GENERATE Block is followed by an ADVANCE Block.) When this is the case, Transactions are always able to move out of their GENERATE Block at the same simulated time they move into it. And so in such cases there is **no simulated time lag** between movement into and execution of the GENERATE Block.

But what if a GENERATE is followed by a Block (such as SEIZE) that can block a Transaction? In such cases, there **may be a simulated time lag** between movement of a Transaction into its GENERATE Block, and eventual execution of the GENERATE Block.

For example, consider the Model File in Figure 8.1. Deterministic interarrival times of 10 are specified at the GENERATE Block. Considered **out of context**, then, it would seem that Xacts would come out of the GENERATE Block at times 10.0, 20.0, 30.0, and so on. This would be the case if each Xact moved into and then out of the Figure 8.1 GENERATE

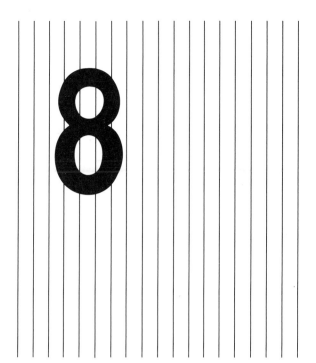

```
          SIMULATE
*
          GENERATE   10
          SEIZE      RESOURCE
          ADVANCE    15
          RELEASE    RESOURCE
          TERMINATE  1
*
          START      25
*
          END
```

Figure 8.1 *A Model That Distorts Arrival Times at a GENERATE Block*

without simulated delay. But **in context**, only the **first** Xact of the simulation will move into and then out of the GENERATE Block without simulated delay. The **second** Xact will **move into** the GENERATE Block at time **20.0**, but won't **move out** until time **25.0** (when the first Xact executes the RELEASE and TERMINATE Blocks). The **third** Xact won't then even be created and scheduled until time 25.0, when its predecessor moves out of the GENERATE. This third Xact won't **move into** the GENERATE until time **35.0** (time of creation 25.0 + interarrival time 10.0 = 35.0), and won't **move out** until time **40.0** (when the second Xact executes the RELEASE and TERMINATE Blocks). And so on. (You're asked to verify these statements in Exercise 1 of Section 8.4.)

In this example, we see that if the Block following a GENERATE can deny entry, then the **realized** times between Xact movement from the GENERATE Block can **exceed** the interarrival times specified with the GENERATE Block's A and B Operands. Xacts after the first move out of the Figure 8.1 GENERATE Block **every 15 time units, not every 10 time units** as the GENERATE Block's A Operand implies.

It's sometimes (although not often) convenient to take advantage of the described GENERATE Block behavior. (See Section 18 of Chapter 11 in this regard and Exercise 1 of Section 11.19.) But what can be done to **avoid** the distortion of interarrival times when it would otherwise be present and isn't wanted? One possibility is to insert between the GENERATE and SEIZE (or whatever type of Block can deny entry to an Xact) **an ADVANCE Block specifying zero holding time** (such as "ADVANCE 0"). An ADVANCE with zero holding time is referred to as a **dummy ADVANCE Block.**

An ADVANCE never denies entry, and so a Transaction can always move from its GENERATE into a dummy ADVANCE without simulated delay. When an Xact moves into a dummy ADVANCE, the Xact remains on the Current Chain and immediately tries to move from the ADVANCE into its Next Block, and so on. And so a dummy ADVANCE can be used to sidestep interarrival time distortions without otherwise affecting the logic of the model.

To illustrate use of a dummy ADVANCE, consider the following problem:

> A single clerk works at an order-filling location in a system. Two types of orders are filled at this location. Orders of the first type arrive every 15 ± 10 minutes. Orders of the second type arrive every 60 ± 20 minutes. Regardless of order type, it takes the clerk 10 ± 5 minutes to fill an order.
>
> The difference between orders is that those of the second type come from preferred customers and are filled with high priority. The service order is therefore "first-come, first-served, within priority class" (see Section 6.2). This means the clerk fills high-priority orders first. Only if there are no high-priority orders waiting will the clerk fill a low-priority order. (However, the clerk won't interrupt the filling of a low-priority order if a high-priority order arrives in the meantime.)

A model for this prioritized order-filling system is shown in Figure 8.2. Order-Xacts of low priority (Priority 5) come into the model from the BLOCK1 GENERATE, move without delay into the following TRANSFER Block, and from there request the clerk, and so on. Order-Xacts of high priority (Priority 10) come into the model from the BLOCK3 GENERATE, move without delay into the following dummy ADVANCE Block, and from there request the clerk, and so on. Filled orders TERMINATE without reducing the value of the model's Termination Counter. The base time unit in the model is 1 minute. The simulation stops at the end of 8 hours (480 minutes).

The importance of the BLOCK4 dummy ADVANCE in the Figure 8.2 model is that its presence permits high-priority order-Xacts to move without delay from their BLOCK3 GENERATE, so there will be no arrival-time distortions. If the dummy ADVANCE were eliminated, "SEIZE CLERK" would follow the BLOCK3 GENERATE, and the realized times of high-priority order arrivals would not correspond to the 60 ± 20 distribution specified at the GENERATE Block.

```
          SIMULATE                      base time unit: 1 minute
*
 BLOCK1   GENERATE  15,10,,,5           low-priority orders arrive
          TRANSFER  ,GETCLERK           go to request/capture the clerk
*
 BLOCK3   GENERATE  60,20,,,10          high-priority orders arrive
 BLOCK4   ADVANCE   0                   no arrival-time distortions
 GETCLERK SEIZE     CLERK               request/capture the clerk
          ADVANCE   10,5                order filling time
          RELEASE   CLERK               let go of the clerk
          TERMINATE 0                   filled order leaves
*
          GENERATE  480                 an Xact comes after 8 hours
          TERMINATE 1                   end the Xact-Movement Phase
*
          START     1                   start the Xact-Movement Phase
          END                           end of Model-File execution
```

Figure 8.2 *A Model That Uses a Dummy ADVANCE BLOCK*

8.3 Using Identical Blocks at Multiple Points in a Model

In the Figure 8.2 model, low-priority orders move from their GENERATE into a TRANSFER, and then to the SEIZE/ADVANCE/RELEASE sequence moved through by high-priority orders. This transfer of low-priority orders isn't necessary, because **it is OK to use identical Blocks at multiple points in a model**. For example, there can be one **or more** "SEIZE CLERK" Blocks in a model, one or more "RELEASE CLERK" Blocks, and so on. This means low-priority orders in the Figure 8.2 model could have moved from their GENERATE Block into an ADVANCE/SEIZE/ADVANCE/ RELEASE/ TERMINATE sequence identical to that used by high-priority orders.

Using identical Blocks at multiple points, an alternative model for the prioritized order-filling system is shown in Figure 8.3. The Figure 8.3 approach provides a degree of flexibility that the Figure 8.2 approach doesn't. For example, suppose high-priority orders take 15 ± 7 minutes to fill. In the Figure 8.3 approach, **their** ADVANCE Block could then be "ADVANCE 15,7" instead of "ADVANCE 10,5". This is just a small example of the convenience that can result from use of identical Blocks at multiple points in a model.

8.4 Exercises

1. The file fig81.gps contains the Figure 8.1 model. Run this model in Test Mode and verify that the second and third Xacts come **into** the GENERATE Block at times 20 and 35, but don't move **out of** the GENERATE Block until times 25 and 40, respectively.

*2. At what time will a simulation performed with the following Model File end?

```
          SIMULATE
*
          GENERATE  25,,0
          SEIZE     KEY
          ADVANCE   25
          RELEASE   KEY
          TERMINATE 0
*
          GENERATE  10
          SEIZE     KEY
          RELEASE   KEY
          TERMINATE 1
*
          START     3
          END
```

```
          SIMULATE                  base time unit: 1 minute
*
          GENERATE   15,10,,,5      low-priority orders arrive
          ADVANCE    0              no arrival-time distortions
          SEIZE      CLERK          request/capture the clerk
          ADVANCE    10,5           order filling time
          RELEASE    CLERK          let go of the clerk
          TERMINATE  0              filled order leaves
*
          GENERATE   60,20,,,10     high-priority orders arrive
          ADVANCE    0              no arrival-time distortions
          SEIZE      CLERK          request/capture the clerk
          ADVANCE    10,5           order filling time
          RELEASE    CLERK          let go of the clerk
          TERMINATE  0              filled order leaves
*
          GENERATE   480            an Xact arrives after 8 hours
          TERMINATE  1              end the Xact-Movment Phase
*
          START      1              start the Xact-Movement Phase
          END                       end of model-file execution
```

Figure 8.3 *A Model Containing Identical Blocks at Multiple Points*

Think through the answer to this question. Then carry out a Test mode simulation with the model (provided in file s84x2.gps) to verify your answer. If the results aren't consistent with your answer, figure out where your reasoning went wrong.

*3. The Figure 8.2 model is in the file fig82.gps. Perform a Batch simulation with this model. What utilization results for the clerk?

Now, using data given in the description of the prioritized order-filling system, compute (by hand) the **expected** utilization (that is, the long-run utilization) of the clerk. Compare the expected utilization with that realized in the simulation. (The utilization realized in the simulation is a **point estimate** of the expected utilization. See Chapter 14 for more details.)

*4. Conduct a Test-Mode simulation with the Figure 8.2 model to determine the earliest time that a high-priority order cuts in line ahead of a low-priority order. At what time does this high-priority order capture the clerk? (This will be the earliest time in the simulation that the priority distinction among orders makes a difference in terms of which order the clerk fills next.)

5. The Figure 8.3 model is in the file fig83.gps. Carry out a Batch simulation with this model. Compare the results with those from the simulation of Exercise 3. Do you think the respective outputs will match? Why, or why not? What are your findings?

6. Repeat Exercise 4, but use the Figure 8.3 model. Do your results match those of Exercise 4, as they should?

7. Suppose service time for high-priority orders in the prioritized order-filling system changes from 10 ± 5 minutes to 15 ± 7 minutes. Compute (by hand) the resulting expected utilization of the clerk.

Now modify the Figure 8.3 model to reflect the changed service time. Perform a Batch simulation with the model. Compare the resulting **estimate** of the clerk's utilization with its **expected value**.

*8. Joe owns and operates a small barber shop in which he cuts hair and gives shaves. Two types of customers come to the shop. Haircut-only customers come every 35 ± 10 minutes to get a haircut. Shave-and-haircut customers come every 60 ± 20 minutes to get both a shave and a haircut. It takes Joe 18 ± 6 minutes to give a haircut and 10 ± 2 minutes to shave a customer. Joe serves customers in the order in which they come into the shop. The shop is open continuously from 9 A.M. until 5 P.M. (Joe eats lunch in bits and snatches when there is no work to be done.)

Using 1 minute as the base time unit, model Joe's operation. Design the model to simulate for one working day. (The simulation is to end at 5 P.M.) Perform a Batch simulation with the model. What is the state of the model when the Xact-Movement Phase ends? Is Joe in the process of serving a customer? If so, is he giving a shave or a haircut? Are there one or more other customers waiting for Joe?

8.5 The Use of Consecutive Blocks That Can Deny Entry

Sometimes a model contains two or more consecutive Blocks of types that can deny entry to a Transaction. To illustrate, let's build a model for this situation:

Type A and Type B ships come to a small harbor to unload cargo. The harbor consists of two berths. One of these berths is used only by Type A ships. The other berth is used only by Type B ships. There is one tugboat at the harbor. The tugboat is used to tug a ship into the berth prior to unloading, and then later to tug the ship back out of the berth after unloading has been completed. The services of the tugboat are not needed while a ship is unloading.

Both ship types compete for use of the one tugboat at the harbor. Service order for tugboat use, and for use of the A and B berths, is FCFS.

When a ship arrives at the harbor, it does these things:

1. It requests the berth of the type it uses.
2. After capturing the berth, it requests the tugboat.
3. After capturing the tugboat, it gets pulled into the berth.
4. It gives up the tugboat.
5. It unloads cargo.
6. It requests the tugboat again.
7. It gets pulled out of the berth.
8. It gives up the tugboat.
9. It gives up the berth.
10. It leaves the harbor.

The interarrival-time and unloading-time distributions for Type A ships are 30 ± 10 hours and 26 ± 8 hours, respectively. The respective interarrival-time and unloading-time distributions for Type B ships are 15 ± 7 hours and 12 ± 4 hours. Berthing and deberthing times are 30 and 15 minutes, respectively, independent of ship type.

You might now try your hand at building a model for this harbor system before reading further.

A model for the harbor system is shown in Figure 8.4, where several Blocks have been labeled for discussion purposes. You should now study the Figure 8.4 model, satisfying yourself that it corresponds to the description of the harbor system.

The Figure 8.4 model contains consecutive SEIZE Blocks in the BLOCK3 and BLOCK4 Locations (and also in the BLOCK15 and BLOCK16 Locations). Now suppose a Type A ship arrives when the A berth is idle (empty) and the tugboat is being used (by a Type B ship). Upon arrival, this Type A ship will then move into (execute) the "SEIZE BERTHA" Block (BLOCK3), **thereby capturing the A berth.** It will then immediately **try** to move into the "SEIZE TUGBOAT" Block (BLOCK4), but will find itself blocked. And so it will remain in the "SEIZE BERTHA" Block (its Current Block) and be put to sleep on the Current Events Chain (unique blocking), waiting its turn to "SEIZE TUGBOAT."

At this point, those learning GPSS/H sometimes ask this question: "The Type A ship is **still in** the "SEIZE BERTHA" Block, and so **has it yet succeeded in capturing the A berth?"** The answer is **yes! Except for GENERATE**, a Block is executed at the time an Xact **moves into** the Block, not at the time it **moves out of** the Block. The Type A ship captured the A berth when it moved into "SEIZE BERTHA." The "SEIZE BERTHA" Block is now simply the Current Block for the Type A ship while it waits its turn to use the tugboat.

```
          SIMULATE             base time unit: 1 hour
*
          GENERATE  30,10      Type A ships arrive, one by one
          ADVANCE   0          no arrival-time distortions
BLOCK3    SEIZE     BERTHA     request/capture the A berth
BLOCK4    SEIZE     TUGBOAT    request/capture the tugboat
          ADVANCE   26,8       unloading time
          SEIZE     TUGBOAT    request/capture the tugboat again
          ADVANCE   0.25       deberthing time
BLOCK10   RELEASE   TUGBOAT    let the tugboat go
BLOCK11   RELEASE   BERTHA     no longer occupying the A berth
          TERMINATE 1          Type A ships leave, one by one
*
          GENERATE  15,7       Type B ships arrive, one by one
          ADVANCE   0          no arrival-time distortions
BLOCK15   SEIZE     BERTHB     request/capture the B berth
BLOCK16   SEIZE     TUGBOAT    request/capture the tugboat
          ADVANCE   0.5        berthing time
          RELEASE   TUGBOAT    let the tugboat go
          ADVANCE   12,4       unloading time
          SEIZE     TUGBOAT    request/capture the tugboat again
          ADVANCE   0.25       deberthing time
BLOCK22   RELEASE   TUGBOAT    let the tugboat go
BLOCK23   RELEASE   BERTHB     no longer occupying the B berth
          TERMINATE 1          Type B ships leave, one by one
*
          START     100        start the Xact-Movement Phase
          END                  end of Model-File execution
```

Figure 8.4 *A Model Containing Consecutive Blocks That Can Deny Entry*

We continue discussion of the Figure 8.4 harbor model in Sections 8.7 and 8.8, and then use the model as the basis for several exercises in Section 8.9.

8.6 Zero-Time Blocks

Some types of Blocks, like RELEASE and "ADVANCE 0", have these three properties:

1. They never deny entry to a Transaction.
2. When an Xact moves into them, the Xact immediately tries to move out of them.
3. The only path out of them leads to the sequential Block.

These types of Blocks are called **zero-time Blocks**, because an Xact executes a sequence of two or more of them in zero simulated time.

Examples of Blocks that are not zero-time Blocks are SEIZE; any ADVANCE at which the holding time exceeds zero; and TERMINATE, TRANSFER, and GENERATE. SEIZE does not satisfy property 1. An ADVANCE with non-zero holding time does not satisfy property 2. TERMINATE does not satisfy property 2. TRANSFER Blocks do not satisfy property 3. And GENERATE is not a zero-time Block, because an error occurs if an Xact tries to move into a GENERATE from some other Block. (See Exercise 2 of Section 3.16.)

When a Transaction moves into a sequence of two or more consecutive zero-time Blocks, each Block in the sequence will be executed at the same **simulated** time. Because the chronological order in which they're executed is unimportant, **consecutive zero-time Blocks can be sequenced in any order.**

Consider the model in Figure 8.4. Two consecutive zero-time Blocks (RELEASE and RELEASE) occupy Locations BLOCK10 and BLOCK11. These two Blocks can be interchanged without affecting the logic of the model in any way. Whether a Type A ship releases the tugboat first, and then the A berth, or releases the A berth first, and then the tugboat, does not matter. Either way, a departing Type A ship releases both the tugboat and the A berth at one and the same simulated time.

The same consideration applies to the two consecutive RELEASE Blocks in Locations BLOCK22 and BLOCK23 in the Figure 8.4 model.

Additional zero-time Blocks will be introduced as we proceed.

8.7 Dummy Facilities

The **--AVG-UTIL-DURING-- TOTAL TIME** statistic in a Facility Report measures the fraction of simulated time the Facility was in a state of capture. But being **captured** is one thing and being **productively used** is another thing. Sometimes it's of interest to measure the fraction of simulated time that a resource is productively used, as contrasted with simply being captured.

As a case in point, suppose a simulation is carried out with the Figure 8.4 model. In the resulting Facility Report, the **--AVG-UTIL-DURING-- TOTAL TIME** statistic for the A berth is **not** the fraction of simulated time the berth was being used to unload cargo. Each Type A ship holds the A berth in a state of capture through each of the following steps:

1. while waiting to capture the tugboat for berthing
2. while berthing
3. while unloading
4. while waiting to capture the tugboat for deberthing
5. while deberthing

And similarly for Type B ships. This means the utilization statistics for the A and B berths in the Figure 8.4 model must be appropriately interpreted. The same need for careful interpretation of Facility (and other) information is called for in general.

Suppose we want the Figure 8.4 model to measure the fraction of simulated time that Type A ships use the A berth **while unloading**. How can we modify the model to accomplish this? All we need do is add another Facility to the model, putting its SEIZE right ahead of the unloading ADVANCE, and its RELEASE right after the unloading ADVANCE, as in the Figure 8.5 Block sequence.

Then this new Facility, named USEANOW ("use A now"), will be captured whenever a Type A ship is unloading cargo, and will be idle otherwise. And so the utilization of the USEANOW Facility will be the fraction of simulated time the A berth was used to unload cargo.

The USEANOW Facility is an example of a **dummy Facility**. A dummy Facility is one whose SEIZE Block **never denies entry** to a Transaction **in the modeling context** in which the Facility is used.

As an exercise, try now to think through the reason why "SEIZE USEANOW" won't ever block a Transaction in the foregoing example. (Hint: What is the maximum number of Xacts that can be in transit at any one time between BLOCK3 and BLOCK11 in Figure 8.4?)

Here's the answer. There can never be more than **one Xact at a time** moving along the path between "SEIZE BERTHA" and "RELEASE BERTHA" in the Figure 8.4 model. This means that when such an Xact tries to move into "SEIZE USEANOW," the Facility must be idle. (In the Figure 8.4 model, no other Xact could possibly have it captured at the time.) And this Xact releases USEANOW before another Xact can "SEIZE BERTHA" and then eventually take "SEIZE USEANOW" as its Next Block. We conclude that "SEIZE USEANOW" is used in the model in such a way that it never denies entry to a Transaction.

```
          ...
          RELEASE   TUGBOAT   let the tugboat go
*
          SEIZE     USEANOW   start to unload
          ADVANCE   26,8      unloading time
          RELEASE   USEANOW   done unloading
*
          SEIZE     TUGBOAT   request/capture the tugboat again
          ...
```

Figure 8.5 *A Segment of the Figure 8.4 Model Extended to Measure the Fraction of the Time the Type A Berth is used to Unload Cargo*

```
         SIMULATE                 base time unit: 1 minute
*
 BLOCK1  GENERATE  50,30          work arrives, unit by unit
         ADVANCE   0              no arrival-time distortions
         SEIZE     STATION1       request/capture Station 1
         ADVANCE   45,10          Station 1 processing time
 BLOCK5  SEIZE     AGV            request/capture the AGV
 BLOCK6  RELEASE   STATION1       free Station 1
         ADVANCE   5,2            move to the next work station
         RELEASE   AGV            let the AGV go
         TERMINATE 1              work leaves the system
*
 BLOCK10 GENERATE  10,3           other AGV users arrive, one by one
         ADVANCE   0              no arrival-time distortions
         SEIZE     AGV            request/capture the AGV
         ADVANCE   6,3            use the AGV
         RELEASE   AGV            let the AGV go
 BLOCK15 TERMINATE 0              other AGV users leave the system
*
         START     50             start the Xact-Movement Phase
         END                      end of Model-File execution
```

Figure 8.6 *A Model Containing Overlapping SEIZE/RELEASE Blocks*

Dummy Facilities aren't used to model scarce system resources. Instead, they are used to force GPSS/H to gather more information during a simulation than would be gathered otherwise. The value of dummy Facilities lies in the Facility Report that is produced for them.

8.8 The Use of Overlapping SEIZE/ RELEASE Blocks

Sometimes a unit of traffic has to be able to capture one resource before it can free another. For example, a Transaction that has executed "SEIZE STATION1" might have to "SEIZE AGV" before it can "RELEASE STATION1". (AGV stands for automated guided vehicle, a type of equipment used to move work-in-process from point to point in a system.) This results in a situation in which the RELEASE Block for STATION1 appears **after** the SEIZE for AGV, and in this sense **overlaps** the "SEIZE AGV" Block. There is nothing wrong with having such overlap in a model. Beginning GPSS/H modelers are sometimes reluctant to introduce such overlapping use of Blocks into their models, however, mistakenly believing that for whatever reason, it would be erroneous to do so. The purpose of this section is to dispel this mistaken idea.

The model shown in Figure 8.6 illustrates the use of overlapping SEIZE/RELEASE Blocks in the situation just referred to. Work arrives from the BLOCK1 GENERATE, has a step performed on it at a workstation (modeled with the STATION1 Facility), and then is removed from the workstation by an automated guided vehicle (modeled with the AGV Facility). The next piece of work cannot be started at the workstation until **after** the most recently finished piece of work has captured the AGV and been removed from the workstation. (The physical presence of a finished piece of work ties up the workstation in such a way that the next piece of work can't be started.) And so a finished piece of work must be able to "SEIZE AGV" before it can "RELEASE STATION1". This explains the BLOCK5/ BLOCK6 pattern in the Figure 8.6 model and provides the occasion for overlapping use of SEIZE/RELEASE Blocks.

The work originating at the BLOCK1 GENERATE isn't the sole user of the AGV. Other AGV users are modeled in Figure 8.6 in BLOCK10 through BLOCK15. Without this contention for use of the AGV, finished work would never have to wait for an AGV at STATION1, and the point of the example would be lost.

```
         SIMULATE
*
         GENERATE  0,,,4     create 4 worker-Xacts at time 0.0
 REPEAT  ADVANCE   30,5      assembly time
         SEIZE     OVEN      request/capture the OVEN
         ADVANCE   8,2       heat-treating time
         RELEASE   OVEN      done with the OVEN
         TRANSFER  ,REPEAT   go start next cycle
*
         GENERATE  2400      control-Xact comes at end of 40th hour
         TERMINATE 1         reduce the TC value by 1,
*                            ending Xact movement
*
         START     1         set the TC = 1 ; start Xact movement
         END                 end of Model-File execution
```

Figure 8.7 *The Case Study 6A Model, with Most Comments Statements Stripped Out*

8.9 Unequal Numbers of Complementary Blocks

As indicated in Chapter 6, SEIZE and RELEASE are complementary Blocks. Many Blocks take the form of complementary pairs. (More complementary pairs are introduced in Chapters 9 and 11, for example.) When modeling with complementary Blocks, the numbers of Blocks of each of the two types making up a pair and referencing a particular entity member are usually equal. (In the model of Figure 8.4, for example, there is one "SEIZE BERTHA" and one "RELEASE BERTHA" Block, and there are two "SEIZE TUGBOAT" and two "RELEASE TUGBOAT" Blocks.) But there is no requirement that this be the case. The only requirement is that the Blocks be used in a logically consistent way.

For an example in which a model contains an unequal number of SEIZE and RELEASE Blocks, let's return to the widget-manufacturing model of Case Study 6A. For convenience, that model is repeated in Figure 8.7 (with most Comments Statements stripped out). When a simulation with the Figure 8.7 model begins, all four worker-Xacts are poised to begin assembling a widget. This starting state is not a state in which the system will ever be found after it has been in operation for some time. (There is no logical way for all the workers to be initiating an assembly at the same time, unless perhaps this happens at the start of a shift.)

For reasons to be considered in Chapter 14, it can be of interest to have a simulation start under conditions more likely to be in effect in a system after it has been operating for a while. Motivated by this consideration, let's build an alternative model for the widget-manufacturing system, designing the model so that the following conditions will be in effect when the simulation starts:

1. Worker 1 is beginning an assembly.
2. Worker 2 will finish heat-treating a widget in 3 minutes.
3. Worker 3 has 10 minutes to go before completing an assembly.
4. Worker 4 is waiting for the oven.

A model corresponding to the changed initial conditions is given in Figure 8.8. Each of the four worker-Xacts has its own GENERATE Block in the model. These GENERATE Blocks have been labeled WORKER1, WORKER2, and so on, corresponding to Worker 1, Worker 2, and so on, in the description of the changed initial conditions. The WORKER1 segment matches that in the Case Study 6A model (except for the inclusion of several Block labels), providing for Worker 1's starting state **and** providing the basic widget-manufacturing Blocks used eventually by all four worker-Xacts during the simulation. The WORKER2, WORKER3, and WORKER4 segments consist of the Blocks that provide the starting-state logic for Workers 2, 3, and 4, respectively. Each of these short segments concludes with an unconditional TRANSFER that puts the corresponding worker-Xact

```
           SIMULATE
*
 WORKER1   GENERATE   0,,,1       create Worker 1 at time 0.0
 REPEAT    ADVANCE    30,5        assembly time
 GETOVEN   SEIZE      OVEN        request/capture the OVEN
           ADVANCE    8,2         heat-treating time
 FREEOVEN  RELEASE    OVEN        done with the OVEN
           TRANSFER   ,REPEAT     go start next cycle
*
 WORKER2   GENERATE   0,,,1       create Worker 2 at time 0.0
           SEIZE      OVEN        capture the oven without delay
           ADVANCE    3           remaining oven-use time
           TRANSFER   ,FREEOVEN   go to the next step
*
 WORKER3   GENERATE   0,,,1       create Worker 3 at time 0.0
           ADVANCE    10          remaining assembly time
           TRANSFER   ,GETOVEN    go to the next step
*
 WORKER4   GENERATE   0,,,1       create Worker 4 at time 0.0
           TRANSFER   ,GETOVEN    go to the next step
*
           GENERATE   2400        control-Xact comes at end of 40th hour
           TERMINATE  1           reduce the TC value by 1,
*                                 ending Xact movement
*
           START      1           set the TC = 1 ; start Xact movement
           END                    end of Model-File execution
```

Figure 8.8 *The Case Study 6A Model, Modified to Provide Different Starting Conditions*

into the appropriate Block provided in the WORKER1 widget-manufacturing segment.

The Figure 8.8 model contains two "SEIZE OVEN" Blocks, but only one "RELEASE OVEN" Block. Such use of an unequal number of complementary Blocks in a model is convenient on occasion, as this example illustrates.

Counting the two-Block control-Xact segment, there are five Block segments in the Figure 8.8 model. Does the order in which the segments are arranged in the Model File matter? In general, the answer is "no." But in the Figure 8.8 model, there is one segment that must precede one of the other segments. The WORKER2 segment must precede the WORKER4 segment. Why? Because the two corresponding worker-Xacts both want the OVEN at time 0.0, and Worker 2 should be the one to get it, per the earlier description of the initial conditions. (See Exercise 10a of Section 8.10.) Except for this requirement, the five Block segments can be arranged in any order, leading to 60 possible arrangements. (The 60 is computed as 5!/2, where 5! is "5 factorial," which is 120.)

Note that the "initial" conditions called for in this exercise aren't yet in effect when Xact movement *begins*, but have been put into effect by the end of the Scan Phase at time 0.0. It's in this sense that arrangements can be made in a model to have specified initial conditions be in effect at the beginning of a simulation.

The modeling approach reflected in the Figure 8.7 model requires less effort than does the approach in the Figure 8.8 model, even though the starting state of the Figure 8.7 model is not one through which the system moves after it has started to operate. Quite a few extra Blocks have been included in the Figure 8.8 model, and they're executed only one time, at or near the start of Xact movement. Trade-offs between these alternative approaches will be put into sharper focus later.

8.10 Exercises

*1. The supplied file fig84.gps contains the model shown in Figure 8.4. Perform a Batch simulation with this model. Discuss and interpret the resulting output.

*2. Using data given in the Section 8.5 description of the harbor system, compute (by hand) the **expected** utilization (that is, the long-run utilization) of the tugboat. Compare the expected utilization with that realized in the Exercise 1 simulation.

3. In the Figure 8.4 model, interchange BLOCK10 with BLOCK11 and BLOCK22 with BLOCK23. Perform a Batch simulation with the modified model. Compare outputs to those from Exercise 1. Do the outputs match, as would be expected?

*4. Add two dummy Facilities to the Figure 8.4 model to measure the fraction of simulated time the A and B berths are, respectively, used to unload cargo. (See Figure 8.5.) Perform a simulation with the resulting model.

   Now use data given in the Section 8.5 description of the harbor to compute (by hand) the **expected** fraction of the time that the A and B berths are, respectively, used actually to unload cargo. Compare the expected values with those realized in the simulation.

5. In the harbor description of Section 8.5, the last several steps a ship goes through are these:
   7. It gets pulled out of the berth.
   8. It gives up the tugboat.
   9. It gives up the berth.
   10. It leaves the harbor.

   (The numbers used in this list match those in Section 8.5.) Suppose these steps are altered as follows:
   7. It gets pulled out of the berth.
   8. It gives up the berth.
   9. It continues to use the tugboat (to get pulled out to open water).
   10. It gives up the tugboat.
   11. It leaves the harbor.

   Assume step 9 in the new list takes 20 ± 5 minutes, independent of ship type. Modify the Figure 8.4 model (contained in the file fig84.gps) to reflect this change in system operation. Perform a Batch simulation with the modified model. Compare the results with those of Exercise 1. How long does it take for 100 ships to move through the harbor in the Exercise 1 and Exercise 5 simulations?

*6. A production system consists of two consecutive workstations, Station 1 and Station 2. There is one worker at each station. Arriving work has a step performed on it at Station 1, and then at Station 2, and then leaves the system.

   There is enough space ahead of Station 1 to hold an unlimited amount of incoming work-in-process (WIP). However, the wait space between Stations 1 and 2 can only hold **one piece** of work-in-process at a time. This situation is pictured in Figure E6.

   The Station 1 worker has to put a finished piece of work into the wait space between Stations 1 and 2 before starting on another piece of work. This sometimes forces the Station 1 worker to be idle, even though there is work to be done by this worker.

   Work arrives at Station 1 every 30 ± 20 minutes. Step times at Stations 1 and 2 are 25 ± 10 and 30 ± 10 minutes, respectively.

   The times required to transfer work-in-process onto Station 1, and from Station 1 into the wait space between Stations 1 and 2, and from the wait space onto Station 2, are assumed to be negligibly small.

   Build a model for the system. Design the simulation to stop after 100 pieces of work have left the system. Perform a simulation with the model. At what time does the simulation stop?

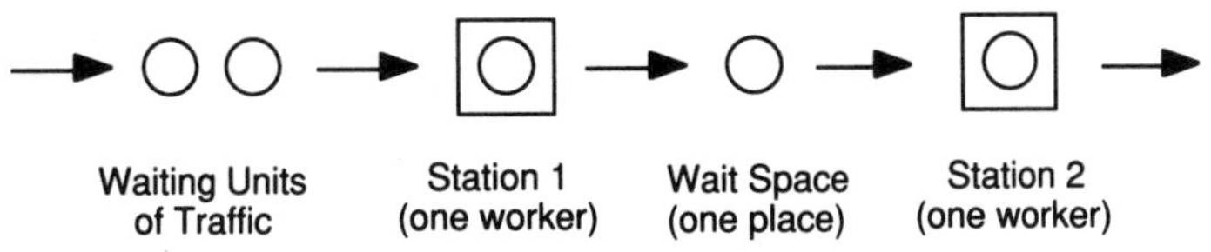

Figure E6

7. Repeat Exercise 6, only now design the model to measure the fraction of simulated time that the Station 1 worker is productive. (The Station 1 worker is not productive when there is no work to be done, or while waiting to put a piece of finished work into the wait-space between Stations 1 and 2.) Perform a simulation with the model. How does the Station 1 worker's productivity compare with the Station 1 utilization statistic reported in the Exercise 6 simulation?

*8. Exercise 6 assumes that WIP transfer times are negligibly small. Eliminate this assumption as follows. Suppose that after a unit of WIP arrives and captures Station 1, it takes 15 seconds to move the WIP into the Station 1 work area before work on it can begin. (The Station 1 worker accomplishes the move.) Similarly, it takes 15 seconds to move a unit of WIP from Station 1 into the wait space between workstations. (The Station 1 worker accomplishes this move, too.) It later takes another 15 seconds to move a unit of WIP from the wait space into the Station 2 work area. (The Station 2 worker accomplishes this move.) Finally, it takes 15 seconds to transfer a unit of WIP from Station 2 to its next destination. (The Station 2 worker accomplishes this move.)

   Build a model for the system as described. Perform a simulation with the model and analyze the resulting output. How long does it take for 100 finished pieces of work to leave the system?

*9. At a small college, students go through these steps to register for courses for the next term:
   1. Accomplish some initial paperwork. This takes 20 ± 10 minutes. Students do not require any assistance for this step.
   2. Go to Window 1 to have the single worker there provisionally OK the paperwork. This takes 7.5 ± 2.5 minutes (not counting any waiting time).
   3. Go to Window 2 to make arrangements with the single worker there for payment of tuition and to get a tuition form stamped. This takes 10 ± 5 minutes (not counting any waiting time).
   4. Go back to Window 1 to get a final OK on the paperwork. This takes 5 ± 2 minutes (not counting any waiting time). After this step, a student is done.

   The system operates from 9 A.M. until 4:30 P.M. and does not close down during the lunch hour. Students arrive every 12.5 ± 10 minutes, independent of the time of day. (In Chapter 13, we'll see that distributions can be made to change as simulated time goes by.)

   Build a model for this system. Use 1 minute as the base time unit. Use the model to perform a one-day simulation. Analyze and discuss the results. Are there any students in the system when the simulation stops? If so, what is their status?

*10. These questions refer to the Figure 8.8 model.
   (a) Explain why putting the WORKER2 segment in the Model File somewhere ahead of the WORKER4 segment is necessary if Worker 2 (not Worker 4) is to capture the OVEN at time 0.0.
   (b) If Worker 2 were given higher Priority (via use of the E Operand on the WORKER2 GENERATE Block) than Worker 4, it wouldn't be necessary to have the WORKER2 segment precede that of WORKER4 in the Figure 8.8 Model File. But then the model would be invalid for other reasons. Explain why.
   (c) Describe a way to eliminate the ADVANCE Block in the WORKER3 segment.

11. In the harbor model of Figure 8.4, show how to change the model so that the following conditions will all be in effect initially:
   (a) A Type A ship is un/loading cargo, and will be finished with this step in 0.5 hours.
   (b) Another Type A ship is waiting to un/load.
   (c) The next arrival of a Type A ship will be at time 0.25 hours. (After this arrival, Type A ships come every 3 ± 1 hours.)
   (d) A Type B ship is deberthing, and will be finished with this step in 0.1 hours.
   (e) The next arrival of a Type B ship will be at time 0.75 hours. (After this arrival, Type A ships come every 1.5 ± 0.75 hours.)

8.11 Bug Clinic

*1. Suppose someone asks you if the logic of the Figure 8.4 model would be affected by interchanging SEIZE Blocks as follows: interchange BLOCK3 and BLOCK4, and interchange BLOCK15 and BLOCK16. What would your answer be? Explain your reasoning. Remember that SEIZE Blocks are not zero-time Blocks.

Make the interchanges in a copy of the fig84.gps file, and perform a Batch simulation with the changed model. What happens? Are the results consistent with your reasoning?

*2. The Figure 8.4 model is contained in the fig84.gps file. In a copy of this file, change the A Operand in BLOCK11 from BERTHA to BERTHB. What problem does this introduce into the model? Initiate a Test-Mode simulation with the changed file. In response to the Ready! prompt, issue a **run** command. When an error condition eventually comes about, what message does GPSS/H issue?

*3. In a copy of the fig84.gps file containing the Figure 8.4 model, delete the RELEASE Block labeled BLOCK10. What is the problem with the resulting model? Do you think GPSS/H will issue a compile-time Warning Message in this regard? What do you think will happen if you simulate with the resulting model? Check out your thinking by initiating a Test-Mode simulation. In response to the Ready! prompt, issue a **run** command. What does happen? In the Block Counts, which Block has the largest Current Count when the simulation stops?

9 Gathering Information About Transactions

9.1 Preview

GPSS/H provides a Facility Report for Facilities used in a model. This report applies to the **servers** that Facilities simulate and not to the **users** of these servers (that Transactions simulate). It can be of interest to gather information about the users of servers or, more generally, about **Transactions** that move between any two modeler-selected points in a model. This chapter introduces a GPSS entity, the **Queue** entity, that can be used for this purpose.

9.2 The Nature of the Queue Entity

Consider Figure 9.1, which shows two arbitrary points, points A and B, on a path traveled by some Xacts as they move through a model. Answers to questions of the following type can be useful at the end of a simulation in helping the modeler come to a better understanding of the system being modeled:

1. **How many** Transactions moved past point A during the simulation?
2. What was the **average number** of Xacts in transit between points A and B?
3. What was the **maximum** number of Xacts in transit between points A and B?
4. What was the **average time** required for an Xact to move from point A to point B?
5. How many Xacts spent **zero simulated time** moving from point A to point B?

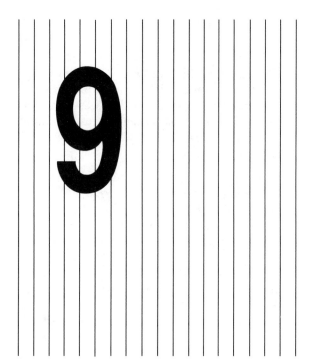

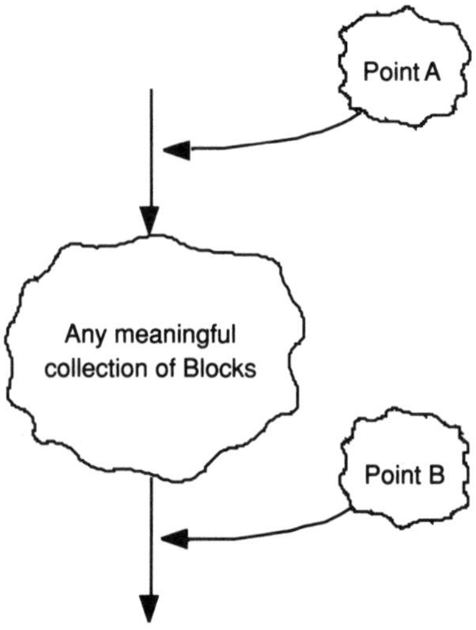

Figure 9.1 *Two Arbitrary Points on a Path in a Model*

GPSS/H provides the **Queue entity** for use in gathering answers to questions of this type. Recall that a GPSS/H entity is a tool (or a set of tools) that can be used to accomplish frequently occurring objectives in modeling and that tools corresponding to most entity types take the form of one or more **types of Blocks**. The Queue entity provides two types of Blocks, the **QUEUE** and **DEPART** Blocks. Use of the Queue entity simply requires placing a QUEUE Block at point A in Figure 9.1 and a corresponding DEPART Block at point B. The use of these Blocks causes GPSS/H to keep track of selected information about Xacts moving between those two points and to provide a summary of this information as part of the output produced at the end of a simulation. (An example of a Queue Report is presented in Section 9.4.)

It's too bad that the word "queue" is used as the name of the Queue entity, and as the Operation word for the QUEUE Block. "Queue" brings to mind the notion of a line of people waiting their turn to be served. If this notion is carelessly carried over into a corresponding interpretation in GPSS/H, then "Queue" brings to mind a set of Xacts all in some Current Block, waiting their turn to move into their Next Block. But this is not what a Queue is. The term "Queue" has a specialized meaning in GPSS/H. Queue is simply the name of the GPSS/H entity class that provides the capability for collecting information of the type suggested earlier. Xacts contribute to the information-gathering process all the while they are in transit between points A and B in a model. While in transit between these points, these Xacts can work their way through arbitrarily complicated Block sequences containing any number of ADVANCE Blocks, SEIZE Blocks, and so on, and in general are **not** "all in some Current Block, waiting their turn to move into their Next Block."

The Queue and Facility entities are similar in several ways. There can be two or more Queues in a model, just as there can be two or more Facilities. This provides the flexibility of being able to work with any number of distinct "point A"/"point B" pairings in a model, with separate and independent sets of information resulting for each such pairing.

Like Facilities, distinctions are made among Queues by giving each Queue its own unique **identifier**, or **name**. As with Facilities, symbolic Queue identifiers consist of from one to eight alphanumeric characters, the first of which must be alphabetic. Examples of such symbolic identifiers are SEGMENT7, FROMATOB, and LINE6J. Symbolic identifiers should (but don't have to) begin with a **minimum of three alphabetic characters** to avoid having them accidentally match or begin with a GPSS/H **reserved word**. (Remember that a reserved word is a sequence of characters which has a predefined meaning.) Queue identifiers can also be positive whole numbers, such as 1, or 3, or 8; however, to promote readability, we will only use symbolic Queue identifiers.

The symbolic identifiers chosen for Queues in a model will usually differ from those chosen for Facilities, but this isn't necessary. For example, a Queue could be named DRILL, and in the same model a Facility could be named DRILL.

The rule for forming Queue and Facility identifiers is the same as for forming Block Labels (Block identifiers). (Caution: Do not use the same identifier for a Queue or a Facility as for a Block. The reason for this, roughly speaking, is that dual use of an identifier for a Block and a Queue or Facility may force GPSS/H to use much more computer memory than would be used otherwise. It is beyond the scope of this book to explain this situation in detail.)

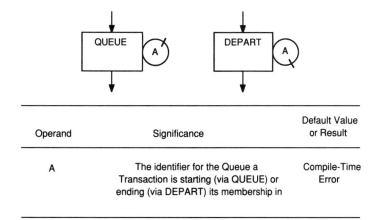

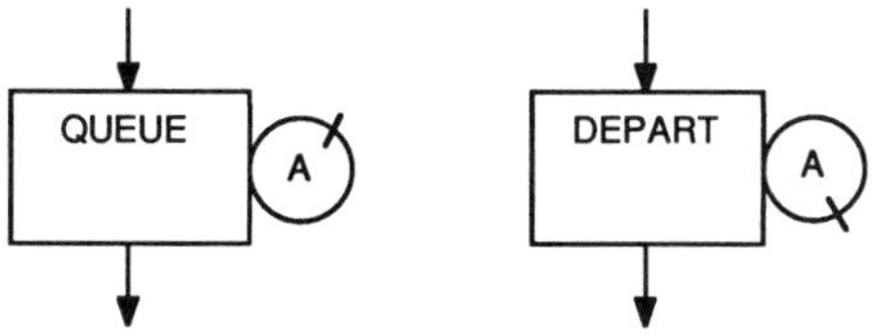

Operand	Significance	Default Value or Result
A	The identifier for the Queue a Transaction is starting (via QUEUE) or ending (via DEPART) its membership in	Compile-Time Error

Figure 9.2 *The QUEUE and DEPART Blocks, and Their A Operand*

A major contrast between Facilities and Queues is that Facilities are used to model system resources (e.g., single servers), whereas Queues are **not** used for this purpose, but are used strictly to gather information. Use of the Queue entity in a model is **optional**. Used correctly, the presence or absence of Queues in a model does not change the logical behavior of the model.

9.3 Starting and Ending Membership in a Queue: QUEUE and DEPART Blocks

Xacts that have moved past point A in Figure 9.1, but haven't yet moved past point B, are said to be **members of a Queue**. A Transaction **starts its membership** in a Queue by executing a QUEUE Block, and then later **ends its membership** in the Queue by executing a DEPART Block. (While an Xact is a member of a Queue, it is sometimes said to be "resident in the Queue.") The QUEUE and DEPART Blocks are shown with their A Operand in Figure 9.2. The A Operand is used to indicate the modeler's choice of an identifier for the relevant Queue.

QUEUE and DEPART (like SEIZE and RELEASE) are complementary. Execution of the second Block in the pair undoes the effect of execution of the first Block in the pair.

Neither QUEUE nor DEPART ever denies entry to a Transaction. (SEIZE is the only Block we've discussed so far which can deny entry to a Transaction.)

QUEUE and DEPART are both zero-time Blocks. (See Section 6 of Chapter 8.)

For a simple example of Queue use, suppose objects are placed on a conveyor every 25 ± 20 time units (uniformly distributed), then spend exactly 100 time units moving to the conveyor's take-off point, where they leave the system. We might use a Queue in modeling this simple situation to estimate what the **largest number** of objects on the conveyor is at any one time. The Figure 9.3 Model File corresponds to this situation:

In this simple model, Xacts start Queue membership when they come into the model, are members during their entire (short) life cycle, and then end their membership just before leaving the model. (More generally, Xacts will be members of a given Queue during just a portion of their life cycle, as later examples in this chapter show.)

So far, we've only indicated in general terms what types of information result from the use of Queues. The specifics of a Queue Report are discussed in the next section.

9.4 Queue Reports

Figure 9.4 provides an example of a Queue Report named TOOLWAIT. (This report was produced at the end of the simulation in Case Study 9A, presented in Section 9.6.) In Figure 9.4, numbers in parentheses have been placed over each of the columns in the report. (These numbers are not part of the report, but have been added to support discussion here.) The information in a Queue Report will now be discussed by column number:

```
          SIMULATE
*
          GENERATE  25,20   objects arrive, one by one,
*                           and are placed on the conveyor
          QUEUE     MOVING  start MOVING Queue membership
          ADVANCE   100     move to the take-off point
          DEPART    MOVING  end MOVING Queue membership
*
          TERMINATE 1       leave the system
*
          START     500     convey 500 objects in total
*
          END               end of Model-File execution
```

Figure 9.3 *A Model Illustrating Use of the Queue Entity*

(1) QUEUE	(2) MAXIMUM CONTENTS	(3) AVERAGE CONTENTS	(4) TOTAL ENTRIES	(5) ZERO ENTRIES	(6) PERCENT ZEROS	(7) AVERAGE TIME/UNIT	(8) $AVERAGE TIME/UNIT	(9) QTABLE NUMBER	(10) CURRENT CONTENTS
TOOLWAIT	6	1.501	146	26	17.8	296.093	360.246		4

Figure 9.4 *An Example of a Queue Report*

(1) The **QUEUE** column identifies the Queue for which information is being reported.

(2) **MAXIMUM CONTENTS** shows the maximum size of the Queue membership. MAXIMUM CONTENTS is the largest value ("high water mark") achieved by the CURRENT CONTENTS (see column 10).

(3) **AVERAGE CONTENTS** shows how many Transactions were members of the Queue on average. AVERAGE CONTENTS is a time-weighted average.

An example will help explain how the AVERAGE CONTENTS is determined. Suppose only two Xacts become members of the TRANSIT Queue during a simulation in which the base time unit is 1 minute. Assume these Xacts spend 20.0 and 30.0 minutes, respectively, as Queue members. Also assume these memberships have expired by time 40.0 (even though the simulation continues to time 100.0). By time 40.0, there will have been 50 "Xact-minutes" (20.0 + 30.0) of Queue membership accumulated. At time 40.0, then, the AVERAGE CONTENTS of the TRANSIT Queue will be 1.25 (50/40.0 = 1.25). At time 50.0, the AVERAGE CONTENTS of the Queue will have dropped to 1.0 (50/50.0 = 1.0). At time 80.0, the AVERAGE CONTENTS will have dropped to 0.6125 (50/80.0 = 0.6125). And by time 100.0, the AVERAGE CONTENTS will have dropped to 0.5. Note that the computation of AVERAGE CONTENTS **does use** the current value of the simulated clock.

(4) **TOTAL ENTRIES** is the total number of Transactions that became Queue members.

If a Queue's TOTAL ENTRIES is zero, **no report** will be produced for that Queue in the standard postsimulation output.

(5) **ZERO ENTRIES** is the number of Queue members whose duration of membership was 0.0 simulated time units. A ZERO entry results when a given Xact executes the QUEUE and DEPART Blocks at one and the same simulated time. Such a Transaction is said to have "passed through the Queue in zero simulated time."

(6) **PERCENT ZEROS** is the percentage of Xacts that passed through the Queue in zero simulated time. PERCENT ZEROS is the percentage of TOTAL ENTRIES that were ZERO ENTRIES.

(7) **AVERAGE TIME/UNIT** indicates how much simulated time Xacts spent on average as Queue members. AVERAGE TIME/UNIT is a time-weighted average.

An example will help explain how AVERAGE TIME/UNIT is determined. Suppose only three Xacts become members of the ENROUTE Queue during a simulation. Assume these Xacts spend 20.0, 0.0, and 30.0 time units, respectively, as Queue members. Also assume that these Queue memberships have expired by simulated time 40.0 (even though the simulation continues to time 100). Then at simulated times 40.0 **and greater**, the AVERAGE TIME/UNIT for the ENROUTE Queue is 16.667 ((20.0 + 0.0 + 30.0)/3 = 16.667). Note that the computation of AVERAGE TIME/UNIT **does not use** the current value of the simulated clock. (Contrast this with the computation of AVERAGE CONTENTS. See 3.)

(8) **$AVERAGE TIME/UNIT** is the average duration of Queue membership, **excluding** cases in which Xacts passed through the Queue in zero simulated time.

In the numeric example just given, the $AVERAGE TIME/UNIT is 25.0, computed as (20.0 + 30.0)/2 = 25.0.

(9) **QTABLE NUMBER** shows the identifier for the "Qtable" (if any) used in conjunction with the Queue. Operational aspects of Qtables, which provide a tabular histogram summarizing the distribution of the "Queue residence time" random variable, will not be discussed in this book.

(10) **CURRENT CONTENTS** shows the number of Xacts that are members of the Queue at the time the Queue Report is produced.

In addition to being provided as part of Postsimulation Reports, Queue Reports can be displayed by the user in Test Mode. This is done by using the **display que** command, where **que** means Queue.

9.5 More Examples of Queue Use

A simple example of Queue use in a model has been shown in Figure 9.3. Now that we know the specifics of Queue Reports, two more examples will be shown of models which use one or more Queues.

Example 1

Suppose cars arrive at the drive-through lane of a fast-food restaurant with interarrival times of 10 ± 10 minutes. It takes 3 ± 1 minutes for the driver of a car to place an order over the intercom. (The intercom is a single server.) The car then spends 15 ± 3 seconds moving from the intercom to the pickup window. (The pickup window is a single server.) A car spends 3 ± 2 minutes at the pickup window while the order is paid for, bagged, and handed over to the car's driver. The car then leaves. Model this system, having each car start membership in a Queue when it arrives, and end its membership in the Queue just before it leaves.

You might try your hand at building this model before reading further.

The Model File shown in Figure 9.5 provides the requested model. The model is straightforward. Notice how a QUEUE Block (labeled BLOCK2) has been placed just after the GENERATE, and a DEPART Block (labeled BLOCK10) has been used just before the TERMINATE.

In the Figure 9.5 model, the order of the RELEASE and DEPART Blocks could be reversed, because both are "zero-time Blocks."

Example 2

Now repeat Example 1, but extend the model so that it will additionally gather Queue information that applies to cars waiting their turn to capture the WINDOW Facility. Just before a car requests the WINDOW, it should start membership in a Queue, and immediately after a car has captured the WINDOW, it should end its membership in that Queue. Consider the interpretation that will apply to information in the corresponding Queue Report. AVERAGE CONTENTS will be the number of cars waiting on average for the WINDOW. MAXIMUM CONTENTS will be the largest number of cars waiting at one and the same time for the WINDOW. ZERO ENTRIES will be the number of cars that were able to capture the WINDOW without having to wait for it. AVERAGE TIME/UNIT will show how long cars spent on average waiting for the WINDOW. And so on. The Model File in Figure 9.6 provides the requested model.

The model repeats that of Figure 9.5, but includes a new QUEUE Block (labeled NEWBLOK1) right before "SEIZE WINDOW"

```
        SIMULATE                 base time unit: 1 minute
*
        GENERATE  10,10          cars arrive, one by one
BLOCK2  QUEUE     SNAKTIME       start SNAKTIME Queue membership
        SEIZE     INTERCOM       request/capture the intercom
        ADVANCE   3,1            place an order
        RELEASE   INTERCOM       done with the intercom
        ADVANCE   0.25,0.05      move to the pickup window
        SEIZE     WINDOW         request/capture the pickup window
        ADVANCE   3,2            pickup time
        RELEASE   WINDOW         leave the pickup window
BLOCK10 DEPART    SNAKTIME       end SNAKTIME Queue membership
        TERMINATE 1              leave the systm
*
        START     50             serve 50 cars in total
        END                      end of Model-File execution
```

Figure 9.5 *A Model for a Drive-Through Restaurant*

and a new DEPART Block (labeled NEWBLOK2) right after "SEIZE WINDOW." (The labels have been removed from the other QUEUE and DEPART Blocks in Figure 9.6.) The Locations chosen for this new pair of QUEUE/DEPART Blocks correspond exactly to the request made in the statement of the problem.

In the Figure 9.6 model, WINDOW is used as an identifier both for a Facility and for a Queue. As mentioned in Section 9.3, it's all right to use the same identifier for members of different entity classes (but **Block** identifiers should only be used to identify Blocks).

During part of their life cycle in the Figure 9.6 model, Xacts are members of two different Queues at one and the same time. This is perfectly fine. In GPSS/H, Xacts can be members of any number of different Queues at one and the same time.

The only Block between "QUEUE WINDOW" and "DEPART WINDOW" in the Figure 9.6 model is "SEIZE WINDOW". A car-Xact starts its membership in the WINDOW Queue by executing the QUEUE Block. The QUEUE Block then serves as its Current Block until it can execute the SEIZE Block. When its turn comes to capture the WINDOW, the car-Xact then ends it membership in the WINDOW Queue and goes on from there. It is true in this case, then, that when Xacts are in the WINDOW Queue, they are "all in some Current Block, waiting their turn to move into their Next Block" (quoted from Section 9.2). But this is clearly a special case of Queue use. In general, Queues can be used in very flexible ways, as we have started to see.

9.6 Case Study 9A: Alternative Service Orders at a Tool Crib

1. Statement of the Problem

In a particular factory, a single clerk works at a tool crib. The clerk checks out tools to mechanics, who use them to repair failed machines. (The tools involved are too expensive and too numerous for each mechanic to have each tool in his or her tool box.) The time between tool requests and the time needed to process a request depend on the type of mechanic involved. The interarrival- and service-time distributions for the two mechanic types are shown in Table 9A.1.

The tool crib clerk has been using an FCFS service order. It has been proposed, however, that an SPT (shortest processing time) service order might lower the average number of mechanics waiting for service at the tool crib. If so, this would result in a cost savings for two reasons: (1) less mechanic time would be wasted because of waiting at the tool crib, and (2) on average, failed machines would be put back into productive use sooner.

```
          SIMULATE                  base time unit: 1 minute
*
          GENERATE  10,10           cars arrive, one by one
          QUEUE     SNAKTIME        start SNAKTIME Queue membership
          SEIZE     INTERCOM        request/capture the intercom
          ADVANCE   3,1             place an order
          RELEASE   INTERCOM        done with the intercom
          ADVANCE   0.25,0.05       move to the pickup window
 NEWBLOK1 QUEUE     WINDOW          start WINDOW Queue membership
          SEIZE     WINDOW          request/capture the pickup window
 NEWBLOK2 DEPART    WINDOW          end WINDOW Queue membership
          ADVANCE   3,2             pickup time
          RELEASE   WINDOW          leave the pickup window
          DEPART    SNAKTIME        end SNAKTIME Queue membership
          TERMINATE 1               leave the system
*
          START     50              serve 50 cars in total
          END                       end of Model-File execution
```

Figure 9.6 *An extended Model for a Drive-Through Restaurant*

Table 9A.1

Interarrival- and service-time distributions for mechanics using the tool crib in Case Study 9A

Type of Mechanic	Interarrival Times (seconds)	Service Times (seconds)
1	420 ± 360	300 ± 90
2	360 ± 240	100 ± 30

Model the tool crib for each of the two alternative service orders. Simulate for one 8-hour workday for each service order. For these specific simulations, does the SPT service order appear to decrease the average number of mechanics in the waiting line?

(Note: there isn't enough information available in two single simulations to draw firm conclusions about the relative merits of an SPT versus FCFS service order in this system. See Chapters 14, 15, and 16 for more particulars.)

Assume that when each simulation starts, no mechanics are waiting their turn for service, and the clerk is idle. Stop the simulation at the end of the eighth hour, even if the clerk is captured and mechanics are waiting to be served at that time.

2. Approach Taken in Building the Model

This model is highly similar to that in Figure 8.3 of Chapter 8. In the Figure 8.3 model, two types of orders arrived at an order-filling system to be filled by a single clerk. In Case Study 9A, two types of mechanics arrive at a tool crib to be served by a single clerk. Just as the two order types come out of two different GENERATE Blocks in Figure 8.3, so too can the two mechanic types come out of different GENERATE Blocks in this case study. For the FCFS service order, both mechanics types can be created with identical Priority Levels. For the SPT service order, type 2 mechanics (which have the lower expected service time, and therefore the higher service priority) can simply be created with a higher Priority than type 1 mechanics. Apart from these priority distinctions, the FCFS and SPT models in this case study are identical to each other.

The case study calls for use of the Queue entity to measure the average number of mechanics waiting their turn for service. In this sense, the models here are enhanced versions of that in Figure 8.3, where the Queue entity hadn't yet been introduced. The enhancement is easily accomplished by putting QUEUE and DEPART Blocks around the "SEIZE CLERK" Blocks in Figure 8.3. The QUEUE Blocks can replace the dummy ADVANCE Blocks of Figure 8.3, which were used there so order-Xacts could move from their respective GENERATE Blocks without simulated delay (GENERATE/dummy ADVANCE/SEIZE). Because a QUEUE Block never denies entry, this same effect is accomplished by a GENERATE/QUEUE/SEIZE sequence.

3. Table of Definitions

The Table of Definitions for Case Study 9A is given in Table 9A.2.

4. Block Diagram

The Block Diagram for the SPT service order model in Case Study 9A is given in Figure 9A.1.

Table 9A.2

Table of definitions for Case Study 9A

Base Time Unit: 1 second

GPSS/H Entity	Interpretation
Transactions	
Model Segment 1	Type 1 mechanics
Model Segment 2	Type 2 mechanics
Model Segment 3	A control-Xact
Facilities	
CLERK	The tool crib clerk
Queues	
TOOLWAIT	The Queue used to gather information on the combined waiting experiences of both types of mechanics

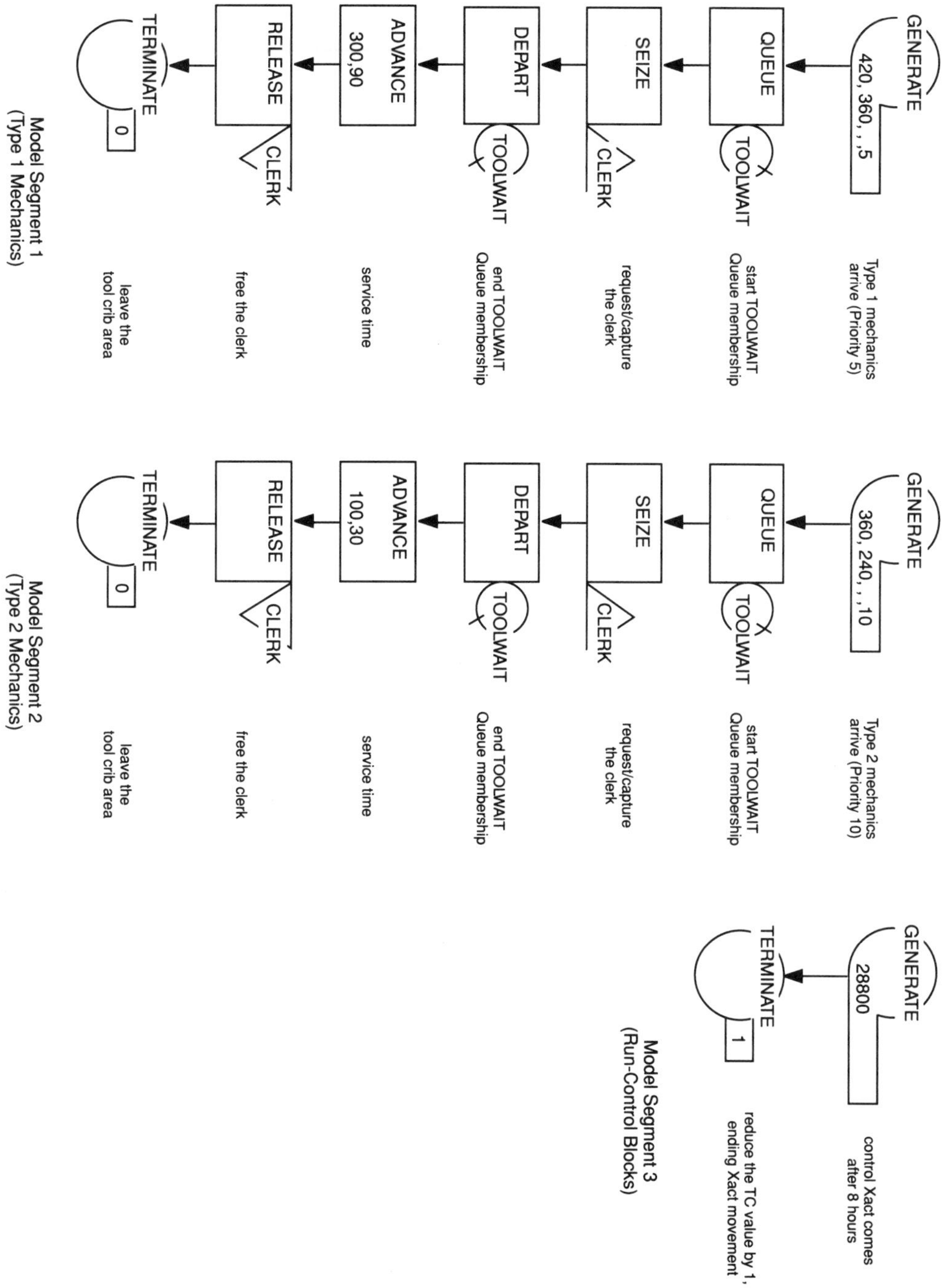

GENERATE
420, 360, , ,5
QUEUE
TOOLWAIT
SEIZE
CLERK
DEPART
TOOLWAIT
ADVANCE
300,90
RELEASE
CLERK
TERMINATE
0
Type 1 mechanics arrive (Priority 5)
start TOOLWAIT Queue membership
request/capture the clerk
end TOOLWAIT Queue membership
service time
free the clerk
leave the tool crib area
Model Segment 1 (Type 1 Mechanics)
GENERATE
360, 240, , ,10
QUEUE
TOOLWAIT
SEIZE
CLERK
DEPART
TOOLWAIT
ADVANCE
100,30
RELEASE
CLERK
TERMINATE
0
Type 2 mechanics arrive (Priority 10)
start TOOLWAIT Queue membership
request/capture the clerk
end TOOLWAIT Queue membership
service time
free the clerk
leave the tool crib area
Model Segment 2 (Type 2 Mechanics)
GENERATE
28800
TERMINATE
1
control Xact comes after 8 hours
reduce the TC value by 1, ending Xact movement
Model Segment 3 (Run-Control Blocks)

Figure 9A.1 *Block Diagram for Case Study 9A (SPT Service Order)*

```
STMT#  BLOCK#  *LOC    OPERATION  A,B,C,D,E,F,G    COMMENTS

  1                    SIMULATE                                    Case Study 9A
  2            *                              A Tool Crib System (SPT Service Order)
  3            *                                           Base Time Unit: 1 Second
  4            **********************************************************************
  5            *       Model Segment 1 (Type 1 Mechanics)                           *
  6            **********************************************************************
  7            *
  8      1             GENERATE   420,360,,,5     Type 1 mechanics arrive
  9            *                                  (Priority 5)
 10      2             QUEUE      TOOLWAIT        start TOOLWAIT Queue membership
 11      3             SEIZE      CLERK           request/capture the clerk
 12      4             DEPART     TOOLWAIT        end TOOLWAIT Queue membership
 13      5             ADVANCE    300,90          service time
 14      6             RELEASE    CLERK           free the clerk
 15      7             TERMINATE  0               leave the tool crib area
 16            *
 17            **********************************************************************
 18            *       Model Segment 2 (Type 2 Mechanics)                           *
 19            **********************************************************************
 20            *
 21      8             GENERATE   360,240,,,10    Type 2 mechanics arrive
 22            *                                  (Priority 10)
 23      9             QUEUE      TOOLWAIT        start TOOLWAIT Queue membership
 24     10             SEIZE      CLERK           request/capture the clerk
 25     11             DEPART     TOOLWAIT        end TOOLWAIT Queue membership
 26     12             ADVANCE    100,30          service time
 27     13             RELEASE    CLERK           free the clerk
 28     14             TERMINATE  0               leave the tool crib area
 29            *
 30            **********************************************************************
 31            *       Model Segment 3 (Run-Control Xact)                           *
 32            **********************************************************************
 33            *
 34     15             GENERATE   28800           control Xact comes after 8 hours
 35     16             TERMINATE  1               reduce the TC value by 1,
 36            *                                  ending Xact movement
 37            *
 38            **********************************************************************
 39            *       Run-Control Statements                                       *
 40            **********************************************************************
 41            *
 42                    START      1               set TC = 1; start Xact movement
 43                    END                        end of Model-File execution
```

Figure 9A.2 *Modified Source Echo of the Case Study 9A Model (SPT Service Order)*

5. Modified Source Echo

The Modified Source Echo for the SPT service order model in Case Study 9A is given in Figure 9A.2.

6. Postsimulation Report

The Postsimulation Report for the SPT and FCFS service orders in Case Study 9A is given in Figure 9A.3.

7. Discussion

Model Implementation. The Model File that led to the Figure 9A.2 SPT Modified Source Echo was run in Batch. Then the E Operand on the Block 8 GENERATE was changed to 5, and a Batch simulation was performed with the resulting FCFS model. This approach is relatively awkward, requiring two separate runs. Methods for automating situations like this are introduced in Chapter 14.

Postsimulation Report. The output of primary interest is the AVERAGE CONTENTS of the TOOLWAIT Queue. The Queue Reports in Figures 9A.3(a) and (b) show that the average number of waiting mechanics for the SPT and FCFS service orders for the 8-hour days simulated were 1.501 and 1.705, respectively. In these specific simulations, then, the SPT service order results in improved

FACILITY	--AVG-UTIL-DURING-- TOTAL TIME	AVAIL TIME	UNAVL TIME	ENTRIES	AVERAGE TIME/XACT	CURRENT STATUS	PERCENT AVAIL	SEIZING XACT	PREEMPTING XACT
CLERK	.903			142	183.097	AVAIL	100.0	145	

QUEUE	MAXIMUM CONTENTS	AVERAGE CONTENTS	TOTAL ENTRIES	ZERO ENTRIES	PERCENT ZEROS	AVERAGE TIME/UNIT	$AVERAGE TIME/UNIT	QTABLE NUMBER	CURRENT CONTENTS
TOOLWAIT	6	1.501	146	26	17.8	296.093	360.246		4

(a)

FACILITY	--AVG-UTIL-DURING-- TOTAL TIME	AVAIL TIME	UNAVL TIME	ENTRIES	AVERAGE TIME/XACT	CURRENT STATUS	PERCENT AVAIL	SEIZING XACT	PREEMPTING XACT
CLERK	.894			141	182.690	AVAIL	100.0	141	

QUEUE	MAXIMUM CONTENTS	AVERAGE CONTENTS	TOTAL ENTRIES	ZERO ENTRIES	PERCENT ZEROS	AVERAGE TIME/UNIT	$AVERAGE TIME/UNIT	QTABLE NUMBER	CURRENT CONTENTS
TOOLWAIT	6	1.705	142	24	16.9	345.867	416.213		1

(b)

Figure 9A.3 *Selected Postsimulation Report Components for Case Study 9A. (a) Facility and Queue Reports, SPT Service Order. (b) Facility and Queue Reports, FCFS Service Order*

system performance in the sense that the average number of waiting mechanics has been decreased by 0.204 (= 1.705-1.501), or by about 12 percent.

It can be argued that the SPT service order was at a slight disadvantage in these two simulations, because 146 mechanics came to the SPT tool crib (TOTAL ENTRIES equals 146 in the Figure 9A.3(a) Queue Report), whereas only 142 mechanics came to the FCFS tool crib (TOTAL ENTRIES equals 142 in the Figure 9A.3(b) Queue Report). Furthermore, the SPT clerk worked somewhat more slowly than the FCFS clerk in these two simulations. (The SPT clerk's AVERAGE TIME/XACT in the Figure 9A.3(a) Facility Report is about 183.1, whereas the equivalent statistic for the FCFS clerk is about 182.7.) In the long run, of course, the average holding time per capture of the clerk is independent of the service order. The SPT service order overcame these small differences and was able to outperform FCFS in these two specific simulations.

In Chapter 16, we'll see possibilities for comparing competing alternatives (such as SPT versus FCFS service orders in this case study) in more rigorous fashion.

9.7 Exercises

1. The file model9a2.gps contains the model for the SPT service order in Case Study 9A. Perform a Batch simulation with this model. Display the Postsimulation Report on your computer screen, or get a listing of it on paper. Compare information in the Facility and Queue Reports to the values given in Figure 9A.3a. Corresponding values should match. You might also want to take note of Block Counts and perhaps the RNG Report for comparison with the Postsimulation Report of Exercise 2.

*2. Change the order of Model Segments 1 and 2 in the model9a1.gps file. Perform a Batch simulation with the resulting model. Compare the information in the Facility and Queue Reports (and Block Counts and the RNG Report from Exercise 1) with the corresponding output in Figure 9A.3. These outputs do not match. Why do you think this might be the case?

(Hint: Only one "random number generator" is used as the starting point for sampling from **all four** distributions in the model. This situation will be explained in detail in Chapter 13.)

*3. By hand, compute the expected holding time per capture of the tool crib clerk in Case Study 9A. Compare this value with the average holding time per capture in Figure 9A.3(a) and (b), and with the corresponding value in Exercise 2.

*4. Both types of mechanics begin and end membership in the TOOLWAIT Queue in Case Study 9A, and so the Queue Report provides information aggregated over both mechanic types. Suppose that, in addition to having this Queue information, you also want a Queue Report specific to the Type 1 mechanics and another Queue Report specific to the Type 2 mechanics. (In other words, you'd like to have the model produce three Queue Reports.) Make the necessary changes in the Case Study 9A SPT model, and perform a simulation with the resulting model. Discuss the three Queue Reports that result.

*5. The Facility Reports produced by the Case Study 9A models provide information that summarizes the aggregate impact of both types of mechanics on the toolcrib clerk. Suppose that, in addition to having this Facility information, you also want a Facility Report specific to the Type 1 mechanics and another Facility Report specific to the Type 2 mechanics. (In other words, you'd like to have the models produce three Facility Reports.) Make the necessary changes in the Case Study 9A SPT model, and perform a simulation with the resulting model. Discuss the three Facility Reports that result.

   Hint: Introduce two dummy Facilities into the Case Study 9A SPT model. Be careful in deciding where to put the corresponding SEIZE Blocks.

*6. File fig93.gps contains the Figure 9.3 model. By hand, compute the expected number of objects on the conveyor. (Use the expected object interarrival time and the known time on the conveyor for this purpose.) Then perform a Batch simulation with the model. In this simulation, what is the average number of objects on the conveyor? How much difference is there between this average and the expected value? What is the maximum number of objects that were on the conveyor?

7. File fig95.gps contains the Figure 9.5 model. Perform a Batch simulation with this model. In this simulation, what are the maximum and average number of cars in the drive-through lane of the fast-food restaurant at any one time? How long does it take a car on average to get through the drive-through lane?

8. File fig96.gps contains the Figure 9.6 model Perform a Batch simulation with this model. In this simulation, how many cars at maximum and on average are waiting their turn to capture the WINDOW? How many cars capture the WINDOW without waiting? On average, how long do cars wait to capture the WINDOW? Among cars which do have to wait for the WINDOW, what is the average waiting time?

9. Show how to extend the Figure 9.6 model so that it will gather Queue information that applies to cars between the time they request the WINDOW and then, having been served at the WINDOW, leave. This involves adding a third Queue to the model. What's your choice of a name for this third Queue? What interpretation will apply to information in the corresponding Queue Report?

   Now make your suggested changes in the Figure 9.6 model. Perform a Batch simulation with the resulting model. Discuss the information in the postsimulation report for the new Queue.

*10. (a) Repeat Exercise 8 of Section 6.12 (Chapter 6), but extend the model so that it will gather Queue information that applies to castings waiting their turn to capture the DRILL. Just before a casting requests the DRILL, it should start membership in a Queue, and immediately after a casting has captured the DRILL, it should end its membership in that Queue. Perform a Batch mode simulation with the extended model, and discuss the information in the Queue Report.

   (b) In the (a) model, castings are put on the conveyor every 9.0 ± 4.5 minutes, conveying time is 6.0 minutes (exactly), and then drilling time is 9.0 ± 1.25 minutes. Suppose castings are put on the conveyor every 9.0 minutes (exactly), and drilling time is 9.0 minutes (exactly). (Conveying time continues to be 6.0 minutes, exactly.) Then what will the AVERAGE CONTENTS and the AVERAGE TIME/UNIT be for the Queue in (a)? Check out your thinking, if necessary, by applying these changes to the model from (a) and carrying out a simulation.

   (c) Now change the model from (a) so that castings are put on the conveyor every 9.0 ± 2.25 minutes, and drilling time is 9.0 ± 0.625 minutes. (Conveying time continues to be 6.0 minutes, exactly.) Suppose a simulation is performed with the changed model. Do you think that the AVERAGE CONTENTS and the AVERAGE TIME/UNIT for the Queue will be less than in (a)? Explain your reasoning. Check out your reasoning by carrying out a simulation and comparing results with the results from (a).

   (d) Consider the following statement: "Variability in systems degrades long-run system performance. The greater the extent to which timings in systems can be controlled, in the sense of being made more predictable, the more efficient can be the use of system resources, in the sense of reducing nonproductive delays." Do you agree or disagree with this statement? Explain your reasoning. The results from (a), (b), and (c) can be referred to in your explanation by way of example.

*11. In a particular shop, a single machine is used to carry out a finishing step on raw castings. The steps required in the overall operation are listed, where the times required are indicated, in minutes, after each step.

1. Fetch a raw casting from a storage area (12 ± 3).
2. Load the raw casting onto the finishing machine (10 ± 4).
3. Carry out finishing process 1 (80 ± 20).
4. Reposition the casting on the finishing machine (15 ± 7).
5. Carry out finishing process 2 (110 ± 30).
6. Unload the finished casting from the machine (10 ± 4).
7. Store the finished casting (12 ± 3).
8. Return to step 1.

The cycle through which a casting moves to have the overall operation performed on it is shown schematically in Figure E11, where boxes have been numbered to match the steps listed, and the step times have been set in parentheses within the boxes.

The castings are too heavy to be handled by the operator of the finishing machine. He or she requires the use of an overhead crane, which he or she operates to accomplish casting movement. The overhead crane is needed at steps 1, 2, 4, 6, and 7.

There is only one overhead crane in the system. The finishing machine operator does not have the exclusive use of this crane. It is also on call to perform service at other machines in the shop. Other calls for the crane occur every 39 ± 10 minutes. The time required for the crane to service one of these other calls is 25 ± 10 minutes.

(a) Using a Facility to simulate the crane, an Xact to simulate the finishing machine operator, and Xacts to simulate "other calls" on the crane, build a model for the crane and castings system. (Note that there is no explicit representation of castings in this modeling approach.) Use 1 minute as the base time unit.

Assume that when the simulation begins, the finishing machine operator has just stored a finished casting and, with the crane under his or her control, is poised to fetch a raw casting from the storage area. (Whenever the operator has obtained the crane to unload and store a finished casting, he or she retains uninterrupted control of the crane for purposes of fetching and loading the next raw casting.) Also assume that when the simulation begins, no "other calls" are waiting for the crane, and the first "other call" will arrive after 39 ± 10 minutes.

Design the model to collect one set of Queue information relative to the finishing machine operator obtaining the crane for step 4, and another set of Queue information relative to obtaining the crane for carrying out the sequence of steps 6, 7, 1, and 2. Also collect Queue

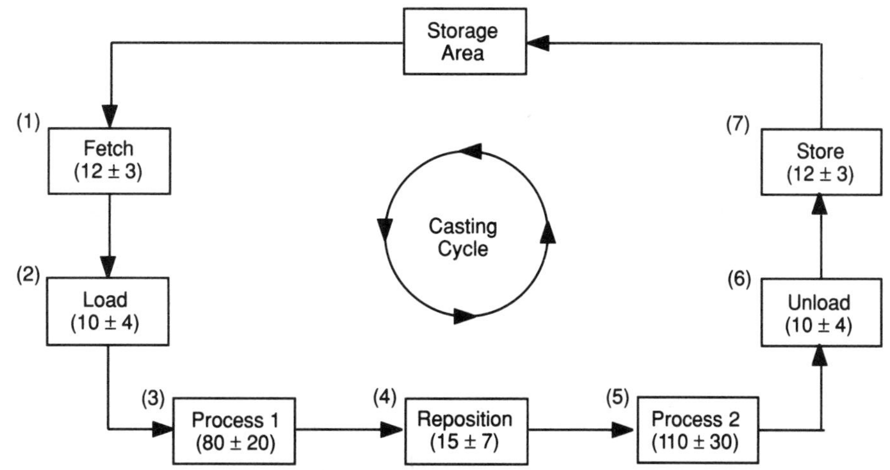

Figure E11 A Schematic for a Casting Cycle in Exercise 11

information relative to other calls obtaining the crane.

Perform a simulation with the model, stopping after 400 simulated hours have elapsed. What is the state of the model at the end of the simulation? What is the crane utilization? How many castings have been finished by the end of the simulation?

(b) There is no easy way for you to know at this point whether your model in (a) has been built correctly. One way to gain some insight into potential model correctness is to ask yourself whether the numbers in the output seem to be reasonable. For example, does the crane utilization in your simulation from (a) seem to be reasonable?
Explore the answer to this question by using hand calculations to estimate the long-run utilization of the crane in the system. Then compare this value to your model-produced value. (Hint: In the long run, what fraction of the time will the crane be used by "other calls"? Other calls arrive every 39 minutes on average, and each uses the crane 25 minutes on average. Hence, if other calls were the only users of the crane, the long-run crane utilization would be 25/39, or about 0.64. Carry out a similar analysis for the contribution of the finishing machine operator to crane utilization, assuming, unrealistically, that he or she never has to wait for the crane. The estimated crane utilization is then the sum of these two estimated utilization components.)

(c) Now modify your model from (a) so that when the simulation starts, one other call is waiting for the crane. (The next other call should arrive in 39 ± 10 minutes.) Carry out a Batch simulation with the modified model. Compare your results with those from the simulation in (a).

(d) Now modify your model from (a) so that when the simulation starts, the crane is being used by one of the "other calls," with 10 minutes of usage time remaining. The next other call should arrive in 39 ± 10 minutes. The finishing machine operator should be waiting to obtain the crane for repositioning purposes (step 4). Carry out a Batch simulation with the modified model. Compare your results with those from the simulations in (c) and (d). How much influence does the starting state of the model seem to have on the final results in this system?

(e) Your model in (a) does not directly provide the machine operator's utilization as part of the Postsimulation Report. Modify the model so that it will do so. (Hint: Use a dummy Facility for this purpose.) Assume the machine operator is being utilized whenever he or she is **not** waiting for the crane. Perform a simulation with the modified model, stopping after 400 hours have elapsed. What is the machine operator's utilization? Note that other numeric results of the simulation should match those produced by the simulation in (a).

(f) Consider changing the service order for crane use from FIFO to one in which the machine operator has higher crane use priority than other calls. Reason out the system conditions under which this change in service order makes a difference in terms of who gets the crane next. In qualitative terms, how frequently do you think the changed service order would make a difference? (Very frequently? With moderate frequency? Or hardly ever?)

Now modify a copy of the model from (e) to reflect this change in service order. Perform a Batch simulation with the modified model, stopping after 400 hours have elapsed. How much impact does the changed service order have on the waiting experiences of the machine operator, and on the other users of the crane? Does the changed service order seem to make as big (or small) a difference as you thought it would?

(g) Now repeat the simulation from (f) in Test Mode and find the first occasion when giving the machine operator high priority for crane use does make a difference in terms of who gets the crane next. On this occasion, at what time does the machine operator begin to wait for the crane? What is the id number of the Xact using the crane at this time? What is the id number of the Xact simulating the "other call" waiting for the crane at that time? (Hint: There is only one of these "other calls" waiting for the crane on this occasion.) At what time did this "other call" begin to wait for the crane? At what time does the machine operator capture the crane?

*12. Mechanics arrive at a tool crib every 300 ± 250 seconds to check out tools for use in repairing broken machines. The clerk who works at the crib requires 280 ± 150 seconds to fill each mechanic's request for a tool.

(a) Build a model for this situation, then simulate with the model for an 8-hour workday. Suppose that, due to lost production attributable to a broken machine, it costs $20 per hour to have a mechanic wait for service at the tool crib.

What is the total waiting cost resulting from the 8-hour day you simulated? (Just include **waiting** time in your calculations. The reason for this is given shortly.)

(b) Now suppose that the clerk described in (a) earns $12 per hour. The clerk can be replaced with another who earns $18 per hour, and who requires 280 ± 50 seconds to fill each mechanic's request for a tool. Model this situation, then simulate with the model for an 8-hour workday. What is the total waiting cost resulting from the 8-hour day you simulated with this alternative clerk? Taking clerk wages and waiting cost into account, was the 8-hour day experienced with the clerk in (a) more or less expensive than with the clerk in (b)?

Note that the expected service time is the same for both clerks. Consequently, the expected time mechanics spend **being served** is the same for both clerks. For purposes of comparing the two clerks, we are interested in the cost **difference**, so the time mechanics spend being served will cancel itself out between the two clerks in the long run. This explains why you were told just to include waiting time in your calculations.

(c) The clerk in (b) has a less variable service-time distribution than does the clerk in (a). This means that the expected number of mechanics in line for the (b) clerk will be less than that for the (a) clerk. (The cost savings might then be great enough to justify the higher wage for the (b) clerk. In this regard, we'll return to this exercise in Chapter 16, after studying techniques for comparing competing alternatives.) As the variability of the service time and/or of the interarrival time in this simple system decreases, the expected number of mechanics in line will also decrease. In the limit, if interarrival time were always exactly 300 seconds, and if service time were always exactly 280 seconds, what would be the expected number of mechanics in line? (Note that no simulation is needed to answer this question.)

13. Repeat Exercise 9 of Section 8.10, but now gather Queue information for the lines which form ahead of Window 1 and Window 2. Discuss the Queue Report that is produced at the end of the simulation.

14. Three types of mechanics arrive at a tool crib to check out tools. Their interarrival times and service time requirements are shown in Table E14. Only one clerk works at the tool crib. Build a model for this situation, designing it to collect Queue information segregated by type of mechanic. (That is, use three Queues in the model.) Perform simulations with each of the three following service orders, simulating in each case until 50 Type 1 mechanics have been served. Discuss the effect of the alternative service orders on the waiting experiences of the three mechanic types.

Table E14

Type of Mechanic	Interarrival Times (minutes)	Service Times (minutes)
1	30 ± 10	12 ± 5
2	20 ± 8	6 ± 3
3	15 ± 5	3 ± 1

(a) FCFS
(b) SPT
(c) Inverse SPT (the higher the expected service time, the higher the priority)

9.8 Bug Clinic

*1. Delete the DEPART Block from a copy of the Figure 9.3 model, then perform a Test-Mode simulation with the modified model. What do you expect might happen? What does happen? Is a Warning Message issued? Is a compile-time or an execution-time Error Message issued?

*2. Delete the QUEUE Block from a copy of the Figure 9.3 model; then perform a Test-Mode simulation with the modified model. What do you expect might happen? What does happen? Is a compile-time or an execution-time Error Message issued?

*3. Interchange the "SEIZE WINDOW" and "DEPART WINDOW" Blocks in a copy of the Figure 9.6 model. How much simulated time do you think cars will spend as members of the WINDOW Queue in the modified model? Perform a Batch simulation with the modified model. Examine and discuss the information found in the WINDOW Queue Report. Is this information consistent with your expectations?

10 Expanding the Set of Test-Mode Capabilities

10.1 Preview

In Chapter 2, use of GPSS/H in Test Mode was introduced, and application of the step command to establish simple interrupt conditions was demonstrated. In Chapter 4, the Test-Mode display command was then provided as a tool for examining the state of a model. In Chapter 5, the somewhat more complicated interrupt conditions corresponding to picking up and dropping Transactions during the Scan Phase, and reaching or exceeding a specified clock value, were introduced. We add further Test-Mode capabilities in this chapter, making it possible to set interrupt conditions on one or more Blocks of choice and on one or more Transactions of choice. Several variations of the display command are also given. Exercises are offered to provide a chance to use this expanded Test-Mode command vocabulary.

10.2 The Test-Mode Un/Break Commands

Sometimes our interest in a Test-Mode simulation centers on one or more Blocks whose execution (or attempted execution) is important to us for one reason or another. We might want to focus attention on such Blocks, having GPSS/H interrupt the simulation during a Scan Phase whenever a Transaction is just about to try to move into such a Block. It's possible to "sensitize" such Blocks in a model by setting what is known as a **breakpoint** on each such Block. The **break** command is used to set Block breakpoints.

In general, the **break** command takes this form,

```
break Location_list
```

where ***Location_list*** is a list of one or more Locations occupied by the Blocks on which breakpoints are to be set. The ***Location_list*** information can consist of Block Labels and/or Block Location Numbers. Block Labels need not be capitalized in the **break** command (although they must be capitalized in a model). Consecutive entries in the list are separated by one or more blanks. Commas are not used. Here's an example of a **break** command:

```
break backup bypass 12 highway1
```

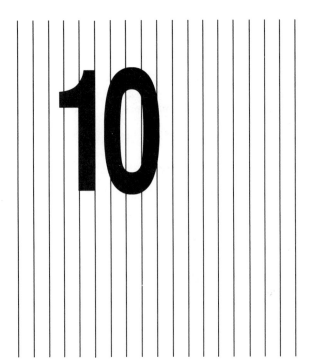

When GPSS/H executes this **break** command, breakpoints will be set on the Blocks labeled **backup**, **bypass**, and **highway1**, and the Block that occupies Location **12** in the model. If the Blocks of interest are labeled, then it's convenient to use those Labels with the **break** command. Otherwise, there's no choice but to use Location Numbers (or to label the Blocks of interest in the Model File **before** starting the Test-Mode simulation). The Location Numbers usually aren't known to us ahead of time, but they can be found in the Source Window when the Test-Mode simulation is taking place. (Remember that the function keys F7 and F9 can be used to scroll up and down, respectively, in the Source Window and that the **ds** command can be used to move around rapidly in the Source Window.)

The minimal abbreviation for the **break** command is **b**.

Suppose a breakpoint has been set on a Block. Then whenever during a Scan Phase an Xact is about to try to move into that Block, GPSS/H temporarily suspends the simulation, issues a message of the following type,

```
XACT 57 POISED AT BLOCK 32 (HIGHWAY1).
RELATIVE CLOCK: 759.3725
```

and then prompts the user for a command.

Issuing a **break** command does not cause the simulation to be started or resumed. After a **break** command is executed, **run** or **step** can be issued to start or resume the simulation.

Block breakpoints set with the **break** command are semipermanent. When a Block breakpoint has been turned on, it remains on until it is turned off with the **unbreak** command. The format of the **unbreak** command corresponds to that of the **break** command. Here's an example of an **unbreak** command:

```
unbreak block231 35
```

When GPSS/H executes this **unbreak** command, the breakpoints on the Block labeled **BLOCK231** and on the Block in Location **35** will be turned off.

The minimal abbreviation for the **unbreak** command is **unb**.

During a Test Mode session, the user may forget which Blocks have breakpoints set on them. The **display** command can be used to ask GPSS/H to list the current Block breakpoints. This **display** command takes the form

```
display breakpoints
```

When a **display breakpoints** command is issued, GPSS/H lists all Block breakpoints **and** all trap conditions that are set. (The trap conditions we've discussed so far are **scan, next, system,** and **clock.**)

The minimal abbreviation for **breakpoints is bre**. Remembering that the minimal abbreviation for **display** is **d**, this means that the **display breakpoints** command can be minimally abbreviated to **d bre**.

10.3 Examples of Break Use

Now suppose we want to apply the **break** command to determine the times when Transactions capture a Facility. We'll use the Figure 10.1 model for discussion purposes.

The goal is to find those times when the SPRAYER Facility in Figure 10.1 is put into a state of capture. Without giving it much thought, we might set a breakpoint on the "SEIZE SPRAYER" Block itself for this purpose. But when we put a breakpoint on a Block, control is returned to us whenever an Xact is about to **try** to execute the Block (whether or not the try will be successful). Of course, not every try to execute a SEIZE will be successful. And so by setting a breakpoint on the SEIZE, interrupts will occur not just prior to what will be a successful try, but also just prior to each unsuccessful try. For example, if an arrival occurs when the SPRAYER is captured, the arriving Xact will try (unsuccessfully) to move into the SEIZE Block, and an interrupt will occur. Worse yet, suppose the RELEASE is executed when there are two or more Xacts asleep in the QUEUE Block, waiting their turn to SEIZE. Then, as we know, **all** these sleeping Xacts will be reawakened by the RELEASE execution. When the scan is restarted,

```
         SIMULATE
*
         GENERATE   50,20
BLOCK2   QUEUE      WAITAREA
BLOCK3   SEIZE      SPRAYER
         DEPART     WAITAREA
         ADVANCE    48,15
BLOCK6   RELEASE    SPRAYER
         TERMINATE  1
*
         START      100
         END
```

Figure 10.1 *A Model to Illustrate Use of the Break Command*

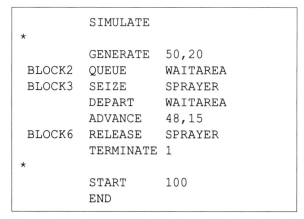

each of these reawakened Xacts will **try**, one by one, to move into the SEIZE, resulting in a number of unwanted interrupts occurring. (See Exercise 1 of Section 10.4.) It's only the successful tries we care about, not the unsuccessful ones.

By now, it should be clear that it may not be a good idea to set breakpoints on SEIZE Blocks. A better way to reach the goal, for example, is to set a breakpoint either on the DEPART or the ADVANCE Block in Figure 10.1. Then **exactly one interrupt will occur** each time a Transaction goes into service.

Now let's discuss applying the **break** command to determine how many Xacts are waiting their turn for a Facility when another Xact releases the Facility. We'll use the Figure 10.1 model for discussion purposes. If we put a breakpoint on "RELEASE SPRAYER," then when the RELEASE is about to be executed, we can issue a **display que** command to see the CURRENT CONTENTS of the WAITAREA Queue. But in a Queue Report, the CURRENT CONTENTS information is "off the screen," and so we have to scroll right to see the CURRENT CONTENTS, which is awkward (because we then probably will want to scroll left again). A less direct but more convenient way to determine how many Xacts are waiting their turn to "SEIZE SPRAYER" is to display **Block Counts**. In this model, all Xacts waiting their turn to "SEIZE SPRAYER" are in the QUEUE Block (BLOCK2). And so the QUEUE Block's **Current Count** equals the number of Xacts waiting their turn for the SPRAYER. We can display the Total and Current Counts of **all** Blocks in a model by issuing this **display** command,

```
display blo
```

where **blo** means "Blocks." We will not have to scroll right to see Block Counts in this small model, and so that step is saved.

We can improve on **display blo** as follows. We really only want to display Block Counts for the QUEUE Block. For our purposes, the other Block Counts are just a distraction. And so we can use a **qualified form** of the **display** command. In the context of Block Counts, a qualified **display** command follows this format:

```
display blo(Location_list)
```

where ***Location_list*** is a list of one or more Locations occupied by the Blocks whose Counts we want displayed. The ***Location_list*** can consist of Block Labels and/or Block Location Numbers. Block Labels need not be capitalized in the qualified **display** command (although they must be capitalized in a model). Consecutive list entries are separated by commas. For our purposes, here's the qualified **display blo** command it would be convenient to use:

```
display blo(block2)
```

Another way to determine how many Xacts are waiting their turn to "SEIZE SPRAYER" when the RELEASE executes is to **display cec** and then inspect the CEC to determine how many Xacts have BLOCK2 as their Current Block (or BLOCK3 as their Next Block). Then we have to do our own counting, but in other situations we might want to look at properties of the waiting Xacts, and **display cec** would be a good way to do this.

The qualified **display** command can be used for types of information other than Block Counts. For example, it can be used when displaying Facility or Queue Reports. We might have many Facilities in a model and might just want to see the Facility report for the MACHINE1 and MACHINE2 Facilities. Then we could issue this qualified **display** command:

```
display fac(machine1,machine2)
```

10.4 Exercises

*1. The s104x1.gps file contains this model:

```
          SIMULATE
*
          GENERATE   0,,,3
          QUEUE      WAITAREA
 BLOCK3   SEIZE      SPRAYER
          DEPART     WAITAREA
          ADVANCE    48,15
          RELEASE    SPRAYER
          TERMINATE  1
*
          START      3
          END
```

Suppose that in a simulation performed with the model, you want to find out at what three times the SPRAYER is put into a state of capture. To do this, suppose you initiate a Test-Mode simulation with the model, set a breakpoint on BLOCK3, and then issue a series of **run** commands repeatedly until the simulation ends. How many interrupts will have occurred by the end of the simulation? Check you prediction by carrying out the indicated Test-Mode simulation.

*2. The file model9a1.gps contains the model for the SPT service order in Case Study 9A. Perform a Test-Mode simulation with this model and determine the times of the first five service initiations for Type1 mechanics.

3. Repeat Exercise 2, only now determine the times of the first five service initiations for Type 2 mechanics.

*4. Repeat Exercise 2, only now determine the times of the first five service initiations for mechanics of either type. Also determine the types of mechanics for whom service is starting at these times.

*5. Repeat Exercise 2, only now determine the times of the first five service completions for mechanics of either type. Also determine the types of mechanics for whom service is completed at these times.

*6. Now combine Exercises 4 and 5 to determine the times of the first five service initiations and service completions for mechanics of either type, and the types of mechanics involved.

*7. Perform a simulation with the model in model9a1.gps and find the earliest time that exactly one mechanic (regardless of type) is waiting for the CLERK when an Xact releases the CLERK.

*8. Repeat Exercise 7, but now find the earliest time that exactly one mechanic of the **other** type is waiting for the CLERK when an Xact releases the CLERK.

*9. Repeat Exercise 7, but now find the earliest time that exactly two mechanics (irrespective of type) are waiting for the CLERK when an Xact releases the CLERK.

*10. Repeat Exercise 9, but now find the earliest time there is at least one mechanic of each type waiting for the CLERK when an Xact releases the CLERK.

*11. Find the earliest time in the Case Study 9A SPT model that a high-priority mechanic cuts in line ahead of a low-priority mechanic. (This will be the earliest time in the simulation when the change in service order from FCFS to SPT alters the order of the waiting line, and therefore changes the order in which mechanics go into service.)

*12. Repeat Exercise 11, but now find the second occasion that a high-priority mechanic cuts in line ahead of a low-priority mechanic.

10.5 The Test-Mode Un/Trap Xact Commands

Sometimes our interest in a Test-Mode simulation centers on one or more **Xacts** whose movement (or attempted movement) in a model is important to us for one reason or another. We might want to focus attention on one or more Xacts, having GPSS/H interrupt the simulation during a Scan Phase whenever it picks up one of these Xacts and is just about to try to move into its Next Block. It's possible to "sensitize" Xacts in a model by setting a trap on them. The **trap** command (which we've already worked with in the forms **trap scan, trap next, trap system**, and **trap clock**) is used for this purpose.

Used to set a trap on a Transaction, the **trap** command takes this form,

```
trap xact id_list
```

where ***id_list*** is a list of one or more id numbers of Xacts on which a trap is to be set. Consecutive entries in the list are separated by one or more blanks. Here's an example of a specific **trap xact** command:

```
trap xact 55
```

When GPSS/H "picks up" a scan-active ("awake") Xact during a Scan Phase and the Xact has a trap set on it, GPSS/H immediately interrupts the simulation, issues a message of the following type,

```
XACT 55 POISED AT BLOCK 26.
RELATIVE CLOCK: 562.7942
```

and gives control to the user. Note that for the trap to be sprung, the Xact **must be scan-active.** CEC Xacts which are scan-inactive (asleep) are "transparent" to GPSS/H during the Scan Phase, even if they have a trap set on them. The presence of such Xacts on the CEC will not cause interrupts to occur during the Scan Phase.

If an attempt is made to set a trap on an Xact that hasn't yet been created, GPSS/H will write out an appropriate message and **will take note of the request**, setting a trap on the Xact when it is later created. However, only one such request can be pending at any one time. (See Exercise 1 of Section 10.7.)

If an attempt is made to set a trap on an Xact that has already been destroyed, GPSS/H will write out an appropriate message. (See Exercise 1 of Section 10.7.)

When a Transaction trap has been set, it remains in force until the Xact is destroyed, or until the trap is turned off with the **untrap xact** command. The format of the **untrap xact** command corresponds to that of the **trap xact** command. Here's an example of an **untrap xact** command:

```
untrap xact 55
```

If an **untrap xact** command refers to an Xact that has already been destroyed, GPSS/H advises the user of this with an appropriate message.

During a Test-Mode session, the user may forget which Xacts have traps set on them. Recall, **display traps** can be used to get a list of all trap conditions in effect. (We've now introduced all five trap conditions in GPSS/H: **scan, next, system, clock,** and **xact.**)

Also recall that when a **display breakpoints** command is issued, GPSS/H lists all Block breakpoints **and** all trap conditions that are set.

The exercises in the Section 10.7 provide a chance to use the **trap xact** command.

10.6 A Summary of Display Modifiers

Modifiers that can be used with the display command were first summarized in Table 4.1 of Chapter 4. Enough additional display modifiers have been introduced in the meantime to make it useful to update this summary. Table 10.1 provides the update.

The one Table 10.1 modifier not previously introduced is **output**. When a **display output** command is issued, GPSS/H displays all components of the standard Postsimulation Report. (This includes clock values, Block Counts, the Facility Report, and the Queue Report, among other things.)

10.7 Exercises

All of the exercises in this section involve Test-Mode use of the SPT service order model in Case Study 9A. This model is in the file model9a2.gps.

1. Start a Test-Mode simulation with the model9a2.gps file.

(a) In response to the Ready! prompt, issue a **trap xact 12** command. Note the message that GPSS/H produces.

Table 10.1

Selected types of information that can be displayed in Test Mode

Display Modifier	Information Displayed
blo	Current and Total Block Counts
breakpoints	a list of Block breakpoints and trap conditions
cec	Current Events Chain
clocks	Absolute and Relative clock values
fac	the Facility Report
fec	Future Events Chain
output	the entire Postsimulation Report
que	the Queue Report
traps	a list of trap conditions
xact=*xact_id*	the properties of the Xact whose id is *xact_id* (e.g., xact=25)

(b) Issue the command **trap xact 12** again. What does GPSS/H say about this?
(c) Now issue a **trap xact 14** command. How does GPSS/H respond?
(d) Issue a **step 5** command, then an **untrap xact 2** command (even though there is no trap set on Xact 2). What does GPSS/H say about this?
(e) Now issue a **step 100** command, then a **trap xact 2** command. (Xact 2 has already come and gone.) What does GPSS/H say about this?
(f) Now set a trap on the Xact whose id number appears in the status window. Does GPSS/H respond with a message or simply issue a colon (:) to prompt for whatever your next choice of a command might be?

*2. Start a Test-Mode simulation with the model9a.gps file. In response to the Ready! prompt, issue a **trap xact 8** command. Now simulate with the objective of following Xact 8 through its life cycle. Does Xact 8 simulate a Type 1 or Type 2 mechanic? At what time does Xact 8 come to the tool crib? How many other mechanics are in line when Xact 8 arrives? What are the id numbers of the Xacts simulating these other mechanics? For each mechanic arriving **after** Xact 8 does, but **before** Xact 8 goes into service (if any), determine the time of arrival, the id number of the Xact, the type of mechanic, and the time the mechanic goes into service (if applicable) and comes out of service. When is service initiated for Xact 8? When is service completed for Xact 8?

*3. Repeat Exercise 2, except with respect to Xact 49.

(Hint: **Four** mechanics arrive at the tool crib **after** Xact 49 does, but **before** Xact 49 goes into service.)

*4. Repeat Exercise 2, except with respect to Xact 91.

*5. Repeat Exercise 2, except with respect to Xact 117.

(Hint: **Eight** mechanics arrive at the tool crib **after** Xact 117 does, but **before** Xact 117 goes into service!)

*6. What is the earliest time in the Case Study 9A SPT model that a low-priority mechanic arrives while a mechanic is being served?

*7. What is the earliest time in the Case Study 9A SPT model that a high-priority mechanic arrives while a mechanic is being served?

*8. What is the earliest time in the Case Study 9A SPT model that two mechanics (regardless of type) arrive while a Type 1 mechanic is being served? When was service initiated for the Type 1 mechanic in service? Was anyone else in line at that time? At what times during ongoing service did the two arrivals come? What types of mechanics are they? When is service completed for the Type 1 mechanic in service?

*9. What is the earliest time in the Case Study 9A SPT model that two mechanics (regardless of type) arrive while a Type 2 mechanic is being served? When was service initiated for the Type 2 mechanic in service? Was anyone else in line at that time? At what times during ongoing service did the two arrivals come? What types of mechanics are they? When is service completed for the Type 2 mechanic in service?

10.8 At-Points and At-Lists

It's possible to automate the issuing of Test-Mode commands when Block breakpoints occur. This is done by associating a list of one or more Test-Mode commands with one or more Blocks on which breakpoints are set. Whenever a break occurs on such a Block, the commands in the associated list will then be executed automatically by GPSS/H.

The Test-Mode **at** command is used both to set a breakpoint on one or more Blocks and to initiate the process of building an associated command list of the type just described. A Block breakpoint that has a command list associated with it is called an **at-point**. The associated command list is called an **at-list**. After the command list has been built, the Test-Mode **end** command is used to terminate the list-building process.

Figure 10.2 shows the complete pattern for use of the **at** and **end** commands.

To establish an **at-point**, the user issues an **at *Location_list*** command in response to a colon prompt. As usual, ***Location_list*** is the list of Locations occupied by Blocks on which the **at-point** is to be set. After the user sends the **at *Location_list***

```
: at Location_list
@     first command
@     second command
        ...
@     last command
@ end
:
```

Figure 10.2 *The Pattern for Use of the At and End Commands*

```
: at block6
@     display blo(block2)
@     run
@ end
:
```

Figure 10.3 *An Example for Establishing an At-Point and an At-List*

command, GPSS/H displays an at-sign (@) to prompt the user for the first command in the **at-list**. (See the first line in Figure 10.2, and the at-sign on the second line.) After the user keys in and sends this first **at-list** command, GPSS/H displays an at-sign again to prompt for the second **at-list** command. (See the second line in Figure 10.2 and the at-sign on the third line.) After the user keys in and sends this second **at-list** command, GPSS/H again displays an at-sign to prompt for the third **at-list** command. And so on. This process continues until the user has keyed in and sent the last command in the **at-list.** When prompted for another **at-list** command, the user keys in and sends either an **end** command (see the next-to-last line in Figure 10.2) or simply sends a null line (keys nothing, but simply presses enter or return). GPSS/H responds with a colon to prompt for another Test-Mode command. (See the last line in Figure 10.2.)

Commands in an **at-list** aren't presented for **immediate** execute, of course; they're presented for **eventual** execution. They'll be executed when a breakpoint occurs on a Block with which the **at-list** is associated.

Figure 10.3 provides a simple example for establishing an **at-list**. The example is motivated by the discussion toward the end of Section 10.3, where it was of interest to determine how many Xacts were waiting their turn to capture the SPRAYER whenever the SPRAYER was released. We saw in Section 10.3 that whenever the RELEASE (in the BLOCK6 Location) was executed, it was of interest to **display blo(block2)**, and then resume the simulation. The pattern in Figure 10.3 shows how to set an **at-point** on the RELEASE Block, then issue the indicated **display** command, and then a **run** command to resume the simulation. The indentation used in Figure 10.3 in keying the **display** and **run** commands is arbitrary, and is provided here just to catch the eye.

Whenever an **at-list** concludes with a **run** command, as in Figure 10.3, the simulation will be resumed automatically after the corresponding interrupt occurs and the commands in the **at-list** have been executed. This can result in situations in which information scrolls across the Dialog Window very rapidly. Under these circumstances, the user may want to "pause" the simulation by pressing the keyboard's Scroll Lock (or equivalent) key. Information on the screen can then be read, after which the "pause" can be turned off so that the simulation can resume. Of course, model execution can be interrupted at any point by pressing the CTRL-BREAK combination. Remember that if this is done in Test Mode, GPSS/H will display ATTENTION! and then issue a colon to prompt for a command.

There is no way to save an **at-list** for later use. When the user quits a Test-Mode simulation, any **at-lists** that may have been in effect are destroyed.

If the user issues a **display breakpoints** command, Locations occupied by Blocks that have **at-points** set on them are specially designated by suffixing them with an at-sign.

The **display** command can be used to display an **at-list**. The pattern for this **display** command takes this form:

```
display atlist Block_location
```

The **unbreak** command is used to turn off an **at-point**. When the **unbreak** is used for this purpose, the **at-list**(s) associated with the corresponding Block(s) are also destroyed.

10.9 Exercises

*1. The file fig101.gps contains the model in Figure 10.1. Initiate a Test-Mode simulation with this model. In response to the Ready! prompt, establish the Figure 10.3 **at-point** and **at-list** with the model. Then issue a **display breakpoints** command, and see how the fact that there is an **at-point** on the Block in the BLOCK6 Location is indicated. Issue a **display atlist block6** command to display the associated **at-list**. Then issue a **run command.** By the time the Xact-Movement Phase stops, what was the largest number of Xacts waiting for the SPRAYER when the RELEASE was about to be executed? At what simulated time(s) was this maximum reached?

*2. Repeat Exercise 1, except set a normal breakpoint on the RELEASE in the BLOCK6 Location first, and then issue an **at** command for the purpose of associating an **at-list** with this Block. How does GPSS/H react to the fact that the RELEASE already has a breakpoint set on it when you issue the **at** command? What would you recommend to solve the resulting problem?

11 Modeling Groups of Identical Servers

11.1 Preview

As pointed out in Chapter 6, a distinction can be made in GPSS/H between single servers and groups of two or more identical servers. The basic details of using the Facility entity to model single servers have been presented in Chapters 6 and 8. Corresponding details about modeling groups of two or more identical servers with the Storage entity are provided in this chapter.

11.2 Single Servers Versus Groups of Identical Servers

Some servers in systems are single servers. For example, there might only be one berth of a particular type at a harbor, or one clerk working at a tool crib, or one drilling machine in a manufacturing system, or one neurosurgeon on the staff of a hospital. In contrast, systems often include two or more identical servers of various types. There might be four berths of a particular type at a harbor, or three clerks working at a tool crib, or eight identical drilling machines in a manufacturing system, or two neurosurgeons on the staff of a hospital. The Facility entity (that is, Facilities) can be used to model single servers in GPSS/H, and the **Storage entity** (that is, **Storages**) can be used to model groups of two or more identical servers.

It's too bad that "Storage" is used for the name of a type of entity in GPSS/H. We have a preconceived notion of what a "storage" is. The word brings to mind the idea of a physical place or space, such as an attic or a cigarbox or a garage, that can be used to store objects. But in GPSS/H, the term Storage is used as the **name of an entity used to model groups of identical servers** and is not a term that describes a physical place or space.

By **identical** servers, we mean servers who (or which) are **indistinguishable** from each other **as servers**. For example, suppose Martha and Tim work as tellers at a bank. Martha and Tim are distinct **as people,** of course, but they might not be distinct **as tellers**. They might both be able to do the same kinds of teller tasks, and they might both work at the same rate. From a customer's point of view, it doesn't matter then if the customer gets Martha or Tim as a teller. As far as a customer is concerned, these two people are identical servers.

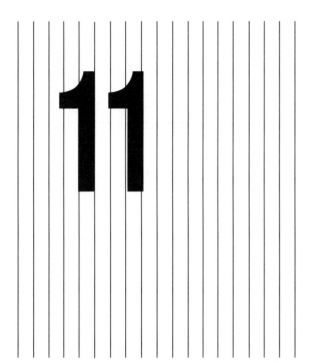

In contrast, suppose Martha and Tim are **not identical as tellers**. Perhaps Martha has been a teller for three years, and Tim is a trainee who has been on the job for three days. Martha works more confidently and, therefore faster, than Tim. Martha also has experience in doing rare tasks, such as handling the paperwork for collecting bond coupons, whereas Tim may have to ask a supervisor for assistance if a customer hands him bond coupons for collection. As far as a customer is concerned, Martha and Tim are not identical as tellers. It does (or can) matter which of them serves a customer.

Only when two or more servers are identical as servers can they be modeled in GPSS/H with a Storage. When distinctions must be made among servers, a Storage can't be used to model them. This is because servers modeled with a Storage **do not have individual identities**. When a Transaction captures one of these servers, the Transaction does not know (and cannot determine) whether it has captured "server 1," or "server 2," and so on.

The usual approach to modeling **nonidentical** servers of the same type is to model each server individually, with a Facility. Simple procedures for using Facilities in this way will be introduced in Chapter 12.

11.3 Using a Server in a Group of Identical Servers: ENTER and LEAVE Blocks

The approach to using a server in a group modeled with a Storage is similar to that for using a single server modeled with a Facility. It is a Transaction that captures such a server, receives service, and then goes on its way. The pattern described in Chapter 6 for the use of a single server also applies here:

1. The Xact arrives at the point where the group of servers is modeled and requests a server.
2. The Xact waits its turn (if necessary) to be served.
3. When its turn comes, the Xact captures a server.
4. The Xact holds its server in a state of capture during some interval of time while the service is performed.

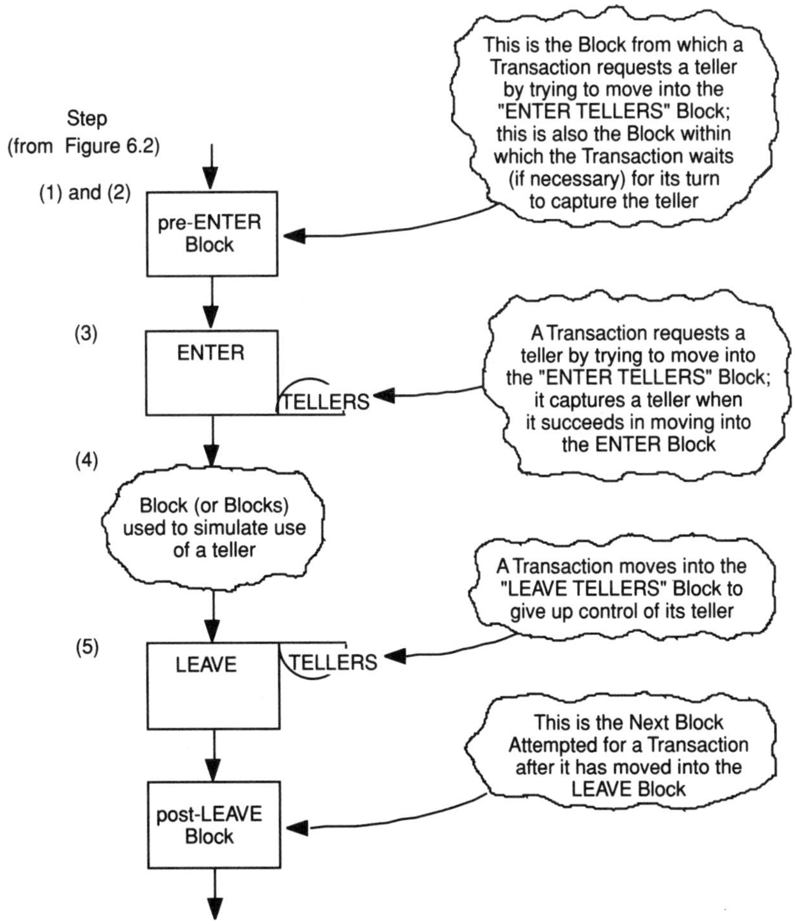

Figure 11.1 *The Role Played by ENTER and LEAVE Blocks in Modeling the Five Steps Involved in Using a Server*

5. Finally, the Xact frees its server and moves on in the model.

This general pattern is pictured in Figure 6.2 of Chapter 6, and then made specific in Figure 6.4 for the Facility entity by use of SEIZE and RELEASE Blocks at Steps 3 and 5, respectively. The general Figure 6.2 pattern is made specific here for the Storage entity by use of **ENTER** and **LEAVE** Blocks in Figure 11.1. Figure 11.1 is set in the context of customers coming to a bank to transact business by capturing a teller. The only **Block** difference between Figures 11.1 and 6.4 is that an ENTER Block is used at step 3 (instead of a SEIZE), and a LEAVE Block is used at step 5 (instead of a RELEASE). ENTER and LEAVE are to Storages as SEIZE and RELEASE are to Facilities. ENTER is the second example we've seen of a Block type that can **conditionally deny entry** to a Transaction.

Note in Figure 11.1 how "TELLERS" has been used with the ENTER and LEAVE Blocks to identify a specific Storage, as explained further shortly. Also note that the comments in Figure 11.1 reflect that the server being used is not a single server, but is one in a group of servers.

The general form of ENTER and LEAVE Blocks is shown in Figure 11.2. Each of these Block types has an A Operand. The role of the A Operand is to indicate the **identity** of a particular **group of servers** ("Storage"), one of whom an Xact requests control of by trying to execute an ENTER Block or gives up control of by executing a LEAVE Block.

Like the A Operand for SEIZE, RELEASE, QUEUE, and DEPART Blocks, the A Operand for ENTER and LEAVE Blocks indicates the **specific** Storage that models the group of servers of interest to Xacts that execute the ENTER and LEAVE Blocks. Like Facilities and Queues, distinctions are made among Storages by giving each Storage its own identifier. Throughout GPSS/H, such identifiers, when symbolic, consist of from one to eight alphanumeric characters, the first of which must be alphabetic. Symbolic Storage identifiers might take such forms as TELLERS, TUGBOATS, CLERKS, RUNWAYS, SPACES, or GROUP26.

Whether used to identify Facilities, Queues, or Storages, or as Block Labels, identifiers should (but don't have to) begin with a minimum of three alphabetic characters to avoid having them accidentally match or begin with a GPSS/H reserved word. Storage identifiers can also be positive whole numbers, such as 2, or 5, or 12; however, to promote readability, only symbolic Storage identifiers will be used in this book.

The symbolic identifiers chosen for Storages in a model will usually differ from those chosen for such other entity types as Facilities and Queues, but this isn't necessary. For example, a Queue could be named TELLERS, and in the same model, a Storage could be named TELLERS. However, the same identifier should **not** be used for a Storage (or a Facility, or a Queue, etc.) as for a **Block**.

It is important to realize that the identifier for a Storage is the name of the **group** of servers (resource units) that the Storage models. There are no identifiers for the **individual** servers in the group. For example, the Storage TELLERS might be used to model a group of five tellers in a bank. TELLERS is the name of the group of five; the five tellers making up the group don't have individual identifiers.

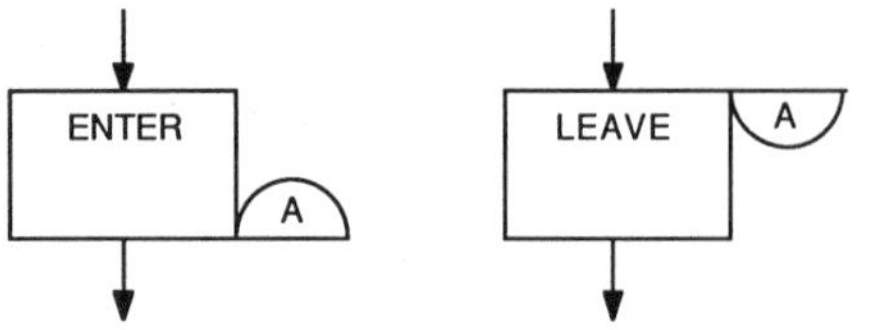

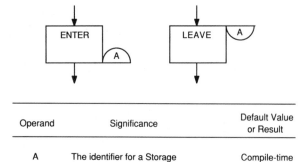

Operand	Significance	Default Value or Result
A	The identifier for a Storage (one of whose servers is being requested/captured at the ENTER, or being given up at the LEAVE)	Compile-time error

Figure 11.2 The ENTER and LEAVE Blocks and Their A Operand

11.4 Specifying Group Size: The STORAGE Control Statement

How many servers, or resource units, are there in a group modeled with a Storage? That's up to the modeler to specify. The number of servers modeled with a particular Storage, referred to as the Storage's **Capacity**, is indicated by including in the Model File a **STORAGE Control Statement** for that Storage.

A form of the STORAGE Control Statement is shown in Figure 11.3. As indicated, the Storage's identifier is entered in the statement's Label field. For this reason, a STORAGE statement in the form of Figure 11.3 is referred to as a **labeled** STORAGE Control Statement. The word STORAGE is entered

Label (2 - 9)	Operation (11 - 20)	Operands (22 - 72) →
see below	**STORAGE**	**A**

Label or Operand	Significance	Default Value or Result
Label	Identifier for the Storage whose Capacity is being defined	Compile-time error
A	The Capacity of the Storage (number of servers modeled)	Compile-time error

Figure 11.3 *The labeled STORAGE Control Statement*

in the Operation field. The A Operand, which usually takes the form of an integer constant, indicates the Capacity of the Storage.

Examples of labeled STORAGE Control Statements are shown in Figure 11.4. In Example 1, the TELLERS Storage has a Capacity of 3. In Example 2, the TUGBOATS Storage has a capacity of 5. In Example 3, a Capacity of 10 is specified for the WAITAREA Storage.

As in the Figure 11.4 examples, comments can be placed on STORAGE statements to the right of the A Operand. (As usual, one or more blanks must separate the A Operand from the first character in the comment.)

The STORAGE statement is only the fourth type of Control Statement introduced up to this point in the book. (The other three types are SIMULATE, START, and END.) Like all Control Statements, a STORAGE statement is **executed** by GPSS/H sometime **after** the Model File has been compiled. Execution of this statement causes the specified Capacity for the indicated Storage to be put into effect.

Where are STORAGE statements placed in a Model File? We want a Storage's Capacity to be put into effect **before** the Xact-Movement Phase begins. After model compilation, GPSS/H goes into Control-Statement execution and executes all Control Statements that appear in the Model File **prior** to the START statement (see Figure 2.19 of Chapter 2). This means that STORAGE statements should be placed in the Model File someplace **ahead of** the START statement. For example, STORAGE statements can be included in a Model File between the SIMULATE statement and the Block statements, as indicated by the "Additional Control Statements (if any)" box in Figure 11.5. (Other types of Control Statements will be introduced later that, like STORAGE statements, can also be placed between the SIMULATE and Block statements, as suggested in Figure 11.5.)

```
TELLERS    STORAGE   3    Example 1
TUGBOATS   STORAGE   5    Example 2
WAITAREA   STORAGE   10   Example 3
```

Figure 11.4 *Examples of Labeled STORAGE Control Statements*

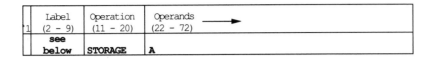

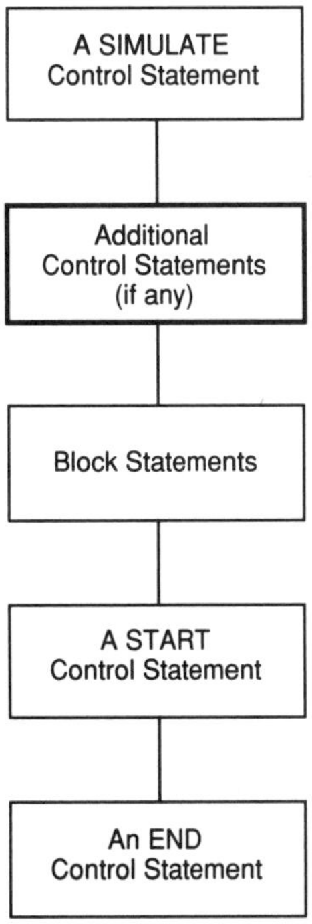

Figure 11.5 *The Top-Down Order of Statements in an Extended Form of a Basic GPSS/H Model File*

The modeler can choose **not to define a Storage's Capacity**. In this case, the Capacity **defaults** in GPSS/H to a value in excess of 2 billion (2,147,483,647, to be exact), which for all practical purposes is the same as infinity. (To support early exploration of system behavior, it is sometimes convenient to let one or more Storages deliberately take their default Capacity. See Section 11.12.)

Only the labeled form of the STORAGE statement will be used here. An alternative form, referred to as the **unlabeled** form, lets the modeler define the capacity of one or more Storages with a single statement. Interested persons should consult the *GPSS/H Reference Manual* for details.

11.5 Facilities Versus Storages with a Capacity of 1

A Facility models a single server. A Storage with a Capacity of 1 also models a single server. And so two alternative approaches are available in GPSS/H for modeling single servers. What are the differences between these two approaches? The differences are briefly summarized here.

Facilities are more sophisticated than Storages. One aspect of this sophistication is that **Facilities can be preempted, whereas Storages cannot**. (As pointed out in Section 6.2, preemption involves a situation in which one Xact comes along and takes a server away from another Xact.) If preemption is to be modeled, the user has no choice but to work with Facilities instead of Storages.

Another aspect of Facility sophistication involves the concept of availability and unavailability. (As indicated in Section 6.2, "available" refers to a server or resource being in a state described with such phrases as "in working order" or "on duty," whereas "unavailable" refers to a server or resource being "broken down," or "down for preventive maintenance," or "off duty.") The available/unavailable concept is supported in GPSS/H both for Facilities and for Storages. But a **much richer set of available/unavailable options** is offered for Facilities than for Storages.

A third difference between Facilities and Storages is that **an ownership concept applies to Facilities, but not to Storages**. When an Xact becomes the current owner of a Facility by executing a SEIZE, GPSS/H records the id number of the capturing Xact. Then, when an Xact executes a RELEASE, GPSS/H checks its id number to be sure the Xact is the current owner of the Facility being released. If it's not, an execution error occurs. In contrast, when an Xact executes an ENTER Block, GPSS/H does **not** record the id number of the Xact. And so there is no record of which Xacts currently own the servers modeled with a Storage. When an Xact executes a LEAVE, GPSS/H cannot check to see if this Xact controls a server in that group, and no error condition can result in this regard. (However, if **all** servers modeled with a Storage are idle when an Xact tries to execute a corresponding LEAVE, an execution error occurs. Why? Because the number of captured servers cannot become **negative**.)

11.6 The Vocabulary Used with Storages

In Section 11.2, we lamented the choice of the term **Storage** as the name of the Storage entity. And we've used the term **Capacity** to indicate how many servers, or resource units, are in the group modeled with a Storage. The term "Capacity" unfortunately reinforces the misleading idea that a Storage is a physical place into which objects can be placed, and from which objects can be taken. Some of the vocabulary additionally used with Storages also reinforces the misleading thought that a Storage is a place where things are stored. Consider the following:

1. A Storage is said to be **Full** if each resource unit (server) in the group it simulates is currently captured.
2. A Storage is said to be **Empty** if each of the resource units (servers) in the group it simulates is currently idle.
3. The **Current Contents** of a Storage is the number of currently captured resource units in the group it simulates. (If a Storage is Empty, its Current Contents is zero.)
4. The **Remaining Capacity** of a Storage is the number of currently idle resource units in the group it simulates. (If a Storage is Full, its Remaining Capacity is zero.)

Remember that these terms have a specialized meaning in GPSS/H, not their general everyday meaning, and that the Storage entity is simply a capability for modeling groups of identical servers with ENTER and LEAVE Blocks, and with the STORAGE Control Statement.

11.7 The Operation of ENTER and LEAVE Blocks

In this section, the operation of ENTER and LEAVE Blocks is discussed in terms of blocking, uniqueness of blocking, a Transaction's Scan-Skip Indicator, and the model's Status Change Flag. ENTER and LEAVE operate much like SEIZE and RELEASE in these regards, and so the ideas presented for Facilities in Chapters 6 and 7 apply quite directly in the following discussion of Storages.

Assume that a Storage is used to model a group of three tellers in a bank and that Transactions representing people come to this bank and use a teller to make checking and savings account deposits and withdrawals, and so on. Using TELLERS as the identifier for the Storage, Figure 11.1 shows how ENTER and LEAVE Blocks can be positioned in a model to provide the logic called for in using a teller. As indicated in Figure 11.1, a Transaction requests **a** teller (any one teller in the group of three) by **trying** to move from its Current Block (the pre-ENTER Block) into the "ENTER TELLERS" Block (its Next Block Attempted). If the TELLERS Storage is **not Full** at the time, the requesting Transaction moves into (executes) the ENTER Block immediately, capturing a teller. This increases the **Current Contents** of the Storage by 1 and decreases the **remaining Capacity** by 1. The capturing Xact then tries to move from the ENTER into the sequential Block, and so on.

But suppose the requesting Xact finds that the TELLERS Storage is **Full**. Then the requesting Xact is denied entry (blocked) by the ENTER Block and stops moving for the time being, remaining in the pre-ENTER Block of Figure 11.1. This Xact (and any others like it) will remain blocked until some other Xact returns a teller to a state of idleness by executing a "LEAVE TELLERS" Block. This waiting Xact/Transaction (and others like it) is **uniquely blocked**, because the only resolution (the **unique** resolution) for the blocking is the execution of a "LEAVE TELLERS" Block. And so, as always in the case of unique blocking, the Xact is **put to sleep** on the Current Chain by turning on its **Scan-Skip Indicator**.

What eventually becomes of an Xact (or Xacts) that have been blocked by an ENTER, and have been put to sleep? Such an Xact (or Xacts) are **reawakened** at the time the cause of the blocking is removed. In the example being discussed, when some Xact executes a "LEAVE TELLERS" Block, GPSS/H wakes up **each** of these sleeping Xacts by turning off each Xact's Scan-Skip Indicator. In addition, GPSS/H **also turns on the model's Status Change Flag** as part of LEAVE-Block execution. After the unblocking Xact can move no farther, GPSS/H then restarts the scan, giving each of the unblocked and reawakened Xacts its turn to try to move into its Next Block, and so on. This logic, identical to that for Facilities, is summarized in the Scan Phase flowchart given in Figure 7.4.

From a **Block-oriented** point of view, Xacts are in a pre-ENTER Block while waiting their turn to take control of one of the servers in a group. From a **chain-oriented** point of view, these Xacts are asleep on the Current Chain, waiting until their blocking condition has been removed. We know that Xacts are arranged on the CEC from front to back in order of decreasing (nonincreasing) Priority. We also know that during a Scan Phase, Xacts on the CEC are dealt with in front-to-back order. The order in which unblocked Xacts retry to move into an ENTER Block determines which Xact is the next to capture one of the servers modeled with the Storage. It follows that retries take place in the order of **first-come, first-served within Priority Level**, which is the default service order for Storages, even as it is for Facilities. (The default GPSS/H service order results from the arrangement of Xacts on the Current Chain and is not directly related to the characteristics of Facilities and Storages as such.)

11.8 The Type of Queuing System that a Storage Models

In general, those waiting for a server in a group of servers can wait in **one line**, or in **two or more lines**. Figure 11.6 shows the geometry of a one-line, multiple-server queuing system. In contrast, Figure 11.7 shows the geometry of a multiple-line, multiple-server queuing system. In Figure 11.7, there is a separate line associated with each server.

One-line, multiple-server systems are often used in such places as banks, airports, post offices, and barbershops. Multiple-line, multiple-server systems are frequently used in such settings as checkout lanes in supermarkets, toll booths on turnpikes, and so on.

An advantage of one-line, multiple-server systems is that service is provided in FCFS order (assuming all requestors have the same priority). This is not necessarily the case in a multiple-line, multiple-server system. If a multiple-line system is used

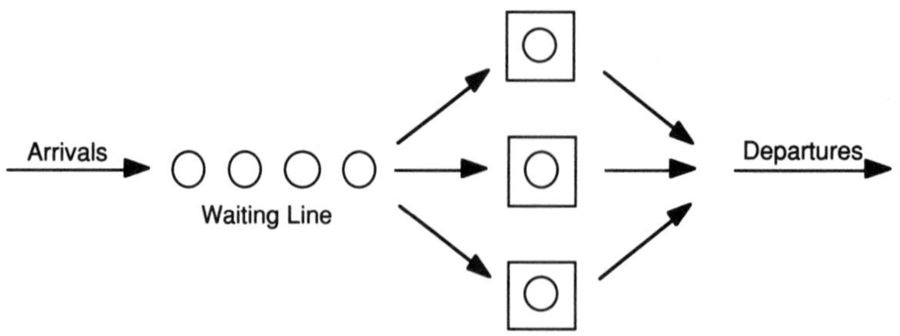

Figure 11.6 *The Geometry of a One-Line, Multiple-Server Queuing System*

in a bank, for example, a person entering the bank selects a teller and then joins the line at **that** teller's window. Some customers might get stuck in line behind a customer with an unusually high service-time requirement (such as a customer opening a new account, for example, or buying and signing traveler's checks). Whether or not these unlucky ones switch to other lines ("jockey"), it's unlikely that customers will be served in the order in which they arrived at the bank. In contrast, the one-line system ensures FCFS service order (assuming equal customer priorities) and also reduces or eliminates cases of extreme waiting times. If there are priority distinctions among the waiting customers, then the service order is FCFS within priority class.

It is a **one-line,** multiple-server system that results when a Storage is used to model a group of servers. This fact follows from the discussion in Section 11.7 leading to the conclusion that **first-come, first-served within Priority Level** is the default service order for Storages.

Modeling a multiple-line, multiple-server system requires that Transactions have some way to **identify** the particular server whose line they are in. But the servers in a group modeled with a Storage don't have individual identities. This rules out the possibility of using a Storage to model a multiple-line, multiple-server system.

How are multiple-line, multiple-server systems modeled in GPSS/H? They're modeled by representing each server in the group with a **Facility.** For example, three Facilities would be used to model the group of three servers in Figure 11.7. Each Facility has a unique identifier, so this approach makes it possible to form an association between Xacts and the particular server for whom they are waiting. This Facility-based approach is taken in GPSS/H to model multiple-line, multiple-server systems, even if the servers in the group are otherwise identical (meaning no distinctions would otherwise have to be made among them). (It is beyond the scope of this book to discuss operational aspects of this Facility-based approach.)

11.9 Requesting/Freeing More than One Server in a Group at a Time

As indicated in Figure 11.8, ENTER and LEAVE Blocks have an optional B Operand. The B Operand indicates **how many** servers are being requested (ENTER Block) and **how many** servers are being freed up (LEAVE Block). The **default value** of this B Operand is **1.**

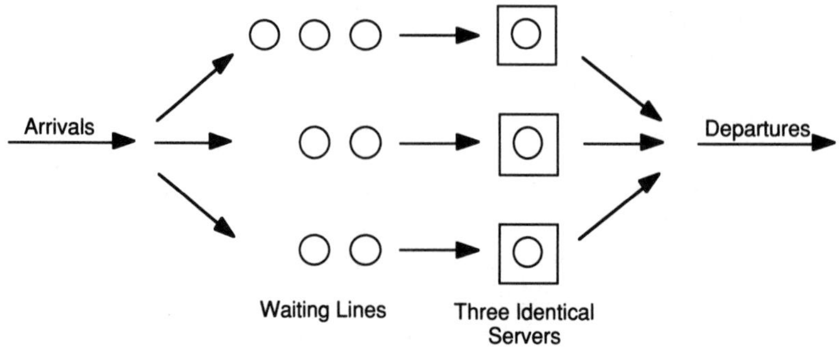

Figure 11.7 *The Geometry of a Multiple-Line, Multiple-Server Queuing System*

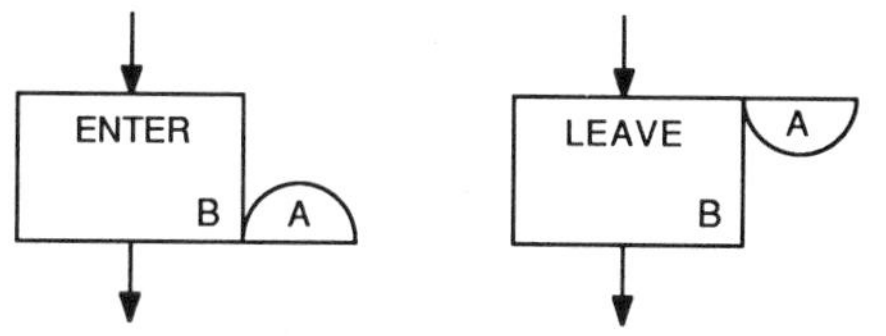

Operand	Significance	Default Value or Result
A	The identifier for a Storage (one or more of whose servers is being requested/captured at the ENTER, or being given up at the LEAVE)	Compile-time error
B	The number of servers being requested/captured at the ENTER, or being given up at the LEAVE	1

Figure 11.8 *The ENTER and LEAVE Blocks and Their A and B Operands*

Consider an occasion for using a **nondefault** B Operand with ENTER and LEAVE Blocks. Suppose the TUGBOATS Storage models a group of tugboats at a harbor. Ship-Transactions come to this harbor to load and unload cargo. Suppose one type of ship needs **three tugboats** for berthing purposes. The corresponding ship-Xacts can request the three needed tugboats by trying to move into an "ENTER TUGBOATS,3" Block, and after berthing is complete can free up these three tugboats by executing a "LEAVE TUGBOATS,3" Block.

When an ENTER Block is executed, the **Current Contents** of the referenced Storage is **increased** by the value of the ENTER Block's B Operand, and the **Remaining Capacity** is likewise **decreased**. Similarly, when a LEAVE Block is executed, the **Current Contents** of the referenced Storage is **decreased** by the value of the ENTER Block's B Operand, and the **Remaining Capacity** is likewise **increased**.

Now suppose the TUGBOATS Storage has a Capacity of 5. Assume a simulation is taking place, and a ship-Xact tries to move into "ENTER TUGBOATS,3" when only two tugboats are idle. What happens then? Will GPSS/H reserve the two idle tugboats on behalf of the requesting ship-Xact, and then make it wait until it can capture another tugboat? The answer is **no**. GPSS/H takes an **all or nothing at all** approach with the ENTER Block. If the number of idle servers is less than the number requested, then no servers are given to the requesting Xact at that time. The requestor will be blocked until its entire request can be satisfied all at one and the same time.

The "all or nothing at all" approach complicates the service order when Storages are involved and some Xacts try to capture two or more Storage servers simultaneously. In the case of the TUGBOATS Storage, suppose two types of ship uses the harbor. The first type of ship needs three tugboats for berthing. Assume the other ship type **only needs two** tugboats for berthing. In the above example, there are two idle tugboats. While a ship of the first type waits until its request for three tugboats can be satisfied all at one and the same time, a ship of the second type can come along, execute an "ENTER TUGBOATS,2" Block, and capture the two idle tugboats. The service order then isn't strictly FCFS.

Maybe the built-in "all or nothing at all" approach used with the ENTER Block isn't acceptable when modeling some systems. In an alternative approach, Xacts can capture one server at a time, one after the other, until they have the number of servers they need. In the harbor example, this could be accomplished by replacing the single "ENTER TUGBOATS,3" Block with a series of three consecutive "ENTER TUGBOATS" Blocks.

Xacts don't have to free up servers in the same sized chunks as they were captured. Consider ships deberthing at a harbor. A ship might need two tugboats to **initiate** deberthing, but after deberthing is partially completed, might be able to free up one tugboat while continuing to use the other tugboat until it has moved into open water. Such a ship could move through the sequence of Blocks shown in Figure 11.9.

```
 ...
ENTER      TUGBOATS,2  get 2 tugboats
ADVANCE    20,10       partial deberthing time
LEAVE      TUGBOATS    give up one tugboat
ADVANCE    15,5        remaining deberthing time
LEAVE      TUGBOATS    give up the other tugboat
 ...
```

Figure 11.9 *An Example for Use of the ENTER Block's B Operand*

11.10 Other Blocks for the Storage Entity

It was mentioned in Section 11.5 that servers modeled with the Storage entity can be moved back and forth between "on duty" ("in working order") and "off duty" ("not in working order") states in GPSS/H. This is done by making use of a logically complementary pair of Blocks for which the Operation words are SAVAIL (for "Storage available") and SUNAVAIL ("Storage unavailable"). (Recall that in GPSS/H, "available" means "on duty" or "in working order," whereas "unavailable" means "not on duty" or "not in working order.") If these types of Blocks are not used in a model, then each Storage in the model is "on duty" ("available") 100 percent of the time. Each Storage in a model is initially in an "Empty and on duty" state. If a model contains no SAVAIL or SUNAVAIL Blocks, then each Storage in the model will be "on duty" 100 percent of the time.

11.11 Storage Reports

During a simulation, GPSS/H gathers information for each Storage in a model, and then produces a Postsimulation Report for each Storage. Figure 11.10 provides an example of a Storage Report for a Storage named TUGBOATS. (This report is produced at the end of the simulation in Case Study 11A, presented in Section 11.13.) In Figure 11.10, parenthesized numbers have been placed over each column in the report. (These column numbers are not part of the report, but have been added to support discussion.) The information in each column will now be discussed by column number:

(1) The **STORAGE** column shows the **identifier** used for the Storage.

(2) **--AVG-UTIL-DURING-- TOTAL TIME** shows the fraction of **total** simulated time the Storage was in a state of capture.

(3) **--AVG-UTIL-DURING-- AVAIL TIME** shows the fraction of **available** simulated time the Storage was in a state of capture. A Storage's "available simulated time" is the amount of simulated time during which the Storage was "on duty" ("in working order"). In this book, each Storage used in a model will **always** be "on duty" ("in working order") throughout a simulation, and so "available simulated time" will equal total simulated time. In such cases, the column 3 entry equals the column 2 entry, and is not printed.

(4) **--AVG-UTIL-DURING-- UNAVL TIME** shows the fraction of **unavailable** simulated time the Storage was in a state of capture. A Storage's "unavailable simulated time" is the amount of simulated time the Storage was "off duty" ("not in working order"). In this book, "unavailable simulated time" for Storages will always be zero. In such cases, the conceptual entry in column 4 of the report for Storages is also zero, but this zero is not printed. The column is left blank instead.

(5) **ENTRIES** indicates the number of server captures that took place during the simulation. For example, if a Transaction executes "ENTER TUGBOATS,2", the number of server captures is increased by 2.

We will sometimes use **Capture Count** as a synonym for ENTRIES.

If ENTRIES for a Storage is zero, **no report will be produced** for that Storage.

(6) **AVERAGE TIME/UNIT** shows the average holding time per server capture. For example, if a Storage's Capture Count (ENTRIES) is 3, and if the Storage was held for 50, 100, and 60 simulated time units during server-captures 1, 2, and 3, respectively, then the average holding time per server-capture is 70 simulated time units ((50 + 100 + 60)/3 = 70).

(7) **CURRENT STATUS** indicates the Storage's "on duty" ("in working order") versus "off duty" ("not in working order") status at the time the report was produced. **AVAIL** means "on duty" ("in working order"), whereas **UNAVAIL** means "off duty" ("not in working order"). For now, Storages will always be "on duty," and so the column 7 entry in Storage Reports will always be AVAIL.

(8) **PERCENT AVAIL** shows the fraction of the total simulated time that the Storage was "on duty" ("in working order"). In models in which Storages are always "on duty," this entry will be

(1) STORAGE	(2) --AVG-UTIL-DURING-- TOTAL TIME	(3) AVAIL TIME	(4) UNAVL TIME	(5) ENTRIES	(6) AVERAGE TIME/UNIT	(7) CURRENT STATUS	(8) PERCENT AVAIL	(9) CAPACITY	(10) AVERAGE CONTENTS	(11) CURRENT CONTENTS	(12) MAXIMUM CONTENTS
TUGBOATS	.439			374	.411	AVAIL	100.0	3	1.316	0	3

Figure 11.10 *An Example of a Storage Report*

100.0 percent, as in Figure 11.10. A value of 100 percent will be displayed in this column throughout this book.

(9) **CAPACITY** shows the Capacity of the Storage.

(10) **AVERAGE CONTENTS** shows how many servers were captured on average during the course of the simulation. AVERAGE CONTENTS equals the product of CAPACITY and --AVG-UTIL-DURING-- TOTAL TIME.

(11) **CURRENT CONTENTS** shows how many of the servers are currently captured.

(12) **MAXIMUM CONTENTS** shows the maximum value attained by the CURRENT CONTENTS.

In addition to being provided as part of postsimulation output, Storage Reports can be displayed by the user in Test Mode. This is done by using the **display sto** command, where **sto** stands for **Sto**rage.

The qualified form of the **display** command can also be used for Storages. For example, issuing the command

```
display sto(tugboats,berths)
```

will cause a Storage Report to be displayed just for the TUGBOATS and BERTHS Storages. (As usual, identifiers such as TUGBOATS and BERTHS need not be capitalized in Test-Mode commands, whereas they must be capitalized in Model Files.)

11.12 Estimating the Minimum and Maximum Number of Servers

Storages can be used to estimate the minimum number of servers of various types needed by a system to keep up with the demands placed on it. They can also be used to estimate the maximum number of servers of various types needed if those servers are to be an unconstrained resource in the system.

The technique involved is to model the system using Storages with default Capacity to represent various types of resources. With a default Capacity in excess of 2 billion, each Storage models an unconstrained resource. After a simulation has been performed, the Storage Report indicates, for each Storage, the **average** (AVERAGE CONTENTS) and the **maximum** (MAXIMUM CONTENTS) number of its servers captured during the simulation.

The next integer larger than the average number of captured servers can be used to estimate the **minimum** number of servers of that type required to keep up with the demand. For example, if the average number of captured servers is 9.7, then it can be estimated that 10 servers are needed to keep up with the demand. (The 9.7 is only a point estimate of the expected number of captured servers, as discussed in Chapter 14. And so it could be appropriate to refine statistically the simple approach being described here.)

Similarly, the **maximum** number of a Storage's captured servers can be used to estimate the level at which the corresponding resource does not impose a constraint on the system. (The foregoing statistical caveat applies here, too, and in stronger terms.) In a series of following simulations, the modeler can then methodically reduce the levels of system resources below the estimated points at which they impose no constraint and study the resulting degradation in system performance.

11.13 Case Study 11A: Ships Un/Loading Cargo at a Harbor

1. Statement of the Problem

Type A and Type B ships come to a harbor to load and/or unload (that is, un/load) cargo. The harbor consists of three berths used only by Type A ships and two berths used only by Type B ships. There are three tugboats at the harbor. The tugboats are used to tug a ship into the berth prior to un/loading, and then later to tug the ship back out of the berth after un/loading has been completed. Tugboat services are not needed while a ship is un/loading.

Type A ships require three tugboats for berthing, and two for deberthing. Type B ships, smaller than Type A ships, only require two tugboats for berthing, and one for deberthing.

When a ship arrives at the harbor, it does these things:

1. It requests a berth of the type it uses.
2. After capturing the berth, it requests the tugboats it needs for berthing.
3. After capturing the tugboats, it gets pulled into the berth.
4. It gives up the tugboats.
5. It un/loads cargo.
6. It requests the tugboat(s) it needs for deberthing.
7. It gets pulled out of the berth.
8. It gives up the tugboat(s).
9. It gives up the berth.
10. It leaves the harbor.

Ships obtain tugboats on an "all or nothing at all" basis, as described in Section 11.9.

The interarrival-time and unloading-time distributions for Type A ships are 3.2 ± 1.5 hours and 8.4 ± 1.5 hours, respectively. The respective interarrival-time and unloading-time distributions for Type B ships are 1.5 ± 0.75 hours and 2.1 ± 0.6 hours. Berthing and deberthing times are 30 and 15 minutes, respectively, independent of ship type.

Build a model for this system, using 1 hour as the base time unit. Gather Queue information by ship type for ships while they are at the harbor, and with respect to the berth-wait process. "By ship type" means that four sets of Queue information should be gathered. One set will be for Type A ships while they are at the harbor. Another set will be for Type A ships with respect to the berth-wait process. Two similar sets of Queue information should be gathered for Type B ships.

Simulate until a total of 100 ships have left the harbor. Interpret the Queue and Storage Reports produced in the Postsimulation Report.

You might try your hand at building the requested model before reading further. (Hint: Refer to Figure 8.4 of Chapter 8.)

2. Approach Taken in Building the Model

The model called for here is a straightforward extension of the model in Figure 8.4 of Chapter 8. In the Figure 8.4 model, there is only one Type A berth, one Type B berth, and one tugboat, so these resources are modeled there as Facilities. In Case Study 11A, these berth and tugboats resources fall into the category of groups of identical servers, and so they are modeled here as Storages. This means that the SEIZE/RELEASE Blocks in the Figure 8.4 model are replaced by ENTER/LEAVE Blocks here and that STORAGE statements are provided to set the Capacities of the corresponding Storages.

Twofold use of the Queue entity for each ship type is also called for in the Case Study 11A model. The Queue for a type of ship *at the harbor* extends from the corresponding GENERATE to the corresponding TERMINATE. (A similar example was given earlier in the model for a drive-through restaurant in Figure 9.5 of Chapter 9.) The QUEUE Block then eliminates the need for the corresponding dummy ADVANCE used in the Figure 8.4 model.

The Queue for a type of ship *waiting for a berth* takes the form of a QUEUE/DEPART pair placed around the corresponding ENTER "berths" Block.

3. Table of Definitions

The Table of Definitions for Case Study 11A is given in Table 11A.1.

Table 11A.1

Table of Definitions for Case Study 11A

Base Time Unit: 1 hour

GPSS/H Entity	**Interpretation**
Transactions	
Model Segment 1	Type A ships
Model Segment 2	Type B ships
Queue	
ABERTH	Queue for Type A ships while waiting for a Type A berth
AINPORT	Queue for Type A ships while at the harbor
BBERTH	Queue for Type B ships while waiting for a Type B berth
BINPORT	Queue for Type B ships while at the harbor
Storages	
ABERTHS	Type A berths
BBERTHS	Type B berths
TUGBOATS	tugboats

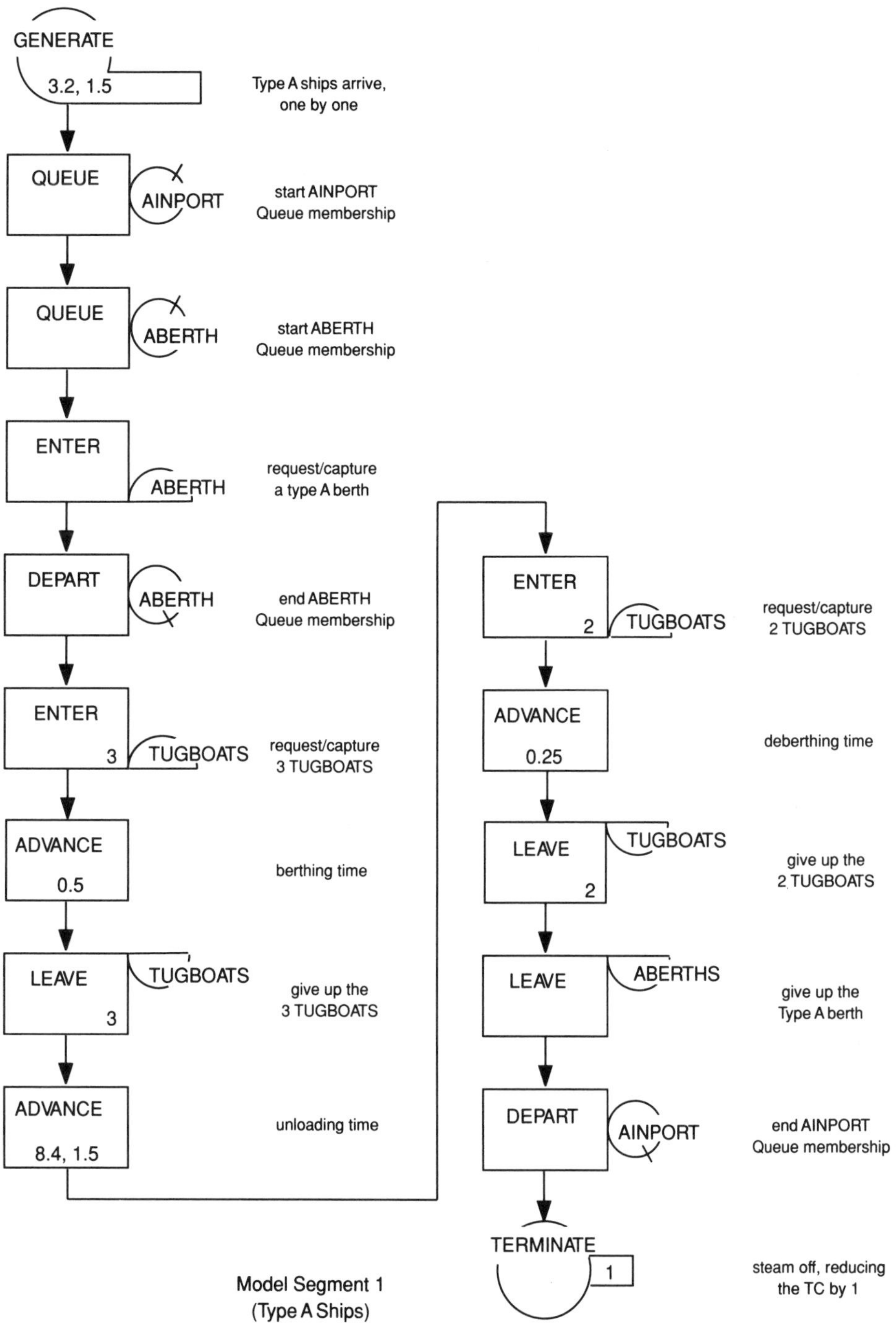

Figure 11A.1 *Block Diagram for Case Study 11A (continued on the next page)*

4. Block Diagram

The Block Diagram for Case Study 11A is given in Figure 11A.1.

5. Modified Source Echo

The Modified Source Echo for Case Study 11A is given in Figure 11A.2.

6. Postsimulation Report

The Postsimulation Report for Case Study 11A is given in Figure 11A.3.

7. Discussion

Model Logic. In the harbor system, Type A ships do not compete with Type B ships for the use of berths

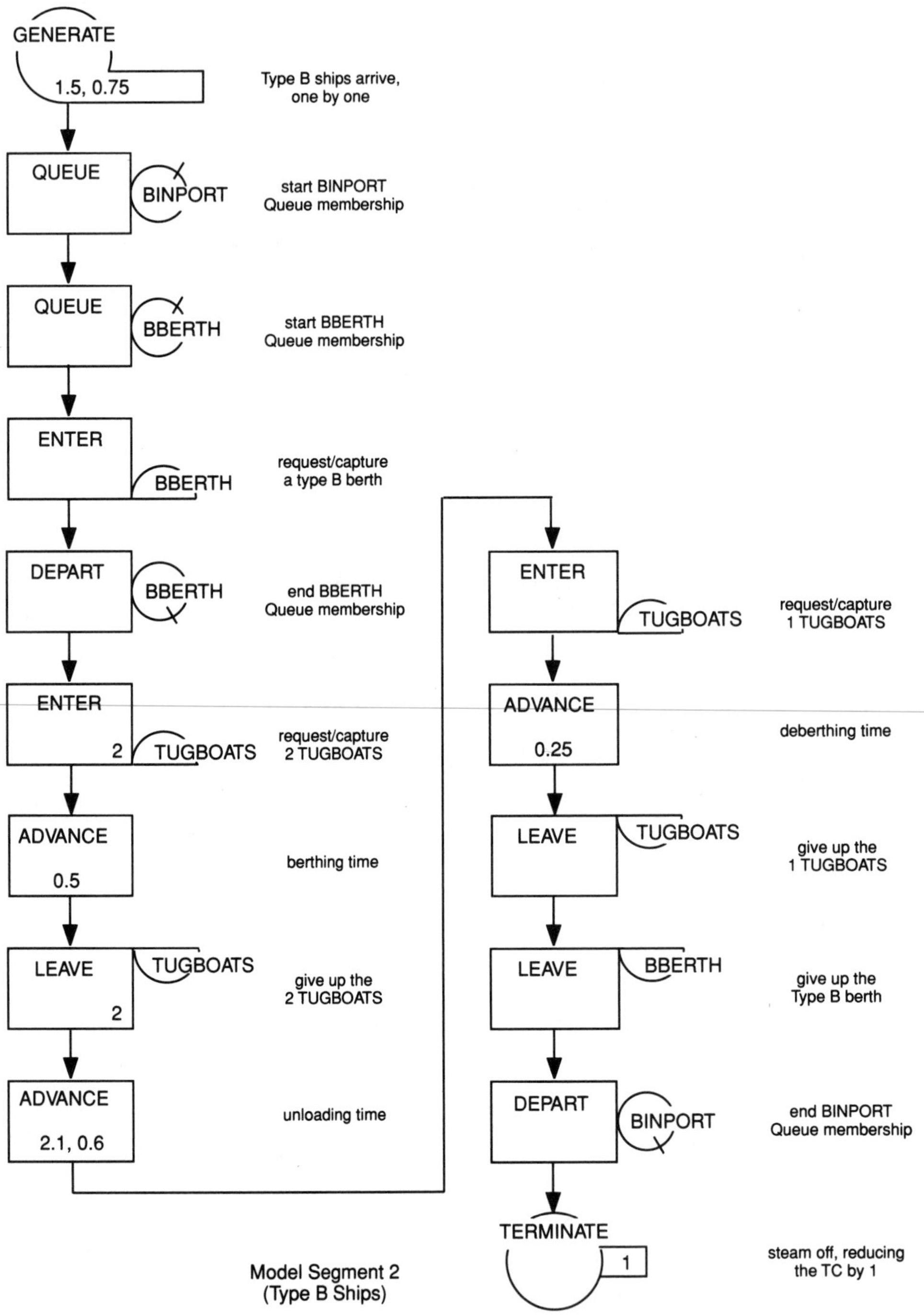

Figure 11A.1 (concluded)

(or vice versa). Type A ships do compete with Type B ships, however (and vice versa), for the use of tugboats. In this sense, the only interaction that takes place between Model Segments 1 and 2 in the Case Study 11A model is in terms of the several "ENTER TUGBOATS" and "LEAVE TUGBOATS" Blocks.

Model Implementation. Note how the STORAGE statements have been positioned toward the top of the Model File. (See Statements 8, 9, and 10 in Figure 11A.2.) This is consistent with the suggested top-down order of Model-File statements shown in Figure 11.5.

Postsimulation Report. As shown in Figure 11A.3(a), it took about 112.0 hours for 100 ships to pass through the harbor.

```
STMT#  BLOCK#  *LOC    OPERATION  A,B,C,D,E,F,G   COMMENTS

   1                   SIMULATE                             Case Study 11A
   2           *                               Ships Un/loading Cargo at a Harbor
   3           *                                            Base Time Unit: 1 Hour
   4           **********************************************************************
   5           *       Control Statements (STORAGE)                                 *
   6           **********************************************************************
   7           *
   8            ABERTHS  STORAGE    3   Type A berths
   9            BBERTHS  STORAGE    2   Type B berths
  10            TUGBOATS STORAGE    3   tugboats
  11           *
  12           **********************************************************************
  13           *       Model Segment 1 (Type A Ships)                               *
  14           **********************************************************************
  15           *
  16       1           GENERATE   3.2,1.5       Type A ships arrive, one by one
  17       2           QUEUE      AINPORT       start AINPORT Queue membership
  18       3           QUEUE      ABERTH        start ABERTH Queue membership
  19       4           ENTER      ABERTHS       request/capture a Type A berth
  20       5           DEPART     ABERTH        end ABERTH Queue membership
  21       6           ENTER      TUGBOATS,3    request/capture 3 tugboats
  22       7           ADVANCE    0.5           berthing time
  23       8           LEAVE      TUGBOATS,3    give up the 3 tugboats
  24       9           ADVANCE    8.4,1.5       un/loading time
  25      10           ENTER      TUGBOATS,2    request/capture 2 tugboats
  26      11           ADVANCE    0.25          deberthing time
  27      12           LEAVE      TUGBOATS,2    give up the 2 tugboats
  28      13           LEAVE      ABERTHS       give up the Type A berth
  29      14           DEPART     AINPORT       end AINPORT Queue membership
  30      15           TERMINATE  1             steam off, reducing the TC by 1
  31           *
  32           **********************************************************************
  33           *       Model Segment 2 (Type B Ships)                               *
  34           **********************************************************************
  35           *
  36      16           GENERATE   1.5,0.75      Type B ships arrive, one by one
  37      17           QUEUE      BINPORT       start BINPORT Queue membership
  38      18           QUEUE      BBERTH        start BBERTH Queue membership
  39      19           ENTER      BBERTHS       request/capture a Type B berth
  40      20           DEPART     BBERTH        end BBERTH Queue membership
  41      21           ENTER      TUGBOATS,2    request/capture 2 tugboats
  42      22           ADVANCE    0.5           berthing time
  43      23           LEAVE      TUGBOATS,2    give up the 2 tugboats
  44      24           ADVANCE    2.1,0.6       un/loading time
  45      25           ENTER      TUGBOATS      request/capture 1 tugboat
  46      26           ADVANCE    0.25          deberthing time
  47      27           LEAVE      TUGBOATS      give up the 1 tugboat
  48      28           LEAVE      BBERTHS       give up the Type B berth
  49      29           DEPART     BINPORT       end BINPORT Queue membership
  50      30           TERMINATE  1             steam off, reducing the TC by 1
  51           *
  52           **********************************************************************
  53           *       Run-Control Statements                                       *
  54           **********************************************************************
  55           *
  56                   START      100           set the TC = 100;
  57                   END                      end of Model-File execution
```

Figure 11A.2 *Modified Source Echo of the Case Study 11A Model File*

```
RELATIVE CLOCK:     112.0387  ABSOLUTE CLOCK:     112.0387
```

(a)

BLOCK	CURRENT	TOTAL	BLOCK	CURRENT	TOTAL	BLOCK	CURRENT	TOTAL
1		36	11		31	21		70
2		36	12		31	22	1	70
3	2	36	13		31	23		69
4		34	14		31	24		69
5		34	15		31	25		69
6		34	16		71	26		69
7		34	17		71	27		69
8		34	18	1	71	28		69
9	3	34	19		70	29		69
10		31	20		70	30		69

(b)

STORAGE	--AVG-UTIL-DURING-- TOTAL TIME	AVAIL TIME	UNAVL TIME	ENTRIES	AVERAGE TIME/UNIT	CURRENT STATUS	PERCENT AVAIL	CAPACITY	AVERAGE CONTENTS	CURRENT CONTENTS	MAXIMUM CONTENTS
ABERTHS	.927			34	9.166	AVAIL	100.0	3	2.782	3	3
BBERTHS	.894			70	2.862	AVAIL	100.0	2	1.788	1	2
TUGBOATS	.457			373	.412	AVAIL	100.0	3	1.370	2	3

(c)

QUEUE	MAXIMUM CONTENTS	AVERAGE CONTENTS	TOTAL ENTRIES	ZERO ENTRIES	PERCENT ZEROS	AVERAGE TIME/UNIT	$AVERAGE TIME/UNIT	QTABLE NUMBER	CURRENT CONTENTS
AINPORT	6	3.449	36	0	0.0	10.732	10.732		5
ABERTH	3	.667	36	12	33.3	2.075	3.113		2
BINPORT	4	2.092	71	0	0.0	3.302	3.302		2
BBERTH	2	.304	71	29	40.8	.480	.812		1

(d)

RANDOM STREAM	ANTITHETIC VARIATES	INITIAL POSITION	CURRENT POSITION	SAMPLE COUNT	CHI-SQUARE UNIFORMITY
1	OFF	100000	100212	212	0.69

(e)

Figure 11A.3 *Postsimulation Report for Case Study 11A. (a) Clock Values. (b) Block Counts. (c) Storage Report. (d) Queue Report. (e) RNG Report*

The sum of Current Counts in Figure 11A.3(b) indicates there are 7 ships at the harbor at the end of the simulation. This is consistent with the sum of the CURRENT CONTENTS of 5 and 2 for the AINPORT and BINPORT Queues in Figure 11A.3(d).

Figure 11A.3(d) indicates that the average number of Type A and Type B ships at the harbor were about 3.4 and 2.1, respectively, during the simulation. (See the AVERAGE CONTENTS for the AINPORT and BINPORT Queues.) The corresponding maximums were 6 and 4. (See the MAXIMUM CONTENTS for the AINPORT and BINPORT Queues.) These fairly large averages and maximums result from the high berth utilizations of 92.7 percent and 89.4 percent for the Type A and Type B berths. (See the --AVG-UTIL-DURING-- TOTAL TIME for the ABERTHS and BBERTHS Storages in Figure 11A.3(c).)

The average time in port for Type A ships in the simulation was about 10.7 hours. (See AVERAGE TIME/UNIT for the AINPORT Queue in Figure 11A.3(d).) If Type A ships never had to wait for a Type A berth or tugboats, their expected time in port would be 9.15 hours (9.15 hours = 0.5 hours berthing + 8.4 hours un/loading + 0.25 hours deberthing). And so the realized time-in-port for Type A ships is about 1.5 hours greater than it would be if the berth and tugboat resources were unlimited in extent. (Carrying out a similar analysis for the Type B ships is left as an exercise.)

In total, 212 random numbers were used during the simulation. (See the SAMPLE COUNT for RANDOM STREAM 1 in Figure 11A.3(e).) This count is consistent with the number of probabilistic GENERATE and ADVANCE Block executions. (Verifying this statement is left as an exercise.)

11.14 Exercises

1. The supplied file model11a.gps contains the Model File for Case Study 11A. Perform a Batch simulation with this Model File. Compare clock times, Block Counts, and informa-

tion in the Storage Report to the values given in Figure 11A.3. Corresponding values should match.

*2. By hand, compute the expected tugboat utilization in the harbor system of Case Study 11A. Compare this expected value against the realized tugboat utilization reported in Figure 11A.3(c).

3. In Case Study 11A, assume that after a Type A ship has deberthed for 0.15 hours, it can give up one of its two tugboats, but must use the other tugboat for an addition 0.10 deberthing hours. Would you expect this small change in system operation to result in much improvement in system performance? Apply this change to a copy of the Case Study 11A model, then carry out a simulation. Compare the results with those in Figure 11A.3.

4. Interchange Model Segments 1 and 2 in a copy of the model11a.gps file, then perform a Batch simulation with the modified Model File. The numeric results differ from those reported in Figure 11A.3. Speculate about the reason why this might be the case. (Clarification is provided in Section 4 of Chapter 13.)

5. In a copy of the model11a.gps file, alter the logic for obtaining tugboats from the "all-or-nothing-at-all" approach used in the case study model to a "one-at-a-time" approach. Perform a Batch simulation with the modified model. Compare the numeric results with those shown in Figure 11A.3. In these two simulations, which approach results in the smaller average in-port residence times for Type A and Type B ships? Does this measure of system performance improve for one type of ship and degrade for the other?

6. Taking the Case Study 11A model as a starting point each time, alter the model in these three ways, each independent of the others:

(a) Add one tugboat to the system.
(b) Add one Type A berth to the system.
(c) Add one Type B berth to the system.

Perform a Batch simulation with each of the three resulting models. Compare the results with those in the case study. Which of the three alternative expansions in harbor resources seems to have the most beneficial effect on system performance in these single simulations? (That is, which expansion has the most beneficial effect on the average in-port residence time?)

*7. In a copy of the Case Study 11A model, give Type A ships higher priority than Type B ships, then perform a Batch simulation with the resulting model. How positive is the resulting effect on the average in-port residence time of Type A ships? How negative is the effect on this measure of system performance for Type B ships?

*8. (a) In Case Study 11A, suppose the interarrival times for Type A and Type B ships become 1.8 ± 0.9 and 0.8 ± 0.4 hours, respectively. Using hand calculations, determine the minimum number of tugboats, Type A berths, and Type B berths needed for the system to be able to respond to the demands placed on it.
(b) Now modify a copy of the Case Study 11A model to reflect these changed interarrival times. Then delete (or "comment out" by putting asterisks in their first character position) the STORAGE statements from the model (so there will be unlimited numbers of Type A and Type B berths and of tugboats). Perform a simulation with the model. Use the results to estimate the minimum number of tugboats and of Type A and Type B berths for the system to be able to respond to the demands placed on it. Are your hand calculations consistent with these results?
(c) The simulation results provide estimates of the maximum number of tugboats and of Type A and Type B berths needed if no ship is ever to have to wait for a berth or tugboats. Speculate about the possibility of obtaining equivalent information by hand calculation.
(d) Now perform a simulation with the estimated minimum number of tugboats and of Type A and Type B berths determined in (b). The simulation results provide estimates of the average in-port residence time for Type A and Type B ships. Speculate about the possibility of obtaining equivalent information by hand calculation.

9. (a) Patients arrive at a doctor's office every 15 ± 10.5 minutes. It takes the doctor 14 ± 5 minutes to serve a patient. Build a model for this system, gathering Queue information for patients between the time they arrive, and the time they start to receive service from the doc-

tor. Perform a simulation with the model, simulating until 50 patients have been served.

(b) In an expanded form of the office in (a), there are three doctors. Patients arrive every 5 ± 3.5 minutes. It takes a doctor 14 ± 5 minutes to serve a patient. A one-line, multiple-server system is used in the office. Model this system, again gathering Queue information for patients between the time they arrive, and the time they start to receive service from a doctor. Simulate with the model until 50 patients have been served.

(c) Compare the Queue Reports from (a) and (b). Do you think the long-run average number of patients waiting to see a doctor in the (a) and (b) system should be equal? Do you think the long-run average waiting time per patient in the (a) and (b) systems should be equal? What is the basis for your thinking? How do these system performance measures compare in your (a) and (b) simulations?

10. Repeat Exercise 7 of Section 8.10 in Chapter 8 (which builds on Exercise 6 there), but now assume there are two workers at Station 1 and two at Station 2. Also assume that work arrives per a 15 ± 10 interarrival time distribution. (The overall effect of these changes is to double the system's resources, and to double the amount of work that the system is expected to accomplish.) Simulate until 100 pieces of work have left the system. Compare the resulting Station 1 productivity measure to that from Exercise 7 of Section 8.10. Would you expect the Station 1 productivity to be the same in the two systems? Why, or why not? Check out your thinking via simulation. If the results are contrary to your reasoning, either defend or change your reasoning.

11. In the widget-manufacturing system of Case Study 6A, assume that there are three ovens instead of one, that there continues to be no limit to the supply of raw material, and that the market for widgets is large enough so that all widgets that can be made can also be sold. Simulate this revised system to estimate how many assemblers there should be if the objective is to maximize the estimated daily profit. For each number of assemblers you try, just perform a single, 40-hour simulation. (This overly simple approach will be refined in Chapter 16.) As in Exercise 5 of Section 6.12, assume a fixed daily cost per oven of $100, a worker's salary (including fringe benefits) of $85 per day, a $20 cost for the material in a widget, and a finished goods value of $30.

*12. Repeat Exercise 11a of Section 9.7, but now assume that there are five finishing machines, each with its own operator and that there are two cranes in the system. Continue to assume, as in that exercise, that there are other calls for use of a crane. After building the model, perform a 400-hour Batch simulation with it. Discuss the information produced in the Postsimulation Report.

13. (a) Repeat the student registration system described in Exercise 11 of Section 8.10, but now provide two workers at Window 1 and two workers at Window 2. Also gather Queue information for students waiting at Window 1 and for students waiting at Window 2. Compare the Queue information with that obtained when there is only one worker at Window 1 and one worker at Window 2.

(b) Suppose there are three workers in the student registration system. There can either be two workers at Window 1 and one at Window 2, or one at Window 1 and two at Window 2. Perform single simulations with each of these two alternatives under the conditions described in Exercise 11 of Section 8.10. Which alternative seems to result in the most favorable Queue information in these single simulations?

14. Read the Statement of the Problem for Case Study 16A of Chapter 16. Build a model for the base-case production system that is described there. That is, model the system for the case of one repairperson and zero leased machines. (Ignore references in the problem statement to the other system alternatives that management wants to consider, and ignore references to the Dudewicz and Dalal methodology for selecting the probable best from two or more competing alternatives.) Perform a Batch simulation with your model, simulating until 25 working weeks (1000 hours) have elapsed. Using economic information given in the statement of the problem, compute the average daily cost experienced in the simulation.

11.15 Bug Clinic

Each of these exercises calls for a Batch simulation. Remember that if an execution error occurs, an Error Message will be displayed on the screen, and GPSS/H will give you control. You can then display additional information of your choice, if you like, before quitting the simulation.

*1. Modify a copy of the Case Study 11A model by eliminating the "ENTER TUGBOATS,3" Block in Model Segment 1. (See Figure 11A.2.) What is wrong with the resulting model? How do you think GPSS/H might respond if a simulation is performed with this model? Carry out a Batch simulation with the modified model and see what happens.

*2. Modify a copy of the Case Study 11A model by eliminating the "LEAVE TUGBOATS,3" Block in Model Segment 1. What is wrong with the resulting model? How do you think GPSS/H might respond if a simulation is performed with this model? Carry out a Batch simulation with the model and see what happens.

*3. Repeat Exercise 2, but now simply delete the 3 from the "LEAVE TUGBOATS,3" Block.

*4. Shift the three STORAGE statements in a copy of the Case Study 11A model (Statements 8, 9, and 10 in Figure 11A.2) so that they follow the START statement. What Storage Capacities will then be in effect during the Xact-Movement Phase? Check your answer by carrying out a Batch simulation with the modified Model File.

*5. Suppose a model contains the statement "SYSTEM STORAGE 5" and the Block "TRANSFER ,SYSTEM", but does not contain a Block labeled SYSTEM (as it shouldn't, given the earlier caution that Block Labels should not be used as identifiers for Storages, Facilities, Queues, etc.). What do you think will happen if an attempt is made to carry out a simulation with the model? Do you think a compile-time or an execution-time error condition will come about? Compose such a model, initiate a simulation with it, and see what happens.

11.16 Dummy Storages

The idea of a dummy Facility was introduced in Chapter 8, where it was explained that a dummy Facility is one whose SEIZE Block **never denies entry** to a Transaction **in the modeling context** in which the Facility is used. Recall that dummy Facilities aren't used to model constrained system resources. Instead, they're used to force GPSS/H to gather more information during a simulation than would be gathered otherwise. The value of dummy Facilities is in the Facility Report that is produced for them.

Dummy Storages are analogous to dummy Facilities. A dummy Storage is one whose ENTER Block never denies entry to a Transaction in the context in which the Storage is used. Instead of modeling constrained system resources, dummy Storages are used to force GPSS/H to gather more information during a simulation than would be gathered otherwise. As with dummy Facilities, the value of dummy Storages is in the Storage Report which is produced for them.

```
AINUSE     STORAGE    3            3 Type A berths (dummy storage)

            ...
OLDBLOK6   LEAVE      TUGBOATS,3   give up the 3 tugboats
*
           ENTER      AINUSE       un/loading now begins
OLDBLOK7   ADVANCE    8.4,1.5      un/loading time
           LEAVE      AINUSE       un/loading now ends
*
OLDBLOK8   ENTER      TUGBOATS,2   request/capture 2 tugboats
            ...
```

Figure 11.11 *Use of a Dummy Storage with the Type A Berths in the Case Study 11A Model*

As an example of a dummy Storage, suppose it's of interest in Case Study 11A to measure the fraction of simulated time that the Type A berths are being used for actual un/loading operations. When a ship is using one of the Type A berths for this purpose, the ship-Xact is in the Block "ADVANCE 8.4,1.5" (see Block 7 in Figure 11A.2). There are three Type A berths, so up to **three** ship-Xacts at a time can be in this ADVANCE. To measure the extent of ADVANCE-Block occupancy, we can introduce a dummy Storage into the model, setting the Storage Capacity to **three** and sandwiching the ADVANCE between a corresponding ENTER/LEAVE pair. This pattern is shown in Figure 11.11, where the name chosen for the dummy Storage is AINUSE (for "Type A berth IN USE"). OLDBLOK6, OLDBLOK7, and OLDBLOK8 in Figure 11.11 correspond to Blocks 6, 7, and 8, respectively, in the Case Study 11A model (see Figure 11A.2). Note that "ENTER AINUSE" in Figure 11.11 will never deny entry to a ship-Xact, because not more than three ship-Xacts at a time are permitted to have access to the Type A berths in the Case Study 11A model. If there are three ship-Xacts in the Figure 11.11 ADVANCE Block, there is no way a fourth ship-Xact can come along and take "ENTER AINUSE" as its Next Block Attempted.

11.17 Overlapping ENTER/LEAVE Blocks

The use of overlapping SEIZE/RELEASE Blocks was discussed in Section 9 of Chapter 8, and illustrated there in the model of Figure 8.6. The basic idea involved is that an Xact may have to capture one Facility as a prerequisite to being able to free up another Facility. As a result, the RELEASE Block for the one Facility comes somewhere **after** the SEIZE Block for the other Facility.

This idea can be extended in straightforward fashion to the use of overlapping ENTER/LEAVE Blocks. Application of this idea is left to the Section 11.18 exercises.

11.18 Exercises

1. Repeat Exercises 6, 7, and 8 of Section 8.10, but now assume that there are two wait spaces between Stations 1 and 2. Compare and contrast the results with those obtained in the Section 8.10 forms of the exercise, when only one wait space was provided between Stations 1 and 2.

*2. By hand, compute the expected berth utilizations in the harbor system of Case Study 11A. For this purpose, assume that a berth is being utilized only when it is being used for ongoing un/loading. Compare these expected values against the realized utilizations reported in Figure 11A.3(c).

3. Modify the Case Study 11A model to measure the fraction of simulated time that the Type A and Type B berths are used for ongoing un/loading. Compare the resulting berth utilizations with the expected utilizations calculated in Exercise 2.

11.19 Admitting Transactions into a Model Only When Needed

Sometimes it's not known at the time of building a model when Transactions should be admitted into the model. This circumstance can arise if Transactions are to be admitted only when specified model conditions are satisfied, but not otherwise. If the specified model conditions come about at probabilistic times, then it's difficult or impossible to structure a conventional GENERATE Block that will introduce Transactions into the model at precisely the right simulated times.

Consider a case in point. Suppose that Transactions simulate raw material that is input to a manufacturing system and that raw material is always available when it's needed. Then a unit of raw material (a Transaction) should be admitted to the system whenever the system is ready to start building another unit of product. Assume the system starts to build the next unit of product whenever a finished unit leaves the system. If there is variability in the manufacturing step times (which is almost bound to be the case), then the times when raw material will be needed won't be known at the time the model is built.

Situations like this can be handled by using a **naked GENERATE Block** followed by a Block capable of conditionally denying entry, such as an ENTER (or SEIZE). A naked GENERATE Block is

```
          SIMULATE
*
 SYSTEM   STORAGE   10         10 units of work-in-process
 AWORKERS STORAGE   5          5 "A" workers
 BWORKERS STORAGE   5          5 "B" workers
*
          GENERATE  0          unlimited raw material
          ENTER     SYSTEM     admit raw material when needed
          ENTER     AWORKERS   capture an A worker
          ADVANCE   35,15      step 1 takes place
          LEAVE     AWORKERS   let go of the A worker
          ENTER     BWORKERS   capture a B worker
          ADVANCE   50,10      step 2 takes place
          LEAVE     BWORKERS   let go of the B worker
          ENTER     AWORKERS   capture an A worker again
          ADVANCE   15,5       step 3 takes place
          LEAVE     AWORKERS   let go of the A worker
          LEAVE     SYSTEM     let more raw material in
          TERMINATE 1          finished unit leaves the model
*
          START     100        build 100 units
          END                  end of Model-File execution
```

Figure 11.12 *A Model That Admits Transactions Only When Needed*

one with no explicitly supplied Operand values (or with the A Operand keyed as zero, which is the default value of the A Operand anyway). The interarrival time at such a GENERATE Block is zero, and with no Limit Count, it would seem that the Block would produce Transactions endlessly at time 0.0. But this doesn't happen, of course, if things eventually reach the point that the next Block denies entry. If this comes about, the Xact currently trying to escape from the GENERATE finds itself blocked, and must remain in the GENERATE. It won't trigger GENERATE-Block execution until it can later escape from the GENERATE Block. When it does eventually escape (at the time another Xact is wanted by the model), it "replaces itself" by executing the GENERATE Block, which means another Xact is created and brought into the GENERATE Block.

Figure 11.12 shows a model that uses a naked GENERATE Block followed by an ENTER Block. The model is for a system consisting of two groups of workers, consisting of five "A" workers and five "B" workers. To transform a unit of raw material into a unit of product requires that an A worker carry out a first step, followed by a B worker carrying out a second step, and then concluded by an A worker carrying out a third step. Ten units of work in process are permitted to be moving through the system at one and the same time. When a unit of product leaves the system, another unit of raw material enters the system to take its place.

Notice how this "when one goes out, another one comes in" effect is achieved in the Figure 11.12 model with a naked GENERATE Block followed by an ENTER Block referencing a Storage (SYSTEM) whose Capacity is 10. There is exactly one Transaction in the GENERATE Block at all times (for all practical purposes). Whenever a unit of product executes the "LEAVE SYSTEM" Block, this has the twofold effect of (1) turning on the model's Status Change Flag and (2) awakening the previously blocked Xact in the GENERATE Block. After the unit of product moves into TERMINATE and destroys itself, the scan is restarted, and the awakened Xact moves from the GENERATE into "ENTER SYSTEM," replacing itself at the GENERATE Block in the process.

11.20 Exercises

*1. Reconsider the widget-manufacturing system model of Case Study 6A. In that model, Xacts simulate workers, a Facility simulates the OVEN, and no GPSS/H elements are used to simulate work-in-process as it is transformed from raw material into finished goods. (Case Study 6A should be reread at this time.)

Now build an alternative model for the widget-manufacturing system. In the alternative model, use a Storage to simulate the workers and Xacts to simulate work-in-process. As before, use a Facility to simulate the OVEN. The starting conditions in the model should match those in Case Study 6A. Remember that there is no shortage of raw material in the system.

Perform a Batch simulation with your model, providing four workers and stopping after 40 hours of simulated time have elapsed. (These stopping conditions match those of Case Study 6A.) If you've built the model correctly, the numeric results will match those of Case Study 6A. (See Figure 6A.5.)

*2. Suppose the widget-manufacturing system of Case Study 6A and Exercise 1 is changed by assigning one of the four workers to do nothing but heat-treat widgets. The other three workers, who previously both assembled and heat-treated widgets, now do nothing but assemble widgets. Modify your model of Exercise 1 to reflect this change in the system. Then perform a simulation with the modified model, stopping after 40 hours of simulated time have elapsed. Compare the number of widgets that are built to the number built under the four-worker system of Case Study 6A and Exercise 1.

*3. In Exercise 2, suppose a new worker is hired to heat-treat widgets and the original four workers are assigned to do nothing but assemble widgets. Assume there is no physical limit to the number of in-process widgets that can be stacked up, waiting to be heat treated. What's the logical flaw in the design of this system? Consider the possibility of verifying your thinking by putting these conditions into effect in the model of Exercise 2 and carrying out a simulation with the model.

*4. In Exercise 3, suppose the staging space at the oven is limited, so that no more than three in-process widgets can be waiting to be heat treated. A worker can't begin assembling another widget until the ones he or she has most recently assembled can be put into this staging space. This eliminates the logical flaw in the design of the system described in Exercise 3. Why?

Model this revised system. Perform a simulation with the model. Compare the resulting production rate with the rate realized for the case of five workers in Exercise 6 of Section 6.12. (In that exercise, instead of having four workers assemble widgets and one worker heat-treat them, each worker was responsible for his or her own assembling and heat treating.)

12 Additional Blocks for Controlling Transaction Direction and Timing

12.1 Preview

In the models presented until now, a Transaction's Next Block has either been the Block sequential to its Current Block or a nonsequential Block pointed to by an unconditional-mode TRANSFER. In this chapter, several additional TRANSFER-Block modes are introduced to provide some flexibility in determining a Transaction's Next Block. Also introduced here is the PRIORITY Block, which is used to change a Transaction's Priority Level and therefore influence the timing of its movement during a Scan Phase.

12.2 The Statistical-Mode TRANSFER Block

It's possible for a Transaction's Next Block to be selected probabilistically from two alternatives. The choice isn't necessarily made on a "50-50" basis, but instead is made on a basis specified by the modeler. For example, Transactions can choose one of the two Blocks 25 percent of the time in the long run (with the other Block then chosen 75 percent of the time).

It's the Statistical-Mode TRANSFER Block that probabilistically splits an incoming stream of Xact traffic into two outgoing streams. Properties of the statistical TRANSFER Block are summarized in Figure 12.1. A **decimal point** is the first character in the Block's A Operand. The **rest** of the A Operand supplies a number, which is interpreted as **parts per thousand**. The B and C Operands are used to "point" to two other Blocks in the model. The pointing is accomplished by (1) labeling each of these two alternative Blocks and (2) repeating those labels in the TRANSFER Block's B and C Operand positions. The B Operand points to what is called the "B-Block" and the C Operand to the "C-Block." The A Operand indicates the fraction of the time (expressed as parts per thousand) that an Xact moving into the TRANSFER will take the C-Block as its Next Block.

When the value of the statistical-TRANSFER's A Operand is supplied as a constant, it is recommended that the value be keyed as a **three-digit constant**. (It's possible to supply Operand values indirectly, as we will see later in the book. For now, however, we'll supply Operand values directly, either as constants or as symbolic identifiers.)

When an Xact executes a statistical TRANSFER, GPSS/H draws a value at random from the population of integers uniformly distributed on the **closed** interval from 0 to 999. (There are 1000 values in this population.) If the sampled value is **less than** the A Operand, the Xact's Next Block will be the C-Block; otherwise, it will be the B-Block.

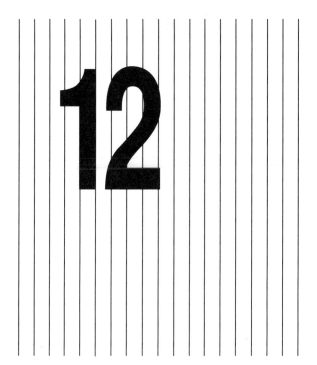

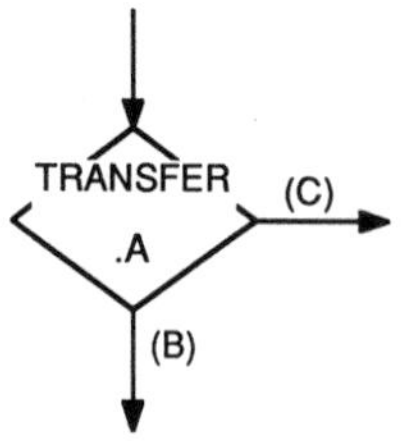

Operand	Significance	Default Value or Result
A	Fraction of the time that the "C-Block" will become the transferring Xact's Next Block [1]	Compile-time error
B	Pointer to a Block[2] (the "B-Block")	The "B-Block" is the sequential Block
C	Pointer to a Block[2] (the "C-Block")	Compile-time error

[1] First character in the A Operand must be a decimal point, e.g. .372; .015; .500
[2] Copy of the Label attached to that Block.

Figure 12.1 *The TRANSFER Block in Statistical Mode*

Here's an example of a statistical TRANSFER Block:

```
TRANSFER .250,WORK,PLAY
```

When a Transaction moves into this Block, there is one chance in four (250 parts out of 1000) that its Next Block will be the one labeled PLAY (the C-Block) and three chances in four that its Next Block will be the one labeled WORK (the B-Block).

Each choice of a Next Block is independent of the previous choices. For example, it's possible that five consecutive Xacts moving into "TRANSFER .250,WORK,PLAY" will take the PLAY Block as their Next Block. It is only **on average** that about 25 percent of them will go to PLAY.

If a statistical TRANSFER Block's A Operand is zero, chances will be "0 in 1000" that it will send Xacts to the C-Block. In other words, Xacts will always be sent to the B-Block. Transactions executing the Block "TRANSFER .0,ROUTE1,ROUTE2," for example, will always take ROUTE1 as their Next Block.

Similarly, if a statistical TRANSFER Block's A Operand is 1000 or greater, Xacts will always be sent to the C-Block.

As indicated in Figure 12.1, a default can be taken on the statistical TRANSFER Block's B Operand. If this is done, then the B-Block is the Block **sequential to the TRANSFER Block**. In such a case, there is no need to label the sequential Block.

Consider this example:

```
TRANSFER .875,,SALTMINE
```

When an Xact moves into this TRANSFER, it will take the Block labeled SALTMINE (the C-Block) as its Next Block with probability 0.875 (875 times out of 1000). The rest of the time, Xacts will "fall through" to whatever Block is sequential to the TRANSFER Block.

The statistical TRANSFER is the second Block we've discussed that uses one or more Operands to point to other Blocks in a model. (Unconditional TRANSFER was the first.) When these Blocks are pictured, as in Figure 12.1, the convention is to put parentheses around the Block-pointer Operands, even though these parentheses are not included in the statement form of the Block.

The statistical TRANSFER Block never denies entry to a Transaction. When an Xact executes the Block, its choice of Next Block is determined for it once and for all. The Xact then immediately tries to move into that Next Block. If its Next Block denies entry, the Xact remains in the TRANSFER Block, which then serves as its Current Block. On some later retry, the Xact presumably will be able to move into its Next Block, and so on. (To put this another way, an Xact "sticks with" its choice of Next Block, even if it is initially refused entry into this Next Block.)

12.3 Case Study 12A: A Quality Control Model

1. Statement of the Problem

Assembled television sets move through a series of testing stations in the final stage of their production. At the last of these stations, the vertical control component on the sets is tested. If the component isn't working correctly, the defective set is routed to an adjustment station, where the component is modified. After adjustment, the set is sent back to the last inspection station, where the component is again inspected. If the set again fails inspection, it is again routed to the adjustment station, and so on. Sets passing the final inspection phase, whether the first time or after one or more routings through the adjustment station, move on to a packing.

The situation is pictured in Figure 12A.1, where circles represent television sets. Open circles are sets waiting for final inspection, whereas X-ed out circles are defective sets that are either being worked on at the adjustment station, or are waiting to be worked on there.

Television sets arrive at the final inspection station from the previous station every 5.5 ± 2 minutes. Two inspectors work side-by-side at the final inspection station. The time required to inspect a set is 10 ± 3 minutes. Because the vertical control component is poorly designed, only 88 percent of the sets pass inspection and continue on to the packing department. (This percentage is assumed to be independent of the number of times attempts have been made to adjust a set. This unrealistic assumption can be relaxed. For instance, see Exercise 4 of Section 12.4. More flexible ways to relax this assumption are possible, but their discussion is beyond the scope of this book.) The other 12 percent are routed to the adjustment station, where there is a single worker. Adjustment of the vertical control component requires 30 ± 10 minutes.

Design a model to simulate the testing-and-adjustment system. Use the model to estimate how much **staging space** should be provided ahead of the inspection station and ahead of the adjustment station. (Staging space is the space occupied by work waiting for service to begin.) Transaction movement should end when television set 100 is sent on to packing. How much simulated time has elapsed when this condition is reached?

2. Approach Taken in Building the Model

This model is easily constructed with use of the Statistical-Mode TRANSFER Block. Television set Xacts move through the usual QUEUE/ENTER/DEPART/ADVANCE/LEAVE sequence simulating the inspection station. From the LEAVE, they move into a statistical TRANSFER, from which 88 percent (on average) fall through to a TERMINATE Block (the B-Block). The remaining 12 percent take the

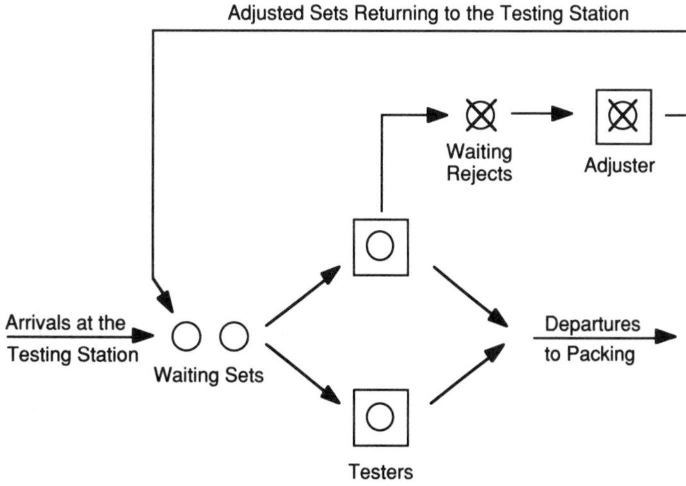

Figure 12A.1 Flow Schematic for Case Study 12A

nonsequential exit (the C-Block) to a QUEUE/SEIZE/DEPART/ADVANCE/RELEASE sequence simulating the adjustment station. After the RELEASE, they unconditionally transfer back to the QUEUE Block associated with the inspection station. The amount of staging space needed at the inspection and adjustment stations can be determined (estimated) from the MAXIMUM CONTENTS statistic for the inspection and adjustment station Queues.

3. Table of Definitions

Table 12A.1 provides the Table of Definitions for Case Study 12A.

4. Block Diagram

Figure 12A.2 shows the Block Diagram for Case Study 12A.

5. Modified Source Echo

Figure 12A.3 shows the Modified Source Echo for Case Study 12A.

6. Postsimulation Report

Figure 12A.4 shows the Postsimulation Report for Case Study 12A.

Table 12A.1
Table of Definitions for Case Study 12A

Base Time Unit: 1 minute

GPSS/H Entity	**Interpretation**
Transactions	
Model Segment 1	Television sets (being tested)
Model Segment 2	Television sets (being adjusted)
Facilities	
ADJUSTER	Worker who adjusts sets that failed the last test
Queues	
ADJUSTQ	Queue for sets waiting to be adjusted
LASTTEST	Queue for sets waiting to be tested
Storages	
TESTERS	Two workers who carry out the last test on sets

7. Discussion

Model Implementation. As is often true, the Block sequential to the statistical TRANSFER in Case Study 12A is the TRANSFER's B-Block. This means a default can be used for the TRANSFER's B Operand, and the sequential Block needn't be labeled. See Blocks 7 and 8 in the Figure 12A.3 Source Echo.

As usual, identification of various subsets of Blocks as "segments" is arbitrary and is not done because of a GPSS/H requirement, but to present a model to a human reader in more rapidly digestible chunks. The banners identifying Model Segments 1, 2, and 3 in the Figure 12A.3 Source Echo have been provided in this spirit.

The order of appearance of the two model segments in the Model File is arbitrary. Model Segment 2 could precede Model Segment 1, and then the first Block in the model would be a QUEUE Block. (See Figure 12A.3.)

Postsimulation Report. From the Queue Report in Figure 12A.4(e), the MAXIMUM CONTENTS of the LASTTEST and ADJUSTQ Queues in this simulation are 6 and 3, respectively. These values suggest that at least this much staging space should be provided ahead of the test and adjustment stations, respectively, if lack of waiting space for sets is not to lead to problems in the system. (See Exercise 3 of Section 12.4.) On the other hand, the AVERAGE CONTENTS of the LASTTEST and ADJUSTQ Queues were less than 2 and 1, respectively, so staging space corresponding to 6 and 3 sets, although needed on occasion, would be underutilized to a considerable extent.

12.4 Exercises

1. The file model12a.gps contains the Model File for Case Study 12A. Perform a Batch simulation with this Model File. Display the postsimulation output on your computer screen, or get a listing of it on paper. Compare clock times, Block Counts, and information in the Facility and Queue Reports to the values given in Figure 12A.4. Corresponding values should match.

2. In Case Study 12A, the staging space required ahead of the adjustment station depends not only on the average service times at the testing and adjustment stations, but also on the amount of variation possible in these service times.

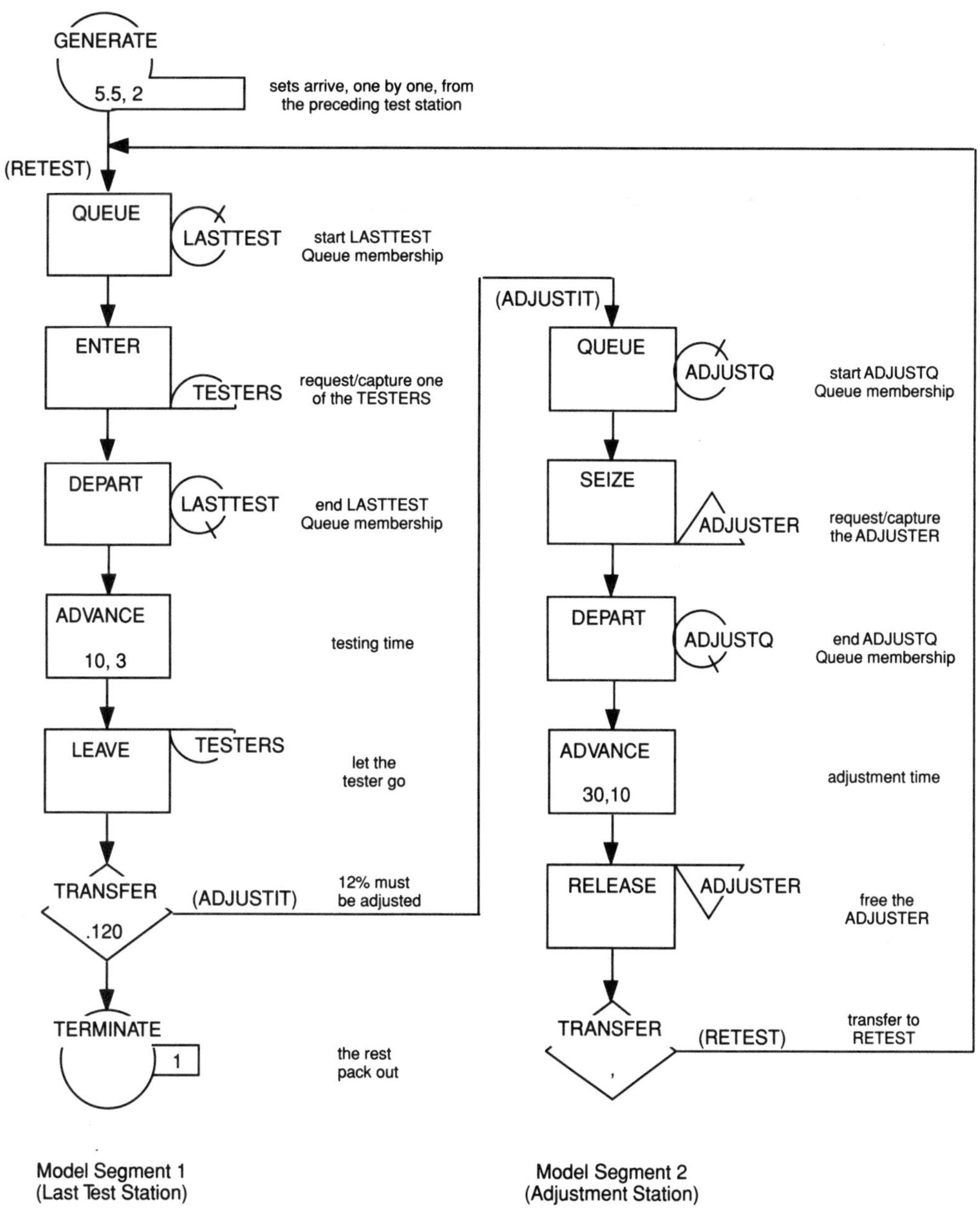

Figure 12A.2 Block Diagram for Case Study 12A

(a) Rerun the Case Study 12A model so that testing and adjustment always require exactly 10 and 30 minutes, respectively. What is the most staging space required during the simulation?

(b) Now rerun Case Study 12A under the assumption that testing time is 10 ± 3 minutes, as before, whereas adjustment of the vertical control setting is now 30 ± 30 minutes. What is the most staging space required in the simulation under these circumstances?

3. Show how to modify the Case Study 12A model so not more than one television set can wait for service at the adjustment station. A worker at the testing station cannot begin to test another set until the preceding set has been sent on to packing or has been transferred to the staging space ahead of the adjustment station. Run the resulting model and compare the behavior of the inspection station's waiting time with the behavior observed in Case Study 12A.

*4. In Case Study 12A, it is unrealistically assumed that even after it has gone through the adjustment station at least one time, the probability a television set will require further adjustment is

```
STMT#  BLOCK#  *LOC    OPERATION  A,B,C,D,E,F,G   COMMENTS

   1                   SIMULATE                                       Case Study 12A
   2           *                                             A Quality Control Model
   3           *                                             Base Time Unit: 1 Minute
   4           ***********************************************************************
   5           *         Control Statements (STORAGE)                               *
   6           ***********************************************************************
   7           *
   8            TESTERS  STORAGE    2   testers at the last test station
   9           *
  10           ***********************************************************************
  11           *         Model Segment 1 (Last Test Station)                        *
  12           ***********************************************************************
  13           *
  14       1             GENERATE   5.5,2            sets arrive, one by one, from
  15           *                                     the preceding test station
  16       2    RETEST   QUEUE      LASTTEST         start LASTTEST Queue membership
  17       3             ENTER      TESTERS          request/capture a tester
  18       4             DEPART     LASTTEST         end LASTTEST Queue membership
  19       5             ADVANCE    10,3             testing time
  20       6             LEAVE      TESTERS          let the tester go
  21           *
  22       7             TRANSFER   .120,,ADJUSTIT   12% must be adjusted
  23           *
  24       8             TERMINATE  1                the rest pack out
  25           *
  26           ***********************************************************************
  27           *         Model Segment 2 (Adjustment Station)                       *
  28           ***********************************************************************
  29           *
  30       9    ADJUSTIT QUEUE      ADJUSTQ          start ADJUSTQ Queue membership
  31      10             SEIZE      ADJUSTER         request/capture the adjuster
  32      11             DEPART     ADJUSTQ          end ADJUSTQ Queue membership
  33      12             ADVANCE    30,10            adjustment time
  34      13             RELEASE    ADJUSTER         free the adjuster
  35      14             TRANSFER   ,RETEST          transfer to retesting
  36           *
  37           ***********************************************************************
  38           *         Run-Control Statements                                     *
  39           ***********************************************************************
  40           *
  41                     START      100              set TC=100; start Xact movement
  42           *
  43                     END                         end of Model-File execution
```

Figure 12A.3 *Modified Source Echo of the Case Study 12A Model File*

still 0.12. Show how to modify the model under the assumption that after one or more visits to the adjustment station, the probability is only 0.01 that a set will have to be adjusted again. Run the resulting model and compare its performance with that in Case Study 12A.

*5. (This exercise is based on one given in Banks and Carson, 1984.) At a fire department in a large city, calls for a firetruck are received every 30 ± 15 minutes. Twelve percent of the calls are false alarms, requiring 30 ± 15 minutes to complete. Twenty percent of the other calls are very serious to the point that they require 200 ± 60 minutes to complete. The other 80 percent of the other calls are less serious ("routine") and only require 90 ± 30 minutes to complete. (In the system, it's not known which category a call is in until a firetruck responds to the call and assesses the situation.)

Assuming there never is a shortage of firetrucks, build a model for this system. Use .120 and .200 as the A Operands for the two statistical TRANSFER Blocks in your model. (Then the numeric results for a correctly built model will

RELATIVE CLOCK: 586.1395 ABSOLUTE CLOCK: 586.1395

(a)

BLOCK	CURRENT	TOTAL	BLOCK	CURRENT	TOTAL
1		107	11		14
RETEST	5	120	12	1	14
3		115	13		13
4		115	14		13
5	1	115			
6		114			
7		114			
8		100			
ADJUSTIT		14			
10		14			

(b)

FACILITY	--AVG-UTIL-DURING-- TOTAL TIME	AVAIL TIME	UNAVL TIME	ENTRIES	AVERAGE TIME/XACT	CURRENT STATUS	PERCENT AVAIL	SEIZING XACT	PREEMPTING XACT
ADJUSTER	.706			14	29.558	AVAIL	100.0	96	

(c)

STORAGE	--AVG-UTIL-DURING-- TOTAL TIME	AVAIL TIME	UNAVL TIME	ENTRIES	AVERAGE TIME/UNIT	CURRENT STATUS	PERCENT AVAIL	CAPACITY	AVERAGE CONTENTS	CURRENT CONTENTS	MAXIMUM CONTENTS
TESTERS	.977			115	9.958	AVAIL	100.0	2	1.954	1	2

(d)

QUEUE	MAXIMUM CONTENTS	AVERAGE CONTENTS	TOTAL ENTRIES	ZERO ENTRIES	PERCENT ZEROS	AVERAGE TIME/UNIT	$AVERAGE TIME/UNIT	QTABLE NUMBER	CURRENT CONTENTS
LASTTEST	6	2.240	120	10	8.3	10.944	11.938		5
ADJUSTQ	3	.603	14	5	35.7	25.243	39.267		0

(e)

RANDOM STREAM	ANTITHETIC VARIATES	INITIAL POSITION	CURRENT POSITION	SAMPLE COUNT	CHI-SQUARE UNIFORMITY
1	OFF	100000	100351	351	0.98

(f)

Figure 12A.4 *Postsimulation Output for Case Study 12A. (a) Clock Values. (b) Block Counts. (c) Facility Report. (d) Storage Report. (e) Queue Report. (f) RNG Report*

match those given in appendix B.) Perform a simulation with the model until 500 calls have been completely handled. Using Block Counts in the output, determine the percentage of calls that were false alarms, the percentage that were very serious, and the percentage that were routine. Compare these realized percentages with those given in the description of the system. How many calls had come in by the end of the simulation? What was the average number of firetrucks in use? What was the maximum number of firetrucks in use?

*6. (a) In Exercise 5, assume there are only five firetrucks available. If all the firetrucks are out when a call comes in, the call must wait its turn (FCFS). Modify the model from Exercise 5 to correspond to this situation. Gather four sets of Queue information for calls waiting their turn for a firetruck: a set for false alarms, a set for very serious calls, a set for less serious calls, and a set for all three types of calls combined. Perform a simulation with the model until 500 calls have been completely handled. What is the largest number of calls waiting all at one and the same time for a firetruck? What is the average utilization of the five firetrucks? What percentages of the three types of calls didn't have to wait at all for a firetruck?

(b) Repeat (a), only now supply one fewer firetruck (four firetrucks).

(c) Repeat (a), only now supply one more firetruck (six firetrucks).

*7. The mean interarrival time of jobs at a work center is 10 ± 5 minutes. Thirty percent of the jobs are of Type A, and the rest are of Type B. Both types of jobs go to Station 1, where a step is performed on them that takes 20 ± 10 minutes. The Type A jobs then go to Station 2, where a step is performed on them that takes 30 ± 10 minutes. After that, they go to Station 4, where a final step requiring 25 ± 10 minutes takes place.

Meanwhile, the Type B jobs go from Station 1 to Station 3, where a step is carried out on them that takes 45 ± 5 minutes. Then they go to Station 4, where their step time is the same as for Type A jobs at Station 4.

(a) Build a model for this system, assuming the service order is FCFS throughout the system. Design the model to gather Queue information for jobs waiting at each of Stations 1 through 4. Assume there is an unlimited number of workers at each of Stations 1 through 4 (so that all Queue entries will be zero entries). Simulate with the model until 100 jobs have left the system. What is the average numbers of workers in use at each station?

(b) Now round up the average numbers of workers in use at Station 1 to the next larger integer. Also do this for Stations 2, 3, and 4. Modify your model to provide the corresponding number of servers at Stations 1 through 4, respectively. Then repeat the simulation. How much longer does it now take (compared to the first simulation) to finish 100 jobs? How many jobs are there on average, and at a maximum, waiting at each of the four stations?

12.5 Bug Clinic

*1. Discuss what happens when a Transaction moves into this Block:

```
TARGET TRANSFER .375,TARGET,SALTMINE
```

*2. Discuss what happens when a Transaction moves into this Block:

```
AGAIN TRANSFER .375,,AGAIN
```

*3. Discuss what happens when a Transaction moves into this Block:

```
ENDLESS TRANSFER .375,ENDLESS,ENDLESS
```

If an Xact moves into the Block during a simulation, what will eventually stop the Transaction-Movement Phase?

*4. Why doesn't the Block "TRANSFER .0,PATH5,PATH7" make sense? Do you think there will be a compile-time or execution-time message (or no message at all) if this Block is included in a model? Try it and see.

*5. Why doesn't the Block "TRANSFER .100,GATEWAY1,GATEWAY2" make sense? Do you think there will be a compile-time or execution-time message (or no message at all) if this Block is included in a model? Try it and see.

12.6 The BOTH-Mode TRANSFER Block

When the statistical TRANSFER Block is used, an Xact's choice of Next Block is made probabilistically. The Xact then sticks with this choice of a Next Block, even if this Next Block initially refuses entry to the Xact. This contrasts with an alternative form of TRANSFER, BOTH-Mode TRANSFER, which sends an Xact to **whichever one of two candidate Blocks will first accept it.**

The general form of the BOTH-Mode TRANSFER Block is shown in Figure 12.2. The A Operand is literally the word BOTH. The B and C Operands are used to "point" to two other Blocks in the model. As is true with statistical TRANSFER, the pointing is accomplished by (1) labeling each of these two alternative Next Blocks and (2) using those labels as the BOTH TRANSFER's B and C Operands. The B Operand points to what is called the "B-Block" and the C Operand to the "C-Block."

An Xact that moves into a BOTH TRANSFER immediately tries to move into the B-Block. If the B-Block denies entry, the Xact then tries to move into the C-Block. If the C-Block also denies entry, the doubly-blocked Xact stops moving for the time being, remaining in the BOTH-Mode TRANSFER Block, and on the Current Chain. The Xact is **not** put to sleep (its Scan-Skip Indicator is **not** turned on), but remains awake (scan active). The Scan Phase then continues in the usual fashion, with the testing of the model's Status Change Flag, and so on (see Figure 7.4 of Chapter 7). When GPSS/H next en-

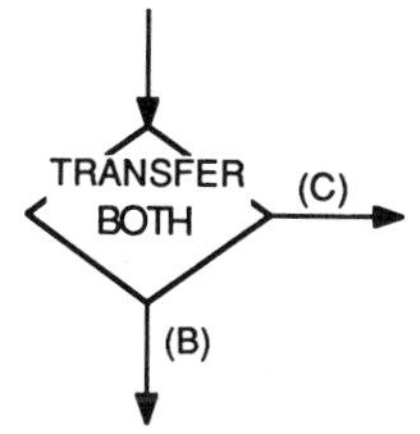

Operand	Significance	Default Value or Result
A	Literally, the word BOTH	Compile-time error
B	Pointer to a Block [1] (the "B-Block")	The "B-Block" is the sequential Block
C	Pointer to a Block [1] (the "C-Block")	Compile-time error

[1] Copy of the Label attached to that Block.

Figure 12.2 *The TRANSFER Block in BOTH Mode*

counters this Xact (either because of a restarted scan at the current time, or after a Clock Update has taken place), the Xact again retrys to move into the B-Block and, if entry is still denied there, into the C-Block. The Xact eventually moves into whichever one of these two Blocks will first accept it.

From a BOTH-Mode TRANSFER, an Xact always tries the B-Block first and then, only if necessary, the C-Block. If both the B- and C-Blocks are willing to accept the Xact, the Xact goes into the B-Block. (The C-Block won't even be tried in this case.) And so in such a case the BOTH-Mode TRANSFER is biased in favor of the B-Block.

If the B Operand is omitted from the BOTH-Mode TRANSFER, then the B-Block is the Block **sequential to the TRANSFER,** as pointed out in Figure 12.2. The statistical and BOTH TRANSFER Blocks are similar in this respect. They are also similar in the sense that neither ever denies entry to an Xact.

12.7 Examples Using BOTH-Mode TRANSFER

This section provides two examples for use of the BOTH-Mode TRANSFER.

Example 1

Suppose there are only two chairs in the waiting area of Joe's barber shop. (Joe is the only barber at the shop.) Potential customers arrive at the shop every 12 ± 7 minutes, but are willing to wait for service only if there is a chair to wait in. Otherwise, they leave and do not return later. Model this system, simulating until 100 *served* customers have left the barbershop.

Using the SEATS Storage to represent the two waiting chairs, the requested model is provided in Figure 12.3. In the model, an arriving customer-Xact moves from the GENERATE to the BOTH-Mode TRANSFER and tries for a waiting chair by trying to move into the B-Block ("ENTER SEATS"). If the SEATS Storage is Full, the customer tries (successfully) to move into the C-Block ("CHIAO TERMINATE 0") and leaves the model. When the C-Block is of a type that never denies entry, as in this example, then there will never be doubly-blocked Xacts that accumulate in the BOTH-Mode TRANSFER.

Example 2

There are two drill presses in a system, a newer model and an older model. These drill presses

```
        SIMULATE
*
SEATS   STORAGE   2               provide 2 waiting chairs
*
        GENERATE  12,7            customers arrive, one by one
        TRANSFER  BOTH,,CHIAO     wait if possible; else, that's it
        ENTER     SEATS           request a waiting chair
        SEIZE     JOE             request/capture Joe
        LEAVE     SEATS           give up a waiting chair
        ADVANCE   18,2            haircutting time
        RELEASE   JOE             let Joe go
        TERMINATE 1               happy customer leaves
*
CHIAO   TERMINATE 0               unhappy potential
*                                 customer leaves
*
        START     100             simulate until 100
*                                 happy customers have left
        END                       end of Model-File execution
```

Figure 12.3 *A First Example for Use of the BOTH-Mode TRANSFER Block*

are used to drill holes in work-in-process (WIP). WIP arrives every 2.8 ± 1.5 minutes. It takes the newer drill press 5 minutes to drill the needed holes in a unit of WIP, whereas it takes the older press 6 minutes to do this same task. (Variations in drilling time are small, and so drilling time is assumed to be deterministic.) Only one waiting line of WIP forms in the drill press area. The WIP unit at the head of the line goes to whichever drill press can first be captured. Because the newer drill press is faster, however, its use is preferred to that of the older press. Model this system, simulating until holes have been drilled in 250 units of WIP. Gather Queue information for WIP units waiting their turn to be drilled.

Note that a one-line, two-server queuing system is involved here. The two servers are identical in type (both are drill presses), but they are not identical in their individual characteristics (they have different service times). And so, instead of modeling the two servers with a Storage of Capacity two, the servers need to be modeled individually, with Facilities.

The requested model is shown in Figure 12.4. The model is straightforward. In contrast with the Figure 12.3 model, Xacts in the BOTH-Mode TRANSFER can experience double blocking in the Figure 12.4 model, and of course will stack up in the TRANSFER Block if and when double blocking occurs.

In the Figure 12.4 model, there is **one** "QUEUE WAITING" Block, but there are **two** "DEPART WAITING" Blocks. This is perfectly all right. There is no reason why there must be an equal number of QUEUE and DEPART Blocks referencing a particular Queue. (Nor is there any reason why there must be an equal number of SEIZE and RELEASE Blocks referencing a particular Facility, as pointed out in Section 8.9 of Chapter 8, or ENTER and LEAVE Blocks referencing a particular Storage, and so on.) What's important is that a model be logically consistent and that requirement is satisfied in the Figure 12.4 model.

12.8 Exercises

1. The fig123.gps file contains the model in Figure 12.3. Perform a simulation with this model. What fraction of potential customers stayed at the barbershop to get their hair cut as of the end of the simulation? How did you compute this fraction?

2. The fig124.gps file contains the model in Figure 12.4. Perform a simulation with this model. What fraction of jobs used the new drill as of the end of the simulation? How did you compute this fraction?

*3. A computer laboratory at a university has a number of microcomputers that are used by students on an FCFS basis. Students arrive

```
          SIMULATE
*
          GENERATE  2.8,1.5        WIP units arrive, one by one
          QUEUE     WAITING        start WAITING Queue membership
          TRANSFER  BOTH,NEW,OLD   try first for the new, then (if
*                                  necessary) the old drill press
 NEW      SEIZE     NEWDRILL       request the new drill press
          DEPART    WAITING        end WAITING Queue membership
          ADVANCE   5              drilling time (new press)
          RELEASE   NEWDRILL       give up the new drill press
          TERMINATE 1              finished WIP unit leaves
*
 OLD      SEIZE     OLDDRILL       request the old drill press
          DEPART    WAITING        end WAITING Queue membership
          ADVANCE   6              drilling time (old press)
          RELEASE   OLDDRILL       give up the old drill press
          TERMINATE 1              finished WIP unit leaves
*
          START     250            simulate until 250
*                                  WIP units have left
          END                      end of Model-File execution
```

Figure 12.4 *A Second Example for Use of the BOTH-Mode TRANSFER Block*

every 10 ± 5 minutes. Microcomputer usage time per student is 90 ± 30 minutes. If all microcomputers are busy, two students out of three will wait. The others leave, then return 60 ± 30 minutes later to try again. Students who try again have assignment deadlines, and have no choice but to wait, if necessary, on their second attempt to get a computer.

(a) Build a model for this system. In your statistical TRANSFER Block, use an A Operand of .333. (Then the results produced by a correctly built model will match those in Appendix C.) Temporarily assume there is an unlimited number of microcomputers. (This means that no students will ever have to leave. In your model, however, provide the possibility that students might choose to leave. This aspect of the model will be used shortly.) Simulate with the model until 250 students have been served. How many microcomputers are in use on average? What is the maximum number of microcomputers ever in use in the simulation at any one time?

(b) Now repeat (a), but set the number of micros to the smallest integer greater than the average number in use in (a). What percentage of the students can't get a micro on their first try? What percentage then leave, to return later?

(c) Repeat (a) again, but set the number of micros to a level one greater than that in (b). What percentage of the students can't get a micro on their first try? What percentage then leave, to return later?

(d) Repeat (a) again, but set the number of micros to a level two greater than that in (b). What percentage of the students can't get a micro on their first try? What percentage then leave, to return later?

4. Suppose units of WIP arrive at a point in a system every 10 minutes to have a turning step performed on them. Two lathes are provided for this purpose, Lathe 1 and Lathe 2. If a unit of WIP goes to Lathe 1, the turning step takes 15 minutes. But if WIP goes to Lathe 2 instead, the turning step takes 30 minutes. (Lathe 1 is newer and has an automated loading and unloading system.) Note that the capacity of the system exactly matches the demands placed on it. (Six units of work arrive per hour. Lathes 1 and 2 handle 4 and 2 units of work per hour, respectively.) Build a model to simulate this system. Assume that at time 0.0, Lathe 1 is in use and has 10 time units to go before finishing, and Lathe 2 is in use and has 20 time units to go before finishing. Assume that WIP units waiting for a lathe form one line and capture one

lathe or the other as soon as they can. Gather Queue information with respect to WIP units waiting to capture a lathe. Simulate until 100 WIP units have been turned. Discuss and explain the resulting Facility and Queue Reports. Why isn't lathe utilization 100 percent? Why is the average WIP waiting time greater than zero?

*5. There are two open teller windows in a bank. Customers arrive at the bank every 1.5 ± 1.0 minutes to transact business at either one of these windows. Service time at one of the windows, where an experienced teller works, is 2.5 ± 1.5 minutes. Service time at the other window, where a trainee works, is 3.25 ± 2.5 minutes. A one-line, multiple-server queuing system is used.

Assume that if both tellers are idle when a customer arrives, the customer chooses a window at random (resulting in a long-run 50-50 split) and goes to that window.

Build a model for this situation. Design the model to gather Queue information for customers waiting to receive service. Simulate with the model until 100 customers have been served. How many customers did not have to wait before service started on them? Is there any way to tell how many customers arrived when both tellers were idle, and of these, how many went to the experienced teller?

6. These exercises each use the model of Figure 12.3 as their starting point unless stated otherwise.

(a) Show how to modify the model so that 20 percent of the potential customers arriving at the shop get a haircut only if they do not have to wait for service. The others remain as long as there is a waiting chair for them.
(b) Show how to include a Queue in the model to gather information on the waiting line which forms ahead of JOE.
(c) Discuss the possibility of using the information in the SEATS Storage Report as an alternative to information in the Queue Report of part (b). In light of this discussion, what additional information, if any, is obtained by using a Queue in the model?
(d) Show how to modify the model to include a shoeshine person. After their haircut is finished, 25 percent of the customers consider the possibility of getting a shoeshine. Among them, 80 percent get a shoeshine only if they don't have to wait for the shoeshine person; otherwise, they leave. The other 20 percent will wait for a shoeshine only if they can sit in a waiting chair; otherwise, they leave. The shop continues to have only two waiting chairs. Shoeshine time is 3.5 ± 0.5 minutes.
(e) Show how to modify the original model so that 40 percent of the customers who leave because there is no chair to wait in come back after 15 ± 5 minutes to try again. Those who are not successful on the second try do not return.

*7. Two types of tankers, Type A and Type B, load oil at a harbor for which a schematic is shown in Figure E6.

These steps are followed by both types of tankers when they come to the harbor:

1. Arrive in open water outside the harbor.
2. Move from open water through the harbor mouth into the harbor when harbor space, the harbor mouth, and tugboat conditions permit (in that order).
3. Move from the harbor into a berth when berth and tugboat conditions permit (in that order).
4. Load oil.
5. Move from the berth back into the harbor when harbor space and tugboat conditions permit (in that order).

The order in which tankers request harbor space, the harbor mouth, and tugboats, *is as listed above*; otherwise, deadlock could come about. (You should be able to think of scenarios in which deadlock would result if any of the indicated orders were not followed.)

Key data are summarized in Table E6.

As indicated in Table E6, tanker loading times are uniformly distributed. Variations in berthing and deberthing times are small, and are treated as deterministic.

Tankers of both types need only one tugboat and require 30 minutes to move from open water into the harbor and another 30 minutes to later move from the harbor back into open water.

Tankers at rest in the harbor do not need tug-

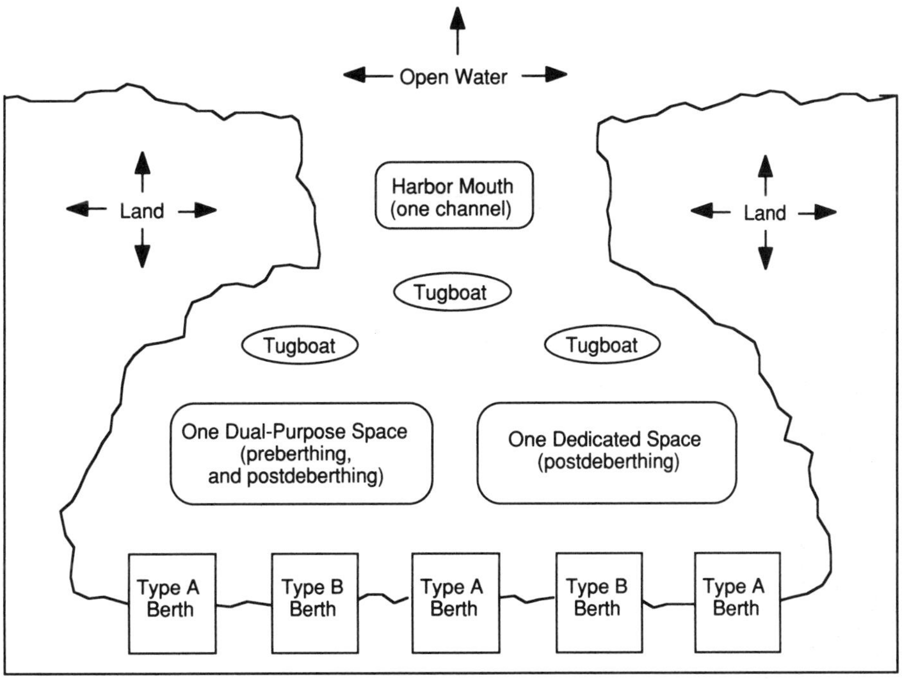

Figure E6

boats. Having moved into the harbor (either having come in from open water, or having moved from a berth back into the harbor), tankers immediately give up control over their tugboat or tugboats, and then request the resources they need to make their next move.

Type A and Type B tankers can only load oil in Type A and Type B berths, respectively.

There are three Type A berths at the harbor and two Type B berths. There is a group of three tugboats. The tugboats are claimed by tankers on an "all-or-nothing-at-all" basis.

Distinguish between tankers that are in a berth, and tankers that are simply in the harbor, either waiting for a berth or waiting to move out to open water. These specifications apply:

1. There can be up to five tankers in berths (because there are five berths).
2. There can only be up to two additional tankers in the harbor (because, in addition to berth space, there are only two other spaces at the harbor).
3. One of the harbor spaces can only be used by tankers waiting for a berth, or waiting to leave the harbor. (This is a dual-purpose space.) The other harbor space can be used only by tankers waiting to leave the harbor. (This is a dedicated space.) If it weren't for the dedicated space, a deadly embrace (deadlock) could come about as follows: No tanker can claim a berth, because they're all occupied, and no tanker can get out of berth, because both harbor spaces are occupied by tankers waiting for berths.

Table E6

Tanker Type	IAT[1] (hours)	Berth Type Needed	Loading Time (hours)	Berthing Time (minutes)	Deberthing Time (minutes)	Number of Tugboats Needed to Berth	Number of Tugboats Needed to Deberth
A	8 ± 6	A	15 ± 2	45	15	3	2
B	4 ± 2	B	6 ± 1	30	12	2	1

[1]IAT: Interarrival time

There is no harbor space for a loaded tanker to deberth into; no tankers can move!)

4. When deberthing, tankers prefer to deberth into the dedicated space rather than into the dual-purpose space.

For all tanker movements in the system, the move must be completed before the space used in the move becomes free. This applies to moves through the harbor mouth, from within the harbor into a berth, and from within a berth back into the harbor. For example, a tanker must move completely into a berth before the space it had occupied within the harbor becomes free for another tanker to use. Similarly, a tanker must move completely through the mouth of the harbor (in either direction) before another tanker can use the mouth.

Build a model for the harbor system. Design the model to gather Queue information describing tanker residence time at the harbor, differentiated by tanker type. A tanker is "at the harbor" between the time it arrives in open water outside the harbor and the time it again reaches open water when leaving the harbor. (For each tanker type, you can compute by hand a "best case" for tanker residence time at the harbor. The best case is computed by assuming tankers never need to wait for constrained resources (i.e., the harbor mouth, harbor space, a berth, tugboats). The purpose of the simulation is to estimate the degree of best case degradation attributable to tanker competition for scarce resources. You might consider how easy or difficult it would be to estimate this degree of degradation by hand.)

Use 1 hour as the base time unit ("implicit time unit") in your model.

Assume that when the simulation starts, there are no ships anywhere in the harbor.

Design the simulation to stop after 100 ships have left the harbor. Discuss the information found in the Postsimulation Report. What degree of degradation was there in the best case residence times of tankers at the harbor?

8. Taking the model for Exercise 7 as a starting point each time, alter the model in these five ways:

   (a) Add one tugboat to the system.
   (b) Add one Type A berth to the system.
   (c) Add one Type B berth to the system.
   (d) Add one dual-purpose space to the harbor.
   (e) Widen the mouth of the harbor to permit two tankers to move through it at the same time.

   In single simulations performed with the resulting models, which addition to harbor resources seems to do the best job of decreasing tanker residence times at the harbor?

9. Taking the model for Exercise 7 as a starting point, alter the model to reflect the occurrence of storms at the harbor under the following conditions:

   1. A storm occurs every 72 ± 24 hours.
   2. When a storm hits, it lasts 4 ± 2 hours.
   3. When a storm is in progress, no tankers can move out of or into open water.

   In a single simulation performed with the resulting model, do the harbor resources appear to be adequate to keep up with the tanker traffic? Or does an explosive situation seem to be developing?

12.9 Modifying a Transaction's Priority Level: The PRIORITY Block

Statistical and BOTH TRANSFER Blocks can be used to help determine **where** a Transaction moves (or tries to move) next. Also important is determining **when** a Transaction moves (or tries to move) relative to other Transactions that also try to move at the same simulated time. The order in which Xacts try to move is determined by their relative position on the Current Chain, and this depends on their Priority.

A Transaction's initial Priority is determined when the Xact is created and is specified with the E Operand at its GENERATE Block. (Recall that a Priority Level is a signed integer that in GPSS/H has a range of about ± 2 billion.) Up to this point in the book, each Transaction has retained this initial Priority throughout its life cycle. It is possible, however, to change a Transaction's Priority one or more times during the course of its life cycle. The PRIORITY Block is used for this purpose.

The PRIORITY Block and its A Operand are shown in Figure 12.5. A PRIORITY Block never denies entry to a Transaction. When a Transaction

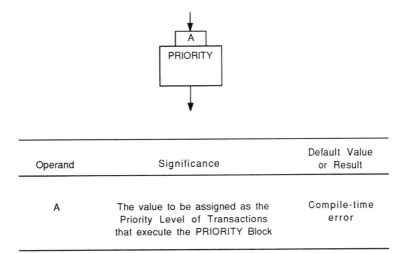

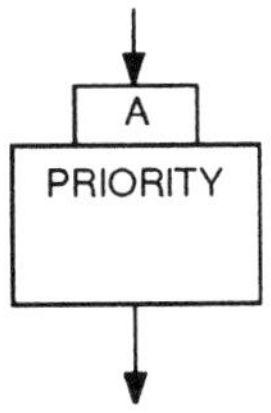

Operand	Significance	Default Value or Result
A	The value to be assigned as the Priority Level of Transactions that execute the PRIORITY Block	Compile-time error

Figure 12.5 The PRIORITY Block and Its A Operand

executes a PRIORITY Block, its Priority is set equal to the value of the Block's A Operand. More specifically, GPSS/H carries out these actions when a Transaction executes a PRIORITY Block:

1. The Transaction is temporarily removed from the CEC.
2. The Transaction's Priority Level is set equal to the value of the PRIORITY Block's A Operand.
3. The Transaction is merged back into the CEC as the last with its new Priority.
4. The model's Status Change Flag (S/C) is turned on.

GPSS/H then immediately moves (or tries to move) the Xact from the PRIORITY Block (its Current Block) into the sequential Block (its Next Block Attempted), and so on. When the Xact can finally move no farther for the time being, GPSS/H restarts the scan of the CEC because PRIORITY execution turned the model's Status Change Flag on.

Why should the model's Status Change Flag be turned on when an Xact executes a PRIORITY Block? The Xact's status relative to other Xacts has changed, true, because of the change in its Priority and by its repositioning on the Current Chain. But why use the S/C to bring about an eventual restart of the scan? Suppose that by executing a PRIORITY Block, an Xact's Priority Level has been **decreased**. Then both the Xact **and the point of the scan** have jumped toward the back of the CEC, possibly **jumping over one or more intermediate CEC Xacts** in the process. If the scan were simply to continue sequentially from that point, the next Clock Update Phase might come about without these intermediate Xacts having been dealt with at the current simulated time. This would be invalid. Turning on the S/C flag brings about an eventual scan restart, sidestepping this potential invalidity.

Figure 12.6 provides an example illustrating the point. In part (a) of the figure, we see Xacts with id numbers 16, 12, 22, 18, and 15 listed on the CEC in that top-down order. These Xacts have Priority Levels of 8, 5, 4, 3, and 0, respectively. (To simplify the figure, the slots for the CURBLK and NXTBLK attributes have been left blank in Figure 12.6.) Now suppose a Scan Phase is taking place, and Xact 12 is being moved. Assume Xact 12 (with Priority Level 5) moves into the Block "PRIORITY 3". Then the actions listed are carried out, with the effect shown in part (b) of the figure. Xact 12 has been given 3 as a Priority Level and has been repositioned on the CEC as last among those with Priority 3. (The pointer in Figure 12.6 connects Xact 12 in its old part (a) CEC position to Xact 12 in its new part (b) CEC position.) In moving toward the back of the CEC, Xact 12 has jumped backward over Xacts 22 and 18, which had been behind it on the CEC when the scan began. When Xact 12 finally can move no farther for the time being, GPSS/H will restart the scan (returning all the way to the front of the CEC, as always), eventually paying attention to intermediate Xacts 22 and 18 when their turn comes.

Suppose an Xact executes a PRIORITY Block with an A-Operand value that **matches** the Xact's Priority at the time the Xact moves **into** the Priority Block. Then the Xact's "new" Priority will equal its "old" Priority, so there will be no net change in its

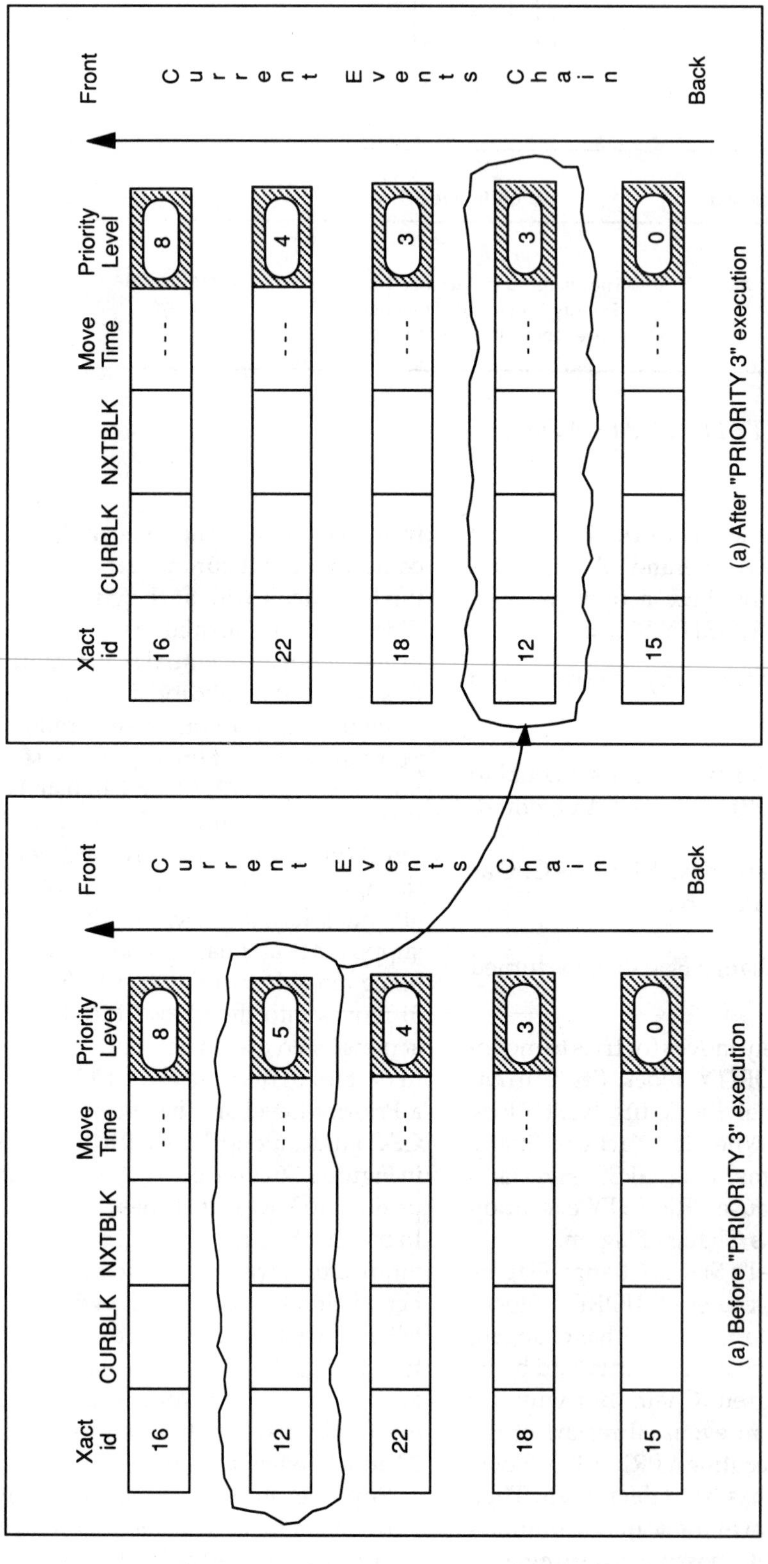

Figure 12.6 *The Repositioning of an Xact on the CEC as a Result of PRIORITY Block Execution*

Priority. Nevertheless, the Xact will be repositioned on the CEC as last among those having its "new" Priority Level, and the model's Status Change Flag will be turned on. In other words, such a Transaction leaps to the back of its Priority Class. (In general, the PRIORITY Block can be used to make Xacts play a game of leapfrog on the CEC.)

12.10 The Correct Location for PRIORITY Blocks in a Model

Consider the simple model shown in Figure 12.7, where Xacts of two different types each use Server 1 and Server 2 in sequence. Xacts of Type 1 and 2 are created at BLOCK1 and BLOCK10 with Priority Levels of 8 and 6, respectively, and retain these initial priorities throughout their life cycle. As a consequence, Type 1 Xacts have higher priority than do Type 2 Xacts for the use of both servers.

Now suppose the model is to be changed so that the service order will be SPT (shortest processing time) everywhere. SPT already is the service order for Server 1. (The expected Server 1 service times for Type 1 and 2 Xacts are 15 and 30, which in terms of SPT is consistent with their respective initial Priority Levels of 8 and 6.) If SPT is also to be the service order for Server 2, then **Type 2 Xacts should have higher priority than Type 1 Xacts for use of Server 2.** (The expected Server 2 service times for Type 2 and 1 Xacts are 10 and 25, respectively.) This means Type 2 Xacts must have their Priority boosted to 9 (or higher) **after** they finish competing for Server 1, but **before** they compete for Server 2. Placement of a "PRIORITY 9" Block

```
         SIMULATE
*
 BLOCK1  GENERATE   30,10,,,8  Type 1 Xacts arrive (Priority 8)
         ADVANCE    0          avoid arrival distortions
*
         SEIZE      SERVER1    request/capture Server 1
         ADVANCE    15,5       service time
         RELEASE    SERVER1    let Server 1 go
*
         SEIZE      SERVER2    request/capture Server 2
         ADVANCE    25,5       service time
         RELEASE    SERVER2    let Server 2 go
*
         TERMINATE 1           done
*
*
 BLOCK10 GENERATE   60,20,,,6  Type 2 Xacts arrive (Priority 6)
         ADVANCE    0          avoid arrival distortions
*
 BLOCK12 SEIZE      SERVER1    request/capture Server 1
 BLOCK13 ADVANCE    30,10      service time
 BLOCK14 RELEASE    SERVER1    let Server 1 go
*
         SEIZE      SERVER2    request/capture Server 2
         ADVANCE    10,5       service time
         RELEASE    SERVER2    let Server 2 go
*
         TERMINATE 1           done
*
         START      100        simulate until 100 Xacts leave
         END                   end of Model-File execution
```

Figure 12.7 A Model in Which the Service Order Is FCFS within Priority Level

between BLOCK12 and BLOCK13 in the foregoing model is therefore indicated.

Locating the "PRIORITY 9" Block **after** the BLOCK12 SEIZE means Type 2 Xacts compete for Server 1 with their initial Priority Level of 6, as should be the case. Locating the "PRIORITY 9" Block **before** the BLOCK13 ADVANCE means that after the Type 2 Xact has gone into the BLOCK13 ADVANCE and **is later returned to the CEC** to free up Server 1 and compete for Server 2, it will be in its proper competitive position on the CEC. (That is, **when the scan begins**, it will be on the CEC **ahead** of any Type 1 Xacts that might be waiting their turn at that time for Server 2. This guarantees that if Server 2 happens to be released at this same simulated time, the next capturer of Server 2 will be a Type 2 Xact, as should be the case.)

It would be **incorrect** to put the "PRIORITY 9" Block **after** the BLOCK13 ADVANCE in the Figure 12.7 model. If this is done, the Type 2 Xact goes to the Future Chain (via the BLOCK13 ADVANCE) with its **outdated Priority Level** of 6. When it is later returned to the CEC to free up Server 1 and compete for Server 2, it will **not be in its proper competitive position** on the CEC when the scan begins. (When the scan begins, it will be on the CEC **behind** any Type 1 Xacts that might be waiting their turn at that time for Server 2. If Server 2 happens to be released at this same simulated time, the next capturer of Server 2 will then be a Type 1 Xact, **resulting in an invalid model.**)

In effect, each ADVANCE Block can be thought of as a **dividing line** in a model. If a Transaction's Priority Level **below** such a dividing line is to differ from its Priority Level **above** the dividing line, then the Priority Level should be changed by placing a PRIORITY Block **just before** the ADVANCE Block, **not** just after the ADVANCE Block.

Section 12.11 presents a case study that demonstrates use of the PRIORITY Block to control service order by repeatedly increasing and then decreasing the Priority Level of looping Transactions as a simulation proceeds.

12.11 Case Study 12B. An Equipment Balancing Problem

1. Statement of the Problem

After rough castings are formed in a manufacturing system, they must pass through a department in which finishing work is done on them. The finishing work consists of a sequence of two processes, Process 1 and Process 2, which are carried out by an operator who uses a finishing machine for this purpose. The finishing department consists of more than one finishing machine. Each machine has its own operator assigned to it.

Assume an operator has just fetched a rough casting from a storage area and has positioned the casting on his or her finishing machine. The steps the operator then follows are shown here, in chronological order.

1. Perform Process 1.
2. Reposition the casting on the machine.
3. Perform Process 2.
4. a. Unload the finished casting from the machine.
   b. Return the finished casting to the storage area.
   c. Fetch the next rough casting from the storage area.
   d. Load this rough casting onto the machine.
   e. Return to step 1.

Because the castings are heavy, the operator needs to obtain and use a crane for steps 2 and 4, which involve movement of the casting. (Note that an operator is single-handedly responsible for carrying out each of the steps listed, not just steps 1 and 2.)

Management wants a two-part study made of the finishing department. First, it wants to know what crane and finishing machine utilizations would result if the number of machines served by a single crane were 3, 4, 5, or 6. Second, management wants to know what the effect would be on these utilizations if two cranes were used to serve a group of 10 machines, or if three cranes were used to serve a group of 15 machines.

Build a model to simulate the finishing department. Then perform single simulations with the model to provide management with preliminary utilization estimates for the various conditions indicated. (Final estimates would require performing more than single simulations. See Chapters 14 and 15.) For each condition, simulate for a 40-hour workweek.

Note: The model presented here does not measure the utilization of the group of finishing machines. Enhancing the model to provide this utilization measure is left to Exercise 2 of Section 12.12.

The service order for crane use is to be SPT. The expected crane capture time for step 2 is 15 minutes, and for step 4 it is 30 minutes. This means a finishing machine operator who needs a crane to carry out step 2 is to have higher priority than one who needs a crane to carry out step 4.

2. Approach Taken in Building the Model

The two constraints in the system are the number of finishing machines and the number of cranes. The problem statement indicates that there is one operator per finishing machine. The "machine constraint" can therefore be viewed as an "operator constraint." By letting an Xact simulate an operator, the number of operators can be controlled through the Limit Count at a GENERATE Block. Having been introduced into the model, these operator-Xacts can then move through a stack of Blocks to simulate the steps listed in the problem statement. After the last step, an operator-Xact can then loop (transfer) back to the first step and repeat the cycle, and so on.

If an Xact simulates an operator, it is natural to use a Storage to simulate the cranes. The utilization of the CRANES Storage will then be the crane utilization.

The matter of defining the meaning of finishing machine utilization, and of enhancing the model to measure this utilization, is left to Exercise 12 of Section 12.12.

Finally, the matter of modeling the SPT service order by making priority distinctions with respect to crane use must be considered. We give crane use for step 2 a Priority of 10, and for step 4 a Priority of 5. (It's the **relative** Priority values that count, of course, not the absolute values. Beyond this consideration, there is nothing special about the choices of 5 and 10 as Priority Levels.) As operator-Xacts cycle repeatedly through the model, their Priority Level must then alternate between 10 and 5.

We assume that when the simulation starts, all the finishing machine operators are poised to begin step 1 (Process 1). (That is, each operator has a casting loaded on his or her finishing machine, and is just starting Process 1, which does not require crane use.) At time 0.0, then, each operator-Xact will come out of a GENERATE Block and move into a Process 1 ADVANCE. Upon return to the CEC, there will be competition to get a crane for high-priority step 2 (intermediate handling, Priority 10). Thinking of the Process 1 ADVANCE as a "dividing line," per the discussion in Section 12.10, we use the Priority Operand at the GENERATE Block to **create** each operator-Xact with a Priority of 10. In the GENERATE/ ADVANCE/ENTER sequence, these operator-Xacts then have their correct Priority when, in the ADVANCE for Process 1, they eventually return from the FEC to the CEC to compete for a crane.

Then the Priority must be downgraded from 10 to 5 prior to competing for a crane for step 4. The Process 2 ADVANCE immediately precedes this point in the operator cycle. This ADVANCE is another "dividing line." And so we precede this ADVANCE with a "PRIORITY 5" Block. In the resulting PRIORITY/ ADVANCE/ENTER sequence, operator-Xacts then have their correct Priority when, in the ADVANCE for Process 2, they eventually return from the FEC to the CEC to compete for a crane.

Finally, the operator Priority must be upgraded from 5 to 10 prior to competing for a crane to use in step 2. The single ADVANCE for steps 4(a) to 4(d) (unload/store/fetch/load) consequently is another "dividing line." And so we precede this ADVANCE with a "PRIORITY 10" Block. Operator-Xacts then have their correct Priority when, in the unload/ store/fetch/load ADVANCE, they return from the FEC to the CEC to compete for a crane.

3. Table of Definitions

Table 12B.1 shows the Table of Definitions for Case Study 12B.

4. Block Diagram

Figure 12B.1 shows the Block Diagram for Case Study 12B.

5. Modified Source Echo

Figure 12B.2 shows the Modified Source Echo for Case Study 12B corresponding to the case of 3 cranes and 15 operators.

Table 12B.1

Table of Definitions for Case Study 12B

Base Time Unit: 1 minute

GPSS/H Entity	Interpretation
Transactions	
Model Segment 1	Finishing operators
Model Segment 2	Control Xact
Storages	
CRANES	The cranes used to handle castings

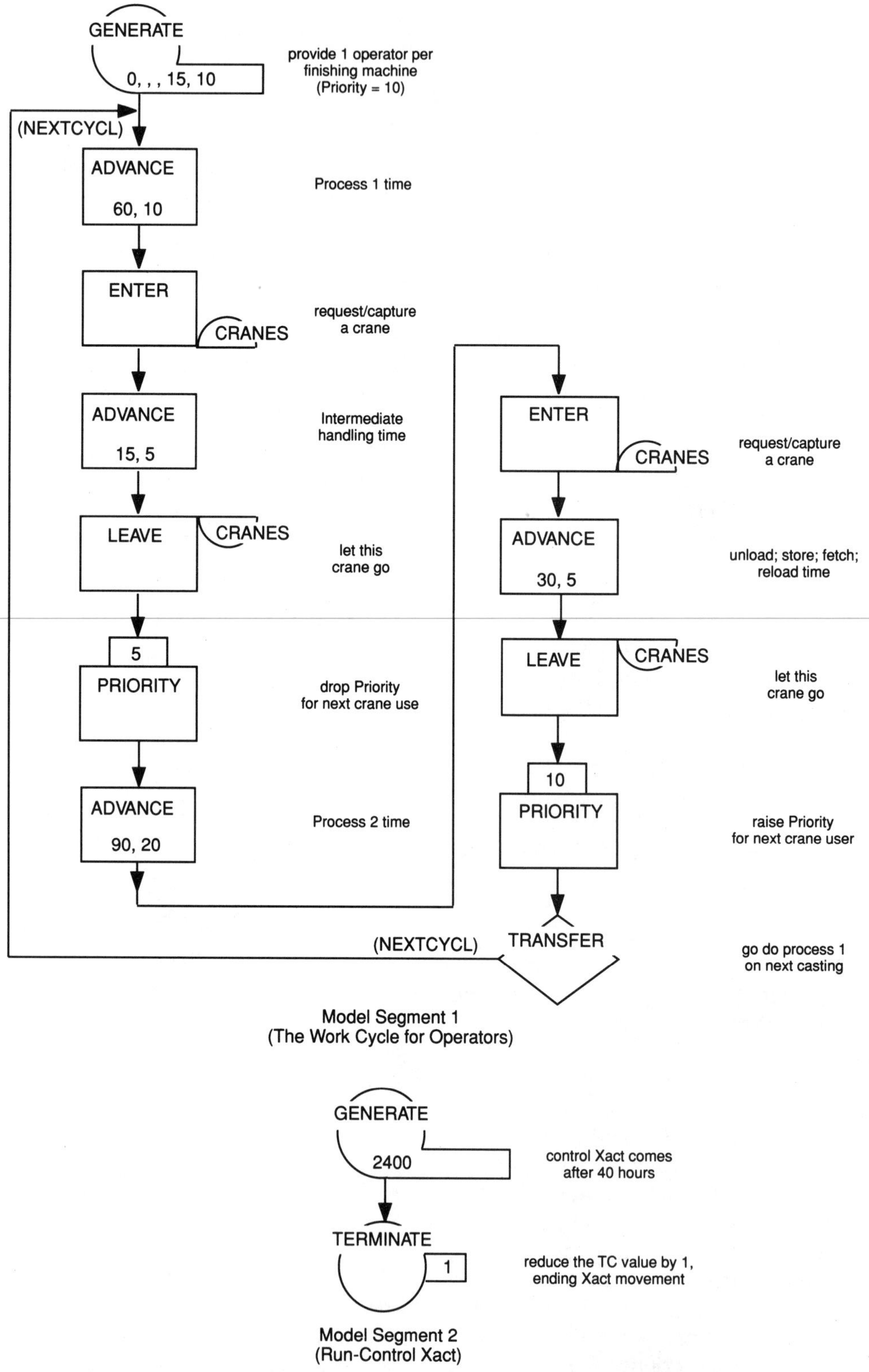

Figure 12B.1 *Block Diagram for Case Study 12B*

```
STMT#  BLOCK#  *LOC     OPERATION  A,B,C,D,E,F,G   COMMENTS

   1           SIMULATE                              Case Study 12B
   2           *                         An Equipment Balancing Problem
   3           *                   (3 Cranes Serving a Group of 15 Machines;
   4           *                  Finishing-Machine Utilization Not Measured)
   5           *                                   Base Time Unit: 1 Minute
   6           **************************************************************
   7           *        Control Statements (STORAGE)                        *
   8           **************************************************************
   9           *
  10            CRANES  STORAGE    3              provide 3 cranes in the system
  11           *
  12           **************************************************************
  13           *        Model Segment 1 (The Work Cycle for Operators)      *
  14           **************************************************************
  15           *
  16       1            GENERATE   0,,,15,10     provide 1 operator per
  17           *                                 finishing machine (Priority = 10)
  18       2    NEXTCYCL ADVANCE   60,10         Process 1 time
  19           *
  20       3            ENTER      CRANES        request/capture a crane
  21       4            ADVANCE    15,5          intermediate handling time
  22       5            LEAVE      CRANES        let this crane go
  23           *
  24       6            PRIORITY   5             drop Priority for next crane use
  25           *
  26       7            ADVANCE    90,20         Process 2 time
  27           *
  28       8            ENTER      CRANES        request/capture a crane
  29       9            ADVANCE    30,5          unload; store; fetch; reload time
  30      10            LEAVE      CRANES        let this crane go
  31           *
  32      11            PRIORITY   10            raise Priority for next crane use
  33           *
  34      12            TRANSFER   ,NEXTCYCL     go do Process 1 on next casting
  35           *
  36           **************************************************************
  37           *        Model Segment 2 (Run-Control Xact)                  *
  38           **************************************************************
  39           *
  40      13            GENERATE   2400          control Xact comes after 40 hours
  41      14            TERMINATE  1             reduce the TC value by 1,
  42           *                                 ending Xact movement
  43           *
  44           **************************************************************
  45           *        Run-Control Statements                              *
  46           **************************************************************
  47           *
  48                    START      1              set TC = 1;  start Xact movement
  49           *
  50                    END                       end of Model-File execution
```

Figure 12B.2 *Modified Source Echo of the Case Study 12B Model File*

6. Postsimulation Reports

No Postsimulation Reports are shown. Results are summarized in the next section.

7. Discussion

Postsimulation Output. The crane and operator utilizations requested in the Statement of the Problem are summarized in Table 12B.2. (The Case Study 12B model of Figure 12B.2 measures the crane utilization. Exercise 2 of Section 12.12 calls for enhancing the model to measure the operator utilization. The model for Exercise 2 has been used to provide the operator utilizations shown in Table 12B.2.)

As shown in Table 12B.2, crane and operator utilizations increase and decrease, repectively, when machine: crane ratios increase in a 3:1, 4:1, 5:1, and 6:1 pattern. (With more machines using a single crane, there is less crane idle time, but machine operators have to wait longer, on average, for the crane.) In contrast, crane and operator utilizations both increase when the machine:crane ratio increases from 10:2 to 15:3. Is this consistent with your intuition? How would you explain this pattern?

Table 12B.2

A summary of crane and operator utilizations realized in Case Study 12B

Machine:Crane Ratio	Crane Utilization	Operator Utilization
3:1	0.640	0.946
4:1	0.802	0.875
5:1	0.940	0.853
6:1	0.972	0.712
10:2	0.954	0.850
15:3	0.995	0.857

12.12 Exercises

For Exercises 1, 2, and 3, the model12b.gps file contains the Case Study 12B model, configured for 15 finishing machines and 3 cranes.

1. Perform a Batch simulation with the Case Study 12B model and compare the resulting crane utilization with that shown in Table 12B.2 for the 15-machines/3-cranes case.

2. (a) The Case Study 12B model does not measure operator utilization. Let's define an operator to be utilized whenever he is **not** waiting to obtain a crane. Modify a copy of the Case Study 12B model so that it will measure and report operator utilization. (Use a dummy Storage for this purpose.) Perform a simulation with the model. The model has been modified correctly if the operator utilization it reports matches the utilization shown in Table 12B.2 for the 15-machines/3-cranes case.
   (b) Now modify the model to correspond to the 6-operator/1-crane case. Perform a simulation with the model. The model is working correctly if the operator utilization it reports for the 6-operator/1-crane case matches the utilization shown for this case in Table 12B.2.

*3. Perform a Test-Mode simulation with the Case Study 12B model and determine the earliest time that the SPT service order makes a difference vis-à-vis a FCFS service order in terms of the type of use to which a crane is next put. (Just determine the earliest time that the service order differs from what it would be in an FCFS model.)

*4. In Case Study 12B, is SPT a better service order than FCFS in terms of minimizing the **average** time finishing-machine operators spend waiting for a crane? Investigate the answer to this question by performing single simulations for each service order, based on the "15 finishing machines, 3 cranes" model provided in the file case12b.gps. How do the average crane-wait times compare with one another? What are your **tentative** findings? (Remember that more than single simulations need be performed with each alternative before drawing firm conclusions, as discussed in Chapters 14, 15, and 16.)

5. In the harbor problem of Case Study 11A, the service order for ships obtaining tugboats is FCFS. Modify a copy of the model for that case (contained in the file model11a.gps) to change the service order to SPT. Perform a simulation with the changed model. Compare and contrast the results with those reported in Case Study 10A.

*6. (This problem is adapted from Banks and Carson, 1984.) Patients arrive for treatment at a hospital's emergency room with interarrival times of 30 ± 30 minutes. Patients begin by seeing a nurse, who classifies 45 percent of them as CW (can wait) and the other 55 percent as NIA (need immediate attention). There is only one nurse who classifies patients. Classification time takes 10 ± 5 minutes.

Two doctors work in the emergency room. NIA patients have **higher priority** for seeing a doctor than do CW patients. An NIA patient sees a doctor for an average of 45 ± 30 minutes. Seventy-five percent of these patients then have to wait while lab tests are performed, whereas the other 25 percent are finished and can go home immediately.

When needed, lab tests take 30 ± 10 minutes. After completion of the lab tests, NIA patients need to see a doctor again (either doctor), but they have lower priority than do CW patients **who haven't yet seen a doctor**. They then receive further treatment from the doctor for 15 ± 5 minutes and are discharged. Note that NIA patients potentially wait to see a doctor on each of two occasions.

Whereas some NIA patients see a doctor twice, CW patients only see a doctor once. As explained, their priority is lower than that of NIA patients who haven't yet seen a doctor at all, but is higher than that of NIA patients waiting to see a doctor for the second time. Treatment of CW patients takes 30 ± 15 minutes.

Build a model for this situation. Design the model to gather Queue information at each of the four points of potential waiting in the system. Simulate with the model through ten 24-hour periods, assuming no changes take place (in the patient interarrival time, the patient classification pattern, the number of doctors on duty, etc.) in the system during this period. (Such an assumption is unrealistic. See Section 14.8.2.) Discuss the results of the simulation.

*7. Consider the model in Figure E7, which is in the s1212x7.gps file:

(a) At time 30.0, the BLOCK1 Xact and the BLOCK6 Xact both try to capture SERVER2. The BLOCK6 Xact has a Priority of 15 for SERVER2 use, and so **should** win the competition at time 30.0. (The BLOCK1 Xact only has Priority 10.) Which of the two Xacts **will** win the competition at time 30.0? What time will the simulation stop? Check out your answers by investigating the behavior of the model in Test Mode.

```
         SIMULATE                    base time unit: 1 second
*
BLOCK1   GENERATE   0,,30,1,10      1 Xact at time 30 (Priority 10)
         SEIZE      SERVER2         request/capture Server 2
         ADVANCE    20              service time
         RELEASE    SERVER2         let Server 2 go
         TERMINATE  0               done
*
BLOCK6   GENERATE   0,,,1,5         1 Xact at time 0 (Priority 5)
         SEIZE      SERVER1         request/capture Server 1
BLOCK8   PRIORITY   15              boost Priority to 15
BLOCK9   ADVANCE    30              service time
BLOCK10  RELEASE    SERVER1         let Server 1 go
         SEIZE      SERVER2         request/capture Server 2
         ADVANCE    70              service time
         RELEASE    SERVER2         let Server 2 go
         TERMINATE  1               done
*
         START      1               start Xact-movement
         END                        end of Model-File execution
```

Figure E7

(b) Repeat part (a), only now suppose the PRIORITY Block is repositioned immediately **after** the BLOCK9 ADVANCE.

(c) Repeat part (a) again, only now suppose the PRIORITY Block is repositioned immediately after the BLOCK10 RELEASE.

12.13 Use of Priority Levels to Control the Order of Model Updating

Priority Levels have two uses in GPSS/H modeling:

1. Priority Levels are used to help structure service order. We've seen that the default service order in GPSS/H is FCFS **within Priority Level**.

2. Priority Levels are also used to control the **chronological order** in which updates are applied to the state of a model **at a given simulated time**. The order in which updates are applied can be of considerable importance when there are interdependencies among various parts of a system.

The first use of Priority Levels is quite straightforward, whereas the second use is more subtle. We'll introduce the spirit of the second type of Priority-Level use by way of a contrived but readily understood example. This example will reinforce the rule of thumb from Section 12.10 for determining **where** to place PRIORITY Blocks in a model.

Consider the following situation. Suppose a customer comes to Joe the barber every 20 minutes. It takes Joe 20 minutes to give a haircut. Joe's shop is very small, too small to have any chairs in which to seat waiting customers. If an arriving *potential* customer cannot capture Joe immediately, the customer goes down the street to another barbershop. But because interarrival time and service time are both 20 minutes, Joe should just be able to keep up with the demand for his services; none of his potential customers should have to go elsewhere.

Now consider the Figure 12.8 model for Joe the barber.

Analyze this model **very** carefully. If a simulation is performed with the model, will any customers ever go BYEBYE???

Yes, **every other potential customer** in the simulation will go BYEBYE! The first customer will capture Joe, the second will go BYEBYE, the third will capture Joe, the fourth will go BYEBYE, and so on. By the end of the simulation, there will have been 100 happy customers and 99 unhappy ones.

Do you see why the second potential customer will go BYEBYE? When the scan begins at time 40, the second potential customer is arriving, and the first customer is coming out of service. And so both of these Xacts are on the Current Chain. The arriving potential customer is on the CEC **ahead of** the customer coming out of service. (The arriving potential customer was created and placed on the FEC **before** the first customer went into ADVANCE and onto the FEC. Both Xacts have the same Priority, and so their relative order on the CEC is the same as it was

```
         SIMULATE
*
         GENERATE   20            a customer arrives every
*                                 20 minutes
         TRANSFER   BOTH,,BYEBYE  get Joe if possible;
*                                 else, go BYEBYE
         SEIZE      JOE           request (maybe capture) Joe
         ADVANCE    20            haircutting time
         RELEASE    JOE           let Joe go
         TERMINATE  1             happy customer leaves
*
BYEBYE   TERMINATE  0             unhappy potential
*                                 customer leaves
         START      100           simulate until 100
*                                 happy customers have left
         END                      end of Model-File execution
```

Figure 12.8 A Model Illustrating the Consequences of Not Controlling the Order of Model Updating

on the FEC.) And so the scan at time 40 starts with the arriving potential customer. Joe is captured, so this potential customer goes BYEBYE. The scan then proceeds to the customer coming out of service, who frees up Joe and terminates. Joe is now idle, but the potential customer has already left. Joe will now be idle for the next 20 minutes, until the next customer arrives. This next customer will stay for service, but his successor will go BYEBYE, and so on.

The situation modeled in Figure 12.8 is contrived, but it does make the point and leads to several insights. If we assume for the moment that it's illogical (or undesirable) for any customers to go BYEBYE in the system described, then we have a problem on our hands. (We might want to assume that an arriving potential customer is alert enough to realize that Joe is just finishing work on the preceding customer.) The "problem" comes about in this case because Transactions on the Future Chain have **matching Move Times and identical Priority Levels** and are in the "**wrong order**" with respect to each other.

Move-Time ties in the model are promoted by the fact that the interarrival and service times in the system are **deterministic** and their relative values are such that the associated events (arrival, and service completion) can occur at identical times. Suppose interarrival times and/or service times in the system are probabilistic. For example, suppose interarrival time is 20 ± 0.01, and let service time continue to be exactly 20. Now over 2 billion distinct interarrival times can occur, and the probability of having an arrival time **exactly** equal a service-completion time, although greater than 0.0, is extremely small.

In general, one might be tempted to assume as a first approximation that Move-Time ties don't occur and simply accept whatever consequences result if they do occur occasionally. But it isn't necessary to make such an assumption, because **Priority Level distinctions** can be made among Xacts to guarantee that **their relative order on the CEC will be correct when the Scan Phase begins**. In the Figure 12.8 model, for example, if service completions occur with higher priority than arrivals, no customer will ever go BYEBYE. The model in Figure 12.9 repeats the Figure 12.8 model modified to give service completions priority over arrivals. Note that a "PRIORITY 5" Block has been put into the model just ahead of the BLOCK5 ADVANCE. This will not affect Xact order on the Future Events Chain, of course. So an "in-service" Xact on the Future Chain will always be **behind** the "arriving" Xact with which it is involved in a Move-Time tie. But when the Clock Update Phase eventually brings these two time-tied Xacts to the Current Chain, the higher-priority in-service Xact will be put onto the CEC ahead of the arriving Xact. When the following Scan Phase takes place, the in-service Xact will first RELEASE and TERMINATE. Then the arriving Xact, finding Joe idle, won't go BYEBYE but will stay for service.

It would be **incorrect** to put the PRIORITY Block **after** the ADVANCE in the model. Why? Because

```
          SIMULATE
*
          GENERATE  20            a customer arrives every
*                                 20 minutes (Priority 0)
          TRANSFER  BOTH,,BYEBYE  get Joe if possible;
*                                 else, go BYEBYE
          SEIZE     JOE           request (maybe capture) Joe
          PRIORITY  5             give high priority to the
*                                 later service completion
 BLOCK5   ADVANCE   20            haircutting time
          RELEASE   JOE           let Joe go
          TERMINATE 1             happy customer leaves
*
 BYEBYE   TERMINATE 0             unhappy potential
*                                 customer leaves
          START     100           simulate until 100
*                                 happy customers have left
          END                     end of Model-File execution
```

Figure 12.9 *The Figure 12.8 Model Revised to Control the Order of Model Updating*

the service-completion Xact must be in the proper relative position on the CEC **when the scan begins**. Repositioning the service-completion Xact on the CEC after the scan has been partially completed has no effect in this case. If an ADVANCE/PRIORITY sequence is used, every other potential customer will still go BYEBYE.

We conclude, as we did in Section 12.10, that when forming a two-Block sequence consisting of PRIORITY and ADVANCE, **the PRIORITY Block should precede the ADVANCE**. This simple rule of thumb is sufficient to model dynamic Priority-Level changes successfully in a very large percentage of the cases that come up in practice.

We finish this section by suggesting that Move-Time ties are not as infrequent as might be thought. (This increases the importance of knowing how to control and resolve them.) Multiple events do sometimes occur at identical times in systems (or at least in models of systems). For example, suppose a workshift begins at 8 A.M. This can mean that worker-Xacts do (or do not, in case of absenteeism) show up at one and the same time in a model of the system. Other events may also occur at the start of a shift. Equipment availability is reviewed. (Previously broken-down equipment might have been fixed overnight.) Schedules are updated to take new orders into account and are acted upon. Workers are given their assignments for the shift. And so on. The chronological order in which various aspects of the state of the model are updated at one and the same simulated time may be important, because of interdependencies in the logic of the system being modeled. For example, the status of a previously broken-down machine should be updated **before** it's decided whether to assign a worker to operate that machine during a shift. This is similar to updating the capture status of Joe the barber in the above example **before** deciding whether an arriving potential customer will remain for service or go BYEBYE.

In conclusion, Priority Levels provide an important tool not just for influencing service order, but also for controlling the order in which updates are applied to the state of a model at a given simulated time.

12.14 Exercises

For Exercises 1 through 8, supplied files fig128.gps and fig129.gps, respectively, contain the Figure 12.8 and 12.9 models of Section 12.13.

1. Run the Figure 12.8 model in Batch mode. Do 99 potential customers go BYEBYE, as the discussion says will happen?

2. Run the Figure 12.8 model in Test Mode. Monitor Transaction movement from the beginning of the simulation until completion of the Scan Phase at time 40.0, displaying the CEC and FEC as the simulation proceeds. Satisfy yourself that the various event sequences will take place in the order indicated in the Section 12.13 discussion.

3. Modify a copy of the Figure 12.8 model, changing "GENERATE 20" to "GENERATE 20,0.01". Run this model in Batch mode. Do the results indicate that any Move-Time ties occurred? On what do you base your statement?

4. Run the Figure 12.9 model in Batch mode. Do all potential customers stay for service, as the discussion says will happen?

5. Modify a copy of the Figure 12.9 model, repositioning the PRIORITY Block to follow rather than precede ADVANCE. Run this model in Batch mode. Does use of the PRIORITY Block in this position have any effect on operation of the model, or do 99 potential customers go BYEBYE, as they would if the PRIORITY Block weren't there at all?

6. Run the Exercise 5 model in Test Mode. Monitor Transaction movement from the beginning of the simulation until completion of the Scan Phase at time 40.0, displaying the CEC and FEC as the simulation proceeds. Satisfy yourself that the presence of the PRIORITY Block **after** the ADVANCE has no practical effect on model behavior.

7. Discuss the possibility of putting the PRIORITY Block in the Figure 12.9 model between the GENERATE and TRANSFER Blocks. If you make this change, how many potential customers will go BYEBYE? Apply this change to a copy of the second model and simulate with the changed model to check out your thinking.

8. Eliminate the TRANSFER Block from a copy of the Figure 12.8 model. (The Block labeled BYEBYE can then also be eliminated, although it doesn't have to be.) Describe the behavior of the resulting model. When do the first five customers arrive? When do they go into ser-

vice? Check out your thinking by carrying out a Test-Mode simulation with the model.

*9. In Exercise 8 of Section 8.11, the workers themselves are responsible for moving WIP. Now suppose that the WIP is too heavy to be moved by hand. It is moved instead by an AGV (automated guided vehicle). There is only one AGV in the system. After a unit of WIP claims the AGV, it takes 30 ± 15 seconds for the AGV to travel to the point where it is needed, and then it takes the AGV another 30 seconds to accomplish the requested move. The AGV is used to transfer WIP from the point of its arrival to Station 1, from Station 1 to the wait space between Stations 1 and 2, from the wait space to Station 2, and from Station 2 to the exit from the system.

   In the movement of WIP from Station 1, the WIP can be taken immediately to Station 2 if Station 2 is idle. This saves time, because a single transfer (from Station 1 to Station 2) accomplishes what otherwise would take two transfers (from Station 1 to the wait space, and, later, from the wait space to Station 2). For this reason, higher priority should be given to the transfer of WIP from Station 2 (to free up that station) than from Station 1.

   The workers do not participate in loading or unloading the AGV, or in AGV movement. They cannot start their next task, however, until the WIP they've most recently worked on has been removed by the AGV.

   Build a model for the system as described. Perform a simulation with the model and analyze the resulting output. How long does it take for 100 finished pieces of work to leave the system? What is the utilization of the AGV?

10. In Exercise 9, suppose higher priority weren't given to the transfer of WIP from Station 2 than from Station 1. Describe a situation in which WIP would then experience a double transfer (from Station 1 to the wait space, and then from the wait space to Station 2), whereas with the priority distinction only a single transfer (directly from Station 1 to Station 2) would have been needed.

11. Repeat Exercise 9, only now assume the AGV is used not just by the portion of the system described in Exercise 8 of Section 8.11, but is also used elsewhere in the overall system. Other needs for the AGV arise every 10 ± 5 minutes. It takes the AGV 4 ± 2 minutes to satisfy these other needs. Furthermore, it takes the AGV longer on average to get to Station 1 or Station 2 when needed there, simply because it often has to travel a longer distance to get from its point of last use to Station 1 or Station 2. Assume it now takes the AGV 75 ± 60 seconds to reach Station 1 or Station 2.

   Build a model for this modified system. Perform a simulation with the model and analyze the resulting output. Now how long does it take for 100 finished pieces of work to leave the system? What is the utilization of the AGV?

12.15 The ALL-Mode TRANSFER Block

ALL TRANSFER is an extended form of BOTH TRANSFER. In BOTH TRANSFER, an Xact waits until it will be accepted by one of two alternative Next Blocks. In ALL TRANSFER, an Xact waits until it will be accepted by one of two **or more** alternative Next Blocks.

The ALL TRANSFER Block is shown in Figure 12.10. In ALL TRANSFER, the Block's A Operand is literally the word ALL. The B Operand points to the B-Block, which is the **first** Block in the set of Next-Block candidates. The C Operand points to the C-Block, which is the **last** Block in the set of Next-Block candidates. **Not all** Blocks between the B- and C-Blocks will necessarily be tried. Instead, **every *n*th Block** between the B- and C-Blocks (inclusive) will be tried. The ALL Block's D Operand supplies the value of n. In terms of **Block Location numbers,** the C-Block must be "greater than" the B-Block, and the C-Block minus the B-Block must be evenly divisible by n.

In ALL TRANSFER, the number of Next-Block candidates equals (C—B)/D+1, where B, C, and D are the values of the B, C, and D Operands. These Blocks are the B-Block, and the Blocks removed n, $2n$, $3n$, and so on Locations from the B-Block (with the C-Block being the last candidate). The candidates are tested in that order, and a Transaction moves into the first candidate Block that does not deny entry to it.

If all candidate Next Blocks deny entry to an Xact in an ALL TRANSFER, the Xact stops moving for

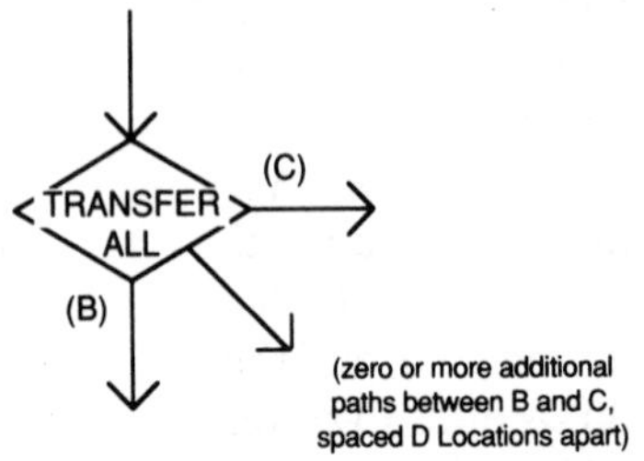

Operand	Significance	Default Value or Result
A	Literally, the word ALL	Compile-time error
B	Pointer to a Block [1] (the "B Block")	The "B-Block" is the sequential Block
C	Pointer to a Block [1] (The "C Block")	Compile-time error
D	An integer indicating the separation between the Blocks lying on the alternative escape routes	Compile-time error

[1] Copy of the Label attached to that Block

Figure 12.10 *The TRANSFER Block in ALL Mode*

the time being, remaining in the ALL-Mode TRANSFER Block and on the Current Chain. The multiply-blocked Xact is **not** put to sleep, but remains scan active. The Scan Phase then continues in the usual way. When GPSS/H next encounters this multiply-blocked Xact (either because of a restarted scan at the current time, or after a Clock Update has taken place), the Xact again retrys to move into the B-Block and, if entry is still denied there, into the B-Block + n, and so on. The Xact eventually moves into the first candidate Next Block that will accept it.

A simple example for ALL-Mode TRANSFER is shown in the Figure 12.11 model. The model is for WIP units that arrive at a point in a system where a hole is to be drilled in them. There are three drill presses, a newer model, a somewhat older model, and a very old model. The newer the model, the faster the drill press can do the job. A single line of WIP forms at this point in the system. The service order is FCFS. WIP goes to whichever drill press will take it next, trying the newer model first, then (if necessary) the somewhat older model, and finally (if necessary) the very old model. These aspects of system operation can be inferred from the Figure 12.11 model of the system.

ALL TRANSFER provides one method, then, for modeling any size group of servers that are similar in type but have differing individual characteris-

```
          SIMULATE
*
          GENERATE  5,1                WIP units arrive, one by one
          TRANSFER  ALL,GET1,GET3,4    check up to 3 drills
*
 GET1     SEIZE     DRILL1             request drill 1
          ADVANCE   10,2               service time
          RELEASE   DRILL1             let drill 1 go
          TERMINATE 1                  finished WIP unit leaves
*
          SEIZE     DRILL2             request drill 2
          ADVANCE   15,3               service time
          RELEASE   DRILL2             let drill 2 go
          TERMINATE 1                  finished WIP unit leaves
*
 GET3     SEIZE     DRILL3             request drill 3
          ADVANCE   30,4               service time
          RELEASE   DRILL3             let drill 3 go
          TERMINATE 1                  finished WIP unit leaves
*
          START     100                drill 100 WIP units
          END                          end of Model-File execution
```

Figure 12.11 *A Model Illustrating Use of ALL-Mode TRANSFER*

tics. Although the ALL-based approach certainly works, there are more efficient ways to accomplish the same effect in GPSS/H. These other ways, whose operational details are beyond the scope of this book, have the advantage that blocked Xacts are put to sleep on the CEC or are even taken off the CEC and put elsewhere (on a User Chain), which generally makes the model execute in less time.

12.16 Exercises

*1. Perform a Test-Mode simulation with the Figure 12.11 model, which is in file fig1211.gps. What is the earliest time that a WIP unit goes to the oldest drill? What is the earliest time that a WIP unit fails to move out of the ALL TRANSFER on its first attempt? How long does it take to drill holes in 100 WIP units? How many WIP units are waiting for a drill press at that time?

2. Modify a copy of the Figure 12.11 model so that after drilling, WIP units proceed to either one of two candidate finishing machines. One of these machines takes 12 ± 3 minutes to polish a WIP unit; the other takes 8 ± 3 minutes. Given a choice, the faster polishing machine is preferred. Assume WIP-movement times are negligibly small. Perform a simulation with the modified model. How long does it take before 100 WIP units have been polished?

3. Repeat Exercise 2, but assume that an AGV is needed to move WIP from the drill press area to the polishing machine area. There is only one AGV in the system. After a WIP unit has captured the AGV, transfer time takes 4 ± 1 minutes. By hand, compute the expected AGV utilization. Perform a simulation with your model. What AGV utilization is achieved in the simulation? Compare the time required to polish 100 WIP units with the time required in the simulation of Exercise 2.

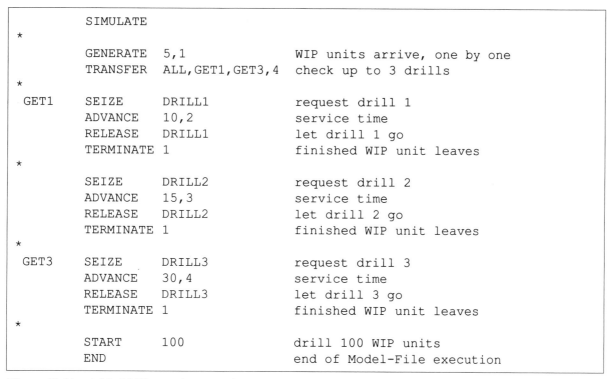

13 Modeling with Nonuniform Probability Distributions

13.1 Preview

In the preceding chapters, 11 types of Blocks have been introduced, and for one of them, TRANSFER, four usage modes have been described. An interesting set of situations can be modeled with this small set of Blocks, as the cases and exercises have indicated. In all models built up to this point, however, it has been assumed that interarrival and service times are uniformly distributed or are deterministic. In this chapter, we take up the topic of modeling with nonuniform probability distributions in GPSS/H.

The chapter begins by introducing built-in GPSS/H functions for sampling from the exponential, normal, and triangular distributions. As we'll see, it's as easy to sample from these distributions as from the uniform. Possibilities for using the uniform, normal, and triangular distributions to interpret limited data are also briefly discussed.

We then introduce the tools provided by GPSS/H for use in describing and sampling from data-based distributions that may be of interest to the modeler, but that may have no theoretical counterpart. These tools take the form of modeler-defined Functions. Two types of modeler-defined Functions, discrete and continuous, are introduced. Examples, cases, and exercises are used throughout the chapter to illustrate the material.

13.2 A Visualization of Simulated Sampling from a Population

Figure 13.1 illustrates a two-step process for sampling from a population consisting of values of a continuous random variable. (A **continuous** random variables can take on any value in some **interval**. Interarrival times and service times usually are continuous random variables.) Shown at the left in the figure is the probability density function (pdf) for a population uniformly and continuously distributed on the interval from 0 to 1. As shown, the pdf for the 0–1 uniform distribution has a value of 1 over the 0–1 interval (and zero otherwise). (In the special case of a 0–1 uniform distribution, the density function forms a square. For the general uniform distribution ranging from a to b, the density function forms a rectangle with height $1/(b\text{–}a)$ over the a–b interval, and zero otherwise. A uniform distribution is consequently referred to as a rectangular distribution.)

At the right of Figure 13.1, the probability density

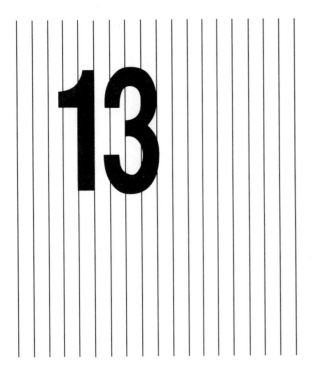

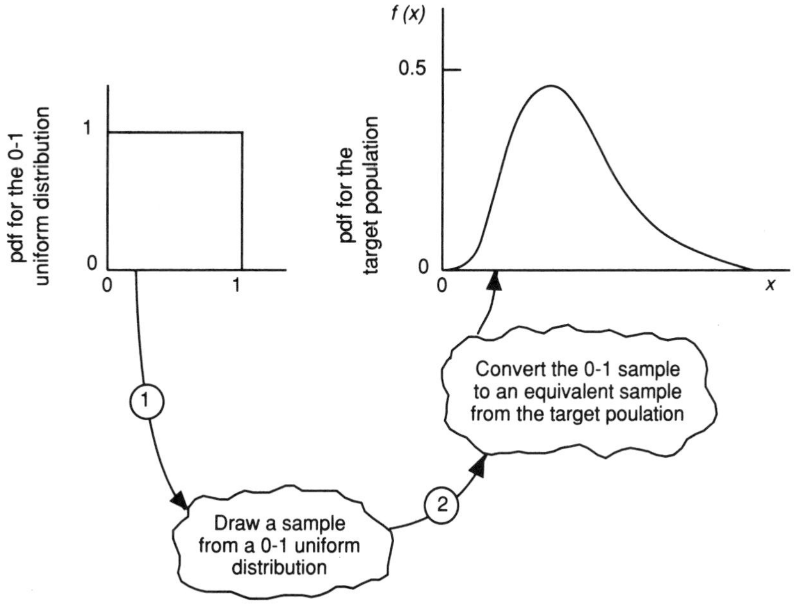

Figure 13.1 *A Two-Step Process for Sampling From a Continuous Distribution*

function $f(x)$ for the target population (the population from which a sample is to be drawn) is shown. (Note that the two vertical scales in Figure 13.1 differ.) The two-step sampling process takes this form:

1. Draw a value from the uniform 0–1 population.
2. Convert this value into an equivalent value from the target population.

To support the two-step process of Figure 13.1, it's necessary to have a source of random numbers uniformly distributed on the 0–1 interval. It's also necessary to specify how to map a random value from a uniform 0–1 source into an equivalent value from the target population. Sources of 0–1 uniform random numbers in GPSS/H will be discussed in Section 13.3 and in Chapter 14. Procedures for mapping a random 0–1 value into an equivalent value from a target population are taken up throughout this chapter.

13.3 The GPSS/H Uniform Random-Number Generators

GPSS/H provides an unlimited number of built-in, independent sources of 0–1 uniform random numbers. We will refer to these sources as **random-number generators**, or **RNGs**. Each of the GPSS/H RNGs produces, on demand, a value sampled at random from the population uniformly distributed on the **open** 0–1 interval. (Recall that an open interval is one that excludes its end points.) The names of these RNGs are RN1, RN2, RN3, and so on. RN1 is referred to as random-number generator 1, RN2 as random-number generator 2, and so on.

Some of the reasons for having more than one RNG will be explained in Chapters 14, 15, and 16, where we discuss statistical experiments with GPSS/H models.

Each of the GPSS/H RNGs has a **nonidentical** default **starting point.** It's possible to override the default starting point for any one or more of the generators by use of a Control Statement to be discussed in Chapter 14.

Suppose we leave RN1 at its default starting point, then call RN1 10 consecutive times. The result is a time series of 10 values produced by RN1. This time series is shown in the RN1 column in Table 13.1, expressed to six decimal places. The columns RN2, RN3, ..., RN8 in Table 13.1 similarly show the time series consisting of the first 10 values produced by random number generators 2 through 8, respectively, when these random-number sources begin at their default starting point.

GPSS/H uses one algorithm (procedure) to produce 0–1 uniform random numbers. (Details are provided in Chapter 14.) The algorithm is deterministic,

Table 13.1

The first 10 values from the first 8 GPSS/H random-number generators

	Generator Called							
Number of the Call	RN1	RN2	RN3	RN4	RN5	RN6	RN7	RN8
1	0.270295	0.985170	0.214159	0.094836	0.567782	0.722544	0.203632	0.045961
2	0.499353	0.445582	0.791699	0.976269	0.677350	0.931816	0.097297	0.990727
3	0.739770	0.675116	0.792091	0.318588	0.352417	0.242655	0.542664	0.605539
4	0.204092	0.454705	0.132872	0.034865	0.496738	0.543981	0.583846	0.032678
5	0.120667	0.834154	0.377848	0.152324	0.724026	0.918246	0.212546	0.369601
6	0.768434	0.559414	0.943256	0.652139	0.135509	0.845153	0.682030	0.707049
7	0.440394	0.634527	0.271380	0.337951	0.530431	0.571151	0.457531	0.196601
8	0.859458	0.617560	0.393878	0.981639	0.897833	0.828790	0.698866	0.094023
9	0.792366	0.960078	0.812006	0.516752	0.414219	0.279809	0.767102	0.295870
10	0.092539	0.255847	0.153557	0.415278	0.598477	0.018436	0.880456	0.554502

so the random numbers it produces are not **truly** random, but are **pseudo**random, which means they are **reproducible.** In other words, if anyone were to build a GPSS/H model to display the first 10 values produced by RN1 beginning at its default starting point, the resulting numbers would match those shown in the RN1 column in Table 13.1. (The reproducibility of random numbers can be taken advantage of in the design of statistical experiments, as will be discussed in Chapters 14, 15, and 16.)

Table 13.1 expresses random numbers only to 6 decimal places. Internally, a random number is represented to somewhat more than 16 decimal places in GPSS/H. (The base 2 number system is used for the internal representation. The magnitude of each random number is represented with 56 binary digits. Those interested are referred to the *GPSS/H Reference Manual.*)

There are in excess of **2 billion** unique values in the open 0–1 population from which the GPSS/H random-number generators sample. To be precise, there are 2,147,483,646 unique values. This fact is consistent with the statement made in Chapter 2 that in GPSS/H, in excess of 2 billion unique values can be sampled from an interval.

13.4 Transparent Sampling at GENERATE and ADVANCE Blocks

When GENERATE and ADVANCE Blocks were introduced in Chapter 2, we saw that their A and B Operands can be used to specify the expected value and half-range of uniformly distributed interarrival times (GENERATE) and service times (ADVANCE). Nothing was said about sources of 0–1 uniform random numbers to support sampling at such GENERATE and ADVANCE Blocks, nor about the procedure used to map a sample from a 0–1 uniform source into an equivalent sample from the uniform distribution of interest. In this sense, the process followed to accomplish this sampling is **transparent** to the modeler.

Consider the GENERATE Block in the general form "GENERATE A,B". Let IAT_{sample} represent an interarrival-time sample from the distribution A ± B. GPSS/H samples transparently from the A ± B population by using **RN1** as the source of random numbers, mapping an RN1 value into an equivalent interarrival time as follows:

```
IATsample = (A - B) + RN1 * (2 * B)
```

where IAT_{sample} is the sampled interarrival time. In other words, the sampled interarrival time is computed by adding to the **largest value excluded from the population at the left**, A - B, a **random fraction**, RN1, of the **range** of values, 2 * B, included in the population. Remember that 0.0 < RN1 < 1.0. We then have (A - B) < IAT_{sample} < (A + B), consistent with the fact that the interarrival times are distributed on the **open** interval A ± B.

If B equals zero in "GENERATE A,B" (either by default, or by keying a zero for B), then the interarrival time is deterministic, not probabilistic. In such cases, no sampling is done, so **no value is drawn from RN1.**

```
STMT#  BLOCK#  *LOC   OPERATION  A,B,C,D,E,F,G   COMMENTS

   1                  SIMULATE                                Case Study 9A
   2             *                          A Tool Crib System (SPT Service Order)
   3             *                                        Base Time Unit: 1 Second
   4             *******************************************************************
   5             *        Model Segment 1 (Type 1 Mechanics)                       *
   6             *******************************************************************
   7             *
   8       1              GENERATE   420,360,,,5     Type 1 mechanics arrive
   9             *                                   (Priority 5)
  10       2              QUEUE      TOOLWAIT        start TOOLWAIT Queue membership
  11       3              SEIZE      CLERK           request/capture the clerk
  12       4              DEPART     TOOLWAIT        end TOOLWAIT Queue membership
  13       5              ADVANCE    300,90          service time
  14       6              RELEASE    CLERK           free the clerk
  15       7              TERMINATE  0               leave the tool crib area
  16             *
  17             *******************************************************************
  18             *        Model Segment 2 (Type 2 Mechanics)                       *
  19             *******************************************************************
  20             *
  21       8              GENERATE   360,240,,,10    Type 2 mechanics arrive
  22             *                                   (Priority 10)
  23       9              QUEUE      TOOLWAIT        start TOOLWAIT Queue membership
  24      10              SEIZE      CLERK           request/capture the clerk
  25      11              DEPART     TOOLWAIT        end TOOLWAIT Queue membership
  26      12              ADVANCE    100,30          service time
  27      13              RELEASE    CLERK           free the clerk
  28      14              TERMINATE  0               leave the tool crib area
  29             *
  30             *******************************************************************
  31             *        Model Segment 3 (Run-Control Xact)                       *
  32             *******************************************************************
  33             *
  34      15              GENERATE   28800           control Xact comes after 8 hours
  35      16              TERMINATE  1               reduce the TC value by 1,
  36             *                                   ending Xact movement
  37             *
  38             *******************************************************************
  39             *        Run-Control Statements                                   *
  40             *******************************************************************
  41             *
  42                      START      1               set TC = 1; start Xact movement
  43                      END                        end of Model-File execution
```

***Figure 13.2** The Modified Source Echo for the SPT Model in Case Study 9A*

The statements just made about transparent sampling at GENERATE Blocks apply without modification to transparent sampling at ADVANCE Blocks.

Now consider the use of RN1 in the context of the Case Study 9A model ("Alternative Service Orders at a Tool Crib"). For convenience, Figure 13.2 repeats the Modified Source Echo for the SPT model from Case Study 9A. In a simulation performed with the model, the first need for sampling comes when the model's GENERATE Blocks are initialized. The GENERATE in Location 1 is initialized first, so RN1 is called **for the first time** for purposes of sampling from the 420 ± 360 population to schedule the first arrival of a Type 1 mechanic. The RN1 value used for this purpose, as we see in Table 13.1, is 0.270295. Evaluating the equation for sampling from a uniform distribution, the first Type 1 mechanic will arrive at time 254.6 (approximately).

The GENERATE in Location 2 is initialized next, so RN1 is called **for the second time** to sample from the 360 ± 240 population to schedule the first arrival of a Type 2 mechanic. Table 13.1 shows that the RN1 value used for this purpose is 0.499353. Evaluating the equation for sampling from a uniform distribution, the first Type 2 mechanic will arrive at time 359.7 (approximately).

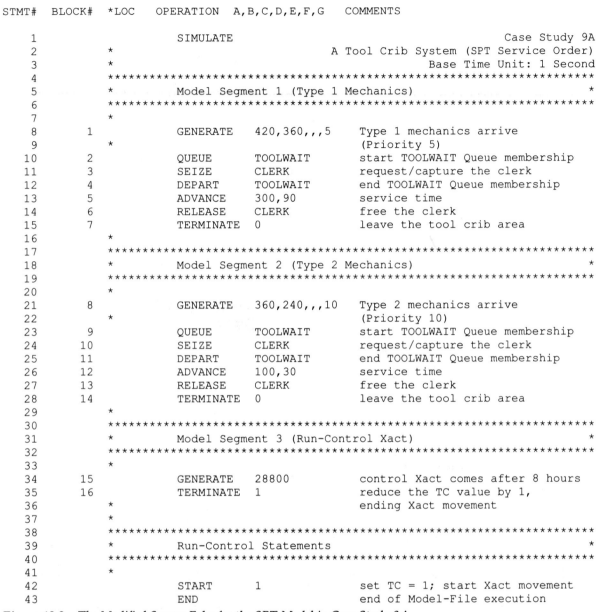

The GENERATE in Location 15 is the next to be initialized. Interarrival times at this Block are deterministic, so **RN1 is not called** to initialize this GENERATE Block.

Then Xact movement begins. A Type 1 mechanic is the first to arrive (at time 254.6, approximately). It executes the Location 1 GENERATE in the process of moving into the Location 2 QUEUE Block. So RN1 is called **for the third time** in the simulation, this time to schedule the arrival of the second Type 1 mechanic. From Table 13.1, the RN1 value used for this purpose is 0.739770. The resulting interarrival time is 472.6 (approximately), and so the second Type 1 mechanic will arrive at time 727.2 (approximately).

The arriving Type 1 mechanic then moves without delay down its path into the Location 5 ADVANCE. So RN1 is called **for the fourth time** in the simulation, to determine the ADVANCE time for the first Type 1 mechanic. From Table 13.1, the RN1 value used for this purpose is 0.204092, and an ADVANCE time is computed accordingly.

And so on. We see that **in the case of transparent sampling** at GENERATE and ADVANCE Blocks, RN1 is used at **all** such Blocks in a model. When transparent sampling takes place at two or more such Blocks, each Block uses only a **subset** of the values produced over time by RN1.

13.5 Use of RN1 at Statistical TRANSFER Blocks

Letting A, B, and C represent Operands, the general form of the statistical-mode TRANSFER Block (introduced in Section 12.2) is "TRANSFER .A,B,C", where B and C point to other Blocks in a model and where the A Operand indicates the fraction of the time that Xacts moving into the TRANSFER Block take the C-Block as their Next Block.

To support execution of this TRANSFER Block, GPSS/H draws a sample from RN1, then uses the sampled value to determine the Next Block for the Xact in the TRANSFER Block. For example, suppose an Xact moves into this TRANSFER Block:

```
TRANSFER .250,ROUTE1,ROUTE2
```

Then RN1 is called, and the value it produces, **converted internally to a three-digit integer** in the closed interval from 0 to 999, will be compared with 250. If the three-digit integer is less than 250, the Xact's Next Block will be ROUTE2; otherwise, it will be ROUTE1.

And so there is transparent use of RN1 at statistical TRANSFER Blocks, as well as for transparent sampling at GENERATE and ADVANCE Blocks. RN1 is also used transparently to support operation of TRANSFER Blocks operating in PICK Mode. (We won't discuss PICK-Mode TRANSFER now or later, except to say it can be used to pick a Block probabilistically from a set of two or more equally likely candidates and uses a sample from RN1 for this purpose. In Section 18 of this chapter, we show how to achieve this effect more flexibly than is possible with the use of PICK TRANSFER. As a result, PICK is not of direct interest to us.) **These are the only four contexts in which GPSS/H uses RN1 transparently.**

13.6 Sampling from the Exponential Distribution: RVEXPO

GPSS/H provides **built-in** functions that can be used to sample from the exponential, normal and triangular distributions. This section discusses the exponential distribution and the built-in function used to sample from it. Following sections similarly discuss the normal and triangular distributions.

The exponential random variable, which is continuous, takes on all values greater than zero. The probability density functions $f(x)$ for the three exponential random variables with expected values (μ) of 0.5, 1.0, and 2.0 are graphed in Figure 13.3.

The exponential random variable is frequently used to model interarrival times when there is little or no control over the arrival process. Examples of such arrival processes potentially include the arrival of patients at the emergency room of a hospital, of ships at a harbor, of orders at an order-filling

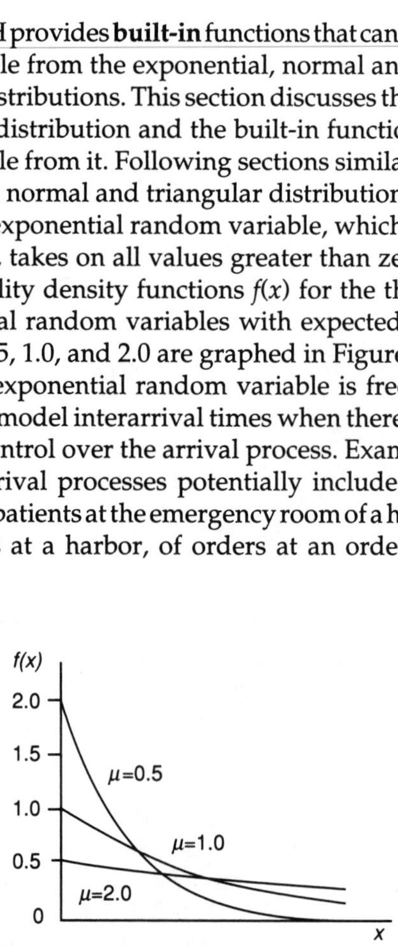

Figure 13.3 *Probability Density Functions for Exponential Distributions With Expected Values (μ) of 0.5, 1.0, and 2.0. (Adapted from Pritsker, 1986.)*

center, of customers at a bank, and of tasks from interactive users' terminals at a computer.

An exponential distribution is completely specified by giving its expected value. For example, to state that interarrival times are exponentially distributed with a mean of 12.6 minutes provides all the information needed to model the corresponding arrival process.

An exponential distribution is sometimes referred to as a **negative** exponential distribution, but will simply be called an exponential distribution here.

A sample from a 0–1 uniform source can be mapped into an equivalent sample from the exponential distribution with mean IAT_{avg} by evaluating this equation,

```
IATsample = IATavg * [-ln(1.0 - RNj)]
```

where ln is the natural logarithm function, and RNj refers to random-number generator *j*, *j* = 1, or 2, or 3, ... (See any general simulation text for development of the equation.)

Even though GPSS/H has a built-in natural logarithm function, (see the *GPSS/H Reference Manual* for details), it's not necessary to work with the arithmetic expression in GPSS/H. Instead, the built-in GPSS/H function **RVEXPO** (for **R**andom **V**ariate **EXPO**nential) can be used to sample from the exponential distribution. RVEXPO takes this form,

```
RVEXPO(j, IATavg)
```

where *j* indicates the modeler's choice of the **number** of a random-number generator and IAT_{avg} can be specified either with or without a decimal point. For example, suppose patients arrive at a hospital's emergency room between 10 P.M. and 1 A.M. on Friday/Saturday with a mean interarrival time of 18.5 minutes, exponentially distributed. Arbitrarily choosing RN4 as the generator that supports sampling from the interarrival time distribution, this GENERATE Block can be used to introduce patient-Xacts into a model:

```
GENERATE RVEXPO(4,18.5)
```

RVEXPO(4,18.5) has been specified as the GENERATE Block's A Operand, and the B Operand has a default value of zero. When the GENERATE Block is executed, the RVEXPO function will be evaluated to determine the current value of the Block's A Operand. This value will then be used as the interarrival time in the ongoing Xact creation-and-scheduling process. (Recall that a GENERATE B Operand defaults to zero, which explains why the value of the A Operand will not be modified in this example.)

The exponential distribution has a high degree of variability. (This is consistent with such relatively uncontrollable processes as, for example, the arrival of patients at a hospital's emergency room.) In fact, its **variance** is equal to the **square** of its mean. For example, an exponential random variable with a mean of 20 has a variance of 400. The exponential random variable has one of the largest variances (relative to its mean) of the more common types of distributions.

One way to appreciate the effect of the high variance of the exponential random variable is to consider that values of -ln(1.0 - RN*j*), which is a **factor** in the above equation, start just greater than zero (for RN*j* arbitrarily close to 0.0); and asymptotically approach infinity (for RN*j* arbitrarily close to 1.0). The larger the values of this factor, the lower their probability of occurrence. For example, the probability that this factor is greater than 1.2 is about 0.3, the probability of being greater than 2.3 is only about 0.1, and the probability of being greater than 8.0 is only about 0.0002. Nevertheless, if the negative logarithm has a value of 8.0 on a given occasion and the mean interarrival time is 20, then the sampled interarrival time will be 8 times 20, or 160.

If interarrival-time observations are available, it's easy to do an informal check to see if they might be exponentially distributed. The check involves listing the interarrival times in increasing order and then plotting these interarrival times on a semilogarithmic scale against their rank on a linear scale. If the interarrival times are exponentially distributed, the points will come close to falling on a straight line. (Such a plot can be found in Gordon, 1975, p. 179.) More formal evaluation can be conducted using goodness-of-fit testing. Interactive software is available that makes such testing fast and straightforward.

Important continuous random variables other than interarrival times are sometimes exponentially distributed. For example, the duration of some types of telephone conversations has been found to be exponentially distributed. So is the life of some electronic components that fail instantaneously (catastrophically), such as light bulbs or semiconductors. RVEXPO can be used as an ADVANCE Block's A Operand, so it's easy to simulate exponentially distributed holding times. For example, if an

Xact simulates a student calling Mom or Dad collect to say "Happy Birthday!" and if the duration of such conversations is exponentially distributed with a mean of 15 minutes, the Xact could move into this ADVANCE Block to simulate talk time:

```
ADVANCE RVEXPO(3,15)
```

The probability density function for the exponential random variable (not shown here) can be handled mathematically with relative ease. Because of this, exponential sources of randomness are often assumed in the mathematical modeling of queuing systems. For example, many of the properties of a queuing system composed of exponential arrivals to an exponential server (a so-called M/M/1 queuing system) have been developed mathematically. (See for example Banks and Carson, 1984, Chapter 5, or any introductory text on operations research or queuing theory for details.)

The discussion here of exponential random variables has been qualitative for the most part. Those who want a more rigorous treatment are referred to the general simulation texts indicated in the references.

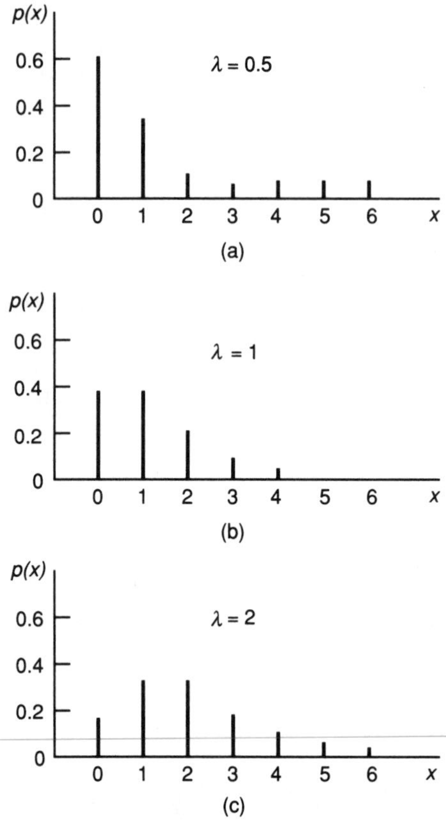

Figure 13.4 *Probability Mass Functions for Poisson Distributions with Expected Values (λ) of (a) 0.5, (b) 1.0, and (c) 2.0*

13.7 The Relationship Between the Exponential and Poisson Random Variables

When an arrival process is discussed, it's possible to talk about **interarrival times,** on one hand, or **arrival rates,** on the other. For example, if an arrival process has a mean **interarrival time** of 20 minutes, then the associated average **arrival rate** is 3 per hour. In simulation, our interest often centers on interarrival times, because it's their distribution from which samples are drawn to schedule future arrivals. (Arrival rates can nevertheless be of interest in their own right, too.)

An interarrival-time random variable is usually **continuous**. (It usually takes on any value in some interval.) In contrast, an arrival-rate random variable is **discrete**. (It only takes on specific values from a limited number of alternatives. The alternatives are integer valued in the case of arrival rates.) For example, an interarrival time can be **any** value in the open interval 10 ± 5, say, whereas an arrival rate (such as the number of arrivals in a given hour) can only be one of the specific values 0, or 1, or 2, or ....

In the case of a **continuous** random variable, one talks about the probability **density** function (**pdf**), denoted here by $f(x)$. In the case of a **discrete** random variable, one talks about the probability **mass** function (**pmf**), denoted here by $p(x)$.

It can be shown that when interarrival times are **exponentially** distributed, the associated arrival rates follow the **Poisson** distribution. The Poisson random variable takes on all integer values greater than or equal to zero. For perspective, the probability mass function $p(x)$ for Poisson random variables with expected values (λ) of 0.5, 1.0, and 2.0 are plotted in Figure 13.4.

Like the exponential, the Poisson random variable is completely characterized by giving its expected value. The expected value of a Poisson random variable is the reciprocal of the expected value of the associated exponential random variable (i.e., $\lambda = 1/\mu$). For example, if exponentially distributed interarrival times have an expected value of 5 minutes (one arrival every 5 minutes on average), then the associated Poisson arrival rate is 1/5, or 0.2 (0.2 arrivals per minute on average). In "per hour" terms, the associated Poisson arrival rate is 60/5, or 12 (12 arrivals per hour on average).

It's sometimes said that an arrival process is Poisson, or arrivals occur in a Poisson stream, or in a Poisson pattern. This is just another way of saying that the interarrival times associated with the arrival process are exponentially distributed.

For an arrival rate to be Poisson distributed, these three assumptions must be satisfied:

1. The probability that an arrival occurs during a small time interval is proportional to the size of the interval. (For example, the probability of an arrival occurring sometime during the next 5 seconds in a Poisson arrival process is twice as great as the probability of an arrival occuring sometime during the next 2.5 seconds.)
2. The probability of two or more arrivals occurring during a sufficiently small time interval is negligibly small. (A consequence of this assumption is that **simultaneous arrivals do not occur** in a Poisson arrival process. In other words, the interarrival time never equals 0.0.)
3. The interarrival times are independent of each other. (For example, suppose that in case 1, an arrival has just occurred, and in case 2, the last arrival occurred 5 minutes ago. To say that interarrival times are independent of each other means the chances of having an arrival occur during the next minute are the same in case 1 as in case 2. This characteristic of a Poisson arrival process is sometimes referred to as the memoryless property of the associated exponential distribution.)

The properties of the Poisson distribution will not be further discussed here. Those interested should consult one of the general simulation texts listed in the References.

13.8 Sampling from the Erlang Distribution

In this section, we point out that two or more samples from an exponential distribution can be added to produce a sample from an Erlang distribution. The Erlang distribution can be of practical use in modeling service times.

An exponential random variable is a special case of an Erlang random variable. An Erlang distribution is characterized by two parameters, known as shape and scale parameters, with the shape parameter being an integer of value 1 or more. The exponential distribution is an Erlang distribution with a shape parameter of 1.

The value of an Erlang distribution's shape parameter is said to be the **order** of the distribution. In these terms, an exponential distribution is an Erlang of order 1, or a "1-Erlang distribution." It's the 2-Erlang distribution (the Erlang of order 2) on which our attention focuses here, because:

> experience has shown that if one collects data on the time to perform some task in the real world, the histogram of these data will often have a shape similar to that of the density function for a 2-Erlang distribution. (Law and Kelton, 1982, p. 87)

It can be shown that one way to sample from a k-Erlang distribution with expected value μ is to form the sum of k samples from an exponential distribution with expected value μ/k. This makes it especially easy in GPSS/H to sample from the Erlang distribution through use of the built-in RVEXPO function. For example, suppose the step time for a job at a machine follows the 2-Erlang distribution with expected value 0.9 hours. Then we can simulate this step time by using this sequence of two ADVANCE Blocks:

```
ADVANCE RVEXPO(3,0.45)
ADVANCE RVEXPO(3,0.45)
```

In this example, the expected value of the exponential random variable is 0.45, which is half the expected value of 0.9 for the 2-Erlang step-time random variable. Random-number generator 3 has been arbitrarily specified in the example.

In GPSS/H, arithmetic expressions can be used in most contexts, including the context of Block Operands. Arithmetic expressions and their use in GPSS/H modeling won't be formally introduced here. It's easy to see on an informal basis, however, that the preceding sequence of **two** consecutive ADVANCE Blocks can be replaced by **one** ADVANCE whose A Operand is expressed as the sum of two values produced by the RVEXPO function. Such an ADVANCE Block is shown below:

```
ADVANCE RVEXPO(3,0.45)+RVEXPO(3,0.45)
```

The variance of a k-Erlang random variable with expected value μ is $(1/k)$th that of an exponential random variable with expected value μ. This means, for example, that if the step time for a job at a machine has a given expected value and follows the 2-Erlang distribution, its variance is only half the variance that would be in effect if the step time were exponentially distributed with the same expected value.

We use the Erlang distribution later in this chapter in Case Study 13B, where it is assumed that step times in a job shop follow Erlang distributions of order 2. Use of the Erlang is also called for in some of the exercises of Section 13.10.

13.9 Case Study 13A: A Model of a Hospital's Emergency Room

1. Statement of the Problem[1]

Patients arrive in Poisson fashion for treatment at a hospital's emergency room. Mean patient interarrival time is 30 minutes. Patients begin by seeing a nurse, who classifies 45 percent of them as CW (can wait), and the other 55 percent as NIA (need immediate attention). There is only one nurse who classifies patients. Classification time is 10 minutes, exponentially distributed.

Two doctors work in the emergency room. NIA patients have **higher priority** for seeing a doctor than CW patients. An NIA patient sees a doctor for an average of 45 minutes (exponentially distributed). Seventy-five percent of these patients then have to wait while lab tests are performed, whereas the other 25 percent are finished and can go home immediately.

When needed, lab tests take 30 minutes (exponentially distributed). After completion of the lab tests, NIA patients need to see a doctor again (either doctor), but they have lower priority than CW patients **who haven't yet seen a doctor**. They receive further treatment from the doctor for 15 minutes (exponentially distributed), and are discharged. Note that NIA patients must (potentially) wait to see a doctor on each of two occasions.

Whereas some NIA patients must see a doctor twice, CW patients only see a doctor once. As explained above, their priority is lower than that of NIA patients who haven't yet seen a doctor at all, but is higher than that of NIA patients waiting to see a doctor for the second time. Treatment of CW patients averages 30 minutes (exponentially distributed).

Build a model for this situation. Design the model to gather Queue information at each of the four points of potential waiting in the system. Simulate with the model through a 240-hour period, assuming no changes take place (in the patient interarrival time, the patient classification pattern, the number of doctors on duty, etc.) in the system during this period. (Such an assumption is unrealistic, of course. See Section 14.8.2.) Discuss the results of the simulation.

[1]Adapted from Banks and Carson, 1984.

Table 13A.1

Table of Definitions for Case Study 13A

Base Time Unit: 1 minute

GPSS/H Entity	**Interpretation**
Transactions	
Model Segment 1	Patients going through classification
Model Segment 2	NIA (need immediate-attention) patients
Model Segment 3	CW (can-wait) patients
Model Segment 4	A run-control Xact
Facilities	
NURSE	The Facility that models the nurse
Queues	
CWLINE	The Queue for can-wait patients waiting to see a doctor
NIALINE1	The Queue for need-immediate-attention patients waiting to see a doctor for the first time
NIALINE2	The Queue for need-immediate-attention patients waiting to see a doctor after lab tests have been performed
NURSE	The Queue for unclassified patients waiting to see the nurse
Storages	
DOCTORS	The Storage that models the doctors

2. Approach Taken in Building the Model

The logic of this model is straightforward. Patients are introduced into the model with one GENERATE Block (Priority 10), go through classification, and then are split into CW and NIA streams with a Statistical-Mode TRANSFER. NIA patients then get a Priority boost (Priority 15) relative to CW patients, see a doctor as soon as possible and then are split into "go home" and "lab testing needed" paths with another Statistical-Mode TRANSFER. On the lab-testing path, they are downgraded in Priority (Priority 5), wait for the lab test, see a doctor again, and then go home. Meanwhile, the CW patients see a doctor on the basis of their original Priority (10), then go home.

3. Table of Definitions

Table 13A.1 shows the Table of Definitions for Case Study 13A.

4. Block Diagram

Figure 13A.1 shows the Block Diagram for Case Study 13A.

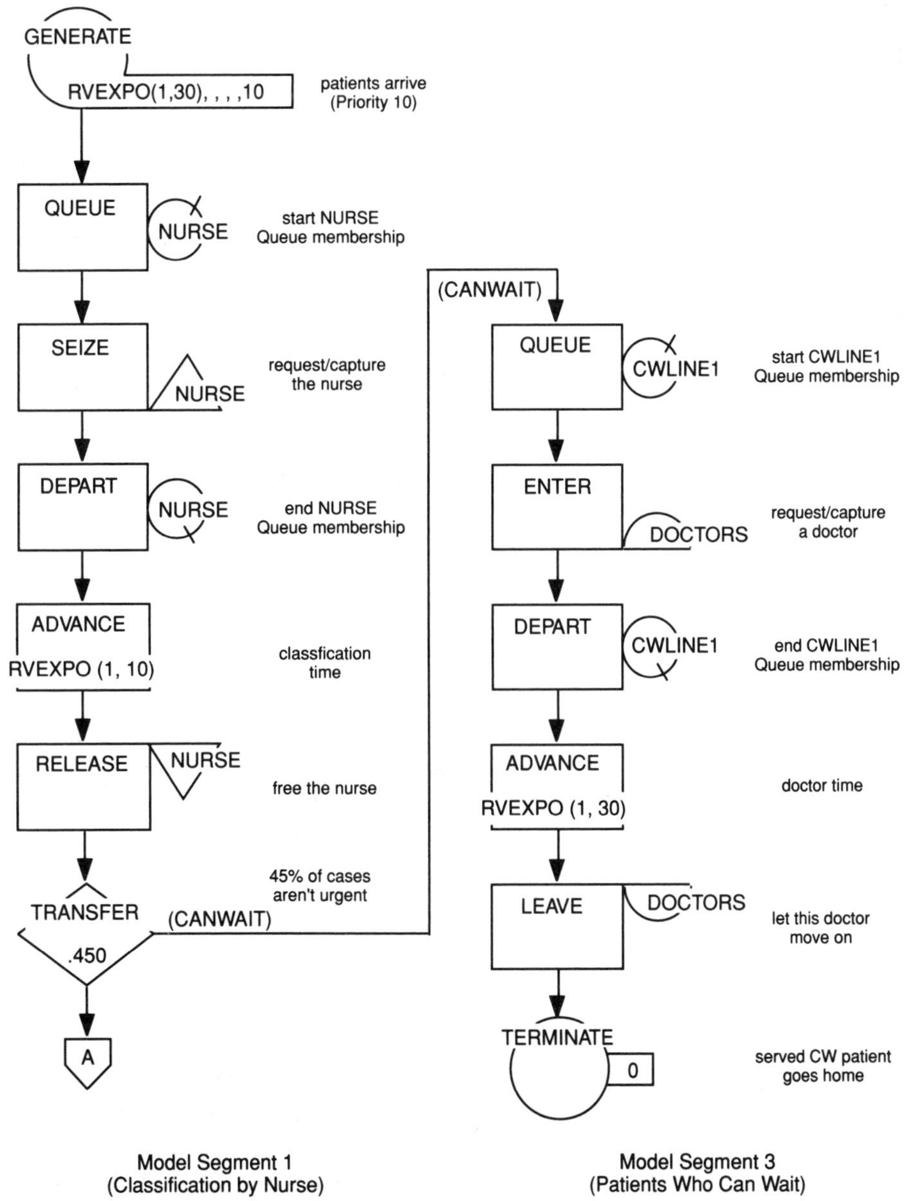

Figure 13A.1 *Block Diagram for Case Study 13A (continued on the next page)*

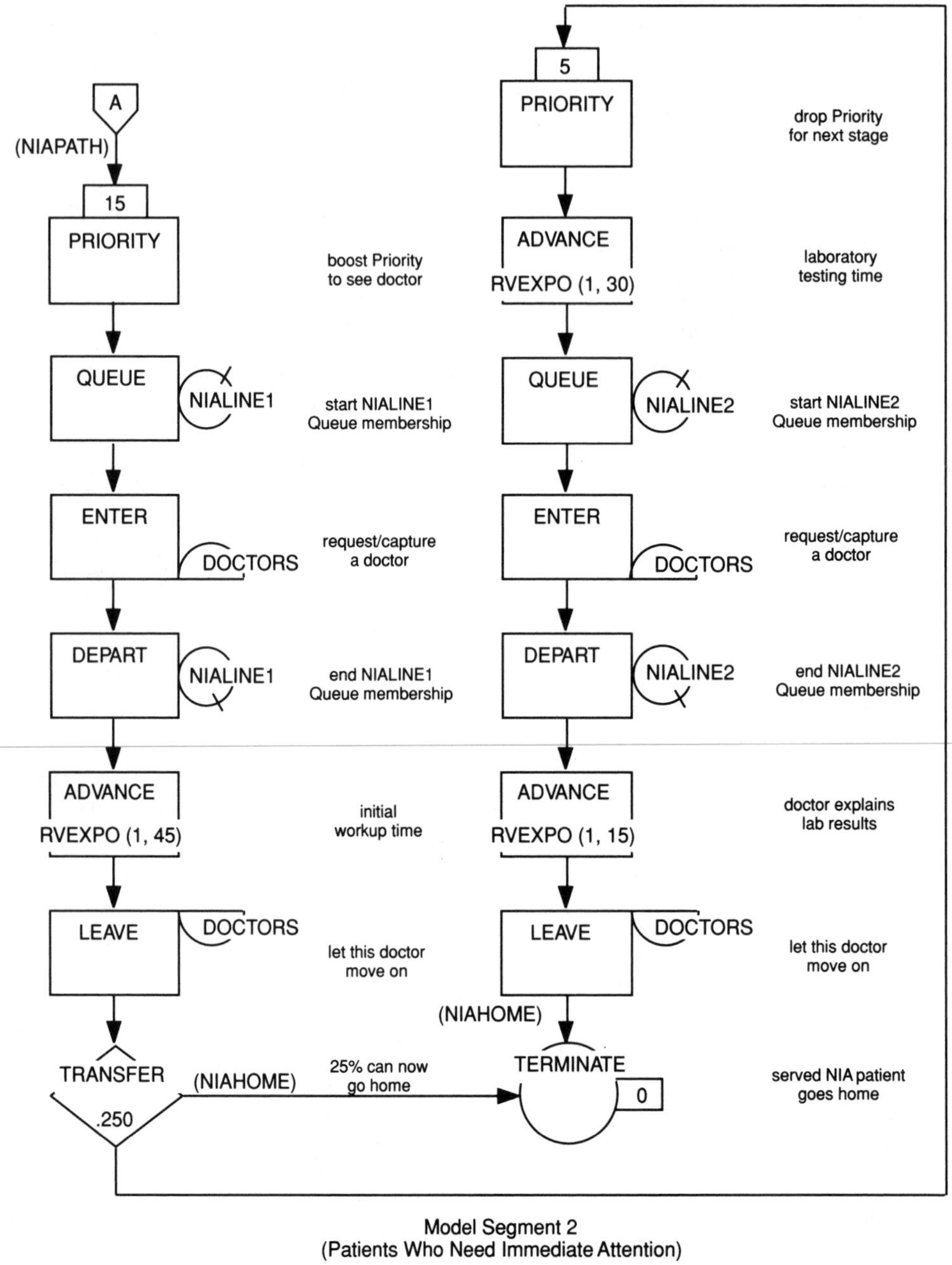

Figure 13A.1 *Block Diagram for Case Study 13A (Run-Control GENERATE/ TERMINATE Blocks Not Shown) (concluded)*

5. Modified Source Echo

Figure 13A.2 shows the Modified Source Echo for Case Study 13A.

6. Postsimulation Report

Figure 13A.3 shows the Postsimulation Report for Case Study 13A.

7. Discussion

Model Logic and Model Implementation. The following features of the model can be noted:

1. RN1 is used to sample from all input distributions throughout the model. Referring to the Modified Source Echo of Figure 13A.2, see how RN1 is specified for RVEXPO in Blocks 1, 5, 12, 16, 20, and

```
STMT#  BLOCK#  *LOC     OPERATION      A,B,C,D,E,F,G   COMMENTS

    1                   SIMULATE                                       Case Study 13A
    2           *                                    Model of a Hospital's Emergency Room
    3           *                                                 Base Time Unit: 1 Minute
    4           **********************************************************************
    5           *         Control Statements (STORAGE)                                *
    6           **********************************************************************
    7           *
    8           DOCTORS  STORAGE    2   doctors at the emergency room
    9           *
   10           **********************************************************************
   11           *         Model Segment 1 (Classification by Nurse)                   *
   12           **********************************************************************
   13           *
   14       1            GENERATE   RVEXPO(1,30),,,,10  patients arrive (Priority 10)
   15       2            QUEUE      NURSE               start NURSE Queue membership
   16       3            SEIZE      NURSE               request/capture the nurse
   17       4            DEPART     NURSE               end NURSE Queue membership
   18       5            ADVANCE    RVEXPO(1,10)        classification time
   19       6            RELEASE    NURSE               free the nurse
   20           *
   21       7            TRANSFER   .450,,CANWAIT       45% of cases aren't urgent
   22           *
   23           **********************************************************************
   24           *         Model Segment 2 (Patients Who Need Immediate Attention)     *
   25           **********************************************************************
   26           *
   27       8   NIAPATH  PRIORITY   15              boost Priority to see doctor
   28           *
   29       9            QUEUE      NIALINE1        start NIALINE1 Queue membership
   30      10            ENTER      DOCTORS         request/capture a doctor
   31      11            DEPART     NIALINE1        end NIALINE1 Queue membership
   32      12            ADVANCE    RVEXPO(1,45)    initial workup time
   33      13            LEAVE      DOCTORS         let this doctor move on
   34           *
   35      14            TRANSFER   .250,,NIAHOME   25% can now go home
   36           *
   37      15            PRIORITY   5               drop Priority for next stage
   38      16            ADVANCE    RVEXPO(1,30)    laboratory testing time
   39           *
   40      17            QUEUE      NIALINE2        start NIALINE2 Queue membership
   41      18            ENTER      DOCTORS         request/capture a doctor
   42      19            DEPART     NIALINE2        end NIALINE2 Queue membership
   43      20            ADVANCE    RVEXPO(1,15)    doctor explains lab results
   44      21            LEAVE      DOCTORS         let this doctor move on
   45           *
   46      22   NIAHOME  TERMINATE  0               served NIA patient goes home
   47           *
   48           **********************************************************************
   49           *         Model Segment 3 (Patients Who Can Wait)                     *
   50           **********************************************************************
   51           *
   52      23   CANWAIT  QUEUE      CWLINE1         start CWLINE1 Queue membership
   53      24            ENTER      DOCTORS         request/capture a doctor
   54      25            DEPART     CWLINE1         end CWLINE1 Queue membership
   55      26            ADVANCE    RVEXPO(1,30)    doctor time
   56      27            LEAVE      DOCTORS         let this doctor move on
   57           *
   58      28            TERMINATE  0               served CW patient goes home
   59           *
   60           **********************************************************************
   61           *         Model Segment 4 (Run-Control Xact)                          *
   62           **********************************************************************
   63           *
   64      29            GENERATE   14400       control Xact comes after 240 hours
   65      30            TERMINATE  1           reduce the TC by 1,
   66           *                               ending Xact movement
   67           *
   68           **********************************************************************
   69           *         Run-Control Statements                                      *
   70           **********************************************************************
   71           *
   72                    START      1               set TC = 1;  start Xact movement
   73           *
   74                    END                        end of Model-File execution
```

Figure 13A.2 *Modified Source Echo of the Case Study 13A Model File*

```
RELATIVE CLOCK: 14400.0000   ABSOLUTE CLOCK: 14400.0000
```

(a)

BLOCK	CURRENT	TOTAL	BLOCK	CURRENT	TOTAL	BLOCK	CURRENT	TOTAL
1		453	11		251	21		174
2		453	12	1	251	NIAHOME		248
3		453	13		250	CANWAIT		202
4		453	14		250	24		202
5		453	15		176	25		202
6		453	16		176	26		202
7		453	17	1	176	27		202
NIAPATH		251	18		175	CWHOME		202
9		251	19		175	29		1
10		251	20	1	175	30		1

(b)

FACILITY	--AVG-UTIL-DURING-- TOTAL TIME	AVAIL TIME	UNAVL TIME	ENTRIES	AVERAGE TIME/XACT	CURRENT STATUS	PERCENT AVAIL	SEIZING XACT	PREEMPTING XACT
NURSE	0.302			453	9.592	AVAIL			

(c)

STORAGE	--AVG-UTIL-DURING-- TOTAL TIME	AVAIL TIME	UNAVL TIME	ENTRIES	AVERAGE TIME/UNIT	CURRENT STATUS	PERCENT AVAIL	CAPACITY	AVERAGE CONTENTS	CURRENT CONTENTS	MAXIMUM CONTENTS
DOCTORS	0.750			628	34.410	AVAIL	100.0	2	1.501	2	2

(d)

QUEUE	MAXIMUM CONTENTS	AVERAGE CONTENTS	TOTAL ENTRIES	ZERO ENTRIES	PERCENT ZEROS	AVERAGE TIME/UNIT	$AVERAGE TIME/UNIT	QTABLE NUMBER	CURRENT CONTENTS
NURSE	5	0.111	453	331	73.1	3.527	13.098		0
NIALINE1	4	0.282	251	88	35.1	16.154	24.875		0
NIALINE2	17	1.726	176	59	33.5	141.204	212.409		1
CWLINE1	8	0.814	202	76	37.6	58.002	92.987		0

(e)

RANDOM STREAM	ANTITHETIC VARIATES	INITIAL POSITION	CURRENT POSITION	SAMPLE COUNT	CHI-SQUARE UNIFORMITY
1	OFF	100000	102414	2414	0.52

(f)

Figure 13A.3 *Postsimulation Report for Case Study 13A. (a) Clock Times. (b) Block Counts. (c) Facility Report. (d) Storage Report. (e) Queue Report. (f) RNG Report*

26. RN1 is also used transparently at the statistical TRANSFER Blocks (Blocks 7 and 14).

2. Patients arrive with a Priority of 10 (Block 1). Patients who "can wait" then retain this Priority throughout the model. Patients who "need immediate attention" have their Priority boosted to 15 (Block 8) before requesting a doctor (Block 10). Among these patients, those who need to see a doctor after lab tests have their Priority dropped to 5 (Block 15) before laboratory testing time elapses. After testing time has been completed, they return to the Current Events Chain and request a doctor (Block 18) on the basis of their Priority of 5.

Note carefully that the Priority boost from 10 to 15 of "need-immediate-attention" patients takes place without sending such patient-Xacts to the Future Events Chain **after** their Priority boost, but **before** they request a doctor on the basis of their updated Priority. This **could** lead to a modeling invalidity (albeit with **extremely** low probability) if one or more "can wait" patients are waiting for a doctor, and a doctor becomes free at exactly the same time the "need-immediate-attention" patient arrives. Here, we assume this probability is zero, for all practical purposes. (See Exercise 4 of Section 13.10.)

Postsimulation Output. In Figure 13A.3(d), note that the doctor utilization is only 75 percent. Despite this 75 percent doctor utilization, the average time patients spend waiting to see a doctor is quite extreme. Figure 13A.3(e) indicates, for example, that "can-wait" patients waited about 1 hour (58 minutes) on average to see a doctor. "Need-immediate-attention" patients waited over 2 hours on average (141 minutes) to see a doctor after having lab tests performed. In fact, the maximum number of such patients reached a level of 17. On the other hand, about one-third of such patients did not have to wait at all to see a doctor after lab tests had been performed. And so the individual patient experiences are highly variable.

13.10 Exercises

*1. These questions involve the use of random numbers coming from Table 13.1.

(a) Using the IAT_{sample} equation of Section 13.4 for sampling from a uniform distribution, verify the statement made in that section that the first arrival of a Type 1 mechanic in the model of Figure 13.2 will take place at time 254.6 (approximately).
(b) Assume Model Segments 1 and 2 in Figure 13.2 are interchanged. What then will be the approximate time of the first arrival of a Type 1 mechanic in the model?
(c) Refer to the Case Study 12A Block Diagram in Figure 12A.2. Approximately when will the first and second television sets be introduced into the model, and what will be the testing time of the first of these television sets?
(d) The model of Figure 13.2 is in the model9a2.gps file. Run the model in Test Mode and verify that the first arrival of a Type 1 mechanic takes place at time 254.6 (approximately), and that the second arrival of a Type 1 mechanic takes place at time 727.2 (approximately) as indicated in Section 13.4.
(e) The Case Study 12A model is in the model12a.gps file. Run the model in Test Mode and verify your answers for part (c) of this Exercise.

*2. These questions involve use of the built-in RVEXPO function.

(a) Show a GENERATE Block that will introduce Xacts into a model with exponentially distributed interarrival times if the mean arrival rate is 15 arrivals per hour. Assume the base time unit in the model is 1 second. Use RN5 as the basis for the sampling.
(b) Repeat (a), but now assume the base time unit in the model is 0.5 minutes, and use RN12 as the basis for the sampling.
(c) A service process is characterized by exponentially distributed service times with a mean of 36 minutes. Show an ADVANCE Block that can be used to model this service time in a model whose base time unit is 1 hour. Use RN2 as the basis for sampling from the service-time distribution.
(d) Repeat part (c), but now assume that the service time is 2-Erlang distributed.

3. (a) The model13a.gps file contains the Model File for Case Study 13A. Carry out a Batch simulation with the model. Compare numbers in the Postsimulation Report with those shown in Figure 13A.2.
(b) Carry out a Batch simulation with the Case Study 13A model with the duration of the simulation doubled. Compare the results with those of Figure 13A.2. How many patients arrived (compared to 453 in the case study)? What fraction of them needed immediate attention (compared to 251 out of 453 in the case study)? What was the Maximum Contents of the NIALINE2 Queue (compared to 17 in the case study)? What was the Average Contents of the CWLINE1 Queue (compared to 0.814 in the case study)?
(c) Repeat the Case Study 13A simulation, but change the exponential service-time distributions in the system to 2-Erlang distributions. Compare the Maximum Contents of the four Queues in the model in the Erlang simulation with those of the case study simulation. Would you expect these to be higher or lower in the Erlang simulation? (A 2-Erlang random variable has a variance that is half that of the exponential random variable having the same expected value.)
(d) Assume the arrival and service processes are deterministic in the Case Study 13A system. (But leave the statistical TRANSFER Blocks intact.) Carry out a simulation with a corresponding model. Compare results (especially Maximum Contents and Average Contents of the four Queues) with those of the case study simulation.

4. (a) In Case Study 13A, it's pointed out in the Model Logic and Implementation discussion that if one or more "can-wait" patients are waiting for a doctor, and a doctor becomes free at exactly the same time a "need-immediate-attention" patient arrives, a modeling invalidity will occur. (The probability of the indicated time tie is extremely small, however, meaning that the modeling invalidity has almost no

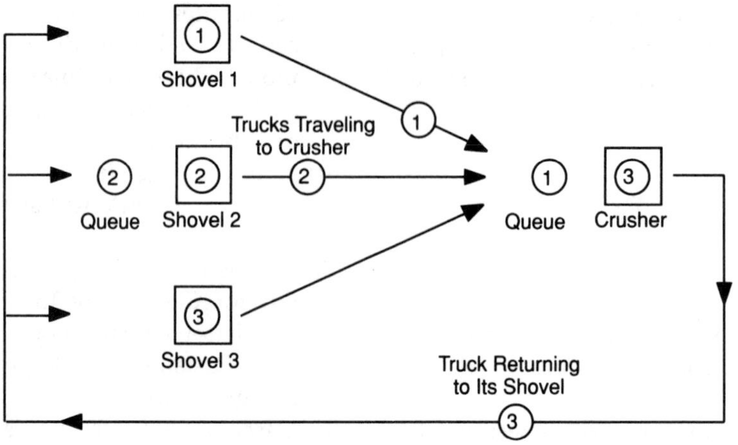

Figure E5

chance of occurring.) Suppose a friend doesn't understand why this circumstance would lead to a modeling invalidity. Explain to your friend what the modeling invalidity would be, and construct a detailed example you can use to show your friend exactly how the invalidity comes about.

(b) The potential modeling invalidity in (a) would be eliminated if "need-immediate-attention" patients had a reason to go to the Future Events Chain **after** their Priority boost to 15, but **before** they request a doctor. (See Section 12.10 in this regard.) Show how to modify the Case Study 13A model so that the "PRIORITY 15" Block can be placed ahead of the "classification time" ADVANCE Block, thereby eliminating any possibility that the modeling invalidity will occur.

5. Figure E5 provides a flow schematic for operations at a quarry. (This exercise is adapted from Pritsker, 1984, pp. 190 et seq.) The principal idea is that ore scooped from an open mine (a strip mine) is loaded onto trucks, to be transported to a crusher. Three shovels load ore onto trucks. Each shovel has three trucks dedicated to carrying ore from that shovel to the crusher. Two of each shovel's trucks are of 20-ton capacity, and the third is of 30-ton capacity.

In Figure E5, each truck is represented by a circled number that matches the number of that truck's shovel. Of the three trucks dedicated to Shovel 1, for example, one is being loaded in Figure E5, one is traveling with a load to the crusher, and one is waiting to unload at the crusher. (Figure E5 does not indicate which trucks are of 20-ton capacity and which are of 50-ton capacity.) Of the three trucks dedicated to Shovel 3, one is unloading at the crusher, one is en route to Shovel 3, and one is being loaded by Shovel 3.

Table E5 provides key data for the system. Loading and unloading times are exponentially distributed, whereas travel times are constant (as a first approximation).

Service order at the crusher is FCFS. Service order at the shovels, however, is "higher capacity, higher priority." (This is the inverse of an SPT service order.)

Build a model for the system as described. Design the model to measure the utilization of each shovel, the utilization of the crusher, and the utilization of the group of three trucks assigned to each shovel. (There will be three independent truck-group utilizations.) Assume

Table E5

	Mean or Constant Activity Time (minutes)			
Truck capacity (tons)	**Loading**	**Travel to Crusher**	**Unloading**	**Return to Shovel**
20	5.0	2.5	2.0	1.5
50	10.0	3.0	4.0	2.0

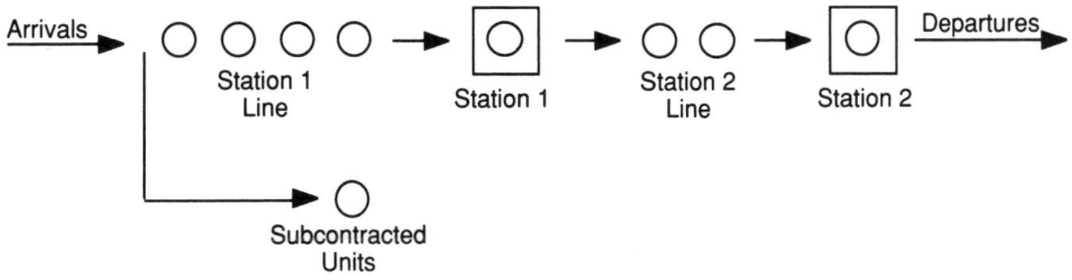

Figure E7

a truck is being utilized whenever it is not waiting for its shovel, or for the crusher. At the start of the simulation, the state of the system should correspond to Figure E5. You are to make up your own "time to go" data for trucks that are part way through activities in Figure E5, and you are to decide which of the trucks in Figure E5 are of 20-ton capacity and which are of 50-ton capacity.

Design the simulation to stop after an 8-hour shift has gone by. Carry out a batch simulation with the model. Discuss the resource utilizations reported in the output, and the extent to which the system seems to be balanced. (Does the system appear to be over capacity with respect to trucks, shovels, or the crusher?)

6. Repeat Exercise 5, only assume that loading and unloading times are 2-Erlang distributed. Compare and contrast the results with those of Exercise 5.

7. Figure E7 provides a flow schematic for a manufacturer's maintenance system. (This exercise is adapted from Pritsker, 1984, pp. 174 et seq.) The system consists of two workstations in series. A work station can only work on one unit at a time. Because of space constraints, the maximum number of units that can be waiting in the system is 6. (Counting units being worked on, then, the system has an 8-unit capacity.) In the Figure E7 configuration, 4 units of waiting space have been assigned to the line at Station 1 and 2 to the line at Station 2. When the system is at capacity (as in Figure E7), any new arrivals are sent to a subcontractor for maintenance.

   A finished unit at Station 1 is blocked (cannot leave Station 1) until there is room for it to move into the Station 2 line. While it is blocked, Station 1 cannot begin work on another unit.

   Arrivals are exponentially distributed with a mean of 0.4 time units. Service times at Stations 1 and 2 are exponentially distributed, with means of 0.25 and 0.50 time units, respectively. Travel times are negligibly small.

   Model this system, measuring station utilization, wait-space utilization, time in system, and the fraction of the time that Station 1 is blocked, and counting the number of units that are sent out for maintenance. Simulate for 300 time units with the model and discuss the Postsimulation Report.

8. Repeat Exercise 7, but now assume that the station activities have been modified, so that the mean times at Stations 1 and 2 are 0.35 and 0.40, respectively. (Note that their sum is still 0.75, as in Exercise 7.) Compare results with those of Exercise 7.

9. Repeat Exercise 7, but now assume the 6 units of waiting capacity are divided evenly between the Station 1 and Station 2 lines. Compare results with those of Exercise 7.

10. Repeat Exercises 7 and 9, but now assume interarrival and service times are 2-Erlang distributed. Compare results with those of Exercises 7 and 9.

13.11 Sampling from the Normal Distribution: RVNORM

The normal random variable, which is continuous and symmetric with respect to its expected value, takes on values ranging from minus infinity to plus infinity. A normal distribution is completely characterized by giving its expected value (μ) and its standard deviation (σ) or variance (σ^2). The probability density functions for normal random variables with expected value 0.0 in each case and standard deviations of 0.5, 1.0, and 2.0 are shown in Figure 13.5. The

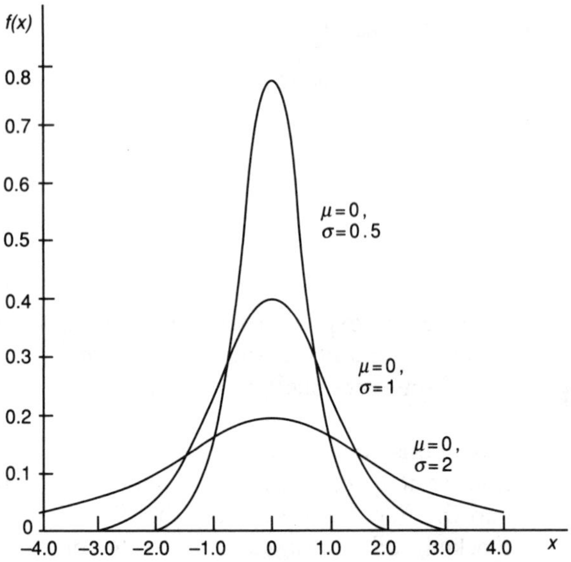

Figure 13.5 *Probability Density Functions for Normal Distributions with Expected Value (μ) 0.0 and Standard Deviations (σ) 0.5, 1.0, and 2.0. (Adapted from Pritsker, 1986.)*

normal random variable with expected value 0.0 and standard deviation (or variance) 1.0 is referred to as the **standard** normal random variable.

Figure 13.6 shows probability density functions for normal random variables with expected values of -1.0, 0.0, and 1.0, and a standard deviation of 1.0 in each case.

Table 13.2 shows the percentage of the values in a normal population falling within the indicated number of standard deviations of the expected value for a number of cases of interest. For example, 68.3 percent of the population falls within one standard deviation of the mean, 95.5 percent within two standard deviations of the mean, and 99.7 percent within three standard deviations of the mean. It's rarely necessary to consider normal values beyond three standard deviations of the mean, because virtually the entire population is included within this range.

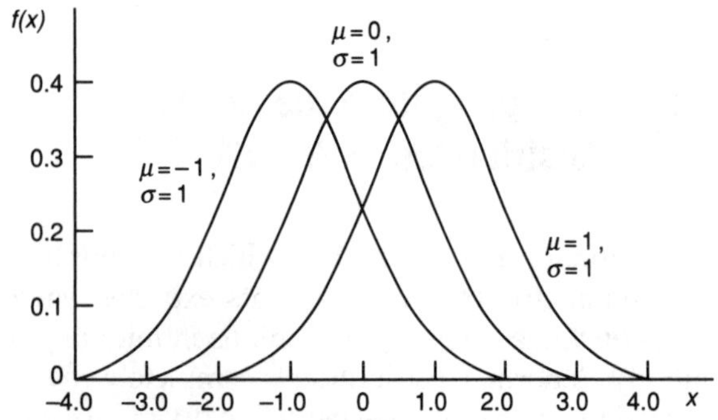

Figure 13.6 *Probability Density Functions for Normal Distributions with Expected Values (μ) -1.0, 0.0, and 1.0, and standard deviation (σ) 1.0. (Adapted from Pritsker, 1986.)*

Table 13.2

Percentage of a normal distribution falling within a specified number of standard deviations of the expected value

Interval	Percentage
$\mu \pm \sigma$	68.3
$\mu \pm 1.28\sigma$	80.0
$\mu \pm 1.65\sigma$	90.0
$\mu \pm 1.96\sigma$	95.0
$\mu \pm 2.0\sigma$	95.5
$\mu \pm 2.33\sigma$	98.0
$\mu \pm 2.575\sigma$	99.0
$\mu \pm 3\sigma$	99.7

A value from any normal distribution can be **standardized** (converted to the equivalent value from the **standard** normal distribution) by subtracting its expected value from it, then dividing this difference by its standard deviation. (Letting z be a value from a standard normal distribution and x be a value drawn from a normal distribution with mean μ and standard deviation σ, $z = (x - \mu)/\sigma$).

The Central Limit Theorem states that under a wide range of conditions, the distribution of the **sum** (or, equivalently, the **average**) of a series of independent, identically distributed random variables **from any distribution** approaches the normal as the number of terms in the sum becomes large. In most cases, the Central Limit Theorem is satisfied when sum of about 30 observations is involved (and is often satisfied for fewer than 30 observations). If the random variables come from a **normal** distribution, then the sum of two or more of these observations is normally distributed.

Simulation output variables are often normally distributed. For example, the time required to manufacture a unit of product may be normally distributed. This can be understood by considering that the time required to make a unit of product is the **sum** of a series of travel times, waiting times, and step (or operation) times, and so on. Similarly, the time to transmit a message in a communication system may be normally distributed, for much the same reason. Or the daily profit in a business may be a sum of various components, and so may be normally distributed.

Gordon points out that a normal distribution

> is characteristic of a variable that should have a specific value but is subject to random errors, usually due to a number of independent minor causes, each of which may equally well be positive or negative. A typical example is provided by a machining operation intended to produce parts of a standard size. Differences in such factors as metal hardness, tool setting, and temperature cause random errors, and in these circumstances it will frequently be found that the size is normally distributed. (Gordon, 1975, pp. 178–179)

A quick graphical check can be made to estimate whether observations might have come from a normal distribution. The check involves working with a special form of graph paper, called probability paper, on which the plot of a cumulative normal distribution will be a straight line. In conducting the check, the observed values are arranged in ascending order, and their relative frequencies in the sample are then used to form the corresponding cumulative frequencies. Using probability paper, the observed values are plotted on the linear-scale vertical axis against their cumulative frequencies on the nonlinear horizontal axis. If the observations are normally distributed, the points will come close to falling on a straight line. (Such a plot can be found in Banks and Carson, 1984, p. 342, and in Gordon, 1975, p. 180.) More formal evaluation can be conducted using goodness-of-fit testing.

A method frequently used to sample from a nonstandard normal distribution is to convert a sample from a 0–1 uniform distribution into a value from a standard normal, and then to convert the standard value into the equivalent value from the nonstandard normal population. The first step can be accomplished in a number of different ways (details are not provided here). The second step is accomplished by using the equation that relates a nonstandard to a standard normal random variable.

GPSS/H provides the built-in function **RVNORM** (**R**andom **V**ariate **NORM**al) for sampling from a normal distribution. RVNORM takes this form,

```
RVNORM(j,μ,σ)
```

where *j* indicates the modeler's choice of the **number** of a random-number generator and the expected value μ and standard deviation σ can be specified either with or without a decimal point. In GPSS/H, RVNORM returns values within plus or minus **43** standard deviations of the expected value, even though it's rarely necessary to consider normal values beyond three standard deviations from the mean.

Now consider the use of RVNORM for modeling normally distributed interarrival times. Interarrival times **cannot be negative**, and so RVNORM must be used with caution in this regard. We suggest these two guidelines:

1. Only assume normally distributed interarrival times if the expected value is at least three times greater than the standard deviation. (As pointed out in Table 13.2, 99.7 percent of a normal population falls within three standard deviations of the expected value. And so no more than 0.15 percent of the values will be negative if the expected value is at least three standard deviations greater than the mean.)
2. Perform an absolute value operation on the values returned by RVNORM, so that the very infrequent negative samples will be converted to their positive equivalents. The small discrepancies resulting from use of this absolute value approach will result in only very small deviations from a truly normal distribution and should be acceptable in light of other approximations and assumptions usually made in building simulation models.

Guideline 2 is accomplished by use of the built-in **ABS** function (**ABS**olute-value function) provided in GPSS/H. The ABS function takes the form

```
ABS(xpr)
```

where *xpr* stands in general for an arithmetic expression. ABS converts the arithmetic expression to its positive value. For example, the value of ABS(–7) is 7, the value of ABS(5.5) is 5.5, the value of ABS(3.2+4.8-10) is 2, and so on. (Formal discussion of arithmetic expressions in GPSS/H is not considered here.)

As an example of the use of RVNORM and ABS, suppose planes arrive in the air space over an airport with normally distributed interarrival times having a mean of 5.5 minutes and a standard deviation of 1 minute. Arbitrarily choosing RN7 as the RNG that supports sampling from the interarrival-time distribution, the following GENERATE Block can be used to introduce plane-Xacts into a model accordingly:

```
GENERATE ABS(RVNORM(7,5.5,1.0))
```

ABS(RVNORM(7,5.5,1.0)) has been specified as the GENERATE Block's A Operand, and the B Operand has a default value of zero. When the GENERATE Block is executed, the RVNORM function will first be evaluated. Next, the absolute value of RVNORM will be formed to determine a current value for the Block's A Operand. This value will then be used as the interarrival time in the ongoing Xact creation-and-scheduling process.

The same considerations that apply to normally distributed interarrival times also apply to normally distributed ADVANCE times. Suppose, for example, that service times are normally distributed with a mean of 250 and a standard deviation of 45. Then this ADVANCE Block could be used to simulate these holding times:

```
ADVANCE ABS(RVNORM(4,250,45))
```

In this example, RN4 has been arbitrarily chosen as the random-number generator used as the basis for the sampling.

13.12 Sampling from the Triangular Distribution: RVTRI

In this section we present the specifics of the triangular distribution, without indicating why the distribution is of interest. In the following section, we indicate the role that the triangular distribution can play in modeling.

The triangular random variable, which is continuous, is so named because its probability density function is triangular in shape. The distribution can be characterized by giving its **minimum**, **modal** (most likely), and **maximum** values. Density functions for three triangular distributions are shown in Figure 13.7. In all three cases, the minimum is 10, and the maximum is 50.

In the first case (Figure 13.7a), the modal (most likely) value is 15, resulting in a distribution skewed to the right. In the second case (Figure 13.7b) the model value, 30, is midway between the minimum and maximum, resulting in a symmetric triangular distribution. In the third case (Figure 13.7c), the modal value is 45, resulting in a distribution skewed to the left. In all three cases, the value of the density function at the modal value is 0.025. In general, this value equals 1/(maximum–minimum).

The **expected value** of a triangular distribution is the **average** of its minimum, modal, and maximum values. If the minimum and maximum are given, the average can be computed from the mode, and vice versa.

Because the density function for the triangular distribution is linear (with a discontinuity at the mode), its mathematical manipulation is straightforward, making it easy to convert a sample from a 0–1 uniform population into an equivalent sample from a specified triangular distribution. (Details can be found in many general simulation texts.)

In GPSS/H, the built-in function **RVTRI** can be used to sample from a triangular distribution. RVTRI takes this form

```
RVTRI(j,min,mode,max)
```

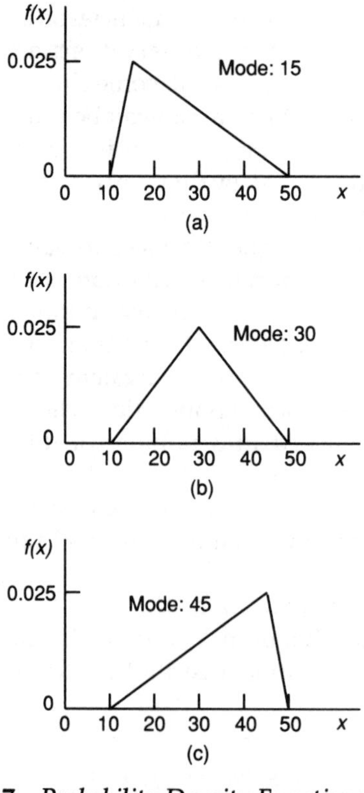

Figure 13.7 *Probability Density Functions for Triangular Distributions with a Minimum of 10, a Maximum of 50, and Modes of (a) 15, (b) 30, (c) 45*

where *j* indicates the modeler's choice of the **number** of a random-number generator, and *min*, *mode*, and *max* are the minimum, modal, and maximum values of the triangular distribution. These values can be supplied with or without a decimal point. (More generally, arithmetic expressions can be used to supply these values in GPSS/H.)

For example, suppose orders arrive at an order-processing point with triangularly distributed interarrival times. The minimum, modal, and maximum interarrival times are 15, 30, and 60 minutes, respectively. Arbitrarily choosing RN1 as the RNG that supports sampling from the interarrival time distribution, the following GENERATE Block can be used to introduce these orders into a model:

```
GENERATE RVTRI(1,15,30,60)
```

When the GENERATE Block is executed, RVTRI will be evaluated and the resulting sampled value will be used as the interarrival time in the ongoing Xact creation-and-scheduling process.

13.13 Using Limited Data to Characterize Distributions

One of the challenges in modeling involves estimating values for the data used in or needed by a model. This challenge comes up in modeling in general and includes a wide range of types of data, for example, costs, timings, reliability, maintainability, accuracy, reproducibility, and quality. These data are sometimes deterministic (or, as a first approximation, are assumed to be deterministic). For example, **how many tugboats** are needed in calm weather to pull an oil tanker of a specified size into a berth at an oil refinery? Perhaps the answer is "4 tugboats."

On the other hand, the situations for which data are needed often involve variability. For example, **how long** does it take in calm weather to pull an oil tanker of a specified size into berth? What is the **minimum** berthing time? What is the **average** berthing time? What is the **maximum** berthing time? (Perhaps the answers are that minimum, average, and maximum berthing times are about 20, 35, and 55 minutes, respectively.) What type of **probability distribution** is followed by the berthing-time random variable?

It is beyond our charter here to survey the issues involved in coming up with the data and distributions used to drive simulation models. General simulation texts and other literature (e.g., Carson, 1986) can be consulted for this purpose. We content ourselves with indicating briefly the simple use of limited data to characterize uniform, normal, and triangular distributions.

It has been suggested that sources of data, ranked in order of decreasing value, are time studies, historical records, vendor's claims, client's best guess (the client is the one for whom the modeling is being done), and modeler's best guess (Carson, 1986). We focus here on the client, assuming that the client (or one of the client's employees) is in a position to provide estimates ("guesstimates") of data values in cases where variability is involved.

As a specific example, suppose it's necessary to specify the distribution of interarrival times for ships coming to an existing harbor. Assume no records (data) are available. The harbor master (or someone familiar with the system) estimates the minimum interarrival time is 1 hour (60 minutes) and the maximum is 5 hours (300 minutes). If we assume the interarrival times are uniformly distributed, then the average interarrival time is 3 hours (180 minutes) and the half-range is 2 hours (120 minutes). If the base time unit in the model is 1 minute, then we can use "GENERATE 180,120" to introduce ship-Xacts into the harbor.

Another possibility would be to use the normal distribution. In this regard, the comments in this paragraph are paraphrased from Stahl (1990). Use of the **uniform** distribution in the above case means interarrival times vary between 60 and 300 minutes, and a value of 60.1, say, is just as likely as the average value of 180, whereas a value of 59.9 is not possible. This sudden drop from a uniform probability to a probability of zero when moving from one value to a very close neighboring value seems quite unrealistic. What the harbor master might mean in saying that interarrival times vary between 1 and 5 hours is that **most** of the values fall within this range. Some chance of realizing values falling outside this range should perhaps also be provided. This makes use of the normal distribution attractive, because then there is some small probability of realizing values that are quite far removed from the average value.

Like the uniform distribution, the normal distribution is symmetric, so we would estimate its expected value in the harbor example to be 180 minutes. One way we can estimate its standard deviation is by assuming that about **95 percent** of all interarrival times fall within the interval from 1 to 5 hours. This means that the **range** from 1 to 5 hours covers about 4 standard deviations. (See Table 13.2.) One standard deviation is then 1 hour, or 60 minutes. We can then use "GENERATE ABS(RVNORM(2,180,60))" to bring ship-Xacts into the harbor. (RNG 2 is specified arbitrary.) Of course, assuming the difference between the estimated minimum and maximum covers four standard deviations is a matter of choice. One could just as easily assume five or even six standard deviations, for example. The assumption made in this regard determines the probability of sampling values beyond the estimated minimum and maximum.

In the example we're working with, suppose the harbor master also estimates the **average** interarrival time is 3.5 hours (210 minutes). Then the interarrival times are not symmetrically distributed. (The estimated average is not midway between the estimated minimum and maximum.) In this case, a triangular distribution can be assumed. This requires that we use the estimated minimum, average, and maximum values to compute the **modal value**. (The harbor master may have a feeling for the **average** interarrival time, but may not have a feeling for the **modal**, or most likely, value.) The mode of a triangular distribution is computed from the minimum, avg, and maximum this way:

```
mode = 3 * avg - (minimum + maximum)
```

In our case, the mode would be 4.5 hours, or 270 minutes. We can then use "GENERATE RVTRI(2,60,270,300)" to bring ship-Xacts into the harbor. (RNG 2 is again specified arbitrarily.)

In a distribution, the mode clearly cannot be less than the minimum or more than the maximum. **Some estimated values of the average lead to a mode for the triangular distribution that violates this requirement**. In the harbor problem, for example, suppose the estimated average had been 4 hours. Then the mode would be 6 hours (3 * 4 – (1 + 5) = 6). But 6 is **outside the range of the distribution,** and so it's not possible to work with a triangular distribution in this case.

It's easy to determine the bound on the values of the **average** for a triangular distribution. The smallest feasible value for the mode is the minimum. This means the **smallest** feasible average is:

$$avg_{min} = (2 * minimum + maximum)/3$$

Similarly, the largest feasible value for the mode is the maximum. This means the **largest** feasible average is:

$$avg_{max} = (minimum + 2 * maximum)/3$$

If the mode equals the minimum, the density function takes the form of a **right triangle** skewed to the right. At the other extreme, if the mode equals the maximum, the density function takes the form of a right triangle skewed to the left. RVTRI can be used to sample from these degenerate forms of a triangular distribution, as well as from the more general form.

If an estimated average is midway between the minimum and maximum, then a uniform, normal, or symmetric triangular distribution can be assumed. A potential advantage of the normal versus the triangular in this case is that values outside the estimated minimum and maximum can occur from time to time, with a controllably small probability. (Sometimes modelers work with a "10–90" triangular distribution, treating the estimated minimum as the tenth percentile, and the estimated maximum as the ninetieth percentile. GPSS/H does not have a built-in function for sampling from the 10–90 triangular distribution.)

The building of simulation models can and often does begin before data collection has been completed, and perhaps before data collection has even started. The logical structure of a model doesn't require that the modeler have data in hand while building the model. The modeler can use reasonable guesstimates and assume simple distributional forms (e.g., uniform) when making trial runs to test the **logic** of the model.

There may be some merit in starting model building **before** starting data collection, because the model itself determines what input data will be needed to drive the model. However, a **permanent** lack of some types of data may place limitations or restrictions on the model, such as impacting the level of detail that can be represented meaningfully in the model.

We conclude this section by pointing out that a model can be used to perform data-related sensitivity analysis without data collection having yet started. A model is a filter that maps sampled values of input variables into observed values of output variables. How sensitive are a model's outputs to assumptions made about its inputs? In a model of a large manufacturing system, how much does it matter whether the running time until failure of a class of machines is assumed to be uniformly distributed between 250 and 400 hours, or uniformly distributed between 300 and 350 hours, or normally distributed with 95 percent of the values falling in the range from 275 to 375 hours? What if it is assumed there is **no** variation in running time until failure? Experiments can be conducted with the model to investigate the answers to questions of this type. The findings may influence the extent of data collection that eventually takes place.

13.14 Exercises

*1. Show a GENERATE Block that will introduce Xacts into a model with triangularly distributed interarrival times when the minimum, average, and maximum interarrival times are 10, 18, and 30 minutes, respectively. Assume a base time unit of 1 minute is being used in the model. Base the sampling on RN7.

*2. Repeat Exercise 1, but now assume that the interarrival times follow a symmetric triangular distribution with minimum and maximum interarrival times corresponding to those in Exercise 1.

*3. Show an ADVANCE Block at which holding times range from 5 to 50 minutes 99.7 percent of the time and are normally distributed. Assume a base time unit of 1 minute is being used in the model. Base the sampling on RN2.

*4. Repeat Exercise 3, but now assume the holding times range from 5 to 50 minutes 98 percent of the time.

5. Repeat Exercise 5 of Section 13.10, except now assume that loading and unloading times are normally distributed, with means equal to those of Exercise 5 and standard deviations equal to 20 percent of the means. Compare the results with those of Exercise 5.

6. Repeat Exercise 7 of Section 13.10, except now assume interarrival times are normally distributed, with standard deviation equal to 35 percent of the mean, and Station 1 and Station 2 times are triangularly distributed, with means equal to those of Exercise 7. Assume minimum and maximum Station 1 times are 75 percent of the mean and twice the mean, respectively. Assume minimum and maximum Station 2 times are 50 percent and 150 percent of the mean, respectively. Compare the results with those of Exercise 7.

13.15 Sampling from Discrete Distributions: D-Functions

In this section, we first show how to define Functions for sampling from discrete distributions. Then we show how GPSS/H interprets and evaluates such Functions. Section 13.16 explains how these Functions are used to supply the values of Block Operands.

Suppose that the time required to drill holes in castings is determined by the number of holes to be drilled and that the number of holes to be drilled depends on the type of casting involved. As shown in Table 13.3, it takes 4 minutes to drill 1 hole in a 1-hole casting, 7.5 minutes to drill 2 holes of a 2-hole casting, and so on. As many as 5 holes may be drilled, which requires 16.5 minutes. (There are some economies of scale in drilling 2 holes instead of 1, and 3 instead of 2, but then it takes an additional 3 minutes to drill a fourth hole and another 3 minutes to drill a fifth.)

As also indicated in Table 13.3, 20 percent of the castings are of the type that need to have 1 hole drilled in them, 35 percent are of the type which need to have 2 holes drilled in them, and so on. Because the number of holes to be drilled depends on the type of casting involved, which varies at random, drilling time itself can be modeled as varying at random. In this case, however, drilling time is a discrete (not continuous) random variable, because the drilling-time variable only takes on specific values from a limited number of possibilities (not any value from some interval).

Figure 13.1 illustrates the process of mapping a sample from a uniform 0-1 distribution into an equivalent value from a **continuous** distribution of interest. Figure 13.8 is similar in spirit to Figure 13.1, but illustrates the idea of mapping a sample from a

Table 13.3

Relative frequencies for the time required to drill holes in castings

No. of Holes to Be Drilled	Drilling Time	Relative Frequency
1	4.0	0.20
2	7.5	0.35
3	10.5	0.15
4	13.5	0.10
5	16.5	0.20

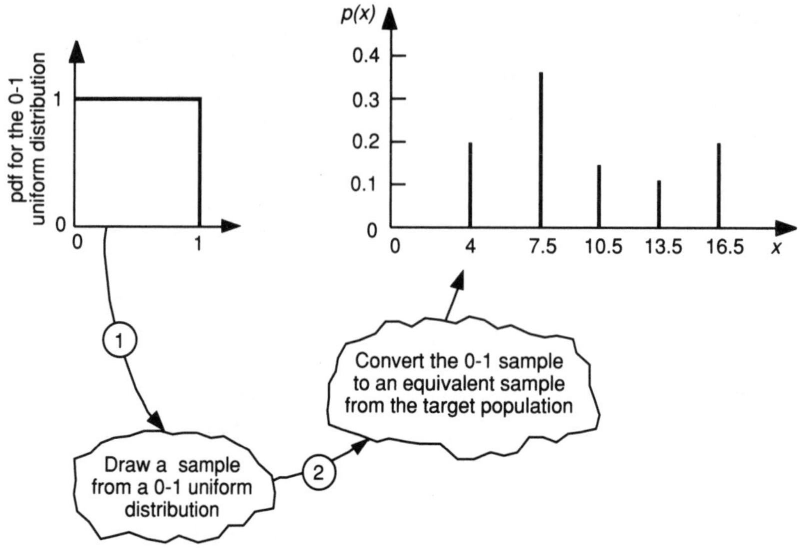

Figure 13.8 *A Two-Step Process for Sampling from a Discrete Distribution*

uniform 0–1 distribution into an equivalent value from a **discrete** distribution, and in particular from the discrete distribution corresponding to Table 13.3. (Note that the two vertical scales in Figure 13.8 differ.)

GPSS/H doesn't have built-in functions for sampling from empirical distributions such as that of Table 13.3. However, GPSS/H does offer the tools needed to define customized discrete functions to sample from whatever empirical distributions may be of interest. In defining such functions, we specify our choice of a random-number generator to be used as the starting point for the sampling process. Defining the function also requires that we indicate both the values that occur in the discrete population, and their frequencies of occurrence. We don't supply the **relative** frequencies, but the **cumulative** frequencies. Table 13.4 repeats Table 13.3, but additionally shows the cumulative frequencies (column 4 in the table) for various drilling-time values. The cumulative frequency for the **first** drilling time in the list equals its relative frequency. The cumulative frequency for the **remaining** j drilling times ($j = 2, 3, 4$, and 5) is the jth relative frequency, plus the sum of the preceding relative frequencies. The first drilling time (4 minutes) has a cumulative frequency of 0.20, the second (7.5 minutes) has a cumulative frequency of 0.55 (0.35 + 0.20), and so on.

A modeler defines GPSS/H Functions with a FUNCTION Control Statement, followed by one or more Function Follower Statements. The format of these statements is shown in Figure 13.9. The first type of statement in Figure 13.9, a FUNCTION Control Statement, always contains five pieces of information, as follows:

1. The required ***Label*** is the modeler's choice of an **identifier** for the Function. Function identifiers are formed the same way as identifiers for Facilities, Queues, Storages, and Blocks.
2. The **Operation** field contains the word **FUNCTION**.
3. The **A Operand** supplies the modeler's choice of an ***argument*** for the Function. A Function maps the value of one variable (the Function's argument) into a value of another variable (the value that the Function produces when it is evaluated). If a Function is being defined to sample from a distribution, then its argument

Table 13.4

Table 13.3 extended to show drilling-time cumulative frequencies

No. of Holes to Be Drilled	Drilling Time	Relative Frequency	Cumulative Frequency
1	4.0	0.20	0.20
2	7.5	0.35	0.55
3	10.5	0.15	0.70
4	13.5	0.10	0.80
5	16.5	0.20	1.0

```
 label   FUNCTION  argument,type_count     FUNCTION Control Statement
x1,y1/x2,y2/x3,y3/.../xcount,ycount        Function Follower Statement
```

Figure 13.9 The Format of a FUNCTION Control Statement and a Function Follower Statement

takes the form of a 0–1 uniform random number generator, for example, RN5.

4. The **first character** in the **B Operand** is a letter that indicates the ***type*** of Function being defined. For example, the letter **D** signals that the Function is a **D**iscrete Function. (In addition to Discrete Functions, there are five other types of Functions in GPSS/H.)

5. The rest of the **B Operand** is an integer that provides the ***count*** of the number of **ordered pairs of points** being supplied to define the Function. In a Discrete Function, this count equals the number of alternative values that the Function can produce. (In a Discrete Function used to sample from a distribution, this count equals the number of values in the population.)

The second statement in Figure 13.9 is a **Function Follower Statement**. One or more statements of this type contain the ordered pairs of points supplied to define the Function. The first member of an ordered pair (x_1, x_2, x_3, etc., in Figure 13.9) is a value of the Function's argument. The second member of the ordered pair (y_1, y_2, y_3, etc., in Figure 13.9) is a value that the Function can produce. If a Function is defined to sample from a distribution, the first member of each ordered pair is a cumulative frequency. The second member is the corresponding value of the random variable.

In a Follower statement, keying begins in **column 1**. As indicated in Figure 13.9, a comma separates the first and second members of an ordered pair. A slash (/) separates consecutive ordered pairs. Blanks are not used. (The first occurrence of a blank causes the GPSS/H compiler to treat any remaining characters in the statement as a **comment**.)

Let x_i be the **first** member of the ith ordered pair, i = 1, 2, 3, ..., as in Figure 13.9. In a Follower statement, it is required that $x_1 < x_2 < x_3$, and so on. (The reason is given shortly.)

Using the format of Figure 13.9, Figure 13.10 shows the definition of a Discrete Function that can be used to sample from the drilling-time distribution of Table 13.4. The Function's identifier is **DRILTIME**. Its argument is **RN7**. It is a **D**iscrete, **5**-point Function. The x and y members of the ordered pairs in Figure 13.10 come from columns 4 and 2, respectively, in Table 13.4.

Note carefully that the argument in the Figure 13.10 FUNCTION Control Statement is not just the number "7," but takes the form "RN7." This differs from the way the supporting random-number generator is specified when using the RVEXPO, RVNORM, and RVTRI Functions in GPSS/H. For example, "RVEXPO(7,25.5)" can be used to sample from the exponential distribution with mean 25.5, using random-number generator 7 as the basis for sampling. Here, just the number "7" (not "RN7") is used in specifying random-number generator 7.

The ordered pairs in a Follower statement cannot extend beyond column 72. However, **more than one** Follower statement can be used to define a Function. For example, the Function of Figure 13.10 could be defined as shown in Figure 13.11, where the first two ordered pairs are on the first Follower statement, the third pair is on a second statement, and the remaining two pairs are on a third statement. (An ordered pair **cannot** be split between two consecutive Follower statements.) Note that the **last** pair in a Follower statement is not followed by a slash, nor is a slash used to start the first pair on the next Follower statement. The slash is only used to separate consecutive pairs entered on the same Follower statement.

When keying values into Follower statements, unnecessary zeros and/or decimal points need not be provided, although they can be. For example, the first pair in Figure 13.10 is keyed as ".2,4," but could have been keyed as "0.20,4.0," and so on.

```
DRILTIME FUNCTION RN7,D5                 FUNCTION Control Statement
.2,4/.55,7.5/.7,10.5/.8,13.5/1,16.5      Function Follower Statement
```

Figure 13.10 A Discrete Function for Sampling from the Table 13.3 Distribution

```
DRILTIME FUNCTION    RN7,D5    FUNCTION Control Statement
.2,4/.55,7.55                  ...first Function Follower Statement
.7,10.5                        ...second Function Follower Statement
.8,13.5/1,16.5                 ...third Function Follower Statement
```

Figure 13.11 *An Alternative Way to Define the Discrete Function of Figure 13.10*

Figure 13.12 provides a graphical interpretation for the Discrete Function of Figure 13.10. Values of the Function's argument, RN7, are shown on the horizontal axis, and values that the function can produce are shown on the vertical axis. The plot of **a Discrete Function consists of a series of horizontal steps**. The height of the first step is y_1, the height of the second step is y_2, and so on. As shown in Figure 13.12, the first step spans the range of argument values from zero to x_1, the second step spans the range from x_1 to x_2, and so on. The leftmost step is **open** on 0.0 (because RN7 is open on 0.0) and **closed** on x_1. The open end of an interval is denoted in Figure 13.12 with an **open** circle; the closed end of an interval is denoted with a **closed** (that is, filled-in) circle. As Figure 13.12 indicates, each step except the rightmost is open on the left and closed on the right. Like the other steps, the rightmost step is open on the left, too, but it's also open on the right (because RN7 is open on 1.0).

Stated another way, the first step in Figure 13.12 covers RN7 values from 0^+ through 0.2, inclusive. The second step covers RN7 values from 0.2^+ through 0.55, inclusive. And so on. The rightmost step covers RN7 values from 0.8^+ through 1.0^-.

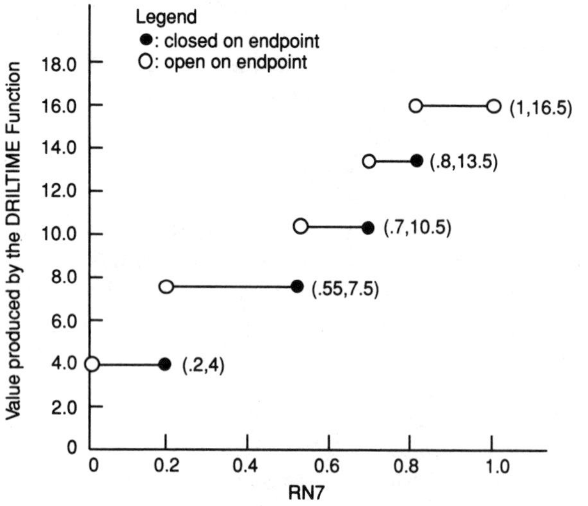

Figure 13.12 *A Graphical Interpretation for the Figure 13.10 D-Function*

Now consider the procedure followed by GPSS/H to evaluate the Figure 13.10 Function. To evaluate any modeler-defined Function, GPSS/H first determines the current value of the Function's argument. The argument of the Figure 13.10 Function is RN7, so GPSS/H fetches a value from RN7. GPSS/H then uses the Function-defining ordered pairs to map this RN7 value into a corresponding value for the DRILTIME Function. A **left-to-right table lookup** is used to do this mapping. If the value of RN7 falls into the interval covered by the **first** step in Figure 13.12, then the Function's value will be 4 on this occasion, or if the value of RN7 falls into the interval covered by the **second** step, then the Function's value will be 7.5 on this occasion, and so on. (Because the table lookup is **left-to-right**, you can see the reason for the requirement stated earlier that $x_1 < x_2 < x_3$, and so on, when defining a Function.)

It's not necessary that the steps making up a Discrete Function form an ascending staircase, as they do in Figure 13.12. The steps will ascend only if the values of the random variable have been arranged in **ascending order** prior to forming their cumulative frequencies and defining the Function. This is the case in Table 13.4. Table 13.5 shows an alternative approach in which the values of the drilling-time variable have been ordered by **decreasing relative frequencies.**

The DRILTIME Function corresponding to the arrangement of information in Table 13.5 is shown in Figure 13.13. If this version of the DRILTIME Function is plotted, the steps making up the Function will form an "up and down" pattern, not an ascending staircase.

Table 13.5
An alternative form of the information in Table 13.4

No. of Holes Being Drilled	Drilling Time	Relative Frequency	Cumulative Frequency
2	7.5	0.35	0.35
1	4.0	0.20	0.55
5	16.5	0.20	0.75
3	10.5	0.15	0.90
4	13.5	0.10	1.0

```
 DRILTIME FUNCTION  RN7,D5                  FUNCTION Control Statement
.35,7.5/.55,4/.75,16.5/.9,10.5/1,13.5       Function Follower Statement
```

Figure 13.13 *A Discrete Function for Sampling from the Drilling-Time Distribution as Arranged in Table 13.5*

The Figure 13.13 version of the DRILTIME Function will take somewhat less computer time to evaluate on average than the version of Figure 13.10. Arranging the variable in order of **decreasing** relative frequencies in Table 13.5 means the first step (interval) in the Function is the **widest**, the second step is the next widest, and so on. In the **left-to-right** procedure used for Function evaluation, not as many steps will have to be examined, on average, to find the interval which covers the current value of RN7. (The small savings in computer time will not be of practical interest unless a Function consists of dozens of ordered pairs of points, which can easily be the case in practice.)

The FUNCTION Control Statement is the fifth type of Control Statement introduced up to this point. (The other four types are SIMULATE, START, END, and STORAGE.) Like all Control Statements, a FUNCTION statement is **executed** by GPSS/H sometime **after** the Model File has been compiled. Execution of this statement causes the specified Function definition to be put into effect.

Where is a FUNCTION statement (and its Follower statement or statements) placed in a Model File? We want a Function's definition made operational **before** Xact movement begins. After model compilation, GPSS/H goes into Control-Statement execution, executing all Control Statements appearing in the Model File **prior** to the START statement (see Figure 2.19 of Chapter 2). This means FUNCTION statements should be placed in the Model File **ahead of** the START statement. For example, FUNCTION statements can be included in a Model File between the SIMULATE statement and the Block statements, as indicated by the "Other Control Statements (if any)" box in Figure 11.5 of Chapter 11.

An example of a model containing FUNCTIONs is given in Case Study 13B.

13.16 Using Discrete Functions at GENERATE and ADVANCE Blocks

The pattern used for referring to a modeler-defined Function takes this form,

```
FN(identifier)
```

where **FN** is the **class name** for modeler-defined Functions and ***identifier*** represents the identifier the modeler has chosen for the Function. The syntax used to refer to the DRILTIME Function of Figure 13.10, for example, is

```
FN(DRILTIME)
```

The Function-referencing pattern uses the Function's identifier to index the class name for Functions. (The syntax is similar to that used with singly subscripted variables in a programming language.)

As with Facilities, Queues, Storages, and so on, Function identifiers can also be positive whole numbers, such as 2, or 5, or 7. This means that Function references such as FN(5) are valid. GPSS/H also supports an alternative referencing pattern in which parentheses aren't used. For example, FN5 is a valid alternative for FN(5). The corresponding nonparenthesized form that applies in the case of symbolic identifiers uses a dollar sign ($) to separate the class name from the symbolic identifier. FN$DRILTIME is an example of this syntax. We stick strictly with the **FN(*identifier*)** form here and use only symbolic identifiers.

If the DRILTIME Function describes the distribution of holding times at an ADVANCE Block, then the ADVANCE takes this form:

```
ADVANCE FN(DRILTIME)
```

FN(DRILTIME) has been specified as the ADVANCE Block's A Operand, and the B Operand has a default value of zero. When the ADVANCE is executed, the DRILTIME Function will be evaluated and the value it produces will be used as the holding time. (Recall that a GENERATE B Operand defaults to zero, which explains why the value of the A Operand will not be modified in this example.)

The procedure for referring to modeler-defined Functions at ADVANCE Blocks similarly applies at GENERATE Blocks.

13.17 Other Applications for Discrete Random Variables

Interarrival times and/or service times don't usually come from a discrete distribution. (Values of these variables are usually determined by sampling from an interval, and so come from a continuous distribution.) There are many other settings, however, in which random variables are discrete. For example, order size (the number of units being ordered) might be a discrete random variable, so might the number of defects in a product, or the number of workers who are absent at the beginning of a shift, and so on. The particulars of these settings will not be discussed here.

13.18 Use of a Function to Determine a Transaction's Next Block at Random

Transactions can use the Statistical-mode TRANSFER Block of Chapter 12 to determine their Next Block at random from a set of two candidates. In this section, we introduce a method for having Xacts select their Next Block at random from a set of two **or more** candidates. The method uses the unconditional TRANSFER, as we will see.

In an unconditional TRANSFER, the B Operand points to the Location occupied by a Transaction's Next Block. The pointing is accomplished by labeling the Next Block, then using the label as the unconditional TRANSFER's B Operand. Until now, we've always supplied the value of this B Operand directly, by putting a Label in the B-Operand position. But the value can be supplied indirectly. For example, the B Operand can refer to a Function, with the value produced by the Function being the label on a Block. The Xact at the unconditional TRANSFER will then take that labeled Block as its Next Block.

Consider the example shown in Figure 13.14. The Discrete Function named JOBPATH has an RNG as its argument, so the value of its argument is determined at random, which means the Function produces a value at random. The y_i's used to define the Function aren't **numbers**, but are **Block Labels.** (When the y_i's used to define Discrete Functions take the form of identifiers, as in Figure 13.14, then these identifiers must be Block Labels.) And so the JOBPATH Function produces a randomly determined Block Label.

Suppose an Xact executes the TRANSFER Block of Figure 13.14. To determine the current value of the Block's B Operand, the JOBPATH Function has to be evaluated. If the Function produces PATH2 as its value, then the Xact at the TRANSFER Block will take the Block labeled PATH2 as its Next Block.

The Figure 13.14 JOBPATH Function will produce PATH1 with probability 0.2, PATH2 with probability 0.6, and PATH3 with probability 0.2. And so the "unconditional" TRANSFER of Figure 13.14 isn't unconditional after all. It determines an Xact's Next Block not deterministically, but at random, per the specifications of the JOBPATH Function.

Figure 13.14 presents the modeler's perspective. Consider the compiler's perspective. When the model is compiled, Location numbers are assigned to all Blocks in the model. If a Label is attached to a Block, the Label becomes a synonym for the number of the Location occupied by the Block. In turn, the y_i values in the JOBPATH Function of Figure 13.14 are just numbers in the compiled version of the model. (For example, the Block Label NIAPATH is a synonym for 2 in the Case Study 13A model. See Statement 27 in Figure 13A.2.) And an Xact's Next Block is just a number. At execution time, the Figure 13.14 TRANSFER Block operates with the numeric equivalent of the Labels.

```
          ...
 JOBPATH  FUNCTION    RN1,D3            ...an RNG is the argument
.2/PATH1/.8,PATH2/1,PATH3               ...the yi's are Block Labels
          ...
          TRANSFER    ,FN(JOBPATH)      ..."unconditional" TRANSFER
          ...
```

Figure 13.14 Example for Use of a Function at a TRANSFER Block

The question springs to mind, could identifiers for Facilities, Queues, Storages, and so on be used in a Discrete Function like that of Figure 13.14? The answer is **no**. Identifiers used in a Discrete Function are **always** Block Labels. (There is another type of GPSS/H Function, however, for which Facility, or Queue, or Storage, and so on, identifiers **can be used** as y elements in the (x,y) pairs of points that define the Function. Particulars are not discussed here.)

13.19 Other Applications for Functions

Modeler-defined GPSS/H Functions can be used in many ways, not just to sample from probability distributions. A Function simply maps the value of one variable (the Function's argument) into another value (the value the Function produces when it is evaluated). A Function whose argument is of the form RNj (j = 1, or 2, or ...) is used to sample from a probability distribution. But Function arguments are not limited to taking the form of a reference to a random-number generator. A Function's argument might refer to the value of the simulated clock, or to the Current Contents of a Queue, or to the Average Holding Time per Capture of a Facility, or to the Capacity of a Storage, and so on. (Operational details will not be discussed here.) A Function's argument can even take the form of a reference to another Function. In general, Functions are a very useful tool in GPSS/H modeling.

13.20 Sampling from Continuous Distributions: C-Functions

The drilling-time variable of Section 13.15 is a case of a **discrete** variable that follows a distribution for which there may be no theoretical counterpart. We've seen that in such cases, the modeler defines a GPSS/H Function to describe **in numeric terms** the distribution followed by the random variable. A Discrete Function (a D-Function) is used for this purpose.

There are also times when a random variable is **continuous** and follows a distribution for which there may be no theoretical counterpart. In such cases, the modeler also defines a GPSS/H Function to describe in numeric terms the distribution followed by the continuous random variable. The type of Function used for this purpose is a **Continuous Function** (a C-Function).

The only **definitional** difference between a C-Function and a D-Function is that the letter **C** (instead of the letter **D**) is used as the first character in the B-Operand of the FUNCTION Control Statement to indicate the Function's ***type***.

The **computational** difference between C- and D-Functions is that GPSS/H interprets a C-Function as consisting of a series of straight-line segments that connect the Function-defining ordered pairs of points (instead of as a series of horizontal steps determined by the Function-defining ordered pairs). To evalute a Continuous Function, GPSS/H first does a left-to-right table lookup (just as with a D-Function) to find the interval that covers the current value of the Function's argument. Then GPSS/H does a linear interpolation over this interval to convert the value of the argument into a value for the C-Function.

Figure 13.15 shows the statements defining a C-Function named BANKSERV. (The context from which the BANKSERV Function comes will be described shortly.) Figure 13.16 shows the graphical interpretation for the Figure 13.15 C-Function. The ordered pairs of points defining the Function are shown as circles in Figure 13.16. Filled circles are used for the interior points, because the corresponding x values can be assumed by the Function's argument, and the corresponding y values can be produced by the Function. Open circles are used for the two outside points, because the x values of 0 and 1 are not assumed by the Function's argument, and the corresponding y values cannot be produced by the Function.

As indicated in Figure 13.16, if the current value of the BANKSERV Function's argument is 0.55, then the value of the Function produced by linear

```
 BANKSERV FUNCTION  RN4,C6      FUNCTION Control Statement
0,60/.07,120/.23,180/.73,240    first Follower statement
.92,300/1,360                   second Follower statement
```

Figure 13.15 *An Example of a Continuous Function*

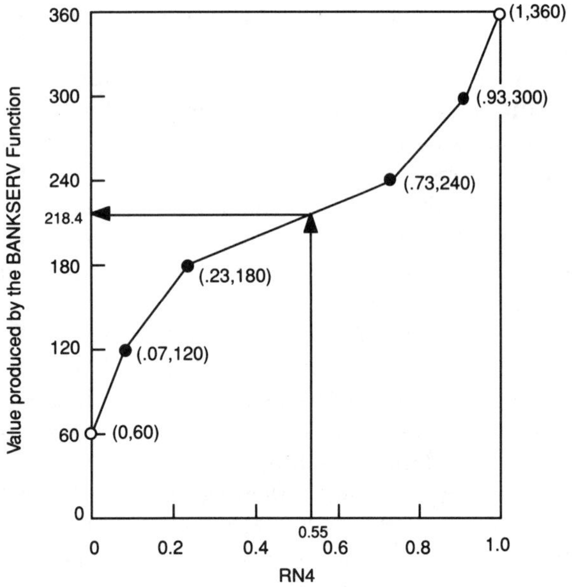

Figure 13.16 A Graphical Interpretation for the Figure 13.15 C-Function

interpolation is 218.4. And so a value falling into an interval on the x-axis is mapped into a value from the corresponding interval on the y-axis.

Within any interval on the x-axis in Figure 13.16, values of the Function's argument are uniformly distributed. With linear interpolation, values from the corresponding y-axis interval also occur with equal likelihood. For example, **if** the current value of the Function's argument falls anywhere within the interval from 0.07 to 0.23, then Function values in the interval from 60 to 120 seconds have equally likely chances of occurring. The Function's value will only fall within the 0.07 to 0.23 interval with probability 0.16, of course (0.16 = 0.23–0.07).

Now consider the situation that leads to the Figure 13.15 Function. Suppose that as part of a study, a bank teller's service times have been observed. The summary resulting from 100 observations is presented in Table 13.6, grouped in 1-minute intervals. The first table row indicates that no customer was served in 1 minute or less. The second row indicates that 7 percent of the customers were served in from 1 to 2 minutes (exclusive of 1, inclusive of 2). The third row indicates that 16 percent were served in from 2 to 3 minutes (exclusive of 2, inclusive of 3). And so on. The last row indicates that service times in the sample of 100 observations were always less than 6 minutes. The relative frequency function for the Table 13.6 service times is shown in the form of a histogram in Figure 13.17, where seconds have been used as the time unit.

Now suppose the information in Table 13.6 is to be used in a model in which the base time unit is 1 second. Service times could be modeled as 90 seconds, 150 seconds, ..., 330 seconds (corresponding to the **midpoints** of the five intervals in Table 13.6.) Such modeling would make use of a D-Function. Or they could be modeled by sampling from **all** values in the sequence of five 60-second intervals in the table. Such modeling makes use of a C-Function. With a C-Function, the values within any given 60-second interval in this example have an equally likely chance of occurring. (In the absence of information about how service times are distributed within any of the 60-second intervals, it is fair to assume that the various service times within an interval occur **with equal likelihood**.)

The steps followed in defining a C-Function are analogous to those in defining a D-Function. As shown in Table 13.6, the relative frequencies for the various service-time intervals are converted to cumulative frequencies. Then these cumulative frequencies are used as first members in a collection of ordered pairs of points. The **upper limits** of the corresponding service time intervals are used as the second members of the ordered pairs. These ordered pairs are then presented on one or more

Table 13.6

A summary of observed service times for a bank teller

Service Time Range (minutes)	Service Time Range (seconds)	Relative Frequency	Cumulative Frequency
≤1	≤60	0.0	0.0
>1 – ≤2	>60 – ≤120	0.07	0.07
>2 – ≤3	>120 – ≤180	0.16	0.23
>3 – ≤4	>180 – ≤240	0.50	0.73
>4 – ≤5	>240 – ≤300	0.19	0.92
>5 – <6	>300 – <360	0.08	1.0
≥6	≥360	0.0	

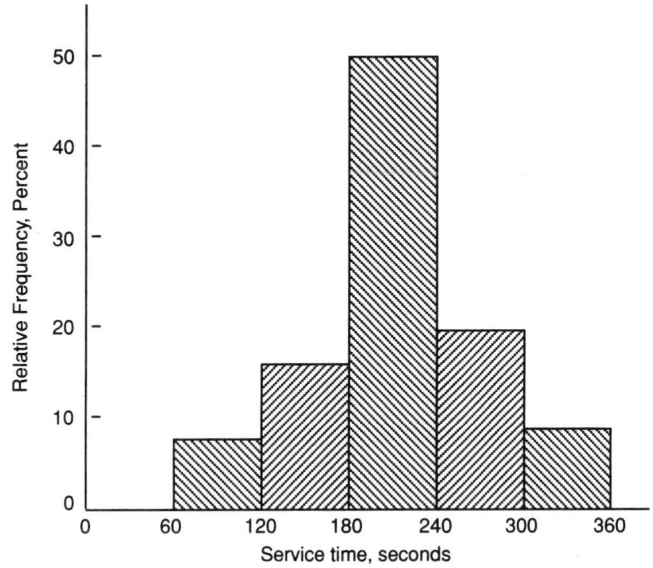

Figure 13.17 *A Relative Frequency Histogram for the Table 13.6 Service Times*

Function Follower Statements, as shown in Figure 13.15. In the associated FUNCTION statement, the modeler provides an identifier for the C-Function, indicates the Function's argument, the type of Function, and the count of the number of ordered pairs supplied to define the Function.

C-Functions and D-Functions are referred to the same way. For example, the Block "ADVANCE FN(BANKSERV)" could be used in a model to simulate the service times for the bank teller of Table 13.6.

13.21 Sampling from Continuous Uniform Distributions with C-Functions

Until now, our only method for sampling from continuous uniform distributions has been by means of what is termed transparent sampling at GENERATE and ADVANCE Blocks. It's also possible to sample from such distributions by using Continuous Functions that are defined with only two pairs of points. There are two things that motivate an interest in using C-Functions for this purpose:

1. In transparent sampling from continuous uniform distributions at GENERATE and ADVANCE Blocks, RN1 is used as the basis for the sampling. When C-Functions are used as an alternative, then any random number generator of the modeler's choice can be used as the basis for the sampling. In Chapters 15 and 16, contexts will be introduced in which it's important for us to be able to control the choice of random number generator used to sample from continuous uniform distributions (and other distributions as well).
2. In modeling, there are contexts outside the use of GENERATE and ADVANCE Blocks in which it is of interest to sample from continuous uniform distributions. And so it is important in general to be able to specify that a sample is to be drawn from a uniform distribution. C-Functions support this need in GPSS/H.

At a GENERATE Block, suppose we want to simulate interarrival times that are uniformly and continuously distributed on the open interval 360 ± 240, and we want to use RN3 as the basis for the sampling. This can be accomplished by using

```
 TYPE2IAT FUNCTION  RN3,C2          A C2 Function for sampling
0,120/1,600                         from a uniform distribution
```

Figure 13.18 *A Continuous, 2-Point Function for Sampling from the Uniform Distribution 360±240*

the Continuous Two-Point Function shown in Figure 13.18. The Function, named TYPE2IAT, has RN3 as its argument. In the two pairs of points used to define the Function, x_1 and x_2 are 0 and 1, respectively. (This will always be the case when defining a C2 Function to sample from a uniform distribution.) The second member of the first ordered pair, y_1, is 120 (= 360—240). (In general, the value of y_1 is *A*—*B*, where the uniform distribution of interest is $A \pm B$.) The second member of the second ordered pair, y_2, is 600 (= 360 + 240). (In general, the value of y_2 is A + B.)

Figure 13.19 provides a graphical interpretation of the Figure 13.18 Function. Because the TYPE2IAT Function is defined with only two pairs of points, its plot takes the form of a single straight-line segment joining these two points. The segment terminates in open circles in Figure 13.19, consistent with the fact that the end points are excluded from the segment (because 0 and 1 are excluded from the values returned by RN3). Thanks to the facts that the values of RN3 are uniformly distributed and that an RN3 value is converted by linear interpolation into the value returned by the Function, all values in the open interval from 120 to 600 (within a precision of about 16 decimal digits) have an equally likely chance of being produced by the TYPE2IAT Function. (In Figure 13.19, an RN3 value of 0.65 is shown being converted into a corresponding Function value of 432.3.) The Function therefore can be used to sample from the population uniformly and continuously distributed on the open interval 360 ± 240.

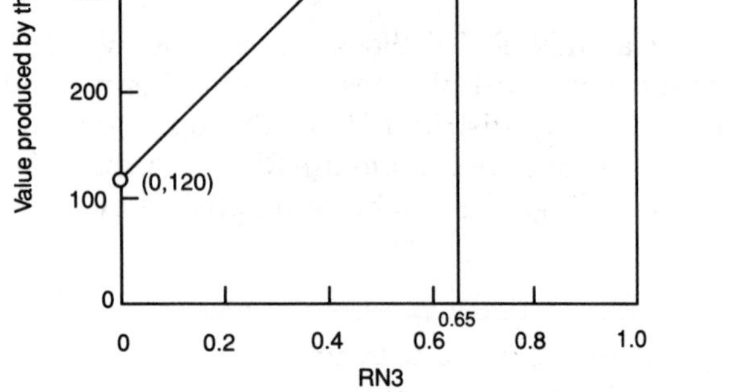

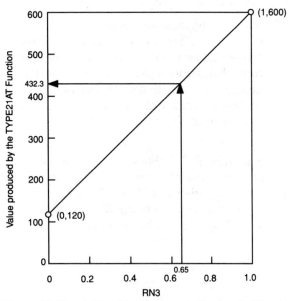

Figure 13.19 *A Graphical Interpretation for the Figure 13.18 C-Function*

13.22 Sampling by the Method of Inversion

In Sections 13.15 and 13.20, similar methods have been illustrated for sampling from discrete and continuous distributions. These methods involve forming the numeric cumulative distribution for the target random variable, then using this distribution as a basis for converting a sample from a 0–1 uniform population into an equivalent sample from the target population. Instead of taking the random variable as the **independent** variable, and the corresponding value of the cumulative distribution as the **dependent** variable, the **inverse** approach is used. That is, a value of the cumulative distribution (the independent variable) is sampled at random from a 0–1 uniform distribution, and the corresponding value of the random variable (the dependent variable) is determined. (This approach is justified because the cumulative distribution for **any** random variable is **uniformly distributed**.) The spirit of this approach is shown graphically for the discrete case in Figure 13.11, and for the continuous case in Figure 13.16.

This sampling approach is referred to as **sampling by the method of inversion.** The method of inversion, as well as alternative sampling methods, is described in most general textbooks on simulation. An important characteristic of the method of inversion is that only **one** sample from a 0–1 distribution is needed to draw a sample from the target population. (In some other sampling methods, the number of samples from a 0–1 distribution needed to draw one sample from a target population **varies at random.**) This characteristic is important in applying the variance reduction techniques discussed in Chapters 15 and 16.

13.23 Case Study 13B: A Job Shop Model

1. Statement of the Problem

A particular job shop is comprised of five different machine groups. Each group consists of a specified number of machines of a given kind, as listed in Table 13B.1. For example, Group 1 consists of three machines, Group 2 consists of two machines, and so on. Within

Table 13B.1

Size of machine groups in the Case Study 13B Job Shop

Group Number	No. of Machines in the Group
1	3
2	2
3	4
4	3

Table 13B.2

Visitation sequences and expected step times for the three job types in Case Study 13B

Job Type	No. of Machines to be Visited	Visitation Sequence	Expected Step Time (hours)
1	4	3	0.50
		1	0.60
		2	0.85
		5	0.50
2	3	4	1.10
		1	0.80
		3	0.75
3	5	2	1.20
		5	0.25
		1	0.70
		4	0.90
		3	1.00

any group, the machines are identical to each other. It does not matter which machine in a group is used to carry out a step on a unit of work-in-process.

Three types of products, or jobs, are produced at the job shop. These job types are designated as Type 1, Type 2, and Type 3. Each job type requires that steps be performed at specified kinds of machines in a specified sequence. The total number and kind of machine groups each job type must visit, and the corresponding visitation sequences, are shown in Table 13B.2. For example, jobs of Type 1 must visit a total of four machines groups, in this order: Group 3, then Group 1, then Group 2, and finally Group 5.

Figure 13B.1 shows a schematic representation of the job shop. Each machine group is pictured as a square, with the parenthesized count of the number of machines in that group indicated within the square. The paths followed by the three types of jobs moving through the shop are also shown in this figure.

Table 13B.2 also lists the expected step times required by each job type at each machine group it must visit. These step times follow Erlang distributions of order 2.

Information summarizing job interarrival times is given in Table 13B.3. The summary results from observations made of actual job interarrival times, grouped in intervals of width 0.2 hours. Interarrival times within the various intervals of Table 13B.3 can be assumed to occur with equal likelihood.

Thirty percent of the jobs are of Type 1, 50 percent of Type 2, and 20 percent of Type 3. The service order at all machine groups is FCFS.

Build a GPSS/H model for the job shop. Design

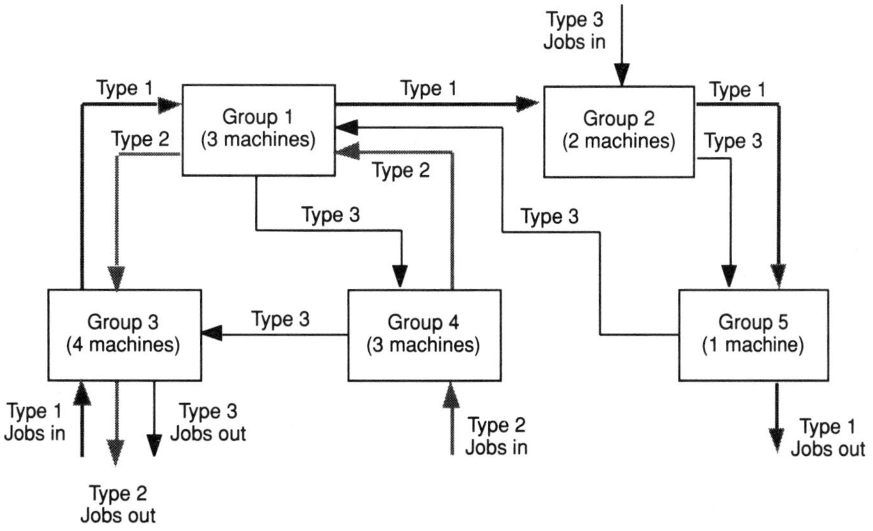

Figure 13B.1 A Schematic of the Job Shop in Case Study 13B

Table 13B.3

A summary of observed job interarrival times

Interarrival Time Range (hours)	Relative Frequency	Cumulative Frequency
≤ 0.0	0.0	0.0
>0.0 – ≤0.2	0.40	0.40
>0.2 – ≤0.4	0.30	0.70
>0.4 – ≤0.6	0.15	0.85
>0.6 – ≤0.8	0.10	0.95
>0.8 – <1.0	0.05	1.0
≥1.0	0.0	

the model to gather Queue information for each machine group. Instead of starting with the model devoid of work-in-process initially, bring eight jobs (of randomly determined types) into the model at time 0.0. Assume that no steps have yet been performed on them.

Simulate the operation of the shop for 25 consecutive 8-hour shifts, assuming any discontinuities that might occur in the transition between shifts can be ignored. Discuss the Queue information that results. Which machine groups appear to be bottlenecks in the job shop? If you could add one more machine to the job shop, what kind of machine would you be inclined to add?

(This problem is similar to one in Schriber, 1974, pp. 295 et seq. The job shop specifications are identical to a job shop problem in Law and Kelton, 1982, pp. 85 et seq., except that their job interarrival time is exponentially distributed with a mean of 0.25 hours, whereas here the interarrival times follow an empirical distribution incorporated into the model in the form of a C-Function and have an expected value of 0.32 hours. Exercise 7 of Section 13.24 calls for modifying this job shop model so that it corresponds exactly to the job shop specified in Law and Kelton.)

2. Approach Taken in Building the Model

The building of the model is straightforward. A C-Function is used to introduce job-Xacts into the model per the specifications of Table 13B.3. A D-Function of the Figure 13.14 variety is used to specify a job's path (and, indirectly, a job's type) at random, with 30 percent of the jobs going down the Type 1 path, 50 percent down the Type 2 path, and the remainder down the Type 3 path. An unconditional TRANSFER Block of the type in Figure 13.14 is used to accomplish the job routing.

After a job's path has been selected, the job moves over time through a stack of Blocks consisting of consecutive QUEUE/ENTER/DEPART/ADVANCE/LEAVE modules. Each module simulates use of a machine of the next type needed by that type of job. Each such stack of Blocks is customized for the type of job in question.

Loading the model with eight jobs initially is easily accomplished by including a GENERATE Block for that purpose, specifying a Limit Count of 8. Job paths are chosen at random for these initial jobs, using the D-

Table 13B.4

Table of definitions for Case Study 13B

Base Time Unit: 1 minute

GPSS/H Entity	Interpretation
Transactions	
Model Segment 1	The eight jobs provided at time 0.0
Model Segment 2	Arriving jobs (of a type to be determined)
Model Segment 3	Type 1 jobs
Model Segment 4	Type 2 jobs
Model Segment 5	Type 3 jobs
Model Segment 6	Run-control Xact
Functions	
JOBPATH	D-Function used to sample from the distribution of job types and route job-Xacts accordingly
JOBIAT	C-Function describing the distribution of job interarrival times
Queues	
GROUP1	The Queues for all
GROUP2	job types waiting
GROUP3	for service at machine
GROUP4	groups 1, 2, 3, 4, and 5,
GROUP5	respectively
Storages	
GROUP1	The Storages
GROUP2	modeling
GROUP3	machine groups
GROUP4	1, 2, 3, 4, and 5,
GROUP5	respectively

Function (and an associated "unconditional" TRANSFER Block) used by jobs that subsequently arrive at the model as the simulation proceeds.

3. Table of Definitions

Table 13B.4 shows the Table of Definitions for Case Study 13B.

4. Block Diagram

In Exercise 6 of Section 13.24, you are asked to sketch a Block Diagram for the Case Study 13B model.

5. Modified Source Echo

The Modified Source Echo for Case Study 13B is given in Figure 13B.2.

6. Postsimulation Report

The Postsimulation Report for Case Study 13B is given in Figure 13B.3.

7. Discussion

Postsimulation Output. Utilizations of the machine groups reported in the Storage Report of Figure 13B.3(c) range from about 57 percent to 80 percent. (In Exercise 5 of Section 13.24, you are asked to hand compute the expected machine-group utilizations and compare them with the simulated results.)

The average number of jobs waiting at the machine groups is small, averaging about 1.9 or fewer, as shown in the Queue Report of Figure 13B.3(d). The maximum number of jobs waiting at the machine groups is high, however, ranging from 5 to 13. This results from the high degree of variability associated with the 2-Erlang machining times.

If another machine were to be added to the job shop, it would seem to be reasonable to consider that the machine be added to Group 2, where both the average and the maximum number of waiting jobs is highest. Such a decision should not be based on the results of a single simulation, however. Techniques for comparing alternative choices are introduced in Chapter 16.

```
STMT#   BLOCK#   *LOC     OPERATION       A,B,C,D,E,F,G   COMMENTS

   1                      SIMULATE                                Case Study 13B
   2             *                                              A Job Shop Model
   3             *                                          Base Time Unit: 1 Hour
   4             *****************************************************************
   5             *         Control Statements (FUNCTION; STORAGE)              *
   6             *****************************************************************
   7             *
   8             JOBPATH  FUNCTION    RN1,D3          job-type distribution
   9             .3,JOBTYPE1/.8,JOBTYPE2/1,JOBTYPE3
  10             *
  11             JOBIAT   FUNCTION    RN1,C6          job interarrival-time dist'n
  12             0,0/.4,.2/.7,.4/.85,.6/.95,.8/1,1
  13
  14             GROUP1   STORAGE     3    Group 1 machines
  15             GROUP2   STORAGE     2    Group 2 machines
  16             GROUP3   STORAGE     4    Group 3 machines
  17             GROUP4   STORAGE     3    Group 4 machines
  18             GROUP5   STORAGE     1    Group 1 machine
  19             *
  20             *****************************************************************
  21             *         Model Segment 1 (Provision for 8 Jobs Initially)    *
  22             *****************************************************************
  23             *
  24     1                GENERATE    0,,,8           provide 8 jobs at time 0.0
  25             *
  26     2                TRANSFER    ,FN(JOBPATH)    route to proper jobpath
  27             *
  28             *****************************************************************
  29             *         Model Segment 2 (Job Arrival and Routing)           *
  30             *****************************************************************
  31             *
  32     3                GENERATE    FN(JOBIAT)      jobs arrive, one by one
  33             *
  34     4                TRANSFER    ,FN(JOBPATH)    route to proper jobpath
  35             *
  36             *****************************************************************
  37             *         Model Segment 3 (Path for Type 1 Jobs)              *
  38             *****************************************************************
  39             *
  40     5      JOBTYPE1 QUEUE       GROUP3          start GROUP3 Queue membership
  41     6                ENTER       GROUP3          request/capture a Group 3 machine
  42     7                DEPART      GROUP3          end GROUP3 Queue membership
  43     8                ADVANCE     RVEXPO(1,.25)   2-Erlang
  44     9                ADVANCE     RVEXPO(1,.25)   machining time
  45    10                LEAVE       GROUP3          let the Group 3 machine go
  46             *
  47    11                QUEUE       GROUP1          start GROUP1 Queue membership
  48    12                ENTER       GROUP1          request/capture a Group 1 machine
  49    13                DEPART      GROUP1          end GROUP1 Queue membership
  50    14                ADVANCE     RVEXPO(1,.3)    2-Erlang
  51    15                ADVANCE     RVEXPO(1,.3)    machining time
  52    16                LEAVE       GROUP1          let the Group 1 machine go
  53             *
  54    17                QUEUE       GROUP2          start GROUP2 Queue membership
  55    18                ENTER       GROUP2          request/capture a Group 2 machine
  56    19                DEPART      GROUP2          end GROUP2 Queue membership

  57    20                ADVANCE     RVEXPO(1,.425)  2-Erlang
  58    21                ADVANCE     RVEXPO(1,.425)  machining time
  59    22                LEAVE       GROUP2          let the Group 2 machine go
  60             *
  61    23                QUEUE       GROUP5          start GROUP5 Queue membership
  62    24                ENTER       GROUP5          request/capture a Group 5 machine
  63    25                DEPART      GROUP5          end GROUP5 Queue membership
  64    26                ADVANCE     RVEXPO(1,.25)   2-Erlang
  65    27                ADVANCE     RVEXPO(1,.25)   machining time
  66    28                LEAVE       GROUP5          let the Group 5 machine go
  67             *
```

Figure 13B.2   *Modified Source Echo of the Case Study 13B Model File (continued on the next page)*

```
68    29              TERMINATE   0              finished Type 1 job leaves
69            *
70            ******************************************************************
71            *          Model Segment 4 (Path for Type 2 Jobs)                *
72            ******************************************************************
73            *
74    30    JOBTYPE2 QUEUE       GROUP4         start GROUP4 Queue membership
75    31             ENTER       GROUP4         request/capture a Group 4 machine
76    32             DEPART      GROUP4         end GROUP4 Queue membership
77    33             ADVANCE     RVEXPO(1,.55)  2-Erlang
78    34             ADVANCE     RVEXPO(1,.55)  machining time
79    35             LEAVE       GROUP4         let the Group 4 machine go
80            *
81    36             QUEUE       GROUP1         start GROUP1 Queue membership
82    37             ENTER       GROUP1         request/capture a Group 1 machine
83    38             DEPART      GROUP1         end GROUP1 Queue membership
84    39             ADVANCE     RVEXPO(1,.4)   2-Erlang
85    40             ADVANCE     RVEXPO(1,.4)   machining time
86    41             LEAVE       GROUP1         let the Group 1 machine go
87            *
88    42             QUEUE       GROUP3         start GROUP3 Queue membership
89    43             ENTER       GROUP3         request/capture a Group 3 machine
90    44             DEPART      GROUP3         end GROUP3 Queue membership
91    45             ADVANCE     RVEXPO(1,.375) 2-Erlang
92    46             ADVANCE     RVEXPO(1,.375) machining time
93    47             LEAVE       GROUP3         let the Group 3 machine go
94            *
95    48             TERMINATE   0              finished Type 2 job leaves
96            *
97            ******************************************************************
98            *          Model Segment 5 (Path for  Type 3 Jobs)               *
99            ******************************************************************
100           *
101   49    JOBTYPE3 QUEUE       GROUP2         start GROUP2 Queue membership
102   50             ENTER       GROUP2         request/capture a Group 2 machine
103   51             DEPART      GROUP2         end GROUP2 Queue membership
104   52             ADVANCE     RVEXPO(1,.6)   2-Erlang
105   53             ADVANCE     RVEXPO(1,.6)   machining time
106   54             LEAVE       GROUP2         let the Group 2 machine go
107           *
108   55             QUEUE       GROUP5         start GROUP5 Queue membership
109   56             ENTER       GROUP5         request/capture a Group 5 machine
110   57             DEPART      GROUP5         end GROUP5 Queue membership
111   58             ADVANCE     RVEXPO(1,.125) 2-Erlang
112   59             ADVANCE     RVEXPO(1,.125) machining time


113   60             LEAVE       GROUP5         let the Group 5 machine go
114           *
115   61             QUEUE       GROUP1         start GROUP1 Queue membership
116   62             ENTER       GROUP1         request/capture a Group 1 machine
117   63             DEPART      GROUP1         end GROUP1 Queue membership
118   64             ADVANCE     RVEXPO(1,.35)  2-Erlang
119   65             ADVANCE     RVEXPO(1,.35)  machining time
120   66             LEAVE       GROUP1         let the Group 1 machine go
121           *
122   67             QUEUE       GROUP4         start GROUP4 Queue membership
123   68             ENTER       GROUP4         request/capture a Group 4 machine
124   69             DEPART      GROUP4         end GROUP4 Queue membership
125   70             ADVANCE     RVEXPO(1,.45)  2-Erlang
126   71             ADVANCE     RVEXPO(1,.45)  machining time
127   72             LEAVE       GROUP4         let the Group 4 machine go
128           *
129   73             QUEUE       GROUP3         start GROUP3 Queue membership
130   74             ENTER       GROUP3         request/capture a Group 3 machine
131   75             DEPART      GROUP3         end GROUP3 Queue membership
132   76             ADVANCE     RVEXPO(1,.5)   2-Erlang
133   77             ADVANCE     RVEXPO(1,.5)   machining time
134   78             LEAVE       GROUP3         let the Group 3 machine go
135           *
```

Figure 13B.2   (*continued on the next page*)

```
   79          TERMINATE  0             finished Type 3 job leaves
      *
      *****************************************************************
      *        Model Segment 6 (Run-Control Transaction)              *
      *****************************************************************
      *
   80          GENERATE   200           control Xact comes after 200 hours
   81          TERMINATE  1             reduce the TC by 1,
      *                                 ending Xact movement
      *
      *****************************************************************
      *        Run-Control Statements                                 *
      *****************************************************************
      *
               START      1             set the TC=1; start Xact movement
      *
               END                      end of Model-File execution
```

Figure 13B.2 *(concluded)*

RELATIVE CLOCK: 200.0000   ABSOLUTE CLOCK: 200.0000

(a)

BLOCK	CURRENT	TOTAL	BLOCK	CURRENT	TOTAL	BLOCK	CURRENT	TOTAL	BLOCK	CURRENT	TOTAL	BLOCK	CURRENT	TOTAL
1		8	11		178	21		178	31		325	41		322
2		8	12		178	22		178	32		325	42		322
3		630	13		178	23		178	33		325	43		322
4		630	14		178	24		178	34	2	325	44		322
JOBTYPE1		178	15		178	25		178	35		323	45		322
6		178	16		178	26		178	36		323	46	1	322
7		178	17		178	27	1	178	37		323	47		321
8		178	18		178	28		177	38		323	48		321
9		178	19		178	29		177	39		323	JOBTYPE3		130
10		178	20		178	JOBTYPE2	5	330	40	1	323	50		130

BLOCK	CURRENT	TOTAL	BLOCK	CURRENT	TOTAL	BLOCK	CURRENT	TOTAL	BLOCK	CURRENT	TOTAL
51		130	61		129	71		124	81		1
52	1	130	62		129	72		124			
53		129	63		129	73		124			
54		129	64	1	129	74		124			
55		129	65	1	128	75		124			
56		129	66		127	76		124			
57		129	67	2	127	77		124			
58		129	68		125	78		124			
59		129	69		125	79		124			
60		129	70	1	125	80		1			

(b)

	--AVG-UTIL-DURING--										
STORAGE	TOTAL TIME	AVAIL TIME	UNAVL TIME	ENTRIES	AVERAGE TIME/UNIT	CURRENT STATUS	PERCENT AVAIL	CAPACITY	AVERAGE CONTENTS	CURRENT CONTENTS	MAXIMUM CONTENTS
GROUP1	0.756			630	0.720	AVAIL	100.0	3	2.268	3	3
GROUP2	0.796			308	1.033	AVAIL	100.0	2	1.591	1	2
GROUP3	0.573			624	0.735	AVAIL	100.0	4	2.293	1	4
GROUP4	0.789			450	1.052	AVAIL	100.0	3	2.366	3	3
GROUP5	0.620			307	0.404	AVAIL	100.0	1	0.620	1	1

(c)

QUEUE	MAXIMUM CONTENTS	AVERAGE CONTENTS	TOTAL ENTRIES	ZERO ENTRIES	PERCENT ZEROS	AVERAGE TIME/UNIT	$AVERAGE TIME/UNIT	QTABLE NUMBER	CURRENT CONTENTS
GROUP1	8	0.764	630	320	50.8	0.243	0.493		0
GROUP2	13	1.853	308	95	30.8	1.203	1.740		0
GROUP3	5	0.164	624	499	80.0	0.052	0.262		0
GROUP4	10	1.267	457	209	45.7	0.554	1.022		7
GROUP5	7	0.611	307	138	45.0	0.398	0.723		0

(d)

RANDOM STREAM	ANTITHETIC VARIATES	INITIAL POSITION	CURRENT POSITION	SAMPLE COUNT	CHI-SQUARE UNIFORMITY
1	OFF	100000	105904	5904	0.97

(e)

Figure 13B.3 *Postsimulation Report for Case Study 13B. (a) Clock Values. (b) Block Counts. (c) Storage Report. (d) Queue Report. (e) RNG Report*

13.24 Exercises

*1. This exercise involves Discrete Functions and is based on the information in Table E1. The table summarizes the time needed to pay for items at the checkout counter of a convenience store, which depends on the number of items being bought.

(a) Show the definition of a Discrete Function that can be used to sample from the checkout time distribution. Use RN5 as the basis for sampling. Do not change the way information is ordered in Table E1. Assume a base time unit of 1 minute.
(b) Using your Discrete Function from (a), show an ADVANCE Block that can be used in a model to simulate checkout time.
(c) Show a plot of your D-Function from (a).
(d) Assume the D-Function from (a) is being evaluated, and RN5 produces a value of 0.35. What value will the D-Function produce?
(e) Repeat (d), but assume that RN5 produces a value of 0.25 (exactly).
(f) From the information in Table E1, what is the expected checkout time?
(g) How would your results in (a) through (f) change if you assumed a base time unit of 0.5 minutes?
(h) Arrange the information of Table E1 in order of decreasing relative frequency, then repeat parts (a) through (e) of the exercise.

*2. This exercise involves Continuous Functions, and is based on the information in Table E2. The table summarizes the interarrival times of planes arriving in the airspace at a major airport. It is assumed that the various interarrival times within the Table E2 intervals occur with equal likelihood.

(a) Show the definition of a Continuous Function that can be used to sample from the interarrival-time distribution. Use RN3 as the basis for sampling. Assume a base time unit of 1 minute.
(b) Using your Continuous Function from (a), show a GENERATE Block that can be used in a model to introduce plane-Xacts into a model with the indicated interarrival times.
(c) Show a plot of your C-Function from (a).
(d) Assume the C-Function from (a) is being evaluated, and RN3 produces a value of 0.40. What value will the C-Function produce?
(e) Repeat (d), but assume that RN5 produces a value of 0.90 (exactly).

Table E1

No. of Items Being Bought	Checkout Time (minutes)	Relative Frequency
1	0.50	0.10
2	0.75	0.15
3	0.95	0.20
4	1.10	0.25
5	1.25	0.15
6	1.40	0.10
7	1.50	0.05

(f) Plot a histogram for the interarrival times of Table E2.
(g) From the information in Table E2, what is the expected interarrival time?
(h) How would your results in (a) through (g) change if you assumed a base time unit of 0.5 minutes?

*3. This exercise involves the definition of Continuous Two-Point Functions for sampling from uniform distributions.

(a) Sampling from the interarrival time distribution at the Block "GENERATE 25,10" makes use of RN1. Suppose (for reasons to be introduced in Chapters 15 and 16) that you want to replace this GENERATE Block with one that will sample from the same interarrival-time distribution, but that uses RN2 as the basis for sampling. Show how to do this. (Show the definition of a C2 Function that can be used for this purpose, then show a GENERATE Block that uses the C2 Function.)
(b) Show a plot of your Function from (a).

Table E2

Interarrival Time Range (minutes)	Relative Frequency
≤ 0	0.0
>0 – ≤1	0.10
>1 – ≤2	0.15
>2 – ≤3	0.20
>3 – ≤4	0.25
>4 – ≤5	0.20
>5 – <6	0.10
≥ 6	0.0

(c) If your Function from (a) is being evaluated, and RN2 produces a value of 0.45, what value will the Function produce?
(d) Repeat (a) through (c), except for the Block "ADVANCE 50,50".

4. The model13b.gps file contains the Case Study 13B Model File. Perform a simulation with this model and compare the results with those of Figure 13B.3.

5. Sketch a Block Diagram for the model of Case Study 13B. When you build a GPSS/H model, do you tend to sketch a Block Diagram first, and then key statements into the Model File, or do you prefer to work immediately at the level of the Model File? (Most experienced modelers take the latter approach, although time can be saved in some cases if a Block Diagram is roughed out at the start. Why? Because better focus may be maintained and oversights may be avoided this way. Some modelers take an intermediate approach, jotting down abbreviated forms of Block Statements (not bothering to show Block geometry) and sketching lines at points where Xacts may take alternative paths.)

*6. Compute the expected job interarrival time in Case Study 13B. Then use this information to compute the expected machine-group utilizations. Compare these expected utilizations with those of Figure 13B.3(c).

*7. (a) Revise the Case Study 13B model so that job interarrival time will be exponentially distributed, with a mean of 0.25 hours. (The mean job interarrival time in Case Study 13B is 0.32 hours. See Exercise 6.) Carry out a simulation with the revised model, which now corresponds to the job shop described in Law and Kelton 1982, pp. 85 et seq. Compare the realized machine-group utilizations with their expected values, which you should compute by hand. Also compare the overall results with those of Case Study 13B.
(b) As the average job interarrival time decreases, the expected machine-group utilizations increase. Compute the job interarrival time for which the expected utilization of a machine group in the Case Study 13B system reaches a level of 100 percent. (That is, decrease the job interarrival time to the extent that among the five machine groups, one of them just reaches an expected utilization of 100 percent, with the other four groups still having expected utilizations below 100 percent. The system is just on the verge of becoming explosive at this point.) Which machine group is the first to reach an expected 100 percent utilization? What are the expected utilizations of the other machine groups at this point? Repeat the simulation in (a), using this interarrival time. Compare the overall results with those in (a). Would you expect more or less variation in job-shop behavior as a result of this increased degree of system loading?

*8. (a) Using the Block Counts in Figure13B.3(b), compute the percentage of each of the three types of jobs which came to the job shop during the Case Study 13B simulation. (Include the eight initial jobs in computing these percentages.)
(b) What was the average level of work-in-process in the Case Study 13B simulation? That is, how many WIP units were in the job shop on average? (This information can be determined from the Postsimulation Report of Figure 13B.3.)
(c) What was the maximum level of work-in-process in the Case Study 13B simulation? (This information can't be determined from the Postsimulation Report of Figure 13B.3, but can only be determined by modifying the model and repeating the simulation. Do this.)

9. (a) The Case Study 13B model assumes unlimited waiting space ahead of each machine group. Assume that the waiting space at each machine group can only hold three units of WIP. Assume further that if a job arrives at the shop and there is no space for it to wait ahead of its first machine group, the job is lost (is routed elsewhere, and does not return). Further assume that if a job that is finished with its current machine is output blocked (that is, cannot move into the wait space associated with its next machine group), the job must remain at its current machine, and so prevents use of the machine for another purpose. Revise the Case Study 13B model to reflect this situation. Perform a simulation with the revised model. Compare the results with those resulting in the original Case Study 13B simulation. How many jobs are lost?
(b) Repeat (a), only now assume that the waiting space at each machine group can only hold two units of WIP.
(c) Repeat (a), only now assume that the waiting

space at each machine group can only hold one unit of WIP.

13.25 Nonzero GENERATE and ADVANCE B Operands When A Operands Are Function References

In the several GENERATE and ADVANCE Blocks used in this chapter to illustrate calls on RVEXPO, RVNORM, RVTRI, and the DRILTIME and BANKSERV Functions, the Block's A Operand has referred to a Function (either built in or modeler defined), and the B Operand has been zero, by default. Would it be acceptable to work with nonzero B Operands at these Blocks? The answer is yes. For instance, consider this ADVANCE Block:

```
ADVANCE FN(DRILTIME),2.5
```

When this ADVANCE is executed, the value of the A Operand will be the value produced by the DRILTIME Function of Figure 13.10. This value will then be used as the **mean of a uniform distribution** whose half-range is 2.5. In other words, the holding-time distribution at the ADVANCE Block is FN(DRILTIME) ± 2.5. And so a value will be sampled from the corresponding uniform distribution, and **this** value will be the applicable holding time on this occasion. This transparent sampling from the uniform will involve obtaining a value from RN1, of course. And so **two** random numbers will be used (one from RN7, the argument of the DRILTIME Function; the other from RN1) to determine the holding time whenever the ADVANCE Block is executed.

ADVANCE and GENERATE Blocks of the above type can be useful in modeling. We'll illustrate this idea in concept here for a GENERATE Block. Suppose patients keeping scheduled appointments come into a hospital with uniformly distributed interarrival times whose half-range is 3 minutes, but whose **mean varies with the time of day**. Figure 13.20 illustrates this situation in specific terms. Mean interarrival times, plotted on the vertical axis, vary with the time of day, plotted on the horizontal axis. (This variation in means is due to variations in laboratory hours, clinic hours, the times when doctors make their rounds in the wards, the times doctors set aside to consult patients in their offices, and so on.) This variation in **mean** interarrival times can be described with a C-Function **whose argument is the value of the simulated clock**. (Such a possibility was pointed out briefly in Section 13.18. Operational details aren't provided here, but further comments are made in Section 5 of Chapter 17.) Suppose a C-Function named MEANIAT has been developed from the information given in Figure 13.20. Then scheduled patients can be introduced

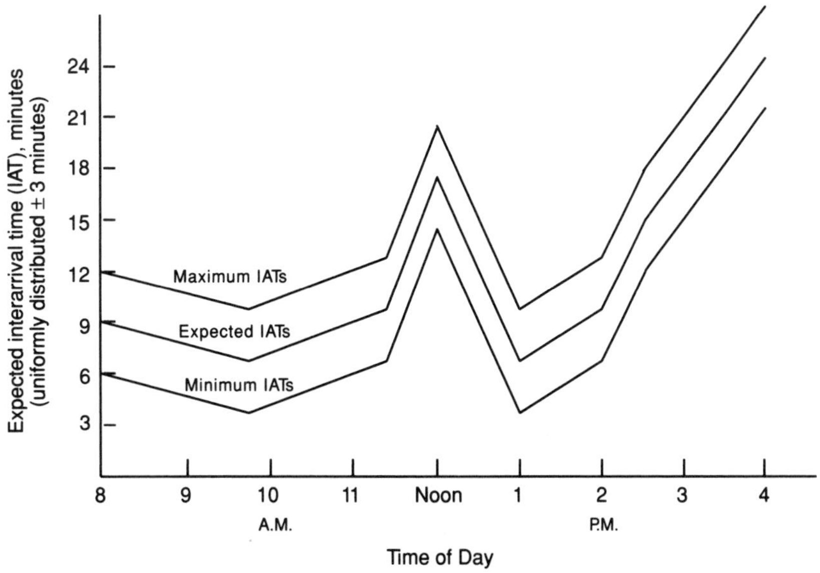

Figure 13.20 Variation in Mean Interarrival Times with the Time of Day

into a hospital model with this GENERATE Block.

```
GENERATE FN(MEANIAT),3
```

Mean interarrival times will vary with the time of day, and realized interarrival times will be determined by sampling from the population uniformly distributed ± 3 minutes about the applicable mean.

13.26 Function-Modified GENERATE and ADVANCE Blocks

Can the B Operand at GENERATE and/or ADVANCE Blocks take the form of a Function reference? The answer is yes. If a GENERATE or ADVANCE B Operand refers to a **modeler-defined** Function, then a **Function-modified** GENERATE or ADVANCE Block is said to be in use. In other words, if a GENERATE or ADVANCE B-Operand begins with **FN**, the Block is said to be Function-modified.

At a Function-modified GENERATE or ADVANCE, interarrival or holding time is computed by **multiplying** the value of the A Operand by the value produced by the B-Operand Function. The result, then, is **not** a sample from the uniformly distributed A ± B population.

Why do Function-modified GENERATE and ADVANCE Blocks exist? These Blocks can be used to model exponentially distributed interarrival and service times in GPSS implementations that don't provide a built-in exponential distribution. (Details won't be given here.) GPSS/H provides RVEXPO, so Function-modified GENERATE and ADVANCE Blocks needn't be used in GPSS/H. (You should **avoid using Function-modified GENERATE and ADVANCE Blocks**; otherwise, you will get the multiplication effect just described, which is an effect you probably do not want.)

13.27 Exercises

*1. Consider the Block "GENERATE RVTRI(3,4.0, 6.0, 9.0), 2".

(a) How many 0–1 uniform random numbers are used to determine an interarrival time at this Block? What random-number generators supply these 0–1 uniform random numbers?

(b) On what interval are the interarrival times at this Block distributed?

*2. Consider the Block "ADVANCE 5, FN(FACTOR)", where FACTOR is a C2 Function defined with the ordered pairs 0, 3 and 1, 6, and having RN7 as its argument.

(a) On what interval are holding times at this Block distributed? What type distribution is followed by the holding times?

(b) What holding time pattern will be in effect if C2 is changed to D2 in the definition of the FACTOR Function?

14 Statistical Experiments with Single-System Models

14.1 Preview

Simulation is a technique for estimating how well a system will perform if it is built or changed in a prescribed way. After a proposed system design has been modeled, experiments are conducted with the model to assess its performance characteristics. The objective is to observe model behavior in specific cases so that inferences can be made about long-run model behavior. These inferences can then be interpreted in terms of the system being modeled. The process of drawing inferences uses methodology from the statistical area of inference.

In this chapter, we introduce possibilities for conducting experiments with GPSS/H models to gather observations for use in making inferences about the expected value of an output variable. For example, we might model the proposed design for a manufacturing system, then experiment with the model to estimate the mean production rate achieved by the system. At the conclusion of our experimentation, we might provide an interval estimate of the mean production rate, stating, for example, that "we are 95 percent confident that the mean production rate will be between 36 and 39 units per 8-hour shift."

Chapter 14 is the first of three that deal with statistical experiments in simulation. Chapter 15 continues the discussion of single-system modeling and Chapter 16 treats situations where it's of interest to investigate the relative performance of two or more alternative (competing) systems.

This chapter provides a blend of GPSS/H capabilities and statistical considerations. No new Blocks are introduced, but several Control Statements are. These provide the capability for performing multiple simulations with a single Model File, and for modifying the settings of the GPSS/H random number generators. The algorithm used in GPSS/H to produce random numbers is introduced, and the RNG Report is discussed. On the statistical side, methodology for forming confidence intervals in the single-system case is reviewed.

14.2 Performing Replications with a Simulation Model

We introduce the concept of replications with a homely example. Suppose you know nothing about dice. A friend gives you a pair of fair dice, and asks you to estimate what the average result will be if you roll them. You decide to experiment and see what happens. The results vary at random from roll to roll. You roll the dice a first time, and a "5" results.

You roll them a second time, and an "8" results. You roll them a third time, and a "4" results. And so on. After carrying out a number of trials like this, you compute the average result (the sample mean) and use it as an estimate of the average result in rolling a pair of fair dice.

Simulating one time is like rolling a pair of dice one time. The result is an observation on the value of the output variable of interest. (We speak here of "the" output variable, but in general there can be many output variables.) Suppose a simulation is carried out **a second time, using a different set of 0–1 uniform random numbers** to sample from the distributions of the model's input variables. Then a **different** value will very likely be observed for the output variable. (This is analogous to rolling the dice a second time.) If the simulation is carried out a third time, a fourth time, and so on, each time using a different set of random numbers, then the observed result will vary from simulation to simulation. The average result produced by carrying out such a series of simulations might then be used to estimate the average value of the output variable.

A **replication** is a simulation run carried out using a series of random numbers unique to that run. By "random numbers," we refer to the 0–1 uniform random numbers used to sample from the distributions of the model's input variables. The **distributions** of the input variables don't vary from replication to replication. It's the series of **values drawn from these distributions** that varies from replication to replication. In turn, the differing combinations of values of the input variables result in differing observed values of the output variable(s) from replication to replication.

For example, consider Case Study 12A ("A Quality Control Model"). A single replication was performed with that model in Chapter 12 to estimate the time required for 100 television sets to pass final inspection. The resulting value was 586.1 minutes. Now suppose an additional 4 replications are performed with the model. (We'll see in the next several sections how easy it is to carry out replications in GPSS/H.) The resulting sample of times required for 100 television sets to pass final inspection is reported in Table 14.1. Values in the sample range from 549.6 to 607.3.

The average time in this sample of size 5 is 584.3 minutes, with a sample standard deviation of 21.2 minutes. The standard deviation is about 4 percent of the mean. (Sample standard deviation will be of use later in computing confidence intervals. The standard deviation is computed by dividing ***n*-1** (not *n*) into the sum of the squares of the differences between the sample mean and the individual sample observations. This results in an **unbiased** estimate of the standard deviation. See an introductory statistics textbook or a general simulation textbook for details.)

Table 14.1

Observed times required for 100 television sets to pass final inspection in Case Study 9A

Replication Number	Time Required, Minutes
1	586.1
2	607.3
3	588.0
4	549.6
5	590.7
Sample mean:	584.3
Sample standard deviation:	21.2

As another example, consider Case Study 9A ("Alternative Service Orders at a Tool Crib"). A single replication was performed with each of **two** models in that case study to determine the average number of mechanics in the waiting line at the tool crib for FCFS and SPT as alternative service orders. The resulting values were 1.705 and 1.501, respectively. Now suppose an additional nine replications are performed with each of the two models. The resulting samples of average number of mechanics in the waiting line are reported in Table 14.2.

The variation in the point estimates in Table 14.2 is quite high, ranging from about 1.4 to 5.5 for FCFS and from just less than 1.0 to about 7.6 for SPT. The sample standard deviations are about 35 percent of the mean for FCFS and 65 percent of the mean for SPT. The average number of mechanics in the waiting line for FCFS is about 8 percent greater than for SPT (3.535 versus 3.268). (We will compare results produced by these two alternative service orders on a more formal basis in Chapter 16.)

The line lengths reported in Table 14.2 are **averages**. (This contrasts with Table 14.1, where the reported values are not averages.) In turn, each of the two sample means in Table 14.2 is an average of averages (or a mean of means, sometimes referred to as a grand mean).

In Tables 14.1 and 14.2, there is only **one** output variable reported for each model. In general, however, a model produces a number of output variables which may be important. For example, in Case Study 11A, "Ships Un/loading Cargo at a Harbor," there are four

Table 14.2

Average number of mechanics in the waiting line for each of two alternative service orders (FCFS and SPT) in Case Study 9A

Replication Number		Average Waiting Line Lengths	
		FCFS	SPT
1		1.705	1.501
2		3.627	2.033
3		2.780	2.456
4		5.502	7.584
5		3.494	2.890
6		4.114	3.060
7		4.704	0.967
8		4.326	5.536
9		1.362	2.489
10		3.737	4.163
	Sample mean:	3.535	3.268
	Sample standard deviation:	1.286	1.999

output variables of interest: average residence time of Type A ships at the harbor, average time spent by Type A ships waiting for a berth, and each of these same two measures for Type B ships.

Table 14.1 provides information about an aspect of the behavior of **one** system. Table 14.2 provides information about an aspect of the behavior of **two** systems (two alternative service orders at a tool crib). The statistical methodology reviewed in this chapter and Chapter 15 applies when it's of interest to make inferences about the performance of one system. The methodology that applies when it's of interest to compare the relative performance of two (or more) alternative systems is taken up in Chapter 16.

The five observations in Table 14.1 form a sample taken from one population (the population of times required for 100 television sets to pass final inspection). Table 14.2 contains observations taken from each of two alternative populations (the populations of average waiting line lengths for FCFS and SPT service orders at a tool crib). In these terms, this chapter (and Chapter 15) deals with "one-population problems," and Chapter 16 deals with "two-population problems," "three-population problems," and so on.

Before discussing the use of information like that in Tables 14.1 and 14.2 to form confidence intervals in one-system settings, we'll first show a number of ways to carry out replications in GPSS/H modeling.

14.3 The CLEAR Control Statement

GPSS/H provides the CLEAR Control Statement as an aid for carrying out two or more consecutive replications with a model when a Model File is executed. A CLEAR Statement is usually executed between replications, to provide a transition from one replication to the next.

In the following subsections, we'll first describe the format of the CLEAR Control Statement, then indicate the position usually occupied by CLEAR Statements in a Model File. Then we'll discuss in detail how CLEAR-Statement execution provides a transition between consecutive replications. Finally, we'll demonstrate the use of CLEAR Statements to perform the five Case Study 12A replications whose ending times are reported in Table 14.1.

14.3.1 The Format of a CLEAR Statement

A CLEAR Control Statement consists of the word **CLEAR** in the statement's Operation field, as shown in Figure 14.1. The statement is never labeled. (In fact, a compile-time error occurs if a label is attached to a CLEAR statement.) And in the form of interest to us here, a CLEAR Statement has no Operands.

	Label (2 - 9)	Operation (11 - 20)	Operands (22 - 72) →
1			
	never used	**CLEAR**	

Label or Operand	Significance	Default Value or Result
Label	Not Applicable	Must Default (Compile-time error otherwise)

Figure 14.1 *The CLEAR Control Statement*

14.3.2 The Positioning of CLEAR Statements in a Model File

When GPSS/H executes a START Statement, Xact movement is initiated and a replication results. If two or more replications are to be performed when a Model File is processed, two or more START-Statement executions must take place (one per replication). Until now, a Model File has only contained one START Statement, and that has been immediately followed by an END Statement. In general, however, there can be additional Control Statements in a Model File between the first START and the eventual END. This possibility is suggested in Figure 14.2, which shows the top-down order of statements in a further extended form of a GPSS/H Model File. The boxes in Figure 14.2 have been numbered for reference. Box 5 corresponds to the additional control statements (if any) which can be placed between the START and END statements (Boxes 4 and 6) in a Model File.

To achieve multiple replications with a Model File, the Box 5 "Additional Control Statements" of Figure 14.2 can include alternating CLEAR and START statements. Such a pattern is shown in Figure 14.3 (where the Box 4 START Statement and the Box 6 END Statement of Figure 14.2 are also shown).

Execution of the first START statement in Figure 14.3 causes GPSS/H to carry out a first replication, then produce a Postreplication Report. GPSS/H then goes back into its Control-Statement Execution Phase, as discussed in Chapter 2 and shown by the return line from Box 4 to Box 2 in Figure 14.4 (which repeats Figure 2.19, except that in Figure 14.4 the term post**replication** is used in Box 4 rather than post**simulation**). Control-statement execution resumes with the Control Statement following the most recently executed START. In the Figure 14.3 pattern, this means that a CLEAR will be executed next. (The effect is to provide a transition into the next replication. Details are spelled out shortly.) Then there will be execution of another START, resulting in another replication. And so on.

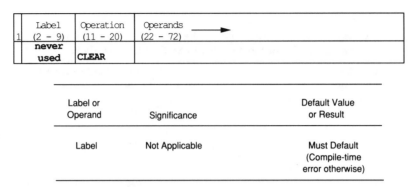

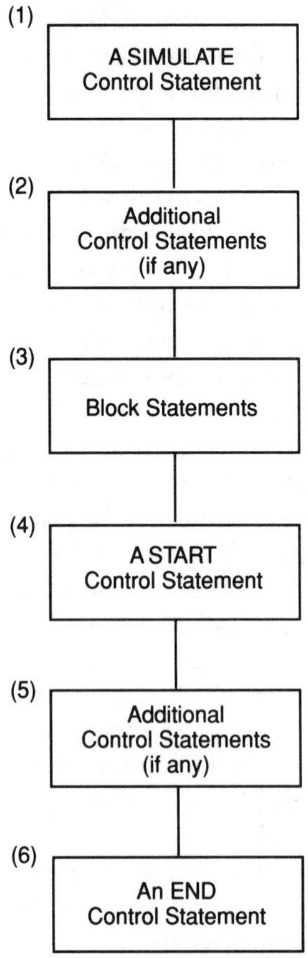

Figure 14.2 *The Top-Down Order of Statements in a Futher Extended Form of a GPSS/H Model File*

```
      ...
    START      100    the first START (Box 4, Fig. 14.2)
    CLEAR             clear the model for the next replication
    START      100    perform the next replication
      ...
    END               the END statement (Box 6, Fig. 14.2)
```

Figure 14.3 *An Example of the Positioning of a CLEAR Statement in a Model File*

14.3.3 The Effect of CLEAR-Statement Execution

What effect does CLEAR-Statement execution have on a model? Clearing a model **almost** returns the model to the state it was in at the beginning of the preceding replication. When a CLEAR is executed, these steps take place:

1. The Relative and Absolute Clocks are set back to zero.

2. All Xacts that were in the model at the end of the preceding replication are destroyed.

3. All Facilities and/or Storages in the model are returned to an idle state. (This is consistent with the destruction of all Xacts in step 2.)

4. The model is reinitialized statistically. This means, for example, that Total and Current Block Counts are set back to zero; entry counts for Facilities, Storages, and Queues are set back to zero; records of maximum contents for Queues and Storages are set back to zero; entry counts for Queues are set back to zero; and so on.

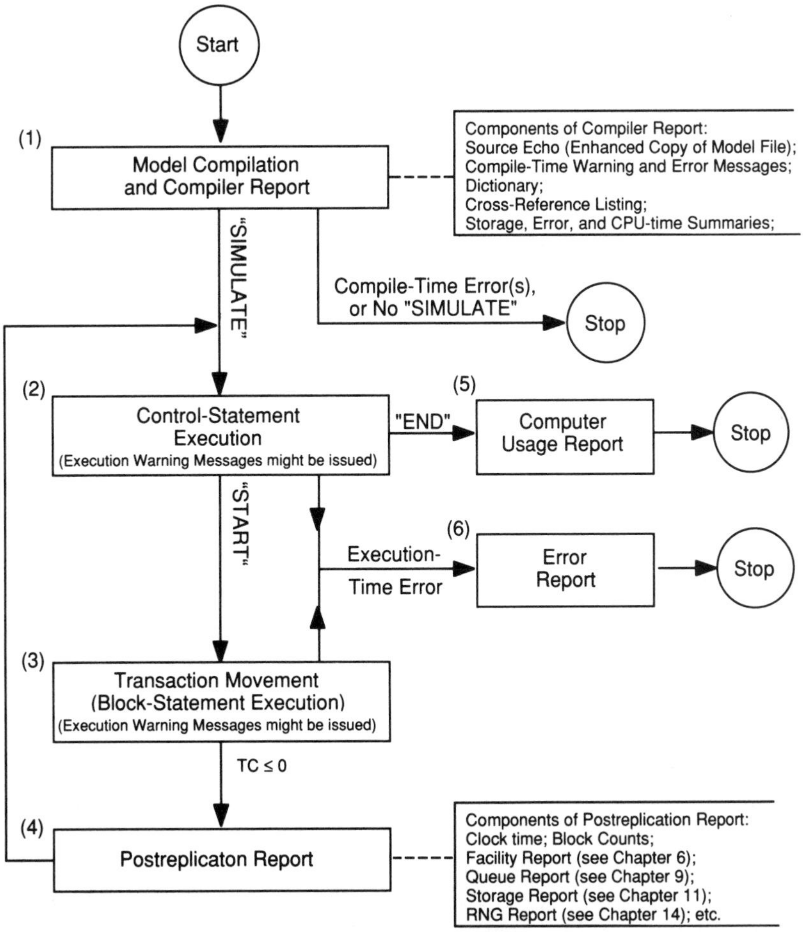

Figure 14.4 *The Steps Followed by GPSS/H in Executing a Model File (a Repetition of Figure 2.19)*

In terms of material discussed so far, there are two ways in which a clearing a model does **not** return it to its state just prior to the preceding replication:

1. **The random number generators are not reinitialized, but are left as is.** When the next replication begins, the random-number generators will pick up where they left off at the end of the preceding replication. In GPSS/H, the 0–1 uniform random numbers used to sample from the distributions of input variables **will therefore differ** from those used during the one or more preceding replications.

2. The counter used to assign Xact id numbers is not reinitialized. When Xacts are created during the next replication, they will be given id numbers that pick up where they left off at the end of the preceding replication. If the last Xact created in the preceding replication was given id number 134, for example, then the first Xact to be created in the next replication will be given id number 135.

It is Item 1 that is important for our purposes here. Because the random-number generators are left as is, clearing a model sets the stage for performing another replication with the model.

14.3.4 Achieving Replications with the Case Study 12A Model

Figure 14.5 shows the Case Study 12A Model File modified so that a sequence of five replications will be performed in a single Batch run when the file is submitted for processing. The only modifications are in the "Run-Control Statements" section at the bottom of the Model File. In the Case Study 12A model, the "Run-Control Statements" section consisted of **one** START statement, followed by an END statement. In contrast, the "Run-Control Statements" section in the Figure 14.5 Model File consists of a series of **five** START statements, with CLEAR statements between them.

Execution of the first START in Figure 14.5 causes the Transaction-Movement Phase to be entered for the first time, initiating replication 1. After this replication has come to an end and the Postreplication Report has been produced, execution of Control Statements resumes. The next Control Statement in Figure 14.5 is a **CLEAR**. Executing this statement, GPSS/H clears the model as described earlier.

GPSS/H then executes the next (second) START in Figure 14.5. This causes the model's GENERATE Blocks and Termination Counter to be initialized and the Transaction-Movement Phase to be entered for the second time, resulting in replication 2.

After replication 2 comes to an end, execution of Control Statements resumes once again (per Figure 14.4), and another CLEAR/START sequence is executed, resulting in the third replication of the overall simulation. This process continues until a fourth and fifth replication have been performed. It's the ending times of these five replications that are reported in Table 14.1.

This is the first example we've seen in which executing a Model File involves moving back and forth repeatedly between Control-Statement execution and Xact movement. The applications of this technique include carrying out replications, as demonstrated here.

14.4 Replicating with DO/ENDDO Control Statements and Integer Ampervariables

Consider the approach taken in Figure 14.5 to achieve replications. If this approach were applied in Case Study 9A to produce either set of results shown in Table 14.2, a sequence of **10** START Statements and **9** interspersed CLEAR Statements would be required. A more compact approach would be to have control loop through a single START/CLEAR sequence ten times. This **looping of control** can be accomplished in GPSS/H by use of a DO/ENDDO Control Statement pair combined with an index used to count and limit the number of times control traverses the loop. The features of GPSS/H used to accomplish this are introduced in this section.

14.4.1 DO/ENDDO Control Statements

GPSS/H provides **DO** and **ENDDO** Control Statements that can be used to structure **control** loops. A control loop is a collection of Control Statements executed repeatedly until some terminating condition is satisfied. For example, we might want to execute the two-statement collection consisting of START and CLEAR repeatedly until the collection has been executed ten times.

The format and setting of DO/ENDDO Control Statements is shown in Figure 14.6. The Operation

```
          SIMULATE                                    Case Study 12A
*                                              A Quality Control Model
*                                             Base Time Unit: 1 Minute
**********************************************************************
*         Control Statements (STORAGE)                               *
**********************************************************************
*
 TESTERS  STORAGE    2   testers at the last test station
*
**********************************************************************
*         Model Segment 1 (Last Test Station)                        *
**********************************************************************
*
          GENERATE   5.5,2             sets arrive, one by one, from
*                                      the preceding test station
 RETEST   QUEUE      LASTTEST          start LASTTEST Queue membership
          ENTER      TESTERS           request/capture a tester
          DEPART     LASTTEST          end LASTTEST Queue membership
          ADVANCE    10,3              testing time
          LEAVE      TESTERS           let the tester go
*
          TRANSFER   .120,,ADJUSTIT    12% must be adjusted
*
          TERMINATE  1                 the rest pack out
*
**********************************************************************
*         Model Segment 2 (Adjustment Station)                       *
**********************************************************************
*
 ADJUSTIT QUEUE      ADJUSTQ           start ADJUSTQ Queue membership
          SEIZE      ADJUSTER          request/capture the adjuster
          DEPART     ADJUSTQ           end ADJUSTQ Queue membership
          ADVANCE    30,10             adjustment time
          RELEASE    ADJUSTER          free the adjuster
          TRANSFER   ,RETEST           transfer to retesting
*
**********************************************************************
*         Run-Control Statements                                     *
**********************************************************************
*
          START      100      set TC=100; start 1st replication
          CLEAR               clear for 2nd replication
          START      100      set TC=100; start 2nd replication
          CLEAR               clear for 3rd replication
          START      100      set TC=100; start 3rd replication
          CLEAR               clear for 4th replication
          START      100      set TC=100; start 4th replication
          CLEAR               clear for 5th replication
          START      100      set TC=100; start 5th replication
*
          END                 end of Model-File execution
```

Figure 14.5 *The Case Study 12A Model File Modified to Perform Five Replications*

words for these statements are DO and ENDDO, respectively. An **optional *label*** can be attached to either or both of the DO/ENDDO statements. This fact is shown in Figure 14.6 with the notation [*label*], where the square brackets indicate that the entry they enclose is **optional**. (This is the first time we've used **square-brackets notation** to indicate optional items in a statement format. The square brackets themselves are **not** part of the statement. There will be additional occasions for use of square-brackets notation.)

The "Control Statements comprising the body of the loop" in Figure 14.6 are the statements that are subject to repeated execution until some terminating condition is satisfied.

As indicated in Figure 14.6, the DO-Statement

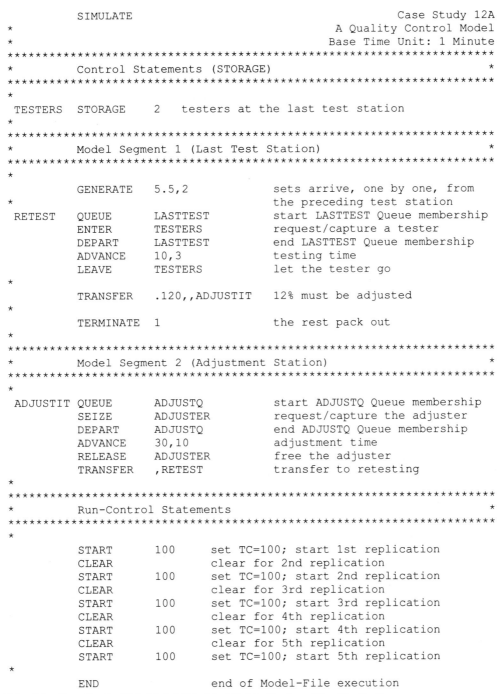

```
[label]  DO          &index=starting_value,limit_value[,increment]
         ...
         Control Statements comprising the body of the loop
         ...
[label]  ENDDO
```

Figure 14.6 *The Format of a DO/ENDDO Control Statement Pair*

Operands specify an ***index***, its ***starting_value***, its ***limit_value***, and an optional ***increment*** for the index. The index must be an **Integer Ampervariable**. (These are discussed in the next section.) Whole numbers are used as the ***starting_value***, ***limit_value***, and optional ***increment*** for the index. The increment must have a value of 1 or more. The **default value** of the increment is 1.

A specific example of a DO statement is

```
DO &I=1,10,1
```

Here, the ***index*** is **I**, its ***starting_value*** is 1, its ***limit_value*** is 10, and its ***increment*** is 1. (The nature of "&I" is discussed in the next section.) When this DO statement is executed, the index I will take on the 10 values ranging from 1 to 10 in steps of 1 (that is, from its *starting_value* to its *limit_value* in steps of its *increment*). The statements in a DO/ENDDO control loop are executed one time for each value of the index. (This assumes that no statements in the body of the loop will cause control to quit the loop.) Execution then continues with the Control Statement following the ENDDO statement in the Model File.

Figure 14.7 shows a complete example of a DO/ENDDO control loop. When this DO-loop is executed, 10 START/CLEAR executions will take place, and 10 replications will be performed with a model as a result.

In the Figure 14.7 DO statement, the increment of 1 is shown explicitly. This isn't necessary, because the default increment is 1.

The START/CLEAR Statements making up the body of the Figure 14.7 loop have been indented to produce a telescoping effect. This arbitrary indentation is possible because free format can be used in GPSS/H. (If such indentation is overdone, a statement's Operation word might extend into the Operands field, which **by default** must start **at least by column 25** of a statement. But this default can be overridden by use of an OPERCOL Compiler Directive. See the *GPSS/H Reference Manual* for details.)

```
DO        &I=1,10,1
    START 1
    CLEAR
ENDDO
```

Figure 14.7 *An Example of a DO/ENDDO Control Loop*

Two cautions are in order with respect to DO/ENDDO control loops. First, DO/ENDDO is used to structure **control loops, not Transaction loops. Only Control Statements (not Block Statements)** are placed in the body of a DO-loop.

Second, remember that in a GPSS/H Statement, the Operands **must be entered in consecutive columns**. The first occurrence of a blank in the Operands field causes the compiler to treat everything to the right of that point as a comment. The following DO Statement is **incorrectly** keyed,

```
DO &I = 1, 10, 1
```

because blanks have been left on either side of the equals sign (=), and after each of the two commas following the starting value and the limit value. (Those new to GPSS/H sometimes have a tendency to key these blanks to make the DO Statement "more readable.")

It's natural to wonder whether nested control loops can be used in GPSS/H. (A nested control loop is one that is contained within one or more other control loops.) The answer is **yes**. Nested control loops will be used in the case study of Chapter 16.

We conclude this subsection by noting that DO/ENDDO Statements are elements of a powerful and flexible **Control Statement Language (CSL)** that is part of GPSS/H. Other elements of this CSL include easily used computational Control Statements (the key word is LET), input and output statements (key words are GETLIST and PUTPIC), conditional branching and case-selection structures (key words are IF, ELSEIF, ELSE, and ENDIF), the ability to call external subroutines (the key word is CALL), and unconditional branching (the key word is GOTO). (Existence of a GOTO explains why it may be of interest to label DO and/or ENDDO Control Statements, per the optional labeling indicated in Figure 14.6.)

14.4.2 Ampervariables

GPSS/H **Ampervariables** are simply variables in the sense of ordinary programming languages, such as Pascal or Fortran. In other words, they are symbolic names for memory locations into which values can be stored and from which values can be fetched. A GPSS/H Ampervariable is prefixed with an ampersand (&), which gives rise to the term **Amper**variable. Excluding the ampersand, an Ampervariable is composed of from one to eight alphanumeric characters, the first of which must be alphabetic. Examples of Ampervariables are &I, &COST, &WORKERS, &OVENS, &DAYWAGE, and &OPTION12.

There are four types of Ampervariables: Integer, Real (that is, floating point), Character, and External. Integer, Real, and Character Ampervariables are, respectively, capable of storing whole numbers, decimal numbers, and character strings. External Ampervariables identify external functions and subroutines that are to be executed as part of GPSS/H model execution.

Except for External Ampervariables, an Ampervariable can be a scalar (that is, it can be the name of exactly **one** memory location), or it can be a linear-list data structure (that is, it can be the name of a list of consecutive memory location). In the case of linear-list Ampervariables, subscripts are used to refer to specific locations in the list. For example, &ITEMCOST(10) refers to the tenth location in the ITEMCOST list and &WAGERATE(&I) refers to the I-th location in the WAGERATE list.

GPSS/H Ampervariables play an integral role in a set of powerful computational capabilities that GPSS/H provides. Our interest in Ampervariables in this chapter is limited to **scalar Integer Ampervariables** used as indices in DO/ENDDO control loops.

If one or more Ampervariables are used in a model, it (or they) must be declared by including **Ampervariable Compiler Directives** in the Model File. The form of the Compiler Directive used to declare scalar Integer Ampervariables is shown in Figure 14.8. The word INTEGER appears in the Compiler Directive's Operation field. The Operands field consists of the names of one or more scalar Integer Ampervariables. If two or more Ampervariables are declared in a single INTEGER Compiler Directive, the consecutive names are separated by commas. As usual, a blank marks the end of the Operands field.

As indicated in Figure 14.8, an Ampervariable Compiler Directive cannot be labeled. (It is illegal throughout GPSS/H to label Compiler Directives. This is not an arbitrary restriction, however. There is no reason to label a Compiler Directive.)

The Figure 14.8 format is illustrated in Figure 14.9, where scalar Integer Ampervariables named I, J, and K are declared in Example 1 and scalar Integer Ampervariables named ONE, TWO, and THREE are declared in Example 2.

1	Label (2 - 9)	Operation (11 - 20)	Operands (22 - 72) →
	never used	**INTEGER**	**A,B,C,...**

Label or Operand	Significance	Default Value or Result
Label	Not Applicable	Must Default (Compile-time error otherwise)
A	The name of a scalar Integer Ampervariable (e.g., &I)	Compile-time error
B,C,...	Names of additional scalar Integer Ampervariables (if any)	End of the Operands field

Figure 14.8 *The Format of a Compiler Directive for Integer Ampervariables*

```
        INTEGER       &I,&J,&K            Example 1
        INTEGER       &ONE,&TWO,&THREE    Example 2
```

Figure 14.9 Examples of INTEGER Compiler Directives

The INTEGER statement is the first example we've seen of a Compiler Directive. Recall, a Compiler Directive provides the GPSS/H compiler with information used in compilation of the model. In contrast with Control and Block Statements, a Compiler Directive is not a type of statement that is subject to execution after a model has been compiled.

The practice here is to place Compiler Directives in a Model File right after the SIMULATE statement. This pattern is shown in Figure 14.10, which indicates the recommended top-down order of statements in a general GPSS/H Model File. (The top-down statement order in a basic Model File was shown in Figure 2.17, then was extended in Figure 11.5, and further extended in Figure 14.2. Figure 14.10 is the most general form we'll use for a Model File.) The Boxes in Figure 14.10 have been numbered for later reference.

We conclude this section by listing four facts about Ampervariables:

1. Integer Ampervariables are all given starting values of zero by the GPSS/H compiler.

2. Ampervariable values are displayed as part of a Postreplication Report.

3. CLEAR-statement execution does not change Ampervariable values. (If it did, the control loop in Figure 14.7 wouldn't work correctly.)

4. When running in Test Mode, the **display** command can be used to display the values of Ampervariables. For example, GPSS/H displays the values of all Ampervariables in a model in response to a **display amp** command.

14.4.3 An Example of the Use of DO/ENDDO for Replications

Figure 14.11 shows the Modified Source Echo for the Case Study 9A SPT model altered for use of a DO/ENDDO Control Statement pair to perform 10 replications with the model. Note the INTEGER Compiler Directive in Statement 8 of Figure 14.11 and the DO/ENDDO control loop in Statements 48 through 53. After the preceding discussion, it should be easy to understand the composition of the Figure 14.11 Model File.

There will be one extra execution of the CLEAR Statement when the Figure 14.11 Model File is processed. After the tenth execution of the START Statement, the CLEAR Statement will be executed a tenth time, and then control will quit the loop and execute the END Statement. This last CLEAR-Statement execution isn't necessary, but isn't harmful, either.

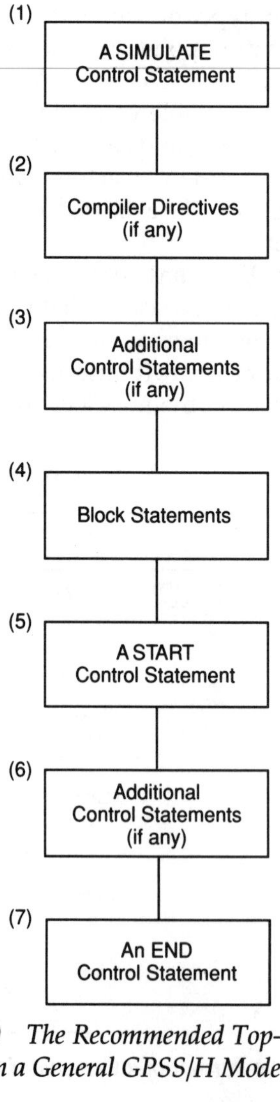

Figure 14.10 The Recommended Top-Down Order of Statements in a General GPSS/H Model File

```
STMT#  BLOCK#  *LOC   OPERATION  A,B,C,D,E,F,G   COMMENTS
    1                    SIMULATE                               Case Study 9A
    2          *                          A Tool Crib System (SPT Service Order)
    3          *                                        Base Time Unit: 1 Second
    4          **********************************************************************
    5          *         Compiler Directives (INTEGER)                              *
    6          **********************************************************************
    7          *
    8                    INTEGER    &I                &I is a DO-loop index
    9          *
   10          **********************************************************************
   11          *         Model Segment 1 (Type 1 Mechanics)                         *
   12          **********************************************************************
   13          *
   14       1            GENERATE   420,360,,,5       Type 1 mechanics arrive
   15          *                                      (Priority 5)
   16       2            QUEUE      TOOLWAIT          start TOOLWAIT Queue membership
   17       3            SEIZE      CLERK             request/capture the clerk
   18       4            DEPART     TOOLWAIT          end TOOLWAIT Queue membership
   19       5            ADVANCE    300,90            service time
   20       6            RELEASE    CLERK             free the clerk
   21       7            TERMINATE  0                 leave the tool crib area
   22          *
   23          **********************************************************************
   24          *         Model Segment 2 (Type 2 Mechanics)                         *
   25          **********************************************************************
   26          *
   27       8            GENERATE   360,240,,,10      Type 2 mechanics arrive
   28          *                                      (Priority 10)
   29       9            QUEUE      TOOLWAIT          start TOOLWAIT Queue membership
   30      10            SEIZE      CLERK             request/capture the clerk
   31      11            DEPART     TOOLWAIT          end TOOLWAIT Queue membership
   32      12            ADVANCE    100,30            service time
   33      13            RELEASE    CLERK             free the clerk
   34      14            TERMINATE  0                 leave the tool crib area
   35          *
   36          **********************************************************************
   37          *         Model Segment 3 (Run-Control Xact)                         *
   38          **********************************************************************
   39          *
   40      15            GENERATE   28800             control Xact comes after 8 hours
   41      16            TERMINATE  1                 reduce the TC value by 1,
   42          *                                      ending Xact movement
   43          *
   44          **********************************************************************
   45          *         Run-Control Statements                                     *
   46          **********************************************************************
   47          *
   48                    DO         &I=1,10,1         control for 10 replications
   49          *
   50                       START      1              start the &I-th replication
   51                       CLEAR                     clear for the next replication
   52          *
   53                    ENDDO                        proceed to the next value of &I
   54          *
   55                    END                          end of Model-File execution
```

Figure 14.11 *The Modified Source Echo for the Case Study 9A SPT Model Altered for Use of a DO/ENDDO Control Loop to Perform 10 Replications*

```
 [label]  PUTPIC   [LINES=line_count][,FILE=file_name][,(output_list)]
c...text and/or editing fields for Picture line 1 ...
c...text and/or editing fields for Picture line 2 ...
         ...
c...text and/or editing fields for Picture line line_count ...
```

Figure 14.12 *A General Form of a PUTPIC/Picture Cluster*

When the Figure 14.11 Model File is submitted for processing, the 10 replications summarized in the SPT column in Table 14.2 result.

14.5 The UNLIST CSECHO Compiler Directive

Suppose a Model File is being processed. After compilation, top-down execution of Control Statements in the Model File begins, and proceeds to the first execution of a START Statement (at which time an Xact-Movement Phase begins). During this first phase of Control-Statement execution, images of the Control Statements are **not** echoed (copied) to the output when the statements are executed.

Then, after the first Xact-Movement Phase has ended, Control-Statement execution resumes. **From this point forward**, as Control Statements are executed, they are **echoed to the output by default**.

This default echoing of Control Statements means copies of them will be interspersed with the Postreplication Reports. On the one hand, these echoes help the modeler navigate through the Postreplication Reports. On the other hand, the echoes sometimes seem to clutter up the reports. As a result, GPSS/H provides an **UNLIST** Compiler Directive that can be used to suppress the echoing of Control Statements when they are executed. This effect is achieved by putting the following Compiler Directive at the point in the Model File beyond which the modeler wants to suppress the echoing of Control Statements:

```
UNLIST CSECHO
```

For example, an **UNLIST CSECHO** statement could be included either before or after the INTEGER Compiler Directive in the Figure 14.11 Model File. Then no Control Statements would be echoed when the Model File is processed.

There are several other forms of the UNLIST Compiler Directive, and there are corresponding LIST Compiler Directives. UNLIST and LIST statements can be used to turn various types of output off and then back on. We only use UNLIST here, and then only to turn off Control-Statement echoes.

14.6 The PUTPIC Control Statement

The 10 replication reports produced when the Figure 14.11 Model File is executed are not individually identified. The only way to find the report for the fifth replication, for example, is to start at the top of the output and count reports until coming to the fifth one (or start at the bottom of the output and count backward). This situation can be remedied by using the GPSS/H **PUTPIC** Control Statement to **print** a labeled replication number (or other identifying information) at the bottom of each replication report.

The PUTPIC (PUT out a PICture) Statement is used to write customized output in GPSS/H (just as WRITE Statements are used in Fortran, PRINT Statements are used in BASIC, and so on). A PUTPIC does not stand alone, but is supported by one or more additional statements known as Picture Statements. Picture Statements present a "picture" of the output. They provide text to be included with the output and indicate where in the output to place the text and any values being written out.

A general form of a PUTPIC/Picture cluster is shown in Figure 14.12. First comes the PUTPIC Statement itself, with **PUTPIC** as the Operation word. Then come one or more consecutive Picture Statements. Let's now go through the steps of analyzing the structure of Figure 14.12.

As indicated by **[*label*]** in Figure 14.12, an **optional** Label can be attached to the PUTPIC Control Statement. The LINES=*line_count*, FILE=*file_name*, and (*output_list*) in the Operands field of the PUTPIC Statement are all **optional**, as use of the square-brackets notation in Figure 14.12 indicates.

```
                PUTPIC      LINES=1,FILE=SYSPRINT,(&I)
           0The above output is for replication number *.
                                   (a)

            The above output is for replication number 5.
                                   (b)
```

Figure 14.13 PUTPIC/Picture Example 1 (a) The PUTPIC and Its One Picture Statement. (b) Output Produced When the PUTPIC Executes and the Value of &I is 5.

LINES=*line_count* provides the count of the number of Picture statements associated with the PUTPIC. The ***line_count*** **defaults to 1**.

FILE=*file_name* indicates the destination of the output that will be produced when the PUTPIC is executed. **FILE=SYSPRINT** will direct the PUTPIC output to the same destination as the Postreplication Report. By default, PUTPIC output is directed to the user's terminal.

In Figure 14.12, **[,(*output_list*)]** is an optional parenthesized list of the variables whose values are to be transmitted to the editing fields in the PUTPIC output. If there are two or more such variables, they are separated by commas.

One or more Picture Statements immediately follow the PUTPIC. Each of these statements corresponds to **one output line** in the output produced when the PUTPIC Control Statement is executed.

In column 1 of each Picture Statement is a character (shown as *c* in Figure 14.12) that **controls the vertical spacing** used for the corresponding output line. A **blank** in this position results in **single spacing**; a **zero** (0) results in **double spacing**, and a **minus sign** (-) results in **triple spacing**.

Except for column 1, the rest of a Picture Statement contains text and/or editing fields. **Text** consists of sequences of characters that are to be copied **verbatim** (exactly as is) to the output when the PUTPIC executes. **Editing fields**, represented by **one or more asterisks** (*) in a Picture Statement, indicate the positions **before, within,** or **following** text into which the values of variables in the *output_list* are to be edited.

An example of a PUTPIC and a one-statement Picture is shown in Figure 14.13(a). The one output line produced when the PUTPIC executes is shown in Figure 14.13(b). Let's go through the steps of analyzing this example, starting with the PUTPIC Statement.

1. The PUTPIC Statement comes first, with PUTPIC as the Operation word. The PUTPIC Statement is unlabeled in this case.
2. LINES=1 in the PUTPIC Operands field indicates that the PUTPIC is supported by a one-statement Picture. (The default *line_count* of 1 could have been used here.)
3. FILE=SYSPRINT directs the PUTPIC output to the SYSPRINT file.
4. &I is the output variable whose value is to be copied to the output when the PUTPIC is executed.

The second (and only other) statement in Figure 14.13(a) is the Picture. Here is a step-by-step analysis of this Picture:

1. The character placed in column 1 of the Picture Statement to control vertical spacing in the output is 0 (zero). This zero results in **double spacing**. (One blank line will be written before the Picture output is written.)
2. Then comes text ("The above output is for replication number "), which will be copied verbatim to the output.
3. Then comes an asterisk (*) indicating the starting column in the output field into which the current value of the output variable, &I, is to be copied.
4. Finally, more text comes in the form of a single character, a period (.)

When the PUTPIC in 14.13a is executed, the line of output shown in Figure 14.13(b) will be produced if the value of &I at the time is 5. This output line will be double-spaced with respect to the preceding output (not shown). Notice that the zero used in column 1 of the Picture Statement to achieve this double spacing is **not** printed in the output.

Figure 14.14a provides an example of a PUTPIC and its associated **three** Picture Statements. If the first and third Picture Statements were eliminated, this PUTPIC/ Picture combination would match that of Figure 14.13(a). Here are the differences in

```
               PUTPIC        LINES=3,FILE=SYSPRINT,(&I)
         0============================================
          The above output is for replication number *.
          ============================================
                                (a)

          ============================================
          The above output is for replication number 5.
          ============================================
                                (b)
```

Figure 14.14 *PUTPIC/Picture Example 2 (a) The PUTPIC and Its Three Picture Statements. (b) Output Produced When the PUTPIC Executes and the Value of &I is 5.*

the two examples:

1. In the PUTPIC statement of Figure 14.14(a), LINES=3 indicates that there are three Picture Statements.

2. The character used to control vertical spacing is **zero** in the first Picture statement of Figure 14.14(a) and is a **blank** in the second and third Picture Statements. (Remember that each Picture Statement has its own vertical spacing control character in column 1 of the statement.)

3. Except for column 1, the first and third Picture Statements consist of nothing but text that is to be copied to the output. The text in both of these Pictures is a row of equals signs (=).

When the PUTPIC in Figure 14.14(a) is executed, the three lines of output shown in Figure 14.14(b) will be produced if the value of &I at the time is 5. The first output line will be double-spaced with respect to the preceding output (not shown). The second and third output lines will be single-spaced with respect to the preceding output line. As always, the Picture characters used to control spacing (the zero in column 1 of the first Picture Statement, and the blanks in column 1 of the second and third Picture Statements) are **not** included as part of the output lines.

The Figure 14.13 and 14.14 examples of PUTPIC/Picture statements are motivated by an interest in **putting a labeled replication number on a Postreplication Report**. In the first example, the labeled replication number is reported in one line. The second example attempts to improve on the first by "highlighting" the labeled replication number in the output. To provide the highlighting, a row of equals signs (=) is written both above and below the labeled replication number.

If the four statements in Figure 14.14(a) are put between the START and CLEAR statements (or between the CLEAR and ENDDO statements) in Figure 14.11, the model will produce labeled replication numbers **at the bottom** of each Postreplication Report.

If the Figure 14.14(a) statements were put between the DO and START statements in Figure 14.11, the model would put labeled replication numbers **at the top of** each Postreplication Report. (In this case, the word "above" in the second Picture of Figure 14.14(a) should be changed to "following.") In some systems, however, a GPSS/H Postreplication Report on paper **starts at the top of a page**. In these cases, the PUTPIC output would appear **on the preceding page**, which would not be desirable.

GPSS/H offers two forms of Picture definition: **immediate** Pictures and **remote** Pictures. Figure 14.12 and the examples in Figures 14.13 and 14.14 use immediate Pictures, so-called because the Picture lines immediately follow the PUTPIC statement. In remote Pictures, the Picture lines are placed elsewhere in the Model File, are labeled, and are referred to in the PUTPIC statement by their label. (Those interested can consult the *GPSS/H Reference Manual* for particulars.)

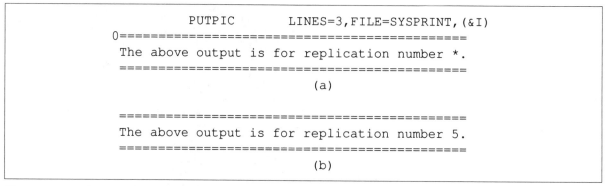

This has been a limited introduction to PUTPIC/Picture statements. These statements have many flexible options and uses, all of which are documented in the *GPSS/H Reference Manual*. For example, these statements can be used to produce customized output reports that take the place of standard postsimulation output. (Standard output can be suppressed by using **NP** (for **N**o **P**rinting) as the B Operand in the START statement.) Such tailored reports make it unnecessary for a person to know how to find and interpret information in the Postreplication Reports. Furthermore, PUTPIC and its input equivalent, GETLIST, can be used to support dialog between an executing GPSS/H model and an interactive user who neither knows nor is interested in the internal details of the simulation model itself. And there is a Block form of the PUTPIC Statement. The Operation word for the Block form is BPUTPIC (Block PUTPIC). By executing BPUTPIC Blocks, Xacts can produce PUTPIC output during Transaction-Movement Phases. (Because PUTPIC itself is a Control Statement, it cannot be executed by Xacts.) The BPUTPIC Block can be of considerable use in tracing model execution.

14.7 Exercises

1. The fig145.gps file contains the Model File of Figure 14.5 (the Case Study 12A Model File modified to perform five replications). Make a Batch run with this file and verify that the ending times of the five replications match those shown in Table 14.1. Note how Control Statements are echoed (copied) to the output after the first execution of a START Statement.

2. Edit a copy of the fig145.gps file so that 10 replications will be performed when it is executed. Make a Batch run with the resulting file. Are any of the ending times in replications 6 through 10 smaller or larger than those in Table 14.1? Compute the mean and standard deviation in the sample of size 10, and compare these with the mean and standard deviation in Table 14.1.

3. The fig1411.gps file contains the Model File of Figure 14.11 (the Case Study 9A SPT model, altered for use of a DO/ENDDO control loop to perform 10 replications). Make a Batch run with this file and verify that the average line lengths in the 10 replications match the SPT average line lengths shown in Table 14.2. Note how Control Statements are echoed to the output after the first execution of a START Statement.

4. Edit a copy of the fig1411.gps file to correspond to the FCFS service order. Put an **UNLIST CSECHO** Compiler Directive after the INTEGER statement. Make a Batch run with this file and verify that the average line lengths in the 10 replications match the FCFS average line lengths shown in Table 14.2. Note that Control Statements are **not** echoed to the output when they are executed.

5. Put the four PUTPIC/Picture statements of Figure 14.14a between the START and CLEAR statements in a copy of the fig1411.gps file. Also put an **UNLIST CSECHO** Compiler Directive after the INTEGER statement in the Model File. Make a Batch run with this file and verify that each of the 10 resulting replications reports is labeled with a replication number.

*6. The model11a.gps file contains the Model File for Case Study 11A ("Ships Un/loading Cargo at a Harbor"). Using INTEGER, UNLIST CSECHO, DO/ENDDO, and a PUTPIC, modify a copy of this file so that 25 replications will be performed when the file is submitted for processing. Make a Batch run with this file. Use the results in the 20 Postreplication Reports to compute the mean and standard deviation of these four output variables: average residence time of Type A ships at the harbor, average time spent by Type A ships waiting for a berth, and each of these same two measures for Type B ships. Save your results for use in Exercise 6 of Section 14.10.

7. The model13a.gps file contains the Model File for Case Study 13A ("A Model of a Hospital's Emergency Room"). Using INTEGER, UNLIST CSECHO, DO/ENDDO, and a PUTPIC, modify a copy of this file so that 20 replications will be performed when the file is submitted for processing. Make a Batch run with this file. Use the results in the 20 Postreplication Reports to compute the mean and standard deviation of these three output variables: average waiting time for patients in NIALINE1, NIALINE2, and CWLINE1. Save your results for use in Exercise 7 of Section 14.10.

8. The model13b.gps file contains the Model File for Case Study 13B ("A Job Shop Model"). Using INTEGER, UNLIST CSECHO, DO/ENDDO, and a PUTPIC, modify a copy of this file so that 20 replications will be performed when the file is submitted for processing. Make a Batch run with this file. Use the results in the 20 Postreplication Reports to compute the mean and standard deviation of these three output variables: percent zero entries for use of the GROUP1, GROUP2, and GROUP3 machines. Save your results for use in Exercise 8 of Section 14.10.

14.8 Types of Simulations

With respect to statistical analysis of simulation output, it is appropriate to distinguish between **terminating** and **steady-state simulations**. In this section, we describe these two types of simulations as a prelude to the later discussion of analysis of output. In addition, we comment qualitatively in this section on various aspects of systems and relate these aspects to terminating and steady-state simulations.

14.8.1 Terminating Simulations

The characteristics of terminating simulations are described in the following quote from Law and Kelton (1982, p. 280):

> A terminating simulation is one for which the desired measures of system performance are defined relative to the interval of simulated time $[0,T_E]$, where T_E is the instant in the simulation when a specified event E occurs. (Note that T_E may be a random variable.) The event E is specified before the simulation begins. Since measures of performance for terminating simulations explicitly depend on the state of the simulated system at time 0, care must be taken in choosing initial conditions.

All the simulations we have considered up to this point are in the category of terminating simulations. Consider the following three examples.

Example 1: Case Study 12A ("A Quality Control Model")

The system simulated in Case Study 12A involves the inspection of television sets. When a simulation (replication) starts at time 0.0, there are no television sets in the model. The specified event E that determines the value of T_E (the time a simulation stops) is the sending of television set 100 to be packed. Here, T_E is a random variable. (Table 14.1 shows five sampled values of this random variable.)

Example 2: Case Study 6A ("Modeling a Widget-Manufacturing System")

The system simulated in Case Study 6A involves transforming raw material into finished goods (widgets). At time 0.0, there is no work-in-process in the model. The specified event E that determines the value of T_E is that simulated time 2400 has been reached. Here, T_E is **not** a random variable, but is a known simulated time.

Example 3: Exercise 11 of Section 8.11

This exercise involves modeling a harbor to which two types of ships come to un/load cargo. At time 0.0, there is ship traffic present in the harbor, with each ship being in a prescribed state (waiting for a berth, berthing, un/loading, or deberthing). The event E that determines the value of T_E (the time a simulation stops) is departure of ship 100 (not counting those initially there) from the harbor. Here, T_E is a random variable.

Other situations introduced so far both in the case studies and in the exercises can be described in terms similar to those in the preceding examples of terminating simulations.

A distinction can be made between systems that are **physically** terminating and those that are not. Systems that "close at the end of the day" are physically terminating, for example, public areas in banks, offices of various kinds, movie theaters, some restaurants, some grocery stores, some pharmacies, some gas stations, manufacturing systems that do not operate around the clock. Other systems are designed to operate or be used continuously, for example, a hospital, a highway system, a restaurant or supermarket that never closes, a telephone system, a student work area in a university computing center, some harbor systems, ATMs (automated teller machines) at banks.

A system does not have to be physically terminating to be studied with terminating simulations. Whether the quality control system of Case Study 12A or the harbor system in Exercise 11 of Section 8.11 are physically terminating or not, both systems have been used as examples for terminating simulations.

Statements made about output variables whose behavior is studied in the setting of terminating simulations are usually couched in terms of the initial conditions and ending event that bracket each replication. For example, consider the inspection system of Case Study 12A. The results reported in Table 14.1 for five replications performed under the Example 1 conditions would be described this way: "Starting with an initially empty system, it took 584.3 minutes on average in a sample of size 5 for 100 television sets to pass final inspection." Similarly worded statements would be made about the Table 14.2 results for the tool crib system, and so on.

A distinction can also be made between systems for which the form and/or the parameters of the distributions of the input variables change with time and those for which this is not the case. Consider the interarrival times of customers coming into a bank. The interarrival times may be exponentially distributed throughout the course of a banking day. If so, then the **form** of the distribution does not change with time. But the **expected value** of the exponentially distributed interarrival times almost certainly changes with time, being relatively small when the bank first opens in the morning, then becoming larger as the bank works its way into the midmorning period, then becoming smaller during the midday period, then larger again during the midafternoon, then smaller again as the bank's closing time approaches. If the behavior of input variables is subject to change such as this, appropriate care must be taken in building the model, in the design of experiments performed with the model, and in the interpretation applied to the observed behavior of the output variable(s).

It is also interesting to distinguish between systems whose resource levels (capacities) change (by design) with time, perhaps cyclically, and those for which this is not the case. In the banking example, for instance, there might be five tellers on duty when the bank opens (to handle the rush of people who come into the bank during the first 20 or 30 minutes). Then, in response to a decreasing arrival rate (increasing interarrival times) during the midmorning period, two or three of these teller windows might be shut down (with the tellers being reassigned to do backoffice paperwork). Later, as the noon-hour rush approaches, the number of open teller windows might be increased to six or seven or eight. Then this same "accordion effect" might be repeated through the afternoon hours.

Terminating simulations can be used to study systems whose input variables and/or resource levels are subject to cyclic behavior of the type described in the bank example. For instance, suppose a bank manager decides to have some fixed number of teller windows open between 11:45 A.M. and 1:15 P.M. to handle the rush of noon-hour business. The manager's criterion might be that at least 95 percent of the customers coming into the bank during this period should start to receive service within 3.5 minutes of arriving. A simulation model could be built for this situation, and then experiments could be performed with the model to study the behavior of the output variable ("percentage of customers for whom service starts within 3.5 minutes of their arrival") for a range of alternative values of the decision variable ("number of open teller windows"). The simulations would not cover the 9 A.M.–5 P.M. banking day, but just the 11:45 A.M.–1:15 P.M. period. The initial condition of the bank (the number of customers in the bank, and their status) when a replication begins at 11:45 A.M. would have to be carefully specified. Whether this would be the same for each replication, or would vary at random from replication to replication, would have to be decided.

In concluding this section, we note that the model of the bank would be driven by input variables that might be difficult to specify, for example, the distribution of customer interarrival time during the 11:45–1:15 period, the types of teller services requested by customers coming in during the 11:45–1:15 period, and the corresponding teller service times, which could depend on the particular teller in question. Nevertheless, reasonable assumptions can be made about the form and parameters of the distributions for these input variables, and a model can be used for sensitivity analysis, with the resulting insights and conclusions conditioned on whatever assumptions have been made.

14.8.2 Steady-State Simulations

The nature of a steady-state simulation is described by Law and Kelton (1982, p. 281) in this quotation:

> A steady-state simulation is one for which the measures of performance are defined as limits as the length of the simulation goes to infinity. Since there is no natural event E to terminate the simulation, the length of one simulation is made large enough to get "good" estimates of the quantities of interest.

The term "steady state" implies a situation in which a system has reached a stable condition of operation and continues to operate indefinitely under these stable conditions. Implicit in the idea of steady state are the assumptions that the distributions of the input variables do not change over time, that the levels of system resources do not change over time, and that the system has been operating so long that current system behavior no longer depends on the conditions under which system operation began initially.

Let's illustrate the spirit of steady-state operation qualitatively. Suppose a new manufacturing plant has been built and is being put into operation. Assume the plant is to operate continuously. Consider the output variable, "level of work-in-pro-

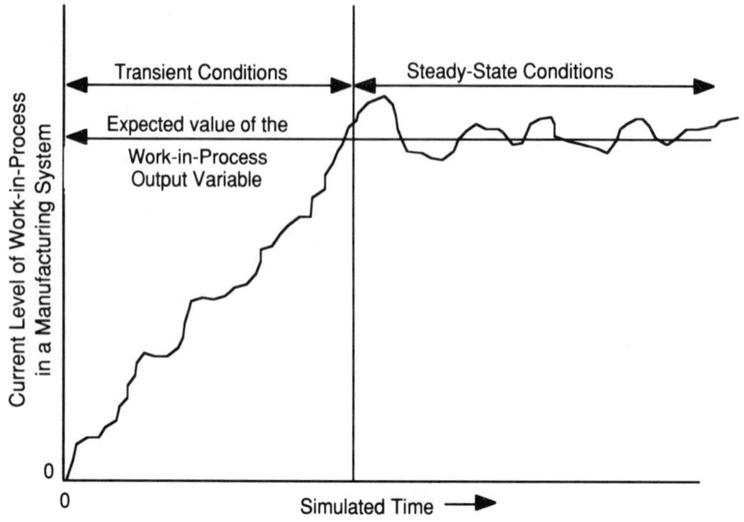

Figure 14.15 Transient vs. Steady-State System Operation

cess" (WIP level). When operation of the plant begins, there is no work-in-process. As the plant operates over time, raw material is steadily introduced into the system, eventually reaches interior points in the system in the form of work-in-process, and then begins to leave the system in the form of finished goods. While this is happening, the level of work-in-process increases, perhaps not in a smooth fashion, until eventually the WIP level no longer shows an increasing trend, but begins to fluctuate probabilistically about its expected value. This process is illustrated in Figure 14.15, where the WIP level is plotted versus simulated time. Starting at zero, the WIP level moves through transient conditions toward steady-state behavior as simulated time elapses. WIP level then eventually begins to fluctuate randomly about its expected-value line.

Several questions about steady-state simulations immediately spring to mind. One of the first questions is whether real systems ever reach and then operate for any significant length of time under steady-state conditions. We won't pursue this question here, but leave the matter to speculation.

A second question about steady-state simulations is how one determines or estimates where the transition is between transient and steady-state behavior. A variety of methods have been proposed for making this determination. (For a review of the literature in this regard, see Pritsker and Wilson, 1978.) This determination is still the subject of research and has been the focus of a number of Ph.D. dissertations during the decade of the 1980s.

A third question raised by Figure 14.15 involves how one goes about factoring out transient behavior statistically when the objective is to make inferences about steady-state behavior. In terms of steady-state behavior, any statistical observations made during transient operation are biased and should be discarded. The GPSS/H approach for discarding biased statistical observations involves use of a Control Statement (RESET) that is outlined in Section 24 of Chapter 17.

Transient behavior of the type suggested in Figure 14.15 is itself often a subject of interest. The behavior of a system during start-up conditions can be an important consideration. It might be appropriate to study alternative start-up strategies to identify the one that best corresponds to stated objectives.

Not suggested in Figure 14.15 is the possibility of studying the reaction of a system to a perturbation (a disturbance) imposed on the system while it is operating at steady state. For example, suppose a machine breaks down in a manufacturing system and is out of service for 48 hours. How long does it take the system to recover from such a perturbation, and what behavior does the system exhibit in the process of recovering from the perturbation and reestablishing steady-state behavior? The answers to these questions can be valid subjects of simulation-based investigation.

A final point motivated by Figure 14.15 is that steady-state behavior is not the same thing as constant, or invariant, behavior. "Steady state" does not imply a single, static system state, but instead corresponds to a set of alternative system states through which a system moves over time. For example, in a one-line, one-server system operating under steady-state conditions, the system is empty of traffic part of the time, contains one unit of traffic part of the time, contains two units of traffic part of the time, and so on. The system migrates from state to state as it operates. This is consistent with the implied fluctuation in Figure 14.15 of the WIP level about its expected value while the manufacturing system operates over time under steady-state conditions.

14.8.3 Summary

We've introduced the idea of terminating versus steady-state simulations and have commented on cyclic simulations as well. The simple experiments we've performed up to this point with GPSS/H models have been for noncyclic simulations of the terminating type. We set aside the topic of steady-state simulations for now and proceed to discuss statistical aspects of simulation in the context of terminating simulations.

14.9 Interval Estimates of Expected Values

In this section, we review the idea of interval estimates of the expected value of an output variable and relate them to the context of simulation. The concept of an interval estimate is first presented. Then the procedures followed to compute small-sample and large-sample interval estimates are described, and the assumptions that must be satisfied for these procedures to be valid are summarized. Some of the means for satisfying these assumptions in the setting of simulation are discussed.

14.9.1 The Meaning of an Interval Estimate

A fundamental objective in observing values of an output variable is to estimate its **expected** value. For example, we might want to estimate the expected production rate resulting from a proposed design for a manufacturing system. Or we might want to estimate the expected time required to fill 100 orders in an order-processing system.

Suppose we build a model for a manufacturing system, then perform **one replication** with the model. Assume our interest focuses on the production rate achieved for the conditions simulated. The production rate resulting from one replication is referred to as a **point estimate** of the expected value of the average production rate. In more general terms, a point estimate is a **single number** used as an estimate of the value of an unknown population parameter (e.g., an estimate of the expected value in the population of production rates achieved by the manufacturing system).

If we perform **two or more replications** with the manufacturing model, then **each replication** produces an independent point estimate of the expected production rate. In these terms, Table 14.1 contains 5 point estimates of the time required for 100 television sets to pass final inspection. Table 14.2 contains 10 point estimates of the average number of mechanics in line at a tool crib when the service order is FCFS, and another 10 point estimates for a SPT service order.

As Table 14.2 illustrates, point estimates can vary widely. Because of this variability, it can be misleading to perform only one replication and then use the resulting single number to estimate an expected value. It is preferable to take the variability of the point estimates into account. This is accomplished by using a sample of two or more point estimates to form an **interval estimate**.

An interval estimate of an expected value is a **pair of numbers** between which we have a **quantified confidence** that the expected value lies. The interval that the pair of numbers determines is called a **confidence interval**. A **confidence coefficient**, such as 90 percent or 95 percent, is attached to this interval to indicate the **confidence level**, or degree of confidence, placed upon the interval. For example, a 90 percent confidence interval for the average number of mechanics in the waiting line for the FCFS service order (based on the 10-point estimates in Table 14.2) is [2.79, 4.28]. (The steps followed to compute this confidence interval are outlined below.) The first number in a confidence interval is the **lower confidence point**, and the second number is the **upper confidence point**.

To understand the meaning of a "confidence level," consider that a given confidence interval either **does or does not** contain the expected value for which the interval estimate is provided. Each number in the pair determining a confidence interval **is a random variable**. (This means that if we performed another 10 replications for the FCFS service order in the tool crib system, then computed the resulting 90 percent confidence interval, it very likely would differ from the above [2.79, 4.28] confidence interval.) Suppose we formed 90 percent confidence intervals **repeatedly** for the FCFS tool crib system, each based on **another** 10 replications. Then, **among all such** 90 percent confidence intervals, 90 percent of them will contain the expected value, and the other 10 percent won't. (In general, we don't know which ones do, and which ones don't.) This is what it means to say we are "90 percent confident" that a 90 percent confidence interval contains the value of the population parameter being estimated.

14.9.2 Small-Sample Confidence Intervals

How are the point estimates in a collection used to compute a confidence interval for an expected value? We summarize the computational steps here, referring the interested person to any introductory text in probability and statistics (or to a general simulation text) for the underlying theory. We deal with the case of small sample sizes (samples of size less than 30) in this subsection, and with the case of large sample sizes in the next subsection.

First, we assume the point estimates are **independent** of each other and come from **identical distributions**. These are the **iid**, or independent and identically distributed assumptions. (We make these assumptions for both small and large sample sizes.)

Second, we assume **for the small-sample case** that the point estimates are **normally distributed**. (This assumption is unnecessary in the large-sample case.)

Table 14.3

Selected values of the *t* statistic for computing small-sample confidence intervals

Sample Size	Confidence Level 80%	90%	95%	98%	99%
5	1.53	2.13	2.78	3.75	4.60
6	1.48	2.02	2.57	3.36	4.03
7	1.44	1.94	2.45	3.14	3.71
8	1.42	1.90	2.36	3.00	3.50
9	1.40	1.86	2.31	2.90	3.36
10	1.38	1.83	2.26	2.82	3.25
11	1.37	1.81	2.23	2.76	3.17
12	1.36	1.80	2.20	2.72	3.11
13	1.36	1.78	2.18	2.68	3.06
14	1.35	1.77	2.16	2.65	3.01
15	1.34	1.76	2.14	2.62	2.98
20	1.32	1.72	2.09	2.53	2.84
25	1.32	1.71	2.06	2.49	2.80
30	1.31	1.70	2.04	2.46	2.76
∞	1.28	1.645	1.96	2.33	2.58

The small-sample confidence interval for an expected value is then computed as

$$\bar{x} \pm t_{\alpha/2}\left(s/\sqrt{n}\right)$$

where $\bar{x}$ is the **average of the point estimates** in a sample of size n, s is the unbiased **sample standard deviation**, and $t_{\alpha/2}$ is the ***t* statistic** for a confidence level of 100(1-α)% based on n-1 **degrees of freedom**. (The value of a *t* statistic depends not only on confidence level, but also on a characteristic known as degrees of freedom, which in this setting is one less than the sample size.)

Extensive tables of the *t* statistics needed for the small-sample confidence-interval computation can be found in any introductory statistics text and in general simulation texts. When working with computers, *t* statistics can also be obtained by calling appropriate functions or subroutines if these are available. For example, the International Mathematical and Statistical Library (IMSL) contains a Fortran subroutine named MDSTI that can be called to obtain *t* statistics.) A selection of useful *t* statistics is given in Table 14.3. For example, the t statistic to use in computing a 95 percent confidence interval for a sample of size 10 is 2.26.

Caution: Table 14.3 takes into account the fact that degrees of freedom is one less than sample size for the purpose at hand. If a sample is of size 10, for example, row "10" (not row "9") should be used in Table 14.3 in looking up the *t* statistic to use at various confidence levels.

As indicated above, a *t* statistic is used as a **multiplier** in computing the half-width of a confidence interval. The narrower a confidence interval, the better (other things being equal). And so we may prefer to work with the smaller *t* values in Table 14.3. Now consider the pattern of *t* values in the table. Moving to the right across any row in Table 14.3, note that as the confidence level **increases**, the *t* statistic (and therefore the width of the confidence interval) **increases**, too. High confidence levels are desirable, but they come at the expense of wide confidence intervals.

On the other hand, moving down any column in Table 14.3, note that as the sample size **increases** (that is, as the amount of information in the sample increases), the *t* statistic (and therefore the width of the confidence interval) **decreases**. Moving down any column, the square root of sample size also **increases**, which **further decreases** the width of the confidence interval. And so a desirable effect results from moving down in Table 14.3.

The changes just described are not linear. The cost (in terms of increased width of the confidence interval) of increasing a confidence level beyond about 95 percent is high, and the width of a small-sample confidence interval shrinks *relatively* slowly beyond sample sizes of about 15 to 20.

14.9.3 Satisfying the iid-Normal Assumptions in Simulation

How good are the assumptions that values of point estimates resulting from replications in terminating simulations are **iid** and are approximately normally distributed as well? By the very nature of a replication, outputs are **independent** from replication to replication. (Remember that a replication is a simulation using a set of random numbers that are unique to and independent of those used in any other run.)

In terminating simulations, point estimates resulting from replications are also identically distributed. This is because each replication starts under statistically comparable initial conditions, uses input variables following distributions that are identical from replication to replication, and terminates when one and the same ending event has occurred. (Rigorously demonstrating that outputs from properly constructed terminating simulations are identically distributed is beyond our charter here. Those interested in a rigorous treatment should consult general simulation texts.)

Finally, how good is the small-sample assumption that the point estimates in simulation are approximately normally distributed? We pointed out in Chapter 13 that important output variables in systems of interest in simulation often result from additive processes, and so may tend to be normally distributed. For example, manufacturing rate may be normally distributed. Consider that the time to make a unit of product is the **sum** of a series of travel times, waiting times, step (or operation) times, and so on. In turn, manufacturing rate (units per 8-hour shift, say) is a count (a sum) of the individual items produced during an interval of time. And so additive processes are often at work in systems, leading in many cases to normal distributions of output variables. (Remember that the hypothesis of normality can be informally examined by plotting data on probability paper, and can be formally examined with goodness-of-fit testing.)

We conclude that point estimates resulting from replications in terminating simulations may often satisfy the **iid normal** assumptions needed to form **small-sample confidence intervals**.

14.9.4 Large-Sample Confidence Intervals

What about **large-sample confidence intervals**? The large-sample case corresponds to samples of size **30 or more**. The **computational pattern** for confidence intervals is the same for large samples as for small samples. But in the large-sample case, we use a **z statistic** (rather than a t statistic) in the confidence-interval formula. (A z statistic is a value of a standard normal random variable. As sample size becomes large, a t distribution converges asymptotically to a z distribution. Extensive tables of z values can be found in statistics books.)

The last row in Table 14.3 contains the z values to which the corresponding t values converge for arbitrarily large samples. This explains why sample size for the last row is shown as ∞ ("infinity"). For operational purposes, we will use these z values for samples of size greater than 30. (The next to last row in Table 14.3 provides t values for samples of size 30. These can be compared with the z values to see the extent to which t values have converged to z values for samples of size 30.)

The **cost** of working with large samples is clear. Doubling sample size from 15 to 30, for example, doubles the computer time and expense. This may or may not be important. If a replication takes 5 CPU **seconds** on a microcomputer, then the personal and computer costs of going from 15 to 30 replications are minuscule. If a replication takes 5 CPU **minutes** on a microcomputer, then the personal cost in going from 15 to 30 replications is noticeable. If mainframe computer use for simulation is limited to overnight runs, and if the size of the simulation model and the cost accounting are such that $500 is billed for each replication, then both the personal and computer costs in going from 15 to 30 replications may make a few people sit up and take notice.

An obvious **benefit** in working with large samples is that as sample size increases, confidence-interval width decreases. But in the case of large samples, the benefit in this regard is only proportional to the square root of sample size. When working with large samples, for instance, it's necessary to increase sample size by a factor of **four** to decrease confidence-interval width by a factor of **two.**

A more subtle benefit in working with large samples is that **point estimates need not be normally distributed** (as they should be for small-sample confidence intervals to be valid). No matter what distribution is followed by the point estimates, **their average** (that is, the mean of the point estimates) will be approximately normally distributed for samples of size 30 or more, thanks to the Central Limit Theorem (CLT). (We are talking here about appealing to the CLT **after** the point estimates have been formed. In the small-sample discussion of Section 14.9.3, we appealed to the applicability of the CLT in some cases **during** the forming of the values of the point estimates.) This means that if we're working with point estimates that aren't approximately normally distributed, one way to cope with the situation is to increase sample size to 30 or more.

14.9.5 Automating the Calculation of Confidence Intervals in GPSS/H

In the GPSS/H discussed so far, only point estimates of output variables are included in Postreplication Reports. This makes it necessary for now for us to compute the means and standard deviations of these point estimates on a postsimulation basis, and then compute the corresponding confidence intervals. The possibilities for automating such computations in GPSS/H are briefly outlined here, but aren't operationalized in this book.

First, GPSS/H provides powerful and flexible computational and reporting capabilities supported by Ampervariables (including External Ampervariables, which make it possible to execute external functions and subroutines under GPSS/H control), LET Control Statements, BLET Blocks (which are the Block equivalent of LET Control Statements), PUTPIC Control Statements, BPUTPIC Blocks, and such built-in GPSS/H functions as SQRT (square root). These capabilities support GPSS/H-based statistical computations and reporting of results.

Second, through use of GPSS/H PUTPIC statements (or their Block equivalent), information can be written directly by an executing GPSS/H model into one or more external files. The information in these files can then be processed in whatever way, using whatever software may be chosen for this purpose by the modeler.

Finally, GPSS/H provides the **Table entity** as an aid in estimating selected aspects of the **distribution** from which observed values of an output variable come. (The Table entity is described in Section 10 of Chapter 17, but isn't otherwise considered in this book.)

14.10 Exercises

1. Compute a 90 percent confidence interval for the FCFS sample of Table 14.2. Does it match the 90 percent confidence interval reported in Section 14.9.1 ([2.79, 4.28]), as it should?

*2. Compute 80 percent and 95 percent confidence intervals for the FCFS sample of Table 14.2. Do you expect these to be wider or narrower than the 90 percent confidence interval? Are your results consistent with your expectations?

*3. Would you expect a 90 percent confidence interval for the SPT sample of Table 14.2 to be wider or narrower than the equivalent confidence interval for the FCFS sample? Why? Compute a 90 percent confidence interval for the SPT sample. Are your results consistent with your expectations?

*4. Compute a 95 percent confidence interval for the output variable of Table 14.1.

*5. Suppose that the sample of Table 14.1 were of size 20, not 5 (but with the same mean and standard deviation of Table 14.1). Would you expect a 95 percent confidence interval for the output variable to be wider or narrow than that of Exercise 4? Why? Now assume that the sample of Table 14.1 is of size 80, not 5, and repeat your reasoning.

6. Use the sample mean and standard deviation resulting from Exercise 6 of Section 14.7 to compute 95 percent confidence intervals for the four output variables of that exercise (average residence time of Type A ships at the harbor, average time spent by Type A ships waiting for a berth, and each of these same two measures for Type B ships.)

7. Repeat Exercise 6, but in the context of Exercise 7, Section 14.7.

8. Repeat Exercise 6, but in the context of Exercise 8, Section 14.7.

The three remaining problems in this section describe systems involving Poisson arrivals to exponential servers in circumstances under which the problems can be solved analytically. In each problem, you're asked to replicate for the purpose of forming confidence intervals, then check to see whether the confidence intervals contain the known expected result (which is provided here with the statement of the problem). See books on operations research or queuing systems for additional problems of this type, and for discussion of their theoretical solutions.

9. Only one car can be washed at a time at a small carwash. Cars arrive in a Poisson stream with an average interarrival time of 5 minutes. Carwashing time is exponentially distributed, with a mean of 4 minutes. Potential customers who find no waiting space available go elsewhere to have their car washed.

   Model this system. Then use the model to simulate for the alternatives of one, two, and three waiting spaces at the carwash. Carry out 20 replications for each alternative, basing each replication on 8 hours of operation. Assume that the queue is empty and the carwash is idle when each replication begins. At time 0.0, schedule the first arrival of a car in the usual way, by sampling from the interarrival-time distribution. For each alternative, form a 90 percent confidence interval for the fraction of arriving cars that remain for service during the course of an 8-hour day. Do these confidence intervals contain the known expected values of 0.738, 0.826, and 0.861, respectively, that result from modeling the situation analytically?

10. One repairperson has been assigned the responsibility of maintaining three machines. Each machine has a mean running time until failure of 9 hours, exponentially distributed. Repair time is exponentially distributed, with a mean of 2 hours.

    Model this system. Then use the model to estimate the expected number of machines that are running. Carry out 20 replications, basing each replication on 250 hours of operation. Assume that when each replication starts, one machine has just broken down, one has 10 hours to go before it will break down, and the third has 3 hours to go before it will break down. Use the replication results to form a 95 percent confidence interval for the number of running machines. Does this confidence interval contain the expected value of 2.28?

11. A company has two tool cribs in its manufacturing area, each with a single clerk. One tool crib handles tools for heavy machinery, whereas the other handles all other tools. Arrivals at each tool crib are exponential with the same expected interarrival time, 3 minutes. The exponentially distributed service time at each tool crib is 2 minutes.

    It has been proposed that these two tool cribs be combined into a single crib in an attempt to decrease the average number of mechanics at the tool crib, and the average time mechanics spend at the tool crib. Both clerks would work (independently of each other) at the combined tool crib. It is thought that interarrival time at the combined tool crib would be exponential, with a mean of 1.5 minutes, and that service time would continue to be exponential, with a mean of 2 minutes.

    Model the system as is, and the proposed new system, for the purpose of estimating the average number of mechanics at the tool crib (including mechanics being served) and the average time spent at the tool crib (service time included). Carry out 20 replications for each alternative, basing each replication on 8 hours of operation. Each replication should begin with idle clerks and with the initial mechanic arrivals (or arrival, in the case of one tool crib) scheduled at times based on sampling from the appropriate interarrival-time distribution. For each alternative, form a 95 percent confidence interval for the average number of mechanics at the tool crib, and for the average time spent at the tool crib. Do the confidence intervals contain the corresponding expected values? (With two tool cribs, the expected number of mechanics at each crib is two and the expected time at each crib is 6 minutes. When the two tool cribs are combined, the total number of mechanics at the tool crib averages 2.4, and the expected time spent at the tool crib is 3.6 minutes.)

14.11 The Use of Pilot Studies to Estimate Required Sample Size

Sometimes an objective in modeling is to estimate an expected value with a specified precision at a stated confidence level. In the SPT tool crib system of Case Study 9A, for example, suppose it is an objective to form an interval estimate for the expected number of mechanics in the waiting line and be 90 percent confident that the maximum error of estimate will not exceed 0.5 mechanics. In other words, the objective is to form a 90 percent confidence interval whose half-width is (approximately) 0.5.

The half-width of a small-sample confidence interval is

$$t_{\alpha/2}\left(s/\sqrt{n}\right)$$

The only variable in this term that we can control is sample size, n. **If we knew the standard deviation,** we could solve for the value of n such that the half-width would be of a specified value. (Trial and error is involved for small samples because

$$t_{\alpha/2}$$

is a function of n. If n is 30 or greater, we substitute z for

$$t_{\alpha/2}.$$

The value of z is fixed for a given confidence level, and so trial and error is not involved for large samples.) But we usually don't know the standard deviation.

What can we do? We can conduct a **pilot study** to estimate the value of the standard deviation. That is, we can carry out some small number of replications with a model and then use the standard deviation of the point estimates of the mean to estimate the standard deviation of the point estimates. We then compute the sample size needed to form an interval estimate that hopefully has the desired precision. Finally, we **perform additional replications**, bringing the sample obtained in the pilot study up to the size that will, it is hoped, achieve the desired precision in the confidence interval.

For example, we might carry out 10 replications with a model, and then estimate that a sample of size 25 is needed to form a confidence interval with the desired precision. We would then perform an additional 15 replications (**independent of the first 10**), combine them with the first 10, and use the resulting sample of size 25 to form a confidence interval (which, we hope, is at least of the desired precision).

It cannot be guaranteed that the final confidence interval will have the desired precision. This is because the pilot study only provides an **estimate** of the standard deviation of the point estimates. If the standard deviation of the combined sample is **larger** than in the pilot study, then the desired confidence-interval precision will not be achieved. On the other hand, precision superior to that desired will be obtained if the combined sample has a standard deviation **smaller** than in the pilot study.

Critical in this discussion is the requirement that when adding replications to an existing sample, the added replications **must be independent of** those already in the sample. How can additional replications be performed that are independent of those already in hand? We can't simply rerun the model, because then the supporting 0–1 uniform random-number generator(s) would have the same default starting point as in the pilot study, and the first "additional" replications would identically match those in the pilot study. And it would be wasteful to have to **repeat** these replications, and then discard them.

What we need is the ability to **specify nondefault starting points** for the 0–1 uniform random-number generators in GPSS/H. With this ability, we can supplement an existing sample with additional replications independent of those already in hand. In this way, we satisfy the requirement that the point estimates in the combined sample be independent, and we are justified in using the confidence interval methodology presented (assuming the other requirements are also satisfied).

The type of Control Statement used to specify the modeler's choice of starting points for the GPSS/H 0–1 uniform random number generators is introduced in the next section.

14.12 Understanding and Controlling the GPSS/H Random-Number Generators

In this section, we comment on the algorithm used in GPSS/H to generate 0–1 uniform random numbers. We describe how the algorithm has been calibrated and indicate the significance of the default starting points for the GPSS/H 0–1 generators. The RNG Report (**R**andom **N**umber **G**enerator report) provided by GPSS/H is then discussed. Finally, the Control Statement used to override the default starting points of one or more of the 0–1 generators is introduced, and its application in extending sample size is illustrated.

14.12.1 The Lehmer Random-Number Generator in GPSS/H

The algorithm used by GPSS/H to generate 0–1 uniform random numbers was first proposed by

Lehmer (Lehmer, 1951) and since has come to be the most commonly used algorithm for generating random numbers in computing. The algorithm is deterministic, which means the random numbers resulting from its use are reproducible. In other words, the random numbers are not **truly** random, but are only **pseudo**random. (For convenience, we will often use the term "random numbers" instead of "pseudorandom numbers.")

Those new to simulation often think that it would be better to use truly random numbers rather than pseudorandom ones. But there are **advantages** that result from the reproducibility of pseudorandom numbers. For example, the ability to exactly reproduce "random" sequences of events at will makes it much easier to troubleshoot a model if it misbehaves during the model development stage. The circumstances under which the model misbehaves can be recreated, the simulation can be "slowed down" at that point, using GPSS/H **Test Mode** and the **step** command, for example, and the exact cause of the misbehavior can be pinpointed and corrected. Another advantage resulting from reproducibility in simulation is the ability to use **variance reduction techniques** when investigating single-system behavior, or when comparing alternative (competing) systems. Briefly, a variance reduction technique is a method for increasing the statistical precision of simulation results, without the need to increase the amount of simulating which needs to be done. (See Chapter 15 and Sections 5 and 6 of Chapter 16 for details.)

It is not our purpose to describe the Lehmer algorithm in detail, but simply to outline it, indicating that it uses three **whole numbers**, here given the names **multiplier** (which is constant), **pseudorandom factor** (which changes each time the algorithm is executed), and **modulus** (which is constant). When the algorithm is executed, it first forms the product of the multiplier and the current value of the pseudorandom factor, and then takes the modulus of this product as the new value for the pseudorandom factor. This new value (which is some whole number in the closed interval from 1 up to, but not including, the modulus) is then divided by the modulus, producing a result that falls within the open 0–1 interval. This result is the 0–1 random number produced by the algorithm on this occasion. In summary, the Lehmer algorithm works with whole numbers, producing a 0–1 decimal number only as a final step. (Those interested in more exacting details of the algorithm are referred to general simulation texts, for example, Fishman, 1978.)

The **modulus** used for the Lehmer algorithm in GPSS/H is $2^{31}-1$ (which is 2,147,483,647). This is a computationally efficient choice of modulus when a computer memory location consists of 32 binary digits (as is often the case with current computers) and otherwise has the property that this modulus is a prime number with a primitive root of 2, which is desirable for theoretical reasons not explored here.

The statistical goodness of the 0–1 uniform random numbers produced by the Lehmer algorithm depends not only on the modulus, but also on the choice of a **multiplier** for the scheme. Furthermore, some multipliers have the desirable property that **all possible values of the pseudorandom factor** (which, as indicated, fall into the closed interval of integers ranging from 1 up to, but not including, the modulus) are produced by the Lehmer algorithm before the series of pseudorandom factors (and hence the series of 0–1 random numbers) begins (necessarily) to repeat itself. These are referred to as **full period-multipliers**.

Fishman and Moore subjected **more than 534 million** full period multipliers for the Lehmer algorithm (with modulus $2^{31}-1$) to empirical analysis with respect to the statistical properties of the 0–1 series of random numbers they produce (Fishman and Moore, 1986). In their work, they identified **five** multipliers that produce 0–1 uniform random numbers best meeting the stringent standards employed in their research. GPSS/H uses the first of these five multipliers. (The multiplier is the first one shown in Table 5, p. 39, of Fishman and Moore, 1986. The value of this multiplier is 742,938,285.)

In addition to a modulus and multiplier, the Lehmer algorithm must be calibrated with an initial value of the pseudorandom factor. This initial value is often referred to as the **base number**, or **seed**, of the random-number generator. The base number built into GPSS/H has been chosen on the basis of unpublished research conducted by the vendor of GPSS/H to find a base producing 0–1 random-number sequences having certain desirable statistical properties described in the following subsection. (The base number built into GPSS/H is 266,301,881.)

Now visualize the time series of 0–1 uniform random numbers produced by repeated application of the Lehmer algorithm as calibrated (in terms of modulus, multiplier, and base number) in GPSS/H. Figure 14.16 provides this visualization. The time series of 0–1 random numbers is represented in the left column in Figure 14.16, not in terms of the **values** of the numbers, but in terms of the **position** occupied by these numbers in the time series. (Selected values of the 0–1 random numbers themselves are shown in Table 13.1.) A random number's position in the time series indicates the extent to which the number is offset from the

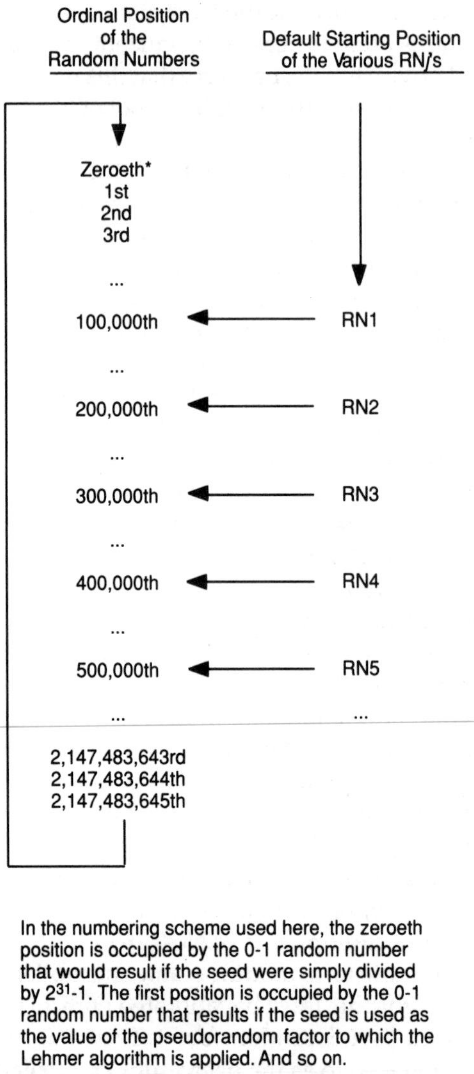
Ordinal Position of the Random Numbers
Default Starting Position of the Various RN/s
Zeroeth*
1st
2nd
3rd
...
100,000th
RN1
...
200,000th
RN2
...
300,000th
RN3
...
400,000th
RN4
...
500,000th
RN5
...
...
2,147,483,643rd
2,147,483,644th
2,147,483,645th
In the numbering scheme used here, the zeroeth position is occupied by the 0-1 random number that would result if the seed were simply divided by 2^31-1. The first position is occupied by the 0-1 random number that results if the seed is used as the value of the pseudorandom factor to which the Lehmer algorithm is applied. And so on.

Figure 14.16 *The Ordinal Position of Random Numbers in GPSS/H, and the Default Starting Positions of RN1, RN2, and so on.*

0–1 number corresponding to the base. For example, the 100,000th random number in the series is offset from the base by 100,000 numbers, the 200,000th random number is offset from the base by 200,000 numbers, and so on.

As indicated in Figure 14.16, the **default offset** for RN1 is 100,000; the default offset for RN2 is 200,000, and so on. In general, the default offset for RN*j* (*j* = 1, 2, 3, ...) in GPSS/H is *j* times 100,000. (In other words, by default each sequence of random numbers is separated from the immediately preceding and immediately following sequences by 100,000 random numbers.) It is these **offsets** that the modeler can control by use of the RMULT Control Statement discussed in the next subsection.

It is not necessary for GPSS/H to start with the initial value of the pseudorandom factor, then compute succeeding values of this factor, one by one, until getting to the starting points for RN1, RN2, and so on. This is because the value of any pseudorandom factor in the series can be directly and efficiently computed for the Lehmer algorithm. No inefficiencies are introduced, then, by having RN1, RN2, and so on be offset by such large amounts from the base.

We see then that GPSS/H uses a random-number algorithm calibrated in only one way. Each of the random-number sources (RN1, RN2, etc.) produces 0–1 uniform random numbers resulting from application of this algorithm as calibrated. The random numbers produced are widely separated **subsequences** drawn from the single time series of 0–1 uniform random numbers computed by this algorithm.

After a **very** large number of 0–1 values have been produced by a GPSS/H pseudorandom number generator, the sequence of values repeats exactly. This fact is illustrated in Figure 14.16. Suppose we start with the first value and produce values from that point forward. After the 2,147,483,645th unique 0–1 value has been produced, the next 0–1 value will be the zeroth value, and the next value after that will again be the first value in the sequence, meaning that after experiencing 2,147,483,646 unique values, we have now wrapped back on our starting point. The number of different random numbers in the time series, 2,147,483,646, is referred to as the **period** of the random-number generator. And so each of the GPSS/H RNGs has a period of 2,147,483,646.

14.12.2 The RNG Report

During a replication, GPSS/H gathers certain types of information for each of the random-number generators used in the replication, and then produces a Postreplication Report for each such generator. Figure 14.17 provides an example of such an RNG (**R**andom **N**umber **G**enerator) report for a replication with a model (not shown) using RN1, RN2, and RN3. In Figure 14.17, parenthesized numbers have been placed over each column in the report. (These numbers are not part of the report, but have been added to support discussion here.) The information in these columns will now be discussed by column number:

(1) The **RANDOM STREAM** column gives the number of the generator to which that row in

the report applies. (In Figure 14.17, RN1, RN2, and RN3 are included in the report.)

(2) The **ANTITHETIC VARIATES** column indicates whether the random numbers themselves **or their antithetic equivalents** were used. (Antithetic variates and their use are discussed in Chapter 15.) Column entries of **OFF** and **ON** are used to indicate whether the random numbers themselves (OFF) or their antithetic equivalents (ON) were used. (For RN1 and RN2 in Figure 14.17, the random numbers themselves were used; for RN3, the antithetic equivalents were used.)

(3 **INITIAL POSITION** indicates the ordinal position (in the time series of random numbers produced by the generator) from which the **first** random number came. (In Figure 14.17, RN1, RN2, and RN3 started from initial positions of 100,000, 125,000, and 150,000, respectively. See Figure 14.16.)

(4) **CURRENT POSITION** indicates the ordinal position from which the generator's **next** random number will come. (The CURRENT POSITIONs for RN1, RN2, and RN3 in Figure 14.17 are 125,048, 125,079, and 150,250, respectively.)

If no samples have been drawn from a random number generator, then its CURRENT POSITION equals its INITIAL POSITION. (In such a case, there will be no report for this generator.)

If the CURRENT POSITION of one generator extends beyond the INITIAL POSITION of another generator in an RNG Report, then **overlapping use of random numbers** has occurred in the simulation. This means that at some point in the simulation, random numbers drawn from the **overlapping** generator were numerically identical to random numbers drawn earlier from the **overlapped** generator. Overlap means there was some unrealistic correlation in sampling from the distributions of the input variables that used the corresponding 0–1 generators as their sampling basis. Whether such unrealistic correlation would be detrimental to the conclusions eventually reached in a simulation study is a matter of speculation. Strictly speaking, the modeler should discard any replications in which overlap has occurred. (If overlap occurs, it can be overcome by increasing the initial separation of the overlapping generators. This is accomplished by use of the RMULT Control Statement, to be discussed in the next subsection.)

In Figure 14.17, note that RN1 has overlapped RN2 by 48 values.

(5) **SAMPLE COUNT** (sample size) indicates how many random numbers were sampled from the generator. (The sample sizes for RN1, RN2, and RN3 in Figure 14.17 are 25,048, 79, and 250, respectively.)

(6) **CHI-SQUARE UNIFORMITY** gives the **achieved significance level** of a Chi-square goodness-of-fit (GOF) test for the uniformity of the random numbers drawn from the generator.

The purpose of the chi-square GOF test is to examine the hypothesis that the sampled random numbers come from a source of random numbers uniformly distributed on the 0–1 interval. For this purpose, GPSS/H divides the 0–1 interval into 16 consecutive, nonoverlapping subintervals, each of width one-sixteenth. In theory, it's expected that one-sixteenth of the values in the sample will fall into each of these subintervals. GPSS/H counts the sampled random numbers that do fall into these subintervals. For each subinterval, the difference between the expected and actual counts is squared (hence the name Chi-**square**); then the squares for the 16 subintervals are summed. The **achieved significance level** of the resulting sum is the **probability** that the sum will take on this value (or a value more improbable under the hypothesis of uniformity) if the random numbers do come from a uniform 0–1 population. In the case of a truly uniform 0–1 population, this probability will be 0.05 or less 5 percent of the time in the long run.

(1) RANDOM STREAM	(2) ANTITHETIC VARIATES	(3) INITIAL POSITION	(4) CURRENT POSITION	(5) SAMPLE COUNT	(6) CHI-SQUARE UNIFORMITY
1	OFF	100000	125048	25048	0.71
2	OFF	125000	125079	79	N/A
3	ON	150000	150250	250	0.34

Figure 14.17 *An Example of an RNG Report*

If replications with achieved significance levels of 0.05 or less occur more than 5 percent of the time in a set of replications, the modeler might choose to discard some of these replications. The modeler could then work with fewer replications or could replace the discarded replications with additional replications.

We said earlier that the **base number** (seed) chosen for the Lehmer algorithm in GPSS/H is based on research conducted by the vendor of GPSS/H. The criterion for choosing this base number was to have random numbers coming from the default settings of RN1 through RN20 show good CHI-SQUARE UNIFORMITY measures.

If fewer than 80 random numbers are drawn from a generator, the entry in the CHI-SQUARE UNIFORMITY column will be **N/A** (**N**ot **A**pplicable). This is because it is inappropriate to use the Chi-square test for uniformity if the expected count per subinterval is less than five.

In Figure 14.17, the samples drawn from RN1 and RN3 show CHI-SQUARE UNIFORMITY measures of 0.71 and 0.34, respectively. These measures are well above the relatively improbable measures of 0.05 or less. The sample drawn from RN2 is of size less than 80, and so the CHI-SQUARE UNIFORMITY measure is N/A.

In this subsection, we've described the RNG Report provided by GPSS/H. We've also indicated how to use the information in the report. The RNG Report lets the modeler steer around the use of overlapping random numbers, and avoid overrepresentation of low-probability random-number samples in replications retained for subsequent analysis. GPSS/H is the only simulation language (as of 1990) that provides such a report for the random numbers used in a replication. (With other languages, the modeler has no way of knowing whether overlapping use of random numbers has taken place, or whether low-probability samples of random numbers have been used in a replication.)

14.12.3 The RMULT Control Statement

The type of Control Statement used to **control the Current Position** (CURRENT POSITION) of one or more of the GPSS/H random-number generators is the RMULT statement. (As pointed out, a generator's CURRENT POSITION is the ordinal position in the time series of random numbers from which that generator's **next** random number will come.)

The general form of an RMULT Control Statement is shown in Figure 14.18. The word RMULT appears in the Operation field. The statement is never labeled. (A syntax error occurs if an attempt is made to label an RMULT statement.) The statement has one (optional) Operand per random-number generator. The A Operand corresponds to RN1; the B Operand to RN2; the C Operand to RN3; and so

1	Label (2 - 9)	Operation (11 - 20)	Operand (22 - 72) →
	never used	**RMULT**	**A,B,C,D,E, etc.**

Label or Operand	Significance	Default Value or Result
Label	Not Applicable	Must default (compile-time error otherwise)
A	The new Current Position for RN1	The Current Position for RN1 is not changed
B	The new Current Position for RN2	The Current Position for RN2 is not changed
C, D, E, etc.	The new Current Position for RN3, RN4, RN5, etc.	The Current Position for RN3, RN4, RN5, etc., is not changed

Figure 14.18 *The RMULT Control Statement*

on. An Operand supplies the value at which the corresponding generator's Current Position is to be set when the RMULT statement is executed.

If a generator hasn't yet been used (for example, if the first replication hasn't yet taken place), then its Current Position is its Initial Position (INITIAL POSITION). In this case, to change the generator's Current Position is to change its default Initial Position.

Several examples of RMULT statements are given in Figure 14.19. When the Example 1 RMULT is executed, the Current Position of RN1 will be set to 50,000. The Current Position of each of the other random number generators will be left "as is." (No Operands are specified for them.)

When the RMULT of Example 2 is executed, the Current Position of RN1 (and RN3, RN4, etc.) will be left as is, and the Current Position of RN2 will be set to 125,000. (Note the use of a leading comma in the Example 2 Operands field to default on the RMULT's A Operand. This results in the Current Position of RN1 being left as is.)

In Example 3 of Figure 14.19, execution of the RMULT statement causes the Current Position of RN1, RN2, and RN4 to be set to 25,000, 50,000, and 100,000, respectively, with the Current Position of the other generators left as is. If the other generators in this example still have their default Initial Position, then RN4's position will be **beyond** that of RN3 (whose default Initial Position is 300,000). There is nothing wrong with this.

Example 4 of Figure 14.19 is motivated by the following scenario. Suppose that starting from their default Initial Positions, RN1 and RN2 have been used to carry out a series of ten replications in a study. Assume that at the end of the tenth replication, the Current Positions of RN1 and RN2 are 123,482 and 202,333. Suppose the decision has now been made to add eight more replications to the set of 10. If the RMULT statement of Example 4 is executed before beginning the first of these 8 additional replications, the random number sequences for RN1 and RN2 will pick up where they left off previously. And so the 8 additional replications will be independent of the first 10. (There are any number of ways to achieve independence of the additional 8 replications in this scenario, of course. For example, RN1 could be set to 300,000, and RN2 to 400,000, before carrying out the additional replications. The RMULT statement would be easier to key this way.)

The position occupied by one or more RMULT statements in a Model File will depend on the relative timing with which the modeler wants to have the statements executed. If one or more generators are to take nondefault Initial Positions, then the corresponding RMULT statement(s) should be executed prior to the first START Statement execution. Their position in the Model File could then be that of Box 2 in Figure 14.10. If the Current Position of one or more generators is to be modified between replications, then the corresponding RMULT(s) should be executed between START executions. Its (or their) position would then correspond to Box 6 in Figure 14.10.

14.13 Case Study 14A: Use of a Pilot Study with the SPT Tool Crib

1. Statement of the Problem

In the system of Case Study 9A ("Alternative Service Orders at a Tool Crib"), estimate the expected number of mechanics in the waiting line for the SPT service order with a targeted precision of ±0.5 mechanics at a 90 percent confidence level. Treating the SPT sample of Table 14.2 as a pilot study, first use information in that sample to estimate the total sample size required to form the requested confidence interval. Then modify a copy of the Case Study 9A SPT Model File (in model9a2.gps) to carry out the additional replications needed to supplement the 10 replications in the pilot study and bring the total sample up to the size estimated to meet the objective.

Note that only RN1 is used in the Case Study 9A SPT model. It's necessary to know (at least approxi-

```
RMULT    50000                    Example 1
RMULT    ,125000                  Example 2
RMULT    25000,50000,,100000      Example 3
RMULT    123482,202333            Example 4
```

Figure 14.19 *Examples of the RMULT Control Statement* mately) the Current Position of RN1 at the end of the pilot study in order to specify an RMULT Control Statement in such a way as to have the supplemental replications be independent of those in the pilot study. The Current Position of RN1 at the conclusion of the pilot study turns out to be 103,262. (It's not necessary to take 103,262 as the Initial RN1 Position in this case study; for keying convenience, simply take 105,000 as the Initial Position.)

Having formed the needed Model File, make a Batch run with it. Using the results to supplement the pilot study, form an interval estimate of the average number of mechanics in the waiting line at a 90 percent confidence interval. Is the targeted precision achieved in this interval estimate? (It won't be if the standard deviation of the supplemented sample is larger than that in the pilot study.)

2. Approach Taken in Building the Model

In making the needed changes in a copy of the Case Study 9A SPT Model File, these two steps were carried out:

1. The sample size estimated to provide the requested confidence interval was computed to be 43.25. Rounded up, this resulted in a total sample size of 44. And so 34 additional replications were needed to supplement the 10 replications in the pilot study.
2. The needed mechanical changes were made in the Model File. See the Modified Source Echo.

3. Table of Definitions

The only new element added to the Case Study 9A SPT Model File is the Integer Ampervariable &I, used as a index in a control loop. No new Table of Definitions is provided to replace the one given for Case Study 9A.

4. Block Diagram

The Block Diagram matches that for the Case Study 9A SPT model and is not repeated here.

5. Modified Source Echo

The Modified Source Echo of the Model File is given in Figure 14A.1. These four aspects of the Model File are to be noted:

1. An INTEGER Compiler Directive has been included for loop index &I. (See statement 9 in Figure 14A.1.)
2. The needed RMULT Control Statement has been placed in the Model File. (See statement 15.)
3. A DO/ENDDO control loop is used to control the replications. (See statements 55 through 66.)
4. PUTPIC/Picture statements have been used to label the Postreplication Reports. (See statements 59 through 62.)

Except for these differences, the Case Study 14A Model File is highly similar to that for the SPT service order in Case Study 9A.

6. Postreplication Reports

The replication reports resulting from execution of the Case Study 14A Model File are not shown, but are summarized in terms of the key output variable in Table 14A.1, where the original 10 Table 14.2 SPT replications from the pilot study are repeated for convenience. The sample mean and standard deviation for the full set of 44 replications are also shown in Table 14A.1, along with the resulting 90 percent confidence interval.

7. Discussion

Postreplication Output. The sample standard deviation in Table 14A.1 is smaller than that in the pilot study (1.62 versus 1.999). This results in more than meeting the targeted precision of ±0.5 mechanics in the waiting line at a 90 percent confidence interval. As shown in Table 14A.1, the 90 percent confidence interval computed from the Table 14A.1 data is [2.2, 3.0], which corresponds to a precision of ±0.4 mechanics in the waiting line. Just as the standard deviation in the supplemented sample is smaller than in the pilot sample by about 20 percent, so too is there an overachievement of about 20 percent in the targeted precision.

```
STMT#  BLOCK#  *LOC    OPERATION  A,B,C,D,E,F,G    COMMENTS
                          SIMULATE                                    Case Study 14A
                *                            A Tool Crib System (SPT Service Order)
                *    (Use of the Case Study 9A Model to Increase the Size of a Sample)
                *                                           Base Time Unit: 1 Second
                **********************************************************************
                *         Compiler Directives (INTEGER)                              *
                **********************************************************************
                *
                          INTEGER    &I       &I is a DO-loop index
                *
                **********************************************************************
                *         Control Statements (RMULT)                                 *
                **********************************************************************
                *
                          RMULT      105000      set RN1 initial position = 105000
                *
                **********************************************************************
                *         Model Segment 1 (Type 1 Mechanics)                         *
                **********************************************************************
                *
          1               GENERATE   420,360,,,5    Type 1 mechanics arrive
                *                                   (Priority 5)
          2               QUEUE      TOOLWAIT       start TOOLWAIT Queue membership
          3               SEIZE      CLERK          request/capture the clerk
          4               DEPART     TOOLWAIT       end TOOLWAIT Queue membership
          5               ADVANCE    300,90         service time
          6               RELEASE    CLERK          free the clerk
          7               TERMINATE  0              leave the tool crib area
                *
                **********************************************************************
                *         Model Segment 2 (Type 2 Mechanics)                         *
                **********************************************************************
                *
          8               GENERATE   360,240,,,10   Type 2 mechanics arrive
                *                                   (Priority 10)
          9               QUEUE      TOOLWAIT       start TOOLWAIT Queue membership
         10               SEIZE      CLERK          request/capture the clerk
         11               DEPART     TOOLWAIT       end TOOLWAIT Queue membership
         12               ADVANCE    100,30         service time
         13               RELEASE    CLERK          free the clerk
         14               TERMINATE  0              leave the tool crib area
                *
                **********************************************************************
                *         Model Segment 3 (Run-Control Xact)                         *
                **********************************************************************
                *
         15               GENERATE   28800          control Xact comes after 8 hours
         16               TERMINATE  1              reduce the TC value by 1,
                *                                   ending Xact movement
```

***Figure 14A.1** Modified Source Echo of the Case Study 14A Model File*
(continued on the next page)

```
         *
         ***********************************************************************
         *          Run-Control Statements                                   *
         ***********************************************************************
         *
                    DO        &I=1,34,1        control for 34 replications
         *
                       START      1            start the &I-th replication
         *
                       PUTPIC  LINES=3,FILE=SYSPRINT,(&I)
         0======================================================================
          The Postsimulation Report above is for supplementary replication *.
          ======================================================================
         *
                       CLEAR                   clear for the next replication
         *
                    ENDDO                      proceed to the next value of &I
         *
                    END                        end of Model-File execution
```

Figure 14A.1 (concluded)

14.14 Exercises

1. The sample size required to form the requested confidence interval in Case Study 14A was computed as 43.25. Repeat this computation to see if your results agree with the 43.25.

2. Repeat Case Study 14A, except for the FCFS tool crib. Note that the FCFS standard deviation in Table 14.2 is over 30 percent smaller than the Table 14.2 SPT standard deviation. This leads to a notably smaller supplementary stage 2 sample when the targeted precision of the stage 2 confidence interval is ±0.5 mechanics. (A total sample of size 20 is needed, so the pilot sample of 10 only needs to be supplemented with 10 additional replications.) What precision do you achieve with the supplemented sample?

3. The 90 percent confidence interval in Exercise 2 turns out to be [2.5, 4.0], which fails to meet the targeted precision of ±0.5 mechanics. Viewing the complete set of 20 replications from Exercise 2 as a pilot study, supplement these with additional replications in an attempt to satisfy the targeted precision of ±0.5 mechanics for a 90 percent confidence interval. Does the confidence interval you compute still fail to satisfy the desired precision, or does it more than satisfy it?

4. For the SPT service order at the tool crib of Case Study 9A, ignore Table 14.2 and Case Study 14A and start all over again, repeating the pilot study and the supplemental study with replications independent of those in Table 14A.1. (This means you'll have to use an RMULT statement even in the pilot study.) Compare the sample standard deviations you obtain at each of the two stages with those of Table 14.2 and Case Study 14A. What precision have you achieved (in the interval estimate of the average number of mechanics in the waiting line) at the end of the second stage?

*5. Suppose someone makes the claim that the SPT results in Table 14.2 are not independent of the FCFS results reported there. Would you support this claim, or would you refute it? Explain.

(Hint: Does the first type 1 mechanic in the first FCFS replication arrive at the same time as the first type 1 mechanic in the first SPT replication? What about the first type 2 mechanic? What about the time at which the third mechanic arrives? What about the service time required by the mechanic who arrives first?)

6. In Exercise 6 of Section 14.7, you performed 20 replications for Case Study 11A ("Ships Un/loading at a Harbor"). Using these 20 replications as a pilot study, decide what precision you would like to have in a 90 percent confidence interval for

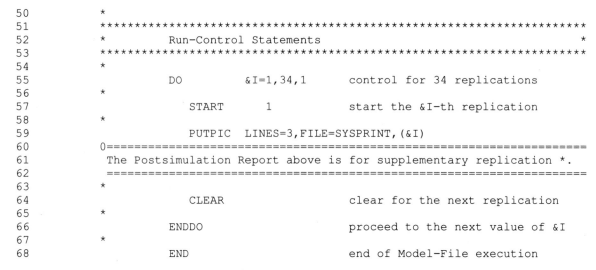

Table 14A.1

Average number of mechanics in the waiting line for each of 44 replications (10 pilot, 34 supplementary) in Case Study 14A

Replication Number	Average Waiting-Line Length	Replication Number	Average Waiting-Line Length
1	1.501	23	1.322
2	2.033	24	1.725
3	2.456	25	4.888
4	7.584	26	3.512
5	2.890	27	1.500
6	3.060	28	1.186
7	0.967	29	1.510
8	5.536	30	3.512
9	2.489	31	1.351
10	4.163	32	4.768
11	1.370	33	5.266
12	4.801	34	1.345
13	1.629	35	1.256
14	0.605	36	1.217
15	1.311	37	4.160
16	2.530	38	3.612
17	3.927	39	1.604
18	1.839	40	1.895
19	0.857	41	0.994
20	2.445	42	5.826
21	1.914	43	3.253
22	1.633	44	1.206
		Sample mean:	2.601
		Sample standard deviation:	1.62
		90% confidence interval:	[2.2, 3.0]

the output variable, "average residence time of Type A ships at the harbor." Then estimate the number of additional replications needed to achieve this objective. Do the modeling necessary to obtain these replications. Compute the corresponding 90 percent confidence interval for the supplemented sample. Have you achieved the targeted precision with this confidence interval?

7. Repeat Exercise 6, except in the context of Exercise 7 of Section 14.7. Base your work on the output variable "average waiting time for patients in NIALINE1."

8. Repeat Exercise 6, except in the context of Exercise 8 of Section 14.7. Base your work on the output variable "percent zero entries for the use of GROUP1 machines."

15 The Use of Antithetic Variates in Single-System Modeling

15.1 Preview

This chapter introduces antithetic modeling, a technique that can significantly increase the statistical precision obtained for a given number of replications when investigating the performance of single systems. First, the concept of antithetic variates is presented. Then the method of providing antithetic inputs in simulation is described. The details of obtaining antithetic random numbers in GPSS/H are provided. The need for synchronized use of random numbers in antithetic modeling is indicated, and the use of dedicated random-number generators to achieve synchronization is explained. Finally, setting up Model Files to automate antithetic modeling is discussed. A case study is presented to show antithetic modeling at work.

15.2 The Concept of Antithetic Variates

The half-width of a confidence interval is directly proportional to the standard deviation in a sample of point estimates. If we can reduce the standard deviation in a sample, then we'll reduce the width of a confidence interval computed from the sample (other things being equal). One way to try to reduce the standard deviation in a single-system model is by the use of antithetic variates.

In general, techniques that attempt to reduce the standard deviation in a sample are known as "variance reduction techniques" (VRTs). The standard deviation is the square root of the variance, of course, which explains use of the term "variance" in the foregoing phrase. Descriptions of such techniques can be found under the category of variance reduction in general simulation texts. Antithetic variates is one of these techniques that is generally fruitful.

The use of antithetic variates involves working with **pairs** of replications, forming the **average** of the two point estimates in the pair. The two replications making up a pair, instead of being independent of each other, are, it is hoped, negatively correlated, with a relatively extreme result in one replication being counterbalanced by a relatively extreme result (but in the opposite direction) in the other replication. (The word "antithetic" means opposed to, or opposite of.) In the averaging process, pairs of opposite, relatively extreme results tend to cancel each other out, resulting in less variability in the average of the pairs. (The same considerations apply to pairs of opposite, nonextreme results, but the potential reduction in variability in nonextreme cases is not as great.)

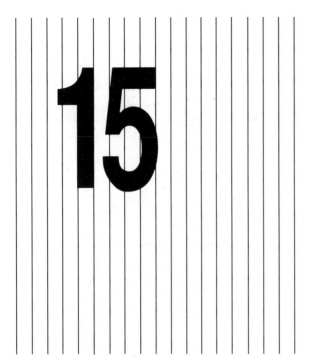

The idea of antithetic replications can be illustrated with the homely example of tossing a pair of fair dice to estimate the expected result. Column 1 in Table 15.1 lists the 11 results that can occur when a pair of dice is tossed. Column 2 lists the relative frequencies with which these results occur for fair dice. Column 3 lists the results that are **antithetic** to those of column 1. Because of symmetry, the relative frequencies in column 2 apply to column 3 as well as to column 1.

Consider the extreme nonantithetic result "2" in row 1 of Table 15.1. Its antithetic equivalent is the opposite extreme result "12." (Both these results occur with relative frequency 1/36th.) These two extreme results counterbalance each other, their average being 7 (shown in column four of Table 15.1), which happens to be the **expected** result in tossing a pair of fair dice. Or consider the nonextreme result "6." Its antithetic equivalent is the opposite nonextreme result "8." (Both of these results occur with relative frequency 5/36th.) These two nonextreme results counterbalance each other, their average being 7, and so on, throughout Table 15.1.

Now suppose you have a model to simulate tossing a pair of fair dice, and you've been authorized to carry out 10 replications with the model to estimate the expected outcome. Would you prefer carrying out 10 independent replications, or 5 paired antithetic replications? The answer is obvious in this example. In fact, you can see from Table 15.1 that when tossing a pair of dice, only 1 antithetic pair of replications would be needed to determine the expected outcome exactly.

Table 15.1 illustrates a case of **perfect negative correlation**. (In perfect negative correlation, the correlation coefficient equals -1. See a statistics text or a general simulation text for details.) The result is that the variance in the paired averages is reduced to **zero**. (In contrast, for **independent** replications the expected variance in tossing a pair of fair dice is **almost 6**, namely, 35/6.) In situations of real interest, the negative correlation will almost certainly not be perfect. Law and Kelton provide examples in which the use of antithetic variates reduces variance on the order of 60 to 65 percent (Law and Kelton, 1982, pp. 356–357). And in the case study in this chapter, variance is reduced by almost 50 percent. These are potentially handsome payoffs, because not much extra effort is needed to work with antithetic variates in GPSS/H, as we'll soon see. (Other things being equal, the higher the variance of the input variables, the greater is the potential reduction in the variance of the output variables in antithetic modeling.)

It is interesting to compare antithetic modeling with the alternative of independent replications in the forming of confidence intervals. **For a given number of replications**, sample size is halved when antithetic pairs rather than independent replications are used. (Each **pair** of antithetic replications produces only **one** average for subsequent use in the confidence-interval computation.) For example, the same effort is required to produce 10 antithetic pairs as to produce 20 independent replications. This reduction in sample size evidences itself in two ways in confidence-interval computation:

Table 15.1

Nonantithetic and antithetic results in tossing a pair of dice

Nonantithetic Result	Relative Frequency	Antithetic Equivalent	Average of the Paired Replications
2	1/36	12	7
3	2/36	11	7
4	3/36	10	7
5	4/36	9	7
6	5/36	8	7
7	6/36	7	7
8	5/36	6	7
9	4/36	5	7
10	3/36	4	7
11	2/36	3	7
12	1/36	2	7

1. For small-sample confidence intervals, the smaller the sample, the larger the value of the t statistic. This leads to wider small-sample confidence intervals, other things being equal. (For large-sample confidence intervals, the z statistic doesn't depend on sample size, and so this is not a large-sample issue.)
2. The width of a confidence interval is inversely proportional to the square root of sample size. And so reducing sample size by a factor of two requires that variance must be reduced by a factor of two, just to break even in terms of antithetic variates versus independent replications. Fortunately, the process of averaging **uncorrelated** pairs of observations **does** reduce variance by a factor of two. (In other words, there is "guaranteed" variance reduction by a factor of two when uncorrelated pairs are averaged. This fact isn't demonstrated here. Interested readers are referred to Law and Kelton, 1982, pp. 334 et seq.) This means that any **further** reduction in variance that results by working with **negatively correlated** pairs is all to the good, even though sample size has been halved.

And so it's just in terms of point 1 that cutting sample size in half has a somewhat detrimental influence on confidence-interval width, and that's only in the small-sample case. Experience suggests that in antithetic modeling, the small detrimental effect of working with a somewhat larger t statistic is strongly offset by the reduction in variance that usually results.

Now consider the spirit of antithetic replications in a simple one-line, one-server system. If the interarrival time for the next arrival is **smaller** than average, and if the service time for its predecessor arrival is **larger** than average, then this next arrival may experience a waiting time **larger** than average. In the paired antithetic replication, if the interarrival time for this same next arrival can be made **larger** than average, and if the service time for its predecessor arrival can be made **smaller** than average, then this next arrival may experience a waiting time **smaller** than average (and may not have to wait at all). And so a larger-than-average waiting time can be counterbalanced by a smaller-than-average waiting time. If similar counterbalancing can be achieved throughout the course of two paired replications, then it is reasonable that waiting times averaged across the two replications will be closer to their expected value than they might be otherwise. In turn, the variance in a sample of such paired averages would show reduced variability, and smaller confidence intervals would result.

The intuition appealed to in the one-line, one-server system is born out mathematically. It's not difficult to show that if an output variable is negatively correlated with itself (that is, has a negative covariance) in paired replications, then the variance of the paired averages is less than when the pairs are uncorrelated. The interested reader is again referred to Law and Kelton (1982, pp. 354 et seq.) for details.

15.3 Providing Antithetic Inputs in Simulation

An attempt is made to achieve negative correlation for the **output** from an antithetic replication by using perfectly negatively correlated 0–1 values as the basis for sampling from the **input** distributions. A random number from a uniform 0–1 population is perfectly negatively correlated with its 1's complement. (This fact is not demonstrated here.) The 1's complement of a number equals 1 minus the number. For example, the 1's complement of 0.25 is 0.75, the 1's complement of 0.05 is 0.95, and so on.

Suppose now that RN2 (say) is used exclusively for sampling from an interarrival-time distribution. In a **nonantithetic** replication, values taken **directly** from RN2 are used for the sampling. If the ith value from RN2 is 0.05, then 0.05 is mapped into the ith interarrival time. (When the method of inversion is used for sampling, a fifth percentile value from RN2 maps into a fifth percentile value from the interarrival-time distribution.) In the paired **antithetic** replication, the ith value from RN2 will be 0.05 again. This value will be used **indirectly** by converting it to its **antithetic equivalent**, 0.95, and then mapping the 0.95 into the ith interarrival time. (A ninety-fifth percentile value from RN2 maps into a ninety-fifth percentile value from the interarrival-time distribution when the sampling is based on the method of inversion.)

When a pair of perfectly negatively correlated 0–1 values is used to sample from an input distribution, will the pair of sampled values be perfectly negatively correlated? Not unless the input distribution is symmetric. For example, if a pair of perfectly negatively correlated 0–1 values is used to sample from an exponential distribution (which is a nonsymmetric distribution), the sampled values will have a correlation coefficient of only about -0.64. And so, in general, corresponding outputs in a nonantithetic-antithetic pair won't be perfectly negatively correlated.

Even if corresponding samples from input distributions in a pair of nonantithetic-antithetic replications were perfectly negatively correlated, this wouldn't guarantee perfectly negatively correlated outputs from the model. A model is a set of rules used to map inputs into outputs. These rules are evidenced in the logical structure of the model, and reflect dependencies among various elements in the system being modeled. A model converts inputs into outputs by a potentially long and complicated process. It's extremely unlikely that perfect negative correlation can be maintained during this process. (In pathological cases, the outputs might even be **positively** correlated, and then the attempted variance reduction would backfire, resulting in **increased** variance. However, there seems to be no evidence of this happening in cases of practical interest.)

15.4 Obtaining Antithetic 0–1 Uniform Random Numbers in GPSS/H

We've seen that an antithetic replication is produced by repeating its nonantithetic counterpart, specifying that antithetic 0–1 uniform random numbers are to be used to drive the antithetic replication. This creates the need to obtain antithetic 0–1 uniform random numbers.

It's easy to produce an antithetic sequence of 0–1 uniform random numbers in GPSS/H. Antithetic random numbers can be obtained from RNj ($j = 1,2,3, \ldots$) in GPSS/H by using the RMULT Control Statement and prefixing the jth Operand with a minus sign (-).

```
RMULT   25000,50000
          (a)

RMULT   -25000,-50000
          (b)
```

Figure 15.1 *RMULT Statements for a Pair of Antithetic Replications (a) RMULT Statement for a Nonantithetic Replication. (b) RMULT Statement for the Paired Antithetic Replication.*

For example, suppose we want to use antithetic modeling in a one-line, one-server system, and suppose that RN1 and RN2 are used to sample from the interarrival and service time distributions, respectively. If the RMULT Statement in Figure 15.1(a) is executed to set the starting points for RN1 and RN2 in a nonantithetic replication, then the RMULT Statement in Figure 15.1(b) can be executed to set the starting points for these two generators in the paired antithetic replication.

As we'll see in Section 15.5, an RMULT Operand in GPSS/H does not have to be a constant, but in general can be an **arithmetic expression**. (A constant is a one-term arithmetic expression.) When an arithmetic expression consisting of two or more terms is used as an RMULT Operand, antithetic random numbers are obtained by **putting parentheses around the expression** and preceding the left parenthesis with a minus sign. (An example is given later, in Figure 15.2.)

15.5 Synchronized Use of 0–1 Uniform Random Numbers

The use of 0–1 uniform random numbers in an antithetic replication must be consistent with their use in the nonantithetic counterpart. For example, if the ith value from RN2 is used to sample an interarrival time in a nonantithetic replication, then its antithetic equivalent should be used to sample the corresponding interarrival time in the paired antithetic replication. This requirement is sometimes described by saying that the use of 0–1 random numbers in the nonantithetic and antithetic replications must be **synchronized**.

Consider an example of **unsynchronized** use of random numbers in an **incorrect** attempt at antithetic modeling. Suppose we want to model a simple one-line, one-server system. The two input variables are interarrival time and service time. Suppose RN1 is used to sample from **both** of the corresponding distributions. Suppose further that, in a **nonantithetic** replication, the ith value from RN1 is used to determine a service time. Assume this RN1 value is relatively large, and consequently results in a relatively long service time. While service is ongoing, the next event might then be an arrival, meaning the $(i + 1)$-st value is used to schedule the **next arrival**.

Now consider the **antithetic** replication, and suppose again the ith antithetic value from RN1 is used to determine a service time. The antithetic equivalent of the ith value will be relatively small, resulting in a relatively short service time. The next event might then be completion of this short service, after which a waiting customer (assuming there is one) will be put into service. This means the $(i + 1)$-st value from RN1 in the antithetic replication will be used to schedule the **next service completion**. And so the use of values from RN1 in the antithetic and nonantithetic replications is not synchronized.

How can synchronized use of 0–1 uniform random numbers be achieved? By working with **dedicated random number generators**, that is, by dedicating to each input variable in a model a random-number generator that is used for the **sole purpose** of sampling from the corresponding distribution. In the one-line, one-server system, for example, suppose RN1 is used solely to determine interarrival times and RN2 is used solely to determine service times. Then the ith nonantithetic value from RN1 is used to determine the ith interarrival time in a nonantithetic replication. And the ith antithetic value from RN1 is used to determine the ith interarrival time in the equivalent antithetic replication. And similarly for the use of RN2 in determining service times in the nonantithetic and antithetic replications. The interplay between interarrival times and service times is not an issue when dedicated random-number generators are used. In other words, dedicated random-number generators decouple the use of random numbers from the order in which events occur in the model.

As we've seen, we specify the number of a 0–1 generator in a model whenever we make reference to one of the GPSS/H built-in Functions (RVEXPO, RVNORM, and RVTRI). And we also specify a random-number generator when defining a C- or D-Function for sampling from a distribution. And so it's easy to dedicate specific generators to sampling from specific distributions in GPSS/H modeling.

Even dedicated random-number generators do not lead in all cases to synchronized use of random numbers in antithetic modeling. There are circumstances in which random numbers need to be deliberately wasted if synchronization is to be maintained. For example, suppose that a **potential** customer in a one-line, one-server system balks (doesn't remain for service) if the waiting line is too long. Assume that the ith customer **does not** balk in a nonantithetic replication, but **does** balk in the corresponding antithetic replication. Then, in the antithetic replication, the random number that would have been used to sample from this potential customer's service-time distribution should be drawn and discarded at the right time. Otherwise, subsequent samples from the antithetic service-time distribution will not be the antithetic equivalent of their correspondents in the nonantithetic replication. (See Exercise 9 of Section 15.7.)

15.6 Computing Operand Values in RMULT Control Statements

The starting point of random-number generators in an antithetic replication must be the same as their starting point in the nonantithetic counterpart. This means it's usually not possible to take the stopping point of the random-number generators in one replication as their starting point in the next replication. Reason: At the end of a replication, the number of draws from a given 0–1 source may depend on whether the nonantithetic or equivalent antithetic replication is involved.

For example, consider Case Study 11A ("Ships Un/loading at a Harbor"), where the terminating condition is having ship 100 leave the harbor. In a non-antithetic replication, 105 arrivals of ships at the harbor might occur by the time ship 100 leaves the harbor. In the antithetic equivalent, only 103 arrivals might occur by the time ship 100 has left the harbor. The number of samples drawn from the generator dedicated to sampling from interarrival times therefore differs in the paired replications. And so the stopping points of this generator for one pair of replications can't be taken as its starting points for the next pair of replications.

The potential problem just described is solved by setting the starting point of various generators to known values prior to the start of **each** replication. This is easily accomplished by using arithmetic expressions to compute values for RMULT Operands. The starting points of the generators for a replication can then depend on the number of the replication and can be made unique to that replication.

Figure 15.2 provides an example of this approach. The first replication (&I = 1) sets the starting point of RN1 and RN2 to 100,000 and 200,000, respectively. These same settings are then used for the paired antithetic replication. The second replication (&I = 2) then sets the starting point of RN1 and RN2 to 101,000 and 201,000, respectively. These same settings are then used for the paired antithetic replication. And so on. (The example assumes that no more

```
        DO     &I=1,10,1                  10 paired replications
*
            RMULT   99000+1000*&I,_       set &I-th non-antithetic RN1
                   199000+1000*&I         set &I-th non-antithetic RN2
*
            START   1                     start non-anti replication
*
            PUTPIC  LINES=1,FILE=SYSPRINT,(&I)
0The above output is for non-antithetic replication number *.
*
            CLEAR                         clear for anti replication
*
            RMULT   -(99000+1000*&I),_    set &I-th anti RN1
                   -(199000+1000*&I)      set &I-th anti RN2
*
            START   1                     start anti replication
*
            PUTPIC  LINES=1,FILE=SYSPRINT,(&I)
0The above output is for antithetic replication number *.
*
            CLEAR                         clear for non-anti rep
*
        ENDDO                             proceed to next value of &I
```

Figure 15.2 *An Example of a DO/ENDDO Control Loop Useful in Producing Antithetic Pairs of Replications*

than 1000 random numbers per replication are drawn from either RN1 or RN2. Otherwise, the use of random numbers would overlap between consecutive replications.)

The RMULT Statements in Figure 15.2 make use of the GPSS/H **continuation character**, which is an **underscore** (_). The continuation character can be used to indicate (to the GPSS/H compiler) that the current GPSS/H statement is continued in the next record in the Model File. This is accomplished by using the continuation character as the last character in the Operands field of the current GPSS/H statement. Notice the use of the continuation character on two occasions in Figure 15.2. After the A Operand has been specified in the RMULT Statement following the DO, the continuation character is used to indicate that the RMULT Statement is continued in the next record (where the B Operand is found). This is similarly done for the other RMULT Statement in Figure 15.2. The motivation here is to spread a long Operands field across two consecutive records, which leaves room on the individual records for comments, and also makes it easier in this case for the eye to pick up the pattern in the arithmetic expressions that supply the Operand values.

Note that in both RMULT Statements of Figure 15.2, the starting column for the B Operand is one to the left of that for the A Operand. The Operands have been keyed this way (arbitrarily) to make it easier for the eye to pick up the pattern in the Operand expressions. With free format in GPSS/H, this kind of flexibility is possible.

The construction and use of arithmetic expressions in GPSS/H won't be formally discussed here. It's nevertheless possible to understand the spirit and motivation for their use in the Figure 15.2 example. The formation of arithmetic expressions in GPSS/H is similar to their formation in programming languages such as Fortran, Pascal, and BASIC. Arithmetic expressions can be used in almost any context in GPSS/H modeling (e.g., as Operands in Block and Control Statements, as Function arguments, and in many other contexts). The rules in GPSS/H for constructing arithmetic expressions are consistent with the law of least astonishment in computing. That is, their construction corresponds to reasonable expectations in this regard.

15.7 Case Study 15A: Antithetic Replications with the SPT Tool Crib

1. Statement of the Problem

In the system of Case Study 9A ("Alternative Service Orders at a Tool Crib"), estimate the expected number of mechanics in the waiting line for the SPT service order at a 90 percent confidence level by pairing 22 replications with their antithetic equivalents.

Dedicate RN1 and RN2 to sampling from the interarrival- and service-time distributions, respectively, of Type 1 mechanics, and use RN3 and RN4 similarly for the Type 2 mechanics.

Compare the width of the resulting confidence interval with that obtained in Case Study 14A, where the same number of replications in total (44) was used to build an independent-replications confidence interval at a 90 percent confidence level. Which approach proves to be more effective in this case, antithetic variates or independent replications?

2. Approach Taken in Building the Model

A copy of the Case Study 14A Model File was taken as a starting point for the work. The techniques presented in Sections 15.3, 15.4, and 15.5 were introduced into the file to build the requested model. The Chapter 13 method of using Continuous Two-Point Functions to sample from uniform distributions was also applied, making it possible to work with dedicated random number generators. The particulars are discussed in terms of the Modified Source Echo of the resulting Model File.

3. Table of Definitions

Except for four Function definitions, there is nothing new in Case Study 15A that would appear in a Table of Definitions. No new Table of Definitions is provided here to replace the one originally given for Case Study 9A.

4. Block Diagram

The Block Diagram is highly similar to that given in Chapter 9 for the SPT service order in Case Study 9A and is not repeated here.

5. Modified Source Echo

Figure 15A.1 shows the Modified Source Echo for Case Study 15A.

6. Postreplication Reports

The 44 Postreplication Reports resulting from execution of the Case Study 15A Model File are not shown, but are summarized in terms of the key output variable in Table 15A.1, columns 2 and 3. In addition, column 4 of Table 15A.1 shows the averages of the paired replications. The sample mean and sample standard deviation are also shown in the table, along with the corresponding 90 percent confidence interval.

7. Discussion

Model Logic and Model Implementation. These four aspects of the Model File (see Figure 15A.1) are to be noted:

1. An UNLIST CSECHO Compiler Directive has been included to suppress the echoing of Control Statements to the output. (See statement 10 in Figure 15A.1.)
2. C-Functions have been introduced to sample from the continuous, uniformly distributed interarrival and service times of Type 1 and 2 mechanics. (See statements 16 through 26.) RN1 through RN4 have been used as the arguments of these Functions, consistent with the request made in the Statement of the Problem. (See Section 21 of Chapter 13 for discussion of C-Functions of this type.) And the Operands at appropriate GENERATE and TERMINATE Blocks in the model have been changed to make reference to these Functions (see Blocks 1, 5, 8, and 12).
3. RMULT Statements have been placed in a DO/ENDDO loop to set the Initial Position for generators RN1 through RN4 just prior to the start of each nonantithetic and antithetic replication. (See statements 68 through 71 and 82 through 85 in Figure 15A.1.) The RMULT pattern is similar to that shown in Figure 15.2. The GPSS/H continuation character (_) has been used in these RMULTs so that each RMULT Operand occupies its own line, for enhanced readability.
4. The GPSS/H continuation character has been used in the Block 1 and 8 GENERATE Blocks to provide room to append comments to these Block statements.

Except for these differences, the Case Study 15A Model File is similar to that for the SPT service order in Case Study 9A.

```
STMT#  BLOCK#  *LOC    OPERATION  A,B,C,D,E,F,G    COMMENTS

    1                    SIMULATE                                    Case Study 15A
    2          *                              A Tool Crib System (SPT Service Order)
    3          *                         (Use of Antithetic Variates with Case Study 9A)
    4          *                                               Base Time Unit: 1 Second
    5          ***********************************************************************
    6          *         Compiler Directives (INTEGER, UNLIST)                        *
    7          ***********************************************************************
    8          *
    9                    INTEGER    &I             &I is a DO-loop index
   10                    UNLIST     CSECHO         don't echo Control Statements
   11          *
   12          ***********************************************************************
   13          *         Control Statements (FUNCTIONs)                               *
   14          ***********************************************************************
   15          *
   16           TYPE1IAT FUNCTION   RN1,C2        interarrival time, Type 1
   17          0,60/1,780
   18          *
   19           TYPE1ST  FUNCTION   RN2,C2        service time, Type 1
   20          0,210/1,390
   21          *
   22           TYPE2IAT FUNCTION   RN3,C2        interarrival time, Type 2
   23          0,120/1,600
   24          *
   25           TYPE2ST  FUNCTION   RN4,C2        service time, Type 2
   26          0,70/1,130
   27          *
   28          ***********************************************************************
   29          *         Model Segment 1 (Type 1 Mechanics)                           *
   30          ***********************************************************************
   31          *
   32      1             GENERATE   FN(TYPE1IAT),_     Type 1 mechanics arrive
   33      1                        ,,,5               (Priority 5)
   34      2             QUEUE      TOOLWAIT           start TOOLWAIT Queue membership
   35      3             SEIZE      CLERK              request/capture the clerk
   36      4             DEPART     TOOLWAIT           end TOOLWAIT Queue membership
   37      5             ADVANCE    FN(TYPE1ST)        service time
   38      6             RELEASE    CLERK              free the clerk
   39      7             TERMINATE  0                  leave the tool crib area
   40          *
```

Figure 15A.1 *Modified Source Echo of the Case Study 15A Model File*
(continued on the next page)

Postreplication Reports. The sample standard deviation in Table 15A.1 is about 35 percent of the corresponding sample standard deviation in Table 14A.1 (0.564 versus 1.62). However, the sample size (number of paired differences) in Table 15A.1 is only 22, whereas in Table 14A.1 it was 44. The 90 percent confidence interval for the Table 15A.1 sample is [2.0, 2.4], which can be compared to the similar confidence interval of [2.2, 3.0] for the Table 14A.1 sample. The width of the confidence interval has decreased by about 50 percent in this case through the use of antithetic variates, going from about 0.8 (44 independent replications) to 0.4 (22 replications paired with 22 antithetic equivalents). This major improvement has required very little additional effort in the modeling process.

Of interest in comparing the [2.2, 3.0] and [2.0, 2.4] confidence intervals is the difference in their midpoints. The midpoint has shifted from 2.6 to 2.2, or by about 15 percent, between independent replications and antithetic-nonantithetic pairs. This shift is not due to a difference in methodology, but is a random shift.

```
          ***********************************************************************
          *         Model Segment 2 (Type 2 Mechanics)                          *
          ***********************************************************************
          *
   8                GENERATE   FN(TYPE2IAT),_      Type 2 mechanics arrive
   8                           ,,,10               (Priority 10)
   9                QUEUE      TOOLWAIT            start TOOLWAIT Queue membership
  10                SEIZE      CLERK               request/capture the clerk
  11                DEPART     TOOLWAIT            end TOOLWAIT Queue membership
  12                ADVANCE    FN(TYPE2ST)         service time
  13                RELEASE    CLERK               free the clerk
  14                TERMINATE  0                   leave the tool crib area
          *
          ***********************************************************************
          *         Model Segment 3 (Run-Control Xact)                          *
          ***********************************************************************
          *
  15                GENERATE   28800          control Xact comes after 8 hours
  16                TERMINATE  1              reduce the TC value by 1,
          *                                   ending Xact movement
          *
          ***********************************************************************
          *         Run-Control Statements                                      *
          ***********************************************************************
          *
                    DO        &I=1,22,1     control for 22 paired replications
          *
                       RMULT       99000+1000*&I,_     &I-th non-antithetic  RN1
                                  199000+1000*&I,_                           RN2
                                  299000+1000*&I,_                           RN3
                                  399000+1000*&I                             RN4
          *
                       START       1           start &I-th non-anti replication
          *
                       PUTPIC      LINES=3,FILE=SYSPRINT,(&I)
          0============================================================
           The Report above is for non-antithetic replication number *.
           ============================================================
          *
                       CLEAR                   clear for the antithetic rep'n
          *
                       RMULT       -(99000+1000*&I),_     &I-th antithetic RN1
                                  -(199000+1000*&I),_                      RN2
                                  -(299000+1000*&I),_                      RN3
                                  -(399000+1000*&I)                        RN4
          *
                       START       1           start &I-th anti replication
          *
                       PUTPIC      LINES=3,FILE=SYSPRINT,(&I)
          0========================================================
           The Report above is for antithetic replication number *.
           ========================================================
          *
                       CLEAR                   clear for next non-anti replication

                    ENDDO                      proceed to the next value of &I
          *
                    END                        end of Model-File execution
```

Figure 15A.1 (concluded)

15.8 Exercises

1. Like Case Study 15A, the purpose of this exercise is to compare a 90 percent confidence interval for the SPT tool crib based on independent replications with a corresponding confidence interval based on an equivalent number of antithetic-nonantithetic pairs. For the independent replications, use the 10 SPT results reported in Table 14.2. For the 5 antithetic-nonantithetic pairs, use pairs 1 through 5 in Table 15A.1. Discuss the extent to which results using the antithetic-nonantithetic pairs are an improvement over those using independent replications.

2. Repeat Exercise 1, but now use pairs 6 through 10 in Table 15A.1 for the 5 antithetic-nonantithetic pairs.

3. Repeat Exercise 1 again, but now use pairs 11 through 15 in Table 15A.1 for the 5 antithetic-nonantithetic pairs. You now have three independent antithetic-nonantithetic confidence intervals. How much variation is there in the midpoints and widths of these three confidence intervals?

4. Repeat Case Study 15A, except for the FCFS tool crib. Do not use RMULT statements identical to those in Case Study 15A, however. Instead, change the RMULT statements to produce paired

Table 15A.1

Nonantithetic and antithetic results for the SPT service order in Case Study 15A (output variable: average number of mechanics in the waiting line)

Replication Pair	Nonantithetic Result	Antithetic Result	Average of the Paired Replications
1	0.937	3.586	2.262
2	2.125	1.049	1.587
3	0.856	4.935	2.896
4	2.244	2.364	2.304
5	3.612	1.163	2.388
6	5.878	0.880	3.379
7	1.888	1.101	1.495
8	0.635	5.939	3.287
9	1.216	2.462	1.839
10	1.710	1.920	1.815
11	1.569	1.826	1.698
12	3.392	1.802	2.597
13	1.104	3.644	2.374
14	2.067	1.340	1.704
15	1.883	2.649	2.266
16	0.789	5.776	3.283
17	3.063	0.973	2.018
18	1.088	2.933	2.011
19	2.715	1.368	2.042
20	2.422	1.131	1.777
21	1.450	2.800	2.125
22	2.060	1.281	1.671
		Sample mean:	2.219
		Sample standard deviation:	0.564
		90% confidence interval:	[2.0, 2.4]

replications that use random numbers other than those in Case Study 15A. Compare the resulting 90 percent FCFS confidence interval with the SPT confidence interval of the case study. Do the two confidence intervals overlap each other?

5. Use the results from Exercise 4 to repeat Exercises 1, 2, and 3 for the FCFS service order.

6. In Exercise 6 of Section 14.7, you were asked to perform 20 replications with the Case Study 11A model ("Ships Un/loading at a Harbor"). Now perform 10 paired antithetic-nonantithetic replications with an appropriately modified version of this model. Use the results to compute the confidence intervals called for in Exercise 6 of Section 14.7. Compare the confidence intervals resulting from the 10 paired antithetic-nonantithetic replications with those resulting from the 20 independent replications of Section 14.7.

7. In Exercise 7 of Section 14.7, you were asked to perform 20 replications with the Case Study 13A model ("A Model of a Hospital's Emergency Room"). Now perform 10 paired antithetic-nonantithetic replications with an appropriately modified version of this model. Use the results to compute the confidence intervals called for in Exercise 7 of Section 14.7. Compare the confidence intervals resulting from the 10 paired antithetic-nonantithetic replications with those resulting from the 20 independent replications of Section 14.7.

8. In Exercise 8 of Section 14.7, you were asked to perform 20 replications with the Case Study 13B model ("A Job Shop Model"). Now perform 10 paired antithetic-nonantithetic replications with an appropriately modified version of this model. Use the results to compute the confidence intervals called for in Exercise 8 of Section 14.7. Compare the confidence intervals resulting from the 10 paired antithetic-nonantithetic replications with those resulting from the 20 independent replications of Section 14.7.

*9. Exercise 9 of Section 14.10 describes a system in which cars balk at a carwash when there is no waiting space for them. Study this system for the case of 4 wait spaces, replicating for 10 antithetic-nonantithetic pairs and then forming a 90 percent confidence interval for the fraction of arriving potential customers who balk. Compare this confidence interval with that formed in Exercise 9 of Section 14.10, which is based on 20 independent replications. Does the antithetic-nonantithetic confidence interval include the correct result as provided by analytic modeling?

Caution: In the case of balking potential customers, you must make arrangements to "waste" the 0–1 random numbers they would otherwise have used to determine their service time, had they stayed for service.

10. Exercise 10 of Section 14.10 describes a machine-maintenance problem. Model this system to replicate for 10 antithetic/ nonantithetic pairs, and then form a 95 percent confidence interval for the average number of operating machines. Compare this confidence interval with that formed in Exercise 10 of Section 14.10, which is based on 20 independent replications. Does the antithetic-nonantithetic confidence interval include the correct result as provided by analytic modeling?

11. Exercise 11 of Section 14.10 describes two alternative ways to design a tool crib system. Model the one-crib design to replicate for 10 antithetic-nonantithetic pairs, and then form 95 percent confidence intervals for the average number of mechanics at the tool crib, and the average time they spend there. Compare these confidence intervals with those formed for the one-crib case in Exercise 11 of Section 14.10, which are based on 20 independent replications. Do the antithetic-nonantithetic confidence intervals include the correct results, as provided by analytic modeling?

16 Statistical Experiments with Models of Competing Alternatives

16.1 Preview

In Chapters 14 and 15, interest centered on operationalizing methods for making inferences about the absolute performance characteristics of single systems. In Chapter 16, we consider situations where it's of interest to investigate the relative performance of two or more alternative (competing) systems. For example, if designs A and B have been proposed for a manufacturing system, we might want to determine which design will produce products at a faster rate.

The new material in Chapter 16 only involves statistical considerations. No additional GPSS/H Blocks or Control Statements are introduced. As in Chapters 14 and 15, terminating simulations are the subject of discussion.

In Chapter 14, we considered the use of independent replications to form interval estimates of the expected value of an output variable. Then, in Chapter 15, a variance reduction technique involving negatively correlated pairs of replications was introduced as a means for trying to improve the statistical precision resulting from a given number of replications. Developments through most of Chapter 16 parallel those in Chapters 14 and 15. First, independent replications for two systems are used to form interval estimates for the difference in expected values of two output variables (one per system). The objective is to estimate which one of the two systems is better (in terms of expected value) for the purpose at hand. Then a variance reduction technique based on positively correlated pairs of replications with two systems is introduced as a means for trying to improve the degree of statistical precision in confidence intervals resulting from a given number of replications.

The techniques introduced up to this point in the chapter are limited to comparison of two alternatives. We conclude the chapter by discussing a method for selecting the probable best from two **or more** alternatives. The method is based on independent replications with the competing alternatives, and involves two-stage sampling. This method is illustrated with a case study set in the context of a production problem.

16.2 Uncorrelated Paired-*t* Comparison of Two Alternatives

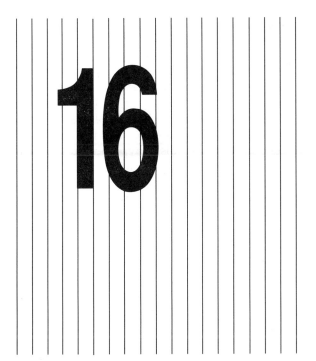

Table 14.2 of Chapter 14 shows results from replications performed with two alternative service orders at a tool crib: FCFS and SPT. In Chapter 14, confidence

intervals were formed to estimate the expected number of mechanics in the waiting line for these alternative service orders. But we may care less about the **absolute** values of the expected number of mechanics in line than we do about their **relative** values. We may want to know which service order results in the **smaller** number of mechanics in line. One way to investigate this matter is to build a confidence interval for the **difference** in the expected line lengths for the two alternatives.

The following procedure provides a straightforward method for comparing two alternatives when the objective is to estimate whether there is a difference in the expected values of two output variables (one output variable per alternative):

1. Replicate n times with each of the two alternatives.
2. Pair replication i from the first alternative with replication i from the second alternative, $i = 1, 2, 3, \ldots, n$.
3. Compute the difference in each pair, then the mean and standard deviation of these differences.
4. Compute a confidence interval for the paired differences at a confidence level of choice. If the confidence interval **excludes** zero, there is reason to believe (at the corresponding significance level in hypothesis testing, discussed shortly) that the output variables **do** differ in their expected values. But if the confidence interval **includes** zero, there is reason to believe the output variables **do not** differ in their expected values.

The replications in step 1 are, by definition of a replication, independent **within** a given alternative (that is, on an **intra**-alternative basis). We assume in this section that the replications are also independent **across** alternatives (that is, on an **inter**alternative basis). In other words, the set of random numbers used for any one of the $2n$ replications should differ from each of the sets used for the other $2n$—1 replications.

Suppose the step 4 confidence interval excludes zero at the confidence level of choice, say, at a 95 percent confidence level. Then this is equivalent to rejecting at a 5 percent significance level the hypothesis that there is no difference in the expected values of the two output variables. On the other hand, if the step 4 confidence interval includes zero at, say, a 95 percent confidence level, then this is equivalent to failing to reject the hypothesis at a 5 percent significance level that there is no difference in the expected values.

We have not discussed hypothesis testing here, nor will we. (The interested reader might choose to review the fundamentals of hypothesis testing in a general simulation text, or in an introductory statistics text.) We content ourselves to offer the comment that whereas a hypothesis test about a difference in expected values results only in rejecting, or failing to reject, the stated hypothesis, a confidence-interval provides the same information (in terms of whether or not the confidence interval contains zero), and in addition provides some quantitative insight into the extent to which the measures of performance may differ in terms of their expected values.

The approach just described requires that the paired differences be iid (independent of each other, and identically distributed). In the case of small sample sizes ($n < 30$), the paired differences must also be normally distributed. Use of the t statistic to compute the step 4 confidence interval is then justified, giving rise to the phrase "uncorrelated paired-t confidence interval." If the replication outputs result from an averaging process (which is often the case), then by a generalization of the Central Limit Theorem that allows for limited kinds of correlation (which may be present within each replication), they may tend to be normal, leading to paired differences which tend to satisfy the normality requirement.

In the case of large sample sizes, neither the replication outputs nor the paired differences need be normally distributed because, by the Central Limit Theorem, the average of the paired differences will tend to be approximately normally distributed as sample size increases, justifying use of the z statistic.

The approach outlined here does not require that the variances in the two output-variable populations (one population per system) be equal. This is an important point, because equality of variances in the populations of two output variables is unlikely.

We assume in this section that the two replications making up each pair are independent (per the **inter**alternative independence described earlier). By way of contrast, we introduce in Sections 16.5 and 16.6 a technique for attempting to induce positive correlation between the replications making up a pair, in the hope of achieving variance reduction.

It's interesting to note that the uncorrelated paired-t approach to comparing **two** populations reduces the problem to a **one**-population problem.

(The one population on which attention focuses is a population of **differences**.) In general, one-population techniques can then be brought to bear on this reduced form of a two-population problem.

Let's illustrate uncorrelated paired-*t* confidence intervals in terms of the FCFS versus SPT service orders at the tool crib. The output variable of interest is "average number of mechanics waiting to be served," and the objective (based on economic motivations) is to identify the service order that has the smallest expected value in this regard. We've replicated with these two models several times on a single-system (noncomparative) basis in Case Studies 9A, 14A, and 15A. Let's now return to the FCFS and SPT models of Case Study 9A, modifying them to do 10 FCFS replications and then another independent set of 10 SPT replications. With all four sources of randomness (two interarrival- and two service-time distributions) based via transparent sampling on RN1, we execute "RMULT 125000" prior to the 10 FCFS replications, and "RMULT 150000" prior to the 10 SPT replications. The resulting outputs are summarized in columns 2 and 3 of Table 16.1. The differences in replication pairs, and the mean and standard deviation of the differences, are shown in column 4. 80, 90, and 95 percent confidence intervals are given at the bottom of the table.

The 80 percent and 90 percent confidence intervals of Table 16.1 exclude zero, providing evidence that the expected line length with the SPT service order is smaller than with the FCFS service order. The 95 percent confidence level includes zero, however, which means we would fail to reject the hypothesis at a 5 percent significance level that there is no difference in the expected line lengths for the two service orders. This situation is further investigated in the exercises of Section 16.4 and via a variance reduction technique introduced in Section 16.6.

16.3 Other Confidence Intervals for the Difference in Expected Values in Two Populations Based on Independent Samples

There are a number of alternative methods for building confidence intervals for the difference in expected values in two populations based on independent (that is, uncorrelated) samples. The methods vary in their assumptions, so one method may be more convenient or useful than another in specific cases. We comment briefly on three alterna-

Table 16.1

Average number of mechanics in the waiting line for each of two alternative service orders (FCFS and SPT) (basis: uncorrelated pairs)

Replication Number	Average Waiting Line Lengths FCFS	SPT	Difference
1	3.826	1.326	2.500
2	1.529	3.668	-2.139
3	1.805	0.737	1.068
4	4.140	1.619	2.521
5	2.116	3.572	-1.456
6	5.010	1.290	3.720
7	5.411	2.723	2.688
8	1.974	2.229	-0.255
9	6.585	1.395	5.190
10	2.550	1.346	1.204
		Sample mean:	1.504
		Sample standard deviation:	2.293
		80% Confidence interval:	[0.50, 2.50]
		90% Confidence interval:	[0.18, 2.83]
		95% Confidence interval:	[-0.14, 3.14]

tives here (the classical two-sample *t* approach, the classical two-sample *z* approach, and Welch confidence intervals), not going into operational details, but providing references.

Two criteria for distinguishing among methods are these:

1. Must the samples from the two populations be of equal size?
2. Must the variances in the two populations be equal?

The uncorrelated paired-*t* method of Section 16.2, for example, requires equal-sized samples from the two populations, but does not require equality of variances. Equality of sample sizes is usually easy to satisfy if both alternatives are **simulated**. But suppose one alternative corresponds to an **existing** system (which has not been modeled) and the other corresponds to a proposed **change** in the existing system (which has been modeled). Only a sample of small size may be available for the existing system, and increasing the sample size may be prohibitive because of cost, and/or time, and/or politics, and/or inconvenience. If the sample is too small, not enough useful information may be available in an uncorrelated paired-*t* confidence interval to support decision making of adequate quality.

The **classical two-sample t** approach is one that does not require equal sample sizes but does require normally distributed output variables and equal variances in the setting of small sample sizes. The approach assumes that both samples are of size less than 30, and so is based on the *t* statistic. The need for equality of variances limits the utility of this approach (although this requirement can be relaxed if the samples are of equal size, but in that case, the uncorrelated paired-*t* approach of Section 16.2 can be used). In any event, the variance assumed common to the two populations is estimated by pooling the two sample variances (that is, by combining the two sample variances, weighting them by sample size). A confidence interval centered on the difference in the two sample means is then formed. (See McClave and Benson, 1988, p. 434, for a convenient summary of the steps involved in computing a classical two-sample *t* confidence interval. Or look into any general simulation text for this purpose.)

The classical two-sample *t* approach can be based on the *z* statistic if both samples are of size at least 30. In this case, normally distributed output variables and equality of variance in the two populations are no longer required. This approach, here called the **classical two-sample** *z* approach, can work well for large samples of unequal size when the modeler is reluctant to discard information by reducing the size of the larger sample to that of the smaller. (See McClave and Benson, 1988, p. 421, for a convenient summary of the steps involved in computing a classical two-sample *z* confidence interval. Or look into any general simulation text for this purpose.)

Finally, a variation of the classical two-sample *t* approach will be mentioned. This variation assumes that the variances in the two populations are unequal and that sample sizes are both less than 30. Sample sizes do not have to be equal. This so-called Behrens-Fisher problem has an approximate solution due to Welch. The approximation involves working with the sample variances to estimate the degrees of freedom used in looking up the *t* statistic for the confidence level of interest. The resulting confidence interval is sometimes referred to as a **Welch confidence interval**. (See Banks and Carson, 1984, p. 456, Section 12.1.2, or Law and Kelton, 1982, p. 321, equation 9.2, for the steps involved in computing a Welch confidence interval.)

Those interested in these other approaches should consult the suggested references for operational details. We content ourselves here with the uncorrelated paired-*t* approach of Section 16.2.

16.4 Exercises

1. Use the uncorrelated paired-*t* approach to compute a 90 percent confidence interval for the paired differences of Table 16.1. Do the lower and upper confidence points you compute match those given in Table 16.1?
2. Repeat the experiment which resulted in Table 16.1, but execute "RMULT 200000" prior to the 10 FCFS replications, and "RMULT 225000" prior to the 10 SPT replications. Use the uncorrelated paired-*t* approach to compute 80 percent, 90 percent, and 95 percent confidence intervals for the FCFS versus SPT differences in average line lengths. Do the 80 percent and 90 percent confidence intervals exclude zero, as in Table 16.1? Does the 95 percent interval include zero?
3. Again repeat the experiment which resulted in Table 16.1, but this time work with 30 paired differences. Execute "RMULT 300000" prior to the 30 FCFS replications, and "RMULT 350000"

prior to the 30 SPT replications. Use what might be called the "uncorrelated paired-*z* approach" to compute 80 percent, 90 percent, and 95 percent confidence intervals for the FCFS versus SPT difference in average line lengths. Do any of these confidence intervals include zero?

4. If you were to compute a classical two-sample *t* confidence interval for the difference in expected values of the two populations sampled to produce Table 16.1, it would have to be true, strictly speaking, that the variances in the two populations be equal. Speculate qualitatively on whether this requirement might be satisfied in this case. For example, compute the variance in the FCFS sample of Table 16.1, then do likewise for the SPT sample. Are the resulting sample variances similar in value, or not? Then compare sample variances for the experiments in Exercises 2 and 3. (Those interested might want to formally test the hypothesis that the variances in the two populations are equal. See McClave and Benson, 1988, pp. 441 et seq., for description and illustration of a methodology for comparing two population variances based on independent random samples from normal populations. Speculate on the likelihood that the two populations are normally distributed.)

5. Using the information in Table 16.1, compute 80 percent, 90 percent, and 95 percent Welch confidence intervals for the difference in FCFS versus SPT expected line lengths. Recall that a Welch confidence interval does not require equality of variances in the two sampled populations. (You will have to look up the Welch confidence-interval methodology in a reference of your choice.) Compare the resulting confidence intervals with those of Table 16.1. Does the 95 percent Welch confidence interval include zero?

6. Using results from Exercise 3, compute 80 percent, 90 percent, and 95 percent classic two-sample *z* confidence intervals for the difference in FCFS vs. SPT expected line lengths. Like a Welch confidence interval, a classic two-sample *z* confidence interval does not require equality of variances in the two sampled populations. (You will have to look up the classic two-sample *z* confidence-interval methodology in a reference of your choice.) Compare the resulting confidence intervals with those of Exercise 3.

7. Read the Statement of the Problem for Case Study 16A ("Selecting the Probable Best from Four Production Systems") in Section 16.9. Suppose you simply want to compare the "1 repairperson, 0 leased machines" versus the "2 repairpeople, 1 leased machine" alternatives in that system, using the uncorrelated paired-t approach. Model the system, basing all sampling on the transparent use of RN1. Do 15 replications for the "1 repairperson, 0 leased machines" case, letting RN1 take its default starting point. Then do 15 replications for the "2 repairpeople, 1 leased machine" case, executing an "RMULT 200000" statement before doing these replications. Use the results to form 80 percent, 90 percent, and 95 percent confidence intervals for the difference in the expected daily costs of the two alternatives. Is there reason to believe at any of these confidence levels (or the corresponding significance levels of hypothesis testing) that there is a cost difference between the two alternatives?

8. Exercises 4 through 10 of Section 16.7 call for comparing pairs of system alternatives through use of a variance reduction technique ("common random numbers") introduced in Section 16.6. For your choice of one or more of these exercises, design and conduct an independent-samples experiment to form an interval estimate of the difference in results corresponding to the two alternatives described in the exercise.

16.5 Correlated Paired-*t* Comparison of Two Alternatives

In this section, we introduce the idea of using positively correlated pairs of observations from two populations to sharpen the contrast in the comparison of alternatives. In the following section, we operationalize this idea in the context of GPSS/H.

Often two or more factors contribute to observed differences between alternatives. One or more of these factors may be controllable, whereas others may not be subject to control. Suppose it's of interest to estimate the extent to which the behavior of an output variable depends on a controllable factor. Then it becomes a challenge to isolate the contribution of the controllable factor while blocking out the the masking effects of the uncontrollable factors.

Consider the following example, taken from outside the context of simulation and motivated by a problem in McClave and Benson (1988, p. 455). Suppose it's of interest to compare the starting salaries of men and women graduating with a bachelor's degree in 1990. Perhaps it's suspected that because of sexual bias, women are given lower starting salaries than men, and this question is to be investigated by sampling. One way to test for a possible difference in expected starting salaries would be to take the uncorrelated paired-t approach of Section 16.2. An iid sample of the starting salaries of women (who graduated in 1990 with a bachelor's degree) could be taken. And an equal-sized iid sample of the starting salaries of men (who graduated in 1990 with a bachelor's degree) could be taken. The salaries of the first woman and the first man chosen for the samples could be paired, and so on, then uncorrelated paired differences and confidence intervals could be formed, and so on.

Now, there are many factors that contribute to the starting salary of a person who graduated with a bachelor's degree in 1990. A person's sex may be such a factor. But factors such as a person's grade point average, a person's major, the perceived quality of the program from which the person graduated, prior work experience, and the cost of living in the part of the country where the person takes a first job, certainly have a potential contribution to make to starting salary. And so if starting salaries are sampled at random, it may be difficult to measure the extent to which starting-salary differences are attributable to the male versus female factor (the factor of interest) versus myriad other factors (the uncontrollable factors).

One way to block out the effect of one or more uncontrollable factors contributing to differences in two populations is to work with **matched pairs**. In the starting-salary context, suppose again that an iid sample of the starting salaries of women (who graduated in 1990 with a bachelor's degree) is taken. Now suppose that for each woman in the sample, a man is found who is equivalent in terms of major and grade point average. (In this discussion, we are just trying to block out the effect of major and grade point average as two uncontrollable factors.) We then use the two starting salaries (the woman's and the man's) to form a pair. We have a **matched** pair, because we have approximately matched the two members of the pair with respect to two otherwise uncontrollable factors. When we compute the paired differences, the contributions of the two "uncontrollable" factors will tend to cancel each other out (by subtraction), with the remaining difference then more directly attributable to the controllable factor.

By working with matched pairs like this, we are trying to induce a **positive correlation** between the members of each matched pair. The objective is to reduce the variability in paired differences, making it possible to sharpen the contrast between opposing alternatives. As was true in working with antithetic variates in single-system modeling, what we are dealing with here is a variance-reduction technique. But with antithetic variates, we try to bring about **negative** correlation between the two members of a matched pair coming from **one** population. In contrast, the goal here is to establish **positive** correlation between the two members of a matched pair coming from **two** populations. In the single-system case, we work with paired **averages**. In the two-system case, we work with paired **differences**.

Now let's interpret the idea of positively correlated matched pairs in the context of simulation. We refer once again to the FCFS versus SPT tool crib, and the corresponding populations of average line lengths. The controllable factors in the two populations are the FCFS versus SPT service orders. The uncontrollable factors are the interarrival and service times. It may not be clear why interarrival and service times are referred to as uncontrollable factors. After all, the interarrival- and service-time **distributions** are the same for both the FCFS and SPT tool cribs. But the **sequence of values** drawn from these distributions very likely isn't the same in an FCFS replication as in the SPT replication with which it might be paired. And the sequence of values sampled in a replication does contribute to the average line length observed for that replication. On a replication-by-replication basis, then, the FCFS and SPT service orders aren't the only factors contributing to observed average line lengths in the tool crib system.

It's true that **short-run** differences in sequences of interarrival times and service times won't lead to **long-run** differences in average line lengths in the tool crib problem. If we work with the uncorrelated paired-*t* approach of Section 16.2, then the effect of short-run differences becomes vanishingly small as the number of replications becomes arbitrarily large. But in practical situations, we may not have the budget needed to work with a large number of replications. And so there is motivation to work with positively correlated matched pairs when comparing competing alternatives.

16.6 Using Common Random Numbers to Induce Positive Correlation

Continuing to use the tool crib system as a basis for illustration, our objective now is to design a simulation experiment to compare the FCFS versus SPT alternatives under otherwise identical conditions. We want to bring about some randomly determined 8-hour day at the tool crib, operate the crib with the FCFS service order on that day, and then operate the crib again **on the identical day** with the SPT service order. Because one and the same day is used in both cases, we can attribute any difference in average line length to the controllable factor, service order.

The four "uncontrollable" factors that characterize a day, and that we want to be able to reproduce so the same day can be experienced by both the FCFS and SPT service orders, are these:

1. The sequence of interarrival times for Type 1 mechanics.
2. The sequence of service times for Type 1 mechanics.
3. The sequence of interarrival times for Type 2 mechanics.
4. The sequence of service times for Type 2 mechanics.

These sequences are determined by sampling from the corresponding distributions. We put ourselves in a position to reproduce these sequences exactly (making it possible to reproduce a given 8-hour day exactly) by using dedicated random-number generators (see Section 5 of Chapter 15) and the method of inversion (see Section 22 of Chapter 13) to sample from the corresponding distributions. (We leave it for you in Exercise 2a of Section 16.7 to explain why it might not be possible to reproduce a given 8-hour day if dedicated random-number generators aren't used.) For example, we might use RN1 and RN2 to sample from the interarrival- and service-time distributions of Type 1 mechanics and RN3 and RN4 to sample from the interarrival- and service-time distributions of Type 2 mechanics. Dedicating to each of the four "uncontrollable" factors its own random-number generator, we wind up using four RNGs.

Figure 16.1 shows the Modified Source Echo for a model designed to simulate for 10 randomly determined 8-hour days with both the FCFS and SPT service orders. Note these aspects of the Figure 16.1 model:

1. Four Continuous, Two-Point Functions have been included to sample from the four uniform distributions in the model. (See Statements 18 through 28 in Figure 16.1.) RNGs 1, 2, 3, and 4 have been respectively dedicated to sampling from the interarrival- and service-time distributions for Type 1 and Type 2 mechanics.
2. The Priority of Type 1 mechanics is fixed at 5. (See Statement 34 in Figure 16.1.) The Priority of Type 2 mechanics is specified as the Integer Ampervariable &TYPE2PR. (This is the first model we've seen in which the value of a Block Operand is supplied indirectly, through an Ampervariable. See Statements 47 and 48.) In turn, &TYPE2PR is used as a DO-loop index, ranging in value from 5 to 10 in steps of 5. (See Statement 68.) The first time through this loop, &TYPE2PR has a value of 5, which means the FCFS service order is being modeled. The second and only other time through this loop, &TYPE2PR has a value of 10, which means the SPT service order is being modeled. Note that all 10 replications are performed first for the FCFS service order, then the 10 SPT replications are carried out.
3. A nested-loop structure is used for run control. The outer loop controls the value of &TYPE2PR, as mentioned above. (See Statement 68.) The inner loop controls the replication count. (See Statement 70.) Statements making up the body of the outer loop have been indented, and those making up the body of the inner loop have been indented even further. (See Statements 68 through 99.) To support this indentation, OPERCOL has been set to 30. (See Statement 11.)
4. For each replication, the Initial Positions of RN1 through RN4 are computed as a function of the value of the replication counter, &I. (See statements 72 through 75.) The computational pattern follows the spirit of that shown in Figure 15.2 of Chapter 15 and used in Case Study 15A (see Statements 68 through 71 in Figure 15A.1).
5. The replications are labeled with both a replication number and a description of the service order. The service order descriptors (FCFS or SPT) are embedded in two alternative Picture Statements. (See Statements 83 and 90.) The correct PUTPIC Statement (Statement 81 or Statement 88) to execute is selected by use of an IF/ELSE/ENDIF structure. (See Statements 79,

```
STMT#  BLOCK#  *LOC   OPERATION  A,B,C,D,E,F,G   COMMENTS

   1                   SIMULATE                     Figure 16.1 of Chapter 16
   2             *                          Common Random Numbers
   3             *              with FCFS vs. SPT Alternatives at the Tool Crib
   4             *                              Base Time Unit: 1 Second
   5             ***********************************************************************
   6             *      Compiler Directives (INTEGER; OPERCOL; UNLIST)          *
   7             ***********************************************************************
   8             *
   9                   INTEGER    &I               &I is a DO-loop index
  10                   INTEGER    &TYPE2PR         Type 2 mechanic Priority Level
  11                   OPERCOL    30               scan to column 30 for A Operands
  12                   UNLIST     CSECHO           don't echo Control Statements
  13             *
  14             ***********************************************************************
  15             *      Control Statements (FUNCTIONs)                         *
  16             ***********************************************************************
  17             *
  18        TYPE1IAT FUNCTION     RN1,C2           Type 1 interarrival time
  19        0,60/1,780
  20             *
  21        TYPE1ST  FUNCTION     RN2,C2           Type 1 service time
  22        0,210/1,390
  23             *
  24        TYPE2IAT FUNCTION     RN3,C2           Type 2 interarrival time
  25        0,120/1,600
  26             *
  27        TYPE2ST  FUNCTION     RN4,C2           Type 2 service time
  28        0,70/1,130
  29             *
  30             ***********************************************************************
  31             *      Model Segment 1 (Type 1 Mechanics)                     *
  32             ***********************************************************************
  33             *
  34     1             GENERATE   FN(TYPE1IAT),,,,5 Type 1 mechanics arrive
  35             *                                 (Priority Level = 5)
  36     2             QUEUE      TOOLWAIT         start TOOLWAIT Queue membership
  37     3             SEIZE      CLERK            request/capture the clerk
  38     4             DEPART     TOOLWAIT         end TOOLWAIT Queue membership
  39     5             ADVANCE    FN(TYPE1ST)      service time
  40     6             RELEASE    CLERK            free the clerk
  41     7             TERMINATE  0                leave the tool crib area
  42             *
  43             ***********************************************************************
  44             *      Model Segment 2 (Type 2 Mechanics)                     *
  45             ***********************************************************************
  46             *
  47     8             GENERATE   FN(TYPE2IAT),,,,_ Type 2 mechanics arrive
  48     8                        &TYPE2PR         (Priority Level = &TYPE2PR)
  49     9             QUEUE      TOOLWAIT         start TOOLWAIT Queue membership
  50    10             SEIZE      CLERK            request/capture the clerk
  51    11             DEPART     TOOLWAIT         end TOOLWAIT Queue membership
  52    12             ADVANCE    FN(TYPE2ST)      service time
  53    13             RELEASE    CLERK            free the clerk
  54    14             TERMINATE  0                leave the tool crib area
  55             *
```

Figure 16.1 Modified Source Echo of the Model used to Produce the Correlated FCFS vs. SPT Pairs Displayed in Table 16.2 (continued on the next page)

```
 56           ************************************************************************
 57           *         Model Segment 3 (Run-Control Xact)                           *
 58           ************************************************************************
 59           *
 60      15             GENERATE   28800           control Xact comes after 8 hours
 61      16             TERMINATE  1               reduce the TC value by 1,
 62           *                                    ending Xact movement
 63           *
 64           ************************************************************************
 65           *         Run-Control Statements                                       *
 66           ************************************************************************
 67           *
 68                      DO         &TYPE2PR=5,10,5  FCFS case first, then SPT case
 69           *
 70                         DO      &I=1,10,1        10 replications for current case
 71           *
 72                            RMULT   99000+1000*&I,_    &I-th RN1 for current case
 73                                   199000+1000*&I,_          RN2
 74                                   299000+1000*&I,_          RN3
 75                                   399000+1000*&I            RN4
 76           *
 77                            START   1          start &I-th current-case replication
 78           *
 79                            IF      &TYPE2PR=5    true => provide FCFS labeling
 80           *
 81                               PUTPIC  LINES=3,FILE=SYSPRINT,(&I)
 82           0======================================================================
 83            The report above is for replication * for the FCFS service order
 84            ======================================================================
 85           *
 86                            ELSE                   else, provide SPT labeling
 87           *
 88                               PUTPIC  LINES=3,FILE=SYSPRINT,(&I)
 89           0======================================================================
 90            The report above is for replication * for the SPT service order
 91            ======================================================================
 92           *
 93                            ENDIF                  end of the if
 94           *
 95                            CLEAR               clear for the next replication
 96           *
 97                         ENDDO                  next value of &I
 98           *
 99                      ENDDO                     next case
100           *
101                      END                       end of model-file execution
```

Figure 16.1 *(concluded)*

86, and 93.) If &TYPE2PR = 5, then the FCFS service order is in effect, and the Statement 81 PUTPIC is executed. If &TYPE2PR ≠ 5, then the SPT service order is in effect, and the Statement 88 PUTPIC is executed. Although we have not discussed IF/ELSE/ENDIF structures formally, and won't do so in this book, use of this structure in the Figure 16.1 model is straightforward, and should be easy to understand.

Table 16.2 displays results produced by executing the Figure 16.1 Model File. The confidence intervals in the table provide strong support for the hypothesis that the expected line content for the SPT service order is less than for the FCFS order. Zero is excluded even from the 99 percent confidence interval, which is equivalent to rejecting at a 1 percent significance level the hypothesis that there is no difference in the expected line lengths.

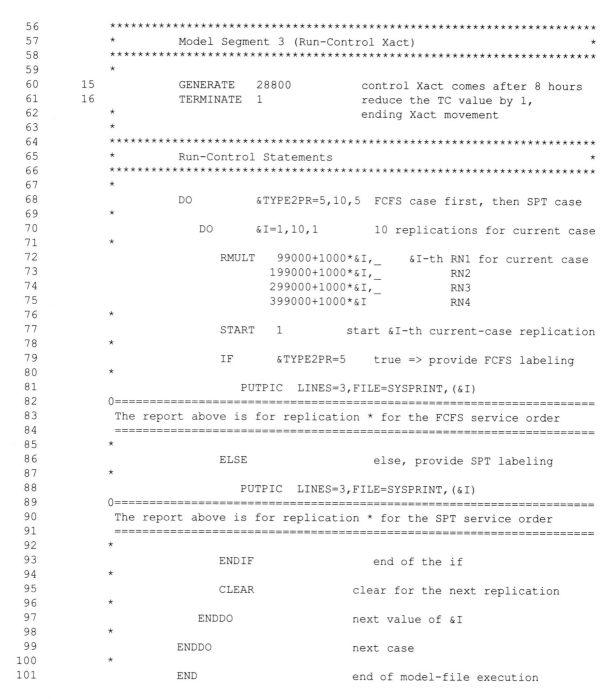

Table 16.2

Average number of mechanics in the waiting line for each of two alternative service orders (FCFS and SPT) (basis: positively correlated pairs)

Replication Number	Average Waiting Line Lengths FCFS	SPT	Difference
1	1.219	0.973	0.246
2	3.065	2.125	0.940
3	1.057	0.856	0.210
4	3.124	2.244	0.880
5	5.084	3.612	1.472
6	8.654	5.878	2.776
7	2.638	1.888	0.750
8	0.745	0.635	0.110
9	1.592	1.216	0.376
10	2.405	1.710	0.695
		Sample mean:	0.845
		Sample standard deviation:	0.796
		80% Confidence interval:	[0.498, 1.192]
		90% Confidence interval:	[0.384, 1.306]
		95% Confidence interval:	[0.276, 1.414]
		98% Confidence interval:	[0.135, 1.555]
		99% Confidence interval:	[0.024, 1.662]

The matched-pair confidence intervals of Table 16.2 should be compared with the uncorrelated-pair confidence intervals of Table 16.1. For the same amount of effort (20 replications in each table), much better statistical precision has been achieved in the matched-pair modeling. The standard deviation in the sample of differences has dropped from 2.293 for the uncorrelated pairs to 0.796 for the matched pairs, a decrease of over 60 percent. (We note that the mean difference has shifted from 1.504 to 0.845. This shift is attributable to randomness, however, and not to the difference in approaches.)

16.7 Exercises

1. The Figure 16.1 Model File is in the fig161.gps file. Initiate a Test Mode simulation with this Model File. On the first FCFS day, when do the first 10 Type 1 mechanics arrive? When do the first 10 Type 2 mechanics arrive? At what times are service initiated for these mechanics? What are the service times?

   Now develop this same information for the first SPT day. For a given mechanic, the time of arrival and the service-time requirement should be the same on the FCFS day as the SPT day. But the time service is initiated for a given mechanic may be different on the FCFS day than on the SPT day. Among the first 10 mechanics of each type, are there any cases for which the time of service initiation for a given mechanic does differ between the two service orders? If not, continue the simulation to find the first such case.

*2. This question deals with the use of dedicated random number generators and with the RMULT Statement in the model of Figure 16.1

(a) Suppose a friend studying this material doesn't understand why a single random number generator (such as RN1) can't be used in the model of Figure 16.1 and still meet the objective of simulating for the same 10 randomly determined 8-hour days with the FCFS and SPT service orders. What would you tell your friend to bring about the needed understanding? (You might postulate a sequence of events in the model to show that the series of interarrival and service times on a given 8-hour day for the FCFS service order won't completely match the series for the SPT service order if a single random-number generator is used.)

(b) Suppose your friend, having seen the light, now claims that only three random number generators need to be used in the Figure 16.1 model to meet the matched-pair objective. Is your friend right? If so, which two sources of randomness in the model could safely use one and the same random-number generator? If only three generators were used, would the results numerically match those of Table 16.2? If not, would this matter?

(c) Now suppose your friend claims that the RMULT Statement in the model (see statements 72 through 75 in Figure 16.1) can be moved to a position right after the first DO Statement (Statement 68) and simplified to "RMULT 100000,200000,300000,400000". Do you agree with your friend? If not, what would you say to try to convince your friend that there is a flaw in his or her thinking?

3. Change the RMULT pattern in the model of Figure 16.1 to some alternative pattern of your choice which will produce random-number sequences differing from those in the Figure 16.1 model. Carry out a Batch simulation using your pattern. Summarize the results in a table like that of Table 16.2. Is the evidence you develop as strongly in favor of the SPT service order as the evidence of Table 16.2?

4. In the widget-manufacturing system of Case Study 6A, design and conduct an experiment using common random numbers to form an interval estimate of the difference in expected daily profits for the cases of four and five assemblers.

5. In Exercise 12 of Section 9.7, it's of interest to determine which of two alternative tool crib clerks minimizes total system cost. Design and conduct an experiment using common random numbers to form an interval estimate of the difference in expected daily system costs for the two alternative clerks.

6. In Exercise 6(a) of Section 11.14, experimentation is requested to determine what effect there would be on the in-harbor residence times of Type A and Type B ships if one additional tugboat were provided at the harbor. Design and conduct an experiment using common random numbers to form interval estimates of the differences in expected in-harbor residence times of Type A and Type B ships with and without the addition of another tugboat.

7. In Exercise 7 of Section 11.14, the effect of changing service order for Type A and Type B ships at a harbor from FCFS to a prioritized alternative is considered. Design and conduct an experiment using common random numbers to form interval estimates of the differences in expected in-harbor residence times of Type A and Type B ships for these alternative service orders.

8. In Exercise 11 of Section 11.14, it's of interest to estimate the number of assemblers maximizing the average daily profit in an expanded form of the widget-manufacturing system. Consider the two best cases determined in doing that exercise. Design and conduct an experiment using common random numbers to form an interval estimate of the difference in expected daily profit for these best two cases.

9. In Exercise 4 of Section 12.12, the question is raised whether FCFS or SPT is a better service order in terms of minimizing the average time finishing-machine operators spend waiting for a crane. Design and conduct an experiment using common random numbers to form an interval estimate of the difference in expected waiting times for these alternative service orders.

10. In Case Study 13B (A Job Shop Model), consider "average time spent by jobs in the job shop" as an output variable. The value of this output variable is not included in the Postreplication Report produced by the Case Study 13B model. Modify the model to include the value of this output variable in Postreplication Reports. What impact would there be on this output variable if one machine were added to Group 2? Design and conduct an experiment using common random numbers to form an interval estimate of the change that would result in this output variable if one machine were added to Group 2.

16.8 Selecting the Probable Best from k Competing Alternatives

We've operationalized two techniques in this chapter for comparing **two** alternatives with the objective of identifying the probable best in terms of a single performance measure. But the number of alternatives may not be limited to two. We may want to select the probable best from k competing alternatives, $k \geq 2$. In such cases, an approach due to Dudewicz and Dalal (originally reported in Dudewicz and Dalal, 1975, but perhaps more readily accessible in Dudewicz and Mishra, 1988) can be used. The Dudewicz/Dalal procedure is described and illustrated computationally in this section and then is set in the context of a GPSS/H case study in the following section.

Two-stage sampling is involved in the Dudewicz/Dalal (D/D) approach. These are the steps followed:

1. First, an identical number of two or more replications is carried out for each alternative. These replications must be independent across the various alternatives. (Common random numbers therefore cannot be used with the Dudewicz/Dalal procedure.) This is the first stage of sampling. (Law and Kelton, 1982, recommend that at least 15 replications per alternative be used for the first-stage sampling.)
2. Various criteria are then applied to compute the number of additional independent replications needed for each alternative. (The number of additional replications usually varies from alternative to alternative, as described shortly.)
3. Next, additional replications are carried out for each alternative. This is the second stage of sampling.
4. For each alternative, the weighted means of the stage one and stage two samples are computed. (The weights are not simply proportional to the first- and second-stage sample sizes, but are computed by a procedure that is described shortly.)
5. The alternative with the smallest or largest weighted sample mean (depending on whether the minimum or maximum value of the performance measure is sought) is then the winner.

The D/D procedure assumes that the output variables are normally distributed, but, importantly, does not assume equality of variances among the various ouput-variable populations. And the procedure can be used for just two alternatives, which arms us with another operationalized method for these situations.

Let's next list and comment on the several factors used in step 2 of the D/D procedure to determine the sizes of the second-stage samples. There are three terms that come into play:

1. **The first-stage sample variance.** The higher the first-stage sample variance, the larger the size of the second-stage sample, other things being equal. Second-stage sample size is directly proportional to the first-stage sample variance, as we will see. Sample variance varies from alternative to alternative, of course, and this explains why the second-stage samples vary in size from alternative to alternative.
2. **The probability of making the correct selection.** Because of randomness, there can be no guarantee that the best alternative will be selected from the competing candidates. However, the modeler does choose the probability, such as 0.90 or 0.95, of making the best selection. The larger this probability, the greater the sizes of the second-stage samples that are needed.
3. **An indifference amount.** The modeler specifies the amount by which a difference in the *expected values* of the output variables is unimportant. For example, the output variable might be the cost, dollars per day, of operating a production system, and the objective might be to select the system design that minimizes this cost. Suppose the lowest cost in the stage-one sampling is on the order of \$500/day. Then the user might specify an indifference amount of, say, \$25/day, which is about 5 percent of the cost estimated to be achievable. This is equivalent to saying that the user will be satisfied if the system picked as the probable best has an expected daily cost within \$25/day of the the best system. The smaller the indifference amount, the larger the sizes of the second-stage samples needed to discriminate among the alternatives. (The sizes of the second-stage samples vary inversely with the square of the indifference amount, as we will see.)

We will now display the governing equations used in steps 2 and 4 and illustrate use of the D/D methodology in an example motivated by the case study in the next section. Suppose we are designing

Table 16.3

Means and standard deviations of the daily costs resulting from the first-stage sampling with a model of a manufacturing system

Number of Repairpeople	Number of Leased Machines: 0	1
1	$413.99 / $39.58	$456.15 / $46.41
2	$402.91 / $7.81	$414.16 / $17.90

Legend: Mean / Std. Dev.

a production system, and as part of the design we need to specify how many repairpeople to hire to fix broken machines, and how many machines of this type to lease to supplement those already owned. The choices involve the four combinations of 1 or 2 repairpeople and 0 or 1 leased machines. From among these four alternatives, we want to select the combination that minimizes the average daily cost of operating the system. A model has been built to simulate the situation, and 15 replications have been performed with each of the alternatives. Results of this first-stage sampling are summarized in Table 16.3, where the rows and columns correspond to the alternative choices of numbers of repairpeople and leased machines, respectively. The upper entry in each cell in Table 16.3 is the average daily cost for the corresponding alternative, and the lower entry is the standard deviation of the average daily cost.

Now we want to compute the size of the second-stage samples required to determine the lowest-cost alternative with probability 0.95, using an indifference amount of $10 per day. Let n_0 be the first-stage sample size and N be the **total** sample size **for any particular alternative**. Then the second-stage sample size for the alternative is $N—n_0$. The value of N is determined as follows,

$$N = \max\{n_0 + 1, \lceil (h_1 s/d)^2 \rceil\}$$

where s is the first-stage standard deviation for the alternative, d is the indifference amount, and h_1 is a value that depends on three factors: the size of the first stage sample, the probability of making the correct selection, and the number of alternatives being considered. (Note that h_1 and d will be the same for all alternatives being considered.) Various values of h_1 can be found in Table 16.4. (Extensive tables of h_1 can be found in Dudewicz and Dalal, 1975. Table 16.4 is based on Dudewicz and Mishra, 1988, Table 9.10-1, pp. 512 et seq., and Table ll.2-2, pp. 588 et seq.)

Table 16.4

Selected values of h_1 for the Dudewicz-Dalal procedure

Probability of Selecting the Best	First-Stage Sample Size, n_0	Number of Alternatives, k: 2	3	4	5	6	7	8	9
0.90	15	1.93	2.39	2.63	2.81	2.93	3.04	3.12	3.20
0.90	20	1.90	2.34	2.58	2.75	2.87	2.97	3.05	3.12
0.90	25	1.88	2.32	2.55	2.72	2.84	2.93	3.01	3.08
0.90	30	1.87	2.30	2.54	2.69	2.81	2.91	2.98	3.05
0.95	15	2.50	2.94	3.17	3.34	3.46	3.57	3.65	3.72
0.95	20	2.45	2.87	3.10	3.26	3.38	3.47	3.55	3.62
0.95	25	2.42	2.84	3.06	3.21	3.33	3.42	3.50	3.56
0.95	30	2.41	2.81	3.03	3.18	3.30	3.39	3.46	3.53
0.99	15	3.64	4.04	4.27	4.43	4.55	4.64	4.73	4.80
0.99	20	3.54	3.92	4.13	4.28	4.39	4.48	4.55	4.62
0.99	25	3.48	3.85	4.05	4.20	4.30	4.39	4.46	4.53
0.99	30	3.45	3.81	4.01	4.14	4.25	4.33	4.40	4.46

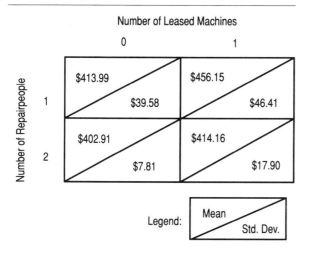

Table 16.5

Values of $(h_1 s/d)^2$ and of the second-stage sample sizes $N - n_0$ for the first-stage samples of Table 16.3, where $n_0 = 15$, $h_1 = 3.101$, and $d = \$10$

Number of Repairpeople	Number of Leased Machines: 0	1
1	158.12 / 144	217.40 / 203
2	6.16 / 1	32.34 / 18

Legend: upper entry $(h_1 s/d)^2$, lower entry $N - n_0$

In the equation, the notation $\lceil x \rceil$ means "the smallest integer greater than or equal to x." Hence $\lceil 31.9 \rceil = 32$, $\lceil 0.05 \rceil = 1$, and so on. As the equation indicates, N is 1 larger than n_0 at a minimum, and equals $\lceil (h_1 s/d)^2 \rceil$ if this value exceeds $n_0 + 1$.

For example, if the first-stage sample n_0 is of size 15 and the value of $\lceil (h_1 s/d)^2 \rceil$ is 31.9, then the total sample size N is 32, and the second-stage sample is of size 17 (=32–15). However, if n_0 is 15 and the value of $\lceil (h_1 s/d)^2 \rceil$ is only 7.1, then N is 16 and the second stage sample is of size 1 (= 16–15).

Let's now compute the size of the second-stage samples for the four alternatives in Table 16.3. With $n_0 = 15$, $d = \$10$, $k = 4$ alternatives, and 0.95 specified as the probability of making a correct selection, h_1 is 3.17 from Table 16.4. The resulting values of $(h_1 s/d)^2$ and of the second-stage sample size, $N–n_0$, are shown for the four alternatives in Table 16.5. The upper entry in each cell in Table 16.5 shows the value of $(h_1 s/d)^2$ for the corresponding alternative, and the lower entry shows the value of $N–n_0$. As indicated in Table 16.5, the sizes of the second-stage samples range from 1 to 203, reflecting a corresponding range of standard deviations in the first-stage samples reported in Table 16.3. These second-stage sample sizes can be decreased by increasing the indifference amount, and/or by decreasing the probability of making a correct selection. (A larger first-stage sample size would also lead to smaller second-stage samples via a smaller h_1 value.)

After the second-stage samples have been taken, their averages are then computed. (The standard deviations of the second-stage samples aren't used, and so don't need to be computed.) Table 16.6 shows the mean costs for the second-stage samples for the four alternatives, based on the Table 16.5 sample sizes.

For each alternative, the averages of the first- and second-stage samples are then weighted and added. The weight W_0 applied to an alternative's first-stage sample mean is computed this way:

$$W_0 = (n_0 / N)\left[1 + \sqrt{1 - (N/n_0)\left[1 - (N - n_0)/(h_1 s/d)^2\right]}\right]$$

The weight W_1 applied to the alternative's second-stage sample mean is then $1 - W_0$.

Table 16.6

Mean daily costs resulting from the second-stage sampling with a model of a production system

Number of Repairpeople	Number of Leased Machines: 0	1
1	\$423.28	\$459.18
2	\$392.93	\$416.80

Table 16.7

Values of the weights W_0 and W_1 applied to the means of the first- and second-stage samples reported in Tables 16.3 and 16.6

Number of Repairpeople	Number of Leased Machines: 0	1
1	0.116 / 0.884	0.082 / 0.918
2	1.243 / - 0.243	0.526 / 0.474

Legend: upper entry w0, lower entry W1

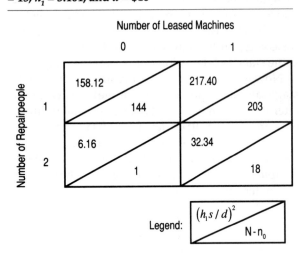

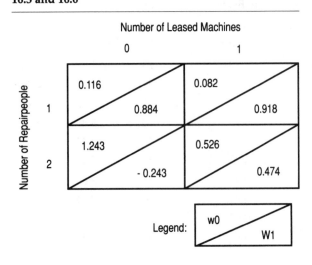

Using the information in Table 16.5, the weights that apply to the four alternatives are summarized in Table 16.7. Note that for the "2 repairpeople, 0 leased machines" alternative, the weight applied to the first-stage sample mean exceeds 1.0, which results in a negative weight being applied to the mean of the second-stage sample. This is the alternative for which the second-stage sample is only of size 1.

Finally, the weights of Table 16.7 are applied to the first- and second-stage sample means of Tables 16.1 and 16.6 to produce the weighted mean daily costs for the four alternatives shown in Table 16.8. With probability 0.95, the least cost alternative is to have 2 repairpeople and 0 leased machines, resulting in an estimated average daily cost of $405.34. This alternative has been selected using an indifference amount of $10 per day in the expected daily cost.

The lowest-cost "2,0" alternative (2 repairpeople, 0 leased machines) of Table 16.8 also happened to be the lowest-cost alternative in the first-stage sampling. (See Table 16.3.) It won't always be true, of course, that the tentative best resulting from the first-stage sampling will be judged to be the ultimate best after the second-stage sampling. In this case, the relatively small standard deviation of the first-stage tentative best (see Table 16.3), combined with the relative superiority of this alternative in first-stage terms, increased the chances that this alternative would be the ultimate best.

The case study in the next section provides the details of the production system used in the above Dudewicz and Dalal example and shows the model that produced the results of Tables 16.3 and 16.5.

Table 16.8

The weighted mean daily costs resulting from application of the Dudewicz and Dalal procedure to four production system alternatives

Number of Repairpeople	Number of Leased Machines: 0	1
1	$422.20	$458.93
2	$405.34	$415.41

16.9 Case Study 16A: Selecting the Probable Best from Four Proposed Production Systems

1. Statement of the Problem

In a particular production system, an objective is to operate 10 machines of a given type 8 hours a day, 5 days a week. Management employs 10 machine operators for this purpose. (The machines do not operate by themselves, but only under the control of an operator, one operator per machine.) Management owns 11 machines of the type in question, and so appears to have slack capacity in this regard. In a perfect world, management's objective of realizing 400 machine operating hours per week could be achieved in straightforward fashion, and there would be an unneeded machine in the system.

But the world is not perfect. Each of the machines is subject to random failure. (In this case study, no other potential operating problems are recognized. For example, it's assumed that there is never absenteeism among the machine operators.) When a machine fails, it is replaced with the machine not in use, either immediately (if the machine not in use is in working order), or as soon as possible (if the machine not in use is in the process of being repaired). Meantime, the failed machine is sent to an in-house repairshop, where it is repaired and then assumes the status of a backup machine ready for use again when needed.

The four stages in the cycle through which machines move are shown in Figure 16A.1 for a hypothetical situation. In the figure, an open square is a machine that is in productive use, or is in operating order. An X-ed out square is a failed machine (being repaired, or waiting to be repaired). One machine is shown in repair. No failed machines are waiting to be repaired. One machine is idle but in operating order, ready to be used again when needed. In total, 12 machines are in the system shown (10 in productive use, 1 in repair, and 1 idle but in operating order). This 12-machine case corresponds to an option that management wants to consider (see below).

There has been a considerable shortfall with respect to the target of realizing 400 machining hours per week. The average number of machines in productive use is estimated to be only about 8, which translates to 64 machining hours per day (contrasted with the target of 80 machining hours per day). The opportunity cost per forgone machining hour is $18.00 This results in an average opportu-

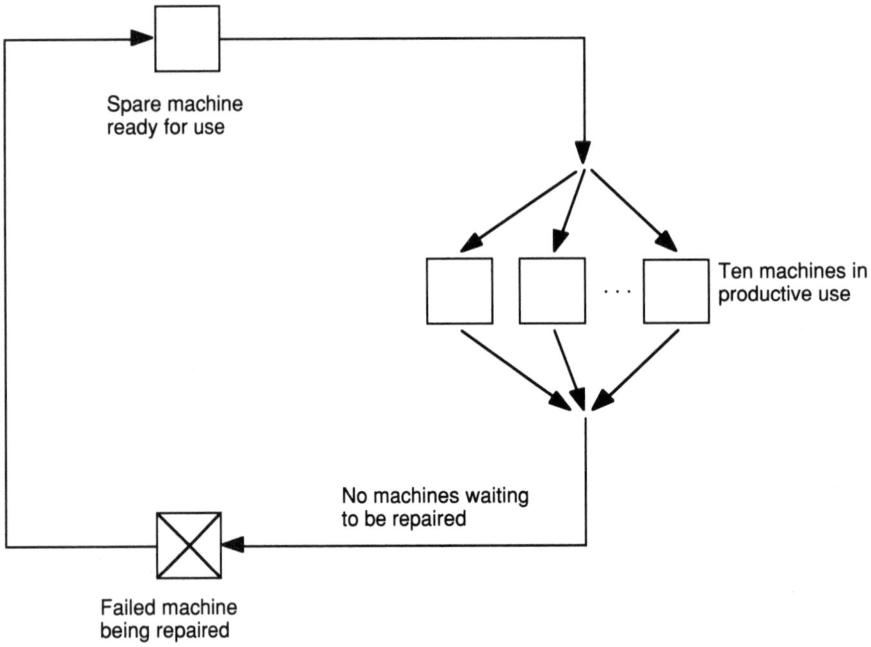

Figure 16A.1 Flow Schematic for Case Study 16A

nity cost of about $288.00 per day (16 forgone machining hours per day on average, each valued at $18) in the current system.

Management only employs one repairperson to fix failed machines, but is willing to hire one more repairperson if this would be cost effective. The overall cost of the additional repairperson (including salary and benefits) would be $15/hour, or $120 per 8-hour day.

Management does not want to hire and train additional machine operators. Furthermore, management does not want to supplement the 11 owned machines by buying additional machines of this type, because of the high capital costs involved and uncertainty in the size of the future market for the product. And for union-related reasons, it is infeasible to have machine operators work overtime to make up the shortfall.

In addition to the possibility of adding a repairperson, management has the opportunity to lease 1 machine on a long-term basis to supplement its 11 owned machines. Leasing charges work out to $100 per 8-hour workday. (The leasing charges would be incurred whether the leased machine is in productive use or not and are independent of the extent of use of the leased machine.) A decision must be made whether to lease a machine.

Based on past experience, the time required for a repairperson to repair a failed machine is 24 ± 8 hours. (This time can't be reduced by having the two repairpeople team up to repair a failed machine. A failed machine is fixed by only one repairperson, even if the other repairperson is idle at the time.) When a machine is put into productive use, its running time before failure is 200 ± 100 hours. The time for a machine operator to switch from a machine that has just failed to one ready to use as its replacement is assumed to be negligibly small.

No distinctions are made among repairpeople, or among machines cycling through the system. That is, the repairtime and running-time-until-failure distributions apply equally to the 11 owned machines and the potentially leased machine. And because the machine leasing charge is independent of machine usage, management has no motivation to distinguish between owned and leased machines in the system.

Model this system; then use the model to investigate the cost consequences of the four options available to management (do nothing; hire a second repairperson, but don't lease another machine; don't hire a second repairperson, but do lease another machine; hire a second repairperson, and, in addition, lease another machine). Use the method of Dudewicz and Dalal to estimate which of the four options is probably the best in terms of minimizing the expected daily cost of the system. Set the probability of selecting the best at 0.95, and use an indifference amount of $10/day. Use 15 replications for each alternative in the first-stage sampling.

In computing average daily costs, take into account payroll for the 1 or 2 repairpeople ($120 per person per day), leasing charges ($100 per day per leased machine), and opportunity cost for forgone production ($18 per machining hour, or $144 per machining day). For the base case (the system as is), for example, both payroll and opportunity cost contribute to the average daily cost measure that is to be used.

Assume that when the simulation starts, 10 owned machines are in productive use. Their remaining lifetime at the start of the simulation is to be 150 ± 140 hours. This range from 10 to 290 hours reflects the fact that at operating equilibrium, some of these machines will have already been in use for a considerable time, and will be near the point of failure, whereas others will have just recently been put back into use, and others will be somewhere between these two extremes. By starting under approximate conditions of operating equilibrium, it won't be necessary to deal with biased observations taken during transient conditions.

Also assume that when the simulation starts, the other owned machine and the leased machine, if any, are in working order, ready for use when next needed.

2. Approach Taken in Building the Model

It is useful to approach the modeling process by first identifying the **constraints** in a system, then deciding on various GPSS/H entities to be used to model these constraints. There are three constraints in the production system:

1. The number of repairpeople.
2. The number of machine operators.
3. The total number of machines in the system.

It is convenient to choose GPSS/H Storages to model the first two constraints, and Xacts to model the third. The reasoning behind these choices, roughly speaking, is that the repairpeople and the machine operators are stationary (within reason), occupying fixed points as suggested in Figure 16A.1. On the other hand, the machines themselves, like Xacts, can be thought of as moving from point to point as they cycle through the system. (Such a simple and "obvious" mapping of system elements into their GPSS/H equivalents is not always the best to take, however. Some mappings are better than others in terms of their implications for the amount of computer time and memory required. Consideration of this matter is outside the scope of this book, however.)

If you've not already modeled this system as Exercise 7 of Section 16.4, you should *try your hand at building the requested model before reading further.*

Consider the history of a typical machine as it makes one complete cycle through the Figure 16A.1 system. Suppose the machine is ready for use, but is idle because 10 other machines are already in productive use. This means the Storage OPRATORS (which models the 10 machine operators) is Full and the idle machine cannot execute its Next Block Attempted, "ENTER OPRATORS". Then one of the machines in productive use fails, executing a "LEAVE OPRATORS" Block and freeing up its operator. The idle machine is then able to execute the "ENTER OPRATORS" Block, and from there moves into an ADVANCE to simulate its running time until failure. When it eventually fails, it executes the "LEAVE OPRATORS" Block, then goes through a repair sequence (ENTER/ADVANCE/LEAVE). It then transfers back to take "ENTER OPRATORS" as its Next Block, waiting until an operator puts it back into productive use. We refer to the sequence of Blocks used for this logic as the mainline model segment.

It's an easy matter to structure the initial conditions in the model. The 10 machines in productive use can come out of their own GENERATE Block, execute an "ENTER OPRATORS" Block, then do the special "ADVANCE 150,140", and transfer from there to the "LEAVE OPRATORS" Block in the mainline model segment described earlier.

The other owned machine can come out of its own GENERATE Block, which can sit on top of the mainline model segment. This other owned machine is, in effect, the typical machine described in the preceding paragraph.

Finally, the leased machine (if any) can come out of its own GENERATE Block, and then transfer to the "ENTER OPRATORS" Block in the mainline segment as its Next Block, waiting until it is needed for productive use.

3. Table of Definitions

Table 16A.1 shows the Table of Definitions for Case Study 16A.

4. Block Diagram

The Block Diagram for Case Study 16A is given in Figure 16A.2.

5. Modified Source Echo

The Modified Source Echo for Case Study 16A is given in Figure 16A.3.

Table 16A.1

Table of Definitions for Case Study 16A

Base Time Unit: 1 hour

GPSS/H Entity	**Interpretation**
Transactions	
Model Segment 1	Machines (the 10 owned machines in productive use initially)
Model Segment 2	Machines (the leased machine, if any, initially waiting to be needed)
Model Segment 3	Machines (the one owned machine initially waiting to be needed; this machine is eventually joined by the owned machines and the leased machine, if there is one; all the machines then loop repeatedly through this segment)
Model Segment 4	A run-control Xact
Ampervariables	
FIXERS	The number of repairpeople (1 or 2)
I	The replication counter
LEASED	The number of leased machines (0 or 1)
Storages	
FIXSHOP	The Storage that models the repairperson or repairpersons
OPRATORS	The Storage that models the 10 machine operators

6. Postreplication Reports

The postreplication output of interest is Average Contents of the OPRATORS Storage, which indicates how many machines were in productive use on average during the preceding Xact-Movement Phase. Using this information, the average daily opportunity cost of having fewer than 10 machines in productive use can be computed. Adding the daily payroll costs and, if applicable, the daily leasing costs to the average daily opportunity cost then provides the average daily cost of the production system.

No postreplication output is shown here. Table 16A.2 summarizes the results of the first-stage sampling in terms of the output variable of interest, average number of machines in productive use. Means and standard deviations for the samples of size 15 are shown in Table 16A.2.

Table 16A.3 summarizes the results of the sec-

Table 16A.2

Means and standard deviations of the average number of machines in productive use in the first-stage sampling with a model of a manufacturing system

Number of Repairpeople	Number of Leased Machines: 0	Number of Leased Machines: 1
1	7.9584 / 0.27484	8.3601 / 0.32232
2	8.8687 / 0.054225	9.4850 / 0.1243

Legend: Mean / Std. Dev.

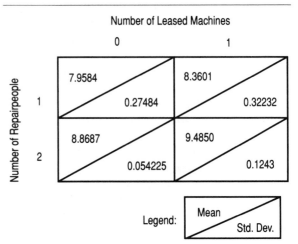

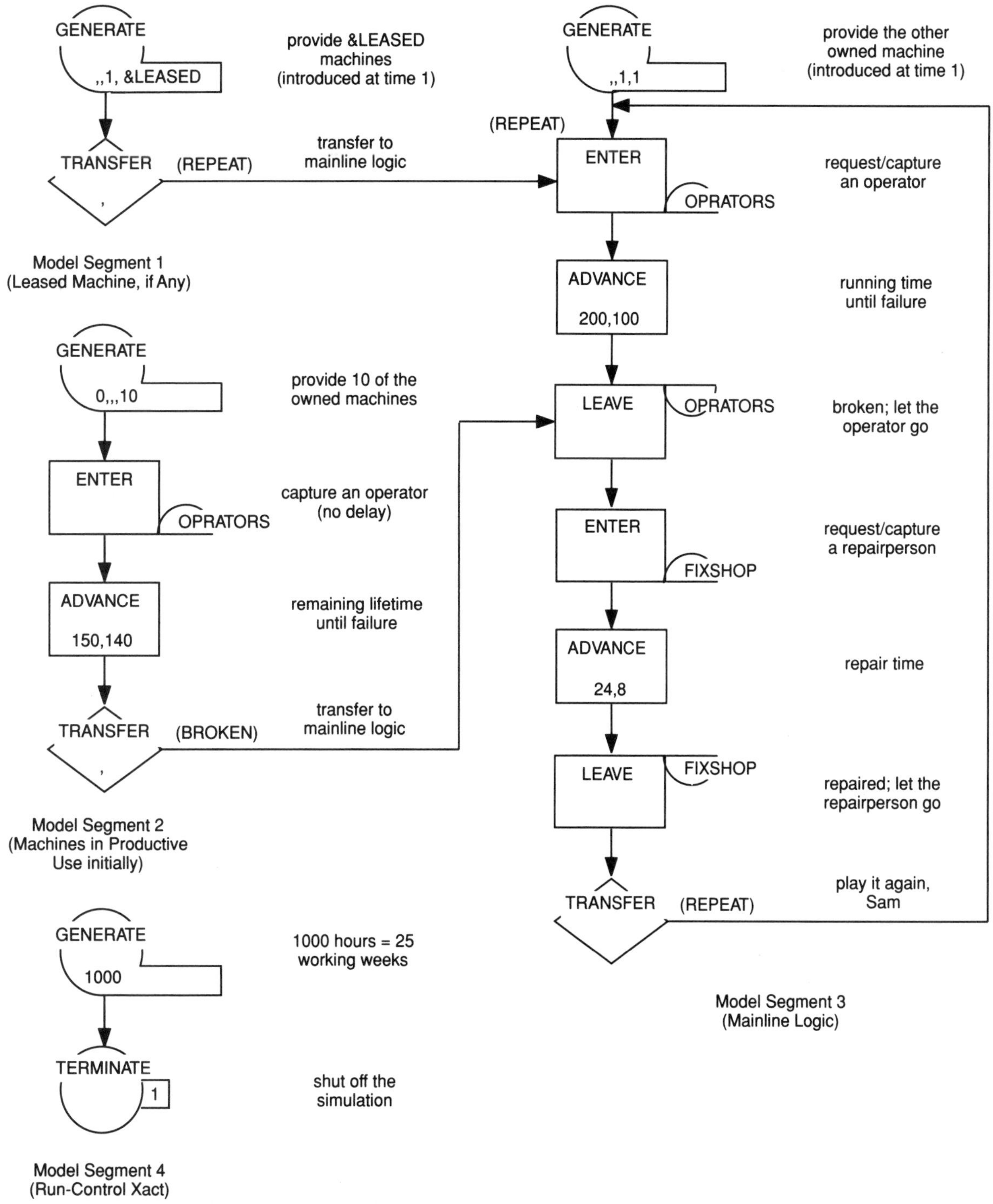

Figure 16A.2 *Block Diagram for Case Study 16A*

ond-stage sampling in terms of the average number of machines in productive use. Only the sample means of Table 16A.3 are needed for the Dudewicz and Dalal computations, but standard deviations are shown in the table as well, so that, as a matter of curiosity, they can be compared with those in Table 16A.2. The "2,0" (2 repairpeople, 0 leased machines) standard deviation in Table 16A.3 is undefined, because the second-stage sample size for this alternative was only 1. (See Table 16.5, which shows the second-stage sample sizes for the various Table 16A.3 alternatives.)

```
STMT#  BLOCK#  *LOC    OPERATION  A,B,C,D,E,F,G    COMMENTS
   1                     SIMULATE                                  Case Study 16A
   2           *                                               Production System
   3           *                                            Base Time Unit: 1 Hour
   4           ********************************************************************
   5           *         Compiler Directives (INTEGER; OPERCOL; UNLIST)            *
   6           ********************************************************************
   7           *
   8                     INTEGER    &FIXERS         number of repairpeople
   9                     INTEGER    &I              &I is a DO-loop index
  10                     INTEGER    &LEASED         number of leased machines
  11                     OPERCOL    30              scan up to column 30 for the
  12           *                                    start of the Operands field
  13                     UNLIST     CSECHO          no control-statement echoes
  14           *
  15           ********************************************************************
  16           *         Control Statements (STORAGE)                              *
  17           ********************************************************************
  18           *
  19            OPRATORS STORAGE    10              10 people to operate machines
  20           *
  21           ********************************************************************
  22           *         Model Segment 1 (Leased Machines, if Any)                 *
  23           ********************************************************************
  24           *
  25      1              GENERATE   ,,1,&LEASED   provide &LEASED machines
  26           *                                  (introduced at time 1)
  27      2              TRANSFER   ,REPEAT       transfer to mainline logic
  28           *
  29           ********************************************************************
  30           *         Model Segment 2 (Machines in Productive Use Initially)    *
  31           ********************************************************************
  32           *
  33           *         GENERATE   0,,,10        provide 10 of the owned machines
  34      3              ENTER      OPRATORS      capture an operator (no delay)
  35      4              ADVANCE    150,140       remaining lifetime until failure
  36      5              TRANSFER   ,BROKEN       transfer to mainline logic
  37           *
  38           ********************************************************************
  39           *         Model Segment 3 (Mainline Logic)                          *
  40           ********************************************************************
  41           *
  42      6              GENERATE   ,,1,1         provide the other owned machine
  43           *                                  (introduced at time 1)
  44      7     REPEAT   ENTER      OPRATORS      request/capture an operator
  45      8              ADVANCE    200,100       running time until failure
```

Figure 16A.3 *Modified Source Echo for Case Study 16A*
(continued on the next page)

The sole purpose of simulating the production system is to estimate the average daily opportunity cost for a given number of repairpeople and leased machines. The simulation model isn't needed to compute the daily payroll and leasing costs. Similarly, for a given number of repairpeople and leased machines, these last two costs aren't variable. The only source of cost variability is the opportunity cost.

7. Discussion

Model Logic. The Case Study 16A model marks the second time we've used an Integer Ampervariable to supply the value of a Block Operand. In particular, the Limit Count at a GENERATE Block (see Statement 25 of Figure 16A.3) is supplied with the Ampervariable &LEASED. (This was done for the first time in the model of Figure 16.1, where an Ampervariable was used to supply the value of a GENERATE Block's Priority Operand.) The technique of supplying Block Operand values indirectly in GPSS/H (whether with Ampervariables, or by using other possibilities not introduced in this book) has important implications for flexible modeling.

```
46       9   BROKEN   LEAVE      OPRATORS     broken; let the operator go
47      10            ENTER      FIXSHOP      request/capture a repairperson
48      11            ADVANCE    24,8         repair time
49      12            LEAVE      FIXSHOP      repaired;  let the repairperson go
50      13            TRANSFER   ,REPEAT      play it again, Sam
51           *
52           **********************************************************************
53           *        Model Segment 4 (Run-Control Transaction)                    *
54           **********************************************************************
55           *
56      14            GENERATE   1000         1000 hours = 25 working weeks
57      15            TERMINATE  1            shut off the simulation
58           *
59           **********************************************************************
60           *        Run-Control Statements                                       *
61           **********************************************************************
62           *
63                    DO         &FIXERS=1,2,1   first 1, then 2 repairpeople
64           *
65            FIXSHOP STORAGE    &FIXERS         put FIXSHOP Capacity into effect
66           *
67                       DO      &LEASED=0,1,1   first 0, then 1 leased machine
68           *
69                          DO   &I=1,15,1       15 replications
70           *
71                             START  1          initiate the &Ith replication
72           *
73                             PUTPIC LINES=6,FILE=SYSPRINT,(&I,&FIXERS,&LEASED)
74           0=====================================================================
75              Shown above is Replication Report * for this configuration:
76
77                            Number of repairpersons:    *
78                          Number of leased machines:    *
79            =====================================================================
80           *
81                             CLEAR              clear for next replication
82           *
83                          ENDDO                 next replication
84           *
85                       ENDDO                    next number of leased machines
86           *
87                    ENDDO                       next number of repairpeople
88           *
89                    END                         end of Model-File execution
```

Figure 16A.3 *(concluded)*

This fact is evident only to a minor extent in the Case Study 16A model.

Model Implementation. Three nested DO loops are used in the Case Study 16A Model File. (See Statements 63, 67, and 69 in Figure 16A.3.) These, respectively, control the number of repairpeople, the number of leased machines, and the number of replications. The potential for using DO loops to cycle methodically through many combinations of decision variables in GPSS/H modeling is evident in this example.

Note how the FIXSHOP STORAGE statement (Statement 65) has been placed in the body of the outer loop in the Figure 16A.3 Model File. Also note how the value of this Control Statement's A Operand is supplied with an Integer Ampervariable (&FIXERS). The output loop controls the value of &FIXERS. It's **after** the value of &FIXERS is set that the STORAGE statement is to be executed, to set the Capacity of the FIXSHOP Storage. (Note that it would make no sense to reposition the FIXSHOP STORGE statement to **precede** the Statement 63 DO, even though GPSS/H would not object if this were done. If this were done, &FIXERS would still have its default value of zero when the STORAGE statement was executed. This means there would be **no** repairpeople for any of the replications.)

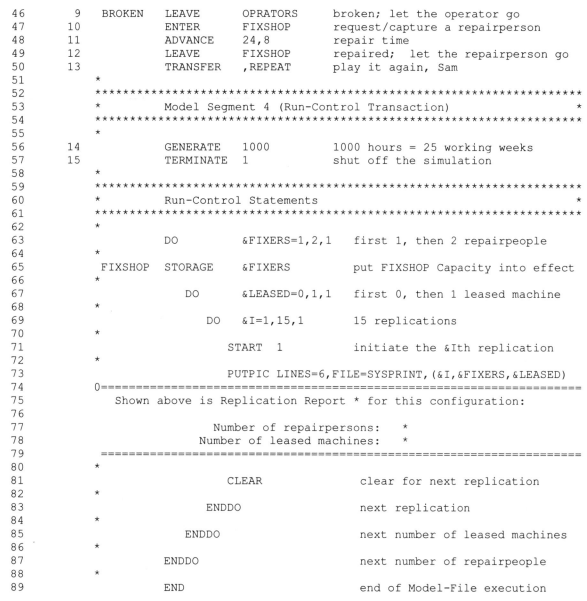

Table 16A.3

Means and standard deviations of the average number of machines in productive use in the second-stage sampling with a model of a manufacturing system

Number of Repairpeople	Number of Leased Machines: 0 (Mean / Std. Dev.)	Number of Leased Machines: 1 (Mean / Std. Dev.)
1	7.8939 / 0.27051	8.3390 / 0.31895
2	8.938 / undefined	9.4667 / 0.080237

Legend: Mean / Std. Dev.

The initial value of &LEASED in the DO of Statement 67 is zero. This means the Limit Count of the Statement 25 GENERATE Block has an initial value of zero. As a result, this GENERATE Block will not create **any** Xacts during the corresponding replications.

As in Figure 16.1, an OPERCOL statement (Statement 11, Figure 16A.3) has been included in the Model File to support the indenting of nested DO loops. (See Statements 63 through 87.)

An "UNLIST CSECHO" statement (Statement 13) has been included in the Model File to eliminate the echoing of Control-Statement images to the output at the time the Control Statements are executed.

Finally, independent replications were achieved for the second-stage replications as follows.

1. An RMULT Statement was put into the Model File after the OPERCOL Statement (Statement 13, Figure 16A.3). This statement took the form "RMULT 200000" for the "1,0" alternative. Later, its A Operand was changed to 300000, 400000, and 500000 for the "1,1," "2,0," and "2,1" alternatives, respectively.
2. The &FIXERS DO Statement (Statement 63) and/or the &LEASED DO Statement (Statement 67) was altered to correspond to the one alternative for which the stage-two sampling was being performed. For the "1,0" alternative, for example, these statements were altered to

   "DO &FIXERS=1,1,1"

   and

   "DO &LEASED=0,0,1".
3. The &I DO Statement (Statement 69) was altered to correspond to the sample size for the one alternative for which the stage-two sampling was being performed. For the "1,0" alternative, for example, this statement was altered to "DO &I=1,144,1".

Batch runs were performed with four separate Model Files, then, to produce the stage 2 samples. This approach was taken because the stage 2 sample sizes were unique to the alternative being considered.

Postsimulation Reports. The Postsimulation Reports, although not shown directly, are indirectly summarized in Tables 16A.1 and 16A.2. The replication means and standard deviations in those tables were **not** computed by rekeying the individual replication means to use with a statistics package or calculator. Instead, an appropriate PUTPIC statement was inserted into the Model File to have the model write the Average Contents of the OPRATORS Storage into a computer file. This Average Contents file was then postprocessed, using an interactive statistical analysis program.

The preceding paragraph implies that a PUTPIC output list can include components of Storage Reports. This is the case. In fact, most elements of a Postreplication Report can be included in PUTPIC output lists. This capability supports analysis of output from GPSS/H models, as well as the preparation of customized reports and real-time dialog with the interactive user of a model, all of which has been mentioned earlier. (This book does not provide the details needed to operationalize these GPSS/H features.)

16.10 Exercises

1. This exercise involves checking some of the Section 16.8 and 16.9 calculations.

(a) Given the information for the "1,0" (1 repairperson, 0 leased machines) alternative in Table 16.3, compute the size of the second-stage sample needed for this alternative under the conditions of Section 16.8. Check your result against the second-stage sample size of 144 reported in Table 16.5.

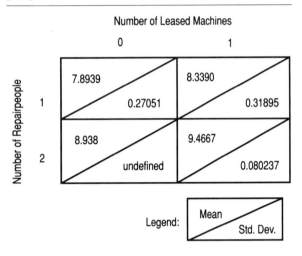

(b) Repeat (a), except for the "2,0" alternative.
(c) Given the information for the "1,0" alternative in Table 16.5, determine the weight W_0 that applies to the first-stage sample mean in determining the overall mean for this alternative. Check your result against the W_0 value reported for this alternative in Table 16.7.
(d) Repeat (c), except for the "2,0" alternative.
(e) Given the information for the "1,0" alternative in Tables 16.3, 16.6, and 16.7, compute the overall mean for this alternative. Check your result against that reported in Table 16.8.
(f) Repeat (e), except for the "2,0" alternative.

2. This exercise involves changing some of the calculations in Sections 16.8 and 16.9.

(a) Suppose the opportunity cost per forgone machine hour in Case Study 16A had been $12, not $18. How would this have changed the entries in Table 16.3 for the "1,0" alternative?
(b) Repeat (a), but for the "2,0" alternative.
(c) For the change described in (a), how would this have changed the entries in Table 16.5 for the "1,0" alternative?
(d) Repeat (c), but for the "2,0" alternative.
(e) For the change described in (a), how would this have changed the entries in Table 16.7 for the "1,0" alternative?
(f) Repeat (e), but for the "2,0" alternative.

3. (a) Recompute the entries in Table 16.5, assuming that the probability of selecting the best alternative is lowered from 0.95 to 0.90.
(b) Repeat (a), but assume that the probability of selecting the best alternative is raised from 0.95 to 0.99.

4. In Case Study 16A, only one repairperson can work on a failed machine, even if there is a second repairperson who is idle. Change this situation by assuming that if a machine fails when two repairpeople are idle, the two people team up to fix the failed machine, with repairtime then being 16 ± 4 hours. (If one or more other machines fail while the two repairpeople are working together on a failed machine, they nevertheless continue to work together until the machine they are working on has been fixed.) Revise the Case Study 16A model to incorporate this change in system logic. Then repeat Case Study 16A for this modified logic. Which alternative now leads to the probable lowest expected daily cost?

5. It is assumed in Case Study 16A that the time required to replace a failed machine with another machine is negligibly small. Change this assumption so that, after a machine fails, it takes 15 minutes to remove the failed machine from the work area (at which time repair of it can begin). Also assume that, after a failed machine has been removed from the work area, it takes another 15 minutes to set up its replacement machine. At a minimum, then, 30 machining minutes are lost every time a machine fails. Revise the Case Study 16A model to incorporate this change in system logic. Then repeat the case study for this modified logic. Which alternative now leads to the probable lowest expected daily cost?

6. Case Study 16A assumes that the lifetime and repairtime distributions of the potentially leased machine are identical to those of the 11 owned machines. Suppose the potentially leased machine reflects a newer design, so that its running time until failure is 300± 50 hours and its repairtime is 16 ± 4 hours. Revise the Case Study 16A model to incorporate this change in system logic, continuing to assume that machines are used and repaired on a FCFS basis. Then repeat Case Study 16A for this modified logic. Which alternative now leads to the probable lowest expected daily cost?

7. Repeat Exercise 6, but now assume the potentially leased machine has higher priority for use and repair than the 11 owned machines.

8. Case Study 16A assumes that leasing charges are $100/day, independent of the utilization of the leased machine. Suppose instead that leasing charges are $20/day, plus $15/hour of leased machine use. Assume that under this circumstance, use and repair of owned machines is given high priority over use and repair of the leased machine (if there is a leased machine). Revise the Case Study 16A model to incorporate this change in system logic. Then repeat Case Study 16A for this modified logic. Which alternative now leads to the probable lowest expected daily cost?

9. In Case Study 16A, suppose the alternatives are expanded to include all combinations of 1, 2, or 3 repairpeople and 0, 1, or 2 leased machines. (There are then 9 possible alternatives.) Independent replications of size 500 have been performed with each of these 9 alternatives. Each alternative has been based on transparent sampling via

Table E11

Means and standard deviations of the average number of machines in productive use in 500 independent replications with each of 9 alternatives

Number of Repair People	Number of Leased Machines: 0 (Mean / Std. Dev.)	1 (Mean / Std. Dev.)	2 (Mean / Std. Dev.)
1	7.92 / 0.252	8.37 / 0.343	8.65 / 0.347
2	9.08 / 0.086	9.72 / 0.087	9.83 / 0.065
3	8.96 / 0.064	9.57 / 0.060	9.87 / 0.041

Legend: Mean / Std. Dev.

RN1. An RMULT statement has been executed at the beginning of each set of 500 replications to set the Initial Position of RN1 at 600000, 700000, 800000, ..., 140000 for the series of 9 alternatives. The resulting means and standard deviations of the Average Contents of the OPRATORS Storage are summarized in Table E11.

(a) Compute 95 percent confidence intervals for the average daily cost for each of the nine alternatives.

(b) Using the classic two-sample z, form a 95 percent interval estimate for the "2,0" (two repairpeople, 0 leased machines) and "2,1" alternatives. Is zero included in this confidence interval? Which of these two alternatives appears to have the lowest expected daily cost associated with it?

(c) Repeat (b), but for the "3,0" and "3,1" alternatives.

(d) Repeat (b), but for the "2,2" and "3,1" alternatives.

(e) Repeat (b), but for the "1,1" and "1,2" alternatives.

10. Repeat Case Study 16A, but assume that machine lifetime is 200 ± 25 hours, and machine repairtime is 24 ± 4 hours. (These uniformly distributed input variables have the same expected values as in Case Study 16A, but smaller variances.) Consistent with the changed lifetime distribution, assume the remaining lifetime for the 10 machines initially in productive use is 110 ± 100 hours. Which of the four competing alternatives is the probable best under this changed set of circumstances?

11. Repeat Case Study 16A, but assume that machine lifetime and machine repairtime are 2-Erlang distributed with means of 200 hours and 24 hours, respectively. Assume the remaining lifetime for the 10 machines initially in productive use is 2-Erlang distributed with a mean of 100 hours. Which of the four competing alternatives is the probable best under this changed set of circumstances? (Recall, the 2-Erlang distribution is used in Case Study 13B.)

12. Use the Dudewicz and Dalal procedure to compare the FCFS versus SPT service-order alternatives in the tool crib system. In the first-stage sampling, replicate 15 times with each of the two alternatives. (Using RN1 as the basis for all sampling, set the RN1 Initial Position to 300000 at the start of the stage 1 FCFS replications and to 400000 at the start of the stage 1 SPT replications.) Then determine stage 2 sample sizes using an indifference amount of 0.25 mechanics in the waiting line and specifying a 0.95

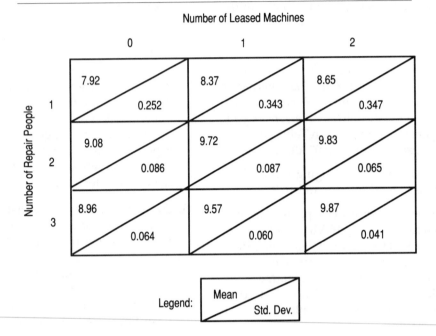

probability of selecting the service order with the smallest expected line content. (Continuing to use RN1 as the basis for all sampling, set the RN1 Initital Position to 500000 at the start of the stage 2 FCFS replications and to 600000 at the start of the stage 2 SPT replications.) Which service order is selected as probably having the smaller expected line length?

13. Exercises 4 through 10 of Section 16.7 call for comparing pairs of system alternatives through use of common random numbers. For your choice of one or more of these exercises, design and conduct an experiment using the methodology of Dudewicz and Dalal (rather than common random numbers) to select the probable best from the two competing alternatives in the pair.

14. In Exercise 11 of Section 11.14, it's of interest to estimate the number of assemblers maximizing the average daily profit in an expanded form of the widget-manufacturing system. Design and conduct an experiment using the methodology of Dudewicz and Dalal to make this determination.

15. In Exercise 6 of Section 11.14, experimentation is requested to determine what effect there would be on the in-harbor residence times of Type A and Type B ships if (a) 1 more tugboat, or (b) 1 more Type A berth, or (c) 1 more Type B berth were provided at the harbor. Introduce economic considerations of your choice into this problem. For example, you might assume that the uniform capital recovery costs associated with resources in the harbor are these:

    1. $1000/day per incremental tugboat
    2. $5000/day per incremental Type A berth
    3. $6500/day per incremental Type B berth

    Also make assumptions about the cost of having ships spend time at the harbor. For example, suppose it costs $1000/hour and $1500/hour, respectively, to have Type A and Type B ships spend time at the harbor. For the economic conditions of your choice, design and conduct an experiment using the methodology of Dudewicz and Dalal to estimate what the total set of harbor resources should be if the objective is to minimize the average daily cost attributable to harbor resources and to ship delay. Do not exclude any possibilities from your consideration. For example, the best harbor configuration might require adding 2 tugboats and 1 berth each of Type A and Type B.

17 Epilogue

17.1 Preview

GPSS/H provides over 65 types of Blocks, 35 types of Control Statements, 20 types of Compiler Directives, and 15 types of Report Statements, for a total in excess of 135 types of statements. Only a subset of this rich collection of GPSS/H capabilities has been introduced in this book. The purpose of this Epilogue is to survey some of the GPSS/H capabilities not covered in the book and to suggest how those interested can proceed in the further study of GPSS/H.

There is some overlap and forward referencing from time to time in the material discussed in various sections in this chapter. This is because the various features of GPSS/H do not exist in isolation, but often involve interplay with other features.

One or two of the capabilities described here may be restricted in DOS GPSS/H. (For example, the SAVE and READ Control Statements are not currently supported in DOS GPSS/H.)

17.2 Availability/Unavailability of Resources

As pointed out in Chapter 6, it's possible in GPSS/H to move resources back and forth between states of availability ("in working order," "on duty") and unavailability ("broken down," "not on duty"). This is done with use of the complementary FUNAVAIL and FAVAIL Blocks for resources modeled with Facilities, and with use of the complementary SUNAVAIL and SAVAIL Blocks for resources modeled with Storages.

What becomes of an Xact that is using a Facility, say, at the time the Facility becomes unavailable? For example, what happens to a piece of work-in-process if it is using a machine, and the machine breaks down? A number of alternatives are offered in this regard. The Xact can simply wait until the resource is eventually returned to a state of availability, and then resume using the resource, or it can be routed along some alternative path in the model. In case the Xact waits for the resource, its remaining resource usage time can be modified (increased, for example) to take into account the disruptive effect of the resource becoming temporarily unavailable while the Xact was using it.

If an Xact is using a Facility when it becomes unavailable, and the Xact waits to resume use of the Facility, the Xact waits on an Interrupt Chain. Each Facility has an associated Interrupt Chain that is used for this purpose. And so there are as many Interrupt Chains in a model as there are Facilities. Like the Current and Future Chains, Interrupt Chains are used by GPSS/H as aids in the management of Xacts.

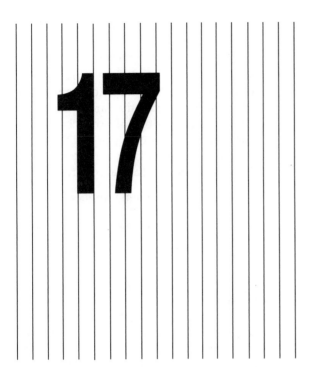

There is not as great a set of options provided with Storage un/availability as with Facility un/availability. To take advantage of flexible Facility un/availability, the servers in a group are sometimes modeled individually with Facilities rather than collectively with Storages.

17.3 Preemptive Use of Facilities

As mentioned in Chapter 6, an Xact can make preemptive use of a resource modeled with a Facility. In preemptive use, one Xact takes a resource away from another Xact, even though the other Xact isn't yet finished with the resource. Preemption is modeled with use of the complementary PREEMPT and RETURN Blocks.

What becomes of the Xact that has had a Facility taken away from it by another Xact? GPSS/H offers a number of alternatives. The Xact displaced from use of the Facility can wait until it can later resume use of the Facility, or it can disassociate itself from the Facility and be routed along some alternative path in the model. In case the Xact waits to resume control of the Facility, its remaining Facility usage time can be modified (increased, for example) to take into account the disruptive effect that might result from having the Facility taken away from it temporarily.

If an Xact has a Facility taken away from it, and decides to wait to resume use of the Facility when the preemptive user is finished, the Xact waits on the Interrupt Chain associated with the Facility. Interrupt Chains are used by GPSS/H not just to support Facility un/availability, but also to support Facility preemption.

17.4 Logic Switches

Logic Switches are two-state switches (on-off switches) provided by GPSS/H in the form of the Logic Switch entity. Logic Switches are used to signal the state of affairs with respect to certain types of conditions in the system being modeled. In a model of a harbor, for example, a Logic Switch might be used to signal whether or not a storm is in progress. (Perhaps ships can't leave the harbor while a storm is in progress.) Or a Logic Switch might be used to signal that a period of low tides is in effect. (Perhaps ships can't move through the mouth of the harbor during periods of low tides.)

The LOGIC Block is provided to control the setting of specified Logic Switches. For example, an Xact might execute a LOGIC Block to turn a specified Logic Switch on, signaling that a storm has just started. The same Xact might later execute another LOGIC Block to turn the same Logic Switch back off, signaling that the storm has now subsided.

Xacts use GATE Blocks to test the setting of specified Logic Switchs. GATE Blocks are described in Section 17.7.

All Logic Switches are off initially, by default. The INITIAL Control Statement is provided as a means of turning one or more Logic Switches on before Xact movement begins in a replication.

In summary, use of the Logic-Switch entity involves the LOGIC and GATE Blocks and the INITIAL Control Statement.

17.5 Standard Numerical and Logical Attributes

Facilities, Storages, Queues, and Blocks (and other aspects of a model, too) have numerical properties, or attributes (e.g., what is the Capture Count of the CRANE Facility? how many tugboats modeled with the TUGBOATS Storage are currently idle? what is the Current Contents of the LONGLINE Queue? what is the Total Count at the Block labeled SOURCE?) These attributes are displayed in Facility, Storage, Queue, and Block reports at the end of a replication and their values can also be obtained by a model on a dynamic basis during the course of Model-File execution. These values are available in the form of Standard Numerical Attributes (SNAs). Specified syntax is used to refer to these values [e.g., FC(CRANE) refers to the Capture Count of the CRANE Facility; R(TUGBOATS) refers to the Remaining Capacity of the TUGBOATS Storage; Q(LONGLINE) refers to the Current Contents of the LONGLINE Queue; N(SOURCE) refers to the Total Count at the Block labeled SOURCE]. Standard Numerical Attributes can be used in Block Operand positions, as Function arguments, as Table arguments (see Section 17.10), and in the construction of arithmetic expressions (see Section 17.13), and can serve in a variety of other ways.

There are also Standard Numerical Attributes for the simulated clocks. The syntax C1 and AC1 is used to refer to the current values of the Relative and

Absolute Clocks, respectively. (See Section 17.24 for the distinction between these clock types.) If a Function's argument is specified as C1, for example, then the value produced by the Function will depend on the simulated time at which the value is produced. And, by constructing arithmetic expressions (see Section 17.13) that make appropriate reference to the current simulated time, desirable cyclic effects can be achieved in the pattern of values that a Function produces.

In addition to having numeric properties, Facilities, Storages, and Logic Switches also have logical (that is, true/false) properties or attributes. Specified syntax is used to refer to these Standard Logical Attributes [e.g., LS(STORM) is true if the STORM Logic Switch is on, and is false otherwise; FNU(CRANE) is true if the CRANE Facility is Idle, and is false otherwise; SNE(TUGBOATS) is true if the TUGBOATS Storage is Not Empty and is false otherwise]. Standard Logical Attributes can be tested by Xacts at GATE Blocks (see Section 17.7), and can be used in the construction of Boolean expressions (see Section 17.14). They can also support modeling in a number of other ways.

17.6 Transaction Attributes

Like Facilities, Storages, Queues, and Blocks, and so on, Xacts have numerical properties, or attributes (Standard Numerical Attributes). Xact attributes include Priority Level (referred to with the syntax PR). Furthermore, each Xact in a model can be the owner of up to four lists of singly subscripted variables known as **Parameters**. Each Parameter list is composed of a sequence of memory locations, or elements, into which signed numeric values can be stored, and from which copies of values can be fetched. One of the four lists is used to record floating-point values, and the other three lists are used to record integer values (fullword, halfword, byte). The types of Parameter lists which an Xact owns, and the number of elements (memory locations) in these lists, is specified by use of F, G, H, and I Operands at the GENERATE Blocks whose execution creates Xacts. (These Operands have default values, which explains why it hasn't been necessary to use these Operands in the book.)

Xacts use the ASSIGN Block to store a value into a specified element in a specified Parameter list. Alternatively, a BGETLIST Block can be used for this purpose. (BGETLIST is the Block form of the GETLIST Control Statement. See Sections 17.15 and 17.17.) By executing a BGETLIST Block, an Xact can cause one or more data values found in one or more records in an external file or keyed in by an interactive user, to be copied into one or more memory locations in one or more of its Parameter lists.

The values in Parameter lists are referred to by using syntax designed for this purpose. For example, PL(STEPTIME) refers to the value found in the STEPTIME element of the floating-point Parameter list of the moving Xact. Similarly, PF(JOBCODE) refers to the value found in the JOBCODE element of the fullword integer Parameter list of the moving Xact. (In these examples, STEPTIME and JOBCODE are simply identifiers for elements in Xact Parameter lists, even as DRILL might be an identifier for a Facility, TUGBOATS might be an identifier for a Storage, etc.)

To what use are an Xact's Parameters put? Xacts often model units of traffic having individual characteristics that need to be represented in a model. Xact Parameter lists can be used to record information about these characteristics of the traffic they model. For example, a unit of work-in-process might have a due date, a customer designation, a customer order number, an internal order number, a routing sequence, and alternative routing information. The Xact modeling the WIP unit could carry this information in one of its Parameter lists. This information could then be referred to by the Xact as it moves through a model. For example, if the next machine needed by the WIP unit is broken, the alternative routing information could be used to send the WIP unit to another machine that is to be used as an alternative under the circumstances.

17.7 Explicit Testing

Only two of the Block types introduced in this book have a flavor of testing associated with them. These two Block types, SEIZE and ENTER, both involve implicit testing of the "wait until" variety. (An Xact must *wait* at such a Block *until* it can capture a server.) And the type of test being conducted is limited to examining the Idle versus Captured status of a server (SEIZE) or servers (ENTER). (BOTH TRANSFER doesn't directly provide a testing capability; it's the B- and/or C-Blocks pointed to by the BOTH TRANSFER that provide the testing capability.)

The modeler can incorporate custom-designed tests into GPSS/H models by using GATE and/or

TEST Blocks. The GATE Block can be used by Xacts either to wait at a point until a specified logical condition is satisfied (e.g., a Storage is now Full, a Facility is now Idle, a Logic Switch has now been turned on), or to select one of two alternative paths in a model (e.g., if the Logic Switch is off, take the sequential path from the GATE; otherwise, take the nonsequential path). These alternative GATE modes are called "wait until" and "path-selection" modes.

Whereas GATE Blocks are used to examine the **logical** status of a Facility (e.g., Idle versus Captured), a Storage (e.g., Full versus Not Full), or a Logic Switch (e.g., on versus off), TEST Blocks are used to compare pairs of **numbers** (e.g., Are the Current Contents of this Queue greater than 10? Is the average utilization of this Facility less than or equal to 50 percent? Does this Storage have at least two idle servers? Is the value of this Ampervariable equal to zero?). Like the GATE Block, the TEST Block can be used in either of two modes: "wait until" mode (meaning that Xacts must wait at the TEST Block until the condition being tested becomes true) or "path-selection" mode (meaning that an Xact moves either sequentially or nonsequentially out of the TEST Block, depending on whether the comparison being made is true or false).

17.8 Selection of Qualifying Entity Members

Xacts sometimes need to scan a set of members of an entity class to determine if at least one of them satisfies a stated *logical* condition. For example, an Xact might scan a set of Facilities to determine if at least one of them is Idle, or a set of Storages to determine if at least one of them is Not Full, or a set of Logic Switches to determine if at least one of them is on. Such scans are accomplished by using the SELECT Block in logical mode. If it's determined in such a scan that at least one entity member satisfies the condition specified, then a qualifying entity member's identifier is copied into a specified element of a Parameter list of the Xact executing the SELECT Block.

Sometimes Xacts need to scan a set of entity members to determine if at least one of them satisfies a stated *numeric* condition. For example, an Xact might scan a set of Queues, to determine if at least one of them has zero Current Contents, or a set of Facilities, to determine if at least one of them has a utilization less than 50 percent. Such scans are accomplished by using the SELECT Block in comparison mode.

If a SELECT Block is used in logical or comparison mode and an entity member satisfies the specified logical or numeric condition, the Xact moves from the SELECT sequentially. If none of the scanned entity members satisfy the specified condition, the Xact moves from the SELECT nonsequentially. The nonsequential path supplies the logic followed by an Xact when no scanned entity members currently satisfy the condition of interest.

Xacts sometimes need to scan a set of entity members to determine which of them has the *smallest or largest numeric attribute* of a specified type. For example, an Xact might scan a set of Queues to determine which of them has the minimum Current Contents (or to determine one of them involved in a tie for minimum Current Contents). Similarly, an Xact might scan a set of Storages to determine which of them has the minimum Capture Count. Scans of this type are accomplished by using the SELECT Block in MIN/MAX mode.

17.9 Counting Qualifying Entity Members

There are occasions when an Xact needs to scan a set of entity members and *count* the number satisfying a specified logical or numeric condition. The COUNT Block can be used for this purpose. COUNT is highly similar to SELECT. With the COUNT Block, the count that is formed is put into a specified element in a Parameter list owned by the Xact at the COUNT Block.

17.10 The Table Entity

An objective in simulation is to observe and record over time the values of output variables of interest. For example, the Current Contents of a Storage might be observed from time to time during a replication. The mean of the observed values can be used as a point estmate of the expected Current Contents of the Storage, the sample standard deviation can be used to estimate the standard deviation of the Current Contents, and the observed values can be counted and relative frequencies can be determined to estimate the distribution followed by the Current Contents variable. (If the observed values are not independent of each other, the sample standard deviation and relative frequencies are biased estimates of the population standard deviation and relative frequencies, so care must be taken in this regard.)

This simulation objective is supported in GPSS/H by the Table entity. A GPSS/H Table is a collection of observed values of a variable of interest. Before such a collection can be formed, a TABLE Control Statement must be executed. The TABLE statement indicates which variable is to be observed. This variable is known as the Table's argument. The argument can simply be a Standard Numerical Attribute or, more generally, can be an arithmetic expression (see Section 17.13). The TABLE statement also indicates the modeler's choice of frequency classes that are to be used for the purpose of forming frequency class counts and computing relative frequencies.

To record the current value of a Table's argument, an Xact must execute a TABULATE Block. And so the Table entity involves both a type of Control Statement (TABLE) and a type of Block (TABULATE). (This is similar to the Storage entity, which involves the STORAGE Control Statement, and the ENTER and LEAVE Blocks.)

If a model contains one or more Tables, a Table Report is included as part of postreplication output. The Table Report provides the sample mean, the sample standard deviation, frequency class counts, relative frequencies, and cumulative frequencies for each Table.

There are Standard Numerical Attributes for Tables. These make it possible for a model to refer to the Table mean, the Table standard deviation, and the Table count (sample size) during an ongoing simulation. Table SNAs can be used in all the ways in which SNAs can be used in general in GPSS/H.

17.11 Ampervariables

As mentioned in Chapter 14, Ampervariables are simply variables in the sense of ordinary programming languages. There are four types of Ampervariables in GPSS/H: Integer, Real (that is, floating point), Character, and External. Integer, Real, and Character Ampervariables are, respectively, capable of storing whole numbers, decimal numbers, and character strings. External Ampervariables identify functions and/or subroutines in external libraries which are to be executed as part of overall GPSS/H model execution.

Except for External Ampervariables, an Ampervariable can be a scalar (that is, correspond to exactly one memory location), or it can be a linear-list data structure (that is, correspond to a singly subscripted variable).

Scaler/Integer Ampervariables have been used in this book as DO-loop indices, as elements in PUTPIC statements, to provide values for Block Operands and to assist in computing values for RMULT Operands. More generally, GPSS/H Ampervariables play an integral role in a set of computational capabilities that GPSS/H provides.

17.12 Computational Capabilities

GPSS/H has the computational capabilities of a conventional programming language. Computation is accomplished with the use of arithmetic expressions (see the next section), and can be supported by the use of built-in functions, and functions and subroutines available in external libraries, or written by the modeler in languages such as Fortran and C. Use of modeler-written functions and subroutines, and those from external libraries, is accomplished by declaring these to be External Ampervariables.

17.13 Arithmetic Expressions

Arithmetic expressions can be constructed in GPSS/H and used at will in Block Operand positions, as Function arguments, as Table arguments, and in virtually any other context in GPSS/H in which a number is required. (We've seen the use of arithmetic expressions to a limited extent in this book, in the context of RMULT Operands.) Arithmetic expressions are formed, in part, by using arithmetic operators to join references to numeric values. The numeric values, in turn, can be supplied via Standard Numerical Attributes, or other arithmetic expressions. The usual arithmetic operators are available (for addition, subtraction, multiplication, conventional division, and modulus division). Arithmetic expressions can also include references to such built-in GPSS/H functions as square root and the trigonometric functions and, via External

Ampervariables, can include references to functions found in external libraries, or written by the modeler in languages such as Fortran and C.

Values of arithmetic expressions are computed and put to immediate use when these expressions are specified as Block Operands, Function arguments, Table arguments, and as elements of output lists in PUTPIC Control Statements or BPUTPIC Blocks (see Section 17.15).

Values of arithmetic expressions are computed and stored in Ampervariables (for later use) with the LET Control Statement (see Section 17.16) and/or with the BLET Block (see Section 17.17). The values of arithmetic expressions can also be computed and stored into elements of an Xact's Parameter lists with the ASSIGN Block, and into Savevalue elements with the SAVEVALUE and MSAVEVALUE Blocks (see Section 17.18).

17.14 Boolean Expressions

Whereas arithmetic expressions have numeric values, Boolean expressions have true/false values. Boolean expressions are formed by using logical operators to join references to true/false values (truth values) and/or by using comparison operators to compare the values of two arithmetic expressions. True/false values in Boolean expressions are supplied via Standard Logical Attributes. The usual Boolen operators are available (for and-ing, or-ing, and not-ing).

The true/false value of a Boolean expression can be examined at a TEST Block. (True and false are coded as 1 and 0, respectively.) Use of either the wait until or the path-selection mode of the TEST Block with Boolean expressions provides the modeler with a powerful set of tools for controlling the movement of Xacts in a model. For example, a ship might have to anchor outside a harbor until three conditions are satisfied simultaneously: (1) there is no storm in progress, (2) the ship can claim three tugboats, and (3) the ship can claim a berth either of Type A or of Type B. The corresponding ship-Xact can wait at a TEST Block until these conditions are all in effect simultaneously, and then move on from there.

17.15 Input/Output Capabilities

GPSS/H provides input/output capabilities with the GETLIST and PUTPIC Control Statements, respectively (and their Block equivalents, BGETLIST and BPUTPIC; see Section 17.17).

PUTPIC statements have been used to a limited extent in the book to label Replication Reports. More generally, PUTPIC statements (and/or BPUTPIC Blocks) can be used to write customized reports and/or to support dialog with the interactive user of a model in man-in-the-loop simulations.

GETLIST statements (and/or BGETLIST Blocks) are used to read records directly from external sources (from a file, for example, or from an interactive user's terminal). Values can be read into Ampervariables, Xact Parameters, and Matrix and List Savevalues (see Section 17.18).

17.16 The Control-Statement Language

A powerful and flexible Control Statement Language (CSL) is provided by GPSS/H to implement the design of experiments that are to be conducted with GPSS/H models. Types of statements provided as part of the CSL include LET (which supports computation), DO/ENDDO (which support iteration), IF/ ELSEIF/.../ELSE/ENDIF (which support control-path selection), GOTO (which supports unconditional branching), GETLIST and PUTPIC (which support input and output), and CALL (which supports execution of subroutines declared as External Ampervariables). Indeed, it is quite possible to write entire GPSS/H models that **contain no Blocks**, but simply use the CSL in settings which do not involve Transactions. For example, the CSL might be used in conjunction with an external library to build up and then print out a table of *t* statistics.

17.17 Block Forms of Control Statements

Blocks are only executed during Xact movement; Control Statements are only executed during a Control-Statement execution phase. Sometimes it is convenient to have Xacts make moves whose effect corresponds to that of Control-Statement execution. For this reason, GPSS/H provides Block forms for many Control Statements. For example, there are Block forms of RESET, CLEAR, RMULT, STORAGE, PUTPIC, GETLIST, and LET. The Operation words for these Blocks are BRESET, BCLEAR,

BRMULT, BSTORAGE, BPUTPIC, BGETLIST, and BLET, respectively.

17.18 Two-Dimensional Data Structures

One-dimensional data structures (that is, singly subscripted variables) are provided by GPSS/H in the form of singly subscripted integer, floating-point, and character-valued Ampervariables, and in the form of Xact Parameter lists. Two-dimensional data structures (that is, doubly subscripted variables) are provided in the form of Matrix Savevalues.

Signed integer values can be stored in Matrix Savevalues. Four types of matrices are available. One of the four types is used to record floating-point values, and the other three types are used to record integer values (fullword, halfword, byte). Subject to the limitations of computer memory, a model can use any number of these matrices, and they can be of any size.

The MATRIX Control Statement is used to specify an identifier for a Matrix Savevalue and indicate its type and the number of rows and columns of which it is composed. For example, the Control Statement "STOCK MATRIX MX,10,20" specifies that a Matrix Savevalue named STOCK, fullword integer in type, consists of 10 rows and 20 columns.

The MSAVEVALUE Block and/or the GETLIST Control Statement (or its Block equivalent, BGETLIST) can be used to store values into elements in a Matrix Savevalue. With GETLIST (or BGETLIST), one or more values can be copied from external files, or from the interactive user's terminal, into Matrix Savevalues.

The values in specified elements of specified Matrix Savevalues can be referenced in the construction of arithmetic expressions. A standard referencing syntax is used for this purpose. For example,

ML(SEQUENCE,JOBTYPE,STEPNUM)

refers to the value found in the JOBTYPE row and STEPNUM column of the floating-point Matrix named SEQUENCE.

The values in Matrix Savevalues are all initially zero, by default. The INITIAL Control Statement is provided as a means of storing nonzero values into specified elements of specified Matrix Savevalues before Xact movement begins in a simulation. (The GETLIST Control Statement can also be used for this purpose.)

Linear-list Savevalues (that is, singly subscripted Savevalues) also exist in GPSS/H, but only one singly subscripted floating-point and three integer (fullword, halfword, byte) Savevalue lists are provided. Singly subscripted, numeric-valued Ampervariables play the same role as their List Savevalue counterparts and are less restricted because any number of singly subscripted Ampervariable lists can be introduced into a model. Most modelers prefer the use of singly subscripted Ampervariables to that of List Savevalues.

17.19 Extended Possibilities for Supplying Operand Values

In this book, the values of Block Operands have almost always been supplied directly, in the form of symbolic identifiers (e.g., TUGBOATS in "ENTER TUGBOATS") or as constants (e.g., 3 in "ENTER TUGBOATS,3"). The values of Block Operands (and of Function arguments, Table arguments, etc.) can alternatively be supplied indirectly, by the use of arithmetic expressions; or by the use of Functions, or by the use of indirect addressing. This flexibility makes it possible to combine two or more parallel sequences of Blocks that are of corresponding types (but may have different Operand values) into a single Block sequence. This results in models that require fewer Blocks than would otherwise be used, but whose logic is not as self-evident as when Operand values are supplied directly.

17.20 Other Types of Functions

There are six types of Functions in GPSS/H. Two of these types, Discrete and Continuous, have been introduced in this book. The other four types are commented on here.

1. List Functions (L-Functions). List Functions are a special case of Discrete Functions. When the x elements in the (x, y) pairs used to define a Discrete Function form the sequence 1, 2, 3, 4, ..., then the Function can be defined either as a Discrete Function, or as an L-Function. The differences between the two types of Functions

are these: (1) the x-values for L-Functions aren't stored in computer memory (this saves memory); (2) Function evaluation proceeds more rapidly for L-Functions, because no table-lookup is required (the value of the Function's argument is used to index directly into the list of values which the Function produces); (3) the value of an L- Function's argument is tested to be certain that it matches one of the x-values used to define the Function. (This isn't necessary and isn't done for a D-Function.)

2. Symbolic-Identifier Functions (S-Functions). The y elements in the (x, y) pairs used to define S-Functions are symbolic identifiers for members of an entity class (e.g., symbolic identifiers for Facilities, or for Storages, or for Queues, or for Logic Switches). These Functions are of use in supplying entity-member identifiers indirectly in Block Operand positions.
3. SNA Functions (E-Functions). The y elements in the (x, y) pairs used to define E-Functions, instead of being constants or symbolic entity-member identifiers, are Standard Numerical Attributes of the modeler's choice, and/or take the form of arithmetic expressions. E-Functions can be used, for example, to define Functions of two or more variables. This comes about when the y elements in the pairs of points defining an E-Function are references to other Functions.
4. The List Form of SNA Functions (M-Functions). M-Functions are a special case of E-Functions. When the x elements in the (x, y) pairs used to define an E-Function form the sequence 1, 2, 3, 4, ..., then the E-Function can be defined either as an E-Function or as an M-Function. The differences between the two types of Functions are these: (1) the x-values for M-Functions aren't stored in computer memory (this saves memory); (2) M-Function evaluation proceeds more rapidly, because no table-lookup is required (the value of the Function's argument is used to index directly into the list of values which the Function produces); (3) the value of the M-Function's argument is tested to be certain that it matches one of the x-values used to define the Function. (This isn't necessary and isn't done for an E-Function.)

17.21 Modeling Complex Service Orders

In GPSS/H, the use of the Current Events Chain to manage Xacts results in a service order that is FCFS within Priority Level. If service orders more complex than this are to be modeled, User Chains are brought into play for this purpose. There can be any number of User Chains in a model. As their name suggests, User Chains are defined by the user (the modeler) and are then used in ways prescribed by the user, such as to model service orders other than FCFS within Priority Level.

Like all of the GPSS/H chains, a User Chain is a list of Xacts. For example, a particular User Chain might be composed of Xacts waiting to capture the SUPPORT Facility. Suppose a Scan Phase is taking place, and the next requirement on the part of the moving Xact is to capture SUPPORT. Instead of trying to move into a "SEIZE SUPPORT" Block, the Xact uses a GATE Block to determine whether the SUPPORT Facility is Idle. If SUPPORT is Idle, the Xact moves sequentially from the GATE into a "SEIZE SUPPORT" Block, captures SUPPORT without delay, and goes on from there. But if SUPPORT is not Idle, then the Xact moves nonsequentially from the GATE into a LINK Block. Execution of the LINK Block causes the moving Xact to be removed from the Current Chain and placed on a specified User Chain, where the Xact joins others on the User Chain who are waiting for the SUPPORT Facility. The newcomer to the User Chain can be put at the front of the chain, or at the back of the chain, or it can be merged into the chain on the basis of the value found in a specified element in one of its Parameter lists.

Eventually, the current user of SUPPORT executes a "RELEASE SUPPORT". It is then the responsibility of this Xact to select one of the Xacts on the associated User Chain to replace it in the use of SUPPORT. The releasing Xact executes an UNLINK Block for this purpose. This causes an Xact to be removed from the specified User Chain and be put back onto the Current Chain, with its Next Block Attempted being the "SEIZE SUPPORT" Block. Later in the Scan Phase, this Xact will then take control of SUPPORT and begin to use it.

Five alternative ways can be specified at an UNLINK Block for deciding that Xact to unlink from a User Chain and transfer to the Current Chain. For example, the Xact at the front of the User Chain might be unlinked, or the Xact at the back might be unlinked. These are the simplest possibilities. The most powerful form of unlinking is to specify a Boolean expression at the UNLINK Block. When the UNLINK executes, the User Chain will be scanned from front to back, with the Boolean expression being freshly evaluated for each Xact on the User Chain. The Xact for which the Boolean expression is true is the Xact that will be transferred from the User Chain to the Current Chain. The Boolean expression can make reference to attributes of the Xact on whose behalf it is being evaluated (e.g., Xact Priority, Xact age, one or more values found in elements of the Xact's Parameter lists), so the expression can be false for some Xacts, and true for others.

In conclusion, Xacts can be put onto a User Chain in three different ways, and later removed in five different ways. By appropriate use of these alternatives, arbitrarily complicated service orders can be modeled.

Sometimes User Chains are applied to speed up the rate at which a model executes. The idea is to remove blocked Xacts from the Current Chain and put them onto a User Chain, where they are "hidden from the Scan." This decreases the Scan-Phase overhead, and so can speed up the rate of model execution. Execution of the LINK and UNLINK Blocks consumes computer time too, of course, and so it's not necessarily true that putting blocked Xacts on User Chains will speed up model execution. A trade-off is involved. In general, the greater the extent of blocking in a model on average, the greater the possibility of speeding up model execution by incorporating User Chains into the model for this purpose.

When User Chains are included in a model, a User Chain Report is provided as part of the postreplication output. Information provided for User Chains in this report is highly similar to that in a Queue Report. User Chain information does not include the concept of "zero entries"; except for that, User Chain information is analogous to Queue information. As a result, QUEUE and DEPART Blocks often can be eliminated from points in models at which LINK and UNLINK Blocks are to be used anyway. The overhead of executing LINK and UNLINK Blocks can then be offset by eliminating the need to execute QUEUE and DEPART Blocks.

There are Standard Numerical Attributes for User Chains. These make it possible for a model to refer to such User Chain attributes as Current Contents, Average Contents, Maximum Contents, Entries (the number of times Xacts have been put onto the User Chain), and Average Time/Xact (the average time Xacts spend on the User Chain). User-Chain SNAs can be used in all the ways in which SNAs can be used in general in GPSS/H.

17.22 The Cloning of Transactions

It is convenient in some situations for an Xact to call for the immediate creation of one or more other Xacts. This is accomplished in GPSS/H by use of the SPLIT Block. When an Xact moves into a SPLIT, a specified number of additional Xacts are created and put onto the Current Chain, with the SPLIT Block as their Current Block. These Xacts are clones of the Xact that executed the SPLIT Block. Their properties are identical to those of the Xact that caused them to be created. For example, their Priority Level matches their creator's, their Parameter lists in the default case are copies of those of their creator, and so on. They are unique Xacts, however, each with its own unique Xact id. They are independent of their creator, and of each other. Each can go its own way and do its own thing.

The SPLIT Block can be of use when an event occurs that sets into motion a series of two or more parallel reactions. For example, when a part in an operating machine breaks, this may set at least two parallel activities into motion. On the one hand, it's necessary to remove the failed part from the machine, and perhaps take it to a repair shop (if the part can be repaired). Meanwhile, it's also necessary to check the supply of backup parts of this type, and to install a backup part to get the machine back into useful operation as quickly as possible. The SPLIT Block can be used to structure such situations.

Although an Xact and its clones do operate independently, they also have an affinity for one another. They are members of one and the same Assembly Set. Details are provided in the next section.

17.23 Assembly Sets

When an Xact splits, the Xact and its clones become members of one and the same Assembly Set. If the Xact later splits again one or more times, and/or if any of its clones split, and if any of their clones split, and so on, then the newly created Xacts become members of their immediate creator's Assembly Set. And so the Assembly Set to which an Xact belongs is passed on from generation to generation.

An Assembly Set is a collection of Xacts that are subject to certain types of manipulation by the use of four Blocks designed for this purpose: ASSEMBLE, GATHER, MATCH, and a variation of the GATE Block. The purpose of these Blocks is to help coordinate and synchronize the movement of Assembly Set members as they proceed through a model.

Consider an example for the use of Assembly Sets. A radio consists of parts. When a radio is assembled, one or more of the needed parts must be brought together at an assembly point in a system. A radio is not finished until each of its parts has reached the assembly point, and the parts have been assembled. Suppose a part is modeled with an Xact. After the Xact-parts have reached the assembly point and have been assembled, one Xact (representing the radio itself) moves on from there. And so we have a pattern in which two or more Xacts move into a point, but only one Xact moves out of that point.

The ASSEMBLE Block can be used to model this assembly pattern. When an Xact executes an ASSEMBLE Block, it initiates an assembly operation. The Xact is removed from the Current Chain and put on a type of chain called an Assemble Chain. As simulated time goes by, other members of this Xact's Assembly Set (representing parts for this radio) move into the ASSEMBLE Block, and are destroyed. After a specified number have been destroyed, the original Xact (now representing the assembled radio) is transferred from the Assemble Chain back to the Current Chain, and goes on its way in the model.

The GATHER Block behaves like the ASSEMBLE Block, except that it does not destroy Xacts. Instead, as members of an Assembly Set move into a GATHER Block over time, one by one, they are removed from the Current Chain and put on a Gather Chain. After a specified number have accumulated on the Gather Chain, they are returned at one and the same simulated time to the Current Chain and are permitted to go on their way in the model. The GATHER Block can be used to force members of an Assembly Set to group together in clusters of specified size before they move forward from the clustering point.

MATCH Blocks are used to synchronize the movement of Assembly Set members moving down parallel paths in a model. The idea is to put a MATCH Block on one path, and another MATCH Block on the parallel path. Each of the two MATCH Blocks takes the other as its conjugate. When an Xact reaches one MATCH Block, it is forced to wait until another member of its Assembly Set reaches the conjugate MATCH. The Xact does its waiting on a Matching Chain. When a match is made (when each MATCH Block in the conjugate pair has a member of the same Assembly Set in it), the Xact that started the matching process is returned from its Matching Chain to the Current Chain and is permitted to resume its movement in the model. Meanwhile, the Xact that made the match simply remains on the Current Chain and continues its movement in the model.

We've now seen that Assembly Sets bring into play Matching, Assemble, and Gather Chains. This is the family of chains referred to as MAG chains in Section 2 of Chapter 4 in the book. Like the Current, Future, and Interrupt Chains, MAG Chains are used by GPSS/H as aids in the management of Xacts.

An example for MATCH-Block use involves modeling a tolerance check between two part-components that are being built in parallel and that must eventually come together physically in a larger-scale assembly. First, one of the components reaches the point at which it is ready for the tolerance check (that is, moves into the conjugate MATCH Block on its path). Then the other component eventually reaches the point at which it, too, is ready for the tolerance check (that is, moves into the conjugate MATCH Block on its path). Now both partially completed components have reached the stage at which the tolerance check can take place. After the check is finished, both partially completed components resume their independent motion down their respective paths.

In conclusion, Assembly Sets support the modeling of manufacturing and assembly operations. Like most GPSS/H capabilities, however, their usefulness extends well beyond their immediately intended purpose.

17.24 The RESET Control Statement

The RESET Control Statement is provided as an aid in carrying out statistical experiments in GPSS/H. Execution of a RESET accomplishes a subset of what CLEAR execution accomplishes. Recall, clearing a model does these things: all Xacts in the model are destroyed; statistical aspects of the model are reinitialized; and both the Relative and Absolute clocks are set to 0.0 in value. Resetting a model does not destroy Xacts; it simply reinitializes statistical aspects of the model and, with respect to the clocks, sets the Relative Clock back to 0.0, but leaves the Absolute Clock as is. The effect is to eliminate statistical observations taken up to the point that the model is reset. The Relative Clock is set back to 0.0 so that this clock will measure how much *additional* simulated time has elapsed (since resetting the model) when the *next* Postreplication Report is produced.

Now consider the potential use of the RESET statement when the objective is to investigate model behavior under steady-state conditions. If the model is initially devoid of Xacts, then it probably has to operate initially under transient conditions before moving into steady-state operating conditions. (See Figure 15 of Chapter 14 in this regard.) Statistical observations taken during transient conditions are not typical of steady-state observations, and so should be discarded for purposes of a steady-state investigation. The RESET statement can be executed for this purpose. The idea is to simulate until steady-state operation has set in, then temporarily suspend Xact movement, execute a RESET statement, and resume Xact movement, taking steady-state observations for use in analysis of steady-state behavior.

The RESET statement can also be used to support experimentation to determine how long a simulation with a given model must proceed to move through transient conditions and into a state of operating equilibrium.

An alternative to use of the RESET statement is to design a model so that conditions typical of operating equilibrium will be in effect initially. This approach is taken on some occasions in the book. For example, see the model in Figure 8 of Chapter 8, or see Case Study 16A.

17.25 SAVE and READ Control Statements; Checkpoint and Restore Test-Mode Commands

In a Batch simulation, a SAVE Control Statement can be executed to save a copy of the workspace in a permanent file. The workspace includes the model itself, and everything related to the state of the model at the time the SAVE is executed (e.g., clock time; the model's chains and all Xacts resident on them, statistical aspects of the model, the setting of the random number generators; and so on). In a later Batch simulation, a READ Control Statement can be executed to cause a copy of the previously saved workspace to be put back into the workspace. In effect, a model can be saved in its current state, and then the saved model can later be used as the starting point for one or more replications.

After a large industrial model has been compiled, for example, SAVE can be used to save the compiled model in a file. The need for later recompilation can then be sidestepped with the use of READ.

SAVE/READ can also be used to help deal with transient conditions. After moving through transient conditions and RESETting the model, a copy of the reset model in the state of operating equilibrium can be saved. This copy can later be used as the starting point for each in a series of replications, avoiding the need to simulate repeatedly through transient conditions, replication by replication.

There is a Test-Mode capability similar in function to the Batch-Mode READ/SAVE. In Test Mode, issuing a **checkpoint** command causes a copy of the workspace to be put into a **temporary** file. During the same Test-Mode session, a **restore** command can be issued with the effect that GPSS/H replaces the content of the workspace with a copy of the previously checkpointed-file. This lets the Test-Mode user go back in time to a previous state of the model, and then come forward in time again. The checkpoint and restore commands can be used to avoid the need to recompile large models during a Test-Mode session. They are also of use in letting a modeler easily go back and "recreate past history," perhaps setting interrupt conditions differently than the first time around, displaying information not displayed the first time around, and so on.

17.26 Transaction and Numeric Groups

The Group entity provides a means for having Xacts take up membership in Groups. A given Xact can belong to any number of different Groups at one and the same time. An Xact joins a Group by executing a JOIN Block. It can later end its membership in the Group (and, optionally, can selectively end the membership of other Group members) by executing a REMOVE Block. In addition, through use of the EXAMINE Block, an Xact's Next Block Attempted can be made to depend on whether the Xact belongs to a given Group.

Group members can examine the Priority Level and the Parameter lists of other Xacts in the Group, searching for the first member that satisfies a condition imposed either on its Priority Level or on the value of an element in one of its Parameter lists. The SCAN Block is used for this purpose. In one use of the SCAN Block, the scanning Xact's Next Block Attempted depends on whether the search produces a Group member with an attribute satisfying the stated condition. In an alternative mode, the scanning Xact fetches a copy of the Priority Level, or of the value of an element in a Parameter list, or of the first Group member found to satisfy the stated condition. The fetched copy is stored in an element of one of the scanning Xact's Parameter lists.

Finally, Group members can change the Priority Level and Parameter values of other Group members. The ALTER Block supports this activity. The altering Xact can unconditionally change the Priority Level of all Group members to a given value; or can unconditionally change the value of a specified Parameter element of all Group members to a given value. Alternatively, these changes can be imposed on only a subset of the Group. The subset can consist of the *n* oldest Group members or it can consist of the first *n* Group members whose Priority Level satisfies a stated condition, or that have a specified Parameter element that satisfies a stated condition.

As implied, the REMOVE, SCAN, and ALTER Blocks have optional nonsequential exits, which enhances the utility of Groups in GPSS/H modeling. As further implied, operations with respect to Group members are independent of where those members happen to be in a model. The member-Xact can be on the Current or Future Events Chain, or on a User Chain, or on an Interrupt or MAG Chain, and will nonetheless be included in activities initiated at REMOVE, EXAMINE, SCAN, and ALTER Blocks.

The preceding discussion applies to Groups whose members are Xacts. There can also be Groups whose members are simply numbers, that is, numeric Groups. Of course, numbers do not have attributes such as Priority Level and values of elements in Parameter lists. As a result, the SCAN and ALTER Blocks do not apply to numeric Groups. The JOIN, REMOVE, and EXAMINE Blocks do apply, however, to numeric Groups as well as to Xact Groups.

17.27 Animation

Simulation animation uses computer graphics to produce screen-based displays of the movement of entities through a simulated system. Such animation greatly enhances communications between simulation model builders and second parties (such as higher-level technical people and managers) responsible for the system being simulated. It helps establish credibility for models and the simulation methodology itself, triggers creative ideas about how the system might be modified to improve performance, and can be helpful in model verification. Simulation animation is not a substitute, however, for rigorous model verification, model validation, and statistical analysis of simulation output.

The GPSS/H vendor began shipping its animation product, "Proof," in the third quarter of 1990[1]. PROOF is characterized by MS-DOS execution, using an EGA or VGA display, with full color supported. Proof employs geometry-based data structures for accurate rendering at any scale or orientation. These structures support zooming (viewing of the running animation at any scale, from close in or from far away), panning (use of the display screen as a window to a much larger area of animation activity, with a coordinate system that allows animations of virtually unlimited size), rotating (rotation of the stationary observer at the overhead viewing point), and changes of viewpoint. Proof features fast performance, so that animations run smoothly. It provides a user-friendly run-time environment for hands-on demonstrations, and offers an open architecture that supports animations based on virtually any simulation package (not just GPSS/H).

For further information about Proof, get in touch with the GPSS/H vendor.

17.28 Further Study of GPSS/H

You can learn more about GPSS/H by studying the textbook literature, and/or the *GPSS/H Reference Manual*, and/or by taking a professional development course.

In the textbook literature, only this book and Banks, Carson, and Sy (1989) directly deal with GPSS/H. Neither of these books covers all aspects of the language.

The *GPSS/H Reference Manual* is the ultimate guide to the content and operational details of GPSS/H. It is well written, and should be of immediate use to those who have finished this book. It is a reference manual, however (as contrasted with a conventional textbook), so working with it might require more effort than using a textbook.

GPSS/H is a superset of GPSS V, so the GPSS V

[1]Remaining material in this paragraph is adapted, often verbatim and with permission, from the GPSS/H vendor's quarterly newsletter, *CHECKPOINT*, Volume 5, No. 4, Fall 1989.

textbook literature can be read meaningfully in terms of GPSS/H. In this regard, Gordon (1975) and Bobillier, Kahan, and Probst (1976) can be considered.

GPSS V, in turn, is a modest extension of GPSS/360, so the GPSS/360 literature can be related directly to GPSS/H. Schriber's (1974) GPSS/360 textbook is fairly comprehensive and covers details of such GPSS/360 language features as Standard Numerical Attributes, Standard Logical Attributes, Tables, TEST and GATE, SELECT, arithmetic and Boolean expressions, Savevalues, indirect addressing, E-, L-, and M-Functions, User Chains, preemption, and Assembly Sets.

Caution: When reading about GPSS V and GPSS/360, remember that in addition to providing the described capabilities, GPSS/H often provides additional related capabilities, and is often more flexible than the GPSS V and GPSS/360 implementations.

Other books dealing with GPSS (but not with GPSS/H as such) are Solomon (1983), Kavian and Dudewicz (1990), and Stahl (1990).

Perhaps the most time- and energy-efficient way to cover a range of topics in GPSS/H is to take a professional development course. Such a 5-day course is taught several times a year by me at various locations, and similar courses may be taught by others as well. Written information about all of these courses can be requested of me by phone (313-764-1398), by electronic mail (tjs@umichub.bitnet), or by conventional mail (University of Michigan, Ann Arbor MI 48109-1234).

17.29 Epilogue to the Epilogue

In the Epilogue, we've described many GPSS/H characteristics and capabilities that go above and beyond the scope of this book. The idea has been to help you understand better the characteristics of a major general-purpose/discrete-event simulation language and to judge for yourself how relevant the use of GPSS/H might be in modeling the types of systems you later encounter. We've also pointed out possible paths that you who have a further interest in GPSS/H can follow to help yourself grow into operational mastery of some or all these intermediate and advanced GPSS/H capabilities.

A Installing and Testing Student DOS GPSS/H[1]

This appendix contains instructions for installing and checking out Student GPSS/H on a microcomputer running under DOS. Files containing Student DOS GPSS/H come with this book, compressed both on one 3 1/2-inch 720K disk and on one 5 1/4-inch 360K disk. (Both disks have identical contents. The two sizes are supplied for convenience.) In the discussion that follows, whichever of these disks is of appropriate size for your system is referred to as the "Supplied Disk."

Student DOS GPSS/H is a full-feature version of Commercial GPSS/H, with the exception that models run under Student DOS GPSS/H cannot exceed either 100 Blocks or 200 statements in size. In addition, the total number of lines in a Student DOS GPSS/H Model File cannot exceed 255. (A GPSS/H statement can extend across two or more lines, which explains this latter qualification.)

Each of the two Supplied Disks also carries compressed files containing 10 GPSS/H case-study models and other GPSS/H models presented in the book. The names and contents of these model files are indicated and discussed at appropriate points in the book.

Section A.1 summarizes the minimum hardware and system software required to run Student DOS GPSS/H. Section A.2 explains how to install and test Student DOS GPSS/H on systems equipped with a hard disk and a floppy drive. Section A.3 describes use and testing of Student DOS GPSS/H on systems that do not have a hard disk but do have two floppy drives. Sections A.2 and A.3 are both self-contained.

A.1 Minimum Hardware and System Software Requirements

Student DOS GPSS/H requires the following minimum hardware and system software:

1. Any IBM PC or compatible
2. PC-DOS or MS-DOS, Version 3.0 or higher
3. 512K RAM
4. A hard disk drive and one 360K or larger floppy disk drive, or a two-floppy system with at least one 720K or larger floppy drive

[1]Appendix A is adapted, in part verbatim and with permission, from the GPSS/H DOS System Guide supplied by the GPSS/H vendor, Wolverine Software Corporation.

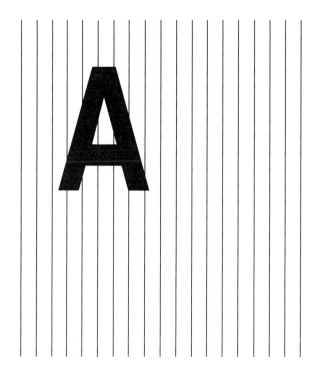

The following configuration is strongly recommended:

1. 640K RAM
2. A hard disk drive and one 360K or larger floppy disk drive
3. An 80x87 math coprocessor (important only for long-running models)

About 700K is required to hold the three decompressed files used to run Student DOS GPSS/H. This is why at least one storage device with a capacity of 720K (or more) is needed. Although not required, the math coprocessor chip is recommended. With a math chip, models run about three times faster than otherwise.

If your system has a hard disk, proceed with Section A.2; otherwise, go directly to Section A.3.

A.2 Installing and Testing Student DOS GPSS/H on a Hard Disk System

The process of installing and testing Student DOS GPSS/H on a system equipped with a hard disk is simple and brief, as described in the following steps. These steps assume that you have a 360K (or larger) 5 1/4-inch drive known to DOS as a: and a hard disk drive known as c:.

1. Set the current drive to c: and the current directory to the main (root) top level directory.
2. It is recommended that Student DOS GPSS/H be placed in its own subdirectory. Assuming that for this purpose you want to use the hard-drive subdirectory named gpssh, issue these two DOS commands:

```
mkdir  gpssh
cd  gpssh
```

   (Either lower or UPPER case may be used in the DOS commands.) You are now in the gpssh subdirectory, where you will remain throughout the following steps in Section A.2.

3. Put the Supplied Disk of appropriate size into drive a: and issue the DOS command

```
copy  a:*.*
```

   DOS will then copy the compressed files from the Supplied Disk into the gpssh subdirectory.

4. When the step 3 copy command has been executed, issue the DOS command

```
hinstall
```

   Execution of this command decompresses the compressed files in the gpssh subdirectory. The decompressed files replace their compressed equivalents in this subdirectory.

5. Now issue the DOS command

```
dir
```

   to obtain on your screen the names of the files in the gpssh subdirectory. The following names should be among those displayed:

```
gpssh.exe
gpssherr.msg
profile.hdb
hinstall.exe
model6a.gps
fig84.gps
s124x4.gps
```

   In total, the names of about 75 files will appear on the screen. The first three files in the preceding list (gpssh.exe, gpssherr.msg, and profile.hdb) are those needed to run Student DOS GPSS/H. The fourth file (hinstall.exe) is the command file executed in step 4. The fifth, sixth, and seventh files in the preceding list (model6a.gps, fig84.gps, and s124x4.gps) are representative of the three classes of files containing GPSS/H models that are discussed in the book.

6. Now issue the DOS command

```
gpssh  model6a.gps  type
```

   This command causes GPSS/H to execute the model contained in the model6a.gps file.

   After a brief pause, information similar to the following will appear on your screen.

```
GPSS/H DOS STUDENT/DEMO RELEASE 2.0
FILE: model6a.gps
Compilation begins.
```

```
Pass 1...
Pass 2...
Simulation begins.
```

There will then be another brief pause while a Batch-Mode simulation takes place. At the conclusion of the simulation, a Postsimulation Report and Computer-Usage Report will be displayed on your screen. The information in a Postsimulation Report isn't discussed in this appendix but is discussed at appropriate points in the book. (The Postsimulation Report and Computer-Usage Report are typed on your screen because you included the **type** option on the **gpssh** DOS command line. See Appendix B for more particulars about **type** and other options that can be specified on a **gpssh** command line. Also see step 8 that follows.)

When the output has finished scrolling by and the DOS prompt has appeared, examine the screen for the number of TOTAL BLOCK EXECUTIONS, which should be 1207.

You have now installed GPSS/H on your hard disk and have successfully run a GPSS/H model in Batch Mode, with the Postsimulation Report displayed on your screen. Congratulations!

7. Assuming all has gone well, you can now (optionally) delete the hinstall file from the gpssh subdirectory on your hard disk. This can be done by issuing the DOS command

```
erase  hinstall.exe
```

8. In this concluding step, you'll run another GPSS/H model in Batch Mode, but output will be put into a DOS file instead of coming to your screen.

Issue the DOS command

```
gpssh  model9a1.gps
```

Note that the **type** option is not specified in this DOS command, as it was in the step 6 command. As a result, except for brief messages, the GPSS/H Postsimulation Report and Computer-Usage Report will not be typed at your screen. Instead, DOS will create a file named **model9a1.lis** in the gpssh subdirectory and will put the Source Echo, Dictionary, Cross-Reference Listing, Postsimulation Report, and Computer-Usage Report into this **lis** file. (See Section 2.19 in Chapter 2 for comments on the Source Echo and Dictionary, etc.)

To display the contents of the **model9a1.lis** file on your screen, issue the DOS command

```
type  model9a1.lis
```

The contents of the **model9a1.lis** file will then be scrolled onto your screen. Any output lines that are more than 80 columns wide might wrap around to the next line. (As with other implementations of GPSS/H, the DOS version assumes that 132 columns of screen and printer width are available. Use of an editor that supports 132 columns via left-and-right scrolling is recommended for viewing listing files on the screen, as is use of a printer that supports 132 columns for printing them.)

When the output has finished scrolling by and the DOS prompt has appeared, examine the screen for the number of TOTAL BLOCK EXECUTIONS, which should be 989.

You have now successfully run a second GPSS/H model in Batch Mode, with the Source Echo, Dictionary, Cross-Reference Listing, Postsimulation Report, and Computer-Usage Report going into a listing file and then later being displayed by you on your screen. Congratulations!

A.3 Use of Student DOS GPSS/H on a Two-Floppy System Without a Hard Disk

As indicated in Section A.1, Student DOS GPSS/H can be run on a two-floppy system without a hard disk. One of the floppy drives must have a capacity of 720K (or more), because the three files needed to run Student DOS GPSS/H occupy about 700K in their decompressed form. The other floppy drive, which only has to have a capacity of 360K, is for the disk containing about 75 GPSS/H models presented and discussed in the book, and/or for the GPSS/H models that you will build and run.

The overall objective in carrying out the following steps is to prepare the two disks just described: the 720K (or larger) "GPSS/H Disk" that contains the three decompressed files needed to run Student

DOS GPSS/H; and the 360K (or better) "Book-Models Disk" that contains about 75 decompressed GPSS/H models presented in the book.

In the following steps, we refer to the two floppy disk drives as the a: and b: drives and assume that drive b: is the 720K (or larger) drive. To prepare and check out the GPSS/H Disk and the Book-Models Disk, perform the following steps.

1. Put the Supplied Disk of appropriate size into drive a:. Put a blank but formatted disk into drive b:. (This drive b: disk will become the GPSS/H Disk.)

   If the current drive is not already a:, set it to a: by issuing the DOS command

   ```
   a:
   ```

   Then issue this sequence of DOS commands

   ```
   hinstall  b:  gpssh.exe
   hinstall  b:  gpssherr.msg
   hinstall  b:  profile.hdb
   ```

   Execution of these commands decompresses the three a:-drive files named gpssh.exe, gpssherr.msg, and profile.hdb, putting them in their decompressed form on the GPSS/H Disk in the b: drive.

2. Now issue the DOS command

   ```
   dir  b:
   ```

   to obtain on your screen the names of the files on the GPSS/H Disk. The file names in the directory should be gpssh.exe, gpssherr.msg, and profile.hdb.

3. Remove the GPSS/H Disk from the b: drive, reserving it for later use in steps 7 and the following ones. Put another blank but formatted disk into the b: drive. (This drive b: disk will become a 720K-or-larger version of the Book-Models Disk. In step 5 that follows, you'll make a 360K-or-larger version of this Book-Models Disk for eventual use in the a: drive.)

   Then issue this sequence of DOS commands

   ```
   hinstall  b:  mod*.gps
   hinstall  b:  fig*.gps
   hinstall  b:  s*.gps
   ```

   Execution of these commands decompresses about 75 a:-drive files containing GPSS/H models from the book and puts them in their decompressed form on the 720K-or-better version of the Book-Models Disk in the b: drive.

4. Now issue the DOS command

   ```
   dir  b:
   ```

   to obtain on your screen a listing of the names of the files on the 720K-or-larger version of the Book-Models Disk. The directory should contain the names of about 75 files. Check to see that the files named model6a.gps, model9a1.gps, fig84.gps, and s124x4.gps are in this directory.

5. Remove the Supplied Disk from the a: drive. Put another blank but formatted disk into the a: drive. (This drive-a: disk will become the 360K-or-larger version of the Book-Models Disk.)

   Change the current drive to b: by issuing the DOS command

   ```
   b:
   ```

   Then issue this sequence of DOS commands

   ```
   copy  mod*.gps  a:
   copy  fig*.gps  a:
   copy  s*.gps  a:
   ```

   These commands copy the book models from the 720K-or-larger b:-drive Book-Models Disk to the 360K-or-larger a:-drive Book-Models Disk.

6. Now issue the DOS command

   ```
   dir  a:
   ```

   to obtain on your screen a listing of the names of the files on the 360K-or-larger version of the Book-Models Disk. The directory should contain the same file names as those obtained in step 4. Check to see that the files named model6a.gps, model9a1.gps, fig84.gps, and s124x4.gps are in this directory.

7. Remove the 720K-or-larger Book-Models Disk from the b: drive. You won't need it again. Put the GPSS/H Disk (prepared in step 2) into the b: drive.

This is the configuration you will use henceforth to run Student DOS GPSS/H. The GPSS/H Disk is in the 720K (or larger) drive, the Book-Models Disk (or an alternative disk on which you want to store models you create) is in the 360K (or larger) drive, and the drive containing the GPSS/H Disk is the current drive.

8. The purpose of this step is to perform a simulation with one of the GPSS/H models on the Book-Models Disk.

   Issue the DOS command

   ```
   gpssh  a:model6a.gps  type
   ```

   This command causes Student DOS GPSS/H to execute the model named model6a.gps and located on the a:-drive Book-Models Disk.

   After a brief pause, information similar to the following will appear on your screen.

   ```
   GPSS/H DOS STUDENT/DEMO RELEASE 2.0
   FILE: a:model6a.gps
   Compilation begins.
   Pass 1...
   Pass 2...
   Simulation begins.
   ```

   There will then be another brief pause while a Batch-Mode simulation takes place. At the conclusion of the simulation, a Postsimulation Report and Computer-Usage Report will be displayed on your screen. The information in a Postsimulation Report isn't discussed in this appendix, but is discussed at appropriate points in the book. (The Postsimulation Report and Computer-Usage Report are typed on your screen because the **type** option is included on the preceding **gpssh** DOS command line. See Appendix B for more particulars about **type** and other options that can be specified on a **gpssh** command line. Also see step 9 that follows.)

   When the output has finished scrolling by and the DOS prompt has appeared, examine the screen for the number of TOTAL BLOCK EXECUTIONS, which should be 1207.

You have now successfully created the GPSS/H Disk and the Book-Models Disk and have run a GPSS/H model in Batch Mode, with the Postsimulation Report displayed on your screen. Congratulations!

9. In this concluding step, you'll run another GPSS/H model in Batch Mode, but output will be put into a DOS file instead of coming to your screen.

   Issue the DOS command

   ```
   gpssh  a:model9a1.gps
   ```

   Note that the **type** option is not specified in the preceding DOS command, as it was in step 8. As a result, except for brief messages, the GPSS/H Postsimulation Report and Computer-Usage Report will not be typed at your screen. Instead, DOS will create a file named **model9a1.lis** *on the Book-Models Disk* in the a: drive and will put the Source Echo, Dictionary, Cross-Reference Listing, Postsimulation Report, and Computer-Usage Report into this **lis** file. (See Section 2.19 in Chapter 2 for comments on the Source Echo and Dictionary, etc.)

   To display the contents of the **model9a1.lis** file on your screen, issue the DOS command

   ```
   type  a:model9a1.lis
   ```

   The contents of the a:-drive **model9a1.lis** file will then be scrolled onto your screen. Any output lines that are more than 80 columns wide might wrap around to the next line. (As with other implementations of GPSS/H, the DOS version assumes that 132 columns of screen and printer width are available. Use of an editor that supports 132 columns via left-and-right scrolling is recommended for viewing listing files on the screen, as is use of a printer that supports 132 columns for printing them.)

   When the output has finished scrolling by and the DOS prompt has appeared, examine the screen for the number of TOTAL BLOCK EXECUTIONS, which should be 989.

You have now successfully run a second GPSS/H model in Batch Mode, with the Source Echo, Dictionary, Cross-Reference Listing, Postsimulation Report, and Computer-Usage Report going into a listing file and then later being displayed by you on your screen. Congratulations!

B Commands and Options for Running GPSS/H Models Under DOS[1]

The first section in this appendix discusses composing command lines and specifying various options for running GPSS/H models under DOS. The second section briefly discusses memory considerations as a prelude to describing an option for increasing in some circumstances the maximum number of Transactions that can simultaneously exist in a Student DOS GPSS/H model.

B.1 Forming DOS Command Lines to Run GPSS/H Models

A DOS command to compile and execute a GPSS/H model takes the form

```
gpssh file_name.ext [options]
```

Here, ***file_name*** is the name of the file containing the GPSS/H Model File, and ***ext*** is the extension on this file name. If no file extension is specified, an extension of **gps** will be assumed. For the command-line form given, DOS assumes that both **gpssh** and the ***file_name*** file are contained in the current directory.

In the foregoing command line, **[*options*]** represents zero or more options that can be specified in the command. (The form such options take, and their resulting effect, are discussed below.)

Here are three examples of **gpssh** command lines with *no options specified.*

```
gpssh model1.tjs
gpssh model2
gpssh model3.gps
```

In the first example, the GPSS/H model is in the file named **model1** and having the extension **tjs**. In the second example, the model is in the file named **model2**. Because no extension is specified, an extension of **gps** is assumed. In the third example, the model is in the file named **model3**, and a **gps** extension is specified explicitly.

If there are no options on a **gpssh** command line, the resulting simulation takes place in *Batch Mode.* (See Section 2.18 in Chapter 2 for discussion of Batch-Mode versus Test-Mode simulations in GPSS/H.) Output resulting from a Batch-Mode simulation is placed in a file having the same name as ***file_name***, but having **lis** as an extension. The **lis** file will be

[1]Appendix B is adapted, in part verbatim and with permission, from the GPSS/H DOS System Guide supplied by the GPSS/H vendor, Wolverine Software Corporation.

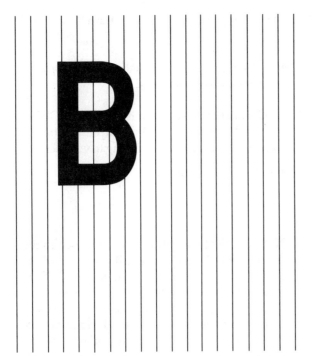

automatically created (if it doesn't already exist) in the directory containing the ***file_name*** file. In the first of the three preceding **gpssh** command-line examples, the simulation output will be put into the **model1.lis** file. In the second and third examples, the simulation output will be put into the **model2.lis** and **model3.lis** files, respectively. (As indicated below, selected output can alternatively be directed to the screen instead of the **lis** file. See the **type** option.)

If options are specified on a **gpssh** command line, these are entered on the line to the right of ***file_name.ext***, with one or more blanks separating them from each other and from ***file_name.ext***. Here are three examples of **gpssh** command lines with options specified. (The effect of the various options is discussed below.)

```
gpssh model1.tjs type
gpssh model2 tv type nowarn
gpssh model3.gps tvtnw
```

In the first example, the single option **type** has been specified. In the second example, the three options **tv**, **type**, and **nowarn** have been specified. In the third example, the option **tvtnw** has been specified. (It turns out that **tvtnw** is an abbreviation for the three options **tv, type,** and **nowarn**, as explained below. In other words, the second and third command lines in the examples have identical options.)

Having shown examples of **gpssh** command lines in which one or more ***options*** are specified, we now proceed to discuss the effect of various options.

Perhaps the most important ***option*** in a **gpssh** command takes the form of the word **test**. If **test** is specified (and there are various ways to do this, as detailed below), then a GPSS/H simulation takes place in *Test Mode;* otherwise, it takes place in *Batch Mode.* (See Section 2.18 in Chapter 2 for discussion of the distinction between Test and Batch Mode use of GPSS/H.)

The **test** option can be specified directly by spelling out the full word **test** or indirectly by choosing the **tv** option. If **test** is specified, the entire computer screen becomes a Dialog Window in the Test-Mode simulation. Alternatively, if **tv** is specified, the computer screen is split into Source, Status, and Dialog Windows in the Test-Mode simulation. (See Section 2.22 in Chapter 2 for particulars about these three windows.)

If the **tv** option is specified on a **gpssh** command line, it's possible to switch back and forth between a screen whose use is split among the Source, Status, and Dialog Windows and a screen used entirely as a Dialog Window. Such switching is accomplished by using the Test-Mode commands **set tv off** and **set tv on** during a Test-Mode simulation. (See Section 4.9 of Chapter 4 for demonstrated use of the **set tv off** and **set tv on** commands.)

In addition to **test** and **tv**, another useful option in a **gpssh** command is **type**. When the **type** option is specified, the GPSS/H Postsimulation Report will be typed on the user's screen, whereas this would not otherwise be the case in either a Test-Mode or a Batch-Mode simulation.

Two abbreviated forms are available for expressing frequently occurring combinations of options. The **tvtnw** abbreviation stands for **tv type nowarn**. The **tv** and **type** options result in a Test-Mode, split-screen simulation, with postsimulation output directed to the screen. The **nowarn** option suppresses the display of Compile-Time Warning Messages on the screen. (The **tvtnw** abbreviation is used in all Test-Mode demonstrations in this book.)

The other available abbreviation is **ttnw**, which stands for **test type nowarn**. The **test**, **type**, and **nowarn** options result in a Test-Mode simulation in which the entire screen is used for the Dialog Window, postsimulation output is directed to the screen, and the display of Compile-Time Warning Messages on the screen is suppressed.

Another option is **source**, and its reverse option, **nos** (for "**no** source"). The word **source** refers to the compiler-produced Source Echo of a Model File. (See Chapters 2 and 6 in the book for more details.) Whether *by default* the GPSS/H compiler will output a Source Echo or not depends on the destination to which the Source Echo would be directed. If the destination is the screen, the Source Echo *will not* be displayed unless the user asks to see it by specifying **source** as a **gpssh** command-line option. If the destination is a disk file, on the other hand, a Source Echo *will* be written to the file unless it is indicated, by specifying **nos** as a **gpssh** command-line option, that this is *not* to be done.

A Source Echo is often lengthy. In light of this, consider the philosophy implied in the preceding paragraph. "By default, suppress sending high-volume material to the screen. By default, do not suppress sending high-volume material to a disk file."

Options similar in structure and spirit to **source** and **nos** are **dict** and **nodict** and **xref** and **noxref**. "Dict" and "xref" refer, respectively, to the Dictionary and Cross-Reference Listing that the GPSS/H compiler is capable of producing. (See the comments attached to Box 1 in Figure 2.19, Chapter 2.) Whether *by default* the GPSS/H compiler will out-

Table B.1

Selected Options for the gpssh Command Line

Option	Effect
DICT NODICT	The DICT option causes the GPSS/H compiler to output a Dictionary for the model. The NODICT option is used to suppress outputting the Dictionary. DICT is in effect by default when the destination to which the Dictionary would be directed is a disk file; otherwise, NODICT is in effect by default. (Details of the GPSS/H Dictionary are not discussed in this book.)
SOURCE NOS	The SOURCE option causes the GPSS/H compiler to output a Source Echo of the Model File. The NOS option is used to suppress outputting the Source Echo. SOURCE is in effect by default when the destination to which the Source Echo would be directed is a disk file; otherwise, NOS is in effect by default. (The Source Echo is discussed in Chapter 6.)
TEST	The TEST option can be used to specify that a Test-Mode simulation is to take place. (The TV, TVTNW, and TTNW options also have this effect.) With the TEST option, the entire screen is used as a Dialog Window. (See Section 2.18 for discussion of Test-Mode versus Batch-Mode simulations and Sections 2.22 et seq. for discussion and demonstration of Test-Mode simulations.)
TTNW	TTNW is an abbreviation for the three options TEST TYPE NOWARN.
TV	The TV option can be used to specify that a Test-Mode simulation is to take place. With the TV option, the screen is split into three windows: Source, Status, and Dialog. (See Section 2.22 for details.) When a Test-Mode simulation is initiated with use of the **tv** (or **tvtnw**) option, the **set tv on** and **set tv off** commands can be used to toggle between the split screen and use of the entire screen as a Dialog Window.
TVTNW	TVTNW is an abbreviation for the three-option sequence TV TYPE NOWARN.
TYPE	The TYPE option causes Compile-Time Warning Messages and the Postsimulation Report to be typed on the screen. The Source Echo, Dictionary, and Cross- Reference Listing will not be typed on the screen when the TYPE option is specified, because NOS, NODICT, and NOXREF defaults are in effect with the TYPE option. These defaults can be overridden by specifying the SOURCE, DICT, and XREF options, respectively, to the right of the TYPE option in a **gpss** command.
WARN NOWARN	The WARN option causes the GPSS/H compiler to display Compile-Time Warning Messages. The NOWARN option is used to suppress displaying these messages. In Test-Mode simulations initiated by specifying TEST or TV, WARN is in effect by default. In Test-Mode simulations initiated by specifying TVTNW or TTNW, NOWARN is in effect. In Batch-Mode simulations, WARN is in effect by default.

put a Dictionary and Cross-Reference Listing or not depends on the destination to which this material would be directed. If the destination is the screen, the Dictionary and Cross-Reference Listing *will not* be displayed unless the user asks to see them by specifying **dict** and/or **xref** as **gpssh** command-line options. If the destination is a disk file, on the other hand, a Dictionary and Cross-Reference Listing *will* be written to the file unless it is indicated, by specifying **nodict** and/or **noxref** as **gpssh** command-line options, that this is *not* to be done.

We now summarize and list various **gpssh** command-line options. Table B.1 shows the form and effect of selected options in alphabetic order.

Table B.2

Examples of gpssh Command Lines for Test-Mode Simulations

Example 1	**gpssh model6a.gps tvtnw** Comments: This is perhaps the most frequently used **gpssh** command-line form for a Test-Mode simulation. The screen is split into Source, Status, and Dialog Windows, Compile-Time Warning Messages are suppressed, and the Postsimulation Report is directed to the screen.
Example 2	**gpssh model6a.gps tv** Comments: In this Test-Mode simulation, the screen is split into Source, Status, and Dialog Windows, Compile-Time Warning Messages are directed to the screen, and no Postsimulation Report will come to the screen.
Example 3	**gpssh model11a.gps test** Comments: In this Test-Mode simulation, the entire screen is used as a Dialog Window; Compile-Time Warning Messages are directed to the screen; and no Postsimulation Report will come to the screen.

The options are shown in UPPER case in the table, but can be specified in either lower or UPPER case in **gpssh** command lines.

Table B.2 shows some examples of **gpssh** command lines for Test-Mode simulations. A Test-Mode simulation is in effect whenever **test**, **tv**, **tvtnw**, or **ttnw** is specified as an option.

Table B.3 shows some examples of **gpssh** command lines for Batch-Mode simulations. In each case, a Batch-Mode simulation is in effect because none of **test**, **tv**, **tvtnw**, or **ttnw** is specified as an option.

B.2 Memory Considerations

This section begins by commenting on computer memory in the context of Commercial DOS GPSS/

Table B.3

Examples of gpssh Command Lines for Batch-Mode Simulations

Example 1	**gpssh model12b.gps** Comments: This is perhaps the most frequently used **gpssh** command-line form for a Batch-Mode simulation. Defaults of **source**, **dict**, **xref**, and **warn** are in effect. The Source Echo, Warning and Error Messages, Dictionary, Cross-Reference Listing, Postsimulation Report, and Computer-Usage Report will all be put into the **model12b.lis** file.
Example 2	**gpssh model13b.gps nodict noxref** Comments: Example 2 is similar to Example 1, except that defaults of **dict** and **xref** are overridden. The Source Echo, Warning and Error Messages, Postsimulation Report, and Computer-Usage Report will all be put into the **model13b.lis** file.
Example 3	**gpssh model14a.gps type** Comments: The simulation will take place in Batch Mode, but with **type** specified, output is directed to the screen, not to the **model14a.lis** file. Defaults of **warn**, **nos**, **nodict**, and **noxref** are in effect. The Source, Dictionary, and Cross-Reference Listings will be suppressed, and the Postsimulation Report will be typed on the screen.

H. Memory considerations for Student DOS GPSS/H are then considered. Finally, an option that can be used in some circumstances to increase the number of Transactions that can exist simultaneously in a GPSS/H model is described.

The 640K limitation on available memory is a well-known fact of the DOS operating system. The 640K limitation means that some large-scale GPSS/H models that run on other machines will not run under Commercial (or Student) DOS GPSS/H.[2]

The total amount of memory needed by Commercial DOS GPSS/H for compiled code and data, combined, cannot exceed the "total available memory," which consists of the total installed memory usable by DOS (640K, hopefully), minus the following:

1. The memory taken up by DOS itself (about 55K for DOS Version 3.3).
2. The memory set aside in the CONFIG.SYS file for buffers, drivers, and so on.
3. The memory taken up by any user-installed terminate-and-stay-resident programs.
4. The peak amount of memory needed by GPSS/H itself at run time (about 385K).

The most memory that is likely to be available for compiled code and data under Commercial DOS GPSS/H is thus about 215K.

By way of contrast, the total memory pool in Student DOS GPSS/H is deliberately fixed at about 50K.

The class of memory known as COMMON defaults to a value of 10,000 bytes under Student DOS GPSS/H. The importance of COMMON, for our purposes, is that it provides the memory needed to support the existence of Transactions (as well as some other things) in a model. If an executing model runs out of COMMON memory, Error Message 411, *"Limits of COMMON Exceeded,"* is issued. (Exercise 5 in Section 6.13 leads to this Error Message.) With 10,000 bytes of COMMON, not more than about 85 Transactions can exist under the most favorable circumstances with Student DOS GPSS/H before an executing model will run out of COMMON, whereas the equivalent number of Transactions under Commercial DOS GPSS/H is about 2600. (In non-DOS implementations of Commercial GPSS/H, this number can be much larger.)

Subject to the limitation on the total memory pool, the default amount of memory for COMMON in Student DOS GPSS/H can be increased by using the REALLOCATE Compiler Directive. (Compiler Directives are introduced in Chapter 14 of this book.) For example, the following REALLOCATE Compiler Directive could be included in a Model File to request that COMMON be set (if possible) at 20,000 bytes

```
REALLOCATE COM,20000
```

In no case can the level of COMMON under Student DOS GPSS/H be set higher than about 32,000 bytes.

Those interested in further details about the REALLOCATE Compiler Directive should see Section 6.39 in Chapter 6 of the *GPSS/H Reference Manual* (Henriksen and Crain 1989).

[2]As we go to press, Wolverine Software Corporation has just announced the availability of GPSS/H 386. This implementation incorporates 32-bit DOS-extender technology (not the same as "Expanded Memory," otherwise known as EMS) for using all available memory installed in the PC. Users of GPSS/H 386 need an 80386 PC with math coprocessor (or an 80486), at least two megabytes of main memory, and DOS 3.0 or later. Those with four megabytes often can run very large models previously runnable only on a mainframe platform. And as for speed, models run 80 to 90 percent faster under GPSS/H 386 than under DOS GPSS/H (which is now known as Personal GPSS/H), and according to the vendor's claim can run four or more times faster than the same models would if implemented on the same hardware in current alternative PC simulation software. Those interested should contact the vendor for details (4115 Annandale Road, Annandale, VA 22003-2500). (This footnote has been adapted, in part verbatim and with permission, from the vendor's quarterly newsletter, *CHECKPOINT*, Vol. 6, no. 2, Spring, 1990.

C Solutions to Selected Exercises[1]

Chapter 2

Section 2.24

4. Results are supplied in Table E4.

Table E4

Xact id	Time Out of GENERATE Block
3	45.0
4	57.4
5	69.0

5. Results are supplied in Table E5.

Table E5

Xact id	Time Out of GENERATE Block
1	3.1
2	6.9
3	11.2
4	14.2
5	17.0

[1]Throughout most of this appendix, times are expressed to one decimal place, unrounded.

6. Xacts come out of the GENERATE Block at times 100.0, 200.0 and 300.0 The simulation will stop at time 300.0.

7. Results are supplied in Table E7.

Table E7

Xact id	GENERATE Block (1st or 2nd)	Time Out
2	2nd	35.0
1	1st	50.0
3	2nd	70.0

The simulation stops at time 70.0.

8. Results are supplied in Table E8.

Table E8

Xact id	GENERATE Block (1st or 2nd)	Time Out
2	2nd	35.0
1	1st	50.0
3	2nd	70.0
4	1st	100.0
5	2nd	105.0
7	2nd	140.0
6	1st	150.0

The simulation stops at time 150.0.

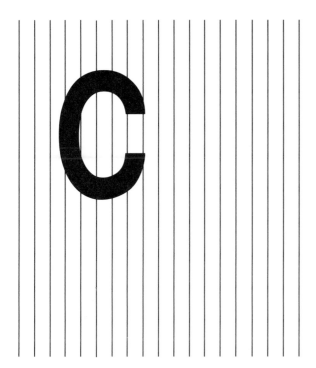

```
          SIMULATE
*
          GENERATE  25,10    Xacts come, one by one
          TERMINATE 0        Xacts are destroyed
*                            without reducing the TC value
*
          GENERATE  480      an Xact comes at time 480
          TERMINATE 1        reduce the TC by 1,
*                            ending Xact movement
*
          START     1        set the TC = 1;
*                            start Xact movement
          END
```

Figure E9

9. A Model File for this exercise is shown in Figure E9 and is given in the file s224x9.gps.

   Nineteen Xacts have come out of the "GENERATE 25,10" Block by the time the Transaction-Movement Phase ends at time 480.

10. Results are supplied in Table E10.

Table E10

Xact id	GENERATE Block (1st or 2nd)	Time Out
1	1st	46.2
2	2nd	49.9
4	2nd	85.1

The value of the model's Termination Counter when the simulation stops is 0 (zero).

Section 2.26

1. The interarrival time distribution specified at the GENERATE Block, 20 ± 30, provides the possibility of sampling negative interarrival times, which are illegal. GPSS/H will not roll the clock back to earlier simulated times. The clock is only allowed to move forward. At the time of attempted model compilation, GPSS/H determines that the specified interarrival time distribution is illogical and issues an Error Message that says, in part,

   "B Operand (modifier) exceeds A Operand (mean)."

   This is an example of a Compile-Time Error.

2. This is an example of a "runaway simulation." The model provides no means for reducing the value of its Termination Counter to zero. No Compile-Time Warning or Error Message will be issued. In DOS (and other operating systems that do not impose a time limit on runs), no Execution-Time Error Message will be issued, either. The simulation will simply continue until the user interrupts it. In DOS GPSS/H, this can be done by pressing the keyboard's CTRL and BREAK keys simultaneously.

3. In response to a **step** command, this message is displayed: "Xact 2 poised at Block ? (indeterminate Block). Relative Clock: 19.9871."

   Then, in response to the next **step** command, this Error Message is issued:

   "Xact 2 has caused execution error 408 at Block ? (indeterminate Block). Remaining Block Step Count = 1. Relative Clock: 19.9871. Execution has "run off the end" of the model."

4. This execution-time Error Message is issued:

   "Xact 1 has caused execution error 409 at Block 2. Relative Clock: 28.1089. Attempt to enter a GENERATE Block."

5. With no START statement to execute, GPSS/H never initializes the GENERATE Blocks and enters the Xact-Movement Phase. In terms of Figure 2.19, GPSS/H moves from Box 1 to Box 2, executes the END Statement, and stops. This situation is not interpreted as involving an error condition. This message is displayed by GPSS/H at the end of the "simulation":

   "Simulation terminated in control statement number 9. Relative Clock: 0. Remaining Block Step Count = 1."

Chapter 3

Section 3.5

2. The simulation stops at time 210.0. "TERMINATE 1" is first executed at time 110.0; then at time 160.0; and finally at time 210.0.

3. The largest number of Xacts ever in the ADVANCE Block at any one time is 5. This level is reached at times 150.1, 190.7, and 205.8. The simulation stops at time 220.3.

4. Results are supplied in Table E4.

Table E4

Xact id	Time into TERMINATE Block
1	185.1
4	302.0
5	310.3
2	349.6
3	519.8

Xacts going into the TERMINATE Block have id's 1, 4, 5, 2, and 3, in that order. When an Xact moves into the TERMINATE Block in this model, it has passed any smaller-numbered Xacts that haven't yet moved into the TERMINATE Block. The information in Table E4 indicates that Xact 4 passed Xacts 2 and 3, and Xact 5 passed Xacts 2 and 3 as well.

6. "ADVANCE 200,150" is not logically equivalent to the two consecutive ADVANCE Blocks in Exercise 5. When two uniform distributions are combined, the result is not itself a uniform distribution. Consult a book on probability and statistics for further details.

7. Xacts with id's 1, 2, and 3 move into the TERMINATE Block at times 100, 200, and 300, respectively. The simulation stops at time 300.

8. The simulation stops at time 150.0. Xact 2 moves out of "GENERATE 75" into "TERMINATE 1" at time 75.0, reducing the model's TC value from 3 to 2; Xact 1 moves out of "ADVANCE 50" into "TERMINATE 1" at time 100.0, reducing the TC value from 2 to 1; and then Xact 4 moves out of "GENERATE 75" into "TERMINATE 1" at time 150.0, reducing the TC value from 1 to 0 and stopping the simulation.

   There are two Xacts scheduled to move at time 150.0: Xact 4 (which does move) and Xact 5 (which doesn't move, because the simulation stops before it has a chance to move). Section 3.9 talks about "when two or more Xacts move at the same simulated time."

9. A Model File for this exercise is shown in Figure E9 and is given in the file s35x9.gps.

   Results are supplied in Table E9.

Table E9

Xact id	Time of Arriving at the Take-off Point
1	677.0
2	876.9
3	1100.9
4	1271.3
5	1433.4

The simulation stops at time 1433.4.

11. The simulation stops at time 10255.8.

Section 3.7

1. No value is supplied explicitly for the GENERATE Block's B Operand, so the value is zero, by

```
         SIMULATE
*
         GENERATE  200,50    casting-Xacts arrive, one by one
         ADVANCE   500       conveying time
         TERMINATE 1         casting-Xact leaves the conveyer
*                            and leaves the model
         START     5         convey 5 castings in total
         END
```

Figure E9

default. What's illustrated here is the general technique of keying consecutive commas to take a default value for an intermediate Operand and a nondefault value for a later Operand.

Xacts come out of the GENERATE Block at times 25.0, 125.0, and 225.0. (Note that when the first Xact comes out at time 25.0, a deterministic interarrival time of 100 is applied to its successor, so its successor comes out at time 125.0 (25.0 + 100.0 = 125.0), and so on). The simulation stops at time 225.0.

2. The value of the GENERATE Block's B Operand is zero by default, as in Exercise 1. A first Xact comes out of the GENERATE Block at time 25.0 (because the Offset Interval is 25). After that, another Xact comes out of the GENERATE every 25 time units (because the interarrival time is 25, deterministically). The Xact that comes out of the GENERATE at time 75.0 stops the simulation.

3. Results are supplied in Table E3.

Table E3

Xact id	Time out of the GENERATE Block
1	25.0
2	124.9
3	248.9

The simulation stops at time 298.9 (=248.9+50).

4. Results are supplied in Table E4.

Table E4

Xact id	Time out of the GENERATE Block
1	0.0
2	100.0
3	200.0
4	300.0

The simulation stops at time 300.0.

There are two Xacts scheduled to move at time 300.0, Xacts 3 and 4. Of these, Xact 4 moves first (from the GENERATE into the ADVANCE). Then Xact 3 moves (from ADVANCE into TERMINATE, stopping the simulation). Section 3.9 talks about "when two or more Xacts move at the same simulated time."

5. An Xact comes out of the first GENERATE Block at time 100.0. Because a Limit Count of 1 is specified for this Block, no additional Xacts are produced by it. (Note how three consecutive commas have been used to take default values for this GENERATE Block's B and C Operands while specifying a nondefault value for the Limit Count.) Xacts come out of the second GENERATE Block at times 250.0, 500.0, and 750.0. The simulation stops at time 750.0. When the simulation stops, the Xact that came out of "GENERATE 100,,,1" at time 100.0 is still in the "ADVANCE 700" Block, where it is scheduled to remain until time 800.0.

6. Results are supplied in Table E6.

Table E6

Xact id	GENERATE Block (1 or 2)	Time Out
1	1	5.0
2	2	20.0
3	1	30.0
4	2	40.0
5	2	60.0

The simulation stops at time 60.0.

Section 3.8

1. The smallest value that the simulated clock registers is 0.0. As a result, an Offset Interval cannot be negative. At the time of attempted model compilation, GPSS/H reacts to the GENERATE Block's negative C Operand by issuing a compile-time Error Message that says, in part: "GENERATE: offset (C Operand) is negative."

2. A Limit Count of 4 is used on the GENERATE Block, so it only produces four Xacts in total. After the fourth of these Xacts has come into the model and been destroyed, the model's Termination Counter hasn't yet been reduced to zero in value, so the simulation tries to continue. But nothing else has been scheduled for future simulated time. In response, GPSS/H prints out Error Message 410, "No Next Event in System," and gives control to the interactive user. The user can then "quit quickly," revise the model, and start again.

3. The holding-time distribution specified at the ADVANCE Block, 10 ± 15, provides the possibility of sampling negative holding times, which are illegal. (GPSS/H will not roll the clock back to earlier simulated times. The clock is only

allowed to move forward.) At the time of attempted model compilation, GPSS/H determines that the specified holding-time distribution is illogical and issues an Error Message that says, in part, "B-Operand (modifier) exceeds A-Operand (mean)."

Section 3.10

1. Results are supplied in Table E1.

Table E1

Clock Time	id of First Xact to Move	id of Second Xact to Move
25.0	1	2
50.0	3	4
75.0	5	6

Xacts with id numbers 1 and 2 come from the first and second GENERATE Blocks, respectively, at time 25.0. Xact 1 moves first, then Xact 2 moves. Xacts with id numbers 3 and 4 come from the first and second GENERATE Blocks, respectively, at time 50.0. Xact 3 moves first, then Xact 4 moves. Xacts with id numbers 5 and 6 come from the first and second GENERATE Blocks, respectively, at time 75.0. Xact 5 moves first, then Xact 6 moves. These results are consistent with the fact that Xacts are numbered serially, in the order of their creation, and time-tied Xacts are moved in the order in which their moves have been scheduled, "other things being equal."

2. At time 100.0, the Xact with id number 7 comes out of the first GENERATE Block and is destroyed, reducing the value of the model's Termination Counter to zero. The simulation then stops immediately. Even though the Xact with id number 8 is also scheduled to come out of the second GENERATE Block at time 100.0, no attempt is made to move this Xact. This illustrates the point that the Transaction-Movement Phase of a simulation stops as soon as the model's Termination Counter is reduced in value to zero, whether or not every Xact scheduled to move at that time has actually yet been given a chance to move.

   (You should now review Exercise 8 of Section 3.5 and Exercise 4 of Section 3.7. Time ties occur in the models corresponding to these two exercises.)

3. Two Xacts are scheduled to move at time 100.0. The Xacts involved are Xact 3 (coming from "GENERATE 50") and Xact 2 (coming from "GENERATE 100"). Xact 2 will be the first of these two to move. Its movement will stop the simulation, so Xact 3 won't be given a chance to move. The first TERMINATE Block will have been executed one time when the simulation stops.

4. Results are supplied in Table E4.

Table E4

Clock Time	id's of Time-Tied Xacts	id of First Xact to Move
50.0	1; 2	2
75.0	2; 3	3

The fact that Xact 2 moves before Xact 1 at time 50.0 can be reasoned out as follows. At time 25.0, Xact 1 moves from the GENERATE, causing its successor, Xact 2, to be created and scheduled to come into the model at future time 50.0. Continuing to move at time 25.0, Xact 1 then goes into the ADVANCE, where it is scheduled to remain until future time 50.0. And so Xacts 1 and 2 are both scheduled to move at time 50.0. Xact 2's scheduling preceded that of Xact 1. Xact 2 is therefore the first of these two Xacxts to move at time 50.0.

Similar reasoning applies to the order of movement of Xacts 2 and 3 at time 75.0.

Section 3.12

1. Results are supplied in Table E1.

Table E1

Clock Time	id's of Time-Tied Xacts	id of First Xact to Move
25.0	1; 2	2
50.0	3; 4	3
75.0	5; 6	5

When the GENERATE Blocks were initialized, Xact 1 was first created and scheduled to come out of the first GENERATE at time 25.0; then Xact 2 was created and scheduled to come out of the second GENERATE at time 25.0. But these two Xacts don't make their moves at time 25.0 in the order in which they were scheduled, because Xact 2 has higher Priority (10) than Xact 1 (5), which overrides the order in which their moves were scheduled.

Similar reasoning applies to the time-tied Xacts which move at times 50.0 and 75.0.

2. Xacts 7 and 8 are involved in a time tie at time 100.0. Xact 8 has the higher Priority (10), and so moves first, with the effect of stopping the simulation. As a result, Xact 7 is not given a chance to move at time 100.0.

3. Results are supplied in Table E3.

Table E3

Xact id	Coming from Which GENERATE	Time out of GENERATE
2	2	25.0
3	2	50.0
1	1	50.0
4	2	75.0
6	2	100.0
5	1	100.0

The simulation stops at time 100.

Section 3.15

1. The simulation ends at time 625.0. When Xact movement ends, 21 objects have been put on the conveyor at source 1, and another 20 have been put on at source 2. There are 16 objects on the conveyor at the end of the simulation.

2. When Xact movement ends, 32 objects have been put on the conveyor at source 1, and another 33 have been put on at source 2. There are 17 objects on the conveyor at the end of the simulation.

3. Results are supplied in Table E3, where Xact moves are summarized in chronological order.

Table E3

Time	Xact id	Move	Total Count at ADVANCE
10.0	1	into ADVANCE	1
20.0	3	into ADVANCE	2
30.0	4	into ADVANCE	3
40.0	5	into ADVANCE	4
45.4	1	from ADVANCE	4
45.4	1	into ADVANCE	5
59.9	3	from ADVANCE	5
59.9	3	into ADVANCE	6
74.0	5	from ADVANCE	6
74.0	5	into ADVANCE	7
74.7	4	from ADVANCE	7
74.7	4	into ADVANCE	8

The Xacts do not necessarily leave the ADVANCE in the order in which they went into it. For example, Xact 5 leaves before Xact 4.

Table E3 shows the times at which the Total Count at the ADVANCE becomes 5, 6, 7, and 8.

4. GPSS/H issues a compile-time Warning Message which says, in part:

Warning: The following entities have been defined but not explicitly referenced: Blocks: WHYDOIT

Section 3.16

1. The trouble with deleting the TRANSFER from the Figure 3.10 model is that the Block following the first GENERATE is then another GENERATE. An Xact can take a GENERATE as its **First** Block Attempted, but not as its **Next** Block Attempted. The execution-time Error Message which GPSS/H issues says, in part,

"Attempt to enter a GENERATE Block."

2. The problem here is similar to the problem in Exercise 1. The same Error Message is produced.

3. GPSS/H does not issue either a compile-time or an execution-time Warning Message for either of these models. Both models run to completion.

(In larger-scale models, it's a good idea to look at Total Block Counts in the Postsimulation Report. These counts are a measure of the traffic intensity along the corresponding paths in the model. If the Total Counts for a series of consecutive Blocks are zero, then no Xacts moved through those Blocks during the preceding Xact-Movement Phase. The modeler can then ponder whether this result seems reasonable or not. If the result isn't reasonable, then a closer look at the model is indicated.)

4. Xacts execute Blocks, they don't execute Control Statements! A compile-time Error Message

is issued in the case of this Model File. The message says, in part:

The following entities are undefined:
Blocks: ZAPPO.

There is no Block labeled ZAPPO, and so the model can't even compile successfully.

5. See Exercise 4 in this section.

6. The compile-time Error Message that results says, in part:

   A user-supplied symbol cannot start with a (built-in) SNA/SLA/SCA name.

   "SNA" is short for Standard Numerical Attribute. (SNAs are commented on in Chapter 17.) The random number generators (discussed in Chapters 13 and 14) are SNAs, and so the special syntax used to refer to them can't form the first or only characters in a user-supplied symbol, such as a Block Label or a Facility identifier.

7. The Error Message that results here matches the one in Exercise 6.

Chapter 4

Section 4.11

2. The BLOCK1 and BLOCK3 GENERATEs will be initialized with Xacts having id's 1 and 2, respectively. Both of these initialization Xacts have Move Times greater than zero, and so these Xacts will be on the Future Chain. The *minimum* feasible Move Time for Xact 1 exceeds 25, and the *maximum* feasible Move Time for Xact 2 is less than 15, so Xact 2 will be ahead of Xact 1 on the FEC.

3. The BLOCK1 and BLOCK3 GENERATEs will be initialized with Xacts having id's 1 and 2, respectively. Both of these initialization Xacts have Move Times greater than zero, and so these Xacts will be on the Future Chain. Xact 1 will be ahead of Xact 2 on the FEC. (The *maximum* feasible Move Time for Xact 1 is slightly less than 15, and the *minimum* feasible Move Time for Xact 2 is slightly more than 25.)

4. The BLOCK1, BLOCK3, and BLOCK5 GENERATEs will be initialized with Xacts having id's 1, 2, and 3, respectively. With Move Times of zero, Xacts 1 and 3 will be on the Current Chain after GENERATE-Block initialization. Xact 1 will be ahead of Xact 3. (These two Xacts each have a default Priority of zero, so their CEC order corresponds to the chronological order in which the GENERATE Blocks were initialized.) With its Move Time exceeding zero, Xact 2 will be on the Future Chain.

5. The BLOCK1, BLOCK3, and BLOCK5 GENERATEs will be initialized with Xacts having id's 1, 2, and 3, respectively. With Move Times of zero, Xacts 1 and 3 will be on the Current Chain after GENERATE-Block initialization. Xact 3 will be ahead of Xact 1. (Xact 1 was already on the CEC when Xact 3 was placed there, but with its Priority of 5, Xact 3 was inserted into the CEC ahead of Xact 1, which has a default Priority of zero.) With its Move Time exceeding zero, Xact 2 will be on the Future Chain.

6. The BLOCK1, BLOCK3, and BLOCK5 GENERATEs will be initialized with Xacts having id's 1, 2, and 3, respectively. Each of these Xacts will be on the Future Chain with a Move Time of 75.0. Xact 1 will be at the head of the FEC, with Xacts 2 and 3 behind it. (With their Move-Time ties, the FEC order of these Xacts corresponds to the chronological order in which the Xacts were placed on the FEC.)

7. The BLOCK1, BLOCK3, and BLOCK5 GENERATEs will be initialized with Xacts having id's 1, 2, and 3, respectively. Each of these Xacts has a Move Time of 0.0 (because an Offset Interval of 0 has been specified at each of the GENERATE Blocks), and so will be on the Current Chain. Xact 3 is at the front of the CEC (Priority 20), Xact 2 is behind it (Priority 15), and Xact 1 is last on the CEC (Priority 5). Except for Xact 2, the order of these Xacts on the CEC differs from the chronological order in which they were placed there.

8. The BLOCK1, BLOCK3, BLOCK5, and BLOCK7 GENERATEs will be initialized with Xacts having id's 1, 2, 3, and 4, respectively. Xacts 1 and 2 will be on the Future Chain, with Xact 2 preceding Xact 1. (Xact 2's *maximum* feasible Move Time is slightly less than 35, whereas Xact 1's *minimum* feasible Move Time is slightly greater than 50.) Xacts 3 and 4 will be on the Current Chain. Xact

Table E2

Clock	Total Blocks Executed	CEC Xacts id	CEC Xacts CURBLK	CEC Xacts NXTBLK	FEC Xacts id	FEC Xacts CURBLK	FEC Xacts NXTBLK	Move Time
0.0	0	1	"BIRTH"	BLOCK1		Empty		
0.0	1	1	BLOCK1	BLOCK2	2	"BIRTH"	BLOCK1	99.9
0.0	2		Empty		1	BLOCK2	BLOCK3	22.3
					2	"BIRTH"	BLOCK1	99.9
22.3	2	1	BLOCK2	BLOCK3	2	"BIRTH"	BLOCK1	99.9
22.3	3		Empty		2	"BIRTH"	BLOCK1	99.9
99.9	3	2	"BIRTH"	BLOCK1		Empty		
99.9	4	2	BLOCK1	BLOCK2	3	"BIRTH"	BLOCK1	170.3
99.9	5		Empty		2	BLOCK2	BLOCK3	116.1
					3	"BIRTH"	BLOCK1	170.3
116.1	5	2	BLOCK2	BLOCK3	3	"BIRTH"	BLOCK1	170.3
116.1	6		Empty		3	"BIRTH"	BLOCK1	170.3
170.3	6	3	"BIRTH"	BLOCK1		Empty		
170.3	7	3	BLOCK1	BLOCK2	4	"BIRTH"	BLOCK1	297.1
170.3	8		Empty		3	BLOCK2	BLOCK3	189.7
					4	"BIRTH"	BLOCK1	297.1
189.7	8		Empty		3	BLOCK2	BLOCK3	189.7
					4	"BIRTH"	BLOCK1	297.1
189.7	9		Empty		4	"BIRTH"	BLOCK1	297.1

3 is there because the Offset Interval is 0 at its GENERATE Block. Xact 4 is there because interarrival times at its GENERATE Block are zero. Xact 4 precedes Xact 3 on the Current Chain. (Xact 3 was already on the Current Chain when Xact 4 was placed there, but with its Priority of 25, Xact 4 goes ahead of Xact 3, which has a default Priority of 0.)

9. The user will be put into control at the beginning of each Scan Phase.

10. If the user issues a **run** command when no interrupt conditions have been established, then the simulation will proceed without interruption until the model's Termination Counter has been reduced in value to zero (or less). GPSS/H will then display an "output pending" message and give control to the user.

11. The answers to the questions in this exercise are valid for any model, not just for the model of Exercise 5. If the user sets a **scan** trap in response to the Ready! prompt, then no matter what command is issued to resume the simulation, the user will *always* be put back into control just as the Scan Phase is about to begin at time 0.0. This will be true whether or not the Current Chain is empty at that time. (Time 0.0 is the only time that the Current Chain could possibly be empty when a Scan Phase is about to start, by the way. The reasoning behind this statement is provided in Section 4.13.) No Blocks will have been executed yet, because no Xacts will have yet tried to move along their path in the model.

Section 4.15

2. Assuming **step 1** and **display cec fec** are used in strictly alternating fashion throughout the simulation, the resulting chain displays are summarized in Table E2.

   Note that Table E2 contains one display of the Current and Future Chains for *each Block execution* and for each *start of a Scan Phase.* Whenever two consecutive entries in the Total Blocks Executed column are identical, a Clock Update Phase has occurred (between the chain displays for the first and second of the two identical Total Blocks Executed counts). For example, there are two consecutive Total Blocks Executed counts of 2 in the table. The chains displayed for the first of these 2s

Table E3

Clock	Total Blocks Executed	CEC Xacts id	CEC Xacts CURBLK	CEC Xacts NXTBLK	FEC Xacts id	FEC Xacts CURBLK	FEC Xacts NXTBLK	Move Time
0.0	0		Empty		1	"BIRTH"	BLOCK1	75.0
75.0	0	1	"BIRTH"	BLOCK1		Empty		
75.0	1	1	BLOCK1	BLOCK2	2	"BIRTH"	BLOCK1	174.9
75.0	2		Empty		1	BLOCK2	BLOCK3	97.3
					2	"BIRTH"	BLOCK1	174.9
97.3	2	1	BLOCK2	BLOCK3	2	"BIRTH"	BLOCK1	174.9
97.3	3		Empty		2	"BIRTH"	BLOCK1	174.9
174.9	3	2	"BIRTH"	BLOCK1		Empty		
174.9	4	2	BLOCK1	BLOCK2	3	"BIRTH"	BLOCK1	245.3
174.9	5		Empty		2	BLOCK2	BLOCK3	191.1
					3	"BIRTH"	BLOCK1	245.3
191.1	5	2	BLOCK2	BLOCK3	3	"BIRTH"	BLOCK1	245.3
191.1	6		Empty		3	"BIRTH"	BLOCK1	245.3
245.3	6	3	"BIRTH"	BLOCK1		Empty		
245.3	7	3	BLOCK1	BLOCK2	4	"BIRTH"	BLOCK1	372.1
245.3	8		Empty		3	BLOCK2	BLOCK3	264.7
					4	"BIRTH"	BLOCK1	372.1
264.7	8		Empty		3	BLOCK2	BLOCK3	264.7
					4	"BIRTH"	BLOCK1	372.1
264.7	9		Empty		4	"BIRTH"	BLOCK1	372.1

correspond to the end of the Scan Phase at time 0.0. The chains displayed for the second of these 2s correspond to the beginning of the Scan Phase at time 22.3. Between these two 2s, the first Clock Update Phase has taken place.

Consider using the format of Table E2 as a mechanism for organizing and summarizing your results for the remaining exercises in this section.

3. Assuming **step 1** and **display cec fec** are used in strictly alternating fashion throughout the simulation, the resulting chain displays are summarized in Table E3.

   Table E3 and E2 are highly similar. The actions taking place in the Exercise 3 model match those in the model of Exercise 2, except that the timing of these actions in Exercise 3 is displaced by +75.0 time units relative to the corresponding actions in Exercise 2. This of course results from changing the Offset Interval at the GENERATE Block from 0 to 75.

7. In a sense, this model barely gets going before the Xact-Movement Phase ends at time 100.0. (Note that Xact 2 will come out of the BLOCK4 GENERATE at time 100.0 and reduce the model's TC value to 0, ending the Xact-Movement Phase.)

   Xact 1 comes out of the BLOCK1 GENERATE at time 0 (because of the Offset Interval of 0), but then its successor, Xact 3, doesn't come out of the BLOCK1 GENERATE until time 99.9, just before Xact movement stops. In the meantime, Xact 1 comes out of and then TRANSFERs right back into the BLOCK2 ADVANCE ("loops the loop") at times 22.3, 39.4, 55.6, 78.3 and 97.7.

Section 4.20

5. Assuming **step 1** and **display cec fec** are used in strictly alternating fashion throughout the simulation, the resulting chain displays are summarized in Table E5.

   The answers to the specific questions in the exercise can be derived from this table and take the following form.

Table E5

Clock	Total Blocks Executed	CEC Xacts id	CEC Xacts CURBLK	CEC Xacts NXTBLK	FEC Xacts id	FEC Xacts CURBLK	FEC Xacts NXTBLK	Move Time
0.0	1	1	"BIRTH"	BLOCK1		Empty		
		2	"BIRTH"	BLOCK3				
		3	"BIRTH"	BLOCK1				
0.0	2	2	"BIRTH"	BLOCK3		Empty		
		3	"BIRTH"	BLOCK1				
0.0	3	2	BLOCK3	BLOCK4		Empty		
		3	"BIRTH"	BLOCK1				
		4	"BIRTH"	BLOCK3				
0.0	4	3	"BIRTH"	BLOCK1		Empty		
		4	"BIRTH"	BLOCK3				

(a) After one Block execution, the successor to Xact 1 has been created. The successor is Xact 3. Xact 3 is on the Current Chain with a Move Time of zero. (See the composition of the Current Chain in the "Total Blocks Executed: 1" section of Table E5.) Note that Xact 3 is behind Xact 2. And so, as the Scan Phase continues at time 0.0, the first BLOCK3 GENERATE arrival will occur before the second BLOCK1 GENERATE arrival occurs.

(b) When a **step 2** has been executed, the successor to Xact 2 will have been created. The successor, Xact 4, is on the back of the Current Chain with a Move time of 0.0. (See the composition of the Current Chain in the "Total Blocks Executed: 3" section of Table E5.) Of the two additional Block executions (bringing the Total Blocks Executed from 1 to 3), the first takes place when Xact 1 moves into the BLOCK2 TERMINATE and is destroyed. The second takes place when Xact 2 moves into the BLOCK3 GENERATE and, because of its imminent escape from BLOCK3 into BLOCK4, triggers execution of the BLOCK3 GENERATE to create and schedule its successor, Xact 4.

(c) Executing another **step 1** command reduces the value of the model's Termination Counter to zero, ending the Xact-Movement Phase. The requested additional Block execution is achieved when Xact 2 moves into the BLOCK4 TERMINATE and is destroyed. See the composition of the resulting Current Chain in the "Total Blocks Executed: 4" section of Table E5.

6. By the end of the simulation, three Xacts will have come out of the BLOCK1 GENERATE. These Xacts have id numbers 1, 3, and 5. Two Xacts will have come out of the BLOCK3 GENERATE. These Xacts have id numbers 2 and 4. When the simulation stops, Xacts 6 and 7 will be on the Current Chain. Xact 6 is the successor to Xact 4 at the BLOCK3 GENERATE. Xact 7 is the successor to Xact 5 at the BLOCK1 GENERATE. Xact 6 is ahead of Xact 7.

   These statements can be derived from a table similar to that shown in Exercise 5. If necessary, clarify your thinking by constructing such a table.

7. By the end of the simulation, three Xacts will have come out of the BLOCK3 GENERATE. These Xacts have id numbers 2, 3, and 4. No Xacts will have come out of the BLOCK1 GENERATE. When the simulation stops, Xacts 5 and 1 will be on the Current Chain. Xact 5 is the successor to Xact 4 at the BLOCK3 GENERATE. Xact 1 is the pending first arrival at the BLOCK1 GENERATE. Xact 5 is ahead of Xact 1. Xact 1 (Priority 5) was already on the Current Chain when Xact 5 (Priority 8) was put there. With its higher Priority, however, Xact 5 was inserted into the chain ahead of Xact 1.

   These statements can be derived from a table similar to that shown in Exercise 5. If necessary, clarify your thinking by constructing such a table.

Chapter 5

Section 5.3

5. (a) The **scan** trap will cause control to be returned to the user for the first time. The **scan** interrupt will occur at the beginning of the first Scan Phase, at time 0.0, whether or not the Current Chain is empty at that time. GPSS/H will issue the usual "SCAN" TRAP TAKEN message. (Note that the **next** trap couldn't possibly trigger the first interrupt, because a Scan Phase has to pick up an Xact before a **next** trap is sprung, and the starting of a Scan Phase causes a **scan** trap to spring even before an attempt is made to pick up an Xact. These remarks are consistent with the Figure 5.1 Scan Phase flowchart.)

(b) A series of **scan**, **next**, and **system** interrupts will occur. None of these will occur at the same time, because the beginning of a Scan Phase (**scan**) is distinct from picking up an Xact during a Scan Phase (**next**), and both of these Scan Phase junctures are distinct from dropping an Xact during a Scan Phase (**system**).

6. (a) A **next** interrupt will occur first. An Xact must be picked up as a prelude to executing a Block. There is no way that the first Block execution of the simulation could precede the first picking up of an Xact in the simulation.

In addition to displaying the usual "why picked up" (POISED AT) message, GPSS/H will point out that REMAINING STEP COUNT = 1.

(b) A series of **next**, **step**, and **system** interrupts will occur. For reasons just explained, **next** and **step** interrupts never occur at the same time. And it goes without saying that **next** and **system** interrupts never occur at the same time. However, **step** *and* **system** interrupts can occur at the same time, doing so whenever the moving Xact executes a Block that forces GPSS/H to drop the Xact (e.g., nonzero ADVANCE and TERMINATE, in terms of material we've covered so far).

Whenever a **next** interrupt occurs, there will be a "why picked up" message (POISED AT), and then a REMAINING STEP COUNT = 1 message. Whenever a **step** interrupt occurs in isolation (that is, without an accompanying **system** interrupt), there will be a POISED AT message. Whenever a **step** and **system** interrupt occurs, there will be a "why dropped" message (either PLACED ON FEC or DESTROYED, in terms of material we've covered so far).

Section 5.5

6. Figure E6 provides a type of model in which there are Priority distinctions and plenty of Move-Time ties. If you want to experiment with this model, it's in the file s55x6.gps. Note that the model does not provide the wherewithal for eventually reducing the model's Termination Counter to a value of zero, so a Test-Mode user can go as far into the simulation as desired before issuing a **qq** (quit quickly) command.

```
          SIMULATE
*
 BLOCK1   GENERATE   10,,0,4,250
 BLOCK2   ADVANCE    10
 BLOCK3   ADVANCE    5
 BLOCK4   TRANSFER   ,BLOCK2
*
 BLOCK5   GENERATE   5,,0,2,500
 BLOCK6   ADVANCE    10
 BLOCK7   ADVANCE    5
 BLOCK8   TRANSFER   ,BLOCK6
*
 BLOCK9   GENERATE   5,,0,2,750
 BLOCK10  ADVANCE    10
 BLOCK11  ADVANCE    5
 BLOCK12  TRANSFER   ,BLOCK10
*
          START      1
          END
```

Figure E6

Section 5.7

6. There are several similarities and differences between **clock** and **scan** traps, as summarized in the following list.

   1. Like a **scan** trap, a **clock** trap is sprung at the beginning of a Scan Phase. A **scan** trap is sprung at the beginning of *every* Scan Phase, however. (See Figure 5.6.) In contrast, a **clock** trap is only sprung at the beginning of the

first Scan Phase at which the clock time equals or exceeds the clock-trap time.

2. Related to 1 is the fact that a **scan** trap remains in effect unless it is turned off by issuing an **untrap scan** command. (The springing of a **scan** trap does not disable it.) A **clock** trap only remains in effect until it is sprung (the springing of a **clock** trap disables it), or until an **untrap clock** command is executed.

3. Suppose the Current Chain is empty when the first Scan Phase takes place at time 0.0. A **scan** trap will be sprung at this time. But a **clock** trap specifying a trap time of 0.0 will *not* be sprung at this time. As indicated by the position of Box A in Figure 5.6, the springing of a **clock** trap requires that there be an Xact on the CEC.

7. In response to the Ready! prompt, issue a **trap clock=0** command. Then, when this **clock** trap is sprung (either at the beginning of the time 0.0 Scan Phase if the Current Chain is not empty, or at the beginning of the second Scan Phase), issue another **trap clock=*clock_time*** command, specifying a ***clock_time*** just marginally greater than the current time. Then repeat this process when this new **clock** trap is sprung at the beginning of the third Scan Phase, and so on.

For example, suppose that a **trap clock=0** command is sprung at time 23.4567. (This means the Current Chain was empty at time 0.0, and the second Scan Phase is beginning at time 23.4567.) The user then issues a **trap clock=23.4568** command. (Note that the new trap time, 23.4568, is 0.0001 greater than the current time, 23.4567.) This new **clock** trap will then be sprung at the beginning of the third Scan Phase, say at time 45.6789. The user then issues a **trap clock=45.6790** command. (This new trap time is 0.0001 greater than the current time, 45.6789.) And so on.

The procedure just described assumes that consecutive entries in the series of clock times are never less than 0.0001. This assumption should be satisfied in most simulations. If this assumption isn't satisfied, then there could be one or more "transparent" Scan Phases taking place in a simulation. That is, Scan Phases could occur that aren't called to the attention of the user. Of course, instead of using 0.0001 as the increment for current time, 0.00001 could be used, or 0.000001, and so on. This is not an issue with a **scan** trap, however, and if a user wants to be put in control at the beginning of each Scan Phase, a **scan** trap is superior in this regard. Furthermore, a **scan** trap is semipermanent, so the user doesn't have to issue **trap** commands repeatedly when the **trap scan** approach is used.

We'll conclude by commenting on another difference between a **scan** trap on the one hand, and use of a **clock** trap to simulate a **scan** trap on the other hand. It's pointed out in Chapter 4 that the Figure 4.9 flowchart shows a *simplified* form of the Scan Phase Logic. In the complete form of the Scan Phase logic in Chapter 7, we'll see that there are occasions when a Scan Phase is *restarted*. That is, there are occasions during a Scan Phase when GPSS/H returns to the front of the Current Chain (without going through a Clock Update Phase first) and starts again to scan the Current Chain from front to back. On such occasions, a **scan** trap is sprung if one is set. And so a **scan** trap may be sprung *two or more times* at a given clock time, whereas a **clock** trap can be sprung only once at a given clock time.

Chapter 6

Section 6.12

3. The only detectable numeric difference in the output is that the Average Time/Xact of the OVEN Facility is 16.001, which is slightly more than twice the Average Time/Xact of 8.000 in Case Study 6B. Nevertheless, it's interesting to consider the implications of working with alternative base time units. Comments follow.

The number of alternative values that GPSS/H can sample from an interval, although large, is finite. (GPSS/H can sample 2,147,483,646 values from an interval, as explained in Chapter 14.) And so, as an interval becomes wider, the spacing (or gap) between values that can be sampled from the interval becomes larger. When the Case Study 6A Block "ADVANCE 30,5" is changed to "ADVANCE 60,10" (to reflect a change in the base time unit from 1 minute to 0.5 minutes), the spacing between realizeable assembly times doubles. This change in spacing (and the similar doubling in the size of the gap between realizable heat-treat times) reflects itself to a small extent numerically in the operation of the model and leads to numeric outputs that differ in unimportant ways from those produced when different spacing is in effect.

As for the influence of the basic time unit on the size of the gap, consider the following scaled-down, base 10 example. Assume GPSS/H can only sample 19 alternative values from an interval. Then the 19 values it could sample from the open 30 ± 5 interval would be the set of 19 values ranging from 25.5 to 34.5, inclusive, in steps of 0.5 (25.5, 26.0, 26.5, 27.0, and so on). Here, the gap between consecutive values is 0.5. In contrast, the 19 values it could sample from the open 60 ± 10 interval would be the set of 19 values ranging from 51.0 to 69.0, inclusive, in steps of 1.0 (51.0, 52.0, 53.0, and so on). Here, the gap between consecutive values is 1.0.

4. (a) Results are shown in Table E4.

Table E4

Xact id	Time Finished with First Widget Assembly
1	27.7
3	29.9
4	32.3
5	27.0

(b) The second worker who finishes a widget assembly, simulated by Xact 1, begins to wait for the oven at time 27.7, and captures the oven at time 33.5.

(c) The worker simulated by the Xact with id number 5 finishes his or her third widget assembly at time 107.4.

(d) There are no Move-Time ties at time 480.0.

(e) Of the three worker-Xacts in the Block 3 ADVANCE at the end of the simulation, all are on the FEC. None is on the CEC, waiting his or her turn to use the OVEN Facility.

5. The total count at "RELEASE OVEN" is 239, so the average number of widgets built per day is 47.8. The average daily revenue, net of the material in a widget, is then $10 times 47.8, or $478. Subtracting the daily oven cost of $100, and the daily payroll of $340 (= 4 times $85), the average daily profit is $38.

6. Three workers produce 184 widgets in 40 hours, resulting in an average daily profit of $13. Five workers produce 285 widgets, resulting in an average daily profit of $45. And so five workers maximize the estimated average daily profit in these specific simulations.

8. A model for this exercise is shown in Figure E8 and is given in the file s612x8.gps.

   In terms of Figure 6.4, the pre-SEIZE Block is the ADVANCE used to simulate conveying time. The post-RELEASE is the TERMINATE that removes drilled casting-Xacts from the model. A simulation performed with the model ends at time 4627.2.

9. At the end of the simulation, two Xact-castings (Xact id's = 501 and 502) have reached the end of the conveyor and are waiting for the drill, and one Xact-casting (Xact id = 503) is still in the process of being conveyed.

```
         SIMULATE                  base time unit: 1 minute
*
         GENERATE  9.0,4.5         objects arrive, one by one,
*                                  and are placed on the conveyer
         ADVANCE   6.0             conveying time
*
         SEIZE     DRILL           request/capture the DRILL
         ADVANCE   9.0,1.25        drilling time
         RELEASE   DRILL           done with the drill
*
         TERMINATE 1               drilled casting leaves the model
*
         START     500             drill 500 objects in total
         END                       end of Model-File execution
```

Figure E8

```
         SIMULATE                 base time unit: 1 minute
*
         GENERATE  9.0,4.5        objects arrive, one by one,
*                                 and are placed on the conveyer
         ADVANCE   6.0            conveying time
*
         SEIZE     DRILL          request/capture the DRILL
         ADVANCE   9.0,1.25       drilling time
         RELEASE   DRILL          done with the drill
*
         ADVANCE   2.5            conveying time
*
         SEIZE     DEBURR         request/capture the DEBURR machine
         ADVANCE   7.5,2.5        deburring time
         RELEASE   DEBURR         deburring is finished
*
         TERMINATE 1              drilled and deburred
*                                 casting leaves the model
*
         START     500            drill/deburr 500 objects in total
*
         END                      end of Model-File execution
```

Figure E10

10. A model for this exercise is shown in Figure E10 and is given in the file s612x10.gps.

    A simulation performed with the Figure E10 model stops at time 4574.4. The number of castings completely drilled by this time is 501. Of the 3 casting-Xacts in the model when the Xact-Movement Phase ends, 1 is being conveyed to the drill, 1 is being drilled, and 1 is being conveyed to the deburring machine.

Section 6.13

1. It's evident to **us** that without the RELEASE Block, the model doesn't make sense logically, but this logical flaw isn't detected by GPSS/H. The model compiles successfully, and then execution begins. The first assembler to capture the heat-treat oven never subsequently releases it, and so no assemblers can capture the oven from that point forward. After all four assemblers have become blocked at "SEIZE OVEN" (this happens early in the simulation), the next Clock Update Phase advances the clock to a value of 2400.0, and the simulation stops. From the point of view of the software, all is right with the world.

   A lesson learned in miniature terms from this example is that the modeler should never take anything for granted, but should always critically examine a model and its output, not simply assuming that "because the model executed to completion, it must be right." It is easy to build models that make no sense logically, but that nevertheless compile successfully and then execute to completion. Every Postsimulation Report should be looked at in terms of such questions as "Do these results make sense?"

2. When the first casting-Xact to be drilled tries to TERMINATE, an Execution Error ("*Transaction being destroyed controls or is in contention for a Facility*") results. This Execution Error always results if an Xact tries to destroy itself while it is still in control of one or more Facilities. (The possibility of having an Xact control two or more Facilities simultaneously is discussed in Chapter 8.)

3. When the first assembler to finish heat treating tries to "RELEASE OVEN" without being in control of the OVEN Facility, an Execution Error ("RELEASing Transaction did not SEIZE the Facility") results. An Xact can RELEASE a Facility only if it is the current owner (capturer) of the Facility.

4. When the control-Xact comes out of its GENERATE Block at time 2400.0, there is no Block to be its Next Block Attempted. At this point in the Xact-Movement Phase, an Execution Error (*"Execution has "run off the end" of the model"*) results.

5. Before the planned end of the Xact-Movement Phase, Student DOS GPSS/H exceeds its self-imposed limit on the number of Xacts simultaneously permitted in a model. Execution-time Error Message 411 is then issued: *"Limits of COMMON storage exceeded."* (COMMON is the supply of computer memory used, in part, to support the existence of Xacts.) When this error condition occurs, there are 82 casting-Xacts waiting to be drilled. See Section B.2 in Appendix B in this regard.

Chapter 7

Section 7.7

2. (a) Xact 1 will be in the "ADVANCE 10" Block and on the Future Events Chain. Its Move Time will be 10. Xacts 2, 3, 4, and 5 will be in the "ADVANCE 0" Block, and on the Current Events Chain. They will be asleep (scan inactive), waiting their turn to "SEIZE POWER". Their Move Time will be 0.0 numerically, and ASAP conceptually.
(b) This statement is true. Xact 1 is on the Future Chain, where it has a known Move Time of 10. (There is no way to put an Xact on the Future Chain without it having a known Move Time.) Xacts 2, 3, 4, and 5, by contrast, are on the Current Chain, and GPSS/H does not know at what simulated time they will be able to move. (It's always true of any Xact on the Current Chain that GPSS/H does not know the simulated time at which it will be able to move.)
(c) The model's Status Change Flag will be on. (Execution of the RELEASE Block turned it on.) Xacts 2, 3, 4, and 5 will still be in the "ADVANCE 0" Block, and each of them will be awake. (Execution of "RELEASE POWER" caused them to be awakened.)
(d) Xact 2 will be in the "ADVANCE 10" Block, and on the Future Chain. Its Move Time will be 20. Xacts 3, 4, and 5 will be in the "ADVANCE 0" Block, and on the Current Chain. They will be asleep (scan inactive), waiting their turn to "SEIZE POWER".

3. False. Execution of a RELEASE turns the model's Status Change Flag on. This sets a signal for an **eventual** restart of the scan. The Xact that executed the RELEASE continues to move as far as it can, **then** GPSS/H tests the Status Change Flag and, finding it on, turns it back off and restarts the scan. (See Figure 7.3 or 7.4.)

4. True. See the answer to 3.

5. True. GPSS/H **could** have been designed to leave the model's Status Change Flag off in such a case (if no Xacts have become unblocked as a result of RELEASE execution, then why eventually restart the scan of the CEC?), but hasn't been. RELEASE execution unconditionally turns on the model's Status Change Flag.

6. False. When a RELEASE executes, then **all** Xacts that have been asleep, waiting for the corresponding Facility to be released, are reawakened. This happens even though, in general, only one of the reawakened Xacts will be able to capture the now-idle Facility, and the others, having experienced a "false alarm," will go back to sleep.

7. True. The Block sequential to an ADVANCE might be of a type (such as SEIZE) that can deny entry to an Xact. If an Xact moves into an "ADVANCE 10" Block, it goes to the FEC for 10 units of time, then is returned (by a Clock Update Phase) to the CEC. If the Block sequential to this ADVANCE denies entry to the Xact for, say, another 5 units of time, then the Xact will remain in the ADVANCE and on the CEC for those 5 units of time.

   If an Xact moves into an "ADVANCE 0" Block, it does not go to the FEC at all, but remains on the CEC, and immediately tries to move into the Block sequential to the ADVANCE. If the Block sequential to this ADVANCE denies entry to the Xact for, say, another 20 units of time, then the Xact will remain in the ADVANCE and on the CEC for those 20 units of time.

8. False. An ADVANCE Block **never** denies entry to an Xact. Any number of Xacts can "stack up" in an ADVANCE Block (subject to the limits of computer memory and other bounds that GPSS/H may impose in this regard).

Chapter 8

Section 8.4

2. The simulation stops at time 75.0.

3. At the end of a simulation performed with the fig82.gps Model File, the clerk's utilization is 0.784.

   The contribution of low-priority orders to the clerk's long-run utilization is 0.667 (that is, 2/3), and of high-priority orders is 0.167 (that is, 1/6). These utilizations are additive, so the expected long-run utilization is 0.834 (that is, 5/6).

4. Surprise! A high-priority order never does cut in line ahead of a low-priority order during the fig82.gps simulation. (Eight high-priority and thirty low-priority orders arrive during the simulation, but there is never a low-priority order waiting when a high-priority order arrives.) If the simulation is allowed to continue beyond time 480.0, a high-priority order (Xact 58) does eventually cut in line ahead of a low-priority order (Xact 63). This happens at time 790.0.

8. When the Xact-Movement Phase ends, Joe is at work, giving a haircut to a haircut-only customer (Xact 22). Both a haircut-only customer, and a shave-and-haircut customer, are waiting for Joe. The haircut-only customer, Xact 23, has been waiting since time 474.6. The shave-and-haircut customer, Xact 21, has been waiting since time 476.4.

Section 8.10

1. The simulation stops at time 1032.9 The reported tugboat utilization is 0.063. The reported utilizations of the Type A and Type B berths are 0.881 and 0.795, respectively.

2. The expected tugboat utilization is 0.075. One way to arrive at this figure is to consider that on average, 1 Type A ship arrives every 30 hours, using the tugboat for 0.75 hours; and 2 Type B ships arrive every 30 hours, each using the tugboat for 0.75 hours. And so the total tugboat use for an average 30-hour period is 2.25 hours. Dividing 2.25 hours by 30 hours results in the expected tugboat utilization of 0.075. This 0.075 figure can be compared with the realized tugboat utilization of 0.063 in Exercise 1.

4. The fractions of simulated time the A and B berths are, respectively, used in the actual unloading of cargo in the simulation are 0.859 and 0.752.

   The expected fraction of the time that the A and B berths are, respectively, used in the actual unloading of cargo are 0.867 and 0.800. (For the A berth, a ship comes on average every 30 hours and uses the berth on average 26 hours. Dividing 26 hours by 30 hours results in the expected unloading utilization of 0.867. For the B berth, a ship comes on average every 15 hours and uses the berth on average 12 hours. Dividing 12 hours by 15 hours results in the expected unloading utilization of 0.800.)

6. A model for this exercise is shown in Figure E6 and is given in file s810x6.gps.

   Notice how the "RELEASE STATION1" Block has been positioned **after** the "SEIZE THESPACE" Block. In other words, the ability of a WIP-Xact to free up the Station 1 worker is conditioned on its prior ability to move into the wait space. (The intended effect would be lost if "RELEASE STATION1" were put **before** "SEIZE THESPACE".)

   Similarly, notice that the "RELEASE THESPACE" Block has been positioned **after** the "SEIZE STATION2" Block. The ability of a WIP-Xact to free up the wait space is conditioned on its prior ability to capture the Station 2 worker. (The intended effect would be lost if "RELEASE THESPACE" were put **before** "SEIZE STATION2".)

8. A model for this exercise is shown in Figure E8 and is given in the file s810x8.gps.

   The one assumption made in building the model involves the position of BLOCK10 relative to BLOCK11. The Figure E8 positioning assumes that the wait space isn't available for use on the part of another WIP-Xact until **after** the transfer from the wait space has taken place. If the wait space becomes available (for all practical purposes) as soon as the transfer **starts** to take place, then BLOCK10 and BLOCK11 should be interchanged.

9. A model for this exercise is shown in Figure E9

```
          SIMULATE                    base time unit: 1 minute
*
          GENERATE   30,20            WIP arrives
          ADVANCE    0                avoid arrival distortions
*
          SEIZE      STATION1         request/capture STATION1
          ADVANCE    25,10            Station 1 time
          SEIZE      THESPACE         request/capture the space
          RELEASE    STATION1         no longer at STATION1
*
          SEIZE      STATION          request/capture STATION2
          RELEASE    THESPACE         no longer in the space
          ADVANCE    30,10            Station 2 time
          RELEASE    STATION2         deburring is finished
*
          TERMINATE  1                finished WIP leaves the model
*
          START      100              finish 100 WIP units

          END                         end of Model-File execution
```

Figure E6

```
          SIMULATE                    base time unit: 1 minute
*
          GENERATE   30,20            WIP arrives
          ADVANCE    0                no arrival-time distortions
*
          SEIZE      STATION1         request/capture STATION1
          ADVANCE    0.25             15 seconds transfer time
          ADVANCE    25,10            Station 1 time
          SEIZE      THESPACE         request/capture the space
          ADVANCE    0.25             15 seconds transfer time
          RELEASE    STATION1         no longer at Station 1
*
          SEIZE      STATION2         request/capture STATION2
 BLOCK10  ADVANCE    0.25             15 seconds transfer time
 BLOCK11  RELEASE    THESPACE         no longer in the space
          ADVANCE    30,10            Station 2 time
          ADVANCE    0.25             15 seconds transfer time
          RELEASE    STATION2         no longer at STATION2
*
          TERMINATE  1                finished WIP leaves the model
*
          START      100              finish 100 WIP units
*
          END                         end of Model-File execution
```

Figure E8

```
          SIMULATE              base time unit: 1 minute
*
          GENERATE   12.5,10    students arrive
          ADVANCE    20,10      initial paperwork time
*
          SEIZE      WINDOW1    request/capture WINDOW1
          ADVANCE    7.5,2.5    initial OK-ing time
          RELEASE    WINDOW1    done for now at WINDOW1
*
          SEIZE      WINDOW2    request/capture WINDOW2
          ADVANCE    10,5       easy come, easy go
          RELEASE    WINDOW2    done for now at WINDOW2
*
          SEIZE      WINDOW1    request/capture WINDOW1 again
          ADVANCE    5,2        final OK-ing time
          RELEASE    WINDOW1    done at last
*
          TERMINATE 0           finished student leaves
*
          GENERATE   450        control-Xact comes after 7.5 hours
          TERMINATE 1           reduce the TC by 1,
*                               ending Xact movement
*
          START      1          set the TC = 1;
*                               start Xact movement
          END                   end of Model-File execution
```

Figure E9

and is given in the file s810x9.gps.

There are seven students in the system when the simulation stops. Of the seven, three are doing initial paperwork, one is waiting to use WINDOW1 for the first time, one is using WINDOW2, one is waiting to use WINDOW1 for the second time, and one is using WINDOW1 for the second time.

10. (a) GENERATE Blocks are initialized in the top-down order of their appearance in a Model File. And all worker-Xacts in the model have the same Priority (zero, by default). So if the Worker 2 GENERATE precedes that of Worker 3 in the Model File, the Worker 2 Xact will be ahead of the Worker 3 Xact on the CEC after GENERATE initialization. Worker 2 will then be the first of these two Xacts to try for the OVEN, and will be successful. If the Worker 3 GENERATE preceded that of Worker 2, the opposite would be true, and Worker 3 would be the first to capture the OVEN, which is contrary to the conditions that are to be in effect initially.

(b) The workers are supposed to use the heat-treat oven in FCFS order. If the Worker 2 Xact has higher Priority than the Worker 3 Xact, then throughout the entire simulation, these two workers won't use the oven in FCFS order with respect to each other, which is inconsistent with the way the system is described (in Case Study 6A) as operating.

(c) Change the WORKER3 GENERATE to "GENERATE 10,,,1", and then the "ADVANCE 10" can be eliminated.

Section 8.11

1. Interchanging the "SEIZE BERTHA" and "SEIZE TUGBOAT" Blocks (and/or interchanging the "SEIZE BERTHB" and "SEIZE TUGBOAT" Blocks) would result in a model in which deadlock could occur. Consider the following scenario. Suppose that while a Type A ship is unloading, another Type A ship comes along, captures the tugboat, and starts to wait for the Type A berth. Can you see the problem here?

When the Type A ship in berth finishes unloading, it can't get the tugboat to get pulled out of its berth, and so can't give up the berth. Meanwhile, the other Type A ship won't let the tugboat go until sometime after it has captured the berth, which it can't do. Each of these two ship-Xacts controls something that the other wants, and neither can give up control over what it has until the other gives up control over what it has!

GPSS/H is not capable of detecting deadlock when it comes about in a model. And so, in the case just described, the simulation would simply continue. Type A ships would continue to arrive at the harbor, of course, but they would simply stack up in their "ADVANCE 0" Block. GPSS/H eventually would not be able to create any more Xacts, an Error Message would be issued, and the simulation would stop. (This statement assumes that this situation would come about before the Termination Counter had been reduced in value to zero. If the Type A SEIZEs were interchanged, but not the Type B, the Type-B ship departures might succeed in shutting down the simulation before the Xact limit is reached. In this case, the large Current Count at the Type A "ADVANCE 0", and the small Total Counts along the path following that Block, would alert the modeler to the fact that something went wrong in the simulation.)

2. The requested change leads to a situation in which an Xact tries to RELEASE a Facility that it doesn't control. We've already seen that this results in an Execution Error ("RELEASing Transaction did not SEIZE the Facility").

3. The requested change leads to a situation in which an Xact that controls a Facility tries to TERMINATE. We've already seen that this results in an Execution Error (*"Transaction being destroyed controls or is in contention for a Facility"*).

Chapter 9

Section 9.7

2. Interchanging the order of Model Segments 1 and 2 changes the order in which samples are drawn from the interarrival time and service time distributions in the model. For example, the GENERATE Blocks in Case Study 9A are initialized in the order "GENERATE 420,360,,,1" and "GENERATE 360,240,,,2". In contrast, these two GENERATE Blocks are initialized in the reverse order in Exercise 2. Only one "random number generator" is used as the starting point for sampling from **all four** distributions in the model. Interchanging the model segments changes the order in which numbers from this random number generator are used, which results in different sampled values. This point will be explained in much more detail when sampling from distributions is discussed in Chapter 13.

3. The tool crib clerk's expected holding time per capture is 192.3 seconds. One way to compute this value is as follows. Consider a 15,120-second span of time. The expected numbers of Type 1 and Type 2 mechanic arrivals during this time span are 36 (= 15,120/420) and 42 (= 15,120/360), respectively. With an expected service time of 300 seconds per mechanic, the 36 Type 1 arrivals will hold the clerk for an expected 10,800 seconds. With an expected service time of 100 seconds per mechanic, the 42 Type 2 arrivals will hold the clerk for an expected 4,200 seconds. In terms of averages, then, 78 captures (78 = 36 + 42) will consume 15,000 seconds (15,000 = 10,800 + 4,200) of clerk time. Dividing 15,000 by 78 results in an expected holding time per capture of 192.3 seconds.

4. A model for this exercise is shown in Figure E4 and is given in the file s97x4.gps.

   Figure E4 repeats the Case Study 9A model for the SPT service order, with the Comments statements eliminated and with the four new Blocks labeled NEW1 through NEW4 added (and with OLD1 through OLD4 labels added to four Blocks that were already in the Case Study 9A model). The OLD1 and NEW1 Blocks could be interchanged (because QUEUE Blocks are zero-time Blocks). The OLD3 and NEW3 Blocks could likewise be interchanged. And similarly for the OLD2 and NEW2 DEPART Blocks; and the OLD4 and NEW4 DEPART Blocks. Any of these interchanges could be made independently of or in combination with the others.

5. A model for this exercise is shown in Figure E5 and is given in the file s97x5.gps.

   Figure E5 repeats the Case Study 9A model for the SPT service order, with the Comments state-

```
          SIMULATE                          base time unit: 1 second
*
          GENERATE   420,360,,,5            Type 1 mechanics arrive
*                                           (Priority 5)
OLD1      QUEUE      TOOLWAIT               start TOOLWAIT Queue membership
NEW1      QUEUE      TYPE1Q                 start TYPE1Q membership
          SEIZE      CLERK                  request/capture the CLERK
NEW2      DEPART     TYPE1Q                 end TYPE1Q membership
OLD2      DEPART     TOOLWAIT               end TOOLWAIT Queue membership
          ADVANCE    300,90                 service time
          RELEASE    CLERK                  free the CLERK
          TERMINATE  0                      leave the toolcrib area
*
          GENERATE   360,240,,,10           Type 2 mechanics arrive
*                                           (Priority 10)
OLD3      QUEUE      TOOLWAIT               start TOOLWAIT Queue membership
NEW3      QUEUE      TYPE2Q                 start TYPE2Q membership
          SEIZE      CLERK                  request/capture the CLERK
NEW4      DEPART     TYPE2Q                 end TYPE2Q membership
OLD4      DEPART     TOOLWAIT               end TOOLWAIT Queue membership
          ADVANCE    100,30                 service time
          RELEASE    CLERK                  free the CLERK
          TERMINATE  0                      leave the toolcrib area
*
          GENERATE   28800                  control-Xact comes after 8 hours
          TERMINATE  1                      reduce the TC value by 1,
*                                           ending Xact movement
          START      1                      set TC = 1; start Xact movement
          END                               end of Model-File execution
```

Figure E4

ments eliminated and with the four new Blocks labeled NEW1 through NEW4 added (and with OLD1 through OLD4 labels added to four Blocks that were already in the Case Study 9A model). The OLD1 and NEW1 Blocks **cannot** be interchanged (SEIZE Blocks are not zero-time Blocks). The OLD3 and NEW3 Blocks likewise **cannot** be interchanged. However, the OLD2 and NEW2 RELEASE Blocks could be interchanged (the order in which the two Facilities are RELEASEd doesn't matter). Similarly, the OLD4 and NEW4 RELEASE Block could be interchanged. Either valid interchange could be made independently of or in combination with the other.

6. The expected number of objects on the conveyor is 4. In the requested Batch simulation, the average number of objects on the conveyor is 3.971, and the maximum number on the conveyor is 8.

10. (c) As the degree of randomness in a system decreases (or, to put it differently, as the degree of control increases), the use of system resources can become more efficient. For example, in a one-line, one-server system, if a customer arrives every 15 minutes (exactly), and if service requires 14 minutes (exactly), then no customer need ever have to wait to go into service. (No customer ever waits, for example, if the first customer arrives and finds an idle server at time 15, the second arrives at time 30, the third arrives at time 45, and so on, because service completions occur at times 29, 44, and so on, always prior to the arrival of the next customer.) But if customers arrive every 15 ± 5 minutes, and if service requires 14 ± 4 minutes, then the average number of waiting customers will exceed zero. And if customers arrive every 15 ± 10 minutes, and if service requires 14 ± 8 minutes, then the average number of waiting customers will be even greater than in the preceding case.

Applying these ideas to the conveying-and-drilling system, note that the variability in (c) is

```
          SIMULATE                       base time unit: 1 second
*
          GENERATE  420,360,,,5          Type 1 mechanics arrive
*                                        (Priority 5)
          QUEUE     TOOLWAIT             start TOOLWAIT Queue membership
OLD1      SEIZE     CLERK                request/capture the CLERK
NEW1      SEIZE     TYPE1HIT             capture the TYPE1HIT dummy
          DEPART    TOOLWAIT             end TOOLWAIT Queue membership
          ADVANCE   300,90               service time
NEW2      RELEASE   TYPE1HIT             free the TYPE1HIT dummy
OLD2      RELEASE   CLERK                free the CLERK
          TERMINATE 0                    leave the toolcrib area
*
          GENERATE  360,240,,,10         Type 2 mechanics arrive
*                                        (Priority 10)
          QUEUE     TOOLWAIT             start TOOLWAIT Queue membership
OLD3      SEIZE     CLERK                request/capture the CLERK
NEW3      SEIZE     TYPE2HIT             capture the TYPE2HIT dummy
          DEPART    TOOLWAIT             end TOOLWAIT Queue membership
          ADVANCE   100,30               service time
NEW4      RELEASE   TYPE2HIT             free the TYPE2HIT dummy
OLD4      RELEASE   CLERK                free the CLERK
          TERMINATE 0                    leave the toolcrib area
*
          GENERATE  28800                control-Xact comes after 8 hours
          TERMINATE 1                    reduce the TC value by 1,
*                                        ending Xact movement
          START     1                    set TC = 1; start Xact movement
          END                            end of Model-File execution
```

Figure E5

less than in (a). As a result, we would expect that AVERAGE CONTENTS and the AVERAGE TIME/UNIT for the Queue would be less in (c) than in (a).

(d) See (c) above.

11. (a) Here are some results produced by a correctly built model:

Crane utilization:	0.864
Average step 4 crane-wait time:	12.644
Average step 6 et seq. crane-wait time:	8.724
Average "Other Calls" crane-wait time:	11.533
Number of "Other Calls" that arrived:	616

(The times are given in minutes.) You can compare these results with those from the model you built and, in this indirect way, check the correctness of your model. (Even though the model's outputs are probabilistic, the system is simple enough so that there is no room for variation in results produced by a correctly built model.) The model that produced the foregoing results contains 27 Blocks.

(b) Under the conditions described in the exercise, the estimated long-run crane utilization is 0.877. This value results from adding the 0.64 contribution of "other calls" to crane utilization and an 0.237 contribution of the finishing-machine operator. The value 0.237 is computed as follows. The time required for a deterministic, "no waiting required" casting cycle is 249 minutes, which equals the sum of expected step times in a cycle (i.e., 12 + 10 + 80 + 15 + 110 + 10 + 12). The operator's expected crane-use time during such a cycle is 59 minutes (i.e., 12 + 10 + 15 + 10 + 12). Dividing 59 by 249 produces 0.237.

The estimate of 0.237 is actually somewhat high, because the operator's expected crane-wait time per casting cycle is nonzero, and this, in turn, means expected casting-cycle time will exceed 249 minutes. Let "cw" be the operator's expected crane-wait time per casting cycle. From the part (a) results, we can estimate the value of cw to be about 21.3 minutes (= 12.6 + 8.7). Then the operator's estimated contribution to the crane utilization can be refined by computing 59/(249+"cw"), which is about 0.218.

(e) The machine-operator's utilization output by the model is 0.922.

(f) The following conditions must all be in effect for the machine operator to benefit from having higher priority than "other calls" for crane use:

1. The crane must be captured.
2. The machine operator must be waiting for the crane. (This means the capturer of the crane must be of the "other call" type.)
3. One or more "other calls" must be waiting for the crane.
4. At least one of the "other calls" must have been waiting for the crane longer than the machine operator.

These conditions do come about from time to time, but not with high frequency. (The model was modified to monitor the state of affairs in this regard, and in a long simulation it was found that these conditions were in effect on about 10 percent of the occasions when the machine operator requested the crane.)

When a simulation was performed with a model that put the changed service order into effect, these results were produced:

Crane utilization:	0.874
Machine operator utilization:	0.924
Average step 4 crane-wait time:	10.930
Average step 6 et seq. crane-wait time:	9.702
Average "Other Calls" crane-wait time:	11.773
Number of "Other Calls" that arrived:	619

(The times are given in minutes.) These results can be compared with those under (a). The machine operator's average crane-wait time per casting cycle, 20.632 (= 10.930 + 9.702), has dropped slightly from 21.3, and the average crane wait for "other calls" has increased slightly, from 11.533 to 11.773. But these differences are not significant, based only on single simulations as they are. (See Chapter 14 et seq. for more elaboration.)

(g) The machine operator begins to wait for the crane at time 329.7. Xact 10 is using the crane at this time. The "other call" already waiting for the crane at this time is simulated by Xact 11. It began to wait for the crane at time 324.3. The machine operator captures the crane at time 333.6.

This information was developed as follows. A trap was set on Xact 1, the machine operator. Then the run command was used to walk through the simulation. Whenever an interrupt occurred, a **display fac** command was issued **if** the machine operator was about to begin membership in the step 4 or step 6 et seq. crane Queue and request the crane. If the CRANE Facility was in a state of capture (as determined from the Facility Report), then a **display que** command was issued. When the Current Contents of the Queue was 1 or more (with the machine operator having not yet checked into the Queue himself), then this is the condition we were waiting to have come about. Then issuing a **display cec** command and inspecting the CEC, we can see who the "other call" already waiting for the crane is (and, from its Mark Time value, when it came into the model and began to wait). From the Facility Report, we see who the current user of the crane is. Issuing another run command then lets us know when the machine operator captures the crane.

12. (a) The average number of mechanics waiting at the tool crib in the requested simulation is 2.543. The total waiting cost resulting from the 8-hour day is $406.88.

(b) The average number of mechanics waiting at the tool crib in the simulation with the $18.00/hour clerk is 1.297. Taking clerk wages and waiting costs into account, the day simulated with the $18/hour clerk is $151.36 less expensive than the day simulated with the $12/hour clerk. (The savings in mechanic waiting time is $207.52. But the $18/hour clerk costs $48 more per day than the $12/hour clerk. The net savings is $151.36.) Also see Exercise 5 in Section 16.7.

(c) No mechanic would ever have to wait to go into service.

Section 9.8

1. The model compiles successfully, and then goes into execution. When the first object-Xact moves into the TERMINATE Block, a Warning Message (*"Transaction being destroyed belongs to one or more Queues."*) is issued, and the simulation

continues. This message is issued on a "one time only" basis. That is, when subsequent object-Xacts TERMINATE, the Warning Message is not reissued.

Why is only a Warning Message issued, and not an Error Message? Why is the simulation permitted to continue? The idea is that the modeler might still be able to obtain useful information from the Postsimulation Report (from the Facility Report component, for example, or from Block Counts, or from other components to be introduced later in the book), even though some of the information in the Queue Report may be meaningless.

2. The model compiles successfully, and then goes into execution. When the first object-Xact moves into the DEPART Block, a Warning Message (*"DEPARTing Transaction not a member of the Queue"*) is issued. And then an Error Message (*"Queue contents have been decremented to less than zero"*) is immediately issued, and the simulation is stopped.

3. With the SEIZE no longer sandwiched between them, the QUEUE and DEPART will be consecutive Blocks in the model. This means that each Xact that begins membership in the Queue will end its Queue membership without simulated delay, thereby passing through the Queue in zero simulated time. One hundred percent of the Queue entries will be Zero Entries.

Chapter 10

Section 10.4

1. By the end of the simulation, six interrupts will have occurred.

2. Results are supplied in Table E2.

Table E2

No. of Type 1 Service Initiation	Time of Initiation
1	254.6
2	847.2
3	1477.7
4	2163.1
5	2773.6

The Table E2 information was developed by setting a breakpoint on the ADVANCE Block for Type 1 mechanics, then issuing repeated run commands.

4. Results are supplied in Table E4.

Table E4

Type of Mechanic	Time of Service Initiation
1	254.6
2	501.3
2	617.4
1	847.2
2	1073.9

The Table E4 information was developed by setting breakpoints on both ADVANCE Blocks, then issuing repeated run commands.

5. Results are supplied in Table E5.

Table E5

Type of Mechanic	Time of Service Completion
1	501.3
2	617.4
2	739.0
1	1073.9
2	1164.0

Note that the Table E5 and Table E4 information are consistent in the sense that in three cases, the time of service completion matches the time another service is initiated.

The Table E5 information was developed by setting breakpoints on both RELEASE Blocks, then issuing repeated run commands.

7. There is a mechanic waiting for the CLERK when the first service completion occurs, which is at time 501.3. It is a Type 1 mechanic (simulated by Xact 1) that is coming out of service, and a Type 2 mechanic (simulated by Xact 2) that is waiting to go into service. (This information was determined by setting breakpoints on both RELEASE Blocks, then issuing a **run** command. When the first interrupt occured, a **display blo** command was issued. The Current Count of 1 at Block 9 indicated that a Type 2 mechanic was waiting to capture the clerk. The CEC was then displayed to determine the id numbers of the releasing and waiting Xacts, although these id numbers weren't asked for as part of the exercise.)

8. The earliest time that exactly one mechanic of the other type (Type 1) is waiting its turn to capture the CLERK when the CLERK is released is 2163.1, corresponding to the tenth service completion of the simulation. The releasing Xact (Xact 12) simulates a Type 2 mechanic. The waiting Type 1 mechanic is simulated by Xact 11. This information was determined by setting breakpoints on both RELEASE Blocks, then repeatedly issuing **run** and **display blo** commands in sequence. When the Current Counts at Blocks 2 and 9 showed values of 1 and 0, respectively, this indicated that one mechanic of Type 1 was waiting for the CLERK (who was in the process of being released), and that no other mechanic was waiting at the same time. The CEC was then displayed to determine the id numbers of the releasing and waiting Xacts, although these id numbers weren't asked for as part of the exercise.)

9. At time 1073.9, a Type 1 mechanic releases the clerk. There are two Type 2 mechanics waiting at this time.

10. At time 3067.4, a Type 1 mechanic releases the clerk. There is one mechanic of each type waiting at this time.

11. At time 5599.0, a Type 2 mechanic cuts in line ahead of a Type 1 mechanic for the first time in the simulation.

12. At time 6152.8, a Type 2 mechanic cuts in line ahead of a Type 1 mechanic for the second time in the simulation.

Section 10.7

2. Results are provided in the following list:

Time of arrival:	1020.5
Type of mechanic:	2 (high priority)
id numbers of any Type 1 mechanics already in line:	None
id numbers of any Type 2 mechanics already in line:	6
Time of service initiation:	1164.0
Time of service completion:	1287.4

There are no subsequent arrivals before Xact 8 goes into service.

The foregoing information was developed as follows. A trap was set on the Xact of interest, then a **run** command was issued. When an interrupt occurred, the message indicated the time of arrival of the Xact of interest and, from the context of the first Block Attempted, the type of mechanic. A display of the CEC was then examined to determine the id numbers and types of any mechanics already in line at the time. The trap was then taken off the Xact of interest, and breakpoints were put on the two QUEUE Blocks (to be told about subsequent arrivals), on the two ADVANCE Blocks (to be told about subsequent service initiations), and on the two RELEASE Blocks (to be told about subsequent service completions). Run commands were then issued repeatedly until the Xact of interest came out of service. Information was squibbed from the interrupt messages to provide answers to the questions in the exercise. This same approach was used in following Exercises 3, 4, and 5.

3. Results are provided in the following list:

Time of arrival:	9584.2
Type of mechanic:	2 (high priority)
id numbers of any Type 1 mechanics already in line:	50
id numbers of any Type 2 mechanics already in line:	None
Time of service initiation:	9629.3
Time of service completion:	9737.8

There are no subsequent arrivals before Xact 8 goes into service.

4. Results are provided in the following list:

Time of arrival:	18,048.6
Type of mechanic:	1 (low priority)
id numbers of any Type 1 mechanics already in line:	89
id numbers of any Type 2 mechanics already in line:	90
Time of service initiation:	18,848.9
Time of service completion:	19,199.4

Data on Subsequent Arrivals Before Xact 91 Goes into Service

Arrival Time	Mechanic Type	Xact ID	Time into Service	Time out of Service
18,178	2	92	18,257.1	18,336.5
18,386	1	93	N/A	
18,457	2	94	18,648.9	18,777.4
18,756	2	96	18,777.4	18,848.9

5. Results are provided in the following list:

Time of arrival:	22,846.3
Type of mechanic:	1 (low priority)
id numbers of any Type mechanics already in line:	111, 113, 115
id numbers of any Type mechanics already in line:	None
Time of service initiation:	24,424.0
Time of service completion:	24,690.1

Data on Subsequent Arrivals Before Xact 117 Goes into Service

Arrival Time	Mechanic Type	Xact ID	Time into Service	Time out of Service
22,978.7	2	116	23,246.5	23,349.8
23,185.5	2	119	23,349.8	23,434.6
23,440.5	1	118	N/A	
23,674.9	2	120	23,786.8	23,888.7
23,847.6	1	121	N/A	
23,932.0	2	122	24,260.4	24,332.5
24,206.6	2	124	24,332.5	24,424.0
24,238.3	1	123	N/A	

6. The earliest time a low-priority mechanic arrives while another mechanic is being served is 2119.2.

7. The earliest time a high-priority mechanic arrives while another mechanic is being served is 359.6.

8. Service is initiated for Xact 4 (Type 1) at time 847.2. The waiting line is empty at the time. While Xact 4 is in service, a Type 2 mechanic, Xact id 6, arrives at time 868.9, and then another Type 2 mechanic, Xact id 8, arrives at time 1020.5. Service is completed for Xact 4 at time 1073.9.

9. Service is initiated for Xact 30 (Type 2) at time 6058.4. The waiting line is empty at the time. While Xact 30 is in service, a Type 1 mechanic, Xact id 29, arrives at time 6061.0, and then a Type 2 mechanic, Xact id 31, arrives at time 6152.8. Service is completed for Xact 30 at time 6185.9.

Section 10.9

1. The largest number of Xacts waiting for the SPRAYER when the RELEASE was about to be executed was 4. This maximum was reached at these eight times: 4563.0, 4621.8, 4684.0, 4717.8, 4760.1, 4819.5, 4901.3, and 5096.9.

2. GPSS/H displays a message saying that *"BLOCK6 is already an active breakpoint."* This situation can be handled by issuing an **unbreak block6** command, and then issuing the **at block6** command.

3. The Maximum Contents of the TOOLWAIT Queue first becomes 6 at time 24,238.4. The Current Contents then drops from 6 to 5 at time 24,260.4. The Current Contents never again becomes 6.

   Here are the details of how the Maximum Contents reaches its level of 6. At time 23,888.7, service begins on Xact 115 (Type 1). There are three waiting mechanics at the time. While Xact 115 is in service, Xact 122 (Type 2) arrives at time 23,932.0; Xact 124 (Type 2) arrives at time 24,206.6, and Xact 123 (Type 1) arrives at time 24,238.4. It is the arrival of Xact 123 that sets a new high-water mark for Current Contents. Service ends for Xact 115 at time 24,260.4, and the next service initiated at that time drops Current Contents from 6 to 5.

   This information was developed as follows. Atpoints were set on the two QUEUE Blocks, with the corresponding Atlist consisting of the two commands **display blo(2,9)** and **run**. Then the simulation was initiated by issuing a **run** command. This put the simulation into nonstop mode, because each time an interrupt occurred, another **run** command was issued automatically. The trick then is to inspect the Current Counts at Blocks 2 and 9 (perhaps pausing the simulation from time to time if necessary) and mentally form their sum. In the context of this model, the sum of these two Current Counts equals the Current Contents of the Queue. These Block Counts are displayed when an Xact is poised to execute one or the other of the two Queue Blocks, with the effect of increasing that Block's Current Count (and therefore the Current Queue Contents) by 1. When the sum of the displayed Current Counts is 5, then that sum is about to become 6, corresponding to the Queue reaching its Maximum Contents of 6.

Chapter 11

Section 11.14

2. The expected tugboat utilization is 0.486. This can be computed as follows. On average, a Type A ship arrives every 3.2 hours and consumes 2 tugboat-hours worth of tugboat resource during its stay (2 = 0.5 times 3 for berthing, plus 0.25 times 2 for deberthing). This provides a contribution of 0.208 on the part of Type A ships to tugboat utilization.

Similarly, a Type B ship arrives every 1.5 hours on average and consumes 1.25 tugboat-hours worth of tugboat resource during its stay (1.25 = 0.5 times 2 for berthing, plus 0.25 times 1 for deberthing). This provides a contribution of 0.278 on the part of Type B ships to tugboat utilization.

Adding the 0.208 and 0.278 (which is justified because Type A and Type B ships can't be using the same tugboats at the same time), we come up with an expected overall tugboat utilization of 0.486.

7. The average in-port residence time of Type A ships drops from 11.494 hours in the Case Study 11A simulation to 9.623 hours when Type A ships have high priority for tugboat use. The average in-port residence time of Type B ships rises from 3.302 hours in the Case Study 11A simulation to 4.551 hours when Type B ships have low priority for tugboat use.

8. (b) The average numbers of tugboats and of Type A and Type B berths in use in the requested simulation are 4.704, 3.331, and 2.566, respectively. And so we estimate that the respective minimum numbers of these resources needed if the system is to be able to respond to the demands place on it are 5, 4, and 3.
(c) The maximum numbers of tugboats and of Type A and Type B berths in use in the (b) simulation are 8, 6, and 9, respectively. These, of course, are only estimates of the maximums, and are based on a single simulation. (See Chapters 14 et seq. for more details.) It would be tedious to work out by hand the conditions that would maximize the number of tugboats in use simultaneously.
(d) The resulting average in-port residence times for Type A and Type B ships are 10.306 and 4.120, respectively. These, of course, are only estimates of the expected in-port residence times, and are based on a single simulation. (See Chapters 14 et seq. for more details.) It would be tedious to try to compute the expected in-port residence times by hand.

12. (a) Here are some results produced by a correctly built model:

Crane utilization:	0.870
Average step 4 crane-wait time:	10.171
Average step 6 et seq. crane-wait time:	8.988
Average "Other Calls" crane-wait time:	9.710
Number of "Other Calls" that arrived:	613

(The times given are in minutes.) You can compare these results with those from the model you built and, in this indirect way, check the correctness of your model. (Even though the model's outputs are probabilistic, the system is simple enough so that there is no room for variation in results produced by a correctly built model.)

Section 11.15

1. When the first Type A ship tries to execute "LEAVE TUGBOATS,3", the Current Contents of the TUGBOATS Storage will be less than three. (At most, the Current Contents would only be two, which would be the case if a Type B ship were using two tugboats at the time for berthing purposes.) This attempt to decrement the record of Current Contents by three then leads to a negative Current Contents, triggering an error condition and resulting in an Error Message (*"Storage contents have been decremented to less than zero"*). (No error would result if the LEAVE execution did not produce a negative Current Contents for the Storage. Recall, GPSS/H does not check the id of an Xact at a LEAVE Block to see if it currently "owns" one or more of the servers in the group modeled by the referenced Storage. Whereas ownership information is maintained for Facilities, this is not done for Storages.)

2. The problem is that the first Type A ship eventually captures all three of the harbor's tugboats, but then does not put them back into a state of idleness when finished using them. As a result, it can't get the two tugboats needed to deberth (it can't "ENTER TUGBOATS,2" after un/loading), nor can any Type B ships subsequently get one or two tugboats for their purposes. Movement of Type A and Type B ships down their respective paths therefore stops. Ships continue to come to the harbor, however, find themselves blocked (the first several because they can't get tugboats, the rest because they can't get a berth), and are put to sleep on the Current Chain. GPSS/H eventually reaches the point that it can't create any more Xacts (either because it has reached an internally imposed GPSS/H limit, or because of the limits of computer memory) and issues an Error Message (Error 411: *"Limits of COMMON storage exceeded"*; see further remarks in the solution to Exercise 5 of Section 6.13.)

3. The same thing happens here as in Exercise 2, but somewhat more slowly. The first Type A ship eventually captures all three of the harbor's tugboats, but only puts one of them back into a state of idleness when finished using them. This net deficit leads to a situation in which movement of ships down their paths eventually stops, and so on.

4. If the STORAGE statements appear anywhere **after** the START statement in the Model File, they won't have yet been executed at the time START execution initiates Xact movement. (See Figure 6.6.) The default Storage capacities in excess of 2 billion (2,147,483,647, to be exact) will consequently be in effect during Xact movement.

5. A Control Statement is not a Block, and so cannot be an Xact's Next Block Attempted. If the B Operand of an unconditional TRANSFER "points" to a nonexistent Block in a model, a compile time Error Message results. See the solution to Exercise 4 of Section 3.16.

Section 11.18

2. Type A and Type B berths will be used for the actual un/loading of cargo 87.5 percent and 70.0 percent of the time, respectively. (A Type A ship comes every 3.2 hours on average and, of the 9.6 hours of Type A berth resource available during a 3.2 hour period, consumes 8.4 hours of the resource on average for actual un/loading. Dividing 8.4 by 9.6 gives 0.875, or 87.5 percent, and similarly for Type B ships and Type B berths.) These figures can be compared with the respective Type A and Type B berth utilizations of 92.7 percent and 89.4 percent, respectively, reported in Figure 11A.3(c).

Section 11.20

1. A model for this exercise is shown in Figure E1 and is given in the file s1120x1.gps. (Ignore the BLOCK3 and BLOCK7 Labels in Figure E1 for now. They're referred to in the discussion of Exercise 2.)

   In a simulation performed with the model of Figure E1, numeric results are identical to those produced in the Case Study 6A simulation.

   In the Case Study 6A model, workers were modeled "actively," with Xacts, and there was no explicit representation of widgets. (In this view, it is workers themselves who initiate assembly and who use the oven resource.) In the Figure E1 model, workers are modeled "passively," with use of the Storage entity, and there is explicit representation of widgets with Xacts. (In this view, material initiates its own assem-

```
         SIMULATE                base time unit: 1 minute
*
 WORKERS STORAGE    4            provide 4 workers
*
         GENERATE   0            unlimited raw material
         ENTER      WORKERS      request/capture a worker
 BLOCK3  ADVANCE    30,5         assembly time
         SEIZE      OVEN         request/capture the OVEN
         ADVANCE    8,2          heat-treat time
         RELEASE    OVEN         done with the OVEN
 BLOCK7  LEAVE      WORKERS      done with the worker
         TERMINATE  0            finished widget leaves
*
         GENERATE   2400         control Xact comes after 40 hours
         TERMINATE  1            reduce the TC by 1,
*                                ending Xact movement
         START      1            set the TC = 1;
*                                start Xact movement
         END                     end of Model-File execution
```

Figure E1

bly when it can capture a worker and initiates its own heat-treating after assembly when it can capture the heat-treat oven.)

2. To build the requested model, simply change the Capacity of the WORKERS Storage in the Figure E1 model from 4 to 3, and move BLOCK7 so that it immediately follows BLOCK3. Then a widget-in-process will put the worker who assembled it back into a state of idleness just before requesting the heat-treat oven (and, by implication, the worker who operates the oven).

   Numeric results from a simulation performed with the resulting model will not match those from Case Study 6A. Only one "random-number generator" is used as the basis for sampling from both distributions in the model. The model change requested in this exercise changes the order in which samples are drawn from the assembly and heat-treat distributions, and this accounts for a change in numeric results. (This point is explained in much more detail when sampling from distributions is discussed in Chapter 13.)

3. Four workers can assemble widgets faster than one worker can heat-treat them! (With four workers assembling widgets, one widget will be assembled every 7.5 minutes, on average. But it takes 8 minutes, on average, to heat-treat a widget.) This results in an explosive queuing situation at the oven.

4. A model for this exercise is shown in Figure E4 and is given in the file s1120x4.gps.

   Constrained waiting space at the oven has been modeled in Figure E4 with the Storage named WIPSPACE. The STORAGE statement sets the Capacity of this Storage to 3. The BLOCK4 ENTER is used to force an assembled widget to obtain a wait space at the oven before it can put the worker who assembled it into a state of idleness. Similarly, the BLOCK7 LEAVE is placed after "SEIZE OVEN" to force a widget to capture the oven before it can vacate the wait space it had been occupying at the oven. Note that there is no explicit modeling of the worker who runs the oven.

Chapter 12

Section 12.4

4. A model for this exercise is shown in Figure E4 and is given in the file s124x4.gps.

```
          SIMULATE                 base time unit: 1 minute
*
 WIPSPACE STORAGE   3              staging space at the oven
 WORKERS  STORAGE   4              provide 4 workers
*
          GENERATE  0              unlimited raw material
          ENTER     WORKERS        request/capture a worker
          ADVANCE   30,5           assembly time
 BLOCK4   ENTER     WIPSPACE       request/capture a wait space
          LEAVE     WORKERS        done with this worker
          SEIZE     OVEN           request/capture the OVEN
 BLOCK7   LEAVE     WIPSPACE       done with this wait space
          ADVANCE   8,2            heat-treat time
          RELEASE   OVEN           done with the OVEN
          TERMINATE 0              finished widget leaves
*
          GENERATE  2400           control Xact comes after 40 hours
          TERMINATE 1              reduce the TC by 1,
*                                  ending Xact movement
          START     1              set the TC = 1;
*                                  start Xact movement
          END                      end of Model-File execution
```

Figure E4

```
          SIMULATE                               base time unite: 1 minute
*
 TESTERS  STORAGE    2                           testers at the last test station
*
          GENERATE   5.5,2                       sets arrive, one by one, from
*                                                the preceding test station
 RETEST   QUEUE      LASTTEST                    start LASTTEST Queue membership
          ENTER      TESTERS                     request/capture a tester
          DEPART     LASTTEST                    end LASTTEST Queue membership
          ADVANCE    10,3                        testing time
          LEAVE      TESTERS                     let the tester go
*
          TRANSFER   .120,,ADJUSTIT              12% must be adjusted
*
          TERMINATE 1                            the rest pack out
*
 ADJUSTIT QUEUE      ADJUSTQ                     start ADJUSTQ Queue membership
          SEIZE      ADJUSTER                    request/capture the adjuster
          DEPART     ADJUST                      Qend ADJUSTQ Queue membership
          ADVANCE    30,10                       adjustment time
          RELEASE    ADJUSTER                    free the adjuster
*
 NEW1     QUEUE      LASTTEST                    start LASTTEST Queue membership
 NEW2     ENTER      TESTERS                     request/capture a tester
 NEW3     DEPART     LASTTEST                    end LASTTEST Queue membership
 NEW4     ADVANCE    10,3                        testing time
 NEW5     LEAVE      TESTERS                     let the tester go
*
 NEW6     TRANSFER   .010,,ADJUSTIT              now only 1% must be adjusted
*
 NEW7     TERMINATE 1                            the rest pack out
*
          START      100                         set TC=100; start Xact movement
          END                                    end of Model-File execution
```

Figure E4

The solution in Figure E4 repeats the Case Study 12A model (with the banner statements stripped out) and includes seven new Blocks, labeled NEW1 through NEW7. These Blocks are simply a copy of the original stack of testing Blocks, but this stack leads to a statistical TRANSFER Block whose A Operand specifies a probability of 0.01 instead of 0.12.

5. In a model using statistical TRANSFER Blocks whose A Operands were .120 and .200, 65 out of 500 calls (13.0 percent) were false alarms, 88 out of the remaining 347 (20.2 percent) were serious, and the rest of the 347 were routine (79.8 percent). A model using these same TRANSFER Operands will result in this same breakdown of alarm types if it has been properly built. Only 500 calls have come in by the time call 500 has been completed. The maximum and average number of firetrucks in use are 6 and 3.413, respectively.

6. (a) The maximum number of calls waiting for a firetruck is three. The utilization of the five firetrucks is 68.5 percent. The percentage of routine, serious, and false alarms that didn't have to wait for a firetruck were 86.1 percent, 84.3 percent, and 92.3 percent, respectively. (Your model should produce results for Exercise 6 identical to those reported here if your TRANSFER Blocks follow the pattern described in Exercise 5.)

(b) The maximum number of calls waiting for a firetruck is five. The utilization of the four firetrucks is 82.6 percent. The percentage of routine, serious, and false alarms that didn't have to wait for a firetruck were 58.0 percent, 63.5 percent, and 60.0 percent, respectively.
(c) The maximum number of calls waiting for a firetruck is one. The utilization of the six firetrucks is 56.9 percent. The percentage of routine, serious, and false alarms that didn't have to wait for a firetruck were 97.4 percent, 97.7 percent, and 100 percent, respectively.

7. In the 35-Block model used to produce the following numeric results, arriving jobs were first split into two streams with a "TRANSFER .300,,APATH" Block. (In an alternative model, job-Xacts could first go through the Station 1 logic and then be split into two separate job streams. Because of the different uses to which random numbers are put in the alternative approaches, numeric results would differ, even though both approaches are correct. See Chapter 13 for more details.)
(a) The simulation stopped at time 1117.5. The average numbers of workers in use at Stations 1 through 4 were 1.837, 0.705, 3.111, and 2.295, respectively.
(b) The simulation stopped at time 1213.5, so it took about 8.5 percent longer to finish 100 jobs in these single simulations. Table E7 provides the remaining results.

Table E7

	No. of Waiting Jobs	
Station	**Average**	**Maximum**
1	1.907	8
2	3.564	8
3	0.010	1
4	0.105	2

Section 12.5

1. Without simulated delay, any Xact moving into the TRANSFER Block of this exercise will take the C-Block as its Next Block. For all practical purposes, the statistical TRANSFER of this exercise behaves as though it were a "TRANSFER ,SALTMINE" Block.

   The problem here is that the TRANSFER Block's B-Block is the TRANSFER Block itself. And so an Xact moving into the TRANSFER will either immediately take SALTMINE as its Next Block (with probability 0.375), or will take the TRANSFER itself as its Next Block. In the latter case, it will immediately reexecute the TRANSFER (which never denies entry; here, we have a case in which an Xact's Next Block Attempted is its Current Block, which does not result in an execution error). The Xact will again either immediately take SALTMINE as its Next Block, or reexecute the TRANSFER Block, etc., etc.

2. Without simulated delay, any Xact moving into the TRANSFER Block of this exercise will take the sequential Block as its Next Block. For all practical purposes, the Block might as well be removed from whatever model it appears in. The Block has no useful purpose. (Also see the comments in the solution to Exercise 1.)

3. Suppose an Xact moves into the TRANSFER Block of this exercise. Then its Next Block will be the TRANSFER Block itself, so the TRANSFER Block will be reexecuted immediately, etc., etc. Nothing will ever cause this moving Xact to stop moving, and so the Xact will repeatedly execute the TRANSFER Block until the user regains control with an Attention Interrupt.

4. The TRANSFER Block of this exercise unconditionally routes Xacts to the PATH5 Block. The Block behaves as though it were a "TRANSFER ,PATH5" Block. No compile-time or execution-time messages are issued. (GPSS/H doesn't pass judgment on the modeler's intelligence in cases like this.)

5. The TRANSFER Block of this exercise unconditionally routes Xacts to the GATEWAY2 Block. The Block behaves as though it were a "TRANSFER ,GATEWAY2" Block. No compile-time or execution-time messages are issued.

Section 12.8

3. (a) The maximum and average number of microcomputers in use are 8.830 and 14, respectively.
(b) Of 267 students who arrive, 179 can't get a micro on the first try. (Sound familiar?) Of these, 61 leave and then come back later.

```
         SIMULATE                          base time unit: 1 minute
*
         GENERATE  1.5,1.0                 customers arrive
         QUEUE     LINE                    start LINE Queue membership
*
         TRANSFER  500,,FAVOR2             which Teller to favor?
*
 FAVOR1  TRANSFER  BOTH,,TRYFOR2           Teller 1 favored here
*
 TRYFOR1 SEIZE     TELLER1                 request Teller 1
         DEPART    LINE                    end LINE Queue membership
         ADVANCE   2.5,1.25                service time
         RELEASE   TELLER1                 done with Teller 1
         TERMINATE 1                       leave the bank
*
 FAVOR2  TRANSFER  BOTH,,TRYFOR1           Teller 2 favored here
*
 TRYFOR2 SEIZE     TELLER2                 request Teller 2
         DEPART    LINE                    end LINE Queue membership
         ADVANCE   3.25,2.5                service time
         RELEASE   TELLER2                 done with Teller 2
         TERMINATE 1                       leave the bank
*
         START     100                     serve 100 customers
         END                               end of Model-File execution
```

Figure E5

(c) Of 260 students who arrive, 66 can't get a micro on the first try. Of these, 20 leave and then come back later.

(d) Of 258 students who arrive, 20 can't get a micro on the first try. Of these, 9 leave and then come back later.

You'll learn in Chapter 13 why the numbers of arriving students aren't identical across all parts of this exercise.

5. A model for this exercise is shown in Figure E5 and is given in the file s128x5.gps.

Zero Entries to the LINE Queue will indicate how many customers didn't have to wait to go into service, but the model provides no way to determine how many of these arrived when both tellers were idle. (Using techniques beyond the scope of this book, it would be easy to count these cases and, among these cases, count the number of customers who went to the experienced teller.)

7. Here are some results produced by a correctly built model:

Clock time at end of Xact movement:	279.7090
Number of Type A tanker arrivals:	35
Number of Type B tanker arrivals:	68
Tugboat utilization:	0.332
Utilization of the harbor's mouth:	0.376
Utilization of the dedicated space:	0.216
Utilization of the dual-purpose space:	0.698

These results assume only that the GENERATE Block for Type A tankers precedes that for Type B tankers. You can compare these results with those from the model you built and, in this indirect way, check the correctness of your model. (Even though the model's outputs are probabilistic, the system is simple enough so that there is no room for variation in results produced by a correctly built model, given that the GENERATE Blocks have been ordered as indicated.) The model that produced the foregoing results contains 82 Blocks.

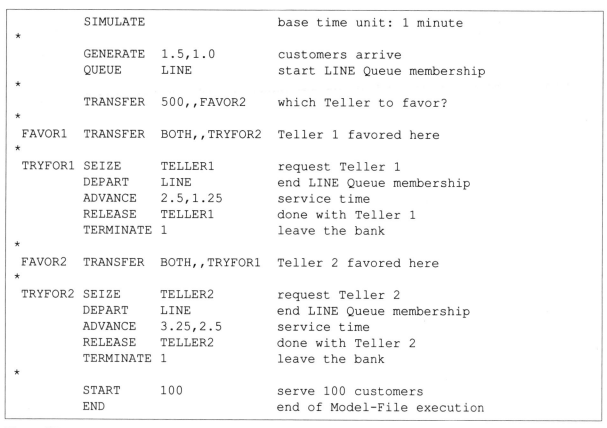

Section 12.12

3. The earliest time SPT service order makes a difference vis-à-vis FCFS service order in terms of the type of use to which a crane is next put is time 271.09. At this time, Xact 6 captures the crane to use for intermediate handling, whereas, with an FCFS service order, Xact 3 would have captured the crane to use for the unload, store, fetch, and reload step.

4. In single simulations, the average crane-wait time per cycle with the SPT service order is 31.554 minutes. (This is the sum of 8.640 minutes spent waiting on average to get a crane for intermediate handling, and 22.914 minutes spent waiting on average to get a crane for the unload, store, fetch, and reload step.) With the FCFS service order, the average crane-wait time per cycle is 35.113 minutes. (This is the sum of 19.451 minutes spent waiting on average to get a crane for intermediate handling, and 15.662 minutes spent waiting on average to get a crane for the unload, store, fetch, and reload step.) And so in these simulations, use of the SPT service order lowered the average crane-wait time per cycle by about 13 percent. The difference between SPT and FCFS can be investigated much more carefully in terms of material in Chapters 14, 15, and 16.

6. This emergency-room system is modeled in Case Study 13A, where interarrival and service times are assumed to be exponentially distributed (as contrasted with the assumed uniform distributions in Exercise 6). Changing the distributions in the Case Study 13A model to uniform provides a solution to Exercise 6.

7. (a) The BLOCK6 Xact will win the competition for SERVER2 at time 30.0. The simulation will stop at time 100.
(b) In this case, the BLOCK1 Xact will win the competition for SERVER1 at time 30.0. The BLOCK6 Xact won't be able to capture SERVER2 until time 50, and so the simulation won't stop until time 120.
(c) The result here is the same as in (b).

Section 12.14

9. A model for this exercise is shown in Figure E9 and is given in the file s1214x9.gps.

These features of the model (which is perhaps the most complicated we've seen up to this point in the book) should be noted:

1. WIP doesn't try to capture the AGV until it has determined that there is some place to which it can be transferred (to Station 1, or to the wait space, or to Station 2). If this weren't the case, deadlock could come about in the model. (See the solution to Exercise 1 of Section 8.11 in this regard.) If the BLOCK4 "SEIZE AGV" Block **preceded** the BLOCK3 "SEIZE STATION1" Block, for example, deadlock could come about. ("The WIP that has the AGV wants Station 1, and the WIP that has Station 1 wants the AGV. Each has something the other wants, and neither can or will give up what it has until the other has given up what it has.")
2. At the BLOCK9 BOTHTRANSFER, finished WIP at Station 1 tries **first** to capture Station 2, and only if that isn't possible tries for the wait space as a second choice.
3. As soon as the AGV reaches a pickup point, it's assumed in the model that the resource at that pickup point (Station 1, or the wait space, or Station 2) is immediately freed up for use on the part of another WIP unit. This can be inferred by looking at the position of the RELEASE STATION1, STATION2, and THESPACE Blocks in the model. (This won't do the next WIP unit any good in this model, however, because it will have to wait for eventual use of the AGV anyway. But if there were more than one AGV in the system, this wouldn't necessarily be the case.)
4. The Priority of WIP at Station 2 is boosted at BLOCK16 (to 5, from its default of 0) just before the WIP-Xact goes to the FEC to simulate use of Station 2. Upon its eventual return to the CEC, this WIP then has high Priority for use of the AGV. In cases of competition for the AGV, this WIP will be transferred from Station 2, freeing that station before finished WIP (if any) waiting at Station 1 determines where it can move next.
5. WIP goes to Station 2 either from Station 1 or from the wait space. The last 10 Blocks (beginning with the BLOCK14 Block) in the logic of Station 2 use do not depend on which of these two locations the WIP comes from, and so this stack of Blocks need appear only one time in the model.

```
         SIMULATE                      base time unit: 1 minute
*
         GENERATE  30,20               WIP arrives (Priority = 0)
         ADVANCE   0                   avoid arrival distortions
*
 BLOCK3  SEIZE     STATION1            request/capture Station 1
 BLOCK4  SEIZE     AGV                 request/capture the AGV
         ADVANCE   0.5,0.25            AGV travels to entry point
         ADVANCE   0.5                 30-second transfer to Station 1
         RELEASE   AGV                 done with the AGV for now
         ADVANCE   25,10               Station 1 time
*
 BLOCK9  TRANSFER  BOTH,,WAIT          try for Station 2 or wait space
*
         SEIZE     STATION2            request/capture Station 2
         SEIZE     AGV                 request/capture the AGV
         ADVANCE   0.5,0.25            AGV travels to Station 1
 BLOCK13 RELEASE   STATION1            no longer at Station 1
 BLOCK14 ADVANCE   0.5                 30-second transfer to Station 2
         RELEASE   AGV                 done with the AGV for now
 BLOCK16 PRIORITY  5                   boost Priority for later
*                                      transfer from Station 2
         ADVANCE   30,10               Station 2 time
         SEIZE     AGV                 request/capture the AGV
         ADVANCE   0.5,0.25            AGV travels to Station 2
         RELEASE   STATION2            no longer at Station 2
         ADVANCE   0.5                 30-second transfer to exit
         RELEASE   AGV                 done with the AGV
         TERMINATE 1                   finished WIP leaves model
*
 WAIT    SEIZE     THESPACE            request/capture the wait space
         SEIZE     AGV                 request/capture the AGV
         ADVANCE   0.5,0.25            AGV travels to Station 1
 BLOCK27 RELEASE   STATION1            no longer at Station 1
         ADVANCE   0.5                 30-second transfer to wait space
         RELEASE   AGV                 done with the AGV for now
*
         SEIZE     STATION2            request/capture Station 2
         SEIZE     AGV                 request/capture the AGV
         ADVANCE   0.5,0.25            AGV travels to wait space
 BLOCK33 RELEASE   THESPACE            no longer in the wait space
         TRANSFER  ,BLOCK14            use rest of Station 2 logic
*
         START     100                 finish 100 WIP units
         END                           end of Model-File execution
```

Figure E9

Section 12.16

1. A WIP unit goes to the oldest drill for the first time at time 13.9. The earliest time a WIP unit fails to move out of the ALL TRANSFER on its first attempt is time 29.3. It takes 522.6 simulated minutes to drill holes in 100 WIP units. Four WIP units are waiting for a drill press at the end of the simulation.

```
BUYTIME   FUNCTION    RN5,D7    FUNCTION Control Statement
.1,.5/.25,.75/.45,.95.7,1.1     ...first Function Follower Statement
.85,1.25/.95,1.4/1,1.5          ...second Function Follower Statement
```

Figure E1

Chapter 13

Section 13.10

1. (a) IAT_{sample} = (420–360) + (0.270295)(2)(360) = 254.61
(b) IAT_{sample} = (420–360) + (0.499353)(2)(360) = 419.5
(c) The first and second sets arrive at times 4.58 and 10.08 (approximately). The testing time of the first set is 11.44 (approximately).

2. (a) "GENERATE RVEXPO(5,240)"
(b) "GENERATE RVEXPO(12,8)"
(c) "ADVANCE RVEXPO(2,0.6)"
(d) Put the Block "ADVANCE RVEXPO(2,0.3)" in the model two consecutive times.

Section 13.14

1. "GENERATE RVTRI(7,10,14,30)"

2. "GENERATE RVTRI(7,10,20,30)"

3. "ADVANCE ABS(RVNORM(2,27.5,7.5))"

4. "ADVANCE ABS(RVNORM(2,27.5,9.66))"

Section 13.24

1. (a) Figure E1 shows a solution.
(b) "ADVANCE FN(BUYTIME)"
(c) See Figure 13.12 for a similar plot.
(d) The RN5 value of 0.35 falls into the interval ranging from 0.25 to 0.45, and so the BUYTIME Function produces a value of 0.95.
(e) The BUYTIME Function produces a value of 0.75. (Steps in Discrete Functions are inclusive of their rightmost endpoint.)
(f) For each of the seven checkout times in Table E1 in this exercise, multiply the checkout time by its relative frequency. The sum of these seven products is the expected checkout time, which turns out to be 1.03 minutes.

2. (a) Figure E2 shows a solution.
(b) "GENERATE FN(IAT)"
(c) See Figure 13.16 for a similar plot.
(d) Interpolating linearly between the ordered pairs (0.25, 2) and (0.45, 3), the IAT Function produces a value of 2.75 when the value of RN3 is 0.4.
(e) The IAT Function produces a value of 5.
(g) For each of the six intervals in Table E2 in this exercise, multiply the midpoint of the interval by its relative frequency. The sum of these six products is the expected interarrival time, which turns out to be 3.1 minutes.

3. (a) Figure E3 shows a C2 Function that samples from the continuous uniform distribution 25 ± 10, and that specifies RN2 as the basis for sampling. To make use of this Function, replace

```
IAT       FUNCTION    RN3,C7    FUNCTION Control Statement
0,0/.1,1/.25,2/.45,3            ...first Function Follower Statement
.7,4/.9,5/1,6                   ...second Function Follower Statement
```

Figure E2

```
IAT       FUNCTION    RN2,C2    FUNCTION Control Statement
0,15/1,35                       Function Follower Statement
```

Figure E3

"GENERATE 25,10"

with

"GENERATE FN(IAT)".

(b) See Figure 13.19 for a similar plot.
(c) Interpolating linearly between the two pairs of points used to define the IAT Function, the Function will produce a value of 24.0.

6. The expected job interarrival time in the Case Study 13B system is 0.32 hours. (See Exercise 2(g) in this section.) This means that on average, 0.3 Type 1 jobs, 0.5 Type 2 jobs, and 0.2 Type 3 jobs arrive every 0.32 hours. Taking into account their use of the machine resources, the expected machine-group utilizations are summarized in Table E6.

Table E6

Group Number	Expected Utilization
1	75.0%
2	77.3
3	56.6
4	76.0
5	62.5

For example, Type 1 jobs require 0.18 hours of Group 1 machine time on average every 0.32 hours (0.18 = 0.3 times 0.6), Type 2 jobs require 0.4 hours of Group 1 machine time on average every 0.32 hours (0.4 = 0.5 times 0.8), and Type 3 jobs require 0.14 hours of Group 1 machine time on average every 0.32 hours (0.14 = 0.2 times 0.7). Summing, 0.72 machining hours are needed from Group 1 every 0.32 hours, on average. This requires 2.25 Group 1 machines (2.25 = 0.72 divided by 0.32). But there are 3 Group 1 machines. This results in the expected Group 1 utilization of 75.0 percent shown in Table E5.

7. (a) Expected utilizations of Groups 1, 2, 3, 4 and 5 and 96.0 percent, 99.0 percent, 72.5 percent, 97.3 percent, and 80.0 percent, respectively.
(b) Group 2 reaches an expected utilization of 100 percent when the mean job interarrival time has dropped to 0.2475 hours. The expected utilizations of all five machine groups at this point are shown in Table E7.

Table E7

Group Number	Expected Utilization
1	97.0%
2	100.0
3	73.2
4	98.3
5	80.8

As the degree of system loading in a probabilistic system increases, the degree of system variation increases. Variations in system behavior may become especially pronounced as the system approaches the point of becoming explosive. Note that with a mean interarrival time of 0.25 hours, the Law and Kelton version of this job shop system is very close to being explosive.

8. (a) The Total Count at the JOBTYPE1 Block in Figure 13B.3(a) is 178, meaning this many Type 1 jobs arrived during the simulation. In total, 638 jobs arrived. (638 = the Total Count of 630 at Block 3, plus the 8 jobs introduced into the model initially.) And so 27.9 percent of the jobs were of Type 1. Similarly, 51.7 percent of the jobs were of Type 2, and 20.4 percent were of Type 3.
(b) Adding the Average Contents of the machine groups and the Average Contents of the lines of WIP waiting to use machines, the average level of work-in-process in the Case Study 13B simulation was 13.797.

Section 13.27

1. (a) Two 0-1 uniform random numbers are used to determine an interarrival time at the Block "GENERATE RVTRI(3,4.0,6.0,9.0),2". To evaluate the A Operand, a 0-1 value from RN3 is used. Then, to sample from the distribution centered on this A Operand value, and uniformly distributed ±2 about it, a 0-1 value from RN1 is used.
(b) The interarrival times are distributed on the open interval ranging from 2.0 to 11.0.

2. (a) The FACTOR Function returns values uniformly distributed on the open interval ranging from 3 to 6. These values are then multiplied by 5 to determine holding times at the ADVANCE Block. The holding times are therefore uniformly distributed on the open interval ranging from 15 to 30.

(b) Defined as a D2 Function, FACTOR always returns the value 3. (RN7 is open on 1.0, so FACTOR can never return the value 6.0.) This value is then multiplied by 5 to determine holding times at the ADVANCE Block. The holding times are therefore always 15, deterministically.

Chapter 14

Section 14.7

6. Results (rounded to one decimal place) are summarized in Table E6, where 90 percent confidence intervals are also shown.

Section 14.10

2. Other things being equal, we expect an 80 percent confidence interval to be narrower than a 90 percent confidence interval. (We are less confident that an expected value lies within a narrower interval.) We similarly expect a 95 percent confidence interval to be wider than one of 90 percent. (We are more confident that an expected value lies within a wider interval.) For the FCFS sample of Table 14.2, the 80 percent interval is [2.97, 4.10], and the 95 percent interval is [2.62, 4.45]. Compared with the 90 percent interval of [2.79, 4.28], these results are consistent with our expectations.

3. We expect a 90 percent confidence interval for the SPT sample of Table 14.2 to be wider than the 90 percent interval for the FCFS sample. The sample sizes and confidence levels are identical, but the SPT sample standard deviation, 1.999, is larger than that of the FCFS sample, 1.286, resulting in a wider confidence interval. The 90 percent SPT confidence interval is [2.11, 4.42], contrasted with that of [2.79, 4.28] for FCFS.

4. A 95 percent confidence interval for the output variable of Table 14.1 is [557.9, 610.7].

Table E6

Replication Number	Average Harbor Residence Time (hours, by ship type) Type A	Type B	Average Berth-Wait Time (hours, by ship type) Type A	Type B
1	10.7	3.3	2.1	0.5
2	11.7	5.0	3.1	2.0
3	11.3	4.6	2.3	1.7
4	9.0	3.9	0.4	1.1
5	12.9	3.8	4.3	0.9
6	10.4	4.5	1.3	1.6
7	9.4	4.0	0.6	1.1
8	9.3	3.8	0.6	0.9
9	10.7	3.4	1.8	0.5
10	9.7	5.7	0.7	2.9
11	13.2	3.9	4.8	1.0
12	9.7	4.8	1.1	1.9
13	9.6	5.4	0.6	2.5
14	11.6	6.8	2.7	3.9
15	9.7	4.1	0.8	1.2
16	12.8	4.4	3.9	1.6
17	9.1	3.4	0.5	0.5
18	13.6	3.9	4.8	1.0
19	10.0	3.7	1.1	0.7
20	9.9	3.8	1.2	0.9
Mean:	10.7	4.31	1.94	1.42
Std. Dev.:	1.46	0.888	1.50	0.879
90% Conf. Int.:	[10.1, 11.3]	[4.0, 4.7]	[1.2, 2.5]	[1.1, 1.8]

5. If the size of the Table 14.1 sample were larger than five, a confidence interval at a given confidence level would be narrower than the one for a sample of size five. In the expression used to compute confidence-interval half-width,

$$t_{\alpha/2}\left(s/\sqrt{n}\right),$$

both a smaller t statistic and/or a larger sample size contribute to a narrower confidence interval when the sample size increases. If the sample were of size 20, the 95 percent confidence interval would be [574.4, 594.2]. If the sample were of size 80, the 95 percent confidence interval would be [579.7, 588.9]. The corresponding confidence interval for the sample of size five is [557.9, 610.7].

Section 14.14

5. The SPT results in Table 14.2 are not completely independent of the FCFS results reported there. The models producing the two sets of results both use RN1 for transparent sampling at GENERATE and ADVANCE Blocks, and use the default Initial Position of RN1. When the respective simulations begin, each of the first three (or more) mechanic arrivals are identical in time and type, irrespective of the service order in use; similarly, the same type of mechanic is the first into service and has the same service time requirement, irrespective of the service order in use. In other words, the uses to which RN1 values are put start out identically in both models. This lock-stepping use of values from RN1 is finally broken when the difference in service orders causes the next mechanic into service to differ between the two models. (In Exercise 11 of Section 10.4, you were asked to determine the earliest time in the SPT model that a high-priority mechanic cuts in line ahead of a low-priority mechanic. It is this occurrence that changes the order in which mechanics go into service.) From that point forward, values from RN1 are used for the same purpose (such as to schedule the arrival of the next Type 2 mechanic) in both models some of the time, but not all of the time.

   Speaking from the high plateau of principle, these interdependencies between the two sets of results in Table 14.2 mean that the results shouldn't be used for statistical comparison of the alternative service orders per the methods introduced for this purpose in Chapter 16. (Whether these weak interdependencies would be of any practical consequence in the final analysis is another question.) Fortunately, it's not necessary to accept unwanted interdependencies; as we have seen, the RMULT Statement can be used to model in such a way that independent sets of results can be produced.

Chapter 15

Section 15.7

9. The Block subset (and several Control Statements) of a Model File for this exercise is shown in Figure E9, and given in the file s157x9.gps.

   Figure E9 demonstrates how to handle the need for a balking customer to waste, or "burn up," the random number that this customer would otherwise have used, had the balk not taken place.

Chapter 16

Section 16.7

2. (b) Your friend is right. The GENERATE Blocks from which the Type 1 and Type 2 mechanics come could share a 0-1 uniform generator. Reason: the order in which mechanics **arrive** is not dependent on the order in which mechanics are **served**.

   (c) Your friend is wrong this time. The starting point of the generators has to be known at the beginning of each **replication**; it's not enough just to know the starting point at the beginning of each **service order**. As a result, the RMULT statement must be in the inner loop (the replication loop) in the Model File.

```
         SIMULATE
*                                    base time unit: 1 minute
 SPACES  STORAGE   4                 4 wait spaces

         GENERATE  RVEXPO(1,5)       cars arrive
         TRANSFER  BOTH,,BALK        get wait space or balk
         ENTER     SPACES            capture a wait space
         SEIZE     CARWASH           request/capture the carwash
         LEAVE     SPACES            no longer in the wait space
         ADVANCE   RVEXPO(2,4)       washing time
         RELEASE   CARWASH           done with the carwash
         TERMINATE 0                 washed car leaves
*
 BALK    ADVANCE   0                 dummy ADVANCE accepts balkers
         SEIZE     CARWASH           capture carwash when what would
*                                    have been your turn comes
         RELEASE   CARWASH           let go right away (the balker is
*                                    not really at the carwash anyway!)
         ADVANCE   RVEXPO(2,4)       waste the draw from RN2
         TERMINATE 0                 task accomplished
*
         GENERATE  480               control Xact comes after 8 hours
         TERMINATE 1                 shut down the replication
*
         START     1                 set TC = 1, start Xact movement
         END                         end of Model-File execution
```

Figure E9

References

ANDERSON, DAVID R., DENNIS J. SWEENEY, AND THOMAS A. WILLIAMS (1990). *Quantitative Methods for Business*, 4th ed. West, St. Paul, MN.

BANKS, JERRY, AND JOHN S. CARSON II (1984). *Discrete Event System Simulation.* Prentice Hall, Englewood Cliffs, NJ.

BANKS, JERRY, JOHN S. CARSON, AND JOHN N. SY (1989). *Getting Started with GPSS/H.* Wolverine Software Corporation, Annandale, VA.

BOBILLIER, P. A., B. C. KAHAN, AND A. R. PROBST (1976). *Simulation with GPSS and GPSS/V.* Prentice Hall, Englewood Cliffs, NJ.

BRATLEY, PAUL, BENNETT L. FOX, AND LINUS E. SCHRAGE (1986). *A Guide to Simulation*, 2nd ed. Springer-Verlag, New York.

BUDNICK, FRANK S., DENNIS MCLEAVEY, AND RICHARD MOJENA (1988). *Principles of Operations Research for Management.* Richard D. Irwin, Homewood, IL.

CARSON, JOHN S. (1986). "Convincing Users of Model's Validity Is Challenging Aspect of Modeler's Job." *Industrial Engineering*, June 1986, pp. 74–85.

COOK, THOMAS J., AND ROBERT A. RUSSELL (1990). *Introduction to Management Science*, 4th ed. Prentice Hall, Englewood Cliffs, NJ.

COOK, THOMAS M., AND ROBERT A. RUSSELL (1976). "A Survey of Industrial OR/MS Activities in the 70's." *Proceedings of the 8th Annual Conference of The American Institute for Decision Sciences*, Decision Sciences Institute, Atlanta, GA, pp. 122–128.

DAVIS, SAMUEL G., ET AL. (1986). "Strategic Planning for Bank Operations with Multiple Check-Processing Locations." *Interfaces*, Vol. 16, no. 6, November–December 1986, pp. 1–12. (Also summarized in Knowles, 1989, pp. 903–904.)

DUDEWICZ, EDWARD J., AND SATYA M. MISHRA (1988). *Modern Mathematical Statistics.* John Wiley, New York.

FISHMAN, GEORGE S., AND LOUIS R. MOORE III (1986). "An Exhaustive Analysis of Multiplicative Congruential Random Number Generators with Modulus 2^{31}-1." *SIAM Journal for Scientific and Statistical Computing*, Vol. 7, no. 1, January 1986, pp. 24–45.

FISHMAN, GEORGE S. (1978). *Principles of Discrete Event Simulation.* Wiley-Interscience, John Wiley , New York.

FISHMAN, GEORGE S. (1983). *Concepts and Methods in Discrete Event Digital Simulation.* Wiley-Interscience, John Wiley, New York.

GOLOVIN, LEWIS B. (1979). "Product Blending: A Simulation Case Study in Double-Time." *Interfaces*, Vol. 9, no. 5, November 1979, pp. 64–76.

GOLOVIN, LEWIS B. (1985). "Product Blending: A Simulation Case Study in Double Time: An Update." *Interfaces*, Vol. 15, no. 4, July–August 1985, pp. 39–40. (Also summarized in Knowles, 1989, pp. 839–840.)

GORDON, GEOFFREY (1975). *The Application of GPSS V to Discrete Systems Simulation*. Prentice Hall, Englewood Cliffs, NJ.

GORDON, GEOFFREY (1978). "The Development of the General Purpose Simulation System (GPSS)." *Proceedings of the ACM SIGPLAN History of Programming Languages Conference*, published as *SIGPLAN Notices*, Vol. 13, no. 8, pp. 183–198. (These *Proceedings* were subsequently published in a hard-cover edition by the Association for Computing Machinery, New York.)

GRANT, JOHN W., AND STEVEN A. WEINER (1986). "Factors to Consider in Choosing a Graphically Animated Simulation System." *Industrial Engineering*, August 1986, pp. 37–40, 65–68.

HAIDER, S. WALI, AND JERRY BANKS (1986). "Simulation Software Products for Analyzing Manufacturing Systems." *Industrial Engineering*, July 1986, pp. 98–103. (Also see the errata for this article appearing on pp. 98–103 of *Industrial Engineering*, September 1986.)

HARPELL, JOHN L., MICHAEL S. LANE AND ALI H. MANSOUR (1989). "Operations Research in Practice: A Longitudinal Study." *Interfaces*, Vol. 19, no. 3, May–June 1989, pp. 65–74.

HENRIKSEN, JAMES O. (1983). "The Integrated Simulation Environment (Simulation Software of the 1990s)." *Operations Research*, Vol. 31, no. 6, November–December 1983, pp. 1053–1073.

HENRIKSEN, JAMES O., AND ROBERT C. CRAIN (1989). *GPSS/H Reference Manual*, Wolverine Software Corporation, Annandale, VA.

HILLIER, FREDERICK S., AND GERALD J. LIEBERMAN (1990). *Introduction to Operations Research*, 5th ed. McGraw-Hill, New York.

HUBBARD, HERBERT B. (1978). "Terminal Airspace/Airport Congestion Delays." *Interfaces*, Vol. 8, no. 2, February 1978, pp. 1–14. (Also summarized in the 3rd edition of Cook and Russell, 1990, pp. 520–521.)

KAVIAN, ZAVEN A., AND EDWARD J. DUDEWICZ (1990). *Modern Statistical, Systems GPSS Simulation: The First Course*. W. H. Freeman, New York.

KELTON, W. DAVID (1986). "Statistical Analysis Methods Enhance Usefulness, Reliability of Simulation Models." *Industrial Engineering*, September 1986, pp. 74–84.

KNOWLES, THOMAS W. (1989). *Management Science: Building and Using Models*. Richard D. Irwin, Homewood, IL.

KOLESAR, PETER (1984). "Stalking the Endangered CAT: A Queueing Analysis of Congestion at Automatic Teller Machines." *Interfaces*, Vol. 15, no. 6, November–December 1984, pp. 16-26. (Also summarized in Budnick, McLeavey, and Mojena, 1988, pp. 801–810.)

LAW, AVERILL M. (1986). "Introduction to Simulation: A Powerful Tool for Analyzing Complex Manufacturing Systems." *Industrial Engineering*, May 1986, pp. 46–63.

LAW, AVERILL M., AND W. DAVID KELTON (1982). *Simulation Modeling and Analysis*. McGraw–Hill, New York. (2nd edition forthcoming, 1990).

LEE, SANG M., LAURENCE J. MOORE, AND BERNARD W. TAYLOR III (1990). *Management Science*, 3rd ed. Allyn & Bacon, Needham Heights, MA.

LEHMER, DONALD H. (1951). "Mathematical Methods in Large-Scale Computing Units." *Annals of the Computational Laboratory* (Harvard University), Vol. 26, pp. 141–146.

MARKLAND, ROBERT E. (1970). "A Simulation Model for Determining Scrap Decision Rules in the Metal Processing Industry." *Production and Inventory Management*, Vol. 11, no. 1, 1st Quarter 1970, pp. 29–35. (Also summarized in Markland, 1989, pp. 620–631.)

MARKLAND, ROBERT E. (1989). *Topics in Management Science*, 3rd ed. John Wiley, New York.

MCCLAVE, JAMES T., AND P. GEORGE BENSON (1988). *Statistics for Business and Economics*, 4th ed. Dellen, San Francisco.

MCHUGH, MARY LYNN (1989). "Computer Simulation as a Method for Selecting Nurse Staffing Levels in Hospitals." *Proceedings of the 1989 Winter Simulation Conference*, Society for Computer Simulation, San Diego, CA, pp. 1121–1129.

MONARCHI, DAVID E., THOMAS E. HENDRICK, AND DONALD R. PLANE (1977). "Simulation for Fire Department Deployment Policy Analysis." *Decision Sciences*, Vol. 8, no. 1, January 1977, pp. 211–227. (Also summarized in Watson and Blackstone, 1989, pp. 46–47.)

MUSSELMAN, KENNETH J., AND DAVID L. MARTIN (1984). "Simulation in the Life Cycle of Flexible Manufacturing Systems." *Proceedings of the First ORSA/TIMS Special Interest Conference on Flexible Manufacturing Systems* (The Institute of Management Sciences, Providence, RI), pp.154–167.

PRITSKER, A. ALAN B. (1984). *Introduction to Simulation and SLAM II*, 2nd ed. Halsted Press, John Wiley, New York.

PRITSKER, A. ALAN B. (1986). *Introduction to Simulation and SLAM II*, 3rd ed. Halsted Press, John Wiley, New York.

RAVINDRAN, RAVI, DON T. PHILLIPS, AND JAMES J. SOLBERG (1987). *Operations Research: Principles and Practice*, 2nd ed. John Wiley, New York.

RICCIO, LUCIUS J., AND ANN LITKE (1986). "Making a Clean Sweep: Simulating the Effects of Illegally Parked Cars on New York City's Mechanical Street-Cleaning Efforts." *Operations Research*, Vol. 34, no. 5, September–October 1986, pp. 661–666. (Also elaborated on in the form of a parallel problem in Shogan, 1988, pp. 764–770.)

SCHERER, WILLIAM T., AND CHELSEA C. WHITE III (1986). "A Planning and Decision-Aiding Procedure for Purchasing and Launching Spacecraft." *Interfaces*, Vol. 16, no. 3, May–June 1986, pp. 31–40. (Also summarized in Budnick, McLeavey, and Mojena, 1988, p. 863.)

SCHRIBER, THOMAS J. (1974). *Simulation Using GPSS*. Krieger Books (407-724-9542). (Russian translation, 1980, edited by Michael Feinberg, Ph.D. Mashinostroyenie Press, Moscow.)

SCHRIBER, THOMAS J. (1989). "Perspectives on Simulation Using GPSS." *Proceedings of the 1989 Winter Simulation Conference*, Society for Computer Simulation, San Diego, pp. 115–128.

SCHRIBER, THOMAS J., AND KATHRYN E. STECKE (1988). "Machine Utilizations Achieved Using Balanced FMS Production Ratios in a Simulated Setting." *Annals of Operations Research*, Vol. 15, 1988, pp. 229–267.

SHANNON, ROBERT E., RICHARD MAYER, AND HEIMO H. ADELSBERGER (1985). "Expert Systems and Simulation." *Simulation*, Vol. 44, no. 6, June 1985, pp. 275–284.

SHOGAN, ANDREW W. (1988). *Management Science*. Prentice Hall, Englewood Cliffs, NJ.

SOLOMON, SUSAN L. (1983). *Simulation of Waiting-Line Systems*. Prentice Hall, Englewood Cliffs, NJ.

STÅHL, INGOLF (1990). *Introduction to Simulation with GPSS*. Prentice Hall International, London.

SWART, WILLIAM, AND LUCA DONNO (1981). "Simulation Modeling Improves Operations, Planning and Productivity of Fast Food Restaurants." *Interfaces*, Vol. 11, no. 6, December 1981, pp. 35–47. (Also summarized in Watson and Blackstone, 1989, pp. 41–43.)

TAHA, HAMDY A. (1987). *Operations Research*, 4th ed. Macmillan, New York.

TAYLOR III, BERNARD W. (1990). *Introduction to Management Science*, 3rd ed. Allyn & Bacon, Needham Heights, MA.

TURBAN, EPHRAIM (1972). "A Sample Survey of Operations Research Activities at the Corporate Level." *Operations Research*, Vol. 20, no. 3, May–June 1972, pp. 708–721.

WAGNER, HARVEY M. (1988). "Operations Research: A Global Language for Business Strategy." *Operations Research*, Vol. 36, no. 5, September–October 1988, pp. 797–803.

WATSON, HUGH J., AND JOHN H. BLACKSTONE, JR. (1989). *Computer Simulation*, 2nd ed. John Wiley, New York.

WILSON, JAMES REED, AND A. ALAN B. PRITSKER (1978). "A Survey of Research on the Simulation Startup Problem." *Simulation*, Vol. 41, no. 8, August 1978, pp. 55–58.

WYMAN, F. PAUL (1977). "Simulation of Tar Sands Mining Operations." *Interfaces*, Vol. 8, no. 1, part 2 (Special Practices issue), November 1977, pp. 6–20. (Also summarized in Watson and Blackstone, 1989, pp. 38–40.)

Author Index*

*This index lists each person mentioned in the text.

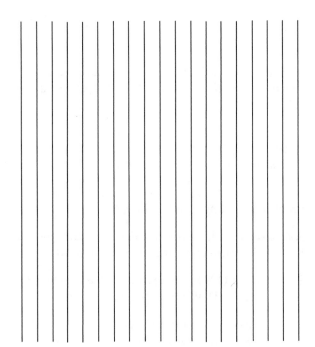

Subject Index*

*Throughout this index, keywords and output labels are shown in **boldface**.

T

U